THE THIRD BOOK OF MOSES, CALLED

LEVITICUS

THE
PREACHER'S
OUTLINE & SERMON
BIBLE®

THE THIRD BOOK OF MOSES, CALLED

LEVITICUS

THE
PREACHER'S
OUTLINE & SERMON
BIBLE®

OLD TESTAMENT

KING JAMES VERSION

Leadership Ministries Worldwide
Chattanooga, TN

THE PREACHER'S OUTLINE & SERMON BIBLE® - LEVITICUS

KING JAMES VERSION

Please address all requests for information or permission to:

Leadership Ministries Worldwide
Ph.# (800) 987-8790   E-Mail: info@lmw.org
Web: lmw.org

Library of Congress Catalog Card Number: 96-75921
International Standard Book Number: Softbound Edition: 978-1-57407-110-8

Printed in the United States of America

LEADERSHIP MINISTRIES WORLDWIDE

DEDICATED

To all the men and women of the world
who preach and teach the Gospel of
our Lord Jesus Christ and
to the Mercy and Grace of God

&

- Demonstrated to us in Christ Jesus our Lord.

  "In whom we have redemption through His blood, the forgiveness of sins, according to the riches of His grace." (Ep.1:7)

- Out of the mercy and grace of God, His Word has flowed. Let every person know that God will have mercy upon him, forgiving and using him to fulfill His glorious plan of salvation.

  "For God so loved the world, that he gave His only begotten Son, that whosoever believeth in Him should not perish, but have everlasting life. For God sent not his son into the world to condemn the world, but that the world through him might be saved." (Jn.3:16-17)

  "For this is good and acceptable in the sight of God our Saviour; who will have all men to be saved, and to come unto the knowledge of the truth." (1 Ti.2:3-4)

10/22

The Preacher's Outline & Sermon Bible®

is written for God's servants to use in their study, teaching, and preaching of God's Holy Word...

- to share the Word of God with the world.
- to help believers, both ministers and laypersons, in their understanding, preaching, and teaching of God's Word.
- to do everything we possibly can to lead men, women, boys, and girls to give their hearts and lives to Jesus Christ and to secure the eternal life that He offers.
- to do all we can to minister to the needy of the world.
- to give Jesus Christ His proper place, the place the Word gives Him. Therefore, no work of Leadership Ministries Worldwide will ever be personalized.

ACKNOWLEDGMENTS AND BIBLIOGRAPHY

Every child of God is precious to the LORD and deeply loved. And every child as a servant of the LORD touches the lives of those who come in contact with him or his ministry. The writing ministries of the following servants have touched this work, and we are grateful that God brought their writings our way. We hereby acknowledge their ministry to us, being fully aware that there are so many others down through the years whose writings have touched our lives and who deserve mention, but whose names have faded from our memory. May our wonderful LORD continue to bless the ministries of these dear servants—and the ministries of us all—as we diligently labor to reach the world for Christ and to meet the desperate needs of those who suffer so much.

THE REFERENCE WORKS

Archer, Gleason L. Jr. *A Survey of Old Testament Introduction*. Chicago, IL: Moody Bible Institute of Chicago, 1974.

Baker's Dictionary of Theology. Everett F. Harrison, Editor-in-Chief. Grand Rapids, MI: Baker Book House, 1960.

Brown, Francis. *The New Brown-Driver-Briggs-Gesenius Hebrew-English Lexicon*. Peabody, MA: Hendrickson Publishers, 1979.

Cruden's Complete Concordance of the Old & New Testament. Philadelphia, PA: The John C. Winston Co., 1930.

Dake's Annotated Reference Bible, The Holy Bible. Finis Jennings Dake. Lawrenceville, GA: Dake Bible Sales, Inc., 1963.

Elwell, Walter A., Editor. *The Evangelical Dictionary of Theology*. Grand Rapids, MI: Baker Book House, 1984.

Encyclopedia of Biblical Prophecy. J. Barton Payne. New York, NY: Harper & Row, Publishers, 1973.

Funk & Wagnalls Standard Desk Dictionary. Lippincott & Crowell, Publishers, 1980, Vol.2.

Geisler, Norman. *A Popular Survey of the Old Testament*. Grand Rapids, MI: Baker Book House, 1977.

Good News Bible. Old Testament: © American Bible Society, 1976. New Testament: © American Bible Society, 1966, 1971, 1976. Collins World.

Good, Joseph. *Rosh HaShanah and the Messianic Kingdom to Come*. Pt. Arthur, TX: Hatikva Ministries, 1989.

Harrison, Roland Kenneth. *Introduction to the Old Testament*. Grand Rapids, MI: Eerdmans Publishing Company, 1969.

Josephus, Flavius. *Complete Works*. Grand Rapids, MI: Kregel Publications, 1981.

Kelley, Page H. *Exodus: Called for Redemptive Mission. January Bible Study*. Nashville, TN: Convention Press, 1977.

Kohlenberger, John R. III. *The Interlinear NIV Hebrew-English Old Testament*. Grand Rapids, MI: Zondervan Publishing House, 1987.

Life Application® Bible. Wheaton, IL: Tyndale House Publishers, Inc., 1991.

Lindsell, Harold and Woodbridge, Charles J. *A Handbook of Christian Truth*. Westwood, NJ: Fleming H. Revell Company, A Division of Baker Book House, 1953.

Lipis, Joan R. *Celebrate Passover Haggadah*. San Francisco, CA: Purple Pomegranate Productions, 1993.

Living Quotations for Christians. Edited by Sherwood Eliot Wirt and Kersten Beckstrom. New York, NY: Harper & Row, Publishers, 1974.

Lockyer, Herbert. *All the Books and Chapters of the Bible*. Grand Rapids, MI: Zondervan Publishing House, 1966.

———— . *All the Men of the Bible*. Grand Rapids, MI: Zondervan Publishing House, 1958.

———— . *The Women of the Bible*. Grand Rapids, MI: Zondervan Publishing House, 1967.

Martin, Alfred. *Survey of the Scriptures, Part I, II, III*. Chicago, IL: Moody Bible Institute of Chicago, 1961.

McDowell, Josh. *Evidence that Demands a Verdict*, Vol.1. San Bernardino, CA: Here's Life Publishers, Inc., 1979.

Miller, Madeleine S. & J. Lane. *Harper's Bible Dictionary*. New York, NY: Harper & Row Publishers, 1961.

Nave's Topical Bible. Orville J. Nave. Nashville, TN: The Southwestern Company. Copyright © by J.B. Henderson, 1921.

Nelson's Expository Dictionary of the Old Testament. Merrill F. Unger & William White, Jr. Nashville, TN: Thomas Nelson Publishers, 1980.

New American Standard Bible, Reference Edition. La Habra, CA: The Lockman Foundation, 1975.

New International Version Study Bible. Grand Rapids, MI: Zondervan Bible Publishers, 1985.

New Living Translation, Holy Bible. Wheaton, IL: Tyndale House Publishers, Inc., 1996.

NIV Exhaustive Concordance. Grand Rapids, MI: Zondervan Corporation, 1990.

Orr, William. *How We May Know That God Is*. Wheaton, IL: Van Kampen Press, n.d.

Owens, John Joseph. *Analytical Key to the Old Testament*, Vols.1, 2, 3. Grand Rapids, MI: Baker Book House, 1989.

Pilgrim Edition, Holy Bible. New York, NY: Oxford University Press, 1952.

Ridout, Samuel. *Lectures on the Tabernacle*. New York, NY: Loizeaux Brothers, Inc., 1914.

Roget's 21st Century Thesaurus, Edited by Barbara Ann Kipfer. New York, NY: Dell Publishing, 1992.

Rosen, Ceil and Moishe. *Christ in the Passover*. Chicago, IL: Moody Press, 1978.

Slemming, C.W. *Made According To Pattern*. Fort Washington, PA: Christian Literature Crusade, 1983.

Soltau, Henry W. *The Holy Vessels and Furniture of the Tabernacle*. Grand Rapids, MI: Kregel Publications, 1971.

———— . *The Tabernacle the Priesthood and the Offerings*. Grand Rapids, MI: Kregel Publications, 1972.

Stone, Nathan J. *Names of God*. Chicago, IL: Moody Press, 1944.

Strong's Exhaustive Concordance of the Bible. James Strong. Nashville, TN: Thomas Nelson, Inc., 1990.

Strong, James. *The Tabernacle of Israel*. Grand Rapids, MI: Kregel Publications, 1987.

The Amplified Bible. Scripture taken from THE AMPLIFIED BIBLE, Old Testament copyright © 1965, 1987 by the Zondervan Corporation. The Amplified New Testament copyright © 1958, 1987 by The Lockman Foundation. Used by permission.

The Hebrew-Greek Key Study Bible, New International Version. Spiros Zodhiates, Th.D., Executive Editor. Chattanooga, TN: AMG Publishers, 1996.

ACKNOWLEDGMENTS AND BIBLIOGRAPHY
REFERENCE WORKS
(continued)

The Holy Bible in Four Translations. Minneapolis, MN: Worldwide Publications. Copyright © The Iversen-Norman Associates: New York, NY, 1972.

The Interlinear Bible, Vol.1, 2, & 3, Translated by Jay P. Green, Sr. Grand Rapids, MI: Baker Book House Company, 1976.

The International Standard Bible Encyclopaedia, Edited by James Orr. Grand Rapids, MI: Eerdmans Publishing Company, 1939.

The NASB Greek/Hebrew Dictionary and Concordance. La Habra, CA: The Lockman Foundation, 1988.

The New Compact Bible Dictionary, Edited by T. Alton Bryant. Grand Rapids, MI: Zondervan Publishing House, 1967. Used by permission of Zondervan Publishing House.

The New Scofield Reference Bible, Edited by C.I. Scofield. New York, NY: Oxford University Press, 1967.

The New Thompson Chain Reference Bible. Indianapolis, IN: B.B. Kirkbride Bible Co., Inc., 1964.

The Open Bible. Nashville, TN: Thomas Nelson Publishers, 1975.

The Zondervan Pictorial Encyclopedia of the Bible, Vol.1. Merrill C. Tenney, Editor. Grand Rapids, MI: Zondervan Publishing House, 1982.

Theological Wordbook of the Old Testament, Edited by R. Laird Harris. Chicago, IL: Moody Bible Institute of Chicago, 1980.

Vine's Complete Expository Dictionary of Old and New Testament Words. W.E. Vine, Merrill F. Unger, William White, Jr. Nashville, TN: Thomas Nelson Publishers, 1985.

Webster's Seventh New Collegiate Dictionary. Springfield, MA: G. & C. Merriam Company, Publishers, 1971.

Wilson, William. *Wilson's Old Testament Word Studies*. McLean, VA: MacDonald Publishing Company, n.d.

Wood, Leon. *A Survey of Israel's History*. Grand Rapids, MI: Zondervan Publishing House, 1982.

Young's Analytical Concordance to the Bible. Robert Young. Grand Rapids, MI: Eerdmans Publishing Company, n.d.

Young, Edward J. *An Introduction to the Old Testament*. Grand Rapids, MI: Eerdmans Publishing Company, 1964.

Zehr, Paul M. *Glimpses of the Tabernacle*. Lancaster, PA: Mennonite Information Center, 1976.

THE COMMENTARIES

Barclay, William. *The Old Law & The New Law*. Edinburgh, Scotland: The Saint Andrew Press, 1972.

Barnes' Notes, Exodus to Esther. F.C. Cook, Editor. Grand Rapids, MI: Baker Book House, n.d.

Bonar, Andrew. *A Commentary on the Book of Leviticus*. Grand Rapids, MI: Baker Book House, 1978.

Bush, George. *Leviticus*. Minneapolis, MN: Klock & Klock Christian Publishers, Inc., 1981.

Demarest, Gary. *The Preacher's Commentary on Leviticus*. Dallas, TX: Word Publishing, 1990.

Gaebelein, Frank E. *The Expositor's Bible Commentary*, Vol.2. Grand Rapids, MI: Zondervan Publishing House, 1990.

Gill, John. *Gill's Commentary*, Vol.1. Grand Rapids, MI: Baker Book House, 1980.

Harrison, R.K. PH.D, D.D. *Leviticus*. "The Tyndale Old Testament Commentaries." Downers Grove, IL: InterVarsity Press, 1980.

Henry, Matthew. *Matthew Henry's Commentary*, 6 Volumes. Old Tappan, NJ: Fleming H. Revell Co., n.d.

Hewitt, Thomas. *The Epistle to the Hebrews*. "Tyndale New Testament Commentaries." Grand Rapids, MI: Eerdmans Publishing Co., Began in 1958.

Kellogg, D.D. *Leviticus*. Minneapolis, MN: Klock & Klock Christian Publishers, Inc., 1978.

Keil-Delitzsch. *Commentary on the Old Testament*, Vol.1. Grand Rapids, MI: Eerdmans Publishing Company, n.d.

Maclaren, Alexander. *Expositions of Holy Scripture*, 11 Vols. Grand Rapids, MI: Eerdmans Publishing Company, 1952-59.

McGee, J. Vernon. *Thru The Bible*, Vol.1. Nashville, TN: Thomas Nelson Publishers, 1981.

Olford, Stephen. *The Tabernacle, Camping With God*. Neptune, NJ: Loizeaux Brothers, 1971.

Pfeiffer, Charles F. *The Book of Leviticus*. "Shield Bible Study Series." Grand Rapids, MI: Baker Book House, 1957.

Pink, Arthur W. *The Ten Commandments*. Grand Rapids, MI: Baker Books, 1994.

Seiss, Joseph A. *Gospel in Leviticus*. Grand Rapids, MI: Kregel Publications, n.d.

The Interpreter's Bible, 12 Vols. New York, NY: Abingdon Press, 1956.

The Pulpit Commentary. 23 Volumes. Edited by H.D.M. Spence & Joseph S. Exell. Grand Rapids, MI: Eerdmans Publishing Company, 1950.

Thomas, W.H. Griffith. *Through the Pentateuch Chapter by Chapter*. Grand Rapids, MI: Eerdmans Publishing Company, 1957.

Wenham, Gordon J. *The Book of Leviticus*. "The New International Commentary on the Old Testament." Grand Rapids, MI: Eerdmans Publishing Co., 1979.

ABBREVIATIONS

&	= and		O.T.	= Old Testament
Bc.	= because		p./pp.	= page/pages
Concl.	= conclusion		Pt.	= point
Cp.	= compare		Quest.	= question
Ct.	= contrast		Rel.	= religion
e.g.	= for example		Rgt.	= righteousness
f.	= following		Thru	= through
Illust.	= illustration		v./vv.	= verse/verses
N.T.	= New Testament		vs.	= versus

THE BOOKS OF THE OLD TESTAMENT

Book	Abbreviation	Chapters	Book	Abbreviation	Chapters
GENESIS	Gen. or Ge.	50	Ecclesiastes	Eccl. or Ec.	12
Exodus	Ex.	40	The Song of Solomon	S. of Sol. or Song	8
Leviticus	Lev. or Le.	27	Isaiah	Is.	66
Numbers	Num. or Nu.	36	Jeremiah	Jer. or Je.	52
Deuteronomy	Dt. or De.	34	Lamentations	Lam.	5
Joshua	Josh. or Jos.	24	Ezekiel	Ezk. or Eze.	48
Judges	Judg. or Jud.	21	Daniel	Dan. or Da.	12
Ruth	Ruth or Ru.	4	Hosea	Hos. or Ho.	14
1 Samuel	1 Sam. or 1 S.	31	Joel	Joel	3
2 Samuel	2 Sam. or 2 S.	24	Amos	Amos or Am.	9
1 Kings	1 Ki. or 1 K.	22	Obadiah	Obad. or Ob.	1
2 Kings	2 Ki. or 2 K.	25	Jonah	Jon. or Jona.	4
1 Chronicles	1 Chron. or 1 Chr.	29	Micah	Mic. or Mi.	7
2 Chronicles	2 Chron. or 2 Chr.	36	Nahum	Nah. or Na.	3
Ezra	Ezra or Ezr.	10	Habakkuk	Hab.	3
Nehemiah	Neh. or Ne.	13	Zephaniah	Zeph. or Zep.	3
Esther	Est.	10	Haggai	Hag.	2
Job	Job or Jb.	42	Zechariah	Zech. or Zec.	14
Psalms	Ps.	150	Malachi	Mal.	4
Proverbs	Pr.	31			

THE BOOKS OF THE NEW TESTAMENT

Book	Abbreviation	Chapters	Book	Abbreviation	Chapters
MATTHEW	Mt.	28	1 Timothy	1 Tim. or 1 Ti.	6
Mark	Mk.	16	2 Timothy	2 Tim. or 2 Ti.	4
Luke	Lk. or Lu.	24	Titus	Tit.	3
John	Jn.	21	Philemon	Phile. or Phm.	1
The Acts	Acts or Ac.	28	Hebrews	Heb. or He.	13
Romans	Ro.	16	James	Jas. or Js.	5
1 Corinthians	1 Cor. or 1 Co.	16	1 Peter	1 Pt. or 1 Pe.	5
2 Corinthians	2 Cor. or 2 Co.	13	2 Peter	2 Pt. or 2 Pe.	3
Galatians	Gal. or Ga.	6	1 John	1 Jn.	5
Ephesians	Eph. or Ep.	6	2 John	2 Jn.	1
Philippians	Ph.	4	3 John	3 Jn.	1
Colossians	Col.	4	Jude	Jude	1
1 Thessalonians	1 Th.	5	Revelation	Rev. or Re.	22
2 Thessalonians	2 Th.	3			

HOW TO USE
The Preacher's Outline & Sermon Bible®
Follow these easy steps to gain maximum benefit from The POSB.

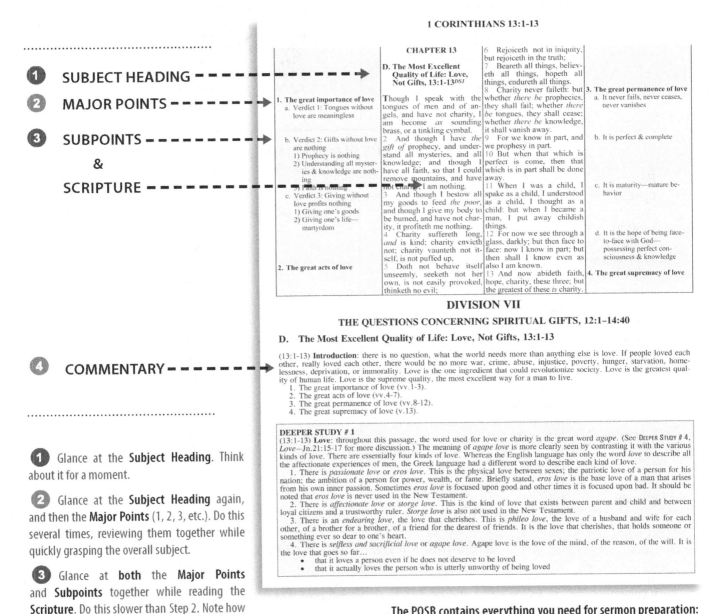

1. **SUBJECT HEADING**

2. **MAJOR POINTS**

3. **SUBPOINTS**
   &
   SCRIPTURE

4. **COMMENTARY**

CHAPTER 13

D. The Most Excellent Quality of Life: Love, Not Gifts, 13:1-13[DS1]

1. The great importance of love
   a. Verdict 1: Tongues without love are meaningless
   b. Verdict 2: Gifts without love are nothing
      1) Prophecy is nothing
      2) Understanding all mysteries & knowledge are nothing
      3) Faith is nothing
   c. Verdict 3: Giving without love profits nothing
      1) Giving one's goods
      2) Giving one's life—martyrdom

2. The great acts of love

Though I speak with the tongues of men and of angels, and have not charity, I am become as sounding brass, or a tinkling cymbal.
2 And though I have the gift of prophecy, and understand all mysteries, and all knowledge; and though I have all faith, so that I could remove mountains, and have not charity, I am nothing.
3 And though I bestow all my goods to feed the poor, and though I give my body to be burned, and have not charity, it profiteth me nothing.
4 Charity suffereth long, and is kind; charity envieth not; charity vaunteth not itself, is not puffed up,
5 Doth not behave itself unseemly, seeketh not her own, is not easily provoked, thinketh no evil;

6 Rejoiceth not in iniquity, but rejoiceth in the truth;
7 Beareth all things, believeth all things, hopeth all things, endureth all things.
8 Charity never faileth: but whether there be prophecies, they shall fail; whether there be tongues, they shall cease; whether there be knowledge, it shall vanish away.
9 For we know in part, and we prophesy in part.
10 But when that which is perfect is come, then that which is in part shall be done away.
11 When I was a child, I spake as a child, I understood as a child, I thought as a child: but when I became a man, I put away childish things.
12 For now we see through a glass, darkly; but then face to face: now I know in part; but then shall I know even as also I am known.
13 And now abideth faith, hope, charity, these three; but the greatest of these is charity.

3. The great permanence of love
   a. It never fails, never ceases, never vanishes
   b. It is perfect & complete
   c. It is maturity—mature behavior
   d. It is the hope of being face-to-face with God—possessing perfect consciousness & knowledge

4. The great supremacy of love

DIVISION VII
THE QUESTIONS CONCERNING SPIRITUAL GIFTS, 12:1–14:40
D. The Most Excellent Quality of Life: Love, Not Gifts, 13:1-13

(13:1-13) **Introduction:** there is no question, what the world needs more than anything else is love. If people loved each other, really loved each other, there would be no more war, crime, abuse, injustice, poverty, hunger, starvation, homelessness, deprivation, or immorality. Love is the one ingredient that could revolutionize society. Love is the greatest quality of human life. Love is the supreme quality, the most excellent way for a man to live.
1. The great importance of love (vv.1-3).
2. The great acts of love (vv.4-7).
3. The great permanence of love (vv.8-12).
4. The great supremacy of love (v.13).

DEEPER STUDY # 1
(13:1-13) **Love:** throughout this passage, the word used for love or charity is the great word *agape*. (See Deeper Study # 4, *Love*—Jn.21:15-17 for more discussion.) The meaning of *agape* love is more clearly seen by contrasting it with the various kinds of love. There are essentially four kinds of love. Whereas the English language has only the word *love* to describe all the affectionate experiences of men, the Greek language had a different word to describe each kind of love.
1. There is *passionate love* or *eros* love. This is the physical love between sexes; the patriotic love of a person for his nation; the ambition of a person for power, wealth, or fame. Briefly stated, *eros love* is the base love of a man that arises from his own inner passion. Sometimes *eros love* is focused upon good and other times it is focused upon bad. It should be noted that *eros love* is never used in the New Testament.
2. There is *affectionate love* or *storge* love. This is the kind of love that exists between parent and child and between loyal citizens and a trustworthy ruler. *Storge love* is also not used in the New Testament.
3. There is an *endearing love*, the love that cherishes. This is *phileo love*, the love of a husband and wife for each other, of a brother for a brother, of a friend for the dearest of friends. It is the love that cherishes, that holds someone or something ever so dear to one's heart.
4. There is *selfless and sacrificial love* or *agape love*. Agape love is the love of the mind, of the reason, of the will. It is the love that goes so far...
   - that it loves a person even if he does not deserve to be loved
   - that it actually loves the person who is utterly unworthy of being loved

---

① Glance at the **Subject Heading**. Think about it for a moment.

② Glance at the **Subject Heading** again, and then the **Major Points** (1, 2, 3, etc.). Do this several times, reviewing them together while quickly grasping the overall subject.

③ Glance at **both** the **Major Points** and **Subpoints** together while reading the **Scripture**. Do this slower than Step 2. Note how these points sit directly beside the related verse and simply restate what the Scripture is saying—in Outline form.

④ Next read the **Commentary**. Note that the *Major Point Numbers* in the Outline match those in the Commentary. A small raised number (**DS1**, **DS2**, etc.) at the end of a Subject Heading or Outline Point, directs you to a related **Deeper Study** in the Commentary.

Finally, read the **Thoughts** and **Support Scripture** (not shown).

As you read and re-read, pray that the Holy Spirit will bring to your attention exactly what you should preach and teach. May God bless you richly as you study and teach His Word.

The POSB contains everything you need for sermon preparation:

1. **The Subject Heading** describes the overall theme of the passage, and is located directly above the Scripture (keyed *alphabetically*).

2. **Major Points** are keyed with an outline *number* guiding you to related commentary. Note that the Commentary includes *"Thoughts"* (life application) and abundant Supporting Scriptures.

3. **Subpoints** explain and clarify the Scripture as needed.

4. **Commentary** is fully researched and developed for every point.
   - **Thoughts** (in bold) help apply the Scripture to real life.
   - **Deeper Studies** provide in-depth discussions of key words.

"Woe is unto me, if I
preach not the gospel"
(1 Co.9:16)

TABLE OF CONTENTS
LEVITICUS

LEVITICUS

INTRODUCTION

AUTHOR: Moses, the great lawgiver of Israel. Moses was the great leader who led Israel from Egyptian bondage and through the wilderness wanderings. The evidence is strong—very strong—that Moses is the author. The great *Pulpit Commentary* says this in its Introduction to *Genesis*:

> *There does not appear, however, to have been any serious questioning on the subject of the Mosaic authorship of the Pentateuch as a whole, or of Genesis as a part of that larger work, until the sixteenth century, when it began to be insinuated by Masius (1574), Spinoza (1670), and Anton Van Dale (1696), that not Moses, the Hebrew lawgiver, but Ezra, the priest-prophet of the Restoration, was the first composer of those parts of sacred Scripture.*[1]

This means, of course, that the earlier Biblical commentators—those who lived and wrote before the *sixteenth century*—held that Moses was the author. Any serious suggestion that he might not be did not arise until the sixteenth century.

For several centuries now there has been a popular theory that is called "the documentary hypothesis." This theory says there are four major sources for the Pentateuch, each of which was written sometime between 900–400 B.C. These sources are said to be...

- *J* (for Jehovah or Yahweh). This represents the writer or source that used the Hebrew name *Jehovah* or *Yahweh* for God throughout the Pentateuch.
- *E* (for Elohim). This represents the writer or source that used the Hebrew name *Elohim* for God.
- *D* (for Deuteronomist). This represents the writer or source that recorded the different accounts of the law throughout the Pentateuch.
- *P* (for Priestly). This represents the writer or source that recorded the information dealing with the *priests*.

Since *Leviticus* deals primarily with the Levitical priesthood and worship of Israel, the author of the book is said to be from the Priestly source. The first person to suggest the theory of "the documentary hypothesis" was a French physician, Jean Astruc, in 1752. Note that he was a physician, not a theologian. The theory was later picked up by the German historian and Biblical writer, J.G. Eichhorn in 1787. However, "the documentary hypothesis" was not thoroughly developed and popularized until Julius Wellhausen who lived in 1844–1918 (Victor Hamilton. *The Book of Genesis*, Chapters 1–17, p.13).

The NIV Study Bible has an excellent statement in answer to the critics of the Mosaic authorship:

> *Modern criticism has attributed practically the whole book to priestly legislation written during or after the exile. But this is without objective evidence, is against the repeated claim of the book to be Mosaic, is against the traditional Jewish view, and runs counter to other OT and NT witness (Ro 10:5). Many items in Leviticus are now seen to be best explained in terms of a second-millennium B.C. date, which is also the most likely time for Moses to have written the Pentateuch (see Introduction to Genesis: Author and Date of Writing). There is no convincing reason not to take at face value the many references to Moses and his work.*[2]

The great weight of evidence points to Moses as the author of *Leviticus*. The evidence can be summarized in the following points.

1. The book of *Leviticus* actually opens and closes with the statement that God gave the instructions or material of *Leviticus* to Moses. In fact, *Leviticus* declares that the LORD spoke to Moses some fifty-six times.

> **"And the LORD called unto Moses, and spake unto him out of the tabernacle of the congregation" (Le.1:1).**
> These *are* the commandments, which the LORD commanded Moses for the children of Israel in mount Sinai" (Le.27:34).

2. Ezra the scribe referred to Moses as the author of *Leviticus* when he dedicated the rebuilt Temple. *Leviticus* is the book that covers the procedure that was to be followed in dedicating the Temple, the actual installation of the priests and Levites in their various divisions and groups.

> **"And they set the priests in their divisions, and the Levites in their courses, for the service of God, which is at Jerusalem; as it is written in the book of Moses" (Ezr.6:18).**

3. Jesus Christ Himself, after healing a leper, set His seal of approval upon *Leviticus* and referred to Moses as its author.

> **"And, behold, there came a leper and worshipped him, saying, Lord, if thou wilt, thou canst make me clean. And Jesus put forth his hand, and touched him, saying, I will; be thou clean. And immediately his leprosy was cleansed. And Jesus saith unto him, See thou tell no man; but go thy way, show thyself to the priest, and offer the gift that Moses commanded, for a testimony unto them" (Mt.8:2-4).**

---

[1] "The Pulpit Commentary," Vol.1, ed. by HDM Spence and Joseph S. Exell. (Grand Rapids, MI: Eerdmans Publishing Co., 1950), p. 88.
[2] *The NIV Study Bible*. Kenneth Barker, General Editor. (Grand Rapids, MI: The Zondervan Corporation, 1985), p.147.

4. The Old Testament always refers without exception to Moses as the author of the Pentateuch (Jos.1:7-8; 8:31-32; 1 K.2:3; 8:9, 53; 2 K.10:31; 14:6; Ezr.6:18; Ne.13:1; Da.9:11-13; Mal.4:4).

5. The New Testament always refers to Moses as the author of the Pentateuch which includes *Leviticus* (Mt.8:4; 19:7-8; 23:2; Mk.1:44; 7:10; 10:3-4; 12:19, 26; Lu.5:14; 16:29-31; 20:37; 24:27, 44; Jn.1:17; 3:14; 5:45-46; 6:32; 7:19, 22-23; Acts 3:22; 13:39; 15:1, 5, 21; 26:22; 28:23; Ro.10:5, 19; 1 Co.9:9; 2 Co.3:15). The weight of the Scriptural evidence is that Moses is the author of the whole Pentateuch including *Leviticus*.

6. Several prophets quote or refer to *Leviticus*:
   ⇒ Amos 2:7 quotes Le.20:3.
   ⇒ Hosea 4:10 refers to Le.26:26.
   ⇒ Joel 1:13-16; 2:1, 14-27 refer to *Leviticus* Chapter 26.
   ⇒ Ezekiel 34:25-31 refers to *Leviticus* Chapter 26; Eze.22:26 to Le.10:10; Eze.20:11 to Le.18:5.

7. The discovery of the Ras shamra Tablets (about 1500–1300 B.C.) along the Syrian coast supports the authorship of Moses. Terminology used in the tablets closely parallel that of *Leviticus*. "Terms such as 'burnt offering,' and 'peace offering' appear in the [tablets]."[3]

DATE: Moses obviously wrote *Leviticus* some time between 1445–1406 B.C., perhaps closer to 1406 B.C.

God gave the laws and instructions of *Leviticus* to Moses when Israel was camped at Mt. Sinai. This was about 1445 B.C. However, all the events covered by *Leviticus* were compiled by Moses into a book at a later date. Perhaps they were recorded toward the end of the wilderness journey, sometime close to 1406 B.C. (see *Introduction, Date—Genesis* for more discussion).

TO WHOM WRITTEN: Israel in particular and all people in general. The Israelites as well as all succeeding generations needed to understand two basic facts about life:
   ⇒ First, there is only one way to become acceptable to God.
   ⇒ Second, God's people are to live holy lives. They are to keep pure bodies and pure spirits.

This is the message of *Leviticus*. This is a message that needs to be taught to all people of all generations.

PURPOSE: three purposes are clearly seen in the great book of *Leviticus*.
   1. The Historical Purpose: to give people a handbook on day to day behavior, a handbook that covers two basic subjects:
      a. How to approach God and become acceptable to Him (1:1–10:20).
      b. How to live a clean, holy life...
         • a life of love, joy, and peace
         • a life of purpose, meaning, and significance
         • a life of fulfillment, satisfaction, and completion (11:1–27:34)

   2. The Doctrinal or Spiritual Purpose: to learn more and more about God and about what it means to be a true believer. There are two major teachings in *Leviticus*.
      a. First, there is the teaching about God: God is holy. This means that God is completely different and set apart from man. Therefore, a person can approach God only as God dictates (1:1–10:20):
         ⇒ through the death or shed blood of the perfect sacrifice (a symbol of Christ's atoning sacrifice)
         ⇒ through the ministry of the perfect High Priest, the Mediator who stands between God and man (a symbol of Christ)

      b. Second, there is the teaching about the need to live a holy, clean life. Since God is holy, a person must be holy. A person must live a holy, clean life (11:1–27:34).
   3. The Christological or Christ-centered Purpose: the great book of *Leviticus* points to Jesus Christ...
      • as the perfect Sacrifice, the Lamb of God who takes away the sin of the world (1:1–7:38; see Jn.1:29)
      • as the perfect High Priest, the Mediator who represents man before God (8:1–10:20)
      • as the One who has the power to cleanse a person and the power to help a person live a clean, holy life (11:1–27:34)

SPECIAL FEATURES:
   1. *Leviticus* is "A Great Book Written to Be a Schoolmaster or Guardian" to bring us to Christ. The Law of the Old Testament was the guardian or schoolmaster put in charge of the human race for the purpose of bringing people to Christ. *Leviticus* is a part of that law; therefore *Leviticus* serves the purpose of a schoolmaster or guardian, written to bring us to Christ.
   2. *Leviticus* is "A Great Book on Holiness." The words "holy," "sanctify," "clean," "unclean," and their derivatives or equivalents occur more than 350 times in *Leviticus*. God reveals one basic truth: He is holy; therefore He demands that His people live holy, clean lives.
   3. *Leviticus* is "The Great Book Covering the Sacrificial Offerings." In order to become acceptable to God, a person had to approach God through the offering of an animal sacrifice, an animal without defect, that is, perfect. The death of the unblemished sacrifice was a type of the death of Jesus Christ, the Lamb of God who takes away the sins of the world (Jn.1:29). By His death, Jesus Christ paid the penalty for sin. The death of the sacrifice was *substitutionary*. Jesus Christ, the perfect Sacrifice, died as our Substitute—died for us, in our behalf, in our stead—once-for-all.

---

3   Charles F. Pfeiffer. *The Book of Leviticus*. "Shield Bible Study Series." (Grand Rapids, MI: Baker Book House, 1957), p.5.

INTRODUCTION TO LEVITICUS

"And walk in love, as Christ also hath loved us, and hath given himself for us an offering and a sacrifice to God for a sweetsmelling savour" (Ep.5:2).

"Who gave himself for us, that he might redeem us from all iniquity, and purify unto himself a peculiar people, zealous of good works" (Tit.2:14).

"For Christ is not entered into the holy places made with hands, *which are* the figures of the true; but into heaven itself, now to appear in the presence of God for us: Nor yet that he should offer himself often, as the high priest entereth into the holy place every year with blood of others; For then must he often have suffered since the foundation of the world: but now once in the end of the world hath he appeared to put away sin by the sacrifice of himself" (He.9:24-26).

"For by one offering he hath perfected for ever them that are sanctified" (He.10:14).

"Who his own self bare our sins in his own body on the tree, that we, being dead to sins, should live unto righteousness: by whose stripes ye were healed" (1 Pe.2:24).

"For Christ also hath once suffered for sins, the just for the unjust, that he might bring us to God, being put to death in the flesh, but quickened by the Spirit" (1 Pe.3:18).

4. *Leviticus* is "The Great Book on Atonement (Reconciliation with God)." The word "atonement" (kipper) means to pay a ransom or the ransom price paid (for a person's life). It is used about forty-five times in *Leviticus*. It can also mean to cleanse or wash away or to cover. The blood of animal sacrifices did not take away sin. They only pictured or symbolized the perfect sacrifice of Christ who was to take away the sin of the world. The offering of His sinless, perfect life was the Ideal Sacrifice, the Ideal Ransom. Therefore, the ransom price He paid—the Perfect, Ideal Sacrifice—makes atonement, reconciling us to God. J. Vernon McGee has an excellent statement on atonement that is well worth quoting in full:

> *Atonement means to "cover up." The blood of bulls and goats did not actually take away sin. It covered over sin until Christ came to take away all sins. This is what Paul is referring to in Romans 3:25: "Whom God hath set forth to be a propitiation through faith in his blood, to declare his righteousness for the remission of sins that are past, through the forbearance of God."*
>
> *The sins that are past are the sins back in the Old Testament. You see, God never accepted the blood of bulls and goats as the final payment for sin, but He required that blood be shed. It was an atonement to cover over the sins until Christ came. In other words, God saved 'on credit' in the Old Testament. When Christ came, as the hymn accurately states it, "Jesus paid it all." This is true as far as the past is concerned, and as far as the present is concerned, and as far as the future is concerned.*[4]

"For the life of the flesh *is* in the blood: and I have given it to you upon the altar to make an atonement for your souls: for it *is* the blood *that* maketh an atonement for the soul" (Le.17:11).

"For if, when we were enemies, we were reconciled to God by the death of his Son, much more, being reconciled, we shall be saved by his life. And not only *so*, but we also joy in God through our Lord Jesus Christ, by whom we have now received the atonement" (Ro.5:10-11).

5. *Leviticus* is "The Great Book that Covers 'the Great Day of Atonement'" (see outline and notes—16:1-34 for discussion).

6. *Leviticus* is "The Great Book on Substitution, the Substitute Sacrifice" (see points 3 and 4 for discussion).

7. *Leviticus* is "A Great Book Symbolizing the Atoning Sacrifice of Christ." Jesus Christ is the Lamb of God who was to come and take away the sins of the world (Jn.1:29). (See outline and notes—Le.1:1–7:38.)

8. *Leviticus* is "A Great Book Revealing the Terrible Tragedy of Sin." Man rejects God: curses, denies, questions, and rebels against God. Man disobeys God and His commandments in every conceivable way. Man sins against God, and the consequence of sin is separation, alienation from God and death—both physical and spiritual death. Sin and its terrible consequences were the reason why God instituted...

• the way for a person to become acceptable to Him (1:1–10:20)
• the way for a person to live a holy life before Him (11:1–27:34)

9. *Leviticus* is "A Great Book Revealing the Only Way to Approach God." This is one of the major purposes for the book of *Leviticus*. The outline clearly shows this:

⇒ THE WAY TO BECOME ACCEPTABLE TO GOD (PART 1): BY THE OFFERING OF A PERFECT SACRIFICE, A SUBSTITUTE (1:1–7:38)
⇒ THE WAY TO BECOME ACCEPTABLE TO GOD (PART 2): BY THE PRIESTHOOD, A PERFECT MEDIATOR (8:1–10:20)

10. *Leviticus* is "A Great Book on the High Priest, the Perfect Mediator." *Leviticus* could be called "The Handbook of the Priests" because the duties and ministry of the priests are covered. The ordination of the priests is also recorded. The importance of the High Priest in representing the people before God is clearly seen in the sacrificial offerings. The absolute necessity for the High Priest—a mediator—to stand before God in behalf of the people runs throughout *Leviticus*. The High Priest is a striking picture of Jesus Christ, our Great High Priest.

"But Christ being come an high priest of good things to come, by a greater and more perfect tabernacle, not made with hands, that is to say, not of this building; Neither by the blood of goats and calves, but by his own blood he entered in once into the holy place, having obtained eternal redemption for us. For if the blood of bulls and of goats, and the ashes of an heifer sprinkling the

---

4   J. Vernon McGee. *Thru The Bible*, Vol.1. (Nashville, TN: Thomas Nelson Publishers, 1981), p.322.

unclean, sanctifieth to the purifying of the flesh: How much more shall the blood of Christ, who through the eternal Spirit offered himself without spot to God, purge your conscience from dead works to serve the living God?" (He.9:11-14).

11. *Leviticus* is "A Great Book of Symbols and Types," (see Chart on Types, Symbols, and Pictures). A large number of symbols and types are clearly seen, focusing upon two major subjects:
> ⇒ the sacrifice, High Priesthood, and mission of Jesus Christ (1:1–10:20)
> ⇒ the desperate need of man for cleansing and holiness (11:1–27:34)

12. *Leviticus* is "The Great Book Covering the Institution of the Feasts or Festivals of Israel" (23:1-44). It is here in *Leviticus* where God instructed the Israelites to celebrate certain feasts or festivals on a regular basis. (See outline and note—Le.3:1-44 for more discussion.)

13. *Leviticus* is "The Great Book that Gives 'the Prophetic Picture of Salvation'" (see chart at the end of outline and notes—Le.23:1-44 for discussion).

14. *Leviticus* is "A Great Book on Sanctification, Consecration, and Separation from the World" (11:1–27:34). This is one of the major themes of *Leviticus*: God's people are to live lives of separation, lives that are different from the immoral and lawless of this earth, lives that are sanctified or consecrated to God. The believer's body and spirit are to be totally given over to God (11:1–27:34).

15. *Leviticus* is "A Great Book on Social Justice—Proclaiming Liberty throughout the Land (25:1-55). It is here that God instituted the great *Year of Jubilee,* the year when all debts were declared paid in full and all property was returned to its original owner and all slaves were given their freedom. The Year of Jubilee was instituted by God to assure social justice among God's people. The great declaration chiseled on America's famous Statue of Liberty was taken from this striking passage: "Proclaim liberty throughout all the land to all the inhabitants" (Le.25:10).

16. *Leviticus* is "A Great Book Revealing God's Word to His People." The very first Hebrew word of this great book is *wayyigra,* which means "and he [God] called." (1:1). Phrases such as "the LORD spoke to Moses" are used over fifty-six times in *Leviticus* (see 1:1; 4:1; etc.). Up to this point, God had been speaking to the Israelites from Mt. Sinai; but now, throughout *Leviticus,* He spoke from the Tabernacle

17. *Leviticus* is "A Great Book on the Abiding Presence of God." There is, of course, the general, permanent presence of God that always dwells with His people. But in Israel's case, there was far more than this: there was a special manifestation of the LORD's presence dwelling continually above the ark in the Tabernacle. All the sacrifices were performed "before the LORD" (1:5, 11; etc.). The offerings were "a sweet aroma for the LORD" (1:9, 13, 17; 2:9; etc.). The LORD spoke over and over to Moses from the Tabernacle (1:1; 4:1; etc.). The abiding presence of God—God with His people—is one of the underlying themes of *Leviticus.*

OUTLINE OF LEVITICUS

THE PREACHER'S OUTLINE AND SERMON BIBLE® is unique. It differs from all other Study Bibles and Sermon Resource Materials in that every Passage and Subject is outlined right beside the Scripture. When you choose any *Subject* below and turn to the reference, you have not only the Scripture but also an outline of the Scripture and Subject *already prepared for you—verse by verse.*

For a quick example, choose one of the subjects below and turn over to the Scripture; you will find this to be a marvelous help for more *organized* and *streamlined* study.

In addition, every point of the Scripture and Subject is *fully developed in a Commentary with supporting Scripture* at the end of each point. Again, this arrangement makes sermon preparation much simpler and more efficient.

Note something else: the Subjects of *Leviticus* have titles that are both Biblical and *practical*. The practical titles are often more appealing to people. This benefit is clearly seen for use on billboards, bulletins, church newsletters, etc.

A suggestion: for the *quickest* overview of *Leviticus*, first read all the Division titles (I, II, III, etc.), then come back and read the individual outline titles.

OUTLINE OF LEVITICUS

I.   THE WAY TO BECOME ACCEPTABLE TO GOD (PART 1): BY THE OFFERING OF A PERFECT SACRIFICE, A SUBSTITUTE, 1:1–7:38

    A.   The Burnt Offering (a Picture of Christ's Atoning Sacrifice): The Only Way to Approach God, to Become Reconciled and Acceptable to God, 1:1-17

    B.   The Grain or Meal Offering (a Picture of Christ, the Bread of Life): The Way to Give Thanks and to Show One's Dedication to God, 2:1-16

    C.   The Fellowship or Peace Offering (a Picture of Christ's Atoning Sacrifice): The Way to Grow in the Peace and Fellowship of God—Seeking a Deeper Life with God, 3:1-17

    D.   The Sin Offering (a Picture of Christ's Atoning Sacrifice): The Way to Secure Forgiveness of Sin, 4:1–5:13

    E.   The Guilt Offering (a Picture of Christ's Atoning Sacrifice): The Way to Be Set Free from the Weight and Anguish of Guilt, the Pricking of Conscience, 5:14–6:7

    F.   The Special Duties of the Priests in Conducting the Offerings: The Duties of Ministers, 6:8–7:38

II.   THE WAY TO BECOME ACCEPTABLE TO GOD (PART 2): BY THE PRIESTHOOD, A MEDIATOR, 8:1–10:20

    A.   The Ordination of the Priests: The Steps to Ordination, 8:1-36

    B.   The Work and Ministry of the Ordained Priest (Minister): Showing People How to Become Acceptable to God, 9:1-24

    C.   The Judgment of God upon Two Priests (Nadab and Abihu) for Their False Worship: Fate of All Who Approach God in a Wrong Way, 10:1-20

III.   THE WAY TO LIVE A HOLY LIFE BEFORE GOD (PART I): BY A CLEAN BODY (SEPARATION), 11:1–16:34

    A.   Laws That Govern Clean and Unclean Animals: Symbolizes Physical and Spiritual Purity—by Eating the Right Foods, 11:1-47

    B.   Laws That Protect Mother and Child Right After Childbirth: Symbolizes the Need for Cleansing from the Sinful Nature, 12:1-8

    C.   Laws That Protect People From Leprosy or Infectious Skin Disease: Symbolizes the Disease of Sin and the Need to Prevent the Spread of Sin, 13:1-59

    D.   Laws That Cleanse and Restore People from Leprosy, from All Forms of Infectious Skin Disease: Symbolizes the Need for Spiritual Cleansing, 14:1-57

    E.   Laws That Protect and Cleanse People from Diseases of Sexual Impurity: Symbolizes How Defiling Sin Is and the Need to Be Cleansed from Sin, 15:1-33

    F.   The Great Provision of God to Make a Person Holy, the Great Day of Atonement: Symbolizes the Only Way to Approach God—Through the Shed Blood of the Atoning Sacrifice, 16:1-34

IV. THE WAY TO LIVE A HOLY LIFE BEFORE GOD (PART 2): BY A PURE SPIRIT (SANCTIFICATION), 17:1–27:34

A. Laws Necessary to Preserve the Atonement: Two Strong Prohibitions, One Against Idolatry and One Against Abusing the Shed Blood of the Sacrifice, 17:1-16

B. Laws That Govern Sexual Behavior: The Prohibition Against Illicit Sex and Sexual Perversion, 18:1-30

C. Laws That Govern Day-to-Day Behavior, Personal Conduct: The Duty to Live a Life of Separation, a Life of Real Devotion to God, 19:1-37

D. Laws That Spell Out the Punishment for Terrible Crimes, 20:1-27

E. Laws That Govern the Priests, the Ministers of God (Part 1): The Basic Requirements and Qualifications for the Minister of God, 21:1-24

F. Laws That Govern the Priests, the Ministers of God (Part 2): The Basic Duties of the Minister of God, 22:1-33

G. Laws That Govern the Annual Feasts or Festivals of Worship: The Prophetic Picture of Salvation, 23:1-44

H. Laws That Govern the Lampstand, the Holy Bread, and the Cursing of God: The Availability of God and the Judgment Against Cursing God, 24:1-23

I. Laws That Govern the Use of Property and the Treatment of the Poor: Social Justice—Proclaim Liberty Throughout the Land, 25:1-55

J. The Exhortations to Obey God: God's Promises and Warnings to His People, 26:1-46

K. Laws That Govern Vows and Commitments Made to God: The Critical Importance of Keeping Sacred Vows, 27:1-34

DIVISION I

THE WAY TO BECOME ACCEPTABLE
TO GOD (PART 1): BY THE OFFERING OF
A SACRIFICE, A SUBSTITUTE, 1:1–7:38

(1:1–7:38) **DIVISION OVERVIEW**: from the very beginning of human history, man has sensed his alienation (separation) from God and the need to be reconciled to God. People who are knowledgeable and who are spiritually-minded and honest have acknowledged that they could never reach God, never secure reconciliation with Him, not on their own. They have confessed the obvious truth...

- that God is Spirit, of the spiritual world, and man cannot penetrate the spiritual world: the physical just cannot enter the spiritual world, not in and by its own strength nor by its own power.
- that God is perfect and man is imperfect, that man's imperfection can never be allowed to enter God's presence lest his imperfection taint the perfection of God and the spiritual world.

What then can man do? Is he hopelessly lost and separated from God forever? This is where the Burnt Offering entered.

1. The Burnt Offering is the offering that symbolized or pictured the atonement, the offering that symbolized the perfect sacrifice—the sacrificial substitute that would take the place of man, bear his sins and the judgment of God against sins. Simply stated, atonement means to ransom, to pay the price for. The perfect sacrifice, the substitute without defect and without blemish, is Jesus Christ, God's very own Son. Jesus Christ paid the price, the penalty of sin for man. He is the perfect sacrifice and substitute who died...

- for man
- in behalf of man
- in the place of man
- instead of man

Before Christ, God instructed people to approach Him through the Burnt Offering, through the sacrifice of an animal without defect or blemish, an animal that was considered perfect, an animal that symbolized or pictured the *promised seed* who was yet to come. But when Christ came, note what happened:

⇒ "But when the fullness of time came, God sent forth His Son, made of a...woman, made under the law, to redeem them that were under the law....that we might receive the adoption of sons" (Ga.4:4-5).

The LORD Jesus Christ, the Son of God...

- was "the Lamb of God who takes away the sin of the world" (Jn.1:29).
- was the fulfillment of the Burnt Offering, the perfect Sacrifice and Substitute who died for man, who redeemed man.

The Burnt Offering was the very first approach man ever made to seek reconciliation with God. No doubt God told the very first family, the family of Adam, to seek reconciliation through the Burnt Offering. Thus, Adam's son Abel is seen seeking God through the sacrifice of an animal, obviously the Burnt Offering (Ge.4:4). Scripture tells us time and again that believers—those who truly followed God—sought to be reconciled with God through the Burnt Offering. This is seen from the very beginning of human history:

⇒ Abel (Ge.4:4)
⇒ Noah (Ge.8:20)
⇒ Abraham (Ge.22:9)
⇒ Jacob (Ge.46:1)
⇒ Moses demanded that Israel be freed from Egypt so they could worship the LORD through sacrifices and Burnt Offerings (Ex.10:25).

2. But note this fact: there are at least two factors that necessitated more than one offering, more than the sacrifice offered in the Burnt Offering. These two factors are clearly seen within the nature of man and the plan of God in sending His Son to be the Savior of the world.

First, man has several very basic needs that must be met through his worship of God. All of these needs cannot be met through one type of offering or sacrifice. For example, man has a need to express thanksgiving and dedication to God, the need to have his sins forgiven, and the need to have his guilt removed. All these needs are not fully pictured or symbolized in the Burnt Offering. Man just needs other offerings to picture and symbolize how God meets his needs, offerings that fully express his worship of God.

Second, man needs to understand the complete ministry of Jesus Christ. Scripture clearly says that all the offerings and sacrifices—even the Tabernacle and the Priesthood—were all a symbol or type of Jesus Christ: His perfect life, ministry, and sacrifice (see Hebrews, chapters 5–10).

This is the reason for the offerings, to meet the basic needs of man and help him understand God's Son, the Lord Jesus Christ. This is, in fact, the very purpose for the entire book of Leviticus: to reveal the holiness of God and the need for man to live a holy and righteous life before God. Moreover, one of the ways God reveals man's need to be holy is through the offerings, the offerings that so clearly symbolize the sacrificial death of Jesus Christ.

⇒ Through the offerings, man's need to approach God for acceptance, and to worship and live before God is symbolized.

⇒ Through the offerings, man's need to see and grasp the full ministry of Jesus Christ is met (see the next point, point three).

> **"And walk in love, as Christ also hath loved us, and hath given himself for us an offering and a sacrifice to God for a sweetsmelling savour" (Ep.5:2).**

3. The offerings picture the believer's life and walk before the LORD. When we look at the offerings, we see a sequence, an overview of the believer's life with God.

a. The Burnt Offering: pictured the atonement, the ransom price paid so that man might escape the death penalty demanded by God's holiness. To say it another way, the Burnt Offering pictured the atonement, the ransom price paid to reconcile and make the person acceptable to God (Le.1:3-4). In today's terms, this is a picture of salvation, of Jesus Christ dying for us, of His paying the ransom price so that we might escape the penalty of death and live forever with God.

b. The Grain Offering: pictured the believer's thanksgiving to God both for the atonement and for God's provision of food and all the other necessities of life. It also pictured dedication when the Grain Offering was being laid upon the sacrifice of the Burnt Offering. The person was symbolizing that he was laying his life and dependence upon God. In today's terms, this is a picture of thanksgiving and dedication being offered to God for salvation and for God's goodness in meeting all of our needs.

c. The Fellowship or Peace Offering: pictured the way to grow in peace and fellowship with God. Once a person was reconciled to God, he immediately gave thanks to God (the Grain Offering). He was then to walk forth seeking to *grow* in the fellowship and peace of God. When sensing a special need for God's presence and spiritual growth, he was to offer the Fellowship or Peace Offering.

d. The Sin Offering: pictured the way to secure forgiveness of sins. As the believer walked about growing in fellowship and peace with God, he found himself faced with a barrage of temptations and trials. In fact, the more he grew in fellowship and peace with God, the more he saw just how short he was of God's glory, just how much he disobeyed God. He needed forgiveness of sins—continual forgiveness. The Sin Offering met his need, gave him a way to secure forgiveness of sin as he walked in open confession day by day.

e. The Guilt Offering: pictured the way to be set free from the weight and anguish of guilt, the pricking of conscience. Suppose a believer refused to confess and ask forgiveness for his sin. His standing, his position before God, was guilty. He was to be judged and condemned unless he repented. The Guilt Offering met his need. When a person approached God through the Guilt Offering, God forgave his sin and removed the guilt. He was set free, ready to begin his life and walk with the LORD anew, in a spirit of thanksgiving and rededication (the symbol of the Grain Offering).

Note how the life and walk of the believer are progressive. Note also how the offerings give an overview of the life and walk of the believer. In simple statements, the believer…

• is saved through the atonement of Jesus Christ upon the cross (the Burnt Offering)
• gives thanks and dedicates his life to God immediately (the Grain Offering)
• begins to walk and grow in the fellowship and peace of God (the Fellowship Offering or Peace Offering)
• walks in open confession of sin throughout the day in order to maintain fellowship with God (the Sin Offering)
• experiences the pricking of conscience, the weight and anguish of guilt, if he refuses to repent of sin. He not only suffers guilt but he also stands guilty before God until he confesses and turns back to God (the Guilt Offering).

THE SACRIFICES OR OFFERINGS OF THE OLD TESTAMENT
SYMBOLS POINTING TO JESUS CHRIST AS THE SUBSTITUTE SACRIFICE[1]

THE OFFERING & ITS PURPOSE	THE ELEMENTS & HOW ONE SECURED THE PROMISE OF THE OFFERING	THE SYMBOLISM: HOW THE OFFERING POINTS TO JESUS CHRIST
The Burnt Offering: To provide the atonement or reconciliation with God. The Burnt Offering was the only way to approach God, to become reconciled, acceptable to God, Le.1:1-17	A person secured atonement or reconciliation with God through the substitute sacrifice: ⇒ The rich person by offering the sacrifice of a male bull without defect	The Burnt Offering is a type of Christ, a picture of Christ dying as the substitute sacrifice for us. By dying for us: ⇒ Christ bore the full justice and judgment of God against sin—paid the ransom price to deliver us from sin and death

THE SACRIFICES OR OFFERINGS OF THE OLD TESTAMENT

THE OFFERING & ITS PURPOSE	THE ELEMENTS & HOW ONE SECURED THE PROMISE OF THE OFFERING	THE SYMBOLISM: HOW THE OFFERING POINTS TO JESUS CHRIST
OTHER SCRIPTURE REFERENCES: Le.6:8-13; 8:18-21; 9:2; 16:24; Ex.29:18; Nu.28:3-15; 29:6; De.33:8-10; Jos.8:31; 1 S.6:15; 7:9; 2 S.24:25; 1 K.3:4; 1 Chr.16:40; 2 Chr.13:11; Ezr.3:3; Ps.40:6; Ep.5:2	⇒ The average person by offering the sacrifice of a male sheep or goat without defect ⇒ The poor person by offering the sacrifice of a dove or young pigeon Note: The sacrifice was totally consumed by fire. This is a symbol that the sacrifice paid the full ransom to free the believer from sin and death; the sacrifice bore the full punishment of God's justice and judgment that was due the sinner.	⇒ Christ secured the atonement or reconciliation with God for us "...by whom [Christ] we have now received the atonement" (Ro.5:11).
The Grain or Meal Offering: To provide the way to express thanksgiving and the dedication of one's life to God, Le.2:1-15 OTHER SCRIPTURE REFERENCES: Le.6:14-23; 9:17; 10:12; 23:18; Nu.15:4; 28:5	A person expressed his thanks and the dedication of his life to God by giving the best of his grain. The offering... • was to be of fine flour mixed with olive oil and some incense and without yeast or honey • could be cooked in an oven, a griddle, or a pan • was seasoned with salt Note: the Grain Offering was offered on top of the Burnt Offering of the daily sacrifice. This was... • a declaration of thanksgiving to God for the atonement (reconciliation) and for all else God had done • a declaration of laying one's life upon God—all one was and had—and dedicating oneself totally to God	The Grain or Meal Offering is a type of Christ, a picture of Christ as the Bread of Life. Jesus Christ is the Bread of Life... • Who satisfies the hunger of our souls for God and for purpose, meaning, and significance • Who satisfies us so much that we break out in joy, giving thanks to God for the atonement (reconciliation) and for all else God has done • Who satisfies us to the point of dedication, committing all we are and have to God "I am the bread of life: he that cometh to me shall never hunger; and he that believeth on me shall never thirst" (Jn.6:35).
The Fellowship or Peace Offering: To provide the way to grow in the peace and fellowship of God—seeking a deeper life with God, Le.3:1-17 OTHER SCRIPTURE REFERENCES: Le.7:11-34; 9:4; 9:18; 17:1-9; 19:5-8; Ex.20:24; 24:5; 29:28; Nu.6:14; 7:17; 10:10	The believer sought to grow in the peace and fellowship of God through the substitute sacrifice. He had... • the option of offering a bull or cow without defect. The bull (an animal of service) focused his attention upon service, the dedication of his life to God. • the option of offering a lamb without defect. The lamb (the animal most used in sacrifice) focused a person's attention upon the sacrifice, dying to self and following God totally. • the option of offering a goat. The goat (the animal that bore away the judgment of sin) focused his attention upon God's judgment. Note: the sacrifice was burned on top of the Burnt Offering. This symbolizes that the peace and fellowship of God is based upon the atonement, based upon being reconciled with God. A person has to experience the atonement, be reconciled with God before he can know the peace and fellowship of God.	The Fellowship or Peace Offering is a type of Christ... ⇒ A picture of Christ as the Perfect Servant of God "Even as the Son of man came not to be ministered unto, but to minister, and to give his life a ransom for many" (Mt.20:28). ⇒ A picture of Christ as the Lamb of God "The next day John seeth Jesus coming unto him, and saith, Behold the Lamb of God, which taketh away the sin of the world" (Jn.1:29). ⇒ A picture of Christ as the Substitute Sacrifice who died on the cross bearing the judgment of sin for us, as the Sacrifice who removed and took away our sin "Who his own self bare our sins in his own body on the tree, that we, being dead to sins, should live unto righteousness: by whose stripes ye were healed" (1 Pe.2:24).

1 **Substitute Sacrifice:** Note how clearly the sacrifice symbolizes Jesus Christ. Jesus Christ died as our substitute: in our behalf, in our stead, in our place. He died for us. There is only one way any of us can be delivered from sin and death and escape the judgment to come. We must approach God through the substitute sacrifice which is the Lord Jesus Christ. He is the only Perfect Sacrifice, the one and only sacrifice acceptable to God. Forgiveness of sins comes only through Him: He is the one and only acceptable sacrifice.

THE SACRIFICES OR OFFERINGS OF THE OLD TESTAMENT

THE OFFERING & ITS PURPOSE	THE ELEMENTS & HOW ONE SECURED THE PROMISE OF THE OFFERING	THE SYMBOLISM: HOW THE OFFERING POINTS TO JESUS CHRIST
The Sin Offering: *To secure the way to receive continual forgiveness of sins,* Le.4:1-5:13 OTHER SCRIPTURE REFERENCES: Le.6:24-30; 8:14-17; 9:2; 9:15; 10:17; 16:3-22; Ex.29:14; 30:10; Nu.6:11; 8:8; 15:27; 2 K. 12:16; He.9:13; 10:11	God provided the way for every person to secure forgiveness of sins through the substitute sacrifice of a sin offering: ⇒ The anointed priest had to offer a young bull without defect. ⇒ The community or society had to offer a young bull without defect. ⇒ A leader had to offer a male goat without defect. ⇒ An individual person had to offer a female goat or lamb without defect. ⇒ The poor person had to offer two doves or two young pigeons. ⇒ The poorest of the poor had to offer a tenth of an ephah (two quarts; two liters) of fine flour. The substitute sacrifice paid the penalty of sin that was due the sinner; the substitute sacrifice set the believer free from the condemnation and judgment of sin.	The Sin Offering is a type of Christ, a picture of Christ. It is through Jesus Christ—through His blood, His death upon the cross—that we receive forgiveness of sins. By walking throughout the day in *open confession*, Christ continually forgives us and cleanses us from all unrighteousness. **"In whom we have redemption through his blood, the forgiveness of sins, according to the riches of his grace" (Ep.1:7).** **"If we confess our sins, he is faithful and just to forgive us *our* sins, and to cleanse us from all unrighteousness" (1 Jn.1:9).**
The Guilt Offering: *To provide the way to be set free from the weight and anguish of guilt, the pricking of conscience,* Lev.5:14-6:7 OTHER SCRIPTURE REFERENCES: Le.7:1-6; 14:12; 19:21; 1 S.6:3; 2 K.12:16; Ezr.10:19	The believer secured freedom from the weight and anguish of guilt, the pricking of conscience through the substitute sacrifice. This he did... • by offering a ram without defect and of true value • by making restitution plus 20% Note the result: the sacrifice made atonement, reconciliation with God—the guilty person was forgiven and the weight and anguish of guilt was removed.	The Guilt Offering is a type of Christ, a picture of Christ. Jesus Christ bore our guilt, bore the judgment and condemnation of our guilt when He died upon the cross. Through the death of Christ, we are set free from the guilt of our sin. We are able to stand before God free from all condemnation and accusation. **"*There is* therefore now no condemnation to them which are in Christ Jesus" (Ro.8:1).** **"Who shall lay any thing to the charge of God's elect? It is God that justifieth. Who is he that condemneth? It is Christ that died, yea rather, that is risen again, who is even at the right hand of God, who also maketh intercession for us" (Ro.8:33-34).**
The Ordination Offering:[2] *To provide the way for a person to be set apart to the priesthood, set apart to God and His service,* Le.8:22-32	A person was ordained, set apart to the ministry of God, by offering a ram as a substitute sacrifice. The person identified with the substitute sacrifice in the following ways: ⇒ by laying his hands on the sacrifice's head ⇒ by placing the shed blood of the sacrifice on the priests right ears, thumbs, and big toes, symbolizing the dedication of one's whole being to God ⇒ by sprinkling all sides of the altar with blood, symbolizing the dedication of the altar ⇒ by offering certain parts of the sacrifice as a wave offering to the LORD Note: the ordination ceremony was consummated with the sprinkling of oil and blood upon the priests. This symbolized that God's anointing (the giving of His Spirit) was based upon the blood, based upon being cleansed from sin.	The Ordination Offering is a type of Christ, a picture of the sacrifice and death of the Lord Jesus Christ. ⇒ It is Christ who died so that we might become acceptable to serve God. ⇒ It is the death of Christ—the demonstration of God's love—that compels us to serve God, that compels us to dedicate all we are and do to God. **"For the love of Christ constraineth us; because we thus judge, that if one died for all, then were all dead" (2 Co.5:14).** **"I beseech you therefore, brethren, by the mercies of God, that ye present your bodies a living sacrifice, holy, acceptable unto God, *which is* your reasonable service" (Ro.12:1).**

2   **The Ordination Offering:** The Ordination Offering is being included in this chart because of its importance to the ministers of God, those who are set apart for the special service of God.

THE WAY TO BECOME ACCEPTABLE TO GOD (PART 1): BY THE OFFERING OF A SACRIFICE, A SUBSTITUTE, 1:1–7:38

A. The Burnt Offering (a Picture of Christ's Atoning Sacrifice): The Only Way to Approach God, to Become Acceptable and Reconciled to God, 1:1-17

B. The Grain or Meal Offering (a Picture of Christ, the Bread of Life): The Way to Give Thanks and to Show One's Dedication to God, 2:1-16

C. The Fellowship or Peace Offering (a Picture of Christ's Atoning Sacrifice): The Way to Grow in Peace and Fellowship with God—Seeking a Deeper Life with God, 3:1-17

D. The Sin Offering (a Picture of Christ's Atoning Sacrifice): The Way to Secure Forgiveness of Sin, 4:1–5:13

E. The Guilt Offering (a Picture of Christ's Atoning Sacrifice): The Way to Be Set Free from the Weight and Anguish of Guilt, the Pricking of Conscience, 5:14–6:7

F. The Special Duties of the Priests in Conducting the Offerings: The Duties of Ministers, 6:8–7:38

LEVITICUS

CHAPTER 1

I. THE WAY TO BE- COME ACCEPTABLE TO GOD (PART 1): BY THE OFFERING OF A SACRIFICE, A SUB- STITUTE, 1:1–7:38

A. The Burnt Offering (a Picture of Christ): The Only Way to Approach God, to Become Ac- ceptable & Reconciled to God, 1:1-17

1. **God, not man, determined the way**
2. **God appointed a mediator (Moses) to reveal the way**
3. **God opened the way for all: To seek reconciliation through sacrifice**
   a. The rich: To bring an offering from the herd
   b. The average & the poor: To bring an offering from the flocks (sheep, goats, or birds)
4. **God told the rich how to ap- proach Him**
   a. Must approach God through the sacrifice (a symbol of Christ)
      1) A male without defect (a sym- bol of Christ's perfection)
      2) The purpose: To secure God's acceptance
   b. Must identify with the sacrifice
      1) By laying one's hands on its head
      2) By making atonement, rec- onciliation: An absolute es- sential for acceptance
   c. Must put the sacrifice to death before the LORD
      1) To slaughter the sacrifice before the LORD: Have the priests present the blood by sprinkling it against the al- tar on all sides
      2) To skin & cut the sacrifice into pieces
   d. Must have the priests prepare the altar & offer the sacrifice
      1) To put wood on the fire
      2) To lay the animal sacrifice on the altar: All its pieces including the head & fat

And the LORD called unto Moses, and spake unto him out of the tabernacle of the congregation, saying,
2 Speak unto the children of Israel, and say unto them, If any man of you bring an offering unto the LORD, ye shall bring your offering of the cattle, *even* of the herd, and of the flock.
3 If his offering *be* a burnt sacrifice of the herd, let him offer a male without blem- ish: he shall offer it of his own voluntary will at the door of the tabernacle of the congregation before the LORD.
4 And he shall put his hand upon the head of the burnt offering; and it shall be accepted for him to make atonement for him.
5 And he shall kill the bul- lock before the LORD: and the priests, Aaron's sons, shall bring the blood, and sprinkle the blood round about upon the altar that *is* by the door of the tabernacle of the congregation.
6 And he shall flay the burnt offering, and cut it into his pieces.
7 And the sons of Aaron the priest shall put fire upon the altar, and lay the wood in order upon the fire:
8 And the priests, Aaron's sons, shall lay the parts, the head, and the fat, in order upon the wood that *is* on the

fire which *is* upon the altar:
9 But his inwards and his legs shall he wash in water: and the priest shall burn all on the altar, *to be* a burnt sacrifice, an offering made by fire, of a sweet savour unto the LORD.
10 And if his offering *be* of the flocks, *namely*, of the sheep, or of the goats, for a burnt sacrifice; he shall bring it a male without blemish.
11 And he shall kill it on the side of the altar north- ward before the LORD: and the priests, Aaron's sons, shall sprinkle his blood round about upon the altar.
12 And he shall cut it into his pieces, with his head and his fat: and the priest shall lay them in order on the wood that *is* on the fire which *is* upon the altar:
13 But he shall wash the inwards and the legs with water: and the priest shall bring *it* all, and burn *it* upon the altar: it *is* a burnt sacri- fice, an offering made by fire, of a sweet savour unto the LORD.
14 And if the burnt sacrifice for his offering to the LORD *be* of fowls, then he shall bring his offering of turtledoves, or of young pi- geons.
15 And the priest shall bring it unto the altar, and wring off his head, and burn *it* on the altar; and the blood thereof shall be wrung out at the side of the altar:
16 And he shall pluck away his crop with his feathers, and cast it beside the altar on the east part, by the place of the ashes:
17 And he shall cleave it with the wings thereof, *but* shall not divide *it* asunder: and the priest shall burn it upon the altar, upon the wood that *is* upon the fire: it *is* a burnt sacrifice, an offering made by fire, of a sweet savour unto the LORD.

3) To wash the inner parts & legs with water
4) To burn the entire sacrifice on the altar
e. The result: The sweet aroma of the sacrifice pleased the LORD—was acceptable to Him

5. **God told the average person how to approach Him**
   a. Must approach God through the sacrifice: A sheep or goat without defect (a symbol of Christ)
   b. Must put the sacrifice to death before the LORD
      1) To have the priests present the blood by sprinkling it against the altar on all sides
      2) To cut it into pieces
   c. Must have the priests offer the sacrifice
      1) To lay the sacrifice—all of it—on the altar
      2) To wash the inner parts & legs with water
      3) To burn the entire sacrifice on the altar
   d. The result: The sweet aroma of the sacrifice pleased the LORD—was acceptable to Him

6. **God told the poor how to ap- proach Him**
   a. Must approach God through the sacrifice (a symbol of Christ)
   b. Must have the priest take a dove or young pigeon to the altar
      1) Put it to death & burn it on the altar
      2) Drain the blood out on the sides of the altar
      3) Remove the crop & its feathers & throw it to the east side of the altar (where the ashes were)
      4) Tear off the wings—not severing the rest of the bird
      5) Burn the sacrifice—all of it—on the altar
   c. The result: The sweet aroma of the sacrifice pleased the LORD—was acceptable to Him (a symbol that Christ's sacri- fice was pleasing & accept- able to God)

DIVISION I

THE WAY TO BECOME ACCEPTABLE TO GOD (PART 1): BY THE OFFERING OF A SACRIFICE, A SUBSTITUTE, 1:1–7:38

A. The Burnt Offering (a Picture of Christ): The Only Way to Approach God, the Only Way to Become Acceptable and Reconciled to God, 1:1-17

(1:1-17) **Introduction**: there is only one way to approach God, only one way to become acceptable to God. Man on his own is not acceptable to God. The Bible declares an awful, tragic fact: a great gulf separates man from God, a gulf so vast that it cannot be crossed. Man simply cannot reach God on his own. Why?

⇒ Because man curses, rejects, and denies God; man ignores, neglects, and forgets God.

⇒ Because man—even at the summit of his goodness and righteousness—is sinful, short of perfection, far, far short of living in a world of absolute perfection.

⇒ Because man lives selfishly: seeking and hoarding more and more, shutting his ears to the needs of the poor, the hungry, the suffering, and the lost.

⇒ Because man lives in self-righteousness and pride, feeling that he is good enough and religious enough to approach God, that he can approach God in his own righteousness and strength.

God is perfect, living in absolute perfection; and heaven is perfect, a place of absolute perfection. No imperfection—no imperfect being, not even man—can ever live in God's holy presence. There is a terrible gulf separating man from God, the tragic gulf of sin and imperfection.

How, then, can man approach God, become acceptable to God? How can man be reconciled, brought to God? This is the glorious message of this passage: there is a way to approach God. The way is through the Burnt Offering. Keep in mind that the Burnt Offering pictured the atonement, the ransom price paid so that man might escape the death penalty demanded by God's holiness. To say it another way, the Burnt Offering pictured the atonement, the ransom price, paid to reconcile and make man acceptable to God (Le.1:3-4). In today's terms, this is a picture of salvation, of Jesus Christ dying for us, of His paying the ransom price so that we might escape the penalty of death.

This is the great message of—*The Burnt Offering (a Picture of Christ): The Only Way to Approach God, to Become Acceptable and Reconciled to God*, 1:1-17.

1. God, not man, determined the way (v.1).
2. God appointed a mediator (Moses) to reveal the way (v.1).
3. God opened the way for all: To seek reconciliation through sacrifice (v.2).
4. God told the rich how to approach Him (vv.3-9).
5. God told the average person how to approach Him (vv.10-13).
6. God told the poor how to approach Him (vv.14-17).

1 (1:1) **Way, The—Acceptance—Reconciliation**: God, not man, determined the way to approach and to become acceptable to Him.

OUTLINE	SCRIPTURE
1. God, not man, determined the way	And the LORD called unto Moses, and spake unto him out of the tabernacle of the congregation, saying

Note that it was God who *called* (qara). The word means to speak in a loud, clear, distinct voice. It indicates that something of importance and significance is about to be declared.

The point is this: God is the Person speaking, not man. God is the One who determines...

• how He is to be approached

• who is acceptable to Him

Thought 1. This strikes a forceful blow against self-righteousness. Only God—the only living and true God, the great Creator and Sovereign Majesty of the universe—determines how He is to be approached and who is acceptable to Him. No person can ever reach God unless he approaches God exactly as God declares.

⇒ We have no right to stand before God and declare, "God, this is the way You and I are to be reconciled. This is the way I am going to approach You. This is the way You must accept me."

⇒ We, mere human beings, have no right to stand up before the Creator of the universe and declare anything, much less tell Him how He must accept us.

"I said therefore unto you, that ye shall die in your sins: for if ye believe not that I am *he*, ye shall die in your sins" (Jn.8:24).

"Jesus saith unto him, I am the way, the truth, and the life: no man cometh unto the Father, but by me" (Jn.14:6).

"Neither is there salvation in any other: for there is none other name under heaven given among men, whereby we must be saved" (Ac.4:12).

"For other foundation can no man lay than that is laid, which is Jesus Christ" (1 Co.3:11).

"There is a way which seemeth right unto a man, but the end thereof *are* the ways of death" (Pr.14:12; cp. 16:25).

"Every way of a man *is* right in his own eyes: but the LORD pondereth the hearts" (Pr.21:2).

"*There is* a generation *that are* pure in their own eyes, and *yet* is not washed from their filthiness" (Pr.30:12).

2 (1:1) **Way, The—Mediator—Reconciliation—Acceptance**: God appointed a Mediator to reveal the way to approach and become acceptable to Him.

OUTLINE	SCRIPTURE
2. God appointed a mediator (Moses) to reveal the way	And the LORD called unto Moses, and spake unto him out of the tabernacle of the congregation, saying,

The mediator—the person who stood between the people and God—was Moses. Throughout the Old Testament, God spoke to His people through visions and dreams. But now, during this particular period of human history, God began to speak face-to-face with His mediator, Moses. God appointed Moses to stand as the mediator between Him and the people.

"With him will I speak mouth to mouth, even apparently, and not in dark speeches; and the similitude of the LORD shall he behold: wherefore then were ye not afraid to speak against my servant Moses?" (Nu.12:8).

Thought 1. Moses was the mediator who stood between God and the people. He was to reveal the way to God, declaring exactly how man was to approach God. In this, Moses was a clear type of Christ. Jesus Christ is the appointed Mediator who stands between God and us, revealing and declaring the way to God.

"For *there is* one God, and one mediator between God and men, the man Christ Jesus" (1 Ti.2:5).

"God, who at sundry times and in divers manners spake in time past unto the fathers by the prophets, Hath in these last days spoken unto us by *his* Son, whom he hath appointed heir of all things, by whom also he made the worlds; Who being the brightness of *his* glory, and the express image of his person, and upholding all things by the word of his power, when he had by himself purged our sins, sat down on the right hand of the Majesty on high" (He.1:1-3).

"But now hath he [Christ] obtained a more excellent ministry, by how much also he is the mediator of a better covenant, which was established upon better promises" (He.8:6).

"And for this cause he is the mediator of the new testament, that by means of death, for the redemption of the transgressions *that were* under the first testament, they which are called might receive the promise of eternal inheritance" (He.9:15).

"For Christ is not entered into the holy places made with hands, *which are* the figures of the true; but into heaven itself, now to appear in the presence of God for us" (He.9:24).

"And to Jesus the mediator of the new covenant, and to the blood of sprinkling, that speaketh better things than *that of* Abel" (He.12:24).

"My little children, these things write I unto you, that ye sin not. And if any man sin, we have an advocate [Mediator] with the Father, Jesus Christ the righteous" (1 Jn.2:1).

3 (1:2) **Way, The—Reconciliation—Acceptance**: God opened the way for every person to approach Him.

OUTLINE	SCRIPTURE
3. God opened the way for all: To seek reconciliation through sacrifice a. The rich: To bring an offering from the herd a. The average & the poor: To bring an offering from the flocks (sheep, goats, or birds)	2 Speak unto the children of Israel, and say unto them, If any man of you bring an offering unto the LORD, ye shall bring your offering of the cattle, *even* of the herd, and of the flock.

Note that the people were to seek acceptance and reconciliation through the sacrifice of an animal. The animal sacrifice was to be offered to the LORD. Just why will be made clear in the next point. But for now, note that the animal was to come from either the herd or the flock. Only the wealthy would own or could purchase large animals from the herd, such as cattle or oxen. The average person would usually be able to secure only animals from the flocks such as sheep and goats. If a person were poverty-stricken, he could at least offer the sacrifice of a bird.

The concern of God for every human being is clearly seen in this provision. God wants the poor as well as the rich to approach Him.

Thought 1. The wonderful truth is just this fact: God has made a way for the poor to come as well as for the rich and the average person. Every human being can approach God, no matter how rich or how poverty-stricken. The way to God is open, open for all to enter. Whoever calls upon the name of the LORD will be saved, no matter who he is.

"Also I say unto you, Whosoever shall confess me before men, him shall the Son of man also confess before the angels of God" (Lu.12:8).

"For God so loved the world, that he gave his only begotten Son, that whosoever believeth in him should not perish, but have everlasting life" (Jn.3:16).

"To him give all the prophets witness, that through his name whosoever believeth in him shall receive remission of sins" (Ac.10:43).

"For whosoever shall call upon the name of the Lord shall be saved" (Ro.10:13).

"Whosoever believeth that Jesus is the Christ is born of God: and every one that loveth him that begat loveth him also that is begotten of him" (1 Jn.5:1).

"Behold, I stand at the door, and knock: if any man hear my voice, and open the door, I will come in to him, and will sup with him, and he with me" (Re.3:20).

"And the Spirit and the bride say, Come. And let him that heareth say, Come. And let him that is athirst come. And whosoever will, let him take the water of life freely" (Re.22:17).

4 (1:3-9) **Way, The—Atonement—Reconciliation—Acceptance—Sacrifice, Animal—Substitution—Symbol—Type**: God told the rich person how to approach Him.

OUTLINE	SCRIPTURE	SCRIPTURE	OUTLINE

4. God told the rich how to approach Him
a. Must approach God through the sacrifice (a symbol of Christ)
  1) A male without defect (a symbol of Christ's perfection)
  2) The purpose: To secure God's acceptance
b. Must identify with the sacrifice
  1) By laying one's hands on its head
  2) By making atonement, reconciliation: An absolute essential for acceptance
c. Must put the sacrifice to death before the LORD
  1) To slaughter the sacrifice before the LORD: Have the priests present the blood by sprinkling it against the altar on all sides
	3 If his offering *be* a burnt sacrifice of the herd, let him offer a male without blemish: he shall offer it of his own voluntary will at the door of the tabernacle of the congregation before the LORD.
	4 And he shall put his hand upon the head of the burnt offering; and it shall be accepted for him to make atonement for him.
	5 And he shall kill the bullock before the LORD: and the priests, Aaron's sons, shall bring the blood, and sprinkle the blood round about upon the altar that *is by* the door of the taber-
		nacle of the congregation
		6 And he shall flay the burnt offering, and cut it into his pieces.
		7 And the sons of Aaron the priest shall put fire upon the altar, and lay the wood in order upon the fire:
		8 And the priests, Aaron's sons, shall lay the parts, the head, and the fat, in order upon the wood that *is* on the fire which *is* upon the altar:
		9 But his inwards and his legs shall he wash in water: and the priest shall burn all on the altar, *to be* a burnt sacrifice, an offering made by fire, of a sweet savour unto the LORD.
			2) To skin & cut the sacrifice into pieces
			
			d. Must have the priests prepare the altar & offer the sacrifice
			  1) To put wood on the fire
			
			  2) To lay the animal sacrifice on the altar: All its pieces including the head & fat
			
			  3) To wash the inner parts & legs with water
			  4) To burn the entire sacrifice on the altar
			e. The result: The sweet aroma of the sacrifice pleased the Lord—was acceptable to Him

a. The rich person must approach God through the symbol of the Burnt Offering just like everyone else (v.3). The rich person had to approach God by offering a male from his herd of cattle or oxen. Note that the animal had to be a male and perfect, with no defect or blemish whatsoever.

Thought 1. The sacrifice pointed toward the coming sacrifice of Christ. The Burnt Offering was a type of Christ, a symbol or picture of Christ.

(1)   The sacrifice had to be a male symbolizing strength, the strength of our LORD to save. Jesus Christ is *mighty to save* and *able to save* completely, to the utmost.

> "Wherefore he is able also to save them to the uttermost that come unto God by him, seeing he ever liveth to make intercession for them" (He.7:25).

(2)   The sacrifice had to be perfect, without any defect or blemish whatsoever. This symbolized the sinlessness, the perfection, and the righteousness of the Lord Jesus Christ.

> "And ye know that he was manifested to take away our sins; and in him is no sin" (1 Jn.3:5).
> "For he hath made him to be sin for us, who knew no sin; that we might be made the righteousness of God in him" (2 Co.5:21).
> "For we have not an high priest which cannot be touched with the feeling of our infirmities; but was in all points tempted like as we are, yet without sin" (He.4:15).
> "For such an high priest became us, who is holy, harmless, undefiled, separate from sinners, and made higher than the heavens" (He.7:26).
> "Forasmuch as ye know that ye were not redeemed with corruptible things, as silver and gold, from your vain conversation received by tradition from your fathers; But with the precious blood of Christ, as of a lamb without blemish and without spot" (1 Pe.1:18-19).

(3)   Jesus Christ was a male and lived a perfect, sinless life. This declares that Jesus Christ is the fulfillment of the Burnt Offering. Jesus Christ is the true Sacrifice—the only sacrifice—that God accepts in behalf of man.

> "While he yet spake, behold, a bright cloud overshadowed them: and behold a voice out of the cloud, which said, This is my beloved Son, in whom I am well pleased; hear ye him" (Mt.17:5; see Mt.3:17; Mk.1:11; 9:7; Lu.3:22; 9:35).
>
> "Forasmuch as ye know that ye were not redeemed with corruptible things, as silver and gold, from your vain conversation *received* by tradition from your fathers; But with the precious blood of Christ, as of a lamb without blemish and without spot" (1 Pe.1:18-19).

b. The rich person must identify with the sacrifice (Le.1:4). How? By laying his hands on the head of the sacrifice. This symbolized that the animal was taking the place of the person, being substituted for the person. A person's guilt—his sins and condemnation—were being transferred to the sacrifice.

> *When hands are laid on the animal and sins are confessed, the sins are in symbol transferred to the animal.* [1]
> *It [the laying on of hands] symbolized a transfer...an obligation to suffer for sin, from the offerer to the innocent victim.* [2]

Once a person identified with the sacrifice, God clearly says that He accepted the sacrifice...
- accepted it on the person's behalf—in his stead, in his place
- accepted it to make atonement for the person (See DEEPER STUDY # 1, *Atonement*—Le.1:4 for discussion.)

Thought 1. The person who placed his hand on the head of the sacrifice was identifying with the sacrifice. But as it is now, so it was then: some believed what God said and some did not believe. Some truly trusted God and some did not. To the person who truly believed, God did a wonderful thing: God counted his faith in the sacrifice as righteousness. The person believed God; therefore he obeyed God: he offered a male sacrifice that was perfect, and he laid his hands on its head...
- identifying himself with the animal
- believing that God would do just what He said: accept the animal sacrifice as atonement, as a ransom, as a substitute for him. He believed that God accepted the sacrifice as the substitute for him, to bear his sins and punishment. And because he believed God, God did accept the sacrifice on his behalf, in his stead, in his place—as his substitute

Note how this symbolizes exactly what Jesus Christ did for us: Jesus Christ...
- took our place
- became our substitute
- became the perfect sacrifice for us

> "For he hath made him *to be* sin for us, who knew no sin; that we might be made the righteousness of God in him" (2 Co.5:21).
> "Christ hath redeemed us from the curse of the law, being made a curse for us: for it is written, Cursed *is* every one that hangeth on a tree" (Ga.3:13).
> "But when the fulness of the time was come, God sent forth his Son, made of a woman, made under the law, To redeem them that were under the law, that we might receive the adoption of sons" (Ga.4:4-5).
> "But we see Jesus, who was made a little lower than the angels for the suffering of death, crowned with glory and honour; that he by the grace of God should taste death for every man" (He.2:9).
> "Who his own self bare our sins in his own body on the tree, that we, being dead to sins, should live unto righteousness: by whose stripes ye were healed" (1 Pe.2:24).
> "For Christ also hath once suffered for sins, the just for the unjust, that he might bring us to God, being put to death in the flesh, but quickened by the Spirit" (1 Pe.3:18).
> "But he *was* wounded for our transgressions, *he was* bruised for our iniquities: the chastisement of our peace *was* upon him; and with his stripes we are healed" (Is.53:5).

c. The rich person must put the sacrifice to death before the LORD (vv.5-6). The phrase "before the LORD" stresses that a person must be sincere, genuine in approaching God. The sacrifice must be put to death before the LORD, not haphazardly nor unthoughtfully.

Once the sacrifice was slain, the priests were to sprinkle the blood against all sides of the altar (v.5). Then the person was to skin and cut the sacrifice into pieces (v.6).

Thought 1. Note three clear symbols and lessons for us.
(1) The sinner put the victim to death.

> "The wages of sin is death" (Ro.6:23).
> "The soul that sinneth shall die" (Eze.18:4, 20).

(2) The innocent died for the guilty.

---

[1] Frank E. Gaebelein, General Editor. *The Expositor's Bible Commentary*, Vol.2. (Grand Rapids, MI: The Zondervan Corporation, 1990), p.537.
[2] J. Vernon McGee. *Thru The Bible*, Vol.1, p.327.

"Who his own self bare our sins in his own body on the tree, that we, being dead to sins, should live unto righteousness: by whose stripes ye were healed" (1 Pe.2:24).

"For Christ also hath once suffered for sins, the just for the unjust, that he might bring us to God, being put to death in the flesh, but quickened by the Spirit" (1 Pe.3:18).

(3) The shed blood of the sacrifice covered the altar of sacrifice, the altar where the fires of judgment consumed the victim. The shed blood kept the judgment from consuming the sinner, the person seeking atonement (reconciliation). The blood of Jesus Christ redeems us, delivers us from the consuming judgment and wrath of God.

"Much more then, being now justified by his blood, we shall be saved from wrath through him" (Ro.5:9).

"How much more shall the blood of Christ, who through the eternal Spirit offered himself without spot to God, purge your conscience from dead works to serve the living God?" (He.9:14).

"Forasmuch as ye know that ye were not redeemed with corruptible things, *as* silver and gold, from your vain conversation *received* by tradition from your fathers; But with the precious blood of Christ, as of a lamb without blemish and without spot" (1 Pe.1:18-19).

d. The rich must have the priests prepare the altar and offer the sacrifice (vv.6-9). This involved four functions:
⇒ The priests put the wood on the fire (v.7).
⇒ The priests laid the animal sacrifice—all of it including the head and fat—on the altar (v.8).
⇒ The priests washed the inner parts and legs with water (v.9).
⇒ The priests burned the entire sacrifice on the altar (v.9).

Thought 1. This is a picture of the sharp, painful sufferings of Christ and of the full and complete sacrifice He was making.
⇒ The entire animal was completely and fully sacrificed. So Christ completely and fully gave Himself up to be *the Sacrifice* for man.
⇒ The animal bore the full judgment of God against sin. So it was with Christ. Jesus Christ sacrificed Himself and suffered for man. He gave Himself totally—in the entirety of His Being—to bear the full judgment of God against sin, all for man.

"But God commendeth his love toward us, in that, while we were yet sinners, Christ died for us" (Ro.5:8).

"Much more then, being now justified by his blood, we shall be saved from wrath through him" (Ro.5:9).

"He was oppressed, and he was afflicted, yet he opened not his mouth: he is brought as a lamb to the slaughter, and as a sheep before her shearers is dumb, so he openeth not his mouth" (Is.53:7).

e. The result of the rich person's Burnt Offering: the sweet aroma of the sacrifice pleased the LORD. The sacrifice was acceptable to God (v.9). The rich person did two significant things that pleased God:
⇒ He believed and obeyed God: approached God exactly as God said.
⇒ He offered the sacrifice of the Burnt Offering before the LORD. By so doing, God saw the sacrifice, the picture, of His dear Son who was to die for the sins of the world. Seeing His Son symbolized in the sacrifice pleased God. The aroma of the person's faith in the sacrifice and his obedience in approaching God exactly as God said—this pleased God. It was like a sweet aroma to God. God accepted the person: atonement was made; the person was reconciled to God.

Note this fact: the Hebrew word for the burnt sacrifice (olah) means that which ascends, that which goes up. This is most likely a symbol of the person's faith in the sacrifice ascending up like a sweet aroma to the LORD. The LORD accepts the person's faith in the sacrifice as atonement, as reconciliation—as righteousness by which he becomes reconciled to God (see Ge.15:6; Ro.4:9; 2 Co.5:21).

"And walk in love, as Christ also hath loved us, and hath given himself for us an offering and a sacrifice to God for a sweetsmelling savour" (Ep.5:2).

"For God so loved the world, that he gave his only begotten Son, that whosoever believeth in him should not perish, but have everlasting life" (Jn.3:16).

"Forasmuch as ye know that ye were not redeemed with corruptible things, *as* silver and gold, from your vain conversation *received* by tradition from your fathers; But with the precious blood of Christ, as of a lamb without blemish and without spot" (1 Pe.1:18-19).

DEEPER STUDY # 1

(1:4) **Atonement (kipper)**: to wipe clean; to pay a ransom; to cover. Atonement means to reconcile by wiping clean, paying a ransom and covering the differences (sins) that alienate and separate a person from God, arousing His justice. The atonement propitiates or satisfies God's wrath; it appeases, placates, cancels, annuls God's anger against sin. Atonement means to ransom or deliver by the means of a substitute. The substitute takes the place of the sinner and bears the punishment due the sinner. Through the atonement, a person is set free from sin and its punishment. A person is ransomed from sin and the punishment of death, ransomed to live eternally with God. In one very simple statement, the atonement means reconciliation: the atonement reconciles a person to God and makes a person acceptable to God. (See note—Ex.25:17-21 for more discussion.) Two important facts need to be noted about the great subject of atonement.

1. The atonement secured by animals was only a type, only a symbol and picture of the atoning sacrifice of Christ. Jesus Christ died as the perfect sacrifice to ransom us from sin, death, and hell (separation from God). This fact must always be remembered: justice demands that a person pay for the crime he has committed. A person cannot get off in court just by apologizing and saying "I'll try my best not to do it again." This is not enough, not in a true court of justice. This is especially true when dealing with God. God's justice demands that a person pay for breaking the law of God. But note: God is perfect; therefore, His justice demands that a perfect payment be made for man's disobedience or crime against God. But in this fact there is a major problem, for no person is perfect. Consequently, no person can make the perfect payment to satisfy God's justice. What then can man do? This is where Jesus Christ enters the picture. Jesus Christ—His death upon the cross—is the perfect payment, the perfect atonement, that satisfies God's justice. He offered Himself up as the perfect sacrifice for our crimes or sins against God. He and He alone is the true atoning sacrifice, the true Lamb of God who takes away the sins of the world.

"The next day John seeth Jesus coming unto him, and saith, Behold the Lamb of God, which taketh away the sin of the world" (Jn.1:29).

"And not only *so*, but we also joy in God through our Lord Jesus Christ, by whom we have now received the atonement [reconciliation]" (Ro.5:11).

"In whom we have redemption through his blood, the forgiveness of sins, according to the riches of his grace" (Ep.1:7).

"Neither by the blood of goats and calves, but by his own blood he entered in once into the holy place, having obtained eternal redemption *for us*. For if the blood of bulls and of goats, and the ashes of an heifer sprinkling the unclean, sanctifieth to the purifying of the flesh: How much more shall the blood of Christ, who through the eternal Spirit offered himself without spot to God, purge your conscience from dead works to serve the living God?" (He.9:12-14).

"For *it is* not possible that the blood of bulls and of goats should take away sins....But this man, after he had offered one sacrifice for sins for ever, sat down on the right hand of God; From henceforth expecting till his enemies be made his footstool. For by one offering he hath perfected for ever them that are sanctified" (He.10:4, 12-14).

"Forasmuch as ye know that ye were not redeemed with corruptible things, *as* silver and gold, from your vain conversation *received* by tradition from your fathers; But with the precious blood of Christ, as of a lamb without blemish and without spot" (1 Pe.1:18-19).

2. The atoning (reconciling) death of Jesus Christ was made once-for-all; therefore, His sacrifice is the only sufficient sacrifice ever made. The Burnt Offering finds its fulfillment in the death of Jesus Christ. His death makes animal sacrifice obsolete. We no longer have a need to offer Burnt Offerings for the atonement of our sins. We are reconciled to God by the death of the Lord Jesus Christ. His sacrifice was the perfect ransom demanded by God for the cursing of His name, for the rejection and hostility of our behavior toward Him. Jesus Christ bore the judgment of God's anger and wrath against sins. This He did to atone for our sins so that we might become reconciled and acceptable to Him. As stated, because of Jesus Christ, we no longer have to offer Burnt Offerings to become acceptable to God. We are acceptable when we approach God through the sacrifice of the Lord Jesus Christ. It is His sacrifice that atones for our sins, that reconciles us to God—His sacrifice that makes us acceptable to God once-for-all.

"For in that he died, he died unto sin once: but in that he liveth, he liveth unto God" (Ro.6:10).

"Wherefore he is able also to save them to the uttermost that come unto God by him, seeing he ever liveth to make intercession for them. For such an high priest became us, *who is* holy, harmless, undefiled, separate from sinners, and made higher than the heavens; Who needeth not daily, as those high priests, to offer up sacrifice, first for his own sins, and then for the people's: for this he did once, when he offered up himself" (He.7:25-27).

"So Christ was once offered to bear the sins of many; and unto them that look for him shall he appear the second time without sin unto salvation" (He.9:28).

"By the which will we are sanctified through the offering of the body of Jesus Christ once *for all*. And every priest standeth daily ministering and offering oftentimes the same sacrifices, which can never take away sins: But this man, after he had offered one sacrifice for sins for ever, sat down on the right hand of God" (He.10:10-12).

"For by one offering he hath perfected for ever them that are sanctified" (He.10:14).

"For Christ also hath once suffered for sins, the just for the unjust, that he might bring us to God, being put to death in the flesh, but quickened by the Spirit" (1 Pe.3:18).

5 (1:10-13) **Way, The—Atonement—Reconciliation—Acceptance—Sacrifice, Animal—Substitution—Symbol—Type—Person, Average—Middle Class**: God told the average person how to approach Him. The average person was to approach God just like the rich man, through the sacrifice of the Burnt Offering. There was only one difference: since he was not wealthy, he could offer the sacrifice of a sheep or goat. The Scripture and outline clearly show that the average person was to approach God in the very same way as the rich:

OUTLINE	SCRIPTURE	SCRIPTURE	OUTLINE

5. God told the average person how to approach Him
a. Must approach God through the sacrifice: A sheep or goat without defect (a symbol of Christ)
b. Must put the sacrifice to death before the Lord
  1) To have the priests present the blood by sprinkling it against the altar on all sides
  2) To cut it into pieces
	10 And if his offering *be* of the flocks, *namely*, of the sheep, or of the goats, for a burnt sacrifice; he shall bring it a male without blemish.
	11 And he shall kill it on the side of the altar northward before the LORD: and the priests, Aaron's sons, shall sprinkle his blood round about upon the altar.
	12 And he shall cut it into
		his pieces, with his head and his fat: and the priest shall lay them in order on the wood that *is* on the fire which *is* upon the altar:
		13 But he shall wash the inwards and the legs with water: and the priest shall bring *it* all, and burn *it* upon the altar: it *is* a burnt sacrifice, an offering made by fire, of a sweet savour unto the LORD.
			c. Must have the priests offer the sacrifice
			  1) To lay the sacrifice—all of it—on the altar
			  2) To wash the inner parts & legs with water
			  3) To burn the entire sacrifice on the altar
			d. The result: The sweet aroma of the sacrifice pleased the LORD—was acceptable to Him

Thought 1. The middle class or average person has no excuse in failing to approach God. God has made it just as possible for him to approach God as He has for anyone else to be delivered from the judgment of God. The average person could be delivered from the fire of God's judgment, the judgment that was symbolized in the consuming fire upon the altar. He could be delivered through the sacrifice of the Burnt Offering—all symbolized in the sacrifice of the Lord Jesus Christ.

"The next day John seeth Jesus coming unto him, and saith, Behold the Lamb of God, which taketh away the sin of the world" (Jn.1:29).

"I am the good shepherd: the good shepherd giveth his life for the sheep" (Jn.10:11).

"Who gave himself for our sins, that he might deliver us from this present evil world, according to the will of God and our Father" (Ga.1:4).

"Christ hath redeemed us from the curse of the law, being made a curse for us: for it is written, Cursed *is* every one that hangeth on a tree" (Ga.3:13).

"Who gave himself for us, that he might redeem us from all iniquity, and purify unto himself a peculiar people, zealous of good works" (Tit.2:14).

"Forasmuch then as the children are partakers of flesh and blood, he also himself likewise took part of the same; that through death he might destroy him that had the power of death, that is, the devil; And deliver them who through fear of death were all their lifetime subject to bondage" (He.2:14-15).

"But he *was* wounded for our transgressions, *he was* bruised for our iniquities: the chastisement of our peace *was* upon him; and with his stripes we are healed" (Is.53:5).

6 (1:14-17) **Way, The—Atonement—Reconciliation—Acceptance—Poor, The—Sacrifice, Animal—Substitution—Symbol—Type**: God told the poor how to approach Him. The door into God's presence was and still is just as open for the poor as it is for anyone else. The poor are to approach God just like the rich and average person: through *the sacrifice*. But note the difference in the animal sacrifice: the poor could offer a dove or young pigeon, and the priest, not the poor person, was to put it to death. The bird was just not large enough to be cut up nor was there enough blood to cover the altar. The blood was simply drained out by the side of the altar. If the poor person did not have the money to purchase a bird, he could easily catch one and offer it.

The point is clear: there is nothing to keep the poor person from approaching God, no excuse whatsoever: nothing was required, nothing except to come through the sacrifice of the Burnt Offering. Note how clearly the outline shows this:

OUTLINE	SCRIPTURE	SCRIPTURE	OUTLINE

6. God told the poor how to approach Him
a. Must approach God through the sacrifice (a symbol of Christ)
b. Must have the priest take a dove or young pigeon to the altar
  1) Put it to death & burn it on the altar
  2) Drain the blood out on the sides of the altar
  3) Remove the crop & its feathers & throw it to the
	14 And if the burnt sacrifice for his offering to the LORD *be* of fowls, then he shall bring his offering of turtledoves, or of young pigeons.
	15 And the priest shall bring it unto the altar, and wring off his head, and burn *it* on the altar; and the blood thereof shall be wrung out at the side of the altar:
	16 And he shall pluck away his crop with his feathers,
		and cast it beside the altar on the east part, by the place of the ashes:
		17 And he shall cleave it with the wings thereof, *but* shall not divide *it* asunder: and the priest shall burn it upon the altar, upon the wood that *is* upon the fire: it *is* a burnt sacrifice, an offering made by fire, of a sweet savour unto the LORD.
			east side of the altar (where the ashes were)
			  4) Tear off the wings—not severing the rest of the bird
			  5) Burn the sacrifice—all of it—on the altar
			c. The result: The sweet aroma of the sacrifice pleased the LORD—was acceptable to Him (a symbol that Christ's sacrifice was pleasing & acceptable to God)

Thought 1. Poverty is no excuse for not coming to God. All a poor person has to do is approach God through the sacrifice of His dear Son, the Lord Jesus Christ. Jesus Christ died for the poor as well as for the rich and average person. Jesus Christ died as our sacrifice, our substitute, the sacrifice and substitute for every living person. Jesus Christ fulfilled the type—the symbol and picture—of the Burnt Offering.

"For he hath made him *to be* sin for us, who knew no sin; that we might be made the righteousness of God in him" (2 Co.5:21).

"But we see Jesus, who was made a little lower than the angels for the suffering of death, crowned with glory and honour; that he by the grace of God should taste death for every man" (He.2:9).

"For Christ also hath once suffered for sins, the just for the unjust, that he might bring us to God, being put to death in the flesh, but quickened by the Spirit" (1 Pe.3:18).

"For the zeal of thine house hath eaten me up; and the reproaches of them that reproached thee are fallen upon me" (Ps.69:9).

"But he *was* wounded for our transgressions, *he was* bruised for our iniquities: the chastisement of our peace *was* upon him; and with his stripes we are healed" (Is.53:5).

TYPES, SYMBOLS, AND PICTURES
Leviticus 1:1-17

Historical Term	Type or Picture (Scriptural Basis for Each)	Life Application for Today's Believer	Biblical Application
The Burnt Offering Le.1:1-17; 6:8-13; 8:18-21; 16:24	*A symbol of atonement, reconciliation with God.* *The Burnt Offering is a type of Christ, a symbol or picture of Christ dying as the substitute sacrifice for us. By dying for us:* ⇒ *Christ bore the full justice and judgment of God against sin—paid the ransom price to deliver us from sin and death* ⇒ *Christ secured the atonement for us, reconciling us to God* **"And he shall put his hand upon the head of the burnt offering; and it shall be accepted for him to make atonement for him" (Le.1:4).** **"...by whom [Christ] we have now received the atonement" (Ro.5:11).**	Jesus Christ died for us as our substitute sacrifice. He died to secure the atonement or reconciliation with God for us. A person can now approach God and be reconciled with God; a person can now become acceptable to God. How? By approaching God through the sacrifice of Christ.	*"But God commendeth his love toward us, in that, while we were yet sinners, Christ died for us. Much more then, being now justified by his blood, we shall be saved from wrath through him. For if, when we were enemies, we were reconciled to God by the death of his Son, much more, being reconciled, we shall be saved by his life. And not only so, but we also joy in God through our Lord Jesus Christ, by whom we have now received the atonement." (Ro.5:8-11).* *"Wherefore he is able also to save them to the uttermost that come unto God by him, seeing he ever liveth to make intercession for them. For such an high priest became us, who is holy, harmless, undefiled, separate from sinners, and made higher than the heavens; Who needeth not daily, as those high priests, to offer up sacrifice, first for his own sins, and then for the people's: for this he did once, when he offered up himself" (He.7:25-27; see 2 Co.5:21).*
Moses Le. 1:1; 8:1-5	*A clear type of Jesus Christ, the appointed Mediator, who stood between man and God, revealing and declaring the way to God. Moses was the mediator appointed by God to stand between the Israelites and God, revealing and declaring the way to God.*	It is Jesus Christ who is the appointed Mediator. It is Christ, and Christ alone. • who stands in the gap between God and man. • who proclaims the way to God • who opens the way into God's presence	*"For there is one God, and one mediator between God and men, the man Christ Jesus" (1 Ti.2:5).* *"God, who at sundry times and in divers manners spake in time past unto the fathers by the prophets, Hath in these last days*

TYPES, SYMBOLS, AND PICTURES
Leviticus 1:1-17

Historical Term	Type or Picture (Scriptural Basis for Each)	Life Application for Today's Believer	Biblical Application
	"And the LORD called unto Moses, and spake unto him out of the tabernacle of the congregation..." (Le.1:1).		*spoken unto us by his Son, whom he hath appointed heir of all things, by whom also he made the worlds; Who being the brightness of his glory, and the express image of his person, and upholding all things by the word of his power, when he had by himself purged our sins, sat down on the right hand of the Majesty on high" (He.1:1-3).* "My little children, these things write I unto you, that ye sin not. And if any man sin, we have an advocate with the Father, Jesus Christ the righteous" (1 Jn.2:1; see Jn.14:6).*
The Animal Sacrifice That Had to Be a Male Le. 1:3	*The fact that the animal sacrifice had to be a male symbolized strength, the strength of our LORD to save.* "If his offering be a burnt sacrifice of the herd, let him offer a male without blemish: he shall offer it of his own voluntary will at the door of the tabernacle of the congregation before the LORD" (Le.1:3).	Jesus Christ is mighty to save and able to save completely, to the utmost.	"Who needeth not daily, as those high priests, to offer up sacrifice, first for his own sins, and then for the people's: for this he did once, when he offered up himself" (He.7:27). "Wherefore he is able also to save them to the uttermost that come unto God by him, seeing he ever liveth to make intercession for them" (He.7:25).
The Animal Sacrifice That Had to Be Perfect, Without Defect or Blemish Le. 1:3; 4:3-12	*The fact that the sacrifice had to be perfect—without defect or blemish—symbolized the sinlessness, the perfect righteousness of the Lord Jesus Christ.* "If his offering be a burnt sacrifice of the herd, let him offer a male without blemish: he shall offer it of his own voluntary will at the door of the tabernacle of the congregation before the LORD" (Le.1:3).	By living a perfect, sinless life, Jesus Christ secured righteousness for man—the *Ideal Righteousness*. As the Ideal Righteousness, His righteousness can cover or stand for every person of all generations. When a person believes in Jesus Christ, the *Ideal Righteousness* of Christ covers the person, makes him acceptable to God.	"And ye know that he was manifested to take away our sins; and in him is no sin" (1 Jn.3:5). "For he hath made him to be sin for us, who knew no sin; that we might be made the righteousness of God in him." (2 Co.5:21) "Forasmuch as ye know that ye were not redeemed with corruptible things, as silver and gold, from your vain conversation received by tradition from your fathers; But with the precious blood of Christ, as of a lamb without blemish and without spot" (1 Pe.1:18-19).
The Laying of One's Hands on the Head of the Animal Sacrifice Le. 1:4; 8:14	*This is a symbol of identifying with the sacrifice. To the person who truly believed, God did a wonderful thing: God counted his faith in the symbol as righteousness. The person believed God; therefore he obeyed God: he offered a male sacrifice that was perfect, and he laid his hands on its head...*	Note how identification with the substitute sacrifice symbolizes exactly what Jesus Christ did for us: Jesus Christ... • took our place • became our substitute • became our righteousness • became the perfect sacrifice for us	"But he was wounded for our transgressions, he was bruised for our iniquities: the chastisement of our peace was upon him; and with his stripes we are healed" (Is.53:5). "For he hath made him to be sin for us, who knew no sin; that we might be made the righteousness of

TYPES, SYMBOLS, AND PICTURES
Leviticus 1:1-17

Historical Term	Type or Picture (Scriptural Basis for Each)	Life Application for Today's Believer	Biblical Application
	• *identifying himself with the sacrifice* • *believing that God would do just what He said: accept the animal sacrifice as atone-ment, as a ransom, as a substitute for him. He believed that God accepted the sacrifice as the substitute for him, to bear his sins and punish-ment. And because he believed God, God did accept the sacrifice on his behalf, in his stead, in his place—as his substitute.* **"And he shall put his hand upon the head of the burnt offering; and it shall be accepted for him to make atonement for him" (Le.1:4).**	In order to be counted righteous, we must identify with the sacrifice of Jesus Christ. We must believe that God will do just what He says: accept the sacrifice of Christ as the atonement, the ransom, the substitute for us.	*God in him" (2 Co.5:21).* *"Christ hath redeemed us from the curse of the law, being made a curse for us: for it is written, Cursed is every one that hangeth on a tree" (Ga.3:13).* *"But we see Jesus, who was made a little lower than the angels for the suffering of death, crowned with glory and honour; that he by the grace of God should taste death for every man" (He.2:9).* *"Who his own self bare our sins in his own body on the tree, that we, being dead to sins, should live unto righteousness: by whose stripes ye were healed" (1 Pe.2:24).* *"For Christ also hath once suffered for sins, the just for the unjust, that he might bring us to God, being put to death in the flesh, but quickened by the Spirit" (1 Pe.3:18).*
The Shed Blood of the Sacrifice Le. 1:5; 8:19; 17:10-16	*A picture of deliverance from God's judgment upon the sinner. The shed blood of the sacrifice covered the altar of sacrifice. Keep in mind that the altar was the place of judgment, the place where the animal sacrifice died bearing the judgment that was due the sinner. The sacrifice shed its blood on behalf of the believer, delivering the believer from judgment and making him acceptable to God.* **"And he shall kill the bullock before the LORD: and the priests, Aaron's sons, shall bring the blood, and sprinkle the blood round about upon the altar that is by the door of the tabernacle of the congregation" (Le.1:5).**	The blood of Jesus Christ redeems us, delivers us from the consuming judgment and wrath of God.	*"Much more then, being now justified by his blood, we shall be saved from wrath through him" (Ro.5:9).* *"How much more shall the blood of Christ, who through the eternal Spirit offered himself without spot to God, purge your conscience from dead works to serve the living God?" (He.9:14).* *"Forasmuch as ye know that ye were not redeemed with corruptible things, as silver and gold, from your vain conversation received by tradition from your fathers; But with the precious blood of Christ, as of a lamb without blemish and without spot" (1 Pe.1:18-19).*
The Burning and Consuming of the Entire Sacrifice on the Altar of Burnt Offering Le. 1:6-9	*The fire that burns and consumes the entire sacrifice is a picture of two things:* 1. *A picture of the sharp, painful sufferings of Christ, a picture of His awful death on the cross.*	Jesus Christ did two things for us: 1. Jesus Christ suffered for us, bore the painful suffering that was due the sinner. 2. Jesus Christ gave Himself fully, totally, en-	*"He was oppressed, and he was afflicted, yet he opened not his mouth: he is brought as a lamb to the slaughter, and as a sheep before her shearers is dumb, so he openeth not his mouth" (Is.53:7).*

TYPES, SYMBOLS, AND PICTURES
Leviticus 1:1-17

Historical Term	Type or Picture (Scriptural Basis for Each)	Life Application for Today's Believer	Biblical Application
	2. *A picture of the full justice and judgment of God that was borne by the substitute sacrifice.* **"And he shall flay the burnt offering, and cut it into his pieces. And the sons of Aaron the priest shall put fire upon the altar, and lay the wood in order upon the fire: And the priests, Aaron's sons, shall lay the parts, the head, and the fat, in order upon the wood that *is* on the fire which *is* upon the altar: But his inwards and his legs shall he wash in water: and the priest shall burn all on the altar, *to be* a burnt sacrifice, an offering made by fire, of a sweet savour unto the LORD" (Le.1:6-9).**	tirely to be *the Sacrifice* for man. The animal was sacrificed and suffered in man's place—totally. The animal bore the full judgment of God against sin. So it was with Christ. Jesus Christ sacrificed Himself and suffered for man. He gave Himself totally—in the entirety of His Being—to bear the judgment of God against sin.	*"But God commendeth his love toward us, in that, while we were yet sinners, Christ died for us" (Ro.5:8).* *"Much more then, being now justified by his blood, we shall be saved from wrath through him" (Ro.5:9).* *"Christ hath redeemed us from the curse of the law, being made a curse for us: for it is written, Cursed is every one that hangeth on a tree" (Ga.3:13).*
The Sweet Aroma Ascending Upward in the Burnt Offering Le. 1:9; 8:21; 16:27-28	*A symbol of the person's faith (obedience) in the sacrifice ascending up like a sweet aroma to the LORD.* *Note this fact: the Hebrew word for the burnt sacrifice (olah) means that which ascends, that which goes up. Again, this is most likely a symbol of the person's faith in the sacrifice ascending up like a sweet aroma to the LORD. The LORD accepts the person's faith in the sacrifice as atonement, as reconciliation—as righteousness by which he becomes reconciled to God (see Ge.15:6; Ro.4:9; 2 Co. 5:21)* **"But his inwards and his legs shall he wash in water: and the priest shall burn all on the altar, *to be* a burnt sacrifice, an offering made by fire, of a sweet savour unto the LORD" (Le.1:9).**	What can we do to please the LORD? We must have faith in the sacrifice of Christ—obey God, do exactly what God says: approach Him through the sacrifice of Christ. When we approach God through the sacrifice of Christ, God is pleased and He accepts us. God reconciles us to Him.	*"And walk in love, as Christ also hath loved us, and hath given himself for us an offering and a sacrifice to God for a sweetsmelling savour" (Ep.5:2).* *"For God so loved the world, that he gave his only begotten Son, that whosoever believeth in him should not perish, but have everlasting life."(Jn.3:16)*
Oil Used in the Grain Offering Le. 2:1	*A picture of anointing and joy: The Grain Offering was an act of joy and thanksgiving to God as well as an act of dedication and commitment.* **"And when any will offer a meat offering unto**	We are to offer the joy and thanksgiving of our hearts to God for everything: 1. For the joy of the atonement: salvation, redemption, reconciliation 2. For our livelihood: the	*"Enter into his gates with thanksgiving, and into his courts with praise: be thankful unto him, and bless his name" (Ps.100:4).* *"And let them sacrifice the sacrifices of thanksgiving, and declare his works with rejoicing" (Ps.107:22).*

TYPES, SYMBOLS, AND PICTURES
Leviticus 1:1-17

Historical Term	Type or Picture (Scriptural Basis for Each)	Life Application for Today's Believer	Biblical Application
	the LORD, his offering shall be *of* fine flour; and he shall pour oil upon it, and put frankincense thereon" (Le. 2:1).	harvest food, crops, rain, sunshine, housing, clothing	*"Giving thanks always for all things unto God and the Father in the name of our Lord Jesus Christ" (Ep.5:20).* *"In every thing give thanks: for this is the will of God in Christ Jesus concerning you" (1 Th.5:18).*

CHAPTER 2

B. The Grain or Meal Offering (a Picture of Christ, the Bread of Life): The Way to Give Thanks & to Show One's Dedication to God, 2:1-16

1. Give the offering to God
   a. An act of joy & thanksgiving: Take fine flour, pour oil, & put incense on it (oil, a symbol of anointing & joy; incense, a symbol of praise & prayer)
   b. An act of dedication & dependence upon the LORD
      1) A portion to be given as a memorial to God & burned on the Altar of Burnt Offering: Laid upon the sacrifice, thanking God for the atonement (reconciliation)
      2) Is an aroma that God accepts

   c. An act of support for God's servants, the priests: Is a most holy part of the offering (a symbol of Christ, the Bread of Life)

2. Give the offering with careful thought & attention
   a. If one's best is baked in an oven, prepare it carefully
      1) If cakes, use no yeast, but mix with oil
      2) If wafers, use no yeast, but spread with oil
   b. If one's best is cooked on a griddle, prepare it carefully
      1) Make of fine flour mixed with oil, but without yeast
      2) Crumble it and pour oil on it

   c. If one's best is cooked in a pan, prepare it carefully: Make of fine flour & oil

3. Give the offering to the LORD through His representative the priest (minister)
   a. Giving with joy & thanks-

And when any will offer a meat offering unto the LORD, his offering shall be of fine flour; and he shall pour oil upon it, and put frankincense thereon:
2 And he shall bring it to Aaron's sons the priests: and he shall take thereout his handful of the flour thereof, and of the oil thereof, with all the frankincense thereof; and the priest shall burn the memorial of it upon the altar, *to be* an offering made by fire, of a sweet savour unto the LORD:
3 And the remnant of the meat offering *shall be* Aaron's and his sons': *it is* a thing most holy of the offerings of the LORD made by fire.
4 And if thou bring an oblation of a meat offering baken in the oven, *it shall be* unleavened cakes of fine flour mingled with oil, or unleavened wafers anointed with oil.
5 And if thy oblation *be* a meat offering *baken* in a pan, it shall be *of* fine flour unleavened, mingled with oil.
6 Thou shalt part it in pieces, and pour oil thereon: it *is* a meat offering.
7 And if thy oblation *be* a meat offering *baken* in the fryingpan, it shall be made *of* fine flour with oil.
8 And thou shalt bring the meat offering that is made of these things unto the LORD: and when it is pre-

sented unto the priest, he shall bring it unto the altar.
9 And the priest shall take from the meat offering a memorial thereof, and shall burn *it* upon the altar: *it is* an offering made by fire, of a sweet savour unto the LORD.
10 And that which is left of the meat offering *shall be* Aaron's and his sons': it is a thing most holy of the offerings of the LORD made by fire.
11 No meat offering, which ye shall bring unto the LORD, shall be made with leaven: for ye shall burn no leaven, nor any honey, in any offering of the LORD made by fire.
12 As for the oblation of the firstfruits, ye shall offer them unto the LORD: but they shall not be burnt on the altar for a sweet savour.
13 And every oblation of thy meat offering shalt thou season with salt; neither shalt thou suffer the salt of the covenant of thy God to be lacking from thy meat offering: with all thine offerings thou shalt offer salt.
14 And if thou offer a meat offering of thy firstfruits unto the LORD, thou shalt offer for the meat offering of thy firstfruits green ears of corn dried by the fire, *even* corn beaten out of full ears.
15 And thou shalt put oil upon it, and lay frankincense thereon: it *is* a meat offering.
16 And the priest shall burn the memorial of it, *part* of the beaten corn thereof, and *part* of the oil thereof, with all the frankincense thereof: *it is* an offering made by fire unto the LORD.

giving is re-emphasized

   b. Giving with a heart of dedication & dependence is re-emphasized
      1) Is to be burned on the altar: Laid upon the sacrifice, thanking God for the atonement
      2) Is an aroma that God accepts

   c. Giving to support God's servants, the priests, is re-emphasized: Is a most holy part of the offering (a symbol of Christ, the Bread of Life)

4. Give the offering with a pure heart
   a. To be offered with no yeast or honey (a symbol of corruption & worldliness)

      1) Must not burn on the altar
      2) May add yeast & honey to an offering of firstfruits: Must never be offered on the altar—does not please, is not accepted by, the LORD
   b. To be seasoned with salt, the salt that preserves & keeps the covenant or promises of God (the covenant that God will preserve or fulfill if one will obey God)

5. Give the offering of firstfruits as a special offering of thanksgiving & dedication when the need is sensed

   a. To prepare it carefully: Offer crushed heads of new grain mixed with oil & incense

   b. To take a portion & offer it as a memorial to God: Used only in God's service
   c. To be an offering by fire: Laid & burned upon the sacrifice, thanking God

DIVISION I

THE WAY TO BECOME ACCEPTABLE TO GOD (PART 1): BY THE OFFERING OF A SACRIFICE, A SUBSTITUTE, 1:1–7:38

B. The Grain or Meal Offering (a Picture of Christ, the Bread of Life): The Way to Give Thanks and to Show One's Dedication to God, 2:1-16

(2:1-16) **Introduction**: few people are truly dedicated to God, wholly committed and devoted to God. Few people take time to give adequate thanks to God, to really offer thanksgiving and praise to God. For example, how many people do you think spend just ten minutes a day giving thanks to God? How many people actually take time every day to focus upon God long enough to thank and praise Him for His goodness and blessings?

This is shocking! For God is the great Creator and Sustainer of the universe, the One who gives us...

- breath and life
- health and strength
- food and water
- clothing and housing
- land and crops
- rain and sunshine
- sky and space
- the earth, the moon, and the stars (universe)
- knowledge and understanding
- the ability to think and reason
- the mind and ability
- technology and progress
- dreams and hope
- love and joy
- salvation and peace
- deliverance and assurance through all the trials and sufferings of life
- victory over sin and evil, death and hell

When God has given us so much, how can we fail to take time every day to thank Him—to thank God for all He is and has done for us? We need to be honest and ask ourselves several questions:

⇒ Just how dedicated and committed are we to God? Honestly, how devoted are we?

⇒ How often and how much time do we spend daily in thanking God and praying to God? Any?

As stated, honesty is needed in answering these questions, for they expose our true dedication and devotion to God. This is the very picture painted by the Grain Offering. The Grain Offering was actually laid upon the top of the Burnt Offering in the daily sacrifice for the people every morning and evening. Keep in mind that the sacrifice of the Burnt Offering made atonement, paid the ransom and reconciled the person to God. By laying the Grain Offering upon the top of the sacrifice, the person...

- was giving thanks for the atonement (reconciliation) and for all else God had done for him
- was symbolizing that he was laying his life—all he was and had—upon God, dedicating himself to God

The symbol is strong. Moreover, the subject of giving thanks and of dedicating one's life totally to God is of critical importance to all who are pilgrims, pilgrims marching ever forward to the promised land of heaven: *The Grain or Meal Offering (a Picture of Christ, the Bread of Life): The Way to Give Thanks and to Show One's Dedication to God*, 2:1-16.

1. Give the offering to God (vv.1-3).
2. Give the offering with careful thought and attention (vv.4-7).
3. Give the offering to the LORD through His representative the priest (minister) (vv.8-10).
4. Give the offering with a pure heart (vv.11-13).
5. Give the offering of firstfruits as a special offering of thanksgiving and dedication when the need is sensed (vv.14-16).

[1] (2:1-3) **Offering, the Grain—Thanksgiving—Dedication—Commitment—Stewardship—Dependent - Dependence, upon God—Ministers, Support of—Priests, Old Testament, Support of**: give the offering to God. Keep in mind that the five major offerings symbolize or picture the believer's life and walk with the LORD: the Burnt Offering has just been covered (Le.1:1-17). The Burnt Offering was made every morning and evening by the priest on behalf of the people. It was a constant, daily reminder that atonement or reconciliation with God was an absolute necessity. The sacrifice was a symbol of Christ, the Lamb of God, who was sacrificed as the ransom or atonement for man.

Now the Grain Offering is to be made. As stated in the Introduction, the Grain Offering was actually offered upon the top of the Burnt Offering in the daily sacrifice for the people, every morning and evening. The reason for this will be seen in just a moment (point two below). Note the three purposes or reasons for the Grain Offering given in the Scripture and outline:

OUTLINE	SCRIPTURE	SCRIPTURE	OUTLINE
1. Give the offering to God a. An act of joy & thanksgiving: Take fine flour, pour oil, & put incense on it (oil, a symbol of anointing & joy; incense, a symbol of praise & prayer) b. An act of dedication & dependence upon the LORD 1) A portion to be given as a memorial to God & burned on the Altar of Burnt Offer-	And when any will offer a meat offering unto the LORD, his offering shall be *of* fine flour; and he shall pour oil upon it, and put frankincense thereon: 2 And he shall bring it to Aaron's sons the priests: and he shall take thereout his handful of the flour thereof, and of the oil thereof, with	all the frankincense thereof; and the priest shall burn the memorial of it upon the altar, *to be* an offering made by fire, of a sweet savour unto the LORD: 3 And the remnant of the meat offering *shall be* Aaron's and his sons': *it is* a thing most holy of the offerings of the LORD made by fire.	ing: Laid upon the sacrifice, thanking God for the atonement (reconciliation) 2) Is an aroma that God accepts c. An act of support for God's servants, the priests: Is a most holy part of the offering (a symbol of Christ, the Bread of Life)

a. The Grain Offering was an act of joy and thanksgiving to God (v.1). For what? No doubt, for everything:

⇒ For the joy of the atonement: salvation, redemption, reconciliation

⇒ For one's livelihood: the harvest, the grain of the earth—food, crops, rain, sunshine, housing, clothing

Note that a person was to take some fine flour, pour oil on it, and put incense upon it. The oil was a symbol of anointing the grain, of setting it apart for the use of God. The incense, when it was burned off, was a symbol of the believer's praise and prayer ascending up to God and being accepted like the smell of a sweet aroma.

Thought 1. We are to offer the joy and thanksgiving of our hearts to God for everything:
(1) For the joy of the atonement: salvation, redemption, reconciliation
(2) For our livelihood: the harvest, the grain of the earth—food, crops, rain, sunshine, housing, clothing

> **"Enter into his gates with thanksgiving, *and* into his courts with praise: be thankful unto him, *and* bless his name" (Ps.100:4).**
> **"And let them sacrifice the sacrifices of thanksgiving, and declare his works with rejoicing" (Ps.107:22).**
> **"Giving thanks always for all things unto God and the Father in the name of our Lord Jesus Christ" (Ep.5:20).**
> **"Be careful for nothing; but in every thing by prayer and supplication with thanksgiving let your requests be made known unto God. And the peace of God, which passeth all understanding, shall keep your hearts and minds through Christ Jesus" (Ph.4:6-7).**
> **"And let the peace of God rule in your hearts, to the which also ye are called in one body; and be ye thankful" (Col.3:15).**
> **"And whatsoever ye do in word or deed, *do* all in the name of the Lord Jesus, giving thanks to God and the Father by him" (Col.3:17).**
> **"In every thing give thanks: for this is the will of God in Christ Jesus concerning you" (1 Th.5:18).**

b. The Grain Offering was an act of dedication and dependence upon God (v.2). Note that a handful of the offering was to be given as a memorial to God. It was to be laid upon the sacrifice (on the Altar of Burnt Offering) and burned. The symbol was clear: the person was not only offering up the thanksgiving of his heart to the LORD, he was dedicating himself to God and declaring his dependence upon God. By laying his offering upon the atoning sacrifice, he was declaring…
• that he was offering and dedicating himself and his grain to God: his fields, crops, livelihood—all he was and had
• that he—all he was and had—was totally dependent upon God

Note God's response to such an offering of thanksgiving and dedication: He was pleased. God accepted the offering. The person's thanksgiving and renewed dedication were just like a pleasing aroma rising up to Him.

Thought 1. It is God who has given us life. He has given us air, water, sun, moon, stars, crops, food, clothing, housing—all the necessities of life. God created the materials of the universe, everything that sustains our lives and keeps us going. We owe God everything we are and have. We must, therefore, give the offering of dedication to God:
⇒ We must dedicate all we are and have to Him—because of all He has done for us.
⇒ We must declare our dependence upon Him—because of who He is.

> **"I beseech you therefore, brethren, by the mercies of God, that ye present your bodies a living sacrifice, holy, acceptable unto God, *which is* your reasonable service" (Ro.12:1).**
> **"Therefore, my beloved brethren, be ye stedfast, unmoveable, always abounding in the work of the Lord, forasmuch as ye know that your labour is not in vain in the Lord" (1 Co.15:58).**
> **"By him therefore let us offer the sacrifice of praise to God continually, that is, the fruit of *our* lips giving thanks to his name" (He.13:15).**
> **"And thou shalt love the LORD thy God with all thine heart, and with all thy soul, and with all thy might" (De.6:5).**
> **"Trust in the LORD with all thine heart; and lean not unto thine own understanding" (Pr.3:5).**

c. The Grain Offering was an act of support for God's servants, the priests (v.3). Note that the Grain Offering is holy; that is, it has been sanctified, set apart to God. Therefore, the rest of the Grain Offering belonged to the priests, the servants of God. None of it whatsoever could be used for any secular purpose. Note what it was that made the offering holy: the fact that it was offered upon the altar of fire, an offering burned upon the holy altar of God.

Thought 1. God demands that His servants be financially supported. God's people are to give and support the ministers who serve God, the people who feed the Word of Life to them.

> **"Even so hath the Lord ordained that they which preach the gospel should live of the gospel" (1 Co.9:14).**
> **"Let him that is taught in the word communicate [give, support] unto him that teacheth in all good things" (Ga.6:6).**
> **"Let the elders [ministers] that rule well be counted worthy of double honour, especially they who labour in the word and doctrine" (1 Ti.5:17).**

Thought 2. The Grain Offering is a symbol of Christ, the Bread of Life.

"For the bread of God is he which cometh down from heaven, and giveth life unto the world. Then said they unto him, Lord, evermore give us this bread. And Jesus said unto them, I am the bread of life: he that cometh to me shall never hunger; and he that believeth on me shall never thirst" (Jn.6:33-35).

"Verily, verily, I say unto you, He that believeth on me hath everlasting life. I am that bread of life" (Jn.6:47-48).

"I am the living bread which came down from heaven: if any man eat of this bread, he shall live for ever: and the bread that I will give is my flesh, which I will give for the life of the world" (Jn.6:51).

"This is that bread which came down from heaven: not as your fathers did eat manna, and are dead: he that eateth of this bread shall live for ever" (Jn.6:58).

"And as they did eat, Jesus took bread, and blessed, and brake *it*, and gave to them, and said, Take, eat: this is my body" (Mk.14:22).

2 **(2:4-7) Offering, the Grain—Dedication—Commitment—Stewardship—Cooking—Service—Ministering—Best, Doing One's:** give the offering with careful thought and attention. Note that a person had three choices as to how he prepared the Grain Offering:

⇒ It could be baked in an *oven,* baking either cakes or wafers (v.4).
⇒ It could be cooked on a *griddle* (v.5).
⇒ It could be cooked in a *pan* (v.7).

OUTLINE	SCRIPTURE
2. Give the offering with careful thought & attention	4 And if thou bring an oblation of a meat offering baken in the oven, *it shall be* unleavened cakes of fine flour mingled with oil, or unleavened wafers anointed with oil.
a. If one's best is baked in an oven, prepare it carefully	
1) If cakes, use no yeast, but mix with oil	
1) If wafers, use no yeast, but spread with oil	
b. If one's best is cooked on a griddle, prepare it carefully	5 And if thy oblation *be* a meat offering *baken* in a pan, it shall be *of* fine flour unleavened, mingled with oil.
1) Make of fine flour mixed with oil, but without yeast	
2) Crumble it and pour oil on it	6 Thou shalt part it in pieces, and pour oil thereon: it *is* a meat offering.
c. If one's best is cooked in a pan, prepare it carefully: Make of fine flour & oil	7 And if thy oblation *be* a meat offering *baken* in the fryingpan, it shall be made *of* fine flour with oil.

Why did God give a choice as to how a person prepared the Grain Offering? There would have been at least two reasons:

First, a person might become gripped with an immediate, deep sense of need, a need to praise God or to rededicate his life to God. The sense of need would be just as it is with all genuine believers—an immediate need, a need that cannot wait. A person feels that he has to rush to God, get into His presence immediately in order to praise, pray, and seek Him, or to rededicate his life. A person who sensed such urgency would not have time to prepare a cake or wafers nor do any other kind of cooking. But in most cases, a person would already have some grain baked or cooked, some bread, cake, wafer, or something on hand. They could thereby take whatever was already cooked and rush to God, having their needs met. But note this fact as well, just how much God wanted His people to rush into His presence: if a person did not have any food baked or cooked, he could bring raw, uncooked grain (vv.1-2).

Thought 1. We must act and act immediately when the Spirit of God moves in our hearts; we must not delay. When the Spirit of God is arousing, convicting, or stirring us, we must rush to God in prayer, praise, and renewed dedication.

"(...behold, now *is* the accepted time; behold, now *is* the day of salvation)" (2 Co.6:2).

"For every one that asketh receiveth; and he that seeketh findeth; and to him that knocketh it shall be opened" (Lu.11:10).

"For Moses had said, Consecrate yourselves to day to the LORD, even every man upon his son, and upon his brother; that he may bestow upon you a blessing this day" (Ex.32:29).

"Seek ye the LORD while he may be found, call ye upon him while he is near" (Is.55:6).

"And ye shall seek me, and find *me*, when ye shall search for me with all your heart" (Je.29:13).

Second, God gave a choice in preparing the Grain Offering because He wants the very best a person can offer. He is the LORD God, the great Creator and Sustainer of the universe, the Sovereign LORD and Majesty of all.

⇒ God is the One who ultimately gives us food, rain, crops, clothing, housing—all the basic necessities of life.
⇒ God is the One who saves us, who makes atonement and reconciles us to Himself, who ransoms us from sin, death, judgment, and hell yet to come.

⇒ God is the One who is due the very best a person can offer. If a person's best were prepared through baking, then the Grain Offering was to be baked. If a person's best were prepared in a pan or on a griddle, then the Grain Offering was prepared in a pan or on a griddle. A person was to give careful thought and attention to the Grain Offering he was presenting to the LORD, careful thought and attention to his praise and thanksgiving or to the renewed dedication he was offering up to God.

Thought 1. We must always give the best we have to God. As the great hymn says: "Give of your best to the Master."

"And whatsoever ye do in word or deed, *do* all in the name of the Lord Jesus, giving thanks to God and the Father by him" (Col.3:17).
"And whatsoever ye do, do *it* heartily, as to the Lord, and not unto men" (Col.3:23).
"And thou shalt love the LORD thy God with all thine heart, and with all thy soul, and with all thy might" (De.6:5).
"Therefore also now, saith the LORD, turn ye *even* to me with all your heart, and with fasting, and with weeping, and with mourning" (Joel 2:12).

3 (2:8-10) **Offering, the Grain—Dedication**: give the offering to the LORD—through His representative, the priest (minister). These verses show how important the Grain Offering was to the LORD, for they simply repeat verses 1-3, re-emphasizing the purpose for the Grain Offering. Note the purpose in the outline and compare it with verses 1-3:

OUTLINE	SCRIPTURE
3. Give the offering to the LORD through His representative the priest (minister)	8 And thou shalt bring the meat offering that is made of these things unto the LORD: and when it is presented unto the priest, he shall bring it unto the altar.
a. Giving with joy & thanksgiving is re-emphasized	
b. Giving with a heart of dedication & dependence is re-emphasized	9 And the priest shall take from the meat offering a memorial thereof, and shall burn *it* upon the altar: *it is* an offering made by fire, of a sweet savour unto the LORD.
1) Is to be burned on the altar: Laid upon the sacrifice, thanking God for the atonement	
2) Is an aroma that God accepts	
c. Giving to support God's servants, the priests, is re-emphasized: Is a most holy part of the offering (a symbol of Christ, the Bread of Life)	10 And that which is left of the meat offering *shall be* Aaron's and his sons': *it is* a thing most holy of the offerings of the LORD made by fire.

Thought 1. The importance of giving thanks and renewing our dedication to God cannot be over-emphasized. Daily, every day of our lives…
• we must rededicate ourselves to live for God more and more, continuing to grow in holiness
• we must walk about giving thanks and praising God for all He is and for all He does for us

"I beseech you therefore, brethren, by the mercies of God, that ye present your bodies a living sacrifice, holy, acceptable unto God, *which is* your reasonable service" (Ro.12:1).
"Be ye therefore followers of God, as dear children; And walk in love, as Christ also hath loved us, and hath given himself for us an offering and a sacrifice to God for a sweetsmelling savour" (Ep.5:1-2).
"Giving thanks unto the Father, which hath made us meet to be partakers of the inheritance of the saints in light" (Col.1:12).
"And let the peace of God rule in your hearts, to the which also ye are called in one body; and be ye thankful" (Col.3:15).
"In every thing give thanks: for this is the will of God in Christ Jesus concerning you" (1 Th.5:18).
"By him therefore let us offer the sacrifice of praise to God continually, that is, the fruit of *our* lips giving thanks to his name" (He.13:15).
"Enter into his gates with thanksgiving, *and* into his courts with praise: be thankful unto him, *and* bless his name" (Ps.100:4).
"And let them sacrifice the sacrifices of thanksgiving, and declare his works with rejoicing" (Ps.107:22).

4 (2:11-13) **Offering, the Grain—Corruption—Yeast—Leaven—Worldliness-Salt—Honey**: give the offering with a pure heart. Note how emphatically this point is spelled out in the Scripture and outline.

OUTLINE	SCRIPTURE
4. Give the offering with a pure heart a. To be offered with no yeast or honey (a symbol of corruption & worldliness) 1) Must not burn on the altar 2) May add yeast & honey to an offering of firstfruits: Must never be offered on the altar—does not please, is not accepted by, the LORD b. To be seasoned with salt, the salt that preserves & keeps the covenant or promises of God (the covenant that God will preserve or fulfill if one will obey God)	11 No meat offering, which ye shall bring unto the LORD, shall be made with leaven: for ye shall burn no leaven, nor any honey, in any offering of the LORD made by fire. 12 As for the oblation of the firstfruits, ye shall offer them unto the LORD: but they shall not be burnt on the altar for a sweet savour. 13 And every oblation of thy meat offering shalt thou season with salt; neither shalt thou suffer the salt of the covenant of thy God to be lacking from thy meat offering: with all thine offerings thou shalt offer salt.

a. The offering was to be given with no yeast or honey mixed with it (vv.11-12). Why? Because yeast and honey are symbols of corruption, evil, and worldliness. Yeast or leaven sours the bread. Honey is a natural sweetener, but it too will eventually ferment and turn sour. Honey represents natural sweetness or worldliness that eventually ruin the bread or life of a person.

Note that yeast (leaven) and honey must never be burned as an offering to the LORD. But yeast and honey could be included in an offering of the firstfruits because they were never offered upon the altar. The harvest of firstfruits was a required offering legally demanded when harvest first began. The firstfruit harvest given to the LORD went primarily to the priests who often needed the grain in order to replenish their food supplies. But, again, note: no yeast and no honey were ever to be offered on the altar where the sacrifice for atonement (redemption and salvation) was being offered to God. No substance that symbolized corruption, evil, or worldliness could be allowed to lay upon the perfect sacrifice that was being offered to God. The sacrifice was a symbol of the Lord Jesus Christ, the sinless and incorruptible Lamb of God who secured eternal redemption and salvation for us.

Thought 1. Note what Scripture teaches about leaven or yeast (the same could be said about honey):

> **"Then Jesus said unto them, Take heed and beware of the leaven [false teaching] of the Pharisees and of the Sadducees" (Mt.16:6).**
> **"A little leaven leaveneth [corrupts] the whole lump" (Ga.5:9).**
> **"Your glorying *is* not good. Know ye not that a little leaven leaveneth the whole lump? Purge out therefore the old leaven, that ye may be a new lump, as ye are unleavened. For even Christ our passover is sacrificed for us: Therefore let us keep the feast, not with old leaven, neither with the leaven of malice and wickedness; but with the unleavened *bread* of sincerity and truth" (1 Co.5:6-8).**
> **"Hast thou found honey? eat so much as is sufficient for thee, lest thou be filled therewith, and vomit it" (Pr.25:16).**
> **"*It is* not good to eat much honey: so *for men* to search their own glory *is not* glory" (Pr.25:27).**

b. The offering was to be seasoned with salt, the salt that preserves and keeps the covenant of God. Note that salt represents the covenant of God in this verse. In fact, the actual term used is, "the salt of the covenant of God." Salt is a preservative. Salt was never to be left out of the Grain Offering. The picture is clear and graphic: the salt of God's covenant will preserve and keep one's thanksgiving and dedication alive before God. The salt symbolizes—preserves and keeps—the covenant of God alive in a person's mind:

⇒ The salt reminded a person that God would keep His promises, His covenant, with His people; that God would guide and deliver His people to the promised land (a symbol of heaven).
⇒ The salt reminded a person that he was to keep his part of the covenant, his promise to obey God and to keep His commandments.

> **"Ye are the salt of the earth: but if the salt have lost his savour, wherewith shall it be salted? it is thenceforth good for nothing, but to be cast out, and to be trodden under foot of men" (Mt.5:13).**
> **"Salt *is* good: but if the salt have lost his saltness, wherewith will ye season it? Have salt in yourselves, and have peace one with another" (Mk.9:50).**
> **"Salt *is* good: but if the salt have lost his savour, wherewith shall it be seasoned? It is neither fit for the land, nor yet for the dunghill; *but* men cast it out. He that hath ears to hear, let him hear" (Lu.14:34-35).**
> **"Let your speech *be* alway with grace, seasoned with salt, that ye may know how ye ought to answer every man" (Col.4:6; see 1 Pe.3:15).**
> **"...it *is* a covenant of salt for ever before the LORD unto thee and to thy seed with thee" (Nu.18:19).**

5 (2:14-16) **Firstfruits, Offering of—Offering, the Firstfruit—Thanksgiving—Dedication**: give an offering of firstfruit as a special offering of thanksgiving and dedication when the need is felt. This is a special provision the LORD makes for His people. Note the Scripture and outline:

OUTLINE	SCRIPTURE
5. Give the offering of firstfruits as a special offering of thanksgiving & dedication when the need is sensed	14 And if thou offer a meat offering of thy firstfruits unto the LORD, thou shalt offer for the meat offering of thy firstfruits green ears of corn dried by the fire, *even* corn beaten out of full ears.
a. Prepare it carefully: Offer crushed heads of new grain mixed with oil & incense	15 And thou shalt put oil upon it, and lay frankincense thereon: it *is* a meat offering.
b. The priest is to take a portion & offer it as a memorial to God: Used only in God's service	16 And the priest shall burn the memorial of it, *part* of the beaten corn thereof, and *part* of the oil thereof, with all the frankincense thereof: *it is* an
c. Is an offering by fire: Laid & burned upon the sacrifice, thanking God	offering made by fire unto the LORD.

When the firstfruits of the harvest came in, a person might sense not only thankfulness but a real need to rededicate his life—all he was and had—to the LORD. Or during the planting or growing season, a person might want to express a special thanks, dedication, or dependence upon God for the upcoming harvest. In either situation, the person would bring an offering of firstfruits as described in these verses (vv.14-16):

⇒ To prepare it carefully: offer crushed heads of new grain mixed with oil and incense (vv.14-15).
⇒ To take a portion and offer it as a memorial to God: used only in God's service (v.16).
⇒ To be an offering by fire: laid and burned upon the sacrifice, thanking God (v.16).

Note that this special firstfruit offering was laid upon the burning sacrifice on the altar; therefore, it had no yeast nor honey added to it.

Thought 1. God meets the needs of His dear people. He makes every provision for us, providing for our care, taking care of every conceivable need we have.

"**But seek ye first the kingdom of God, and his righteousness; and all these things shall be added unto you**" (Mt.6:33).
"**Give, and it shall be given unto you; good measure, pressed down, and shaken together, and running over, shall men give into your bosom. For with the same measure that ye mete withal it shall be measured to you again**" (Lu.6:38).
"**I am come that they might have life, and that they might have** *it* **more abundantly**" (Jn.10:10).
"**And God** *is* **able to make all grace abound toward you; that ye, always having all sufficiency in all** *things*, **may abound to every good work**" (2 Co.9:8).
"**Now unto him that is able to do exceeding abundantly above all that we ask or think, according to the power that worketh in us**" (Ep.3:20).
"**And ye shall serve the LORD your God, and he shall bless thy bread, and thy water; and I will take sickness away from the midst of thee**" (Ex.23:25).
"**And the LORD thy God will make thee plenteous in every work of thine hand, in the fruit of thy body, and in the fruit of thy cattle, and in the fruit of thy land, for good: for the LORD will again rejoice over thee for good, as he rejoiced over thy fathers**" (De.30:9).
"**Blessed** *be* **the LORD,** *who* **daily loadeth us** *with benefits, even* **the God of our salvation. Selah**" (Ps.68:19).
"**Bring ye all the tithes into the storehouse, that there may be meat in mine house, and prove me now herewith, saith the LORD of hosts, if I will not open you the windows of heaven, and pour you out a blessing, that** *there shall* **not** *be room* **enough** *to receive it*" (Mal.3:10).

TYPES, SYMBOLS, AND PICTURES
Leviticus 2:1-16

Historical Term	Type or Picture (Scriptural Basis for Each)	Life Application for Today's Believer	Biblical Application
Incense Used in the Grain Offering Le. 2:1	*A symbol of the believer's praise and prayer ascending up to God and being accepted like the smell of a sweet aroma.* **"And when any will offer a meat offering unto the LORD, his offering shall be *of* fine flour; and he shall pour oil upon it, and put frankincense thereon"** (Le.2:1).	The most pleasing aroma a believer can offer up to God is that of his prayers and that of placing his trust and hope in the saving grace of God, in the sacrifice of Jesus Christ. Like the incense that drifted continually up to God, our prayers should be constantly ascending up and pleasing God.	*"He shall call upon me, and I will answer him: I will be with him in trouble; I will deliver him, and honour him" (Ps.91:15)* *"And I say unto you, Ask, and it shall be given you; seek, and ye shall find; knock, and it shall be opened unto you" (Lu.11:9).* *"If ye abide in me, and my words abide in you, ye shall ask what ye will, and it shall be done unto you" (Jn.15:7).* *"By him therefore let us offer the sacrifice of praise to God continually, that is, the fruit of our lips giving thanks to his name" (He.13:15).*

Grain Offering Le. 2:3	*The Grain Offering is a symbol of three things:*
	1. A symbol of joy and thanksgiving to God...
	  • *for the joy of atonement: salvation, redemption, reconciliation*
	  • *for one's livelihood: the harvest, crops, rain, sunshine, housing, clothing*
	
	2. A symbol of an act of dedication and dependence upon God
	3. In addition, the Grain Offering was also a symbol of Christ, the Bread of Life.
	
	"And the remnant of the meat offerings *shall be* Aaron's and his sons': it is a thing most holy of the offerings of the LORD made by fire" (Le.2:3).
		The symbol of the Grain Offering teaches us three things:
		
		1. We are to offer the joy and thanksgiving of our hearts to God for everything:
		  • For the joy of the atonement: salvation, redemption, reconciliation
		  • For our livelihood: the harvest food, crops, rain, sunshine, housing, clothing
		
		2. It is God who has given us life: air, water, sun, moon, stars, crops, food, clothing, housing—all the necessities of life. God created the materials of the universe, everything that sustains our lives and keeps us going. We owe God everything we are and have: we must, therefore, give the offering of dedication to God and declare our dependence upon Him.
		3. Jesus Christ is the Bread of Life...
		  • who feeds us
		  • who nourishes us
		  • who sustains us with Himself
			"For the bread of God is he which cometh down from heaven, and giveth life unto the world. Then said they unto him, LORD, evermore give us this bread. And Jesus said unto them, I am the bread of life: he that cometh to me shall never hunger; and he that believeth on me shall never thirst" (Jn.6:33-35).
			
			"Verily, verily, I say unto you, He that believeth on me hath everlasting life. I am that bread of life" (Jn.6:47-48).
			
			"I am the living bread which came down from heaven: if any man eat of this bread, he shall live for ever: and the bread that I will give is my flesh, which I will give for the life of the world" (Jn.6:51).
			
			"This is that bread which came down from heaven: not as your fathers did eat manna, and are dead: he that eateth of this bread shall live for ever" (Jn.6:58).
			
			"And as they did eat, Jesus took bread, and blessed, and brake it, and gave to them, and said, Take, eat: this is my body" (Mk. 14:22).

TYPES, SYMBOLS, AND PICTURES
Leviticus 2:1-16

Historical Term	Type or Picture (Scriptural Basis for Each)	Life Application for Today's Believer	Biblical Application
Yeast and Honey Le. 2:11-12	*Yeast and honey are symbols of corruption, evil, and worldliness. Yeast or leaven sours the bread. Honey is a natural sweetener, but it too will eventually ferment and turn sour. Honey represents natural sweetness or worldliness that eventually ruins the bread or life of a person.* **"No meat offering, which ye shall bring unto the LORD, shall be made with leaven: for ye shall burn no leaven, nor any honey, in any offering of the LORD made by fire"** (Le.2:11).	Jesus Christ delivers us and gives us victory over the world. Note the strong contrasts: 1. The world offers corruption. Christ delivers us from corruption and offers us eternity. 2. The world is the source of evil. Christ—the source of all goodness—gives us victory over evil. 3. The world's consuming passion is the frenzied pursuit of the sinful nature, the flesh. Jesus Christ delivers us from worldliness and fills us with the deep yearning… • to love Him more intimately • to walk with Him more closely • to count all things as loss in order to know Him and to make Him known to the world.	*"Then Jesus said unto them, Take heed and beware of the leaven [false teaching] of the Pharisees and of the Sadducees"* (Mt.16:6). *"A little leaven leaveneth [corrupts] the whole lump"* (Ga.5:9). *"Your glorying is not good. Know ye not that a little leaven leaveneth the whole lump? Purge out therefore the old leaven, that ye may be a new lump, as ye are unleavened. For even Christ our passover is sacrificed for us: Therefore let us keep the feast, not with old leaven, neither with the leaven of malice and wickedness; but with the unleavened bread of sincerity and truth"* (1 Co. 5:6-8). *"Hast thou found honey? eat so much as is sufficient for thee, lest thou be filled therewith, and vomit it"* (Pr.25:16). *"It is not good to eat much honey: so for men to search their own glory is not glory"* (Pr.25:27)

CHAPTER 3

C. The Fellowship or Peace Offering (a Picture of Christ's Atoning Sacrifice): The Way to Grow in Peace and Fellowship of God—Seeking a Deeper Life with God, 3:1-17

1. **Seek more fellowship with God, more of the peace of God**
2. **Offer a bull or cow, an animal of service, to God (a symbol of Christ the Servant): Focus upon the sacrifice of service**
   a. Offer a sacrifice with no defect
   b. Identify with the sacrifice: By laying one's hands on its head
   c. Put the sacrifice to death
   d. Have the priests (ministers) offer the sacrifice
      1) To sprinkle the blood against the altar on all sides
      2) To offer a portion to the LORD by fire on the altar: The fat, liver, & kidneys
      3) To burn on the altar, on top of the burnt offering
   e. The result: The sweet aroma of the sacrifice pleases the LORD
3. **Offer a lamb, the animal most used in sacrifice (a symbol of Christ the Lamb of God): Focus upon dedication to God, dying to self & following God totally (Lu.9:23)**
   a. Offer a sacrifice with no defect (v.6)
   b. Identify with the sacrifice by laying one's hands on its head
   c. Put the sacrifice to death
      Have the priests (ministers) offer the sacrifice

And if his oblation *be* a sacrifice of peace offering, if he offer *it* of the herd; whether *it be* a male or female, he shall offer it without blemish before the LORD.
2 And he shall lay his hand upon the head of his offering, and kill it *at* the door of the tabernacle of the congregation: and Aaron's sons the priests shall sprinkle the blood upon the altar round about.
3 And he shall offer of the sacrifice of the peace offering an offering made by fire unto the LORD; the fat that covereth the inwards, and all the fat that *is* upon the inwards,
4 And the two kidneys, and the fat that *is* on them, which *is* by the flanks, and the caul above the liver, with the kidneys, it shall he take away.
5 And Aaron's sons shall burn it on the altar upon the burnt sacrifice, which *is* upon the wood that *is* on the fire: *it is* an offering made by fire, of a sweet savour unto the LORD.
6 And if his offering for a sacrifice of peace offering unto the LORD *be* of the flock; male or female, he shall offer it without blemish.
7 If he offer a lamb for his offering, then shall he offer it before the LORD.
8 And he shall lay his hand upon the head of his offering, and kill it before the tabernacle of the congregation: and Aar-

on's sons shall sprinkle the blood thereof round about upon the altar.
9 And he shall offer of the sacrifice of the peace offering an offering made by fire unto the LORD; the fat thereof, *and* the whole rump, it shall he take off hard by the backbone; and the fat that covereth the inwards, and all the fat that *is* upon the inwards,
10 And the two kidneys, and the fat that *is* upon them, which *is* by the flanks, and the caul above the liver, with the kidneys, it shall he take away.
11 And the priest shall burn it upon the altar: *it is* the food of the offering made by fire unto the LORD.
12 And if his offering *be* a goat, then he shall offer it before the LORD.
13 And he shall lay his hand upon the head of it, and kill it before the tabernacle of the congregation: and the sons of Aaron shall sprinkle the blood thereof upon the altar round about.
14 And he shall offer thereof his offering, *even* an offering made by fire unto the LORD; the fat that covereth the inwards, and all the fat that *is* upon the inwards,
15 And the two kidneys, and the fat that *is* upon them, which *is* by the flanks, and the caul above the liver, with the kidneys, it shall he take away.
16 And the priest shall burn them upon the altar: *it is* the food of the offering made by fire for a sweet savour: all the fat *is* the LORD's.
17 *It shall be* a perpetual statute for your generations throughout all your dwellings, that ye eat neither fat nor blood.

1) To sprinkle its blood against the altar on all sides
2) To offer a portion to the LORD
   - The entire tail
   - All fat (considered the most choice part of an animal for eating)
   - The kidneys
   - The liver
3) To burn on the altar as food given to the LORD: Symbolizing fellowship with God
4. **Offer a goat, the animal that most symbolizes the bearing of God's judgment (a symbol of Christ upon the cross)**
   a. Identify with the sacrifice
   b. Put the sacrifice to death
   c. Have the priests offer the sacrifice
      1) To sprinkle its blood against the altar
      2) To offer a portion to the LORD
         - All the fat (see v.16)
         - Both kidneys
         - The liver
      3) To burn on the altar as food given to the LORD
   d. The result: The sweet aroma pleases the LORD
5. **Offer the sacrifice faithfully, never abusing—never eating—any of God's portion (the fat or the blood): Keep this law**

DIVISION I

THE WAY TO BECOME ACCEPTABLE TO GOD (PART 1): BY THE OFFERING OF A SACRIFICE, A SUBSTITUTE, 1:1–7:38

C. The Fellowship or Peace Offering (a Picture of Christ's Atoning Sacrifice): The Way to Grow in the Peace and Fellowship of God—Seeking a Deeper Life with God, 3:1-17

(3:1-17) **Introduction**: this is an age of restlessness, an age of uneasiness and disturbance. The soul of man is unsettled: it is not content. It is as restless, as uneasy and disturbed as it has ever been. Most people…

- are usually wanting to be on the move, to be someplace they are not—all because of a restless spirit that grips them
- are usually not satisfied with what they are doing, wanting to change jobs or professions
- are usually hoping for and looking ahead to something else
- are often uneasy and disturbed over the lawlessness and evil of society, over the trends and irresponsibilities of government
- are tragically subjected to distress over sickness, disease, accident, broken relationships, failures, shortcomings—every imaginable trial and temptation—and eventually the death of loved ones

The soul of man is restless and unsettled—in desperate need of peace. We need the peace and fellowship of God. We need God's presence—purpose, rest, comfort, satisfaction, fulfillment, confidence, and assurance—all that comes from the fellowship and peace of God. How can we secure the fellowship and peace of God? There are two kinds of peace that God gives.

⇒ First, there is *peace with God*. Man is separated and alienated from God because of sin. It is man's sin—his evil and lawlessness—that causes so much restlessness and disturbance in his heart and life. But there is an answer: the atonement, that is, reconciliation with God. This was seen in the Burnt Offering discussed in chapter one. Man can make peace with God by turning his life over to Jesus Christ: when we turn away from sin and turn to Christ, God makes peace with us and reconciles us to Himself. Peace with God is established, and we begin to fellowship with God (Ro.5:1; 1 Jn.1:3).

⇒ Second, there is *the peace of God*. Once we have made *peace with God*, the *peace of God* begins to fill our spirits. God's peace settles within us and to give us the peace and fellowship of God's…

- presence
- comfort
- rest
- purpose
- satisfaction
- fulfillment
- confidence
- assurance

Once a believer has secured peace and fellowship with God, how can he experience a continuous flow of God's peace and fellowship? How can he gain a deeper life with God, develop an intimacy with God, grow in the fellowship and *peace of God*?

This Scripture deals with the *peace of God* that fills a believer's heart and life. This is the great subject of this passage: *The Fellowship or Peace Offering (a Picture of Christ's Atoning Sacrifice): The Way to Grow in the Peace and Fellowship of God—Seeking a Deeper Life with God*, 3:1-17.

1. Seek more fellowship with God, more of the peace of God (v.1).
2. Offer a bull or cow, an animal of service, to God (a symbol of Christ the Servant): focus upon the sacrifice of service (vv.1-5).
3. Offer a lamb, the animal most used in sacrifice (a symbol of Christ the Lamb of God): focus upon dedication to God, dying to self and following God totally (vv.6-11).
4. Offer a goat, the animal that most symbolizes the bearing of God's judgment (a symbol of Christ upon the cross) (vv.12-16).
5. Offer the sacrifice faithfully, never abusing—never eating—any of God's portion (the fat or the blood): keep this law (v.17).

1 (3:1) **Fellowship, with God—Peace, of God—Hunger, after God—Thirst, for God—Seeking, after God—Desire, for God**: How was a person to grow in the peace and the fellowship of God? By seeking more fellowship with God, more of the peace of God.

OUTLINE	SCRIPTURE
1. Seek more fellowship with God, more of the peace of God	And if his oblation *be* a sacrifice of peace offering, if he offer *it* of the herd; whether *it be* a male or female, he shall offer it without blemish before the LORD.

Note a fact that is self-evident: if a person wanted more of the fellowship and peace of God, he would offer the Fellowship or Peace Offering to God. This was the very reason God set up and established this offering: to meet the need of His people, their need to grow more and more in fellowship with Him and to experience more and more of His peace. Once a person had experienced the atonement, been reconciled to God, he was to grow in his fellowship with God, experience more and more of God's peace within his heart and life.

Thought 1. How do we grow in fellowship with God? Gain more of the peace of God within our hearts? Very simply, by seeking more of the fellowship and peace of God.

2 (3:1-5) **Offering, the Peace or Fellowship—Fellowship, with God—Peace, of God—Hunger, after God—Thirst, after God—Desire, for God**: How was a person to grow in the fellowship and peace of God? He could offer a bull or a cow to God, an *animal of service*. (Note that this sacrifice is a symbol of Christ, the *Servant of God*.) This particular sacrifice would focus a person's attention upon…

- sacrificing more and more service to God
- serving God more and more

OUTLINE	SCRIPTURE	SCRIPTURE	OUTLINE

2. Offer a bull or cow, an animal of service, to God (a symbol of Christ the Servant): Focus upon the sacrifice of service
a. Offer a sacrifice with no defect
 	
b. Identify with the sacrifice: By laying one's hands on its head
c. Put the sacrifice to death
d. Have the priests (ministers) offer the sacrifice
  1) To sprinkle the blood against the altar on all sides
 	
  2) To offer a portion to the LORD by fire on the altar: The fat, liver, & kidneys
	And if his oblation *be* a sacrifice of peace offering, if he offer *it* of the herd; whether *it be* a male or female, he shall offer it without blemish before the LORD.
	2 And he shall lay his hand upon the head of his offering, and kill it *at* the door of the tabernacle of the congregation: and Aaron's sons the priests shall sprinkle the blood upon the altar round about.
	3 And he shall offer of the sacrifice of the peace offering an offering made by fire
		unto the LORD; the fat that covert the inwards, and all the fat that *is* upon the inwards,
		4 And the two kidneys, and the fat that *is* on them, which *is* by the flanks, and the caulk above the liver, with the kidneys, it shall he take away.
		5 And Aaron's sons shall burn it on the altar upon the burnt sacrifice, which *is* upon the wood that *is* on the fire: *it is* an offering made by fire, of a sweet savor unto the LORD.
			3) To burn on the altar, on top of the burnt offering
			e. The result: The sweet aroma of the sacrifice pleases the LORD

The bull or cow could be taken from either the cattle or oxen. Both were major animals of service used for both work and food. The cow was used to provide milk as well as food, and the bull was used for food and heavy work such as pulling carts, plowing, and pulling huge stones in grinding the grain. Most of the heavy work on farms and in the commerce of that day was placed upon the shoulders of the bull. In sacrificing the bull or cow, the major animal of service, the person was bound to think about the sacrifice of service, focus upon sacrificing more and more of his service to God.

As stated, this sacrifice is a symbol of Christ, the Servant of God. The symbolism of Christ is clearly seen throughout the Fellowship or Peace Offering. If a person seeks more peace and fellowship with God, he has to focus upon Christ, the Perfect Servant of God. Note the clear instructions given in making this sacrifice.

a. A person was to offer a sacrifice with no defect (v.2). The bull or cow was to be without blemish, perfect. This pointed to Christ, the Perfect Servant of God. The person saw in this a perfect sacrifice of service. He was declaring just what genuine believers often declare when they are seeking more and more peace and fellowship with God: his sincerity, that he wanted to serve God more and more, even perfectly.

b. A person was to identify with the sacrifice. How? By laying his hands on the head of the sacrifice (v.2). By so doing, the person was declaring that he was doing just what the animal was doing: giving himself up as a sacrifice of service to God. (See note, pt.2, Le.1:3-9 for more discussion.)

c. A person was to put the sacrifice to death (v.2). The animal was the substitute for the person's sins, bearing the judgment of separation and alienation from God. By the animal's dying for the person, that person was reconciled to God. He was free to stand before God and serve God. He was free from everything that kept him from God, free to serve God and live for God.

d. A person was to have the priests (ministers) offer the sacrifice (vv.2-5).
1) The priest was to sprinkle the blood against the altar on all sides (v.2). The blood appeased, satisfied, the justice of God against sin. It calmed and settled God's anger and wrath against sin. It opened the door or the way into God's presence so that the person could approach God and serve God.
2) The priest was to offer a portion to the LORD by fire. "By fire" means on the altar where the Burnt Offering was always burning before the LORD as a constant reminder of the need for the atoning sacrifice in order to be reconciled with God. The fat, liver, and kidneys were offered to the LORD (vv.3-4). These particular parts were considered the choice parts.
3) The priest was then to actually burn the choice parts on top of the Burnt Offering (v.5). Remember, the Burnt Offering made atonement, reconciled a person, to God. This declared that peace and fellowship with God were *based upon the atonement*, upon reconciliation with God. A person had to understand this: he could never grow in peace and fellowship with God until the atonement, the ransom, was paid for him—until he was reconciled to God by the atonement (the ransom for his sins, alienation and separation from God).

e. The result: the sweet aroma of the sacrifice pleased the LORD. He accepted the sacrifice of the Fellowship or Peace Offering. Therefore, the person seeking more peace and fellowship with God would be filled with more of God's presence, more of His peace and fellowship. The person would grow more and more in his life and walk with God.

Thought 1. Today how do we grow in the peace and fellowship of God? By looking to the Person symbolized by the sacrifice of the bull or cow, the Lord Jesus Christ. Jesus Christ is the Perfect Servant of God. We must focus upon the sacrifice of service, sacrificing more and more of our service to God.
(1) Jesus Christ is the Perfect Servant of God.

"Even as the Son of man came not to be ministered unto, but to minister, and to give his life a ransom for many" (Mt.20:28; see Jn.20:21, pt.2 below).

"For whether *is* greater, he that sitteth at meat, or he that serveth? *is* not he that sitteth at meat? but I am among you as he that serveth" (Lu.22:27).

"He riseth from supper, and laid aside his garments; and took a towel, and girded himself. After that he poureth water into a bason, and began to wash the disciples' feet, and to wipe *them* with the towel wherewith he was girded" (Jn.13:4-5).

"But made himself of no reputation, and took upon him the form of a servant, and was made in the likeness of men" (Ph.2:7).

(2) The more we serve God, the more we grow in the fellowship and peace of God.

"I beseech you therefore, brethren, by the mercies of God, that ye present your bodies a living sacrifice, holy, acceptable unto God, *which is* your reasonable service. And be not conformed to this world: but be ye transformed by the renewing of your mind, that ye may prove what *is* that good, and acceptable, and perfect, will of God" (Ro.12:1-2).

"Then said Jesus to them again, Peace *be* unto you: as *my* Father hath sent me, even so send I you" (Jn.20:21; see Mt.20:28, pt.1 of this thought).

"We then that are strong ought to bear the infirmities of the weak, and not to please ourselves" (Ro.15:1).

3   (3:6-11) **Fellowship, with God—Peace, of God—Hunger, after God—Thirst, after God—Desire, for God**: How was a person to grow in the peace and the fellowship of God? He could offer a lamb to God, the animal most used in sacrifice. (Note that this sacrifice is a symbol of Christ, the Lamb of God.) The sacrifice of a lamb would focus a person's attention...
- upon the sacrificing of oneself more and more to God
- upon dedication, upon the giving up of oneself to God
- upon the sacrifice of one's life completely to God
- upon dying to self and living totally for God

The Scripture and outline show how the sacrifice was to be made. Again, the symbolism of Christ is clearly seen throughout the ritual.

OUTLINE	SCRIPTURE	SCRIPTURE	OUTLINE
3. Offer a lamb, the animal most used in sacrifice (a symbol of Christ the Lamb of God): Focus upon dedication to God, dying to self & following God totally (Lu.9:23) a. Offer a sacrifice with no defect (v.6) b. Identify with the sacrifice by laying one's hands on its head c. Put the sacrifice to death: Have the priests (ministers) offer the sacrifice 1) To sprinkle its blood against the altar on all sides 2) To offer a portion to the LORD	6 And if his offering for a sacrifice of peace offering unto the LORD *be* of the flock; male or female, he shall offer it without blemish. 7 If he offer a lamb for his offering, then shall he offer it before the LORD. 8 And he shall lay his hand upon the head of his offering, and kill it before the tabernacle of the congregation: and Aaron's sons shall sprinkle the blood thereof round about upon the altar. 9 And he shall offer of the sacrifice of the peace	offering an offering made by fire unto the LORD; the fat thereof, *and* the whole rump, it shall he take off hard by the backbone; and the fat that covereth the inwards, and all the fat that *is* upon the inwards, 10 And the two kidneys, and the fat that *is* upon them, which *is* by the flanks, and the caul above the liver, with the kidneys, it shall he take away. 11 And the priest shall burn it upon the altar: *it is* the food of the offering made by fire unto the LORD.	• The entire tail • All fat (considered the most choice part of an animal for eating) • The kidneys • The liver 3) To burn on the altar as food given to the LORD: Symbolizing fellowship with God

The fellowship meal with God symbolized a very special time with God...
- a time of peace: comfort, calm, rest, assurance, agreement, satisfaction, fulfillment
- a time of fellowship: communion, companionship, caring, closeness

Thought 1. How do we grow in the peace and the fellowship of God? By looking to the Person symbolized in the sacrifice of the lamb, the Lord Jesus Christ. Jesus Christ is the Lamb of God, the Lamb who so willingly submitted—dedicated Himself, gave Himself up—to die for us. We must focus upon the *sacrifice of dedication*...
- sacrificing ourselves more and more to God
- giving ourselves totally to grow in the peace and the fellowship of God

"For whosoever will save his life shall lose it: and whosoever will lose his life for my sake shall find it" (Mt.16:25).

"And he said to *them* all, If any *man* will come after me, let him deny himself, and take up his cross daily, and follow me" (Lu.9:23).

"And whosoever doth not bear his cross, and come after me, cannot be my disciple" (Lu.14:27).

"The next day John seeth Jesus coming unto him, and saith, Behold the Lamb of God, which taketh away the sin of the world" (Jn.1:29).

"Yea doubtless, and I count all things *but* loss for the excellency of the knowledge of Christ Jesus my Lord: for whom I have suffered the loss of all things, and do count them *but* dung, that I may win Christ" (Ph.3:8)

"That I may know him, and the power of his resurrection, and the fellowship of his sufferings, being made conformable unto his death" (Ph.3:10).

"Forasmuch as ye know that ye were not redeemed with corruptible things, *as* silver and gold, from your vain conversation *received* by tradition from your fathers; But with the precious blood of Christ, as of a lamb without blemish and without spot" (1 Pe.1:18-19).

"That which we have seen and heard declare we unto you, that ye also may have fellowship with us: and truly our fellowship *is* with the Father, and with his Son Jesus Christ" (1 Jn.1:3).

4 (3:12-16) **Fellowship, with God—Peace, of God—Hunger, after God—Thirst, after God—Desire, for God**: How was a person to grow in the peace and the fellowship of God? He could offer a goat to God, the animal that most symbolized the bearing of God's judgment against sin. (Note that this sacrifice is a symbol of Christ on the cross, bearing the judgment of God.) The sacrifice of a goat would focus a person's attention...

- upon the justice and judgment of God against sin
- upon the atonement, the ransom price demanded by God's anger and wrath against sin
- upon one's deliverance from God's judgment through the substitute sacrifice

OUTLINE	SCRIPTURE	SCRIPTURE	OUTLINE

4. Offer a goat, the animal that most symbolizes the bearing of God's judgment (a symbol of Christ upon the cross)
a. Identify with the sacrifice
b. Put the sacrifice to death
c. Have the priests offer the sacrifice
  1) To sprinkle its blood against the altar
 	
  2) To offer a portion to the LORD
    • All the fat (see v.16)
	12 And if his offering *be* a goat, then he shall offer it before the LORD.
	13 And he shall lay his hand upon the head of it, and kill it before the tabernacle of the congregation: and the sons of Aaron shall sprinkle the blood thereof upon the altar round about.
	14 And he shall offer thereof his offering, *even* an offering made by fire unto the
		LORD; the fat that covereth the inwards, and all the fat that *is* upon the inwards,
		15 And the two kidneys, and the fat that *is* upon them, which *is* by the flanks, and the caul above the liver, with the kidneys, it shall he take away.
		16 And the priest shall burn them upon the altar: *it is* the food of the offering made by fire for a sweet savour: all the fat *is* the LORD's.
			
			• Both kidneys
			• The liver
			
			3) To burn on the altar as food given to the LORD
			d. The result: The sweet aroma pleases the LORD

Again, the ritual of this sacrifice is the same as for the other two sacrifices. Moreover, the symbolism of Christ is just as clearly seen as in the other two offerings.

a. The person was to offer the sacrifice of a goat (v.12).
b. The person was to identify with the sacrifice by laying his hands on the head of the sacrifice (v.13).
c. The person was to put the sacrifice to death (v.13).
d. The person was to have the priests (ministers) offer the sacrifice to the LORD, all the fat, liver, and kidneys (vv.13-15).
e. The result: the sweet aroma of the sacrifice pleased the LORD. God accepted the person seeking more peace and fellowship with Him. God fulfilled His promise: the person was filled with God's presence and experienced more and more of God's peace and fellowship.

Thought 1. How do we grow in the peace and the fellowship of God? By looking to the Person symbolized by the sacrifice of the goat, the Lord Jesus Christ. Jesus Christ is the Sin-Bearer and the Judgment-Bearer for us. When He died upon the cross, Christ bore our sins and the judgment of God against sin—all for us.

"So Christ was once offered to bear the sins of many; and unto them that look for him shall he appear the second time without sin unto salvation" (He.9:28).

"Christ hath redeemed us from the curse of the law, being made a curse for us: for it is written, Cursed *is* every one that hangeth on a tree" (Ga.3:13).

"But we see Jesus, who was made a little lower than the angels for the suffering of death, crowned with glory and honour; that he by the grace of God should taste death for every man" (He.2:9).

"Who his own self bare our sins in his own body on the tree, that we, being dead to sins, should live unto righteousness: by whose stripes ye were healed" (1 Pe.2:24).

"For Christ also hath once suffered for sins, the just for the unjust, that he might bring us to God, being put to death in the flesh, but quickened by the Spirit" (1 Pe.3:18).

"And ye know that he was manifested to take away our sins; and in him is no sin" (1 Jn.3:5).

"But he *was* wounded for our transgressions, *he was* bruised for our iniquities: the chastisement of our peace *was* upon him; and with his stripes we are healed" (Is.53:5).

5 (3:17) **Fellowship, with God—Peace, with God—Obedience—Sacrifices, Animal—Offerings, Laws Governing**: How was a person to grow in the peace and the fellowship of God? He was to offer the fellowship sacrifice faithfully, never abusing—never eating—any of God's portion (the fat or the blood). What belonged to God belonged to God, and it was never to be held back nor kept for oneself. The part that belonged to God, the fat and the blood, was to be sacrificed to God, given to Him and Him alone. Therefore, when a person was making a Peace or Fellowship Offering, he was to keep this one strict law: never abuse, never eat, God's portion (the fat and the blood).

OUTLINE	SCRIPTURE
5. Offer the sacrifice faithfully, never abusing—never eating—any of God's portion (the fat or the blood): Keep this law	17 It shall be a perpetual statute for your generations throughout all your dwellings, that ye eat neither fat nor blood.

Thought 1. What belongs to God belongs to God. It must be given to God. How, then, do we grow in the peace and the fellowship of God? By not holding back anything from God: by sacrificing ourselves totally to God.

"My son, give me thine heart, and let thine eyes observe my ways" (Pr.23:26).

"And he said to them all, If any man will come after me, let him deny himself, and take up his cross daily, and follow me" (Lu.9:23).

"For if ye live after the flesh, ye shall die: but if ye through the Spirit do mortify the deeds of the body, ye shall live" (Ro.8:13).

"I beseech you therefore, brethren, by the mercies of God, that ye present your bodies a living sacrifice, holy, acceptable unto God, which is your reasonable service. And be not conformed to this world: but be ye transformed by the renewing of your mind, that ye may prove what is that good, and acceptable, and perfect, will of God" (Ro.12:1-2).

"Let no man seek his own, but every man another's *wealth*" (1 Co.10:24).

"And they that are Christ's have crucified the flesh with the affections and lusts" (Ga.5:24).

"But what things were gain to me, those I counted loss for Christ. Yea doubtless, and I count all things *but* loss for the excellency of the knowledge of Christ Jesus my LORD: for whom I have suffered the loss of all things, and do count them *but* dung, that I may win Christ" (Ph.3:7-8).

"And the very God of peace sanctify you wholly; and *I pray God* your whole spirit and soul and body be preserved blameless unto the coming of our Lord Jesus Christ" (1 Th.5:23).

TYPES, SYMBOLS, AND PICTURES
Leviticus 3:1-17

Historical Term	Type or Picture (Scriptural Basis for Each)	Life Application for Today's Believer	Biblical Application
The Fellowship or Peace Offering Le. 3:1-17	*The Fellowship Or Peace Offering is a type of Christ, a symbol or picture of Christ, the One who died on the cross bearing the judgment of God for man. The sacrifice of Christ made peace between a holy God and an alienated, fallen, depraved people. The sacrifice of Christ and Christ alone brings peace and fellowship between man and God.* **"And if his oblation *be* a sacrifice of peace offering, if he offer *it* of the herd; whether *it* be a male or female, he shall offer it without blemish before the LORD" (Le.3:1).**	How do we grow in the fellowship and peace of God? Very simply, by seeking more of the fellowship and peace of God. We must stand upon the completed work of Christ's sacrifice on the cross. Because of Christ… • we can enjoy the fellowship of the LORD • we can experience the peace of God	*"Yea doubtless, and I count all things but loss for the excellency of the knowledge of Christ Jesus my LORD: for whom I have suffered the loss of all things, and do count them but dung, that I may win Christ" (Ph.3:8)* *"That I may know him, and the power of his resurrection, and the fellowship of his sufferings, being made conformable unto his death" (Ph.3:10).* *"That which we have seen and heard declare we unto you, that ye also may have fellowship with us: and truly our fellowship is with the Father, and with his Son Jesus Christ" (1 Jn.1:3).*
Bull or Cow Sacrificed in the Fellowship or Peace Offering Le. 3:1-5	*The bull or cow is an animal of service, therefore, this animal would be a picture of the sacrifice of service. This particular sacrifice would focus a person's attention upon…* • *sacrificing more and more service to God* • *serving God more and more*	How do we grow in the peace and fellowship of God? By looking to the Person symbolized by the sacrifice of the bull or cow, the Lord Jesus Christ. Jesus Christ is the Perfect Servant of God. We must therefore focus upon Christ, upon His sacrifice of service. His sacrifice stirs us to sacrifice	*"I beseech you therefore, brethren, by the mercies of God, that ye present your bodies a living sacrifice, holy, acceptable unto God, which is your reasonable service. And be not conformed to this world: but be ye transformed by the renewing of your mind, that ye may prove what is*

TYPES, SYMBOLS, AND PICTURES
Leviticus 3:1-17

Historical Term	Type or Picture (Scriptural Basis for Each)	Life Application for Today's Believer	Biblical Application
	"And if his oblation *be* a sacrifice of peace offering, if he offer *it* of the herd; whether *it be* a male or female, he shall offer it without blemish before the LORD" (Le.3:1).	more and more of our service to God.	*that good, and acceptable, and perfect, will of God" (Ro.12:1-2).* *"Then said Jesus to them again, Peace be unto you: as my Father hath sent me, even so send I you" (Jn.20:21; see Mt.20:28).* *"We then that are strong ought to bear the infirmities of the weak, and not to please ourselves" (Ro.15:1).*
Lamb: The Sacrifice Used in... ⇒ *the Fellowship or Peace Offering, Le. 3:6-11* ⇒ *the Sin Offering, Le. 4:32, 35; 5:6* ⇒ *the First Worship Service of the Priest, Le. 9:3* ⇒ *the Burnt Offering for a Mother's Protection Right After Childbirth, Le. 12:6* ⇒ *the Cleansing That Took Place Inside the Camp, Le. 14:10, 13* ⇒ *the Guilt Offering for the Poorest of the Poor, Le. 14:21, 24-25* ⇒ *the Burnt Offering celebrated during the Festival of Firstfruits, Le.23:12*	*A symbol of sacrifice. In fact, the animal most used in sacrifice was the lamb. The sacrifice of a lamb would focus a person's attention...* • *upon the sacrificing of oneself more and more to God* • *upon dedication, the giving up, of oneself to God* • *upon the sacrifice of one's life completely to God* • *upon dying to self and living totally for God* **"If he offer a lamb for his offering, then shall he offer it before the LORD" (Le.3:7).**	How do we grow in the peace and fellowship of God? By looking to the Person symbolized in the sacrifice of the lamb, the Lord Jesus Christ. Jesus Christ is the Lamb of God, the Lamb who so willingly submitted and dedicated Himself to die for us. We must focus upon the *sacrifice of dedication...* • sacrificing ourselves more and more to God • dedicating ourselves, willingly submitting ourselves more and more to God	*"For whosoever will save his life shall lose it: and whosoever will lose his life for my sake shall find it" (Mt.16:25).* *"And he said to them all, If any man will come after me, let him deny himself, and take up his cross daily, and follow me" (Lu.9:23).* *"And whosoever doth not bear his cross, and come after me, cannot be my disciple" (Lu.14:27).* *"Likewise reckon ye also yourselves to be dead indeed unto sin, but alive unto God through Jesus Christ our LORD" (Ro.6:11).*
The Burning of the LORD's Portion on the Altar As Food Being Offered to God Le. 3:6-11; 7:18	*This food is a picture of having a fellowship meal with God. Having a fellowship meal with God, symbolized a very special time with God...* • *a time of peace: comfort, calm, rest, assurance, agreement, satisfaction, fulfillment* • *a time of fellowship: communion, companionship, caring, closeness* **"And the priest shall burn it upon the altar: *it is* the food of the offering made by fire unto the LORD" (Le.3:11).**	Jesus Christ is the Bread of God who alone can satisfy the hunger of man. Jesus Christ invites His people to fellowship, eat, and commune with Him.	*"Behold, I stand at the door, and knock: if any man hear my voice, and open the door, I will come in to him, and will sup with him, and he with me" (Re.3:20).* *"That which we have seen and heard declare we unto you, that ye also may have fellowship with us: and truly our fellowship is with the Father, and with his Son Jesus Christ" (1 Jn.1:3; see Is.55:2; Jn.6:51; Ph.3:10).*
The Goat: The Sacrifice Used in... ⇒ *the Fellowship or Peace Offering, Le.3:12-16* ⇒ *the First Worship Service of the Priest, Le.9:15*	*The goat most symbolized the bearing of God's judgment against sin. (Note that this sacrifice is a symbol of Christ on the cross, bearing the judgment of God.) The sacrifice of a goat would focus a person's attention*	We must look to the Person symbolized by the sacrifice of the goat, the Lord Jesus Christ. Jesus Christ is the Sin-Bearer and the Judgment-Bearer for us. When He died upon the cross, Christ bore our sins and the	*"So Christ was once offered to bear the sins of many; and unto them that look for him shall he appear the second time without sin unto salvation" (He.9:28).* *"Christ hath redeemed*

TYPES, SYMBOLS, AND PICTURES
Leviticus 3:1-17

Historical Term	Type or Picture (Scriptural Basis for Each)	Life Application for Today's Believer	Biblical Application
⇒ *the Day of Atonement, Le.16:3-10; 15*	*upon...* • *the justice and judgment of God against sin* • *the atonement, the ransom price demanded by God's anger and wrath against sin* • *one's deliverance from God's judgment through the substitute sacrifice* **"And if his offering be a goat, then he shall offer it before the LORD" (Le.3:12).**	judgment of God against sin—all for us.	*us from the curse of the law, being made a curse for us: for it is written, Cursed is every one that hangeth on a tree" (Ga.3:13).* *"But we see Jesus, who was made a little lower than the angels for the suffering of death, crowned with glory and honour; that he by the grace of God should taste death for every man" (He.2:9).* *"Who his own self bare our sins in his own body on the tree, that we, being dead to sins, should live unto righteousness: by whose stripes ye were healed" (1 Pe.2:24; see Is.53:5).*

CHAPTER 4

D. The Sin Offering (a Picture of Christ's Atoning Sacrifice): The Way to Secure Forgiveness of Sin, 4:1–5:13

1. The basic essential: A person must acknowledge the LORD & the need for forgiveness
   a. Seek forgiveness for all sin, even unintentional sin[DS1]
   b. The reason: A person has broken the LORD's commands

2. The way for an anointed priest (minister) to be forgiven
   a. Must confess the truth: He sins
   b. Must approach God thru the sacrifice (a symbol of Christ's atoning sacrifice): Offer a young bull without defect
   c. Must observe the principles of atonement (reconciliation)
      1) Substitution: Present...bull
      2) Identifying with the substitute: Lay his hand on its head
      3) Death of the substitute

   d. Must have the anointed priest (High Priest) offer the sacrifice
      1) To take some of the blood into the Tabernacle

      • Dip his finger into the blood: Sprinkle it seven times in front of the Inner Curtain of the Most Holy Place
      • Put some blood on the horns of the incense altar

      • Pour out the remaining blood at the base of the altar of burnt offering

      2) To remove & offer certain parts of the sacrifice to the LORD
      • All the fat

      • Both kidneys

      • The liver

      • All to be done as in the sacrifice of the Fellowship Offering

And the LORD spake unto Moses, saying,
2 Speak unto the children of Israel, saying, If a soul shall sin through ignorance against any of the commandments of the LORD *concerning things* which ought not to be done, and shall do against any of them:
3 If the priest that is anointed do sin according to the sin of the people; then let him bring for his sin, which he hath sinned, a young bullock without blemish unto the LORD for a sin offering.
4 And he shall bring the bullock unto the door of the tabernacle of the congregation before the LORD; and shall lay his hand upon the bullock's head, and kill the bullock before the LORD.
5 And the priest that is anointed shall take of the bullock's blood, and bring it to the tabernacle of the congregation:
6 And the priest shall dip his finger in the blood, and sprinkle of the blood seven times before the LORD, before the vail of the sanctuary.
7 And the priest shall put *some* of the blood upon the horns of the altar of sweet incense before the LORD, which *is* in the tabernacle of the congregation; and shall pour all the blood of the bullock at the bottom of the altar of the burnt offering, which *is at* the door of the tabernacle of the congregation.
8 And he shall take off from it all the fat of the bullock for the sin offering; the fat that covereth the inwards, and all the fat that *is* upon the inwards,
9 And the two kidneys, and the fat that *is* upon them, which *is* by the flanks, and the caul above the liver, with the kidneys, it shall he take away,
10 As it was taken off from the bullock of the sacrifice of peace offerings: and the priest shall burn them upon the altar of the burnt offering.
11 And the skin of the bullock, and all his flesh, with his head, and with his legs, and his inwards, and his dung,
12 Even the whole bullock shall he carry forth without the camp unto a clean place, where the ashes are poured out, and burn him on the wood with fire: where the ashes are poured out shall he be burnt.
13 And if the whole congregation of Israel sin through ignorance, and the thing be hid from the eyes of the assembly, and they have done *somewhat against* any of the commandments of the LORD *concerning things* which should not be done, and are guilty;
14 When the sin, which they have sinned against it, is known, then the congregation shall offer a young bullock for the sin, and bring him before the tabernacle of the congregation.
15 And the elders of the congregation shall lay their hands upon the head of the bullock before the LORD: and the bullock shall be killed before the LORD.
16 And the priest that is anointed shall bring of the bullock's blood to the tabernacle of the congregation:
17 And the priest shall dip his finger *in some* of the blood, and sprinkle *it* seven times before the LORD, *even* before the vail.
18 And he shall put *some* of the blood upon the horns of the altar which *is* before the LORD, that *is* in the tabernacle of the congregation, and shall pour out all the blood at the bottom of the altar of the burnt offering, which *is at* the door of the tabernacle of the congregation.
19 And he shall take all his fat from him, and burn *it* upon the altar.
20 And he shall do with the bullock as he did with the bullock for a sin offering, so shall he do with this: and the priest shall make an atonement for them, and it shall be forgiven them.
21 And he shall carry forth

3) To take the rest of the bull outside the camp to burn it upon the ash heap (a symbol of judgment, the fact that sin cannot be allowed in God's presence: Sin must be removed, judged, condemned)

3. The way for society—a community, an entire nation—to be forgiven
   a. Must confess the truth: Are guilty of national sin (once sin is brought to their attention, even if they were unaware of the sins)

   b. Must approach God thru the sacrifice when they become aware of the sin: Offer a young bull (without defect)

   c. Must observe the principles of atonement
      1) Substitution: Present...bull
      2) Identification: Lay hands...
      3) Death of the substitute: Slaughter it

   d. Must have the priest (High Priest) offer the sacrifice
      1) To take some of the blood into the Tabernacle
      • Dip his finger into the blood: Sprinkle it seven times in front of the Inner Curtain

      • Put some blood on the horns of the incense altar

      • Pour out the remaining blood at the base of the altar of burnt offering

      2) To remove & offer certain parts of the sacrifice: Just as he did with the sacrifice for the sins of the priests
   e. The result: Brings atonement or reconciliation between the people & God—brings forgiveness of sins

   f. The condemnation of sin

symbolized: To take the rest of the sacrifice outside the camp (a symbol of judgment—that sin can never be allowed in God's presence)

4. The way for a leader to be forgiven

a. Must confess the truth: Is guilty of sin when he breaks any of God's commands, even unintentionally

b. Must approach God thru the sacrifice when made aware of sin

c. Must observe the principles of atonement
   1) Substitution: Offer a male goat without defect
   2) Identification: Lay his hand on its head
   3) Death of the substitute: Slaughter it

d. Must have the priest offer the sacrifice
   1) To take some of the blood
      • Dip his finger in the blood & put it on the horns of the altar of burnt offering
      • Pour out the remaining blood at the base of the altar
   2) To offer all the fat on the altar just as he did the fellowship offering

e. The result: Makes atonement (reconciliation) for the leader's sin—he is forgiven

5. The way for an individual person to be forgiven

a. Must confess the truth: Is guilty of sin when any of God's commands are disobeyed, even unintentional sins

b. Must approach God thru sacrifice when made aware of the sin

c. Must observe the principles of atonement
   1) Substitution: Offer a female goat without defect
   2) Identification: Lay his hand on its head
   3) Death of the substitute: Slaughter it

d. Must have the priest offer the sacrifice
   1) To take some of the blood
      • Dip his finger in the blood & put it on the horns of the altar of burnt offering
      • Pour out the remainder at the base of the altar

the bullock without the camp, and burn him as he burned the first bullock: it *is* a sin offering for the congregation.

22 When a ruler hath sinned, and done *somewhat* through ignorance *against* any of the commandments of the LORD his God *concerning things* which should not be done, and is guilty;

23 Or if his sin, wherein he hath sinned, come to his knowledge; he shall bring his offering, a kid of the goats, a male without blemish:

24 And he shall lay his hand upon the head of the goat, and kill it in the place where they kill the burnt offering before the LORD: it *is* a sin offering.

25 And the priest shall take of the blood of the sin offering with his finger, and put *it* upon the horns of the altar of burnt offering, and shall pour out his blood at the bottom of the altar of burnt offering.

26 And he shall burn all his fat upon the altar, as the fat of the sacrifice of peace offerings: and the priest shall make an atonement for him as concerning his sin, and it shall be forgiven him.

27 And if any one of the common people sin through ignorance, while he doeth *somewhat against* any of the commandments of the LORD *concerning things* which ought not to be done, and be guilty;

28 Or if his sin, which he hath sinned, come to his knowledge: then he shall bring his offering, a kid of the goats, a female without blemish, for his sin which he hath sinned.

29 And he shall lay his hand upon the head of the sin offering, and slay the sin offering in the place of the burnt offering.

30 And the priest shall take of the blood thereof with his finger, and put *it* upon the horns of the altar of burnt offering, and shall pour out all the blood thereof at the bottom of the altar.

31 And he shall take away all the fat thereof, as the fat is taken away from off the sacrifice of peace offerings; and the priest shall burn *it* upon the altar for a sweet savour unto the LORD; and the priest shall make an atonement for him, and it shall be forgiven him.

32 And if he bring a lamb for a sin offering, he shall bring it a female without blemish.

33 And he shall lay his hand upon the head of the sin offering, and slay it for a sin offering in the place where they kill the burnt offering.

34 And the priest shall take of the blood of the sin offering with his finger, and put *it* upon the horns of the altar of burnt offering, and shall pour out all the blood thereof at the bottom of the altar:

35 And he shall take away all the fat thereof, as the fat of the lamb is taken away from the sacrifice of the peace offerings; and the priest shall burn them upon the altar, according to the offerings made by fire unto the LORD: and the priest shall make an atonement for his sin that he hath committed, and it shall be forgiven him.

CHAPTER 5

And if a soul sin, and hear the voice of swearing, and *is* a witness, whether he hath seen or known *of it*; if he do not utter *it*, then he shall bear his iniquity.

2 Or if a soul touch any unclean thing, whether *it be* a carcase of an unclean beast, or a carcase of unclean cattle, or the carcase of unclean creeping things, and *if* it be hidden from him; he also shall be unclean, and guilty.

3 Or if he touch the uncleanness of man, whatsoever uncleanness *it be* that a man shall be defiled withal, and it be hid from him; when he knoweth *of it*, then he shall be guilty.

2) To remove & offer all the fat: Just as he did with the fellowship offering

e. The result
   1) The sweet aroma of the believer's faith in the sacrifice pleases the LORD
   2) The trust (obedience) of the believer makes atonement: He is forgiven (because he trusted what God said, that He would forgive sin thru the sacrifice)

f. The option: May offer a lamb
   1) Must still observe the principles of atonement
      • Substitution: Bring a female
      • Identification: Lay his hand on its head
      • Death of the substitute: Slaughter it
   2) Must have the priest offer the sacrifice
      • To dip his finger in the blood & put it on the horns of the altar of burnt offering & pour out the remaining at the base of the altar
      • To remove & offer all the fat: Just as he did with the fellowship offering
   3) The result: Makes atonement for the person—is forgiven (because he believed God—trusted God—did exactly what God said to do)

6. The way for a person to be forgiven for specific, terrible sins

a. The sins listed
   1) Social & civil injustice: Refusing to stand up for truth & justice when one knows the truth
   2) Religious defilement: Touching or doing anything that defiles one—this makes one unclean religiously or ceremoniously
   3) Human & personal defilement: Touching anything that would make a person unclean or defiled

4) Verbal sin or sins of the tongue: Rash swearing, thoughtless, careless swearing	4 Or if a soul swear, pronouncing with *his* lips to do evil, or to do good, whatsoever *it be* that a man shall pronounce with an oath, and it be hid from him; when he knoweth *of it*, then he shall be guilty in one of these.	upon the side of the altar; and the rest of the blood shall be wrung out at the bottom of the altar: it *is* a sin offering.	3) He must pour out the remaining blood at the base of the altar
b. The remedy: The Sin Offering 1) Must confess the specific sin	5 And it shall be, when he shall be guilty in one of these *things*, that he shall confess that he hath sinned in that *thing*:	10 And he shall offer the second *for* a burnt offering, according to the manner: and the priest shall make an atonement for him for his sin which he hath sinned, and it shall be forgiven him.	c. The poor must then have the priest offer the burnt offering as prescribed (Le.4:14-17; 1 Chr.15:13)
2) Must approach God thru the sacrifice: Offer a female lamb or goat (as spelled out above [4:27-35])	6 And he shall bring his trespass offering unto the LORD for his sin which he hath sinned, a female from the flock, a lamb or a kid of the goats, for a sin offering; and the priest shall make an atonement for him concerning his sin.	11 But if he be not able to bring two turtledoves, or two young pigeons, then he that sinned shall bring for his offering the tenth part of an ephah of fine flour for a sin offering; he shall put no oil upon it, neither shall he put *any* frankincense thereon: for it *is* a sin offering.	d. The poorest of the poor had provision made for them to be forgiven 1) Must offer one tenth of an ephah of fine flour (two quarts; two liters): Not to put oil or incense on it
3) The result: Makes atonement, reconciliation for sin			
7. The way for the poor person to be forgiven a. The poor must offer two doves or two young pigeons: One for the Sin Offering; the other for a burnt offering	7 And if he be not able to bring a lamb, then he shall bring for his trespass, which he hath committed, two turtledoves, or two young pigeons, unto the LORD; one for a sin offering, and the other for a burnt offering.	12 Then shall he bring it to the priest, and the priest shall take his handful of it, *even* a memorial thereof, and burn *it* on the altar, according to the offerings made by fire unto the LORD: it *is* a sin offering.	2) Must have the priest make the offering: To offer a handful to the LORD as a memorial or token portion & to give the remainder to the priests
b. The poor must have the priest first offer the Sin Offering 1) He must put it to death	8 And he shall bring them unto the priest, who shall offer *that* which *is* for the sin offering first, and wring off his head from his neck, but shall not divide *it* asunder:	13 And the priest shall make an atonement for him as touching his sin that he hath sinned in one of these, and it shall be forgiven him: and *the remnant* shall be the priest's, as a meat offering.	3) The result: Makes atonement, reconciles the guilty with God; he is forgiven
2) He must sprinkle the blood against the side of the altar	9 And he shall sprinkle of the blood of the sin offering		

DIVISION I

THE WAY TO BECOME ACCEPTABLE TO GOD (PART 1): BY THE OFFERING OF A SACRIFICE, A SUBSTITUTE, 1:1–7:38

D. The Sin Offering (a Picture of Christ's Atoning Sacrifice): The Way to Secure Forgiveness of Sin, 4:1–5:13

(4:1–5:13) **Introduction—Offering, The Sin—Sin Offering, The—Sin, Definition of—Forgiveness**: What is sin? Sin can be defined in at least two ways.
⇒ Sin is the condition, state, or being of imperfection. Sin is coming short of the glory of God, of His perfection (Ro.3:23).
⇒ Sin is disobedience, the disobeying of God's commandments. There are sins of *omission*: a person just fails to do what God says. And there are sins of *commission*: a person commits some direct act of disobedience, does exactly what God says not to do.

Every person stands before God as a sinner. We are all in the state or condition of sin. We are all guilty of having broken the commandments of God, of having disobeyed God. The terrible tragedy is this: no person can ever live in the presence of God. Why? Because the penalty of sin is death, that is, separation from God. How then can a person approach God and become acceptable to Him? How can a person gain the right to live eternally with God? Through the death of Jesus Christ. Jesus Christ is the sacrifice, the ransom paid to deliver man from the penalty of sin. The most wonderful thing happens when a person trusts Jesus Christ to save him from his sins: his sins are forgiven. God Himself forgives the person's sins. The person is reconciled to God and accepted by God, accepted to live eternally with God—all because Jesus Christ died as the sacrifice for his sins. Jesus Christ paid the ransom price to deliver the person from the penalty of sin.

What about the people before Christ came? Could they be forgiven their sins, and if so, how? God loves man; therefore, He has made provision for every generation to be forgiven their sins—if they will just follow His instructions, approaching Him exactly as He says. In the Old Testament, people were to approach God through the sacrifice of an animal that bore the guilt of his sins. The animal stood as a symbol of the Lord Jesus Christ. Jesus Christ was the Lamb of God that was to take away the sin of the world (Jn.1:29). If a person believed God and approached God through the sacrificed animal, God counted the animal as a picture of Christ, as the person's substitute in bearing the punishment of sin. God counted the sacrifice as the ransom payment to be paid by Christ for the person's sin. The person was counted free from sin, and he stood perfect before God. He was thereby accepted by God. His sins and the penalty for his sins were paid by the substitute sacrifice that symbolized Christ.

This is the subject of the present passage, a discussion of the Sin Offering. The Sin Offering is the provision God made for His people to be forgiven their sins throughout the Old Testament. Once an Old Testament believer had been reconciled to God through the atoning sacrifice of the Burnt Offering, he immediately gave thanks and dedicated his life to God (the Grain Offering). He was then living in the fellowship and peace of God. But as he walked about day by day, he experienced just what we experience: a constant barrage of trials and temptations. He became more and more aware of being short of God's glory and more and more sensitive to disobeying the commandments of God. He sensed what we sense, a deep-seated need for special encounters with God and for special times in seeking the forgiveness of sins. This God knew. Therefore, God made provision for His people and gave them the Sin Offering. This is the much-needed subject of this passage: *The Sin Offering (a Picture of Christ's Atoning Sacrifice): The Way to Secure Forgiveness of Sin*, 4:1–5:13.

1. The basic essential: a person must acknowledge the LORD and the need for forgiveness (vv.1-2).
2. The way for an anointed priest (minister) to be forgiven (vv.3-12).
3. The way for society—a community, an entire nation—to be forgiven (vv.13-21).
4. The way for a leader to be forgiven (vv.14-26).
5. The way for an individual person to be forgiven (vv.27-35).
6. The way for a person to be forgiven for specific, terrible sins (Ch.5:1-6).
7. The way for the poor person to be forgiven (vv.7-13).

---

1 (4:1-2) **Sin—Forgiveness of Sins—Disobedience—Commandments, Breaking the**: How can a person secure forgiveness of sin, a sense of unbroken forgiveness, a constant forgiveness of sin? There is one basic essential: a person must acknowledge the LORD and the need for forgiveness.

OUTLINE	SCRIPTURE
1. **The basic essential: A person must acknowledge the LORD & the need for forgiveness**	And the LORD spake unto Moses, saying,
a. Seek forgiveness for all sin, even unintentional sin	2 Speak unto the children of Israel, saying, If a soul shall sin through ignorance against any of the commandments of the LORD *concerning things* which ought not to be done, and shall do against any of them:
a. The reason: A person has broken the LORD'S commands	

Note that it is the LORD who is giving these instructions, the LORD God Himself (v.1). He and He alone is the true and living God, the great Creator and Sustainer of the universe. The LORD (Jehovah, Yahweh) is the God of salvation, redemption, and deliverance. He alone can save and redeem us, delivering us from our sins and from the judgment to come. He and He alone can continually forgive us from sin as we march day by day toward the promised land of heaven.

But there are some people who do not acknowledge God and even deny the existence of sin. They claim that sin is nothing more than human mistakes or weaknesses. At most, they say sin is simply the violation of human and social laws. They just reject, question, deny, and ignore God, and some even curse Him. Scripture declares that a person who so rebels against God will not be forgiven.

> **"For the wages of sin *is* death; but the gift of God *is* eternal life through Jesus Christ our LORD" (Ro.6:23).**
> **"But the fearful, and unbelieving, and the abominable, and murderers, and whoremongers, and sorcerers, and idolaters, and all liars, shall have their part in the lake which burneth with fire and brimstone: which is the second death" (Re.21:8).**
> **"He, that being often reproved hardeneth *his* neck, shall suddenly be destroyed, and that without remedy" (Pr.29:1).**
> **"The soul that sinneth, it shall die" (Eze.18:20).**

Logic itself tells us this clear fact: a person must acknowledge God and his need for forgiveness if he expects God to forgive his sins. It is foolish, utterly foolish, to think that God will forgive a person's sins and accept him when he dies if the person has rejected God and refused to live for God. To be forgiven, a person must do just what God says in this verse and passage.

a. A person must seek forgiveness for all sins, even for unintentional sins or sins of ignorance (v.2. See DEEPER STUDY #1—Le.4:2 for more discussion.)

DEEPER STUDY # 1
(4:2) **Sin through Ignorance or Unintentional Sin** (hata bishgagah): the words *unintentional* and *through ignorance* give the impression that there is no forgiveness for sins that are intentional or deliberate, sins that a person commits when he willingly gives in to temptation. Just think of all the sins that we commit through the day: sins of thought and sins of behavior, sins that are aroused by worldliness, sins committed through the lust of the flesh, the lust of the eyes, and the

pride of life (1 Jn.2:15-16). Tragically, we sin far too often, and our sin is known by us to be sin. We may genuinely struggle against sin, yet our flesh is so weak and our minds so corrupt that we cave in. As Paul said:

> **"For we know that the law is spiritual: but I am carnal, sold under sin. For that which I do I allow not: for what I would, that do I not; but what I hate, that do I. If then I do that which I would not, I consent unto the law that *it is* good. Now then it is no more I that do it, but sin that dwelleth in me. For I know that in me (that is, in my flesh,) dwelleth no good thing: for to will is present with me; but *how* to perform that which is good I find not. For the good that I would I do not: but the evil which I would not, that I do. Now if I do that I would not, it is no more I that do it, but sin that dwelleth in me. I find then a law, that, when I would do good, evil is present with me. For I delight in the law of God after the inward man: But I see another law in my members, warring against the law of my mind, and bringing me into captivity to the law of sin which is in my members. O wretched man that I am! who shall deliver me from the body of this death? I thank God through Jesus Christ our Lord. So then with the mind [set upon the Lord Jesus Christ] I myself serve the law of God; but with the flesh the law of sin" (Ro.7:14-25).**

Scripture is clear about sin: all sin can be forgiven except the sin of blasphemy against the Holy Spirit (Mt.12:31-32; Mk.3:29-30; Lu.12:4-12). In the Old Testament, this seems to be what is meant by *defiant sin* or sins that are committed in total rebellion against God, with a *high hand* raised against God (be yad ramah, Nu.15:27-30).

In light of these facts, what is meant by *unintentional sins, by sins of ignorance*" Is there no forgiveness for sins that are committed intentionally, deliberately? When a person knows he is sinning and still goes ahead and sins, can he be forgiven? How should the Hebrew, the original language, be translated in this passage? Is *unintentional sin* or *sin of ignorance* the best translation?

⇒ *The Expositor's Bible Commentary* says this:

> *The expression "to sin unintentionally" (hata bisegagah) in v.2 calls for some comment. The NIV reading may give the impression that there was no sacrifice for intentional sins. This would be a problem, for many of our sins are more or less intentional though not necessarily deliberate. The word sagag and its by-form sagah and their cognates basically seem to mean "to err," "go astray," "wander," "stagger." The nouns mean "error," "mistake"....The idea of intent is not basic to the word and ought not to be imported.*
>
> *The sense of the verb sagag will be adequately caught if in all the verses concerned here in Leviticus 4-5, the phrase "sins unintentionally" is rendered by "goes astray in sin" or "does wrong" or the like. In Numbers 15:22-29 the translation "wrong" or "wrongly" or "in error" will better replace "unintentional" or "unintentionally." Indeed, the NIV translates segagah by "wrong" in Numbers 15:25 (second instance) and in Leviticus 5:18. "Unintentional" seems better to fit sagag and its cognates only in the manslaughter passages (Num 35:22-33; Josh 20:3-5), and even there "inadvertently" or "by mistake" would actually fit better.[1]*

⇒ *Barnes' Notes* says *sins through ignorance* means: *"Sin through error; that is, through straying from the right way."[2]*

> **"Before I was afflicted I went astray: but now have I kept thy word" (Ps.119:67).**

⇒ Charles Pfeiffer says this: *"Sins committed 'through ignorance' (bishgagah) are sins arising from human infirmity, or the weakness of 'flesh and blood.' Manslaughter without malice is so designated (Numbers 35:11-23)."[3]*

⇒ The great *Pulpit Commentary* says this:

> *The expression "through ignorance" (bishgagah), is intended to cover all sins except those committed "with a high hand," or defiantly, whether the agent was ignorant that they were sins or was led into them by inconsiderateness or infirmity (cf. Ps.xix.12, 13, 'Who can understand his errors? Cleanse thou me from secret faults. Keep back thy servant also from presumptuous sins')."[4]*

⇒ *The Theological Wordbook of the Old Testament* points out that the verb form (shagaga) is translated elsewhere as "I went astray" (Ps.119:78).[5]

⇒ R.K. Harrison says:

> *Sins...is from the Hebrew hata, a root which means basically "to miss the mark"....What is involved in the committing of offences unwittingly (NEB "inadvertently"; NIV "unintentionally") is doing that which is prohibited in any of the Lord's commands....The translation "unwitting" is rather misleading...because a degree of conscious disobedience was obviously involved....unwitting sin would include both conscious acts of disobedience and offences committed as the result of human weakness and frailty.[6]*

---

1 Frank E. Gaebelein, Editor. *The Expositor's Bible Commentary*, Vol.2, pp.547-548.
2 F.C. Cook, Editor. *Barnes' Notes, Exodus to Esther.* (Grand Rapids, MI: Baker Book House, n.d.), p.118.
3 Charles F. Pfeiffer. *The Book of Leviticus*, p.20.
4 *The Pulpit Commentary*, p.53.
5 *Theological Wordbook of the Old Testament,* Vol.2. Edited by R. Laird Harris. (Chicago, IL: Moody Bible Institute of Chicago, 1980), p.903.
6 R.K. Harrison. *Leviticus.* (Downers Grove, IL: Inter-Varsity Press, 1980), pp.60-61.

The point is this: the meaning of the Hebrew seems to be that all sin can be forgiven with one exception: the sin of *utter defiance and rebellion* against God, the sin committed with "*a high hand*" raised up in God's face. God forgives sin, all sin, except the unpardonable sin. There is a sacrifice for intentional sins, a sacrifice that atones for all sin, the perfect sacrifice of God's Son upon the cross, the Lord Jesus Christ. But note: as this Scripture declares, the sinner must believe God and come to Him through the sacrifice, the atonement or ransom He has provided in the sacrificial offering of the Lord Jesus Christ. There is forgiveness only in Christ.

> "**In whom we have redemption through his blood, the forgiveness of sins, according to the riches of his grace**" (Ep.1:7).
> "**Who his own self bare our sins in his own body on the tree, that we, being dead to sins, should live unto righteousness: by whose stripes ye were healed**" (1 Pe.2:24).

b. The reason we must seek forgiveness is that we have all broken the LORD's commands (v.2).

> "**Who can say, I have made my heart clean, I am pure from my sin?**" (Pr.20:9).
> "**But we are all as an unclean *thing*, and all our righteousnesses *are* as filthy rags; and we all do fade as a leaf; and our iniquities, like the wind, have taken us away**" (Is.64:6).
> "**For all have sinned, and come short of the glory of God**" (Ro.3:23).
> "**If we say that we have no sin, we deceive ourselves, and the truth is not in us**" (1 Jn.1:8).

[2] (4:3-12) **Forgiveness of Sin—Sin, Forgiveness of—Priests, The—Ministers, The**: How can a priest (minister) secure forgiveness of sins, a continual forgiveness of sins, a sense of unbroken forgiveness? God told the anointed priest (minister) how to be forgiven. The anointed priest refers to the High Priest. Four clear steps are spelled out by the Scripture and outline.

OUTLINE	SCRIPTURE	SCRIPTURE	OUTLINE
2. The way for an anointed priest (minister) to be forgiven a. Must confess the truth: He sins b. Must approach God thru the sacrifice (a symbol of Christ): Offer a young bull without defect c. Must observe the principles of atonement (reconciliation) 1) Substitution: Present...bull 2) Identifying with the substitute: Lay his hand on its head 3) Death of the substitute d. Must have the anointed priest (High Priest) offer the sacrifice 1) To take some of the blood into the Tabernacle • Dip his finger into the blood: Sprinkle it seven times in front of the Inner Curtain of the Most Holy Place • Put some blood on the horns of the incense altar • Pour out the remaining blood at the base of the altar of burnt offering	3 If the priest that is anointed do sin according to the sin of the people; then let him bring for his sin, which he hath sinned, a young bullock without blemish unto the LORD for a sin offering. 4 And he shall bring the bullock unto the door of the tabernacle of the congregation before the LORD; and shall lay his hand upon the bullock's head, and kill the bullock before the LORD. 5 And the priest that is anointed shall take of the bullock's blood, and bring it to the tabernacle of the congregation: 6 And the priest shall dip his finger in the blood, and sprinkle of the blood seven times before the LORD, before the vail of the sanctuary. 7 And the priest shall put *some* of the blood upon the horns of the altar of sweet incense before the LORD, which *is* in the tabernacle of the congregation; and shall pour all the blood of the bullock at the bottom of the altar of the burnt offering,	which *is* at the door of the tabernacle of the congregation. 8 And he shall take off from it all the fat of the bullock for the sin offering; the fat that covereth the inwards, and all the fat that *is* upon the inwards, 9 And the two kidneys, and the fat that *is* upon them, which *is* by the flanks, and the caul above the liver, with the kidneys, it shall he take away, 10 As it was taken off from the bullock of the sacrifice of peace offerings: and the priest shall burn them upon the altar of the burnt offering. 11 And the skin of the bullock, and all his flesh, with his head, and with his legs, and his inwards, and his dung, 12 Even the whole bullock shall he carry forth without the camp unto a clean place, where the ashes are poured out, and burn him on the wood with fire: where the ashes are poured out shall he be burnt.	2) To remove & offer certain parts of the sacrifice to the LORD • All the fat • Both kidneys • The liver • All to be done as in the sacrifice of the Fellowship Offering 3) To take the rest of the bull outside the camp & burn it upon the ash heap (a symbol of judgment, the fact that sin cannot be allowed in God's presence: Sin must be removed, judged, condemned)

a. He must confess the truth: he sins (v.3). When the anointed priest (minister) sinned, his sin had enormous repercussions: his sin affected and brought guilt upon the whole community. How? He was their representative before God. He stood before God on their behalf, in their place. He was just like an ambassador who represented a nation or a body of people. Whatever he did was counted as an act on behalf of the people. If he did good, then the people's position and appeal were acceptable; if he did evil, the people were counted guilty. The people were represented in the anointed priest, identified in him before God. Note how this pointed to Jesus Christ. He stands for us, as our perfect representative. Jesus Christ is our great High Priest who represents us before God.

But another factor was also involved in the representative or ambassadorial role of the High Priest before God. The anointed priest was responsible for leading and teaching the Word of God to the people—just how they were to live for God. If he were corrupted by sin, his teaching and leadership were weakened and his example too often caused the weak to stumble and fall. Because of this heavy responsibility, the High Priest was immediately to confess his sin and take steps to correct it. Note: what is said here is true of any priest or minister.

> **"If we confess our sins, he is faithful and just to forgive us *our* sins, and to cleanse us from all unrighteousness" (1 Jn.1:9).**
> **"He that covereth his sins shall not prosper: but whoso confesseth and forsaketh *them* shall have mercy" (Pr.28:13).**
> **"But if the wicked will turn from all his sins that he hath committed, and keep all my statutes, and do that which is lawful and right, he shall surely live, he shall not die" (Eze.18:21).**

b. The priest (minister) must approach God through the sacrifice and offer a young bull without defect (v.3). Note, there is no forgiveness apart from the sacrifice. The sacrifice was a symbol of Jesus Christ, and the bull without defect was a symbol of the sinlessness and perfection of Christ.

Thought 1. Jesus Christ was the Perfect, Sinless Sacrifice. As such, He stands before God as the Perfect, Ideal Man. As the Ideal, Perfect Man, He can represent us before God. This is the reason the sinner (all of us) has to approach God through Christ. We have no other way to secure forgiveness of sin. Priest, minister, and layperson alike—we all have to approach God through the Perfect, Sinless Sacrifice, the Lord Jesus Christ Himself.

> **"For we have not an high priest which cannot be touched with the feeling of our infirmities; but was in all points tempted like as *we are, yet* without sin" (He.4:15).**
> **"For such an high priest became us, *who is* holy, harmless, undefiled, separate from sinners, and made higher than the heavens" (He.7:26).**
> **"Forasmuch as ye know that ye were not redeemed with corruptible things, *as* silver and gold, from your vain conversation *received* by tradition from your fathers; But with the precious blood of Christ, as of a lamb without blemish and without spot" (1 Pe.1:18-19).**
> **"Who did no sin, neither was guile found in his mouth" (1 Pe.2:22).**

c. The priest (minister) must observe the principles of atonement or reconciliation (v.4).
   1) The principle of substitution: he had to present the sacrifice to the LORD, offer it up...
   * on his behalf
   * in his stead
   * in his place
   * as a substitute for him

   2) The principle of identifying with the substitute: this he did by laying his hands on the bull's head. (See note, pt.2—Le.1:3-9 for more discussion.)
   3) The principle of death for the substitute: he had to put the substitute sacrifice to death.

Thought 1. Note how clearly the sacrifice symbolizes Jesus Christ. Jesus Christ died as our substitute: on our behalf, in our stead, in our place. He died for us. There is only one way any of us can be forgiven—whether priest, minister, or layperson: we must present ourselves to God in the substitute sacrifice, in the Lord Jesus Christ. Christ is the only sacrifice acceptable to God. Forgiveness of sins comes only through Him: He is the one and only acceptable sacrifice.

> **"But we see Jesus, who was made a little lower than the angels for the suffering of death, crowned with glory and honour; that he by the grace of God should taste death for every man" (He.2:9).**
> **"Who his own self bare our sins in his own body on the tree, that we, being dead to sins, should live unto righteousness: by whose stripes ye were healed" (1 Pe.2:24).**
> **"For Christ also hath once suffered for sins, the just for the unjust, that he might bring us to God, being put to death in the flesh, but quickened by the Spirit" (1 Pe.3:18).**
> **"But he *was* wounded for our transgressions, *he was* bruised for our iniquities: the chastisement of our peace *was* upon him; and with his stripes we are healed" (Is.53:5).**

d. The priest (minister) must have the anointed priest offer the sacrifice to the LORD (vv.5-12). The ritual was as follows:
   1) The priest was to take some blood into the Tabernacle (v.5).
   ⇒ He was to dip his finger into the blood and sprinkle it seven times in front of the Inner Curtain of the Most Holy Place (v.6). This shows just how serious the sin of a priest (minister) was to God. For laypersons, the blood was sprinkled on the Altar of Burnt Offering, never in front of the Holy Place. This symbolized that a sinning priest (minister) was shut out from God's presence (the Most Holy Place) and could not be readmitted until he was cleansed by the blood.
   ⇒ He was to put some blood on the incense altar (v.7). This was the altar symbolizing the prayers of God's people ascending up to God like the sweet fragrance of burning incense. The symbol is clear: the prayers of

a sinning priest were shut out, rejected. They could not be heard nor answered until he was cleansed by the blood.

⇒ He was to pour out the remaining blood at the base of the Altar of Burnt Offering (v.7). Remember, this altar symbolized the justice and judgment of God against sin. The poured-out blood appeased and satisfied the justice and the wrath of God, fulfilling the judgment of God.

2) The priest (minister) was to remove and offer certain parts of the sacrifice to the LORD (vv.8-10). He was to remove...
- all the fat (v.8)
- both kidneys (v.9)
- the liver (v.9)

All were to be removed just as they were in the Fellowship Offering (v.10; see 3:9-11). The choice parts were to be burned on the altar as the LORD's portion (v.10).

3) The priest was to take the rest of the sacrifice—all of it—outside the camp to burn it upon the ash heap. This was a symbol of God's feelings toward and judgment against sin. Sin cannot be allowed in God's presence; sin must be removed, judged, and condemned in order for the believer to be forgiven, whether priest, minister, or layperson.

Thought 1. It is the death—the blood—of the Lord Jesus Christ that cleanses the priest or minister, that cleanses all of us from sin. He died that we might be cleansed and restored to righteousness. His death, His blood alone, cleanses us. Forgiveness of sins is found in Christ and Christ alone.

"**For this is my blood of the new testament, which is shed for many for the remission of sins**" (Mt.26:28).

"**Much more then, being now justified by his blood, we shall be saved from wrath through him**" (Ro.5:9).

"**For he hath made him** *to be* **sin for us, who knew no sin; that we might be made the righteousness of God in him**" (2 Co.5:21).

"**In whom we have redemption through his blood, the forgiveness of sins, according to the riches of his grace**" (Ep.1:7).

"**Forasmuch as ye know that ye were not redeemed with corruptible things,** *as* **silver and gold, from your vain conversation** *received* **by tradition from your fathers; But with the precious blood of Christ, as of a lamb without blemish and without spot**" (1 Pe.1:18-19).

"**But if we walk in the light, as he is in the light, we have fellowship one with another, and the blood of Jesus Christ his Son cleanseth us from all sin**" (1 Jn.1:7).

---

3 (4:13-21) **Sin—Forgiveness of Sin—Commandments, Breaking the—Society—Nations—Community**: How can society—a community, an entire nation—be forgiven? God told the community of Israel how to be forgiven. The steps to be taken were the same as for the anointed priests (minister). Remember, there were at least two to three million Israelite citizens at this time. There would obviously be times when the entire nation would be guilty of sin and wrongdoing, but there would also be times when a much smaller number of people—small communities—would become involved in a sin. Whatever the case, the remedy—the only way to escape the justice and judgment of God—was to approach God as a community or nation of people and seek His forgiveness. Of course, if the nation as a whole were involved, the leaders would go to the Tabernacle, the place of worship, and approach God on behalf of the people. The people would stay home, praying and seeking God for forgiveness until their leaders returned to their communities or tribes. Note the ritual and steps to be taken by the community or nation in seeking forgiveness.

OUTLINE	SCRIPTURE	SCRIPTURE	OUTLINE
3. **The way for society—a community, an entire nation—to be forgiven** a. Must confess the truth: Are guilty of national sin (once sin is brought to their attention, even if they were unaware of the sins) b. Must approach God thru the sacrifice when they become aware of the sin: Offer a young bull (without defect) c. Must observe the principles of atonement 1) Substitution: "Present...bull"	13 And if the whole congregation of Israel sin through ignorance, and the thing be hid from the eyes of the assembly, and they have done *somewhat against* any of the commandments of the LORD *concerning things* which should not be done, and are guilty; 14 When the sin, which they have sinned against it, is known, then the congregation shall offer a young bullock for the sin, and bring him before the tabernacle of the congregation.	15 And the elders of the congregation shall lay their hands upon the head of the bullock before the LORD: and the bullock shall be killed before the LORD. 16 And the priest that is anointed shall bring of the bullock's blood to the tabernacle of the congregation: 17 And the priest shall dip his finger *in some* of the blood, and sprinkle *it* seven times before the LORD, *even* before the vail. 18 And he shall put *some* of	2) Identification: "Lay hands..." 3) Death of the substitute: Slaughter it d. Must have the priest (High Priest) offer the sacrifice 1) To take some of the blood into the Tabernacle • Dip his finger into the blood: Sprinkle it seven times in front of the Inner Curtain • Put some blood on the

OUTLINE	SCRIPTURE	SCRIPTURE	OUTLINE
horns of the incense altar	the blood upon the horns of the altar which *is* before the LORD, that *is* in the tabernacle of the congregation, and shall pour out all the blood at the bottom of the altar of the burnt offering, which *is at* the door of the tabernacle of the congregation.	20 And he shall do with the bullock as he did with the bullock for a sin offering, so shall he do with this: and the priest shall make an atonement for them, and it shall be forgiven them.	for the sins of the priests
• Pour out the remaining blood at the base of the altar of burnt offering			e. The result: Brings atonement, reconciliation between the people & God—brings forgiveness of sins
		21 And he shall carry forth the bullock without the camp, and burn him as he burned the first bullock: it *is* a sin offering for the congregation.	f. The condemnation of sin symbolized: To take the rest of the sacrifice outside the camp (a symbol of judgment—that sin can never be allowed in God's presence)
2) To remove & offer certain parts of the sacrifice: Just as he did with the sacrifice	19 And he shall take all his fat from him, and burn *it* upon the altar.		

a. The people must confess the truth: they were guilty of national sin once it was brought to their attention, even if they were not previously aware of the sin (v.13).

Thought 1. A desperate need exists for courageous leaders who will make us aware of sin and lead us to confess sin, crying out to God for forgiveness and deliverance. Our communities and nations would suffer far less lawlessness, violence, injustice, and seemingly unsolvable problems if leaders would arise who would be courageous enough to be raw honest and truthful.

b. People must approach God through the sacrifice when they become aware of the sin: offer a young bull (without defect) (v.14).
c. People must observe the principles of atonement (vv.14-15).
d. People must have the priest (High Priest) offer the sacrifice (vv.16-20).
e. The result: God declares that the people's trust in the sacrifice (a symbol of Christ) will bring atonement, reconciliation, between Him and the people. God will forgive them and forgive their sins if they will just approach Him as He says, through the death and shed blood of the sacrifice.
f. The condemnation of sin symbolized: to take the rest of the sacrifice outside the camp (a symbol of judgment—that sin can never be allowed in God's presence) (v.21).

Thought 1. A community or nation of people stands just as guilty of sin before God as individuals do. Whole communities…
• can become involved in sinful or evil acts of war, lawlessness, violence, immoral behavior, abuse, drunkenness, and a host of other evils
• can become guilty by keeping silent and doing nothing to prevent or correct the evil

In such cases, the very ground of a community or nation becomes polluted and corrupt in God's eyes. When the day of judgment comes, leaders and citizens alike will give an account for their sinful acts and/or cowardly silence and inaction.

"**And God looked upon the earth, and, behold, it was corrupt; for all flesh had corrupted his way upon the earth. And God said unto Noah, The end of all flesh is come before me; for the earth is filled with violence through them; and, behold, I will destroy them with the earth**" (Ge.6:12-13).

"**If my people, which are called by my name, shall humble themselves, and pray, and seek my face, and turn from their wicked ways; then will I hear from heaven, and will forgive their sin, and will heal their land**" (2 Chr.7:14).

"**But** *there is* **forgiveness with thee, that thou mayest be feared**" (Ps.130:4).

"**By the blessing of the upright the city is exalted: but it is overthrown by the mouth of the wicked**" (Pr.11:11).

"**Righteousness exalteth a nation: but sin** *is* **a reproach to any people**" (Pr.14:34).

"**When the Son of man shall come in his glory, and all the holy angels with him, then shall he sit upon the throne of his glory: And before him shall be gathered all nations: and he shall separate them one from another, as a shepherd divideth** *his* **sheep from the goats: And he shall set the sheep on his right hand, but the goats on the left**" (Mt.25:31-33).

"**Him hath God exalted with his right hand** *to be* **a Prince and a Saviour, for to give repentance to Israel, and forgiveness of sins**" (Ac.5:31).

"**Be it known unto you therefore, men** *and* **brethren, that through this man is preached unto you the forgiveness of sins**" (Ac.13:38).

4 (4:22-26) **Sin—Forgiveness of Sins—Commandments, Breaking the—Leaders**: How can a leader secure forgiveness of sins? God tells the leader how to be forgiven. The leader must do what the priest and the community or nation does: he must approach God for forgiveness, approach God in the very same way as everyone else. The fact that he is a leader carries no weight with God. The greatest leader ever known among men has no more merit or value before God than the lowest follower, not even an ounce more merit. Note the steps a leader had to take in order to be forgiven his sin.

OUTLINE	SCRIPTURE	SCRIPTURE	OUTLINE
4. The way for a leader to be forgiven a. Must confess the truth: Is guilty of sin when he breaks any of God's commands, even unintentionally b. Must approach God thru the sacrifice when made aware of sin c. Must observe the principles of atonement 1) Substitution: Offer a male goat without defect 2) Identification: Lay his hand on its head 3) Death of the substitute: Slaughter it	22 When a ruler hath sinned, and done *somewhat* through ignorance *against* any of the commandments of the LORD his God *concerning things* which should not be done, and is guilty; 23 Or if his sin, wherein he hath sinned, come to his knowledge; he shall bring his offering, a kid of the goats, a male without blemish: 24 And he shall lay his hand upon the head of the goat, and kill it in the place where they kill the burnt offering	before the LORD: it *is* a sin offering. 25 And the priest shall take of the blood of the sin offering with his finger, and put *it* upon the horns of the altar of burnt offering, and shall pour out his blood at the bottom of the altar of burnt offering. 26 And he shall burn all his fat upon the altar, as the fat of the sacrifice of peace offerings: and the priest shall make an atonement for him as concerning his sin, and it shall be forgiven him.	d. Must have the priest offer the sacrifice 1) To take some of the blood • Dip his finger in the blood & put it on the horns of the altar of burnt offering • Pour out the remaining blood at the base of the altar 2) To offer all the fat on the altar just as he did the fellowship offering e. The result: Makes atonement (reconciliation) for the leader's sin—he is forgiven

a. The leader must confess the truth: he is guilty of sin when he breaks any of God's commands, even unintentionally (v.22).

b. The leader must approach God through the sacrifice when he is made aware of his sin (v.22). The idea involves immediacy: when a person pointed out his sin, he was immediately to approach God for forgiveness. This was an absolute essential because of the leader's responsibility and influence over others. If he continued in sin, he could do enormous damage…

• to his office and area of responsibility
• to his people by leading the weak to stumble and fall

Thought 1. Note how strongly this applies to every generation of leaders.

c. The leader must observe the principles of atonement (vv.22-24).
d. The leader must have the priest offer the sacrifice (vv.25-26).
e. The result: God declared that the leader's faith in the sacrifice made atonement or reconciliation for him (v.26). The sacrifice was counted as his substitute, his ransom. The substitute sacrifice paid the price for sin, the penalty of sin, for the leader. The leader was freed from sin, set free to be reconciled and acceptable to God. God forgave the leader, cleansed him from sin—all because of the sacrifice (a symbol of Christ).

Thought 1. A leader approaches God and receives forgiveness just like everyone else: through the substitute sacrifice, the Lord Jesus Christ. Christ died and shed His blood to make atonement and reconciliation with God possible. A leader's sins are forgiven only through Jesus Christ and through Him alone.

"Then Peter opened *his* mouth, and said, Of a truth I perceive that God is no respecter of persons: But in every nation he that feareth him, and worketh righteousness, is accepted with him" (Ac.10:34-35).
"But unto them that are contentious, and do not obey the truth, but obey unrighteousness, indignation and wrath, Tribulation and anguish, upon every soul of man that doeth evil, of the Jew first, and also of the Gentile; But glory, honour, and peace, to every man that worketh good, to the Jew first, and also to the Gentile: For there is no respect of persons with God" (Ro.2:8-11).
"For there is no difference between the Jew and the Greek: for the same LORD over all is rich unto all that call upon him" (Ro.10:12).
"And whatsoever ye do, do *it* heartily, as to the LORD, and not unto men; Knowing that of the LORD ye shall receive the reward of the inheritance: for ye serve the LORD Christ. But he that doeth wrong shall receive for the wrong which he hath done: and there is no respect of persons" (Col.3:23-25).
"But as he which hath called you is holy, so be ye holy in all manner of conversation; Because it is written, Be ye holy; for I am holy. And if ye call on the Father, who without respect of persons judgeth according to every man's work, pass the time of your sojourning *here* in fear: Forasmuch as ye know that ye were not redeemed with corruptible things, *as* silver and gold, from your vain conversation *received* by tradition from your fathers; But with the precious blood of Christ, as of a lamb without blemish and without spot" (1 Pe.1:15-19).

5 (4:27-35) **Sin—Forgiveness of Sin—Atonement, Principles of—Commandments, Breaking the—Reconciliation—Offerings, the Sin—Sin Offering, the:** How can an individual person secure forgiveness of sin? God tells the individual person how to be forgiven. He or she is to do exactly what everyone else does when they seek forgiveness: the person must approach God exactly like God says. How is an individual person to approach God? Note the Scripture and outline:

OUTLINE	SCRIPTURE	SCRIPTURE	OUTLINE

5. The way for an individual person to be forgiven
a. Must confess the truth: Is guilty of sin when any of God's commands are disobeyed, even unintentional sins
 	
b. Must approach God thru sacrifice when made aware of the sin
c. Must observe the principles of atonement
  1) Substitution: Offer a female goat without defect
  2) Identification: Lay his hand on its head
  3) Death of the substitute: Slaughter it
 	
d. Must have the priest offer the sacrifice
  1) To take some of the blood
   • Dip his finger in the blood & put it on the horns of the altar of burnt offering
   • Pour out the remainder at the base of the altar
  2) To remove & offer all the fat: Just as he did with the fellowship offering
e. The result
  1) The sweet aroma of the believer's faith in the sacrifice pleases the LORD
	27 And if any one of the common people sin through ignorance, while he doeth *somewhat against* any of the commandments of the LORD *concerning things* which ought not to be done, and be guilty;
	28 Or if his sin, which he hath sinned, come to his knowledge: then he shall bring his offering, a kid of the goats, a female without blemish, for his sin which he hath sinned.
	29 And he shall lay his hand upon the head of the sin offering, and slay the sin offering in the place of the burnt offering.
	30 And the priest shall take of the blood thereof with his finger, and put *it* upon the horns of the altar of burnt offering, and shall pour out all the blood thereof at the bottom of the altar.
	31 And he shall take away all the fat thereof, as the fat is taken away from off the sacrifice of peace offerings; and the priest shall burn *it* upon the altar for a sweet sa-
		vour unto the LORD; and the priest shall make an atonement for him, and it shall be forgiven him.
		32 And if he bring a lamb for a sin offering, he shall bring it a female without blemish.
		33 And he shall lay his hand upon the head of the sin offering, and slay it for a sin offering in the place where they kill the burnt offering.
		34 And the priest shall take of the blood of the sin offering with his finger, and put *it* upon the horns of the altar of burnt offering, and shall pour out all the blood thereof at the bottom of the altar:
		35 And he shall take away all the fat thereof, as the fat of the lamb is taken away from the sacrifice of the peace offerings; and the priest shall burn them upon the altar, according to the offerings made by fire unto the LORD: and the priest shall make an atonement for his sin that he hath committed, and it shall be forgiven him.
			2) The trust (obedience) of the believer makes atonement: He is forgiven (because he trusted what God said, that He would forgive sin thru the sacrifice)
			f. The option: May offer a lamb
			  1) Must still observe the principles of atonement
			  • Substitution: Bring a female
			  • Identification: Lay his hand on its head
			  • Death of the substitute: Slaughter it
			  2) Must have the priest offer the sacrifice
			  • To dip his finger in the blood & put it on the horns of the altar of burnt offering & pour out the remaining at the base of the altar
			  • To remove & offer all the fat: Just as he did with the fellowship offering
			  3) The result: Makes atonement for the person—he is forgiven (because he believed God—trusted God—did exactly what God said to do)

a. The individual person is to confess the truth (v.27). Note that a person is guilty of sin when he breaks any of God's commandments—any. Even if he fails to do something he should do—a sin of omission—he is guilty. Or if he unintentionally does something, he is guilty. He has sinned, and his sin separates him from God. He needs to confess his sin and his need for forgiveness.

b. The individual person must approach God through sacrifice when made aware of his sin (v.28).

c. The individual person must observe the principles of atonement (v.28).
  1) Substitution: offer a male goat without defect. Note that a female goat, not a male, was to be sacrificed by the individual person. This was an animal of less value, thereby allowing any average person the privilege of sacrificing a larger animal (see 5:7-13).
  2) Identification: lay his hand on its head.
  3) Death of the substitute: slaughter it.

d. The individual person must have the priest offer the sacrifice (vv.30-31).

e. The result was wonderful: the sweet aroma of the believer's faith and trust in the sacrifice pleased the LORD. The trust (obedience) of the believer in the sacrifice made atonement—ransomed, paid the price—for his sin. God reconciled the person and forgave his sin. The person believed God, believed what God said, trusted that God would forgive sin through the sacrifice; therefore God forgave the person.

f. Note the option: the person could offer a lamb just in case he did not have a goat or had more lambs than goats (vv.32-35). This shows the love and compassion of God, just how much He longs and seeks for man to repent and come to Him. The love of God reaches out to every individual person no matter who they are or what they have done.
  1) The person offering a lamb must still observe the principles of atonement (vv.32-33).
  2) The person must have the priest offer the sacrifice (vv.34-35).
  3) The result for this person was the same wonderful result: the person's faith—his obedience—made atonement for him. The substitute sacrifice paid the ransom, the price for his sin. God reconciled the person to Himself; God forgave the person's sins—all because the person believed and trusted God; all because the person did exactly what God said. He approached God and asked for forgiveness through the sacrifice and its shed blood.

Thought 1. What a beautiful picture and symbol of the Lord Jesus Christ. Jesus Christ is the sacrifice for our sins. Christ is our ransom; He has paid the price, delivered us from the snare of sin and death. Christ has reconciled us to God, and God forgives us through the perfect sacrifice of His shed blood.

"The next day John seeth Jesus coming unto him, and saith, Behold the Lamb of God, which taketh away the sin of the world" (Jn.1:29).

"For when we were yet without strength, in due time Christ died for the ungodly" (Ro.5:6).

"Who gave himself for our sins, that he might deliver us from this present evil world, according to the will of God and our Father" (Ga.1:4).

"In whom we have redemption through his blood, the forgiveness of sins, according to the riches of his grace" (Ep.1:7).

"And walk in love, as Christ also hath loved us, and hath given himself for us an offering and a sacrifice to God for a sweetsmelling savour" (Ep.5:2).

"Who gave himself for us, that he might redeem us from all iniquity, and purify unto himself a peculiar people, zealous of good works" (Tit.2:14).

"Forasmuch as ye know that ye were not redeemed with corruptible things, *as* silver and gold, from your vain conversation *received* by tradition from your fathers; But with the precious blood of Christ, as of a lamb without blemish and without spot" (1 Pe.1:18-19).

6 (5:1-6) **Sin—Forgiveness of Sin—Sin, Terrible**: How can a person secure forgiveness of sin even if he has sinned in some terrible way? Note that God tells the individual person how he can be forgiven, forgiven for any and all sins. Note the outline of the Scripture.

OUTLINE	SCRIPTURE	SCRIPTURE	OUTLINE

6. The way for a person to be forgiven for specific, terrible sins
a. The sins listed
  1) Social & civil injustice: Refusing to stand up for truth & justice when one knows the truth
  2) Religious defilement: Touching or doing anything that defiles one—this makes one unclean religiously or ceremoniously
 	
  3) Human & personal defilement: Touching anything that would make a person unclean or defiled
	And if a soul sin, and hear the voice of swearing, and *is* a witness, whether he hath seen or known *of it*; if he do not utter *it*, then he shall bear his iniquity.
	2 Or if a soul touch any unclean thing, whether *it be* a carcase of an unclean beast, or a carcase of unclean cattle, or the carcase of unclean creeping things, and *if* it be hidden from him; he also shall be unclean, and guilty.
	3 Or if he touch the uncleanness of man, whatsoever uncleanness *it be* that a man shall be defiled withal, and it be hid from him; when he knoweth *of it*, then he shall be guilty.
		4 Or if a soul swear, pronouncing with *his* lips to do evil, or to do good, whatsoever *it be* that a man shall pronounce with an oath, and it be hid from him; when he knoweth *of it*, then he shall be guilty in one of these.
		5 And it shall be, when he shall be guilty in one of these *things*, that he shall confess that he hath sinned in that *thing*:
		6 And he shall bring his trespass offering unto the LORD for his sin which he hath sinned, a female from the flock, a lamb or a kid of the goats, for a sin offering; and the priest shall make an atonement for him concerning his sin.
			4) Verbal sin or sins of the tongue: Rash swearing, thoughtless, careless swearing
			
			b. The remedy: The Sin Offering
			  1) Must confess the specific sin
			
			  2) Must approach God thru the sacrifice: Offer a female lamb or goat (as spelled out above [4:27-35])
			
			  3) The result: Makes atonement, reconciliation for sin

a. The specific sins are listed (vv.1-4). No doubt the sins listed here are only examples of a few terrible sins to show that God forgives all sins no matter what they are and no matter how awful. The particular sins listed cover the scope of human life: social and civil injustices, religions, human and personal behavior, even sins of the tongue.

1) Social and civil injustice: refusing to stand up for truth and justice when one knows the truth (v.1). This is such a serious matter that it could lead to wrong verdicts in court resulting in the execution of an innocent victim. Or, this sin could lead to murder, violence, abuse, and a host of other sins and evil out on the streets. In the case of nations, it could even result in war. Can a person guilty of such horrendous evil be forgiven? God gives the answer below.

2) Religious defilement: touching or doing anything that defiles a person, that makes a person unclean religiously or ceremoniously (v.2).

3) Human and personal defilement: touching or doing anything that would make a person unclean or defiled (v.3).

4) Verbal sin or sins of the tongue: rash swearing, thoughtless, careless swearing (v.4). Far, far too many people stand guilty of this sin. They have sworn and cursed so much—even using the name of God—that they do it with no thought whatsoever. In fact, every other word is a false, foul oath of profanity or vulgarity. (See outline and notes—Ex.20:7 for more discussion.)

b. The remedy for such sins is clearly stated by God: it is the Sin Offering (vv.5-6).

1) The person must confess the specific sin (v.5).

2) The person must approach God through the sacrifice: offer a female lamb or goat (v.6).

3) The result is the very same wonderful experience as for the individual who does not commit such horrendous sins. The person who commits terrible sin—no matter who he is nor how terrible the sin—is forgiven (v.6). He is forgiven if he approaches God through the sacrifice. The sacrifice (a symbol of Christ) made atonement for the terrible sinner. The sacrifice is the ransom, the price paid for his sins. The terrible sinner is reconciled to God and forgiven through the sacrifice.

"And the Pharisees and scribes murmured, saying, This man receiveth sinners, and eateth with them" (Lu.15:2).

"And they which heard *it*, being convicted by *their own* conscience, went out one by one, beginning at the eldest, *even* unto the last: and Jesus was left alone, and the woman standing in the midst. When Jesus had lifted up himself, and saw none but the woman, he said unto her, Woman, where are those thine accusers? hath no man condemned thee? She said, No man, Lord. And Jesus said unto her, Neither do I condemn thee: go, and sin no more" (Jn.8:9-11).

"But God commendeth his love toward us, in that, while we were yet sinners, Christ died for us" (Ro.5:8).

"For whosoever shall call upon the name of the Lord shall be saved" (Ro.10:13).

"This *is* a faithful saying, and worthy of all acceptation, that Christ Jesus came into the world to save sinners; of whom I am chief" (1 Ti.1:15).

7 **(5:7-13) Poor, The—Sin—Forgiveness—God, Love of—God, Compassion of—Offering, The Sin—Sin Offering, The:** How can the poor person secure forgiveness of sin? God tells the poor person how to be forgiven. The poor person is not excluded from forgiveness and salvation. He can be forgiven just as easily as the rich and well-to-do man. The poor person must approach God just like everyone else does.

OUTLINE	SCRIPTURE	SCRIPTURE	OUTLINE
7. The way for the poor person to be forgiven a. The poor must offer two doves or two young pigeons: One for the Sin Offering; the other for a burnt offering b. The poor must have the priest first offer the Sin Offering 1) He must put it to death 2) He must sprinkle the blood against the side of the altar 3) He must pour out the remaining blood at the base of the altar c. The poor must then have the priest offer the burnt offering as prescribed (Le.4:14-17; 1 Chr.15:13)	7 And if he be not able to bring a lamb, then he shall bring for his trespass, which he hath committed, two turtledoves, or two young pigeons, unto the LORD; one for a sin offering, and the other for a burnt offering. 8 And he shall bring them unto the priest, who shall offer *that* which *is* for the sin offering first, and wring off his head from his neck, but shall not divide *it* asunder: 9 And he shall sprinkle of the blood of the sin offering upon the side of the altar; and the rest of the blood shall be wrung out at the bottom of the altar: it *is* a sin offering. 10 And he shall offer the second *for* a burnt offering, according to the manner: and the priest shall make an atonement for him for his sin which he hath sinned, and	it shall be forgiven him. 11 But if he be not able to bring two turtledoves, or two young pigeons, then he that sinned shall bring for his offering the tenth part of an ephah of fine flour for a sin offering; he shall put no oil upon it, neither shall he put *any* frankincense thereon: for it *is* a sin offering. 12 Then shall he bring it to the priest, and the priest shall take his handful of it, *even* a memorial thereof, and burn *it* on the altar, according to the offerings made by fire unto the LORD: it *is* a sin offering. 13 And the priest shall make an atonement for him as touching his sin that he hath sinned in one of these, and it shall be forgiven him: and *the remnant* shall be the priest's, as a meat offering.	d. The poorest of the poor had provision made for them to be forgiven 1) Must offer one tenth of an ephah of fine flour (two quarts; two liters): Not to put oil or incense on it 2) Must have the priest make the offering: To offer a handful to the LORD as a memorial or token portion & to give the remainder to the priests 3) The result: Makes atonement, reconciles the guilty with God; he is forgiven

a. The poor person must offer two doves or two young pigeons: one for the Sin Offering, the other for a Burnt Offering (v.7). Note that the sacrifice of a Burnt Offering is mentioned here. If this were true for the poor, then a Burnt Offering was no doubt required for the wealthier people as well.

b. The poor person must have the priest first offer the Sin Offering (v.8).
1) He must put it to death (v.8).
2) He must sprinkle the blood against the side of the altar (v.9).
3) He must pour out the remaining blood at the base of the altar (v.9).

c. The poor person must then have the priest offer the Burnt Offering as prescribed (Le.4:14-17; 1 Chr.15:13) (v.10).

d. The poorest of the poor even had provision made for them to be forgiven (vv.11-13).
1) Must offer one tenth of an ephah of fine flour (two quarts; two liters): not to put oil or incense on it (v.11).
2) Must have the priest make the offering: to offer a handful to the LORD as a memorial or token portion, giving the remainder to the priests (v.12).
3) The result was just as wonderful for the poorest of the poor as it was for the wealthy: his sacrifice made atonement—ransomed or paid the price—for him to be freed from the penalty and judgment of sin. The poorest of the poor was reconciled to God: he was forgiven all his sins through the sacrifice and its shed blood.

"But God commendeth his love toward us, in that, while we were yet sinners, Christ died for us" (Ro.5:8).

"Purge out therefore the old leaven, that ye may be a new lump, as ye are unleavened. For even Christ our passover is sacrificed for us" (1 Co.5:7).

"For I delivered unto you first of all that which I also received, how that Christ died for our sins according to the scriptures" (1 Co.15:3).

"In whom we have redemption through his blood, the forgiveness of sins, according to the riches of his grace" (Ep.1:7).

"Forasmuch as ye know that ye were not redeemed with corruptible things, *as* silver and gold, from your vain conversation *received* by tradition from your fathers; But with the precious blood of Christ, as of a lamb without blemish and without spot" (1 Pe.1:18-19).

"Who his own self bare our sins in his own body on the tree, that we, being dead to sins, should live unto righteousness: by whose stripes ye were healed" (1 Pe.2:24).

TYPES, SYMBOLS, AND PICTURES
Leviticus 4:1–5:13

Historical Term	Type or Picture (Scriptural Basis for Each)	Life Application for Today's Believer	Biblical Application
The Sin Offering Le. 4:1-5:13. See also Le. 6:24-30; 8:14-17; 9:2; 9:15; 10:17; 16:3-22	*The Sin Offering is a type of Christ, a symbol or picture of Christ. This offering was to secure the forgiveness of sins.* "Speak unto the children of Israel, saying, If a soul shall sin through ignorance against any of the commandments of the LORD *concerning things which ought not to be done, and shall do against any of them: If the priest that is anointed do sin according to the sin of the people; then let him bring for his sin, which he hath sinned, a young bullock without blemish unto the LORD for a sin offering" (Le.4:2-3).	Jesus Christ is the Savior of the world, the One who provides the way of forgiveness for us. This He does through His sacrifice upon the cross. Through His blood we are cleaned from sin, cleansed from all unrighteousness.	"If we confess our sins, he is faithful and just to forgive us our sins, and to cleanse us from all unrighteousness" (1 Jn.1:9). "But we see Jesus, who was made a little lower than the angels for the suffering of death, crowned with glory and honour; that he by the grace of God should taste death for every man" (He.2:9). "Who his own self bare our sins in his own body on the tree, that we, being dead to sins, should live unto righteousness: by whose stripes ye were healed" (1 Pe.2:24). "For Christ also hath once suffered for sins, the just for the unjust, that he might bring us to God, being put to death in the flesh, but quickened by the Spirit" (1 Pe.3:18).
Young Bull Without Defect: The Sacrifice Used in the Sin Offering for the Anointed Priest or Minister Le. 4:3-12; see also Le.1:3	*This sacrifice is a symbol of Christ, and the bull with no defect was a symbol of the sinlessness and perfection of Christ.* "If the priest that is anointed do sin according to the sin of the people; then let him bring for his sin, which he hath sinned, a young bullock without blemish unto the LORD for a sin offering" (Le.4:3).	Jesus Christ is the Perfect, Sinless Sacrifice. As such, He stands before God as the Perfect, Ideal Man. As the Ideal, Perfect Man, He can represent us before God. This is the reason the sinner (all of us) has to approach God through Christ. We have no other way to secure forgiveness of sin. Priest, minister, and layperson alike—we all have to approach God through the Perfect, Sinless Sacrifice of the Lord Jesus Christ Himself.	"For we have not an high priest which cannot be touched with the feeling of our infirmities; but was in all points tempted like as we are, yet without sin" (He.4:15). "For such an high priest became us, who is holy, harmless, undefiled, separate from sinners, and made higher than the heavens" (He.7:26). "Forasmuch as ye know that ye were not redeemed with corruptible things, as silver and gold, from your vain conversation received by tradition from your fathers; But with the precious blood of Christ, as of a lamb without blemish and without spot" (1 Pe.1:18-19).
Blood Sprinkled Seven Times in Front of the Inner Curtain of the Most Holy Place During the Sin	*The blood sprinkled seven times in front of the inner curtain symbolized that a sinning priest (minister) was*	It is the death or the blood of the Lord Jesus Christ that cleanses the priest or minister, that cleanses all of us	"For this is my blood of the new testament, which is shed for many for the remission of sins" (Mt.26:28).

TYPES, SYMBOLS, AND PICTURES
Leviticus 4:1–5:13

Historical Term	Type or Picture (Scriptural Basis for Each)	Life Application for Today's Believer	Biblical Application
Offering for the Anointed Priest or Minister Le.4:5-12	*shut out from God's presence (the Most Holy Place), and could not be readmitted until he was cleansed by the blood. Remember, seven is the number of completion, of fulfillment. The priest was fully, completely cleansed by the blood.* **"And the priest shall dip his finger in the blood, and sprinkle of the blood seven times before the LORD, before the vail of the sanctuary" (Le.4:6).**	from sin. He died that we might be completely and fully cleansed. His death, His blood alone, cleanses us. Forgiveness of sins is found in Christ and Christ alone.	*"Much more then, being now justified by his blood, we shall be saved from wrath through him" (Ro. 5:9).* *"For he hath made him to be sin for us, who knew no sin; that we might be made the righteousness of God in him" (2 Co.5:21).* *"In whom we have redemption through his blood, the forgiveness of sins, according to the riches of his grace" (Ep.1:7).*
Blood Put Upon the Altar of Incense During the Sin Offering for the Anointed Priest or Minister Le. 4:7	*The blood put upon the altar of incense symbolized that the prayers of a sinning priest were shut out, rejected. They could not be heard and answered until he was cleansed by the blood.* **"And the priest shall put** *some* **of the blood upon the horns of the altar of sweet incense before the LORD, which** *is* **in the tabernacle of the congregation: and shall pour all the blood of the bullock at the bottom of the altar of the burnt offering, which** *is* **at the door of the tabernacle of the congregation" (Le.4:7).**	The believer who is living in unconfessed sin cannot be heard until he is cleansed by the blood of the Lamb, the shed blood of Jesus Christ.	*"Forasmuch as ye know that ye were not redeemed with corruptible things, as silver and gold, from your vain conversation received by tradition from your fathers; But with the precious blood of Christ, as of a lamb without blemish and without spot" (1 Pe. 1:18-19).* *"But if we walk in the light, as he is in the light, we have fellowship one with another, and the blood of Jesus Christ his Son cleanseth us from all sin" (1 Jn.1:7).*
The Poured-Out Blood at the Bottom of the Altar of Burnt Offering Le. 4:7	*This poured-out blood is a symbol that appeases and satisfies the justice and demand of God for righteousness. The blood poured out at the foot of the altar fulfilled the judgment of God against sin.* **"And the priest shall put** *some* **of the blood upon the horns of the altar of sweet incense before the LORD, which** *is* **in the tabernacle of the congregation: and shall pour all the blood of the bullock at the bottom of the altar of the burnt offering, which** *is* **at the door of the tabernacle of the congregation" (Le.4:7).**	The only thing that can cleanse us from sin is the shed, poured-out blood of Jesus Christ. It is the blood of Christ… • that appeases and satisfies the justice and demands of God • that justifies us • that brings us near to God, being reconciled to Him.	*"But God commendeth his love toward us, in that, while we were yet sinners, Christ died for us. Much more then, being now justified by his blood, we shall be saved from wrath through him. For if, when we were enemies, we were reconciled to God by the death of his Son, much more, being reconciled, we shall be saved by his life. And not only so, but we also joy in God through our Lord Jesus Christ, by whom we have now received the atonement" (Ro.5:8-11).* *"But now in Christ Jesus ye who sometimes were far off are made nigh by the blood of Christ" (Ep.2:13).*
The Ash Heap Le. 4:12; 9:11	*The ash heap is a symbol of God's feelings and judgment*	Sin cannot be allowed in God's presence; sin must be	*"For the bodies of those beasts, whose blood is*

TYPES, SYMBOLS, AND PICTURES
Leviticus 4:1–5:13

Historical Term	Type or Picture (Scriptural Basis for Each)	Life Application for Today's Believer	Biblical Application
	against sin. The priest was to take the rest of the sacrifice—all of it—outside the camp and burn it upon the ash heap. **"Even the whole bullock shall he carry forth without the camp unto a clean place, where the ashes are poured out, and burn him on the wood with fire: where the ashes are poured out shall he be burnt" (Le.4:12).**	removed, judged, and condemned in order for the believer to be forgiven, whether priest, minister, or layperson.	*brought into the sanctuary by the high priest for sin, are burned without the camp. Wherefore Jesus also, that he might sanctify the people with his own blood, suffered without the gate. Let us go forth therefore unto him without the camp, bearing his reproach" (He.13:11-13).* *"He that covereth his sins shall not prosper: but whoso confesseth and forsaketh them shall have mercy" (Pr.28:13).* *"If we confess our sins, he is faithful and just to forgive us our sins, and to cleanse us from all unrighteousness" (1 Jn.1:9).*
The Bull Sacrificed for Society During the Sin Offering Le.4:21	*The bull sacrificed for society during the sin offering symbolized the condemnation of sin* **"And he shall carry forth the bullock without the camp, and burn him as he burned the first bullock: it *is* a sin offering for the congregation" (Le.4:21).**	A community or nation of people stands just as guilty of sin before God as individuals do. Whole communities... • can become involved in sinful or evil acts of terrorism, war, lawlessness, violence, immoral behavior, abuse, drunkenness, and a host of other evils. • can become guilty by keeping silent and doing nothing. In such cases, the very ground of a community or nation becomes polluted and corrupt in God's eyes. When the day of judgment comes, leaders and citizens alike will give an account for their sinful acts and/or cowardly silence and inaction.	*"By the blessing of the upright the city is exalted: but it is overthrown by the mouth of the wicked" (Pr.11:11).* *"Righteousness exalteth a nation: but sin is a reproach to any people" (Pr.14:34).* *"And I will bring an everlasting reproach upon you, and a perpetual shame, which shall not be forgotten" (Je.23:40).* *"For our transgressions are multiplied before thee, and our sins testify against us: for our transgressions are with us; and as for our iniquities, we know them" (Is.59:12).* *"If my people, which are called by my name, shall humble themselves, and pray, and seek my face, and turn from their wicked ways; then will I hear from heaven, and will forgive their sin, and will heal their land" (2 Chr.7:14).*

1. A person can be set free from guilt—guilt due to sins against the holy things of God

a. Must approach God through the sacrifice (a symbol of Christ)

  1) To offer a ram without defect & of proper or full value

  2) To pay restitution plus 20% for the harm done to the holy things of God

  3) To have the priest offer the sacrifice

b. The result: The sacrifice makes atonement, reconciliation with God—the guilty is forgiven

2. A person can be set free from guilt—guilt due to breaking the commandments of God, doing what is forbidden

a. Must approach God through the sacrifice (a symbol of Christ): A ram without defect & of proper value

b. The result: The sacrifice makes atonement, reconciliation with God—the guilty is forgiven

c. The clear truth restated: Breaking God's commandment is

E. The Guilt Offering (a Picture of Christ's Atoning Sacrifice): The Way to Be Set Free from the Weight & Anguish of Guilt, the Pricking of Conscience, 5:14–6:7

14 And the LORD spake unto Moses, saying,
15 If a soul commit a trespass, and sin through ignorance, in the holy things of the LORD; then he shall bring for his trespass unto the LORD a ram without blemish out of the flocks, with thy estimation by shekels of silver, after the shekel of the sanctuary, for a trespass offering:
16 And he shall make amends for the harm that he hath done in the holy thing, and shall add the fifth part thereto, and give it unto the priest: and the priest shall make an atonement for him with the ram of the trespass offering, and it shall be forgiven him.
17 And if a soul sin, and commit any of these things which are forbidden to be done by the commandments of the LORD; though he wist *it* not, yet is he guilty, and shall bear his iniquity.
18 And he shall bring a ram without blemish out of the flock, with thy estimation, for a trespass offering, unto the priest: and the priest shall make an atonement for him concerning his ignorance wherein he erred and wist *it* not, and it shall be forgiven him.
19 It *is* a trespass offering: he hath certainly trespassed

against the LORD.

CHAPTER 6

And the LORD spake unto Moses, saying,
2 If a soul sin, and commit a trespass against the LORD, and lie unto his neighbour in that which was delivered him to keep, or in fellowship, or in a thing taken away by violence, or hath deceived his neighbour;
3 Or have found that which was lost, and lieth concerning it, and sweareth falsely; in any of all these that a man doeth, sinning therein:
4 Then it shall be, because he hath sinned, and is guilty, that he shall restore that which he took violently away, or the thing which he hath deceitfully gotten, or that which was delivered him to keep, or the lost thing which he found,
5 Or all that about which he hath sworn falsely; he shall even restore it in the principal, and shall add the fifth part more thereto, *and* give it unto him to whom it appertaineth, in the day of his trespass offering.
6 And he shall bring his trespass offering unto the LORD, a ram without blemish out of the flock, with thy estimation, for a trespass offering, unto the priest:
7 And the priest shall make an atonement for him before the LORD: and it shall be forgiven him for any thing of all that he hath done in trespassing therein.

serious, against God Himself

3. A person can be set free from guilt—guilt due to sins against one's neighbors

a. The warning: An act against God

b. The example of some common sins

  1) Lying about borrowed items or trusts left in one's care

  2) Stealing or cheating

  3) Finding lost property & lying about it

  4) Swearing falsely

  5) Committing any sin that a person may or can do

c. The way to be set free from the guilt of sinning against one's neighbor

  1) Must make restitution in full

    • Return what was stolen, extorted, entrusted to one's care, found, or sworn falsely about

    • Pay 20% interest

    • Make restitution on the very day one confesses

  2) Must approach God through the sacrifice (a symbol of Christ): Offer a ram without defect & of proper value

  3) The result: Makes atonement, reconciliation with God

    • The guilty is forgiven

    • The wonderful truth restated: The guilty is forgiven for anything he has done that made him guilty

DIVISION I

THE WAY TO BECOME ACCEPTABLE TO GOD (PART 1): BY THE OFFERING OF A SACRIFICE, A SUBSTITUTE, 1:1–7:38

E. The Guilt Offering (a Picture of Christ's Atoning Sacrifice): The Way to Be Set Free from the Weight and Anguish of Guilt, the Pricking of Conscience, 5:14–6:7

(5:14–6:7) **Introduction—Guilt—Freedom, from Guilt—Liberty, from Guilt**: the weight and anguish of guilt gnaw at millions of people worldwide every day. Guilt pricks the conscience. It eats away at and disturbs some people so much that they become a bundle of nerves. They experience all kinds of emotional, mental, and physical problems, some even having to be institutionalized. When dealing with guilt, we must always keep this one fact in mind: there is a *false guilt* as well as a *true guilt*.

  ⇒ False guilt is aroused when a person fails to keep the impossible standards set by family, friends, or society, and in some cases even by himself. False guilt seldom if ever accepts anything other than perfection and never sees the possibility of complete forgiveness.

⇒ On the other hand, true guilt is healthy and serves as a red warning flag to protect a person. True guilt is aroused when a person breaks a commandment of God, an act of disobedience that threatens to harm the person himself or someone else in society. True guilt keeps people from destroying themselves and their society. True guilt restrains, controls, and corrects a person and his neighbors. True guilt arouses a person to seek forgiveness from both God and man.

The point is this: when guilt strikes a person, he needs to evaluate it. He needs to determine whether the guilt is false or true. If the guilt is false, he needs to accept the fact that it is false and move on with his life. He needs to adopt the true laws of God's Word and of society, living by them and them alone, not by the false standards demanded by loved ones and others. If the person is plagued by true guilt, he needs to confess and repent of his wrong, confessing both to God and to the person wronged. And he needs to make restitution. Restitution will help ease a person's guilt as much as, if not more than, anything else.

Now, note two things about guilt. First, guilt is a feeling, a pricking of conscience, a conviction within the heart that one has done wrong. But guilt is not only a feeling or inner pricking of conscience. Guilt is, second, a standing, a condition, a state of being before God. If a person sins, he stands guilty before God; his condition before God is guilty. A person may be so hardened in a sin that he *never feels guilty*; he never suffers the anguish and weight of guilt. Nevertheless, his condition and standing before God is guilty. He still must give an account and face the judgment of God. In this case, there is only one escape from God's judgment: a person must be set free from the guilt of sin. Once he is set free from guilt he is declared "not guilty." He is able to stand before God without any guilt whatsoever. He is counted as though he is perfect, sinless. No charge can be made against the person because the charges have been borne by Someone else. By whom? By the Lord Jesus Christ.

On the cross, Jesus Christ died for the sins and guilt of man. He took the sins and guilt of man upon Himself to pay the penalty for man. By this act—by dying for man—Jesus Christ sets man free from the guilt of sin. When a person believes and approaches God through the sacrifice of Jesus Christ, God counts the death of Jesus Christ for the person. God counts the person innocent, counts him free of guilt and condemnation. God counts the person sinless and perfect, blameless and guiltless; therefore, the person is acceptable to God. The person is forgiven forever and given the right to live in the presence of God forever.

Now, how about Old Testament believers? How were they delivered from the weight and anguish of guilt? Through the sacrifice, the offering of an animal as a *substitute sacrifice*. God counted the sacrifice as the ransom payment for the person's sin and guilt. God counted the person freed from guilt. This He did for one reason: the substitute sacrifice pointed to the Perfect Sacrifice of the Lord Jesus Christ. This is the much needed subject of this passage: *The Guilt Offering (a Picture of Christ's Atoning Sacrifice): The Way to Be Set Free from the Weight and Anguish of Guilt, the Pricking of Conscience*, 5:14–6:7.

1. A person can be set free from guilt—guilt due to sins against the holy things of God (5:14-16).
2. A person can be set free from guilt—guilt due to breaking the commandments of God, doing what is forbidden (5:17-19).
3. A person can be set free from guilt—guilt due to sins against one's neighbors (6:1-7).

---

1 (5:14-16) **Guilt—Freedom, Spiritual—Liberty, Spiritual—Conscience—Deliverance—Believer, Life and Walk**: a person can be set free from guilt—the guilt arising from sins against the holy things of God. The Hebrew word for *holy things* (qodes) refers to anything that is holy or set apart to God, such things as...

- a sanctuary or any other sacred room, holy ground, or holy place
- furnishings or any other sacred object
- worship or spiritual services, holy days, or spiritual duties
- believers, people who are dedicated and consecrated to God

God declares that any person who sins against the holy things of God is guilty before Him and must face the judgment of God. A person stands guilty before God if he...

- damages a sanctuary or any other sacred room, holy ground, or holy place
- damages church furnishings or any other sacred object
- neglects or abuses worship or spiritual services, holy days, or spiritual duties
- fails to give or keeps back part of the tithe, offerings, or gifts
- ridicules or persecutes believers, people who are dedicated and consecrated to God

Now, when a person sins against the holy things of God, he might feel guilty or he might not. He may or may not be troubled, pricked, or bothered over the wrong he has done. Feelings have nothing to do with the matter. The person's *standing* before God is guilty. His *position* before God is guilty. The person...

- abused the holy things of God
- showed disrespect and dishonor to God
- ignored or neglected the holy things of God

The person is guilty. He is to be judged, to face the condemnation of God. He is hopelessly guilty and condemned unless one thing is done: he must be set free from the awful weight of guilt. How? Note the steps spelled out by God in the Scripture and outline:

OUTLINE	SCRIPTURE	SCRIPTURE	OUTLINE
1. A person can be set free from guilt—guilt due to sins against the holy things of God a. Must approach God through the sacrifice (a symbol of Christ) 1) To offer a ram without defect & of proper or full value	14 And the LORD spake unto Moses, saying, 15 If a soul commit a trespass, and sin through ignorance, in the holy things of the LORD; then he shall bring for his trespass unto the LORD a ram without blemish out of the flocks, with thy estimation by shekels of silver, after the shekel of the	sanctuary, for a trespass offering: 16 And he shall make amends for the harm that he hath done in the holy thing, and shall add the fifth part thereto, and give it unto the priest: and the priest shall make an atonement for him with the ram of the trespass offering, and it shall be forgiven him.	2) To pay restitution plus 20% for the harm done to the holy things of God 3) To have the priest offer the sacrifice b. The result: The sacrifice makes atonement, reconciliation with God—the guilty is forgiven

a. The person must approach God to be set free, approach God through the sacrifice (v.15). Keep in mind that the sacrifice was a symbol of Christ.

   1) The person had to offer a ram sacrifice, a perfect ram, one without blemish or defect. Note that the animal had to be valuable, that is, of such a size and weight that it would be fully valued. This shows how serious this sin is to God. A person who sins against the holy things of God has committed a terrible wrong.
   2) The person must pay restitution for the harm done plus 20 percent interest (v.16). Note that the damage is to be appraised and determined by the priest.
   3) The person must have the priest offer the sacrifice for him (v.16). The person would have identified with the substitute sacrifice by laying his hands on its head. The sacrifice took the place of the guilty person, paying the ransom, the price for the sin against the holy things. (See note, pt.2—Le.1:3-9 for more discussion.)

b. The result was wonderful: the sacrifice made atonement for the guilty person. As stated above, the sacrifice took the place of the guilty person and bore the judgment and condemnation of his guilt for him. The person was reconciled to God: his sin against the holy things of God was forgiven. His guilt was removed. He was set free from the guilt, fully forgiven and fully accepted by God.

Thought 1. Jesus Christ sacrificed Himself for us. He bore our guilt, bore the judgment and condemnation of our guilt. We can now be set free from guilt by approaching God through the Perfect Sacrifice of Christ. If we will believe God, approach Him exactly as He says—through Christ—then God counts the sacrifice of Christ...

- on our behalf
- in our place
- in our stead
- as our substitute

The result is wonderful: through Christ, we are set free from the guilt of our sin against the holy things of God. We are able to stand before God free, set free from sin and guilt—all through the sacrifice of Christ.

> **"Who gave himself for our sins, that he might deliver us from this present evil world, according to the will of God and our Father" (Ga.1:4).**
> **"Christ hath redeemed us from the curse of the law, being made a curse for us: for it is written, Cursed is every one that hangeth on a tree" (Ga.3:13).**
> **"Forasmuch as ye know that ye were not redeemed with corruptible things, as silver and gold, from your vain conversation received by tradition from your fathers; But with the precious blood of Christ, as of a lamb without blemish and without spot" (1 Pe.1:18-19).**
> **"Having a good conscience; that, whereas they speak evil of you, as of evildoers, they may be ashamed that falsely accuse your good conversation [behavior, conduct] in Christ" (1 Pe.3:16).**
> **"That which we have seen and heard declare we unto you, that ye also may have fellowship with us: and truly our fellowship is with the Father, and with his Son Jesus Christ" (1 Jn.1:3).**
> **"But he was wounded for our transgressions, he was bruised for our iniquities: the chastisement of our peace was upon him; and with his stripes we are healed" (Is.53:5).**

2 **(5:17-19) Guilt—Freedom, Spiritual—Liberty, Spiritual—Conscience—Deliverance—Believer, Life and Walk—Commandments, of God**: a person can be set free from guilt—the guilt arising from breaking the commandments of God, from doing what is forbidden. Note what the Scripture declares: the person is guilty and will be held accountable. Note also that a person is guilty and held accountable for all sins, even unintentional sins or sins of ignorance. A person is guilty because of the sins of omission as well as the sins of commission, whether known or unknown. Just think how often we break the commandments of God and sense some guilt because of our disobedience. Some people are so guilt-ridden that they cannot handle the guilty feelings that gnaw at them and prick their consciences.

> **"For mine iniquities are gone over mine head: as an heavy burden they are too heavy for me" (Ps.38:4).**

There is hope—glorious hope—for people who suffer under the heavy weight of guilt, who suffer so much pricking of conscience. There is deliverance, full and complete freedom from guilt, the deliverance found right here in this Scripture. In fact, the very subject of this passage is "How to Be Set Free from the Weight of Guilt, Set Free from the Pricking of

Conscience." All a person has to do is do exactly what the Israelites had to do: follow God's instructions. If a person stood guilty before God, he had to do just what the Scripture says:

OUTLINE	SCRIPTURE	SCRIPTURE	OUTLINE
2. A person can be set free from guilt—guilt due to breaking the commandments of God, doing what is forbidden	17 And if a soul sin, and commit any of these things which are forbidden to be done by the commandments of the LORD; though he wist *it* not, yet is he guilty, and shall bear his iniquity.	tion, for a trespass offering, unto the priest: and the priest shall make an atonement for him concerning his ignorance wherein he erred and wist *it* not, and it shall be forgiven him.	& of proper value b. The result: The sacrifice makes atonement, reconciliation with God—the guilty is forgiven
a. Must approach God through the sacrifice (a symbol of Christ): A ram without defect	18 And he shall bring a ram without blemish out of the flock, with thy estima-	19 It *is* a trespass offering: he hath certainly trespassed against the LORD.	c. The clear truth restated: Breaking God's commandment is serious, against God Himself

a. The person had to approach God through the sacrifice. He had to bring a ram that was perfect, without blemish or defect. Again, note that the ram was to be fully valued, that is, to bring the full market value. The ram was to be a costly offering made to the LORD. Breaking His commandment was a serious offense, a grave wrong, a wrong that caused suffering for the LORD, that literally broke His heart. The guilty law-breaker was to keep this fact before his mind and to symbolize it by offering the most costly sacrifice as a ransom for his guilt.

b. The result was again effective, very effective: the substitute sacrifice bore the law-breaker's guilt, made atonement, paid the ransom price for his deliverance. He was then freed from all guilt, forgiven and reconciled to God. God accepted the person—all because he came to God through the sacrifice.

> **Thought 1**. We are all law-breakers, guilty of breaking God's commandments. The result is tragic:
> ⇒ All of us stand guilty before God and are to give an account for violating His commandments.
> ⇒ Some of us are so heavily burdened with feelings of guilt—so troubled and pricked—that we can hardly bear the emotional pain and anguish.

> God declares a wonderful truth to us: there is deliverance. We can be set free from the anguish of guilt, set free from all guilt. How? Through Jesus Christ: by approaching God through the sacrifice of Christ. Just imagine this wonderful, glorious truth. Jesus Christ died—sacrificed Himself—for our guilt, the guilt of our sins. Jesus Christ paid the ransom, paid the price to set us free. Believe God; trust God; approach God through Jesus Christ. Ask God to forgive you through Christ and take God at His Word. Believe Him, for He means what He says; He forgives you through the death and sacrifice of His Son. He set you free from all guilt through Christ.

> **"The next day John seeth Jesus coming unto him, and saith, Behold the Lamb of God, which taketh away the sin of the world" (Jn.1:29).**
> **"For whosoever shall call upon the name of the LORD shall be saved [delivered and freed from guilt]" (Ro.10:13).**
> **"In whom we have redemption through his blood, the forgiveness of sins, according to the riches of his grace" (Ep.1:7).**
> **"Now the end of the commandment is charity out of a pure heart, and *of* a good conscience, and *of* faith unfeigned" (1 Ti.1:5).**
> **"For Christ also hath once suffered for sins, the just for the unjust, that he might bring us to God, being put to death in the flesh, but quickened by the Spirit" (1 Pe.3:18).**
> **"If we confess our sins, he is faithful and just to forgive us *our* sins, and to cleanse us from all unrighteousness" (1 Jn.1:9).**

3 (6:1-7) **Guilt—Freedom, Spiritual—Liberty, Spiritual—Conscience—Deliverance—Believer, Life and Walk—Commandments, of God—Neighbor—Forgiveness, of Sins**: a person can be set free from guilt—the guilt arising from sins against one's neighbor. Think back over the sins covered in this passage so far:
⇒ the sins against the holy things of God
⇒ the sins of breaking God's commandments
⇒ and now, the sins against one's neighbor

These three classes or areas of sins cover all possible sins. Any sin ever committed by any person can be placed into one of these classes, under one of these three headings. The point is this: no matter what a person stands guilty of—no matter what sin he has committed or how terrible the sin—he can be forgiven, set free from the guilt. There is no need—absolutely no need—for any person to suffer under the weight and anguish of guilt. God loves His people. This is the reason He made a way for His people to be delivered and set free from guilt. Note what He says about the guilt that arises from sins against one's neighbors.

OUTLINE	SCRIPTURE	SCRIPTURE	OUTLINE

3. A person can be set free from guilt—guilt due to sins against one's neighbors
a. The warning: An act against God
b. The example of some common sins
  1) Lying about borrowed items or trusts left in one's care
  2) Stealing or cheating
  3) Finding lost property & lying about it
  4) Swearing falsely
  5) Committing any sin that a person may or can do
c. The way to be set free from the guilt of sinning against one's neighbor
  1) Must make restitution in full
    • Return what was stolen, extorted, entrusted to one's care, found, or
	And the LORD spake unto Moses, saying,
	2 If a soul sin, and commit a trespass against the LORD, and lie unto his neighbour in that which was delivered him to keep, or in fellowship, or in a thing taken away by violence, or hath deceived his neighbour;
	3 Or have found that which was lost, and lieth concerning it, and sweareth falsely; in any of all these that a man doeth, sinning therein:
	4 Then it shall be, because he hath sinned, and is guilty, that he shall restore that which he took violently away, or the thing which he hath deceitfully gotten, or that which was delivered him to keep, or the lost
		thing, which he found,
		5 Or all that about which he hath sworn falsely; he shall even restore it in the principal, and shall add the fifth part more thereto, *and* give it unto him to whom it appertaineth, in the day of his trespass offering.
		6 And he shall bring his trespass offering unto the LORD, a ram without blemish out of the flock, with thy estimation, for a trespass offering, unto the priest:
		7 And the priest shall make an atonement for him before the LORD: and it shall be forgiven him for any thing of all that he hath done in trespassing therein.
			sworn falsely about
			• Pay 20% interest
			• Make restitution on the very day one confesses
			
			2) Must approach God through the sacrifice (a symbol of Christ): Offer a ram without defect & of proper value
			
			3) The result: Makes atonement, reconciliation with God
			• The guilty is forgiven
			• The wonderful truth restated: The guilty is forgiven for anything he has done that made him guilty

a. The warning is clear: a sin against one's neighbor is a sin against the LORD Himself (v.1). Note God's charge: the person trespasses or is *unfaithful* (maal maall) to the LORD. The word means to break faith; to deal treacherously; to commit a terrible transgression; to sin grievously; to commit a painful, severe sin. The pain and severity of the sin matches that of marital unfaithfulness. The person who sins against his neighbor…

- breaks faith with his neighbor
- deals treacherously with his neighbor
- commits a terrible transgression against his neighbor
- sins grievously against his neighbor
- commits a severe, painful sin against his neighbor
- commits an act equal to marital unfaithfulness in the eyes of God

> **"O my God, I am ashamed and blush to lift up my face to thee, my God: for our iniquities are increased over *our* head, and our trespass is grown up unto the heavens" (Ezr.9:6).**

The sin against one's neighbor is a serious sin, counted by God as a sin against God Himself. This is the reason a sin against one's neighbor often troubles and bothers a person so deeply. God's Spirit arouses the disturbance within a person's heart. But keep in mind: a person's conscience can become so conditioned to sin that it becomes hardened, as hard as a rock, well beyond feeling any guilt for sin. Nevertheless, the person is still in the *position* of being guilty before God. His standing before God is "guilty" even if he feels no guilt. He will still be judged and condemned for sin.

> **"And they said one to another, We *are* verily guilty concerning our brother, in that we saw the anguish of his soul, when he besought us, and we would not hear; therefore is this distress come upon us" (Ge.42:21).**
> **"For innumerable evils have compassed me about: mine iniquities have taken hold upon me, so that I am not able to look up; they are more than the hairs of mine head: therefore my heart faileth me" (Ps.40:12).**

b. Now, note some examples of sins committed against one's neighbor. Note how common these sins are (vv.2-3).
  ⇒ lying about borrowed items or trusts left in one's care (v.2)
  ⇒ stealing or cheating (v.2)
  ⇒ finding lost property and lying about it (v.3)
  ⇒ swearing falsely (v.3)
  ⇒ committing any sin that a person may or can do (v.3)

When a person does any of these, he sins against his neighbor. He is guilty. He is condemned by God and is to be judged.
c. How then can a person be freed from the guilt of his sin and from the feelings of guilt that cause so much anguish? God told His people how.
  1) The person must make restitution in full (vv.4-5). What does this mean? Restitution means…
- return what was stolen, extorted, entrusted to one's care, found, or sworn falsely about
- pay 20 percent interest
- make restitution on the very day one confesses

If a person were sincere in seeking forgiveness and freedom from guilt, he would gladly make restitution. He would arrange to make payment against the required restitution. This was a real test of the person's desire for forgiveness, showing just how great his desire was to be free from guilt.

2) The person must approach God through the sacrifice: offer a ram, a perfect ram, one without blemish or defect (v.6). Once again, the sacrifice had to be of full value, a costly sacrifice.

3) The result was wonderful and glorious: the perfect sacrifice made atonement for the guilty person, paid the ransom and price to set him free from guilt. Note exactly what God declares: the person would be forgiven for any of these things he had done that made him guilty. The guilty person was set free from guilt because he believed and trusted God's promise. What promise? The promise that the sacrifice would suffer, would bear the sin and guilt for the person.

Thought 1. The promise of God is real and effective: the guilty person will be forgiven for anything he has done that makes him guilty. There is no need to be weighed down with the anguish of guilt, no need to face the condemnation and judgment of God. All we have to do is approach God through the sacrifice of the Lord Jesus Christ. Jesus Christ was the Perfect Sacrifice who bore the anguish of our sin and guilt for us. We must believe Him, trust Him. We must come to God and ask Him to forgive our sin and remove our guilt. And then arise and accept God's Word; begin following God more diligently than ever before. God never lies; He never has lied. He will forgive our sins and remove our guilt. All we have to do is call upon Him, call upon Him repeatedly until our faith is so strengthened that we sense and know He has forgiven us. We must accept His Word. This is our only hope of being freed from guilt—permanently freed. Again, God does not lie. He will forgive and free us from the anguish and condemnation of guilt.

"For God so loved the world, that he gave his only begotten Son, that whosoever believeth in him should not perish, but have everlasting life" (Jn.3:16).

"He that believeth on him is not condemned: but he that believeth not is condemned already, because he hath not believed in the name of the only begotten Son of God" (Jn.3:18).

"Verily, verily, I say unto you, He that heareth my word, and believeth on him that sent me, hath everlasting life, and shall not come into condemnation; but is passed from death unto life" (Jn.5:24).

"For when we were yet without strength, in due time Christ died for the ungodly....But God commendeth his love toward us, in that, while we were yet sinners, Christ died for us" (Ro.5:6, 8).

"There is therefore now no condemnation to them which are in Christ Jesus, who walk not after the flesh, but after the Spirit. For the law of the Spirit of life in Christ Jesus hath made me free from the law of sin and death. For what the law could not do, in that it was weak through the flesh, God sending his own Son in the likeness of sinful flesh, and for sin, condemned sin in the flesh" (Ro.8:1-3).

"Who shall lay any thing to the charge of God's elect? It is God that justifieth. Who is he that condemneth? It is Christ that died, yea rather, that is risen again, who is even at the right hand of God, who also maketh intercession for us" (Ro.8:33-34).

"Holding faith, and a good conscience; which some having put away concerning faith have made shipwreck" (1 Ti.1:19).

"Who gave himself for us, that he might redeem us from all iniquity, and purify unto himself a peculiar people, zealous of good works" (Tit.2:14).

"For if the blood of bulls and of goats, and the ashes of an heifer sprinkling the unclean, sanctifieth to the purifying of the flesh: How much more shall the blood of Christ, who through the eternal Spirit offered himself without spot to God, purge your conscience from dead works to serve the living God?" (He.9:13-14).

"So Christ was once offered to bear the sins of many; and unto them that look for him shall he appear the second time without sin unto salvation" (He.9:28).

"Who his own self bare our sins in his own body on the tree, that we, being dead to sins, should live unto righteousness: by whose stripes ye were healed" (1 Pe.2:24).

TYPES, SYMBOLS, AND PICTURES
Leviticus 5:14–6:7

Historical Term	Type or Picture (Scriptural Basis for Each)	Life Application for Today's Believer	Biblical Application
The Guilt Offering Le.5:14-6:7	*The Guilt Offering symbolized Jesus Christ. He is the way for a person to be set free from the weight and anguish of guilt, the pricking of conscience.* "And the priest shall offer them, the one *for* a sin offering, and the other *for* a burnt offering; and the priest shall make an	Jesus Christ bore our guilt, bore the judgment and condemnation of our guilt. His sacrifice has made atonement with God, forgiving the guilty person.	"Who gave himself for our sins, that he might deliver us from this present evil world, according to the will of God and our Father" (Ga.1:4). "Christ hath redeemed us from the curse of the law, being made a curse for us: for it is written, Cursed is every one that hangeth on a tree" (Ga.3:13).

TYPES, SYMBOLS, AND PICTURES
Leviticus 5:14–6:7

Historical Term	Type or Picture (Scriptural Basis for Each)	Life Application for Today's Believer	Biblical Application
	atonement for him before the LORD for his issue" (Le.15:15).		"Having a good conscience; that, whereas they speak evil of you, as of evildoers, they may be ashamed that falsely accuse your good conversation in Christ" (1 Pe.3:16).
Ram Without Defect and of True Value Was the Sacrifice Used in the Guilt Offering Le.5:15, 18; 6:6	*The Ram without defect was a type of Christ who was sinless, without blemish or defect.* **"If a soul commit a trespass, and sin through ignorance, in the holy things of the LORD; then he shall bring for his trespass unto the LORD a ram without blemish out of the flocks, with thy estimation by shekels of silver, after the shekel of the sanctuary, for a trespass offering" (Le.5:15).**	Jesus Christ was the sinless, perfect sacrifice who gave Himself for us. As the Perfect Sacrifice, He bore our guilt, bore the judgment and condemnation of our guilt. We can now be set free from guilt by approaching God through the Perfect Sacrifice of Christ. If we believe God, approach Him exactly as He says—through Christ—then God counts the sacrifice of Christ... • on our behalf • in our place • in our stead • as our substitute The result is wonderful: through Christ, we are set free from the guilt of our sin against God. We are able to stand before God free, set free from sin and guilt—all through the sacrifice of Christ.	"Who gave himself for our sins, that he might deliver us from this present evil world, according to the will of God and our Father" (Ga.1:4). "Christ hath redeemed us from the curse of the law, being made a curse for us: for it is written, Cursed is every one that hangeth on a tree" (Ga.3:13). "Having a good conscience; that, whereas they speak evil of you, as of evildoers, they may be ashamed that falsely accuse your good conversation in Christ" (1 Pe.3:16). "That which we have seen and heard declare we unto you, that ye also may have fellowship with us: and truly our fellowship is with the Father, and with his Son Jesus Christ" (1 Jn.1:3).

F. The Special Duties of the Priests in Conducting the Offerings: The Duties of Ministers, 6:8–7:38

8 And the LORD spake unto Moses, saying,
9 Command Aaron and his sons, saying, This *is* the law of the burnt offering: It *is* the burnt offering, because of the burning upon the altar all night unto the morning, and the fire of the altar shall be burning in it.
10 And the priest shall put on his linen garment, and his linen breeches shall he put upon his flesh, and take up the ashes which the fire hath consumed with the burnt offering on the altar, and he shall put them beside the altar.
11 And he shall put off his garments, and put on other garments, and carry forth the ashes without the camp unto a clean place.
12 And the fire upon the altar shall be burning in it; it shall not be put out: and the priest shall burn wood on it every morning, and lay the burnt offering in order upon it; and he shall burn thereon the fat of the peace offerings.
13 The fire shall ever be burning upon the altar; it shall never go out.
14 And this *is* the law of the meat offering: the sons of Aaron shall offer it before the LORD, before the altar.
15 And he shall take of it his handful, of the flour of the meat offering, and of the oil thereof, and all the frankincense which *is* upon the meat offering, and shall burn *it* upon the altar *for* a sweet savour, *even* the memorial of it, unto the LORD.
16 And the remainder thereof shall Aaron and his sons eat: with unleavened bread shall it be eaten in the holy place; in the court of the tabernacle of the congregation they shall eat it.
17 It shall not be baken with leaven. I have given it *unto them for* their portion of my offerings made by fire; it *is* most holy, as *is* the sin offer-

ing, and as the trespass offering.
18 All the males among the children of Aaron shall eat of it. *It shall be* a statute for ever in your generations concerning the offerings of the LORD made by fire: every one that toucheth them shall be holy.
19 And the LORD spake unto Moses, saying,
20 This *is* the offering of Aaron and of his sons, which they shall offer unto the LORD in the day when he is anointed; the tenth part of an ephah of fine flour for a meat offering perpetual, half of it in the morning, and half thereof at night.
21 In a pan it shall be made with oil; *and when it is* baken, thou shalt bring it in: *and* the baken pieces of the meat offering shalt thou offer *for* a sweet savour unto the LORD.
22 And the priest of his sons that is anointed in his stead shall offer it: *it is* a statute for ever unto the LORD; it shall be wholly burnt.
23 For every meat offering for the priest shall be wholly burnt: it shall not be eaten.
24 And the LORD spake unto Moses, saying,
25 Speak unto Aaron and to his sons, saying, This *is* the law of the sin offering: In the place where the burnt offering is killed shall the sin offering be killed before the LORD: it *is* most holy.
26 The priest that offereth it for sin shall eat it: in the holy place shall it be eaten, in the court of the tabernacle of the congregation.
27 Whatsoever shall touch the flesh thereof shall be holy: and when there is sprinkled of the blood thereof upon any garment, thou shalt wash that whereon it was sprinkled in the holy place.
28 But the earthen vessel wherein it is sodden shall be broken: and if it be sodden in a brasen pot, it shall be both scoured, and rinsed in water.
29 All the males among the priests shall eat thereof: it *is* most holy.

1. Duty 1: To help people approach God, become acceptable, reconciled to Him—through the burnt offering

a. Keep the fire of the burnt offering ablaze always, even through the night—never let the sacrifice cease from being offered (a symbol of the sacrifice of Christ: It lasts, is permanent, & is sufficient & adequate)
b. Put on the special linen clothing & undergarments for removing the ashes (a symbol of the righteousness of Christ to remove the ashes or dirt of sin)

c. Take off the special clothing & put on regular clothing to take the ashes outside the camp (a symbol of Christ's bearing sin & taking it away from man)
d. Keep the fire burning & never let it go out: Be sure that the morning functions are performed
1) That wood is added
2) That a new burnt offering is made
3) That the fat of the fellowship offering is burned

e. Remember: The fire on the altar must burn continuously (a symbol of the sufficiency & eternalness of Christ's sacrifice)

2. Duty 2: To help people give thanks & dedicate their lives more fully to God—through the grain offering

a. To offer a handful of grain to the LORD as an act of thanksgiving & dedication
1) To burn it on the altar as the LORD'S memorial
2) The aroma symbolized that the thanksgiving & dedication pleased the LORD

b. To give the remaining grain to the priests as food with two restrictions
1) Must be made without yeast (a symbol of sin, corruption)
2) Must be eaten within the courtyard of the Tabernacle
c. To strictly observe the restriction: Must not be baked with yeast (a symbol of sin, corruption)
1) Because it is part of God's

offering: It is most holy

2) Because it is a gift to the priests from God's offering: It is always to be without yeast (a symbol of corruption)
3) Because touching the grain offering conveys holiness to the priests: Must not be contaminated with yeast (sin)

3. Duty 3: To guide the newly ordained priest to give thanks & to commit his life more fully to God—through the grain offering

a. To begin the daily offering of thanksgiving & commitment on the day of his anointing
1) Offer two quarts (one-tenth an ephah) of fine flour: Half in the morning & half in the evening
2) Mix with oil
3) Result: The aroma symbolized that the offering pleased the LORD: He accepted the daily offering of thanksgiving & dedication

b. To be a permanent offering in the future for all anointed priests
c. To strictly observe this one restriction: The entire offering (one's thanksgiving & commitment) is the LORD's share
1) It is to be completely burned up—totally offered
2) None of it is to be eaten

4. Duty 4: To help people secure forgiveness of sin—through the Sin Offering

a. Must approach God through the sacrifice (a symbol of Christ)
1) The sacrifice was to be put to death in the same place the Burnt Offering was sacrificed: Because the Sin Offering was most holy
2) The priest who offers it has to eat it: But it is to be eaten in the courtyard of the Tabernacle
b. Must observe the holiness of the sacrifice
1) Anything or anyone who touches the sacrifice becomes holy
2) If any blood splattered on clothing, it must be washed in a holy place
3) If a clay pot is used to cook the sacrifice, it must be broken: Never used for anything else
4) If a bronze pot is used, it is to be cleansed thoroughly
5) Only the priests may eat it: Because it is holy, set apart to God

c. Must observe one absolute restriction: The sacrifice must never be eaten if the blood is taken into the Holy Place to make atonement for the nation's or priest's sin—it must be completely burned (4:5, 18)

5. Duty 5: To help people find freedom from the weight & anguish of guilt through the sacrifice of the Guilt Offering, which is most holy
a. Must approach God through the sacrifice (a symbol of Christ)
1) Put the sacrifice to death in the same place the burnt offering is slaughtered
2) Sprinkle the blood against the altar on all sides
3) Offer a portion to the LORD
   • All the fat
   • Both kidneys & the liver

   • Burn all the LORD'S portion

b. Must accept a portion of the offering to provide food for his sons (priests): It must be eaten in a holy place, for it is holy
c. Must accept a portion of several offerings to provide for his family
1) The meat of the Sin Offering & the Guilt Offering

2) The hide of the Burnt Offering

3) The grain of the Grain Offering

4) The uncooked offerings belonged equally to all the priests

6. Duty 6: To help people grow in the peace & fellowship of God through the Fellowship or Peace offering
a. The Fellowship Offering of

30 And no sin offering, whereof *any* of the blood is brought into the tabernacle of the congregation to reconcile withal in the holy *place*, shall be eaten: it shall be burnt in the fire.

CHAPTER 7

Likewise this *is* the law of the trespass offering: it *is* most holy.
2 In the place where they kill the burnt offering shall they kill the trespass offering: and the blood thereof shall he sprinkle round about upon the altar.
3 And he shall offer of it all the fat thereof; the rump, and the fat that covereth the inwards,
4 And the two kidneys, and the fat that *is* on them, which *is* by the flanks, and the caul *that is* above the liver, with the kidneys, it shall he take away:
5 And the priest shall burn them upon the altar *for* an offering made by fire unto the LORD: it *is* a trespass offering.
6 Every male among the priests shall eat thereof: it shall be eaten in the holy place: it *is* most holy.
7 As the sin offering *is*, so *is* the trespass offering: *there is* one law for them: the priest that maketh atonement therewith shall have *it*.
8 And the priest that offereth any man's burnt offering, *even* the priest shall have to himself the skin of the burnt offering which he hath offered.
9 And all the meat offering that is baken in the oven, and all that is dressed in the fryingpan, and in the pan, shall be the priest's that offereth it.
10 And every meat offering, mingled with oil, and dry, shall all the sons of Aaron have, one *as much* as another.
11 And this *is* the law of the sacrifice of peace offerings, which he shall offer unto the LORD.
12 If he offer it for a thanks-giving, then he shall offer with the sacrifice of thanksgiving unleavened cakes mingled with oil, and unleavened wafers anointed with oil, and cakes mingled with oil, of fine flour, fried.
13 Besides the cakes, he shall offer *for* his offering leavened bread with the sacrifice of thanksgiving of his peace offerings.
14 And of it he shall offer one out of the whole oblation *for* an heave offering unto the LORD, *and* it shall be the priest's that sprinkleth the blood of the peace offerings.
15 And the flesh of the sacrifice of his peace offerings for thanksgiving shall be eaten the same day that it is offered; he shall not leave any of it until the morning.
16 But if the sacrifice of his offering *be* a vow, or a voluntary offering, it shall be eaten the same day that he offereth his sacrifice: and on the morrow also the remainder of it shall be eaten:
17 But the remainder of the flesh of the sacrifice on the third day shall be burnt with fire.
18 And if *any* of the flesh of the sacrifice of his peace offerings be eaten at all on the third day, it shall not be accepted, neither shall it be imputed unto him that offereth it: it shall be an abomination, and the soul that eateth of it shall bear his iniquity.
19 And the flesh that toucheth any unclean *thing* shall not be eaten; it shall be burnt with fire: and as for the flesh, all that be clean shall eat thereof.
20 But the soul that eateth *of* the flesh of the sacrifice of peace offerings, that *pertain* unto the LORD, having his uncleanness upon him, even that soul shall be cut off from his people.
21 Moreover the soul that shall touch any unclean *thing, as* the uncleanness of man, or *any* unclean beast, or any abominable unclean *thing*, and eat of the flesh of

thanksgiving
1) Must approach God through the sacrifice (a symbol of Christ)
2) Must also offer several kinds of bread: Cakes, wafers, & loaves—mixed with oil & made without yeast (a symbol of sin, of corruption)
3) Must also offer several loaves of bread made with yeast (were for the priests)
4) Must bring one of each kind as an offering to the LORD: This bread then belongs to the priest who sprinkles the blood of the sacrifice against the altar
5) Must eat the meat on the very day it is offered, leaving none until morning

b. The Fellowship Offering given as a vow or just to show one's desire to grow in the peace & fellowship of God
1) Must approach God through the offering: "If...offering"
2) Must eat within two days
3) Must burn up any meat still left on the third day

4) Must not eat any of the sacrifice on the third day
   • Because God does not accept, does not credit the offering to one's account: Because the meat is spoiled, impure
   • The warning: The person is held accountable to God
5) Must obey the commandment on being spiritually clean
   • Must not eat meat that has touched anything unclean: Must be burned up
   • Must only eat clean meat
   • Must never eat any meat of the sacrifice if one is unclean (spiritually unclean): To be cut off from the community

   • The judgment is re-emphasized: Must be cut off if he is unclean (spiritually unclean), if he abuses the sacrifice

c. The prohibitions governing the Fellowship Offering, as well as all the offerings of life
1) Must never eat any fat of any animal

- Not of dead animals: May be used for any other purpose, but not for eating

- Not of sacrificed animals: This violator is to be cut off from the community

2) Must not eat the blood of any animal: This violator is to be cut off

d. The clear, emphatic instructions governing the support of the priests: To be given part of the Fellowship Offering as their support

1) The believer is to bring part of his sacrifice to the LORD: Bring the fat & the breast—wave the breast before the LORD as a wave offering

- To burn the fat on the altar
- But to keep the breast as

the sacrifice of peace offerings, which *pertain* unto the LORD, even that soul shall be cut off from his people.
22 And the LORD spake unto Moses, saying,
23 Speak unto the children of Israel, saying, Ye shall eat no manner of fat, of ox, or of sheep, or of goat.
24 And the fat of the beast that dieth of itself, and the fat of that which is torn with beasts, may be used in any other use: but ye shall in no wise eat of it.
25 For whosoever eateth the fat of the beast, of which men offer an offering made by fire unto the LORD, even the soul that eateth *it* shall be cut off from his people.
26 Moreover ye shall eat no manner of blood, *whether it be* of fowl or of beast, in any of your dwellings.
27 Whatsoever soul *it be* that eateth any manner of blood, even that soul shall be cut off from his people.
28 And the LORD spake unto Moses, saying,
29 Speak unto the children of Israel, saying, He that offereth the sacrifice of his peace offerings unto the LORD shall bring his oblation unto the LORD of the sacrifice of his peace offerings.
30 His own hands shall bring the offerings of the LORD made by fire, the fat with the breast, it shall he bring, that the breast may be waved *for* a wave offering before the LORD.
31 And the priest shall burn the fat upon the altar: but the breast shall be Aaron's and

his sons'.
32 And the right shoulder shall ye give unto the priest *for* an heave offering of the sacrifices of your peace offerings.
33 He among the sons of Aaron, that offereth the blood of the peace offerings, and the fat, shall have the right shoulder for *his* part.
34 For the wave breast and the heave shoulder have I taken of the children of Israel from off the sacrifices of their peace offerings, and have given them unto Aaron the priest and unto his sons by a statute for ever from among the children of Israel.
35 This *is the portion* of the anointing of Aaron, and of the anointing of his sons, out of the offerings of the LORD made by fire, in the day *when* he presented them to minister unto the LORD in the priest's office;
36 Which the LORD commanded to be given them of the children of Israel, in the day that he anointed them, *by* a statute for ever throughout their generations.
37 This *is* the law of the burnt offering, of the meat offering, and of the sin offering, and of the trespass offering, and of the consecrations, and of the sacrifice of the peace offerings;
38 Which the LORD commanded Moses in mount Sinai, in the day that he commanded the children of Israel to offer their oblations unto the LORD, in the wilderness of Sinai.

food for the priests
2) The believer is to give the right thigh to the priest who offers the blood & the fat to the LORD—all on the believer's behalf

3) The believer gives part of the sacrificed offerings—the breast & thigh—to the priests as part of their support

- Was part of their regular support

- Was part of the very offering made to the LORD Himself: Was begun on the very first day of their service

- Was the commandment of God Himself: To be part of their support throughout the generations

7. **The conclusion: These are the regulations, the duties given to the priest to govern the offerings**
a. The five basic offerings & the Ordination Offering for the priests (or ministers)
b. The regulations were given through God's mediator, Moses
1) Given on Mt. Sinai
2) Given while Israel was camped in the desert

DIVISION I

THE WAY TO BECOME ACCEPTABLE TO GOD (PART 1): BY THE OFFERING OF A SACRIFICE, A SUBSTITUTE, 1:1–7:38

F. **The Special Duties of the Priests in Conducting the Offerings: The Duties of Ministers, 6:8–7:38**

(6:8–7:38) **Introduction**: one of the most important tasks in the world is proclaiming the good news of God, that man's needs—all of his needs—can be met through the mercy and grace of God. Man must have his needs, the basic needs of human life, met. It is when his needs go unmet that stealing, lying, violence, murder, greed, immorality, war—all the evils of the human heart—are acted out in society. But the glorious news of God is that the basic needs of man can be met through His Son, the Lord Jesus Christ. Through the power of His blood, man's sins and condemnation are removed; and through the conquering power of His resurrection, man gains victory over all the trials and temptations of life and eventually over death itself.

But what about the people of ancient history, the people before Christ came? How were their needs met by God? Through the blood of the sacrifice, the sacrifice that was a symbol of the Lord Jesus Christ. Note how their needs were met:
⇒ Man's need to be delivered from the justice and judgment of God, to be reconciled to God, was met through the sacrifice of the Burnt Offering.
⇒ Man's need to give thanks and to have a higher purpose to which he could totally dedicate his life was met through the Grain Offering.
⇒ Man's need to grow in the peace and fellowship of God was met in the Peace or Fellowship Offering.
⇒ Man's need to secure forgiveness of sins was met in the Sin Offering.
⇒ Man's need to be set free from the anguish and very heavy weight of sin was met through the Guilt Offering.

Think of all this. This is the good news of God: the needs of man can be met through the sacrifice of Christ. And the needs of ancient man were met through the symbol that pointed to Jesus Christ, the substitute sacrifice of animals. This was the special duty of the priest, to proclaim the good news of God. This is the special duty of the minister of God today, to proclaim the goodness of God. This is the message of this important passage: *The Special Duties of the Priests in Conducting the Offerings: The Duties of Ministers,* 6:8–7:38.
1. Duty 1: to help people approach God, to become acceptable and reconciled to Him—through the Burnt Offering (vv.8-13).
2. Duty 2: to help people give thanks and dedicate their lives more fully to God—through the Grain Offering (vv.14-18).
3. Duty 3: to guide the newly ordained priest to give thanks and commit his life more fully to God—through the Grain Offering (vv.19-23).
4. Duty 4: to help people secure forgiveness of sin—through the Sin Offering (vv.24-30).
5. Duty 5: to help people find freedom from the weight and anguish of guilt through the sacrifice of the Guilt Offering, which is most holy (ch.7:1-10).
6. Duty 6: to help people grow in the peace and fellowship of God through the Fellowship or Peace Offering (vv.11-36).
7. The conclusion: these are the regulations, the duties given to the priest to govern the offerings (vv.37-38).

1 (6:8-13) **Offering, Burnt—Burnt Offering—Reconciliation—Acceptance—Way, the—Symbol, of Christ—Jesus Christ, Death, Symbol of**: the first duty of the priest or minister is critical: he is to help people approach God, to become acceptable or reconciled to God. How? The priests were to offer the sacrifice of the Burnt Offering every morning and every evening (Nu.28:3-8). The sacrifice of the Burnt Offering was never to cease. Note that clear instructions were given to the priests. (See outline and notes—Le.1:1-17 for more discussion.)

OUTLINE	SCRIPTURE	SCRIPTURE	OUTLINE
1. Duty 1: To help people approach God, become acceptable, reconciled to Him—through the burnt offering a. Keep the fire of the burnt offering ablaze always, even through the night—never let the sacrifice cease from being offered (a symbol of the sacrifice of Christ: It lasts, is permanent, & is sufficient & adequate) b. Put on the special linen clothing & undergarments for removing the ashes (a symbol of the righteousness of Christ to remove the ashes or dirt of sin)	8 And the LORD spake unto Moses, saying, 9 Command Aaron and his sons, saying, This is the law of the burnt offering: It is the burnt offering, because of the burning upon the altar all night unto the morning, and the fire of the altar shall be burning in it. 10 And the priest shall put on his linen garment, and his linen breeches shall he put upon his flesh, and take up the ashes which the fire hath consumed with the burnt offering on the altar, and he shall put them beside the	altar. 11 And he shall put off his garments, and put on other garments, and carry forth the ashes without the camp unto a clean place. 12 And the fire upon the altar shall be burning in it; it shall not be put out: and the priest shall burn wood on it every morning, and lay the burnt offering in order upon it; and he shall burn thereon the fat of the peace offerings. 13 The fire shall ever be burning upon the altar; it shall never go out.	c. Take off the special clothing & put on regular clothing to take the ashes outside the camp (a symbol of Christ's bearing sin & taking it away from man) d. Keep the fire burning & never let it go out: Be sure that the morning functions are performed 1) That wood is added 2) That a new Burnt Offering is made 3) That the fat of the fellowship offering is burned e. Remember: The fire on the altar must burn continually (a symbol of the sufficiency & eternalness of Christ's sacrifice)

a. The priests were always to keep the fire of the Burnt Offering ablaze, even through the night. They were never to let the sacrifice cease from being offered (v.9). This is a clear symbol of the sacrifice of Christ. His sacrifice is lasting; it is permanent, sufficient, adequate for all people and for all generations. Any person of any generation can be reconciled to God, no matter who the person is and no matter what he has done.

> **"Who needeth not daily, as those high priests, to offer up sacrifice, first for his own sins, and then for the people's: for this he did once, when he offered up himself" (He.7:27).**
> **"For Christ also hath once suffered for sins, the just for the unjust, that he might bring us to God, being put to death in the flesh, but quickened by the Spirit" (1 Pe.3:18).**

b. The priests were to put on the special linen clothing and undergarments—the priestly clothing—for removing the ashes of the sacrifice (v.10). This symbolizes the clothing of righteousness, the righteousness of Christ, who removes the ashes or dirt of sin.

69

"For he hath made him *to be* sin for us, who knew no sin; that we might be made the righteousness of God in him" (2 Co.5:21).

"And to her was granted that she should be arrayed in fine linen, clean and white: for the fine linen is the righteousness of saints" (Re.19:8).

c. The priests were then to take off the special clothing and put on regular clothing to take the ashes outside the camp (v.11). This symbolized Jesus Christ bearing and taking away the sins of man. This He did as a man, clothed in the regular flesh of man. Jesus Christ *died and bore* the penalty for man's sin. Through Him and Him alone, sin is removed, taken and *borne away*.

d. The priests were to make sure, absolutely sure, that the fire of the Burnt Offering was kept ablaze, that it never went out (v.12). They were never to fail in the performance of their duties. Every morning they were…
- to add wood to the fire
- to make a new Burnt Offering
- to burn the fat of the Fellowship Offerings

e. The priests were never to forget: the fire of the Burnt Offering was to be kept burning, never allowed to go out (v.13). The frequent re-emphasis of the point is striking: God wanted the sacrifice always before the faces of His people. They were never to forget that atonement or reconciliation with Him was through the sacrifice and the sacrifice alone.

Thought 1. The point is striking. Jesus Christ is the sacrifice that makes atonement for us, that paid the penalty for our sins and reconciles us to God. His sacrifice was once-for-all: it is lasting and permanent, sufficient and adequate:

⇒ His sacrifice is lasting and sufficient. God accepts His sacrifice once-for-all. A sacrifice for sin never again has to be made. The sacrifice that reconciles and makes a person acceptable to God was made by Jesus Christ— once-for-all.

"Who needeth not daily, as those high priests, to offer up sacrifice, first for his own sins, and then for the people's: for this he did once, when he offered up himself" (He.7:27).

"For then must he often have suffered since the foundation of the world: but now once in the end of the world hath he appeared to put away sin by the sacrifice of himself" (He.9:26).

"So Christ was once offered to bear the sins of many; and unto them that look for him shall he appear the second time without sin unto salvation" (He.9:28).

"By the which will we are sanctified through the offering of the body of Jesus Christ once *for all*" (He.10:10).

"For Christ also hath once suffered for sins, the just for the unjust, that he might bring us to God, being put to death in the flesh, but quickened by the Spirit" (1 Pe.3:18).

⇒ His sacrifice is lasting and sufficient: it causes God to reconcile and accept and forgive the sins of any person who comes to Him, any person of any generation.

"The next day John seeth Jesus coming unto him, and saith, Behold the Lamb of God, which taketh away the sin of the world" (Jn.1:29).

"Who gave himself for our sins, that he might deliver us from this present evil world, according to the will of God and our Father" (Ga.1:4).

"And walk in love, as Christ also hath loved us, and hath given himself for us an offering and a sacrifice to God for a sweetsmelling savour" (Ep.5:2).

"But this *man*, because he continueth ever, hath an unchangeable priesthood. Wherefore he is able also to save them to the uttermost that come unto God by him, seeing he ever liveth to make intercession for them. For such an high priest became us, *who is* holy, harmless, undefiled, separate from sinners, and made higher than the heavens; Who needeth not daily, as those high priests, to offer up sacrifice, first for his own sins, and then for the people's: for this he did once, when he offered up himself" (He.7:24-27).

"Forasmuch as ye know that ye were not redeemed with corruptible things, *as* silver and gold, from your vain conversation *received* by tradition from your fathers; But with the precious blood of Christ, as of a lamb without blemish and without spot" (1 Pe.1:18-19).

---

2 (6:14-18) **Offering, the Grain—Grain Offering—Thanksgiving—Dedication—Ministers, Duty of—Priest, Duty of**: the second duty of the priest or minister is an immediate duty, a duty that is performed right after a person has been reconciled to God through the atoning sacrifice. The priest (minister) is to lead the person to give thanks and to dedicate his life more fully to God. How? Through the Grain Offering. (See outline and notes—Le.2:1-16.)

OUTLINE	SCRIPTURE	SCRIPTURE	OUTLINE
2. Duty 2: To help people give thanks & dedicate their lives more fully to God—through the grain offering	14 And this *is* the law of the meat offering: the sons of Aaron shall offer it before the LORD, before the altar.	the meat offering, and of the oil thereof, and all the frankincense which *is* upon the meat offering, and shall burn *it* upon the altar *for* a sweet savour, *even* the memorial of it, unto the LORD.	giving & dedication 1) To burn it on the altar as the LORD'S memorial 2) The aroma symbolized that the thanksgiving & dedication pleased the LORD
a. To offer a handful of grain to the LORD as an act of thanks-	15 And he shall take of it his handful, of the flour of		

OUTLINE	SCRIPTURE	SCRIPTURE	OUTLINE
b. To give the remaining grain to the priests as food with two restrictions 1) Must be made without yeast (a symbol of sin, corruption) 2) Must be eaten within the courtyard of the Tabernacle c. To observe strictly the limitation: Must not be baked with yeast (a symbol of sin, corruption)	16 And the remainder thereof shall Aaron and his sons eat: with unleavened bread shall it be eaten in the holy place; in the court of the tabernacle of the congregation they shall eat it. 17 It shall not be baken with leaven. I have given it *unto them for* their portion of my offerings made by fire; it *is*	most holy, as *is* the sin offering, and as the trespass offering. 18 All the males among the children of Aaron shall eat of it. *It shall be* a statute for ever in your generations concerning the offerings of the LORD made by fire: every one that toucheth them shall be holy.	1) Because it is part of God's offering: It is most holy 2) Because it is a gift to the priests from God's offering: It is always to be without yeast (a symbol of corruption) 3) Because touching the grain offering conveys holiness to the priests: Must not be contaminated with yeast (sin)

a. The priest was to offer a handful of grain to the LORD as an act of thanksgiving and dedication (v.15).
   1) This he did every morning and evening by laying a handful of grain upon the Burnt Offering on the altar. Laying the grain upon the Burnt Offering symbolized two things:
   ⇒ It symbolized thanksgiving to God for all His goodness: for the atonement (reconciliation) through the sacrifice lying upon the altar and for all else that God provided—crops, food, livelihood.
   ⇒ It symbolized dedication, the laying of one's life—all one is and has—upon the sacrifice lying upon the altar. God had reconciled His people to Himself through the sacrifice; therefore, the people owed their lives to God.

   2) Note the result: the aroma of the offering ascending up symbolized that the thanksgiving and dedication pleased the LORD. God accepted the thanksgiving and dedication of the true believer.

b. The priest was to give the remaining grain to the other priests as food, as part of their support. But there were two restrictions governing the grain or food. First, the grain—bread, loaves, cakes—had to be made and eaten without leaven or yeast. Why? Remember that leaven or yeast is a symbol of sin, of corruption. A person's thanksgiving and dedication to God must always be free of sin and corruption.

> "I beseech you therefore, brethren, by the mercies of God, that ye present your bodies a living sacrifice, holy, acceptable unto God, *which is* your reasonable service. And be not conformed to this world: but be ye transformed by the renewing of your mind, that ye may prove what *is* that good, and acceptable, and perfect, will of God" (Ro.12:1-2).
> "If I regard iniquity in my heart, the LORD will not hear *me*" (Ps.66:18).
> "But your iniquities have separated between you and your God, and your sins have hid *his* face from you, that he will not hear" (Is.59:2).

Second, the grain had to be eaten within the courtyard of the Tabernacle, in a holy place. The very place of a person's thanksgiving and dedication is holy, sanctified—set apart to God. (See outline and note—1 Co.3:16 for more discussion.)

Thought 1. Many believers have special places where they meet God, places that might be called *prayer gardens*. The church or sanctuary is certainly one of these places—a very special place of worship, a place where believers meet God.

> "And he said, Draw not nigh hither: put off thy shoes from off thy feet, for the place whereon thou standest *is* holy ground" (Ex.3:5).
> "And the captain of the LORD's host said unto Joshua, Loose thy shoe from off thy foot; for the place whereon thou standest *is* holy. And Joshua did so" (Jos.5:15).
> "Stand in awe, and sin not: commune with your own heart upon your bed, and be still. Selah" (Ps.4:4).
> "Let all the earth fear the LORD: let all the inhabitants of the world stand in awe of him" (Ps.33:8).
> "But the LORD *is* in his holy temple: let all the earth keep silence before him" (Hab.2:20).

c. Note that the priest was to observe strictly the limitation: the grain was not to be baked with leaven or yeast (vv.17-18). Again, keep in mind that leaven or yeast is a symbol of sin and corruption. God gave three reasons for the restriction:
   1) It must not be baked with leaven or yeast because it is a part of God's offering. God's offering is holy; therefore, it must not be contaminated.
   2) It must not be baked with leaven or yeast because it is a gift to the priests from God's offering (v.18). It is a holy offering; therefore, the priests are to keep it holy, make sure it is set apart to God.
   3) It must not be baked with leaven or yeast because touching the Grain Offering conveys holiness to the priests. They must not partake, eat, nor take hold of anything sinful or corrupted.

Thought 1. A believer—minister and layperson alike—must approach God with a pure, clean heart. He must give thanks and dedicate himself with a pure, clean heart. God does not accept a half-hearted dedication or praise, does not accept a person who still seeks to live a sinful, corrupt life.

"Wherefore come out from among them, and be ye separate, saith the Lord, and touch not the unclean *thing*; and I will receive you, And will be a Father unto you, and ye shall be my sons and daughters, saith the LORD Almighty" (2 Co.6:17-18).

"And have no fellowship with the unfruitful works of darkness, but rather reprove *them*. And this is the confidence that we have in him, that, if we ask any thing according to his will, he heareth us" (Ep.5:11).

"Love not the world, neither the things that are in the world. If any man love the world, the love of the Father is not in him. For all that is in the world, the lust of the flesh, and the lust of the eyes, and the pride of life, is not of the Father, but is of the world" (1 Jn.2.15-16).

"Depart ye, depart ye, go ye out from thence, touch no unclean *thing*; go ye out of the midst of her; be ye clean, that bear the vessels of the LORD" (Is.52:11).

[3] (6:19-23) **Offering, the Grain—Grain Offering—Thanksgiving—Dedication—Ministers, Duty of—Priests, Duty of**: the third duty of the priest or minister is to guide the newly ordained priest to give thanks and commit his life daily to the LORD. How? Through the Grain Offering. Note that all the priests were involved in this offering.

OUTLINE	SCRIPTURE	SCRIPTURE	OUTLINE
3. Duty 3: To guide the newly ordained priest to give thanks & to commit his life more fully to God—through the grain offering	19 And the LORD spake unto Moses, saying, 20 This *is* the offering of Aaron and of his sons, which they shall offer unto the LORD in the day when he is anointed; the tenth part of an ephah of fine flour for	in *and* the baken pieces of the meat offering shalt thou offer *for* a sweet savour unto the LORD. 22 And the priest of his sons that is anointed in his stead shall offer it: *it is* a	pleased the LORD: He accepted the daily offering of thanksgiving & dedication
a. To begin the daily offering of thanksgiving & commitment on the day of his anointing			b. To be a permanent offering in the future for all anointed priests
1) Offer two quarts (one-tenth an ephah) of fine flour: Half in the morning & half in the evening	a meat offering perpetual, half of it in the morning, and half thereof at night.	statute for ever unto the LORD; it shall be wholly burnt.	c. To observe strictly this one restriction: The entire offering of one's thanksgiving & commitment is the LORD's share
2) Mix with oil	21 In a pan it shall be made with oil; and when *it*	23 For every meat offering for the priest shall be	1) It is to be completely burned up—totally offered
3) Result: The aroma symbolized that the offering	is baken, thou shalt bring it	wholly burnt: it shall not be eaten.	2) It is not to be eaten, none of it

a. Aaron and his sons were to make the offering of thanksgiving and dedication on the very day he, the High Priest, was anointed (vv.20-21). From the day of his anointing, the offering was thereafter to be made *every day*. The point is clear: the priests were to make a daily offering of thanksgiving and dedication to God.
 1) They were to offer two quarts (one-tenth an ephah) of fine flour: half in the morning and half in the evening (v.20).
 2) They were to mix it with oil (v.21).
 3) The result: the ascending aroma symbolized that the offering pleased the LORD. He accepted the daily thanksgiving and dedication of the priests.
 b. This offering was to be a permanent offering in the future for all anointed priests (v.22).
 c. The priests were to observe this one restriction: the offering of thanksgiving and dedication was the LORD's rightful share; therefore, it was to be totally, wholly burned up. None of it was to be eaten (v.23).

Thought 1. The lesson is clear: a minister of God should make an offering of thanksgiving and dedication to God every day. He should have a daily worship time, a quiet time, a time of daily devotion to the LORD. And he should rededicate himself to the LORD every day of his life.

"And he said to *them* all, If any *man* will come after me, let him deny himself, and take up his cross daily, and follow me" (Lu.9:23).

"I beseech you therefore, brethren, by the mercies of God, that ye present your bodies a living sacrifice, holy, acceptable unto God, *which is* your reasonable service. And be not conformed to this world: but be ye transformed by the renewing of your mind, that ye may prove what *is* that good, and acceptable, and perfect, will of God" (Ro.12:1-2).

"But exhort one another daily, while it is called To day; lest any of you be hardened through the deceitfulness of sin" (He.3:13).

"So will I sing praise unto thy name for ever, that I may daily perform my vows" (Ps.61:8).

"Mine eye mourneth by reason of affliction: LORD, I have called daily upon thee, I have stretched out my hands unto thee" (Ps.88:9).

"Blessed *is* the man that heareth me, watching daily at my gates, waiting at the posts of my doors" (Pr.8:34).

"Now when Daniel knew that the writing was signed, he went into his house; and his windows being open in his chamber toward Jerusalem, he kneeled upon his knees three times a day, and prayed, and gave thanks before his God, as he did aforetime" (Da.6:10).

[4] (6:24-30) **Offering, the Sin—Sin Offering—Forgiveness of Sin—Symbol, of Christ**: the fourth duty of the priest or minister is to help people secure forgiveness of sin. How? By leading them to approach God through the sacrifice. The sacrifice was, of course, a symbol of Jesus Christ. (See outline and notes—Le.4:1-5:13 for more discussion.)

OUTLINE	SCRIPTURE	SCRIPTURE	OUTLINE

4. Duty 4: To help people secure forgiveness of sin—through the Sin Offering
a. Must approach God through the sacrifice (a symbol of Christ)
  1) The sacrifice was to be put to death in the same place the Burnt Offering was sacrificed: Because the Sin Offering was most holy
  2) The priest who offers it has to eat it: But it is to be eaten in the courtyard of the Tabernacle
b. Must observe the holiness of the sacrifice
  1) Anything or anyone who touches the sacrifice becomes holy
	24 And the LORD spake unto Moses, saying,
	25 Speak unto Aaron and to his sons, saying, This *is* the law of the sin offering: In the place where the burnt offering is killed shall the sin offering be killed before the LORD: it *is* most holy.
	26 The priest that offereth it for sin shall eat it: in the holy place shall it be eaten, in the court of the tabernacle of the congregation.
	27 Whatsoever shall touch the flesh thereof shall be holy: and when there is sprinkled of the blood thereof upon any garment,
		thou shalt wash that whereon it was sprinkled in the holy place.
		28 But the earthen vessel wherein it is sodden shall be broken: and if it be sodden in a brasen pot, it shall be both scoured, and rinsed in water.
		29 All the males among the priests shall eat thereof: it *is* most holy.
		30 And no sin offering, whereof *any* of the blood is brought into the tabernacle of the congregation to reconcile *withal* in the holy *place*, shall be eaten: it shall be burnt in the fire.
			2) If any blood splattered on clothing, it must be washed in a holy place
			3) If a clay pot is used to cook the sacrifice, it must be broken: Never used for anything else
			4) If a bronze pot is used, it is to be cleansed thoroughly
			5) Only the priests may eat it: Because it is holy, set apart to God
			c. Must observe one absolute restriction: The sacrifice must never be eaten if the blood is taken into the Holy Place to make atonement for the nation's or priest's sin—it must be completely burned (4:5, 18)

a. The priest was to lead people to approach God through the sacrifice of the Sin Offering (vv.25-26).
  1) The sacrifice is most holy, that is, set apart to God. It was in the sacrifice that a person's sins were to be forgiven (v.25).
  2) The priest who offered the sacrifice was to eat his portion, but he had to eat it in a holy place, that is, in the courtyard of the Tabernacle (v.26).

b. The priest must observe the holiness of the sacrifice (vv.27-29). The sacrifice of the Sin Offering was most holy to God because it symbolized the death of His Son for the sins of the world. Therefore:
  ⇒ If anything or anyone touched the sacrifice, he or it became holy (v.27).
  ⇒ If any blood were splattered on the clothing, the clothing had to be washed in a holy place (v.27).
  ⇒ If a clay pot were used to cook the sacrifice, the pot had to be broken, never used for anything else (v.28).
  ⇒ If a bronze pot were used, it had to be thoroughly cleaned (v.28).
  ⇒ Only the priests were ever allowed to eat a portion of the meat because the meat was holy; that is, the meat that had been set apart to God (v.29).

c. Note the one absolute restriction: the sacrifice of a Sin Offering was never to be eaten if the blood was taken into the holy place to make atonement for the nation's or people's sins (v.30).

Thought 1. Note how this point stresses the holiness of the Sin Offering. The blood of the sacrifice was set apart to God; therefore, it was meaningful and precious to God. Moreover, God demands that people count the blood of His Son holy, meaningful, and precious. It is His blood that cleanses us from sin and makes it possible for us to be forgiven sin.

    "For this is my blood of the new testament, which is shed for many for the remission of sins" (Mt.26:28).
    "In whom we have redemption through his blood, the forgiveness of sins, according to the riches of his grace" (Ep.1:7).
    "And almost all things are by the law purged with blood; and without shedding of blood is no remission" (He.9:22).
    "My little children, these things write I unto you, that ye sin not. And if any man sin, we have an advocate with the Father, Jesus Christ the righteous: And he is the propitiation for our sins: and not for ours only, but also for *the sins of* the whole world" (1 Jn.2:1-2).

5 (7:1-10) **Offering, the Guilt—Guilt Offering—Guilt, Deliverance from—Conscience—Minister, Duties of—Priest, Duty of:** the fifth duty of the priest or minister is to help people find freedom from the weight and anguish of guilt. How? Through the sacrifice of the Guilt Offering. (See outline and notes—Lev.5:14-6:7 for more discussion.) Remember, the sacrifice is a symbol of Christ's dying for the guilt of the world. Note also that this offering is said to be most holy: the sacrifice of Christ for the guilt of people is a sacrifice especially set apart to God. This sacrifice is especially meaningful to God: He clearly wants people—ministers and laypersons alike—freed from the weight and anguish of guilt. Note what the priest was to do:

OUTLINE	SCRIPTURE	SCRIPTURE	OUTLINE
5. Duty 5: To help people find freedom from the weight & anguish of guilt through the sacrifice of the	Likewise this *is* the law of the trespass offering: it *is* most holy.	2 In the place where they kill the burnt offering shall they kill the trespass	**Guilt Offering, which is most holy** a. Must approach God through the sacrifice (a symbol of Christ)

OUTLINE	SCRIPTURE	SCRIPTURE	OUTLINE
1) Put the sacrifice to death in the same place the burnt offering is slaughtered 2) Sprinkle the blood against the altar on all sides 3) Offer a portion to the LORD • All the fat • Both kidneys & the liver • Burn all the LORD's portion	offering: and the blood thereof shall he sprinkle round about upon the altar. 3 And he shall offer of it all the fat thereof; the rump, and the fat that covereth the inwards, 4 And the two kidneys, and the fat that *is* on them, which *is* by the flanks, and the caul *that is* above the liver, with the kidneys, it shall he take away: 5 And the priest shall burn them upon the altar *for* an offering made by fire unto the LORD: it *is* a trespass offering.	7 As the sin offering *is*, so *is* the trespass offering: *there is* one law for them: the priest that maketh atonement therewith shall have *it*. 8 And the priest that offereth any man's burnt offering, *even* the priest shall have to himself the skin of the burnt offering which he hath offered. 9 And all the meat offering that is baken in the oven, and all that is dressed in the fryingpan, and in the pan, shall be the priest's that offereth it.	c. Must accept a portion of several offerings to provide for his family 1) The meat of the Sin Offering & the Guilt Offering 2) The hide of the Burnt Offering 3) The grain of the Grain Offering
b. Must accept a portion of the offering to provide food for his sons (priests): It must be eaten in a holy place, for it is holy	6 Every male among the priests shall eat thereof: it shall be eaten in the holy place: it *is* most holy.	10 And every meat offering, mingled with oil, and dry, shall all the sons of Aaron have, one *as much* as another.	4) The uncooked offerings belonged equally to all the priests

a. He was to approach God through the sacrifice (a symbol of Christ) (v.2).
1) He was to put the sacrifice to death in the same place the Burnt Offering was slaughtered (v.2).
2) He was to sprinkle the blood against the altar on all sides (v.2).
3) He was to offer a portion to the LORD (v.3).
   ⇒ all the fat
   ⇒ both kidneys and the liver
   ⇒ burn all the LORD'S portion

b. He was to accept a portion of the offering to provide food for the other priests. But, again, it had to be eaten in a holy place because it was a holy sacrifice (v.6).
c. Note that the priest was to accept a portion of several offerings to provide for his family (vv.7-10).
1) The meat of the Sin Offering and the Guilt Offering
2) The hide of the Burnt Offering
3) The grain of the Grain Offering

Thought 1. The sacrifice of the Guilt Offering was holy, totally set apart to God. This is a graphic description of Jesus Christ, the sacrifice that was set apart to take away the sin and guilt of the world. The only permanent deliverance from the weight and anguish of guilt is through the Lord Jesus Christ. The only way we can ever be set free from the condemnation and judgment of sin is to be forgiven through the blood of Jesus Christ. Jesus Christ alone can set us free from the weight and anguish of sin and guilt.

"For when we were yet without strength, in due time Christ died for the ungodly....But God commendeth his love toward us, in that, while we were yet sinners, Christ died for us" (Ro.5:6, 8).
"Holding faith, and a good conscience; which some having put away concerning faith have made shipwreck" (1 Ti.1:19).
"Who gave himself for us, that he might redeem us from all iniquity, and purify unto himself a peculiar people, zealous of good works" (Tit.2:14).
"For if the blood of bulls and of goats, and the ashes of an heifer sprinkling the unclean, sanctifieth to the purifying of the flesh: How much more shall the blood of Christ, who through the eternal Spirit offered himself without spot to God, purge your conscience from dead works to serve the living God?" (He.9:13-14).
"If we confess our sins, he is faithful and just to forgive us *our* sins, and to cleanse us from all unrighteousness" (1 Jn.1:9).

6 (7:11-36) **Offering, the Peace or Fellowship—Peace Offering—Fellowship Offering—Believer, Life and Walk—Vows—Judgment, Caused by—Ministers, Support of—Ministers, Duty of—Priest, Duty of**: the sixth duty of the priest or minister is to help people grow in the peace and fellowship of God. How? Through the sacrifice of the Fellowship or Peace Offering. (See outline and notes—Le.3:1-17 for more discussion.) Again, this is a clear symbol of the death of Jesus Christ. Keep in mind that the Burnt Offering made atonement—paid the price—for man's condemnation and judgment, reconciling man with God.
Fellowship with God was secured through the sacrifice of the Burnt Offering. This passage is talking about the *peace and fellowship* of God, about...
• maintaining the *peace and fellowship of God* within one's heart and life
• keeping and letting the *peace and fellowship of God* rule in one's heart and life
• growing in the *peace and fellowship of God*

74

This discussion of the Peace or Fellowship Offering gives several new instructions. Note in particular that a Fellowship Offering could be given in three ways: as an offering of thanksgiving, as a vow, or just as a freewill offering to express one's spiritual hunger to grow in peace and fellowship with God.

Since this offering covers so much detail, it helps us to gain an overview of the discussion by glancing at the four major points of the outline:

⇒ the Peace or Fellowship Offering of thanksgiving (vv.12-15)
⇒ the Peace or Fellowship Offering given as a vow or just to show one's desire to grow in peace and fellowship with God (vv.16-21)
⇒ the prohibitions governing the Fellowship Offering as well as all the offerings of life (vv.22-27)
⇒ the clear, emphatic instructions governing the support of the priests (vv.28-36)

OUTLINE	SCRIPTURE	SCRIPTURE	OUTLINE
6. Duty 6: To help people grow in the peace & fellowship of God through the Fellowship or Peace offering a. The Fellowship Offering of thanksgiving 1) Must approach God through the sacrifice (a symbol of Christ) 2) Must also offer several kinds of bread: Cakes, wafers, & loaves—mixed with oil & made without yeast (a symbol of sin, of corruption) 3) Must also offer with several loaves of bread made with yeast (were for the priests) 4) Must bring one of each kind as an offering to the LORD: This bread then belongs to the priest who sprinkles the blood of the sacrifice against the altar 5) Must eat the meat on the very day it is offered, leaving none until morning b. The Fellowship Offering given as a vow or just to show one's desire to grow in the peace & fellowship of God 1) Must approach God through the offering: "If...offering" 2) Must eat within two days 3) Must burn up any meat still left on the third day 4) Must not eat any of the sacrifice on the third day • Because God does not accept, does not credit the offering to one's account: Because the meat is spoiled, impure • The warning: The person is held accountable to God 5) Must obey the commandment on being spiritually clean • Must not eat meat that has	11 And this *is* the law of the sacrifice of peace offerings, which he shall offer unto the LORD. 12 If he offer it for a thanksgiving, then he shall offer with the sacrifice of thanksgiving unleavened cakes mingled with oil, and unleavened wafers anointed with oil, and cakes mingled with oil, of fine flour, fried. 13 Besides the cakes, he shall offer *for* his offering leavened bread with the sacrifice of thanksgiving of his peace offerings. 14 And of it he shall offer one out of the whole oblation *for* an heave offering unto the LORD, *and* it shall be the priest's that sprinkleth the blood of the peace offerings. 15 And the flesh of the sacrifice of his peace offerings for thanksgiving shall be eaten the same day that it is offered; he shall not leave any of it until the morning. 16 But if the sacrifice of his offering *be* a vow, or a voluntary offering, it shall be eaten the same day that he offereth his sacrifice: and on the morrow also the remainder of it shall be eaten: 17 But the remainder of the flesh of the sacrifice on the third day shall be burnt with fire. 18 And if *any* of the flesh of the sacrifice of his peace offerings be eaten at all on the third day, it shall not be accepted, neither shall it be imputed unto him that offereth it: it shall be an abomination, and the soul that eateth of it shall bear his iniquity. 19 And the flesh that toucheth any unclean *thing* shall not be eaten; it shall be	burnt with fire: and as for the flesh, all that be clean shall eat thereof. 20 But the soul that eateth *of* the flesh of the sacrifice of peace offerings, that *pertain* unto the LORD, having his uncleanness upon him, even that soul shall be cut off from his people. 21 Moreover the soul that shall touch any unclean *thing, as* the uncleanness of man, or *any* unclean beast, or any abominable unclean *thing*, and eat of the flesh of the sacrifice of peace offerings, which *pertain* unto the LORD, even that soul shall be cut off from his people. 22 And the LORD spake unto Moses, saying, 23 Speak unto the children of Israel, saying, Ye shall eat no manner of fat, of ox, or of sheep, or of goat. 24 And the fat of the beast that dieth of itself, and the fat of that which is torn with beasts, may be used in any other use: but ye shall in no wise eat of it. 25 For whosoever eateth the fat of the beast, of which men offer an offering made by fire unto the LORD, even the soul that eateth *it* shall be cut off from his people. 26 Moreover ye shall eat no manner of blood, *whether it be* of fowl or of beast, in any of your dwellings. 27 Whatsoever soul *it be* that eateth any manner of blood, even that soul shall be cut off from his people. 28 And the LORD spake unto Moses, saying, 29 Speak unto the children of Israel, saying, He that offereth the sacrifice of his peace offerings unto the LORD shall bring his oblation unto the LORD of the	touched anything unclean: Must be burned up • Must only eat clean meat • Must never eat any meat of the sacrifice if one is unclean (spiritually unclean): To be cut off from the community • The judgment is re-emphasized: Must be cut off if he is unclean (spiritually unclean), if he abuses the sacrifice c. The prohibitions governing the Fellowship Offering, as well as all the offerings of life 1) Must never eat any fat of any animal • Not of dead animals: May be used for any other purpose, but not for eating • Not of sacrificed animals: This violator is to be cut off from the community 2) Must not eat the blood of any animal: This violator is to be cut off d. The clear, emphatic instructions governing the support of the priests: To be given part of the Fellowship Offering as their support

75

OUTLINE	SCRIPTURE	SCRIPTURE	OUTLINE
1) The believer is to bring part of his sacrifice to the LORD: Bring the fat & the breast—wave the breast before the LORD as a wave offering • To burn the fat on the altar • But to keep the breast as food for the priests 2) The believer is to give the right thigh to the priest who offers the blood & the fat to the LORD—all on the believer's behalf	sacrifice of his peace offerings. 30 His own hands shall bring the offerings of the LORD made by fire, the fat with the breast, it shall he bring, that the breast may be waved *for* a wave offering before the LORD. 31 And the priest shall burn the fat upon the altar: but the breast shall be Aaron's and his sons'. 32 And the right shoulder shall ye give unto the priest *for* an heave offering of the sacrifices of your peace offerings. 33 He among the sons of Aaron, that offereth the blood of the peace offerings, and the fat, shall have the right shoulder for *his* part.	34 For the wave breast and the heave shoulder have I taken of the children of Israel from off the sacrifices of their peace offerings, and have given them unto Aaron the priest and unto his sons by a statute for ever from among the children of Israel. 35 This *is the portion* of the anointing of Aaron, and of the anointing of his sons, out of the offerings of the LORD made by fire, in the day *when* he presented them to minister unto the LORD in the priest's office; 36 Which the LORD commanded to be given them of the children of Israel, in the day that he anointed them, *by* a statute for ever throughout their generations.	3) The believer gives this part of the sacrificed offerings—the breast & thigh—to the priests as part of their support • Was part of their regular support • Was part of the very offering made to the LORD Himself: Was begun on the very first day of their service • Was the commandment of God Himself: To be part of their support throughout the generations

a. The Fellowship Offering of thanksgiving.

   1) The person had to approach God through the sacrifice (v.12). Keep in mind that the sacrifice is a symbol of Christ. A person can grow in the peace and fellowship of God only as he grows in Christ.

   2) The person also had to offer several kinds of bread with the sacrifice: cakes, wafers, and loaves mixed with oil. But note: the bread was to be made without leaven or yeast (v.12). Again, this symbolized sin and corruption. No person can grow in the peace and fellowship of God if he has sin in his life. The offering with leaven or yeast (sin, corruption) is unacceptable to God.

   3) The person must also offer several loaves of bread made with yeast (v.13). These were to go to the priests to be their portion, not the LORD's portion of the offering (see v.14).

   4) The person must bring one of each kind as an offering to the LORD: this bread then belonged to the priest who sprinkled the blood of the sacrifice against the altar (v.14).

   5) The person must eat the meat on the very day it was offered, leaving none until morning (v.15).

b. The Fellowship Offering given as a vow or just to show one's desire to grow in the peace and fellowship of God (vv.16-21).

   1) A person must approach God through the offering (a symbol of Christ) (v.16).

   2) A person must eat the meat within two days (v.16).

   3) A person must burn up any meat left until the third day (v.17).

   4) A person must never eat any meat of the Peace or Fellowship Offering on the third day (v.18). Note why:

     ⇒ Because God does not accept, does not credit, the offering to one's account because the meat would most likely be spoiled, impure (v.18). The word for *impure* (piggul) is probably derived from the root word *to rot* (pagal). Thus the law was given in order to stress that nothing unclean or spoiled was acceptable to God. The spoiled, the unclean, is just not acceptable to God. Therefore, when a person ate or partook of the meat, it had to be pure, for it symbolized that a person was eating with God. He was partaking of God's peace and fellowship, and God's peace and fellowship are pure, unspoiled.

     ⇒ The warning is clear: a person will be held accountable if he partakes of the fellowship meal after it is spoiled (v.18).

   5) A person absolutely must obey the commandment on being spiritually clean (vv.19-21).

     ⇒ He must not eat meat that has touched anything unclean; it must be burned up (v.19).

     ⇒ He must only eat clean meat (v.19).

     ⇒ He must never eat any meat of the sacrifice if he is unclean (v.20). If he did eat it, he was to be cut off: to be disciplined and excommunicated from God's people and to be judged by God.

     ⇒ Note the re-emphasis of the judgment: he must be cut off if he abused the sacrifice (v.21).

c. Note the prohibitions governing the Fellowship Offering as well as all the offerings of life (vv.22-27).

   1) A person was never to eat the fat of any animal (vv.23-25).

     ⇒ Not the fat of dead animals. The fat of a dead animal could be used for any other purpose such as for candles, oil for lamps, and other household purposes (v.24).

     ⇒ Not the fat of sacrificed animals. This fat was to be offered to the LORD as His portion of the sacrifice (v.26). The violator who ate this portion was to be severely judged: cut off by God's people and by God Himself.

   2) A person was never to eat or drink the blood of any animal. Again, the violator was to be severely judged, cut off by the people and by God (v.27).

d. Note the clear, emphatic instructions governing the support of the priests: they were to be given part of the Fellowship Offering as their support (vv.28-36). The outline clearly shows how God's people supported the priests of God.

1) The believer was to bring part of his sacrifice to the LORD: bring the fat and the breast. He was to wave the breast before the LORD as a wave offering:
   ⇒ burn the fat on the altar
   ⇒ keep the breast as food for the priests

2) The believer was to give the right thigh to the priest who offered the blood and the fat to the LORD—all on the believer's behalf

3) This part of the sacrificed offerings—the breast and thigh—was given to the priests as part of their support.
   ⇒ This was part of their regular support.
   ⇒ This was part of the very offering made to the LORD Himself.
   ⇒ This was begun on the very first day of their service.
   ⇒ This was the commandment of God Himself: to be part of their support throughout the generations.

Thought 1. God's instructions are clear: the people of God are to support God's ministers. Feeding and providing a livelihood for the minister of God is the clear duty of God's people. And note: the ministers of God are to lead the people to support God's servants. This is the major subject of this passage: one of the duties of a minister is to give clear, emphatic instructions governing the support of the priests or ministers of God.

> **"The workman is worthy of his meat" (Mt.10:10).**
> **"Even so hath the Lord ordained that they which preach the gospel should live of the gospel" (1 Co.9:14).**
> **"Let him that is taught in the word communicate [give] unto him that teacheth in all good things" (Ga.6:6).**
> **"For the scripture saith, Thou shalt not muzzle the ox that treadeth out the corn. And, The labourer *is* worthy of his reward" (1 Ti.5:18).**

7 (7:37-38) **Offerings, the—Moses, Ministry of**: this is simply a concluding statement covering the first division of Leviticus, a simple declaration that what has just been given are the regulations or duties to govern the offerings of God's people. Remember, the two basic reasons why God gave the offerings to His people: first to meet the many and varied needs of His people; and, second, to symbolize the complete ministry of Jesus Christ. Note how the offerings did both.

OUTLINE	SCRIPTURE
7. **The conclusion: These are the regulations, the duties given to the priest to govern the offerings**	37 This *is* the law of the burnt offering, of the meat offering, and of the sin offering, and of the trespass offering, and of the consecrations, and of the sacrifice of the peace offerings;
a. The five basic offerings & the Ordination Offering for the priests (or ministers)	
b. The regulations were given through God's mediator, Moses	38 Which the LORD commanded Moses in mount Sinai, in the day that he commanded the children of Israel to offer their oblations unto the LORD, in the wilderness of Sinai.
1) Given on Mt. Sinai	
2) Given while Israel was camped in the desert	

a. Note how the offerings met man's needs and symbolized the complete ministry of Jesus Christ (v.37). (See discussion point 3—Division I.)

1) The Burnt Offering met man's need for the atonement, for reconciliation with God. The Burnt Offering pointed to the atoning sacrifice of Jesus Christ. He paid the price for man's sin and condemnation: He alone reconciles man to God.

2) The Grain Offering met man's need for joy and thanksgiving and for the dedication of his life to a higher cause than what can be found in this world—the highest cause of all, the dedication of his life to God (v.37). In laying the grain upon the altar of the Burnt Offering, the person was declaring two things:
   ⇒ his thanks to God for the atoning sacrifice and for his livelihood—the crops, the food—and for all of God's goodness
   ⇒ his dedication to God

3) The Sin Offering met man's need for a constant, unbroken forgiveness of sin (v.37). When a person sensed a deep need for forgiveness of sin, he sacrificed the Sin Offering to God. This was a strong symbol of the sacrifice of Jesus Christ. Through His sacrifice and His sacrifice alone, we receive a constant, unbroken forgiveness of sin.

> **"In whom we have redemption through his blood, the forgiveness of sins, according to the riches of his grace" (Ep.1:7).**

4) The Guilt Offering met man's need for deliverance from the weight and anguish of guilt. This, too, is a strong symbol of the sacrifice of Jesus Christ. Through His death, a person is delivered, set free, from all sin:

⇒ set free from the condemnation of sin
⇒ set free from the punishment of sin
⇒ set free from the weight of sin

⇒ set free from the pricking conscience of sin
⇒ set free to live victoriously and triumphantly over all the temptations and trials of life

5) The Peace of Fellowship Offering met man's need to grow in the peace and fellowship of God. Again, the sacrifice of this offering pointed to the sacrifice of the Lord Jesus Christ. Christ and Christ alone gives us the strength to gain more and more of the peace and fellowship of God.

"That which we have seen and heard declare we unto you, that ye also may have fellowship with us: and truly our fellowship *is* with the Father, and with his Son Jesus Christ" (1 Jn.1:3).

6) The Ordination Offering met man's need for spiritual leaders. The Ordination Offering set men apart to focus upon God and to lead God's people to grow in the knowledge and understanding of God. These men were the priests, the ministers, of God to the people. The priest of the Old Testament pointed to the High Priesthood of Christ, the great Mediator between God and man. (See outline and note—Le.6:19-23 for more discussion.)

b. Note that the regulations were given through God's appointed mediator, Moses. They were given on Mt. Sinai while Israel was camped in the desert (v.38).

Thought 1. Three strong lessons are to be learned from this section of Scripture.

(1) People are to approach God through the sacrifice, the sacrifice of God's only Son, the Lord Jesus Christ.

"I am the door: by me if any man enter in, he shall be saved, and shall go in and out, and find pasture" (Jn.10:9).
"Jesus saith unto him, I am the way, the truth, and the life: no man cometh unto the Father, but by me" (Jn.14:6).
"Neither is there salvation in any other: for there is none other name under heaven given among men, whereby we must be saved" (Ac.4:12).

(2) The priests or ministers of God are to serve God's people by leading them to the only Person who can meet their needs: God Himself. They are to lead God's people...
• to approach God through the sacrifice of the Lord Jesus Christ

"For God so loved the world, that he gave his only begotten Son, that whosoever believeth in him should not perish, but have everlasting life" (Jn.3:16).
"Then Simon Peter answered him, LORD, to whom shall we go? thou hast the words of eternal life" (Jn.6:68).
"For I determined not to know any thing among you, save Jesus Christ, and him crucified" (1 Co.2:2).

• to grow in the knowledge of God through the sacrifice of the Lord Jesus Christ

"Take heed therefore unto yourselves, and to all the flock, over the which the Holy Ghost hath made you overseers, to feed the church of God, which he hath purchased with his own blood" (Ac.20:28).
"But speaking the truth in love, may grow up into him in all things, which is the head, *even* Christ" (Ep.4:15).
"Therefore leaving the principles of the doctrine of Christ, let us go on unto perfection; not laying again the foundation of repentance from dead works, and of faith toward God" (He.6:1).
"As newborn babes, desire the sincere milk of the word, that ye may grow thereby: If so be ye have tasted that the LORD *is* gracious" (1 Pe.2:2-3).
"But grow in grace, and *in* the knowledge of our LORD and Saviour Jesus Christ. To him *be* glory both now and for ever. Amen" (2 Pe.3:18).

(3) People are to learn and understand that the great sacrificial offerings of the Old Testament symbolized the Lord Jesus Christ, God's One and Only Son.

"The next day John seeth Jesus coming unto him, and saith, Behold the Lamb of God, which taketh away the sin of the world" (Jn.1:29).
"For whatsoever things were written aforetime were written for our learning, that we through patience and comfort of the scriptures might have hope" (Ro.15:4).
"Now all these things happened unto them for ensamples: and they are written for our admonition, upon whom the ends of the world are come" (1 Co.10:11; see He. Chs.8–10).
"But Christ being come an high priest of good things to come, by a greater and more perfect tabernacle, not made with hands, that is to say, not of this building; Neither by the blood of goats and calves, but by his own blood he entered in once into the holy place, having obtained eternal redemption *for us*. For if the blood of bulls and of goats, and the ashes of an heifer sprinkling the unclean, sanctifieth to the purifying of the flesh: How much more shall the blood of Christ, who through the eternal Spirit offered himself without spot to God, purge your conscience from dead works to serve the living God?" (He.9:11-14).

TYPES, SYMBOLS, AND PICTURES
Leviticus 6:8–7:38

Historical Term	Type or Picture (Scriptural Basis for Each)	Life Application for Today's Believer	Biblical Application
The Perpetual Fire of the Burnt Offering Le. 6:8-13	*The perpetual fire of the burnt offering is a clear symbol of the sacrifice of Christ. His sacrifice is lasting; it is permanent, sufficient, adequate. The priests were to offer the sacrifice of the Burnt Offering every morning and every evening (Nu.28:3-8). The sacrifice of the Burnt Offering was never to cease. The priests were always to keep the fire of the Burnt Offering ablaze, even through the night. They were never to let the sacrifice cease from being offered.* **"Command Aaron and his sons, saying, This *is* the law of the burnt offering: It *is* the burnt offering, because of the burning upon the altar all night unto the morning, and the fire of the altar shall be burning in it" (Le.6:9).**	The sacrifice that Jesus Christ made is... • perpetual, lasting and permanent • timeless, not bound by time • abiding, always present • enduring, never exhausting its power • immutable, never changing • durable, never wearing out • everlasting, for each and every generation of believers The sacrifice of Jesus Christ was once and for all.	*"Who needeth not daily, as those high priests, to offer up sacrifice, first for his own sins, and then for the people's: for this he did once, when he offered up himself" (He.7:27).* *"For Christ also hath once suffered for sins, the just for the unjust, that he might bring us to God, being put to death in the flesh, but quickened by the Spirit" (1 Pe.3:18).* *"By the which will we are sanctified through the offering of the body of Jesus Christ once for all" (He.10:10).* *"For by one offering he hath perfected for ever them that are sanctified" (He.10:14).*
The Priestly Clothing Le. 6:8-13	*The priestly clothing symbolizes the clothing of righteousness, the righteousness of Christ. Jesus Christ removes the ashes or dirt of sin and clothes a person in righteousness. The priests were to put on the special linen clothing and undergarments (the priestly clothing) for removing the ashes.* **"And the priest shall put on his linen garment, and his linen breeches shall he put upon his flesh, and take up the ashes which the fire hath consumed with the burnt offering on the altar, and he shall put them beside the altar" (Le. 6:10).**	Jesus Christ is our righteousness, the only One who can cleanse us from sin and clothe us in righteousness. Jesus Christ is the only one who can make us acceptable to God, acceptable in His righteousness.	*"But we are all as an unclean thing, and all our righteousnesses are as filthy rags; and we all do fade as a leaf; and our iniquities, like the wind, have taken us away" (Is.64:6).* *"For he hath made him to be sin for us, who knew no sin; that we might be made the righteousness of God in him" (2 Co.5:21).* *"And to her was granted that she should be arrayed in fine linen, clean and white: for the fine linen is the righteousness of saints" (Re.19:8).* *"For Christ is the end of the law for righteousness to every one that believeth" (Ro.10:4).*
The Priest's Regular Clothing Worn When Taking the Ashes of the Sacrifice Outside the Camp Le. 6:8-13	*The priest's regular clothing symbolized the human body or human flesh that Jesus Christ took upon Himself. Jesus Christ became man in order to bear and take away the sins of man. As stated, this He did as a man, clothed in the regular flesh of man.*	Jesus Christ clothed Himself in human flesh—became a man—so that He might die and bear the penalty for man's sin. Through Him and Him alone, sin is removed and taken away—far, far away.	*"Forasmuch then as the children are partakers of flesh and blood, he also himself likewise took part of the same; that through death he might destroy him that had the power of death, that is, the devil; And deliver them who through fear of death were all their lifetime subject to bondage. For verily he took*

79

TYPES, SYMBOLS, AND PICTURES
Leviticus 6:8-7:38

Historical Term	Type or Picture (Scriptural Basis for Each)	Life Application for Today's Believer	Biblical Application
	"And he shall put off his garments, and put on other garments, and carry forth the ashes without the camp unto a clean place" (Le. 6:11).		*not on him the nature of angels; but he took on him the seed of Abraham. Wherefore in all things it behoved him to be made like unto his brethren, that he might be a merciful and faithful high priest in things pertaining to God, to make reconciliation for the sins of the people. For in that he himself hath suffered being tempted, he is able to succour them that are tempted" (He.2:14-18; see 1 Pe.2:24).* *"And ye know that he was manifested to take away our sins; and in him is no sin" (1 Jn.3:5).*
Laying the Grain Upon the Burnt Offering Le. 6:14-18	*Laying the grain upon the Burnt Offering symbolized two things:* 1. *It symbolized giving thanks to God for the atonement (reconciliation) secured by the Burnt offering. It also symbolized giving thanks for all else that God provided—crops, food, livelihood.* 2. *It symbolized dedication, the laying of one's life—all one is and has—upon the sacrifice lying upon the altar. God had reconciled His people to Himself through the sacrifice; therefore, the people owed their lives to God.* **"And he shall take of it his handful, of the flour of the meat offering, and of the oil thereof, and all the frankincense which** *is* **upon the meat offering, and shall burn** *it* **upon the altar** *for* **a sweet savour,** *even* **the memorial of it, unto the LORD" (Le.6:15).**	Once we are saved, by trusting the sacrifice of Jesus Christ, we are compelled to offer thanksgiving to God for everything He has so graciously provided, things such as. • salvation • food • clothing • shelter • livelihood Once we are saved, we are to dedicate our lives to God. Nothing is to be withheld from Him, nothing	*"Enter into his gates with thanksgiving, and into his courts with praise: be thankful unto him, and bless his name" (Ps.100:4).* *"Giving thanks always for all things unto God and the Father in the name of our Lord Jesus Christ" (Ep.5:20).* *"In every thing give thanks: for this is the will of God in Christ Jesus concerning you" (1 Th.5:18).* *"I beseech you therefore, brethren, by the mercies of God, that ye present your bodies a living sacrifice, holy, acceptable unto God, which is your reasonable service. And be not conformed to this world: but be ye transformed by the renewing of your mind, that ye may prove what is that good, and acceptable, and perfect, will of God" (Ro.12:1-2).*
Yeast or Leaven Withheld from the Grain Offering Le. 6:14-18	*Yeast or Leaven is a symbol of corruption, evil, and worldliness.* **"It shall not be baken with leaven. I have given it** *unto them for* **their portion of my offerings made by fire; it** *is* **most holy, as** *is* **the sin offering, and as the trespass offering" (Le.6:17).**	A believer—minister and layperson alike—must approach God with no yeast or leaven in his heart. He must have a pure, clean heart. He must give thanks and dedicate himself with a pure, clean heart. God does not accept a half-hearted dedication or half-hearted praise. He does not accept a	*"Wherefore come out from among them, and be ye separate, saith the LORD, and touch not the unclean thing; and I will receive you, And will be a Father unto you, and ye shall be my sons and daughters, saith the LORD Almighty" (2 Co.6:17-18).* *"And have no fellowship*

TYPES, SYMBOLS, AND PICTURES
Leviticus 6:8–7:38

Historical Term	Type or Picture (Scriptural Basis for Each)	Life Application for Today's Believer	Biblical Application
		person who still seeks to live a sinful, corrupt life.	*with the unfruitful works of darkness, but rather reprove them (1 Jn.5:14).* *And this is the confidence that we have in him, that, if we ask any thing according to his will, he heareth us" (Ep.5:11).* *"Depart ye, depart ye, go ye out from thence, touch no unclean thing; go ye out of the midst of her; be ye clean, that bear the vessels of the LORD" (Is.52:11).*
The Aroma of the Grain Offering Laid Upon the Burnt Offering Le. 6:14-18; 6:19-23	*The aroma is most likely a symbol of the person's faith in the sacrifice ascending up like a sweet aroma to the LORD. The aroma of the Grain Offering ascending up symbolized that the thanksgiving and dedication pleased the LORD. God accepted the thanksgiving and dedication.* **"And he shall take of it his handful, of the flour of the meat offering, and of the oil thereof, and all the frankincense which** *is* **upon the meat offering, and shall burn** *it* **upon the altar** *for* **a sweet savour,** *even* **the memorial of it, unto the LORD" (Le.6:15).** **"In a pan it shall be made with oil;** *and when it is* **baken, thou shalt bring it in:** *and* **the baken pieces of the meat offering shalt thou offer** *for* **a sweet savour unto the LORD" (Le.6:21).**	God accepts our faith in the sacrifice of the Lord Jesus Christ. He accepts our faith as atonement or reconciliation by which we become acceptable to God (see Ge.15:6; Ro.4:9; 2 Co. 5:21).	*"And walk in love, as Christ also hath loved us, and hath given himself for us an offering and a sacrifice to God for a sweet-smelling savour" (Ep.5:2).* *"For God so loved the world, that he gave his only begotten Son, that whosoever believeth in him should not perish, but have everlasting life" (Jn.3:16).* *"Forasmuch as ye know that ye were not redeemed with corruptible things, as silver and gold, from your vain conversation received by tradition from your fathers; But with the precious blood of Christ, as of a lamb without blemish and without spot" (1 Pe.1:18-19).*
The Sin Offering During the Special Duties of the Priests in Conducting the Offerings Le. 6:24-30. See also Le. 4:1–5:13	*The sacrifice of the Sin Offering was most holy to God because it symbolized the death of His Son for the sins of the world.* **"Speak unto Aaron and to his sons, saying, This** *is* **the law of the sin offering: In the place where the burnt offering is killed shall the sin offering be killed before the LORD: it** *is* **most holy" (Le.6:25).**	Jesus Christ was the Perfect, Sinless Sacrifice. As such, He stands before God as the Perfect, Ideal Man. As the Ideal, Perfect Man, He can represent us before God. This is the reason the sinner (all of us) has to approach God through Christ. We have no other way to secure forgiveness of sin. Priest, minister, and layperson alike—we all have to approach God through the Perfect, Sinless Sacrifice of the Lord Jesus Christ Himself.	*"For we have not an high priest which cannot be touched with the feeling of our infirmities; but was in all points tempted like as we are, yet without sin" (He.4:15; see He.7:26).* *"Forasmuch as ye know that ye were not redeemed with corruptible things, as silver and gold, from your vain conversation received by tradition from your fathers; But with the precious blood of Christ, as of a lamb without blemish and without spot" (1 Pe.1:18-19).* *"Who did no sin, neither was guile found in his mouth" (1 Pe.2:22).*

TYPES, SYMBOLS, AND PICTURES
Leviticus 6:8–7:38

Historical Term	Type or Picture (Scriptural Basis for Each)	Life Application for Today's Believer	Biblical Application
The Guilt Offering During the Special Duties of the Priests in Conducting the Offerings Le.7:1-10. See also Le.5:14–6:7	*The sacrifice is a symbol of Christ's dying for the guilt of the world.* **"In the place where they kill the burnt offering shall they kill the trespass offering: and the blood thereof shall he sprinkle round about upon the altar" (Le.7:2).**	The only permanent deliverance from the weight and anguish of guilt is through the LORD Jesus Christ. The only way we can ever be set free from the condemnation and judgment of sin is to be forgiven our sin through the blood of Jesus Christ. Jesus Christ alone can set us free from the weight and anguish of sin and guilt.	*"Who gave himself for our sins, that he might deliver us from this present evil world, according to the will of God and our Father" (Ga.1:4).* *"Christ hath redeemed us from the curse of the law, being made a curse for us: for it is written, Cursed is every one that hangeth on a tree" (Ga.3:13; see 1 Pe.1:18-19).* *"That which we have seen and heard declare we unto you, that ye also may have fellowship with us: and truly our fellowship is with the Father, and with his Son Jesus Christ" (1 Jn.1:3).*

DIVISION II

THE WAY TO BECOME ACCEPTABLE TO GOD (PART 2): BY THE PRIESTHOOD, A PERFECT MEDIATOR, 8:1–10:20

(8:1–10:20) **DIVISION OVERVIEW**: *Leviticus* and *Exodus* are closely connected. This was clearly seen in the first division of *Leviticus*. *Exodus* had ended with the construction and dedication of the Tabernacle; *Leviticus* began with God's instructions governing the offering of sacrifices within the Tabernacle.

Now, this second division of *Leviticus* continues the instructions of God given in *Exodus*. In *Exodus*, God had clearly stated that His priests were to be ordained and faithfully execute their ministry. These three chapters in *Leviticus* cover their ordination and the actual beginning of their ministry on behalf of the people (see Ex.29:4 with Le.8:1-36; 9:1–10:20).

Note a significant fact throughout this division: both Moses and Aaron are clear types of Christ. Moses acted as priest until Aaron, the High Priest, could be ordained (8:1-36). Once ordained, Aaron took over the functions of the High Priest, representing the people before God (9:1-24). The importance of Moses as the priest of God's people until Aaron took over is well stated by *The Expositor's Bible Commentary*:

> It is hard to overemphasize the work of Moses, the man of God. As the greatest of the OT prophets, he was a type of Christ to come (De.18:15-19; Jn.7:40). As the first priest who instituted Israel's worship, Moses is a type of Christ the Great High Priest. Moses, the great lawgiver, received God's revelations face to face and was faithful in all God's house (Nu.12:7-8). Yet even he was but a type and a shadow, far inferior to Christ the High Priest and Son over the house (He 3:1-6). [1]

In reading or studying this passage, just keep in mind that the priest is a type of Christ. Moses was a type of Christ when he acted as priest, then Aaron when he became priest.

THE WAY TO BECOME ACCEPTABLE TO GOD (PART 2): BY THE PRIESTHOOD, A PERFECT MEDIATOR, 8:1–10:20

A. The Ordination of the Priests: The Steps to Ordination, 8:1-36
B. The Work and Ministry of the Ordained Priest (Minister): Showing People How to Become Acceptable to God, 9:1-24
C. The Judgment of God upon Two Priests (Nadab and Abihu) for Their False Worship: The Fate of All Who Approach God in a Wrong Way, 10:1-20

---

[1] *The Expositor's Bible Commentary*, Vol.2, p.559.

CHAPTER 8

II. THE WAY TO BECOME ACCEPTABLE TO GOD (PART 2): BY THE PRIESTHOOD, A PERFECT MEDIATOR, 8:1–10:20

A. The Ordination of the Priests: The Steps to Ordination, 8:1-36

1. **Step 1: The LORD'S call to ordination—He calls through His mediator, Moses (a symbol of Christ)**
   a. The call to the priests (ministers) to prepare: Aaron & his sons

   b. The call to the assembly: To gather for the ordination

   c. The obedience: Everyone obeyed

   d. The declaration: Ordination is God's commandment

2. **Step 2: The washing in water (a symbol of spiritual cleansing)**
3. **Step 3: The putting on of special clothing, the clothing of the High Priest (a symbol of Christ's righteousness & of bringing dignity & honor to the name of God) (Ex.28:1-43)**
   a. The tunic, sash, robe, & ephod

   b. The breastpiece & the Urim & Thummim

   c. The turban for the head & the gold plate or sacred diadem on the front of it

4. **Step 4: The anointing with oil (a symbol of dedication or consecration & of the Holy Spirit)**
   a. Anointed the Tabernacle & its furnishing
   b. Anointed the altar seven times & anointed its utensils, basin, & stand: To dedicate them to God's service

   c. Anointed Aaron's head: To consecrate or set him apart to God

And the LORD spake unto Moses, saying,

2 Take Aaron and his sons with him, and the garments, and the anointing oil, and a bullock for the sin offering, and two rams, and a basket of unleavened bread;

3 And gather thou all the congregation together unto the door of the tabernacle of the congregation.

4 And Moses did as the LORD commanded him; and the assembly was gathered together unto the door of the tabernacle of the congregation.

5 And Moses said unto the congregation, This is the thing which the LORD commanded to be done.

6 And Moses brought Aaron and his sons, and washed them with water.

7 And he put upon him the coat, and girded him with the girdle, and clothed him with the robe, and put the ephod upon him, and he girded him with the curious girdle of the ephod, and bound it unto him therewith.

8 And he put the breastplate upon him: also he put in the breastplate the Urim and the Thummim.

9 And he put the mitre upon his head; also upon the mitre, even upon his forefront, did he put the golden plate, the holy crown; as the LORD commanded Moses.

10 And Moses took the anointing oil, and anointed the tabernacle and all that was therein, and sanctified them.

11 And he sprinkled thereof upon the altar seven times, and anointed the altar and all his vessels, both the laver and his foot, to sanctify them.

12 And he poured of the anointing oil upon Aaron's head, and anointed him, to sanctify him.

13 And Moses brought Aaron's sons, and put coats upon them, and girded them with girdles, and put bonnets upon them; as the LORD commanded Moses.

14 And he brought the bullock for the sin offering: and Aaron and his sons laid their hands upon the head of the bullock for the sin offering.

15 And he slew it; and Moses took the blood, and put it upon the horns of the altar round about with his finger, and purified the altar, and poured the blood at the bottom of the altar, and sanctified it, to make reconciliation upon it.

16 And he took all the fat that was upon the inwards, and the caul above the liver, and the two kidneys, and their fat, and Moses burned it upon the altar.

17 But the bullock, and his hide, his flesh, and his dung, he burnt with fire without the camp; as the LORD commanded Moses.

18 And he brought the ram for the burnt offering: and Aaron and his sons laid their hands upon the head of the ram.

19 And he killed it; and Moses sprinkled the blood upon the altar round about.

20 And he cut the ram into pieces; and Moses burnt the head, and the pieces, and the fat.

21 And he washed the inwards and the legs in water; and Moses burnt the whole ram upon the altar: it was a burnt sacrifice for a sweet savour, and an offering made by fire unto the LORD; as the LORD commanded Moses.

22 And he brought the other ram, the ram of consecration: and Aaron and his sons laid their hands upon the head of the ram.

23 And he slew it; and Moses took of the blood of it, and put it upon the tip of Aaron's right ear, and upon the thumb of his right hand, and upon the great toe of his right foot.

24 And he brought Aaron's sons, and Moses put of the blood upon the tip of their right ear, and upon the thumbs of their right hands,

d. Anointed & clothed the other priests (ministers) (Ex.40:15)

5. **Step 5: Confessing the forgiveness of sins through the Sin Offering (a symbol of Christ)**
   a. Identifying with the sacrifice

   b. Putting the sacrifice to death

   c. Placing some blood on the horns of the altar: To purify or set it apart for God's service
   d. Pouring the remaining blood at the base of the altar: To dedicate the altar for atonement (reconciliation)

   e. Offering certain parts of the sacrifice to God: The fat, liver, kidneys

   f. Taking certain parts of the sacrifice outside the camp & burning them: The hide, flesh, & dung (a symbol of Christ's taking away sin)

6. **Step 6: Confessing the atonement through the Burnt Offering (a symbol of Christ)**
   a. Identifying with the sacrifice
   b. Putting the sacrifice to death
   c. Sprinkling the blood against all sides of the altar

   d. Offering certain parts of the sacrifice to the LORD

   e. Washing & offering the other parts of the sacrifice to the LORD
   f. The result: The sweet aroma pleased the LORD, was acceptable to Him & made atonement (reconciliation, see Le.1:1-17, esp. 4)

7. **Step 7: Dedicating all that one is & does to God—through the ordination sacrifice (a symbol of Christ)**
   a. Identifying with the sacrifice
   b. Dedicating or setting apart one's whole being to God—through the blood of the sacrifice
      1) Symbolized by blood being placed on Aaron's right ear, thumb, & big toe
      2) Symbolized by blood being placed on Aaron's sons, on their right ears, thumbs, & big toes

c. Dedicating the altar of sacrifice: Symbolized by sprinkling blood against all sides of the altar

d. Offering certain parts of the sacrifice to the LORD
1) Moses took all the fat, liver, kidneys, & right thigh: On top of these he placed a loaf of bread made without yeast, a cake made with oil, & a wafer

2) Moses gave all these to Aaron & his sons: To offer a wave offering before the LORD

3) Moses, as God's mediator, then took all the sacrifices from them & offered them on the altar
4) The result: The sweet aroma pleased & was acceptable to the LORD

e. Praising & thanking God for His provision: Moses took the breast—his part of the offering—& gave thanks through the wave offering

f. Consummating the ordination dedication: The whole being of Aaron & his sons were set apart by the anointing oil &

and upon the great toes of their right feet: and Moses sprinkled the blood upon the altar round about.
25 And he took the fat, and the rump, and all the fat that was upon the inwards, and the caul above the liver, and the two kidneys, and their fat, and the right shoulder:
26 And out of the basket of unleavened bread, that was before the LORD, he took one unleavened cake, and a cake of oiled bread, and one wafer, and put them on the fat, and upon the right shoulder:
27 And he put all upon Aaron's hands, and upon his sons' hands, and waved them for a wave offering before the LORD.
28 And Moses took them from off their hands, and burnt them on the altar upon the burnt offering: they were consecrations for a sweet savour: it is an offering made by fire unto the LORD.
29 And Moses took the breast, and waved it for a wave offering before the LORD: for of the ram of consecration it was Moses' part; as the LORD commanded Moses.
30 And Moses took of the anointing oil, and of the blood which was upon the altar, and sprinkled it upon

Aaron, and upon his garments, and upon his sons, and upon his sons' garments with him; and sanctified Aaron, and his garments, and his sons, and his sons' garments with him.
31 And Moses said unto Aaron and to his sons, Boil the flesh at the door of the tabernacle of the congregation: and there eat it with the bread that is in the basket of consecrations, as I commanded, saying, Aaron and his sons shall eat it.
32 And that which remaineth of the flesh and of the bread shall ye burn with fire.
33 And ye shall not go out of the door of the tabernacle of the congregation in seven days, until the days of your consecration be at an end: for seven days shall he consecrate you.
34 As he hath done this day, so the LORD hath commanded to do, to make an atonement for you.
35 Therefore shall ye abide at the door of the tabernacle of the congregation day and night seven days, and keep the charge of the LORD, that ye die not: for so I am commanded.
36 So Aaron and his sons did all things which the LORD commanded by the hand of Moses.

some blood being sprinkled on them & their clothes

g. Demonstrating the financial support of the ordained priests
1) Instructed to cook & eat the priest's portion before the people at the entrance of the Tabernacle: Was commanded by God

2) Instructed to burn up all leftovers

8. **Step 8: Knowing the critical importance of ordination & heeding God's warning**
a. Must repeat the service for 7 days (the complete number): A symbol that a person must complete his ministry
1) Is the commandment of God
2) Is for one purpose: To declare that atonement (reconciliation) is essential
b. Must heed God's warning
1) Observe the ordination for seven days: Complete one's ministry
2) Obey God or die: Do all that God requires or die

c. The obedience: They obeyed God

DIVISION II

THE WAY TO BECOME ACCEPTABLE TO GOD (PART 2): BY THE PRIESTHOOD, A PERFECT MEDIATOR, 8:1–10:20

A. The Ordination of the Priests: The Steps to Ordaining the Ministers of God, 8:1-36

(8:1–10:20) **Introduction—Ordination—Minister, Ordination of**: God calls and God ordains. Ordination is essential if a person is to serve God. In fact, no person should ever try to serve in the ministry unless he has been ordained by God.
⇒ Ordination means to be appointed by God to serve in the ministry of God.
⇒ Ordination means to be called, set apart, and consecrated to the service of God.

The significant fact in ordination is this: it is God who calls, sets apart, and consecrates a person to serve Him. The ministry is God's ministry; therefore, He has the right to decide who will serve in the ministry. God calls and God ordains. No person can serve God, not effectively, not unless he is called and ordained by God. Again, Scripture is clear: God calls and God ordains.

"Ye have not chosen me, but I have chosen you, and ordained you, that ye should go and bring forth fruit, and that your fruit should remain: that whatsoever ye shall ask of the Father in my name, he may give it you" (Jn.15:16).

Aaron and his sons had been called and appointed by God to the priesthood: they were to be the ministers of God to God's people. It was now time for the call and appointment to be demonstrated before the people...
• demonstrated in such a way that their ordination would make a lasting impression upon them, that they would never forget their call and appointment.

- demonstrated in such a way that their ordination would make a lasting impression upon the people, that the people would hold them and their ministry in the highest respect.

This is a subject that needs to be closely studied by every minister of God as well as by every believer: *The Ordination of the Priests: The Steps to Ordaining the Ministers of God*, 8:1-36.
1. Step 1: the LORD's call to ordination—He calls through His mediator, Moses (a symbol of Christ) (vv.1-5).
2. Step 2: the washing in water (a symbol of spiritual cleansing) (v.6).
3. Step 3: the putting on of special clothing, the clothing of the High Priest (a symbol of Christ's righteousness, of bringing dignity and honor to the name of God) (vv.7-9).
4. Step 4: the anointing with oil (a symbol of dedication or consecration and of the Holy Spirit) (vv.10-13).
5. Step 5: confessing the forgiveness of sins through the sin-offering (a symbol of Christ) (vv.14-17).
6. Step 6: confessing the atonement through the Burnt Offering (a symbol of Christ) (vv.18-21).
7. Step 7: dedicating all that one is and does to God—through the ordination sacrifice (a symbol of Christ) (vv.22-32).
8. Step 8: knowing the critical importance of ordination and heeding God's warning (vv.33-36).

1 (8:1-5) **Ordination—Mediator—Jesus Christ, Mediator**: the first step to ordination is the LORD's call to the ministry, His call for a person to serve the people of God.

OUTLINE	SCRIPTURE	SCRIPTURE	OUTLINE
1. Step 1: The LORD's call to ordination—He calls through His mediator, Moses (a symbol of Christ) a. The call to the priests (ministers) to prepare: Aaron & his sons b. The call to the assembly: To gather for the ordination	And the LORD spake unto Moses, saying, 2 Take Aaron and his sons with him, and the garments, and the anointing oil, and a bullock for the sin offering, and two rams, and a basket of unleavened bread; 3 And gather thou all the congregation together unto the door of the tabernacle of	the congregation. 4 And Moses did as the LORD commanded him; and the assembly was gathered together unto the door of the tabernacle of the congregation. 5 And Moses said unto the congregation, This *is* the thing which the LORD commanded to be done.	c. The obedience: Everyone obeyed d. The declaration: Ordination is God's commandment

Note that God's call comes through His mediator Moses. But keep in mind the practical application: Moses was a symbol of Christ. Being ordained to the priesthood or ministry is of critical importance to God. A person is to be ordained only if he has been called of God and willingly submits to that call. This is dramatically pictured in the ordination of Aaron and his sons to the priesthood of Israel. Two calls were issued: there was the call to the priests (ministers) to prepare for the ordination; and there was the call to the people to assemble and gather for the ordination service (vv.2-3). The picture would be this: the elders would have joined Moses and the priests at the entrance of the Tabernacle and all the people would have stood at the entrances to their tents (Ex.33:8).

Note the obedience of everyone (v.4). They did exactly what God commanded. Also note the important declaration made: ordination is God's commandment: "this is what the LORD has commanded" (v.5). Ordination is not of man; it is of God. A person was to be ordained to the priesthood because of God not because of man. God called and God ordained; therefore God's call and ordination were to be symbolized in an ordination service.

Thought 1. Why do people enter the ministry? Some like the profession. They like the idea of serving and ministering to people. Others like the professionalism of the ministry, the opportunity for leadership within the community that the ministry offers. Others like the opportunity for speaking and teaching on a regular basis. Some would like the prestige, image, and respect usually shown the minister. There are many reasons why a person might choose to serve in the ministry. But there is only one legitimate reason: the call and ordination of God. No person should ever serve in the ministry unless he has been called and ordained by God to serve. God calls and God ordains: this is the only legitimate reason for the church's ever ordaining a person to serve God's people.

"Ye have not chosen me, but I have chosen you, and ordained you, that ye should go and bring forth fruit, and that your fruit should remain: that whatsoever ye shall ask of the Father in my name, he may give it you" (Jn.15:16).

"But the Lord said unto him, Go thy way: for he is a chosen vessel unto me, to bear my name before the Gentiles, and kings, and the children of Israel" (Ac.9:15).

"But rise, and stand upon thy feet: for I have appeared unto thee for this purpose, to make thee a minister and a witness both of these things which thou hast seen, and of those things in the which I will appear unto thee" (Ac.26:16).

"And all things are of God, who hath reconciled us to himself by Jesus Christ, and hath given to us the ministry of reconciliation; To wit, that God was in Christ, reconciling the world unto himself, not imputing their trespasses unto them; and hath committed unto us the word of reconciliation. Now then we are ambassadors for Christ, as though God did beseech you by us: we pray you in Christ's stead, be ye reconciled to God" (2 Co.5:18-20).

"And such trust have we through Christ to God-ward: Not that we are sufficient of ourselves to think any thing as of ourselves; but our sufficiency *is* of God; Who also hath made us able ministers of the new testament; not of the letter, but of the spirit: for the letter killeth, but the spirit giveth life" (2 Co.3:4-6).

"Whereof I was made a minister, according to the gift of the grace of God given unto me by the effectual working of his power" (Ep.3:7).

"And I thank Christ Jesus our Lord, who hath enabled me, for that he counted me faithful, putting me into the ministry" (1 Ti.1:12).

"Who hath saved us, and called *us* with an holy calling, not according to our works, but according to his own purpose and grace, which was given us in Christ Jesus before the world began, But is now made manifest by the appearing of our Saviour Jesus Christ, who hath abolished death, and hath brought life and immortality to light through the gospel: Whereunto I am appointed a preacher, and an apostle, and a teacher of the Gentiles" (2 Ti.1:9-11; see Abraham in Ge.12:1; Moses in Ex.3:10; Gideon in Jud.6:14; Elisha in 1 K.19:19; Isaiah in Is.6:8).

2 (8:6) **Washing, Symbol of—Cleansing, Symbol of—Symbol, of Washing—Cleansing, Spiritual**: the second step in ordination is washing in water.

OUTLINE	SCRIPTURE
2. Step 2: The washing in water (a symbol of spiritual cleansing)	6 And Moses brought Aaron and his sons, and washed them with water.

Moses, God's mediator, took the men to be ordained and washed them in water. This is important: it was God's mediator who did the washing and the cleansing. Washing in water was a symbol of their need to be spiritually cleansed. No person can cleanse himself, not spiritually, not from sin. Only God's mediator can wash and cleanse a person spiritually.

Note one other fact as well: the washing and cleansing with water took place right before the putting on of the priestly clothes. The putting on of holy clothes is symbolic of putting on the righteousness of God. A person must be cleansed from sin before he is clothed in the righteousness of God.

Thought 1. It is Jesus Christ who washes us, who cleanses us from sin.

"And now why tarriest thou? arise, and be baptized, and wash away thy sins, calling on the name of the Lord" (Ac.22:16).

"In whom we have redemption through his blood, the forgiveness of sins, according to the riches of his grace" (Ep.1:7).

"How much more shall the blood of Christ, who through the eternal Spirit offered himself without spot to God, purge your conscience from dead works to serve the living God?" (He.9:14).

"But if we walk in the light, as he is in the light, we have fellowship one with another, and the blood of Jesus Christ his Son cleanseth us from all sin" (1 Jn.1:7).

"And from Jesus Christ, who is the faithful witness, and the first begotten of the dead, and the prince of the kings of the earth. Unto him that loved us, and washed us from our sins in his own blood" (Re.1:5).

"And such were some of you: but ye are washed, but ye are sanctified, but ye are justified in the name of the Lord Jesus, and by the Spirit of our God" (1 Co.6:11).

"Husbands, love your wives, even as Christ also loved the church, and gave himself for it; That he might sanctify and cleanse it with the washing of water by the word" (Ep.5:25-26).

"And I said unto him, Sir, thou knowest. And he said to me, These are they which came out of great tribulation, and have washed their robes, and made them white in the blood of the Lamb" (Re.7:14).

"Wash me throughly from mine iniquity, and cleanse me from my sin....Purge me with hyssop, and I shall be clean: wash me, and I shall be whiter than snow" (Ps.51:2, 7).

"Iniquities prevail against me: *as for* our transgressions, thou shalt purge them away" (Ps.65:3).

"Then will I sprinkle clean water upon you, and ye shall be clean: from all your filthiness, and from all your idols, will I cleanse you" (Eze.36:25).

"In that day there shall be a fountain opened to the house of David and to the inhabitants of Jerusalem for sin and for uncleanness" (Zec.13:1).

3 (8:7-9) **Clothing, of the Priest—Clothing, of the High Priest—High Priest, Clothing of—Symbol, of the Clothing of the High Priest—Righteousness in Ministry, Dignity and Honor of**: the third step in ordination involves clothing, the putting on of special clothing. What clothing? The clothing of the High Priest. Remember: the High Priest symbolized the High Priesthood of Jesus Christ, and the clothing symbolized the righteousness of Jesus Christ. A person must put on and be covered with the righteousness of Jesus Christ in order to be acceptable to God. The clothing of the High Priest declared two truths:

⇒ that the High Priest had to wear a different clothing than the people. He had to be covered with the most honorable and perfect clothing possible. This, of course, pointed to the righteousness of Jesus Christ, to His perfection.

⇒ that the High Priest was holy, set apart to God. He was to be respected and honored as the mediator between man and God. This, of course, pointed to the dignity and honor of Jesus Christ, the dignity and honor of His righteousness.

OUTLINE	SCRIPTURE	SCRIPTURE	OUTLINE
3. Step 3: The putting on of special clothing, the clothing of the High Priest (a symbol of Christ's righteousness & of bringing dignity & honor to the name of God) (Ex.28:1-43) a. The tunic, sash, robe, & ephod b. The breastpiece & the	7 And he put upon him the coat, and girded him with the girdle, and clothed him with the robe, and put the ephod upon him, and he girded him with the curious girdle of the ephod, and bound *it* unto him therewith. 8 And he put the breastplate	upon him: also he put in the breastplate the Urim and the Thummim. 9 And he put the mitre upon his head; also upon the mitre, *even* upon his forefront, did he put the golden plate, the holy crown; as the LORD commanded Moses.	Urim & Thummim c. The turban for the head & the gold plate or sacred diadem on the front of it

a. The High Priest was clothed with the tunic, sash, robe, and ephod (v.7).
⇒ The linen tunic was a long, coat-like garment that essentially covered the whole body. It symbolized righteousness, the putting on of God's righteousness. (See outline and note—Ex.28:1-5 for more discussion.)
⇒ The multi-colored sash of fine linen was symbolic of truth, the truth of God's Word. It is comparable to the belt of truth in the armor of God that the believer is to put on (Ep.6:14). The Word of God enlightens and wraps together everything in the believer's spiritual wardrobe. (See outline and note—Ex.28:1-5 for more discussion.)
⇒ The robe was worn by the High Priest as he entered through the veil and ministered to the LORD in the Sanctuary. The robe was called the robe of the ephod and symbolized the intercessory or mediatorial ministry of the High Priest. (See outline and note—Ex.28:31-35 for more discussion.)
⇒ The ephod was a sleeveless, coat-like garment. It had two onyx stones sewn into it with the names of Israel's twelve tribes engraved on them, six names on each stone. The ephod symbolized that the priest carried the names of God's people before the LORD as their mediator and intercessor. (See outline and note—Ex.28:6-14 for more discussion.)

b. The High Priest was clothed with the breastpiece that had the Urim and Thummim placed in its pouch (v.7). The breastpiece or chestpiece was a pouch-like garment that was worn close to the heart, right next to the ephod. The pouch was for the purpose of carrying the Urim and Thummim. This symbolized two things:
⇒ It symbolized that the High Priest represented and carried the names of God's people upon his heart, that he represented them before the LORD continually. (See outline and notes—Ex.28:29-30 for more discussion.)
⇒ It symbolized that the High Priest sought the will of God for the people. The Urim and Thummim were two stones that symbolized the special revelation or guidance that God gave the High Priest. (See outline and note—Ex.28:15-30 for more discussion.)

c. The High Priest was clothed with the turban for the head and the gold plate or sacred diadem on the front of it (v.9).
⇒ The turban was something like a linen headband that covered the head. This symbolized the need for mental righteousness. The mind and thoughts of the High Priest must be subjected to God and His righteousness. (See Types Chart—Ex.28:1-43 for more discussion.)
⇒ The gold plate (medallion) or sacred diadem was attached with a blue ribbon to the headband of the High Priest and was the crowning piece of the High Priest's wardrobe. The words "HOLINESS TO THE LORD" were written upon the medallion.
• The gold medallion symbolized that the High Priest bore the guilt for the shortcomings of the people.
• The gold medallion symbolized that the people must seek the acceptance of a holy God. (See Types Chart—Ex.28:1-43 for more discussion.)

Thought 1. This point is critical: no person should be ordained unless he has put on the righteousness of Jesus Christ. The righteousness of Jesus Christ must clothe a person completely, totally. In fact, two things are absolutely essential before a person should be ordained:
⇒ A person must demonstrate that he has been clothed with the righteousness of Christ, that God has clothed him with the righteousness of Christ.

> **"For he hath made him to be sin for us, who knew no sin; that we might be made the righteousness of God in him" (2 Co.5:21).**
> **"Even as Abraham believed God, and it was accounted to him for righteousness" (Ga.3:6).**
> **"And be found in him, not having mine own righteousness, which is of the law, but that which is through the faith of Christ, the righteousness which is of God by faith" (Ph.3:9).**
> **"Lie not one to another, seeing that ye have put off the old man with his deeds; And have put on the new man, which is renewed in knowledge after the image of him that created him" (Col.3:9-10).**
> **"And he believed in the LORD; and he counted it to him for righteousness" (Ge.15:6).**

⇒ A person must demonstrate that he will walk in the righteousness of Christ, that he will bring dignity and honor to the ministry of God.

> **"For I say unto you, That except your righteousness shall exceed the righteousness of the scribes and Pharisees, ye shall in no case enter into the kingdom of heaven" (Mt.5:20).**
> **"Awake to righteousness, and sin not; for some have not the knowledge of God: I speak this to your shame" (1 Co.15:34).**

"Therefore if any man be in Christ, he is a new creature: old things are passed away; behold, all things are become new" (2 Co.5:17).

"And that ye put on the new man, which after God is created in righteousness and true holiness" (Ep.4:24).

"Stand therefore, having your loins girt about with truth, and having on the breastplate of righteousness" (Ep.6:14).

"Being filled with the fruits of righteousness, which are by Jesus Christ, unto the glory and praise of God" (Ph.1:11).

4 (8:10-13) **Oil, Anointing—Symbol, of the Anointing Oil—Holy Spirit—Consecration**: the fourth step in ordination is the anointing with oil. Throughout Scripture, both people and places were anointed if they were to be consecrated to God. Note that dedication or consecration was the basis for being anointed. If a person was to be consecrated to the service of God, he was to be anointed with oil. The oil is a symbol of consecration and of the Holy Spirit, who anointed a person for service. The points of the Scripture and outline give a clear picture of the anointing service.

OUTLINE	SCRIPTURE	SCRIPTURE	OUTLINE
4. **Step 4: The anointing with oil (a symbol of dedication or consecration & of the Holy Spirit)** a. Anointed the Tabernacle & its furnishing b. Anointed the altar seven times & anointed its utensils, basin, & stand: To dedicate them to God's service	10 And Moses took the anointing oil, and anointed the tabernacle and all that *was* therein, and sanctified them. 11 And he sprinkled thereof upon the altar seven times, and anointed the altar and all his vessels, both the laver and his foot, to sanctify them.	12 And he poured of the anointing oil upon Aaron's head, and anointed him, to sanctify him. 13 And Moses brought Aaron's sons, and put coats upon them, and girded them with girdles, and put bonnets upon them; as the LORD commanded Moses.	c. Anointed Aaron's head: To consecrate & set him apart to God d. Anointed & clothed the other priests (ministers) (Ex.40:15)

a. Moses anointed the Tabernacle and its furnishings, everything in it (v.10). The Tabernacle was consecrated, set apart for the service of God.

b. Moses anointed the altar seven times and anointed its utensils, basin, and stand (v.11). Why was the altar anointed seven times? Remember, the altar was where the atoning sacrifice was offered, the place where the payment or ransom for sin was made. The sacrifice or payment for sin was full and complete. It provided a perfect redemption for man. Throughout the Bible, the number seven symbolizes the idea of completion, fullness, and perfection. The altar was anointed seven times to symbolize that a complete, full, and perfect sacrifice was being made for man's atonement (reconciliation) and redemption.

c. Moses anointed Aaron's head, symbolizing thereby that Aaron was being consecrated, set apart to God and His service (v.12).

d. Moses anointed and clothed the other priests, symbolizing that they also were being consecrated, set apart for the service of God (v.13).

Thought 1. A person being ordained to the ministry must be anointed by the Spirit of God. He must be called by God and led to the point of dedication and consecration to God. The person must be totally dedicated to the service of God through the presence and power of the Holy Spirit.

"And he said to them all, If any man will come after me, let him deny himself, and take up his cross daily, and follow me" (Lu.9:23).

"And when they had prayed, the place was shaken where they were assembled together; and they were all filled with the Holy Ghost, and they spake the word of God with boldness" (Ac.4:31).

"Then tidings of these things came unto the ears of the church which was in Jerusalem: and they sent forth Barnabas, that he should go as far as Antioch. Who, when he came, and had seen the grace of God, was glad, and exhorted them all, that with purpose of heart they would cleave unto the Lord. For he was a good man, and full of the Holy Ghost and of faith: and much people was added unto the Lord" (Ac.11:22-24).

"As they ministered to the Lord, and fasted, the Holy Ghost said, Separate me Barnabas and Saul for the work whereunto I have called them" (Ac.13:2).

"For as many as are led by the Spirit of God, they are the sons of God" (Ro.8:14).

"And Moses took of the anointing oil, and of the blood which *was* upon the altar, and sprinkled *it* upon Aaron, *and* upon his garments, and upon his sons, and upon his sons' garments with him; and sanctified Aaron, *and* his garments, and his sons, and his sons' garments with him" (Le.8:30).

"Then Samuel took the horn of oil, and anointed him in the midst of his brethren: and the Spirit of the LORD came upon David from that day forward. So Samuel rose up, and went to Ramah" (1 S.16:13).

"The Spirit of the Lord GOD is upon me; because the Lord hath anointed me to preach good tidings unto the meek; he hath sent me to bind up the brokenhearted, to proclaim liberty to the captives, and the opening of the prison to them that are bound" (Is.61:1).

5 (8:14-17) **Forgiveness of Sins—Sins, Forgiveness of—Sin Offering—Offerings, the Sin—Believer, Identification with Christ—Identification, with the Sacrifice of the Old Testament**: the fifth step in ordination is confessing the forgiveness of sins. This Aaron and his sons did through the sacrifice of the Sin Offering. Keep in mind that the sacrifice is a symbol of Jesus Christ, of His sacrificial death upon the cross. Through the sacrifice of the Sin Offering, Aaron and his sons made an emphatic declaration: they needed the constant forgiveness of God. They needed God to continually cleanse them from sin. Moreover, as they launched their ministry, they needed a fresh cleansing from sin, a fresh cleansing from being short of God's glory (Ro.3:23). Note the ritual of the Sin Offering in the Scripture and outline.

OUTLINE	SCRIPTURE	SCRIPTURE	OUTLINE
5. Step 5: Confessing the forgiveness of sins through the Sin Offering (a symbol of Christ) a. Identifying with the sacrifice	14 And he brought the bullock for the sin offering: and Aaron and his sons laid their hands upon the head of the bullock for the sin offering.	sanctified it, to make reconciliation upon it. 16 And he took all the fat that *was* upon the inwards, and the caul *above* the liver, and the two kidneys, and their fat, and Moses burned	atonement (reconciliation) e. Offering certain parts of the sacrifice to God: The fat, liver, kidneys
b. Putting the sacrifice to death c. Placing some blood on the horns of the altar: To purify or set it apart for God's service d. Pouring the remaining blood at the base of the altar: To dedicate the altar for	15 And he slew *it*; and Moses took the blood, and put *it* upon the horns of the altar round about with his finger, and purified the altar, and poured the blood at the bottom of the altar, and	*it* upon the altar. 17 But the bullock, and his hide, his flesh, and his dung, he burnt with fire without the camp; as the LORD commanded Moses.	f. Taking certain parts of the sacrifice outside the camp & burning them: The hide, flesh, & dung (a symbol of Christ's taking away sin)

a. There was the identification with the sacrifice (v.14). Aaron and his sons laid their hands upon the head of the sacrifice. This act symbolized substitution, that the sacrifice was taking their place in death. The condemnation and judgment against sin that was due them was being placed upon the sacrifice.

b. There was the putting of the sacrifice to death (v.15). Death was the penalty for sin; therefore, the sacrifice, the substitute, had to die for their sin.

c. There was the placing of blood on the horns of the altar (v.15). Note why this was done: to purify and cleanse the altar, to set it apart as holy for God's service. The altar had to be holy—set apart in a very special way—because the sacrifice for sin was to be offered upon it, offered up to God as the satisfaction for sin. The sacrifice offered upon the altar paid in full the penalty for sin. The sacrificial offering satisfied God completely and fully, satisfied His justice and judgment.

d. There was the remaining blood at the base of the altar being poured out (v.15). Note why this was done: to consecrate the altar so that atonement (reconciliation) could be made upon it. This will be more fully discussed in the next point (pt.6).

e. There was the offering of the best parts of the sacrifice to God (v.16). This included the fat, the liver, and the kidneys. Note that these were burned upon the altar. The aroma of roasted meat ascended up toward heaven, thereby symbolizing the prayer for the forgiveness of sins ascending up to God. As indicated in other Scripture, God was pleased, and He accepted the sacrifice and prayer. He met the need of the person; in this case, He forgave the sins of the priests. He cleansed them. (See Le.1:9, 13,17; 2:2, 9, 12; 3:5, 16; 4:31; 6:15, 21; 8:21, 28; 17:6; 23:13, 18; 26:31.)

f. There was the taking of certain parts of the sacrifice outside the camp and burning them (v.17). This included the hide, the flesh, and the offal (waste, filth). Remember, this is a symbol of Christ taking away the sins of the world. By this act, the sins of the priests were pictured as being removed, taken off, and taken away from them. A substitute sacrifice died for them and took away their sins.

Thought 1. When dealing with sin, the person being ordained must do two things:

(1) He must make a clear-cut confession that his sins are forgiven, that Jesus Christ has cleansed him from sin.

"**And now why tarriest thou? arise, and be baptized, and wash away thy sins, calling on the name of the Lord**" (Ac.22:16).

"**Husbands, love your wives, even as Christ also loved the church, and gave himself for it; That he might sanctify and cleanse it with the washing of water by the word**" (Ep.5:25-26).

"**Who gave himself for our sins, that he might deliver us from this present evil world, according to the will of God and our Father**" (Ga.1:4).

"**How much more shall the blood of Christ, who through the eternal Spirit offered himself without spot to God, purge your conscience from dead works to serve the living God?**" (He.9:14).

"**But if we walk in the light, as he is in the light, we have fellowship one with another, and the blood of Jesus Christ his Son cleanseth us from all sin**" (1 Jn.1:7).

"**Iniquities prevail against me: as for our transgressions, thou shalt purge them away**" (Ps.65:3).

"**Come now, and let us reason together, saith the LORD: though your sins be as scarlet, they shall be as white as snow; though they be red like crimson, they shall be as wool**" (Is.1:18).

"**Then will I sprinkle clean water upon you, and ye shall be clean: from all your filthiness, and from all your idols, will I cleanse you**" (Eze.36:25).

(2) He must declare that he stands in constant need of forgiveness and that the sacrifice of Jesus Christ continually cleanses the believer from sin.

"In whom we have redemption through his blood, the forgiveness of sins, according to the riches of his grace" (Ep.1:7).

"And walk in love, as Christ also hath loved us, and hath given himself for us an offering and a sacrifice to God for a sweetsmelling savour" (Ep.5:2).

"If we [continually, Greek] confess our sins, he is faithful and just to forgive us our sins, and to cleanse us from all unrighteousness" (1 Jn.1:9).

"My little children, these things write I unto you, that ye sin not. And if any man sin, we have an advocate with the Father, Jesus Christ the righteous: And he is the propitiation for our sins: and not for ours only, but also for the sins of the whole world" (1 Jn.2:1-2).

"And ye know that he was manifested to take away our sins; and in him is no sin" (1 Jn.3:5).

6 (8:18-21) **Ordination—Atonement—Reconciliation—Offering, Burnt—Burnt Offering—Acceptance**: the sixth step in ordination is basic, the very foundation of life: it is confessing the atonement, that one has been reconciled with God through the atonement of the sacrifice. Remember that atonement means to ransom or deliver through a substitute. The substitute takes the place of the sinner and bears the punishment of God's justice and judgment due the sinner. Through the atonement, a person is set free from sin and its punishment. He is reconciled to God and made acceptable to Him. Aaron and his sons were confessing just this, that they were being set free from sin and its punishment through the substitutionary sacrifice of the Burnt Offering. Remember, the substitutionary sacrifice is a symbol of Christ dying upon the cross as our atonement, paying the price or ransom to set us free from sin and its punishment.

OUTLINE	SCRIPTURE	SCRIPTURE	OUTLINE
6. **Step 6: Confessing the atonement through the Burnt Offering (a symbol of Christ)** a. Identifying with the sacrifice b. Putting the sacrifice to death c. Sprinkling the blood against all sides of the altar d. Offering certain parts of the sacrifice to the LORD	18 And he brought the ram for the burnt offering: and Aaron and his sons laid their hands upon the head of the ram. 19 And he killed *it*; and Moses sprinkled the blood upon the altar round about. 20 And he cut the ram into pieces; and Moses burnt the	head, and the pieces, and the fat. 21 And he washed the inwards and the legs in water; and Moses burnt the whole ram upon the altar: it *was* a burnt sacrifice for a sweet savour, *and* an offering made by fire unto the LORD; as the LORD commanded Moses.	e. Washing & offering the other parts of the sacrifice to the LORD f. The result: The sweet aroma pleased the LORD, was acceptable to Him & made atonement (reconciliation, see Le.1:1-17, esp. 4)

a. They identified with the sacrifice by laying their hands upon its head (v.18).

b. They put the sacrifice to death (v.19).

c. They sprinkled the blood against all sides of the altar, symbolizing that the very place of the sacrifice was made holy by the blood (v.19).

d. They offered certain parts of the sacrifice to the LORD: the head, some other pieces, and the fat (v.20).

e. They washed and offered the other parts of the sacrifice to the LORD, and they burned the whole sacrifice on the altar. By this act, they declared their belief that God accepted the substitute sacrifice...

- as their atonement
- as their ransom
- as their substitute

f. They believed and their belief was rewarded. Note the result: the sweet aroma of the roasting meat ascended up toward heaven, thereby symbolizing that the LORD was pleased. He accepted their belief in the sacrifice and made atonement for them. He counted the substitute sacrifice as their ransom. God set them free from sin and its punishment. He reconciled them to Himself. (See outline and notes—Le.1:1-17, especially 4 for more discussion.)

Thought 1. The person being ordained must confess the atonement, that he has been reconciled with God through the substitute sacrifice of the Lord Jesus Christ. He must confess that Jesus Christ is the atoning sacrifice, the substitute, the ransom, that has set him free from sin and its punishment. He must confess that Jesus Christ has ransomed him to live eternally with God.

"The next day John seeth Jesus coming unto him, and saith, Behold the Lamb of God, which taketh away the sin of the world" (Jn.1:29).

"And not only so, but we also joy in God through our Lord Jesus Christ, by whom we have now received the atonement" (Ro.5:11).

"Neither by the blood of goats and calves, but by his own blood he entered in once into the holy place, having obtained eternal redemption for us. For if the blood of bulls and of goats, and the ashes of an heifer sprinkling the unclean, sanctifieth to the purifying of the flesh: How much more shall the blood of Christ, who through the eternal Spirit offered himself without spot to God, purge your conscience from dead works to serve the living God?" (He.9:12-14).

"For it is not possible that the blood of bulls and of goats should take away sins....But this man, after he had offered one sacrifice for sins for ever, sat down on the right hand of God; From henceforth expecting till his enemies be made his footstool. For by one offering he hath perfected for ever them that are sanctified" (He.10:4, 12-14).

"Forasmuch as ye know that ye were not redeemed with corruptible things, as silver and gold, from your vain conversation received by tradition from your fathers; But with the precious blood of Christ, as of a lamb without blemish and without spot" (1 Pe.1:18-19).

"Who his own self bare our sins in his own body on the tree, that we, being dead to sins, should live unto righteousness: by whose stripes ye were healed" (1 Pe.2:24).

"For Christ also hath once suffered for sins, the just for the unjust, that he might bring us to God, being put to death in the flesh, but quickened by the Spirit" (1 Pe.3:18).

7 (8:22-32) **Dedication—Consecration—Ordination—Offering, Ordination—Commitment**: step seven in ordination is the dedication of all one is and does to God. This is a special ordination offering, a special sacrifice that was to be offered by a person who was being ordained to the ministry of God. Note the ritual of the sacrifice, how it focused upon dedication, the setting apart of one's whole being to God and His service. Note again that the sacrifice symbolizes the sacrifice and death of the Lord Jesus Christ. It is only through Him that a person can approach and dedicate himself to God. God accepts the dedication of a person only if he approaches Him through the blood of the Lord Jesus Christ. First comes cleansing through the blood of the Lord Jesus Christ, then comes the dedication of one's heart and life to the service of God.

OUTLINE	SCRIPTURE	SCRIPTURE	OUTLINE

7. Step 7: Dedicating all that one is & does to God—through the ordination sacrifice (a symbol of Christ)
a. Identifying with the sacrifice
b. Dedicating or setting apart one's whole being to God—through the blood of the sacrifice
  1) Symbolized by blood being placed on Aaron's right ear, thumb, & big toe
  2) Symbolized by blood being placed on Aaron's sons, on their right ears, thumbs, & big toes
c. Dedicating the altar of sacrifice: Symbolized by sprinkling blood against all sides of the altar
d. Offering certain parts of the sacrifice to the LORD
  1) Moses took all the fat, liver, kidneys, & right thigh: On top of these he placed a loaf of bread made without yeast, a cake made with oil, & a wafer
  2) Moses gave all these to Aaron & his sons: To offer a wave offering before the LORD
	22 And he brought the other ram, the ram of consecration: and Aaron and his sons laid their hands upon the head of the ram. 23 And he slew it; and Moses took of the blood of it, and put it upon the tip of Aaron's right ear, and upon the thumb of his right hand, and upon the great toe of his right foot. 24 And he brought Aaron's sons, and Moses put of the blood upon the tip of their right ear, and upon the thumbs of their right hands, and upon the great toes of their right feet: and Moses sprinkled the blood upon the altar round about. 25 And he took the fat, and the rump, and all the fat that was upon the inwards, and the caul above the liver, and the two kidneys, and their fat, and the right shoulder: 26 And out of the basket of unleavened bread, that was before the LORD, he took one unleavened cake, and a cake of oiled bread, and one wafer, and put them on the fat, and upon the right shoulder: 27 And he put all upon Aaron's hands, and upon his sons' hands, and waved them for a wave offering be-	fore the LORD. 28 And Moses took them from off their hands, and burnt them on the altar upon the burnt offering: they were consecrations for a sweet savour: it is an offering made by fire unto the LORD. 29 And Moses took the breast, and waved it for a wave offering before the LORD: for of the ram of consecration it was Moses' part; as the LORD commanded Moses. 30 And Moses took of the anointing oil, and of the blood which was upon the altar, and sprinkled it upon Aaron, and upon his garments, and upon his sons, and upon his sons' garments with him; and sanctified Aaron, and his garments, and his sons, and his sons' garments with him. 31 And Moses said unto Aaron and to his sons, Boil the flesh at the door of the tabernacle of the congregation: and there eat it with the bread that is in the basket of consecrations, as I commanded, saying, Aaron and his sons shall eat it. 32 And that which remaineth of the flesh and of the bread shall ye burn with fire.	3) Moses, as God's mediator, then took all the sacrifices from them & offered them on the altar
			4) The result: The sweet aroma pleased & was acceptable to the LORD
			
			e. Praising & thanking God for His provision: Moses took the breast—his part of the offering—& gave thanks through the wave offering
			
			f. Consummating the ordination dedication: The whole being of Aaron & his sons were set apart by the anointing oil & some blood being sprinkled on them & their clothes
			
			g. Demonstrating the financial support of the ordained priests
			1) Instructed to cook & eat the priest's portion before the people at the entrance of the Tabernacle: Was commanded by God
			2) Instructed to burn up all leftovers

a. There was the identification with the sacrifice. Aaron and his sons laid their hands on the head of the sacrifice (v.22). They were declaring that they were laying their lives as a living sacrifice upon the altar just as the animal was to be sacrificed.

b. There was the dedication or setting apart of one's whole being to God through the blood of the sacrifice (vv.23-24).

  1) This was symbolized by placing blood on Aaron's right ear, thumb, and big toe. His hearing and the work of his hands and the direction of his feet were all sanctified, set apart, and dedicated to the service of God. His ear was set apart to listen and hear the Word of God, to hear and listen only to clean and holy conversation. His thumb or hand was set apart to touch and do only clean and holy things. His big toe or foot was set apart to walk after God and only where good, clean, and holy things were done.

  2) This was also symbolized by placing blood on Aaron's sons, on their right ears, thumbs, and big toes (v.24).

c. There was the dedication of the altar of sacrifice. The dedication was symbolized by the sprinkling of blood against all sides of the altar (v.24).

d. There was the offering of certain parts of the sacrifice to the LORD (vv.25-28).

1) Moses took all the fat, the liver, the kidneys, and the right thigh. On top of these he placed a loaf of bread made without yeast, a cake made with oil, and a wafer (vv.25-26).

2) Moses then gave all these to Aaron and his sons. They were to offer these as a wave offering before the LORD (v.27).

3) Moses, as God's mediator, then took all the sacrifice back from them and offered it on the altar (v.28).

4) The result was wonderful: the sweet aroma of the roasted meat ascended up toward heaven, symbolizing that it pleased the LORD. The dedication of their lives to God was acceptable to Him.

e. There was the praise and thanksgiving to God for His provision. Moses took the breast, the part of the offering that belonged to him, and gave thanks by waving the breast before the LORD as a wave offering (v.29). Note that he did all this in obedience to the LORD's command.

f. There was the consummation of the ordination dedication: Aaron and his sons, their entire beings, were consecrated, set apart by the anointing oil and some blood being sprinkled on them and their clothes (v.30). The symbol shows the close tie between the anointing of God's Spirit and the blood of the sacrifice. There can be no anointing other than through the blood of the sacrifice. First, a person must be cleansed through the blood, then God anoints him.

g. There was the demonstration of financial support for the ordained servants of God (vv.31-32). (See outline and note—Le.7:11-36, pt. 4 for more discussion.) Note that Aaron and his sons were instructed to cook and eat the priests' portion of the sacrifice at the very entrance of the Tabernacle. Note also that this was a direct commandment from God. Why? To give the people an object lesson about tithing, that they were responsible to support the priests in their livelihood. By eating a portion of the sacrifice at the entrance of the Tabernacle, all the people were able to see them partake of the offering. Part of the offering was their support. Note that after the meal they were instructed to burn up all leftovers (v.32). The food was counted holy by God and was not to be eaten by anyone else nor on any other occasion than the ordination service.

Thought 1. The minister of God, yea every believer, is to be totally dedicated to God. He is to set apart his whole being to God.

"I beseech you therefore, brethren, by the mercies of God, that ye present your bodies a living sacrifice, holy, acceptable unto God, which is your reasonable service. And be not conformed to this world: but be ye transformed by the renewing of your mind, that ye may prove what is that good, and acceptable, and perfect, will of God" (Ro.12:1-2).

"Moreover it is required in stewards, that a man be found faithful" (1 Co.4:2).

"Therefore, my beloved brethren, be ye stedfast, unmoveable, always abounding in the work of the Lord, forasmuch as ye know that your labour is not in vain in the Lord" (1 Co.15:58).

"And thou shalt love the LORD thy God with all thine heart, and with all thy soul, and with all thy might" (De.6:5).

"Be not thou one of them that strike hands, or of them that are sureties for debts" (Pr.22:26).

Thought 2. The commitment of a person's right ear, thumb, and big toe is a descriptive picture of just how dedicated a believer must be. It is a lesson not only for ordained servants of God but also for every believer.

(1) The believer is to dedicate and set apart his ears to God: he is to listen and hear only clean and holy conversation.

"And every one that heareth these sayings of mine, and doeth them not, shall be likened unto a foolish man, which built his house upon the sand" (Mt.7:26).

"But blessed are your eyes, for they see: and your ears, for they hear" (Mt.13:16).

"Mine ears hast thou opened" (Ps.40:6).

"The heart of the prudent getteth knowledge; and the ear of the wise seeketh knowledge" (Pr.18:15).

"The hearing ear, and the seeing eye, the LORD hath made even both of them" (Pr.20:12).

"To whom shall I speak, and give warning, that they may hear? behold, their ear is uncircumcised [sinful, unclean], and they cannot hearken: behold, the word of the LORD is unto them a reproach; they have no delight in it" (Je.6:10).

"Son of man, thou dwellest in the midst of a rebellious house, which have eyes to see, and see not; they have ears to hear, and hear not: for they are a rebellious house" (Eze.12:2).

(2) He is to dedicate and set apart his thumb or hand to God: he is to touch and do only that which is clean and holy.

"Labour not for the meat which perisheth, but for that meat which endureth unto everlasting life, which the Son of man shall give unto you: for him hath God the Father sealed" (Jn.6:27).

"Wherefore come out from among them, and be ye separate, saith the Lord, and touch not the unclean *thing;* and I will receive you, And will be a Father unto you, and ye shall be my sons and daughters, saith the Lord Almighty" (2 Co.6:17-18).

"Let him that stole steal no more: but rather let him labour, working with his hands the thing which is good, that he may have to give to him that needeth" (Ep.4:28).

"And whatsoever ye do in word or deed, *do* all in the name of the Lord Jesus, giving thanks to God and the Father by him" (Col.3:17).

"And whatsoever ye do, do *it* heartily, as to the Lord, and not unto men" (Col.3:23).

"Then I looked on all the works that my hands had wrought, and on the labour that I had laboured to do: and, behold, all was vanity and vexation of spirit, and there was no profit under the sun" (Ec.2:11).

"Wherefore do ye spend money for that which is not bread? and your labour for that which satisfieth not? hearken diligently unto me, and eat ye that which is good, and let your soul delight itself in fatness" (Is.55:2).

"Whatsoever thy hand findeth to do, do it with thy might; for there is no work, nor device, nor knowledge, nor wisdom, in the grave, whither thou goest" (Ec.9:10).

(3) He is to dedicate, set apart, his feet to God: he is to walk only where good, clean, and holy things are done.

"This I say then, Walk in the Spirit, and ye shall not fulfil the lust of the flesh....Now the works of the flesh are manifest, which are these; Adultery, fornication, uncleanness, lasciviousness, Idolatry, witchcraft, hatred, variance, emulations, wrath, strife, seditions, heresies, Envyings, murders, drunkenness, revellings, and such like: of the which I tell you before, as I have also told you in time past, that they which do such things shall not inherit the kingdom of God" (Ga.5:16, 19-21).

"I therefore, the prisoner of the Lord, beseech you that ye walk worthy of the vocation wherewith ye are called" (Ep.4:1).

"And walk in love, as Christ also hath loved us, and hath given himself for us an offering and a sacrifice to God for a sweetsmelling savour" (Ep.5:2).

"See then that ye walk circumspectly, not as fools, but as wise" (Ep.5:15).

"But if we walk in the light, as he is in the light, we have fellowship one with another, and the blood of Jesus Christ his Son cleanseth us from all sin" (1 Jn.1:7).

"He that saith he abideth in him ought himself also so to walk, even as he walked" (1 Jn.2:6).

8 (8:33-36) **Warning—Ordination, Warning About—Ordination, Purpose of—Ministry, Duty to Fulfill—Obedience**: step eight of ordination is imperative: the ordained person must know the critical importance of ordination and heed God's warning. Note what God says in the Scripture and outline.

OUTLINE	SCRIPTURE	SCRIPTURE	OUTLINE
8. Step 8: Knowing the critical importance of ordination & heeding God's warning a. Must repeat the service for 7 days (the complete number): A symbol that a person must complete his ministry 1) Is the commandment of God 2) Is for one purpose: To declare that atonement (reconciliation) is essential	33 And ye shall not go out of the door of the tabernacle of the congregation *in* seven days, until the days of your consecration be at an end: for seven days shall he consecrate you. 34 As he hath done this day, *so* the LORD hath commanded to do, to make an atonement for you.	35 Therefore shall ye abide *at* the door of the tabernacle of the congregation day and night seven days, and keep the charge of the LORD, that ye die not: for so I am commanded. 36 So Aaron and his sons did all things which the LORD commanded by the hand of Moses.	b. Must heed God's warning 1) Observe the ordination for seven days: Complete one's ministry 2) Obey God or die: Do all that God requires or die c. The obedience: They obeyed God

a. The ordination service must be repeated for seven days. Remember that seven is the number of completion, of fulfillment, of perfection. This symbolizes that the ordained person must complete his ministry. This is the very commandment of God. Note one other significant fact. The person was ordained for one primary purpose: to declare the truth; the atonement (reconciliation) is an absolute essential (v.34). The blood of the sacrifice made atonement for him personally, and this was declared loudly and clearly through the ordination service. But the implication is that he was to arise and walk forth from the ordination service to declare the glorious message of atonement through the substitute sacrifice. He was to lead people to approach God through the substitute sacrifice of the offerings.

b. The person being ordained must heed God's warning (v.35). He must observe the ordination service for seven days. The truth of their ordination must be driven home to their hearts and lives, driven so deeply that they would never fail to complete their ministry. Note the warning God gave: they must complete the ordination service and obey God, doing all that He requires—or else they would die. The severity of the warning is clearly understood in one fact: approaching God is a serious matter. Approaching God through the blood of the sacrifice is a serious matter, the most serious matter in all the world. Why? Because the blood of the sacrifice pointed toward the blood of God's own Son being shed for the atonement (reconciliation) of the world. The one thing that God most certainly will not tolerate from any creature is the abuse or the trampling underfoot of the blood of His Son. Even more so, God will not tolerate the abuse of His Son by an ordained servant set apart to serve Him. The sacrifices made in the ordination service of Aaron and his sons were important to God, important because they symbolized the sacrifice of His Son.

c. Note their obedience: Aaron and his sons obeyed God and did everything exactly as the LORD commanded (v.36).

Thought 1. The minister must know the great importance of his ordination. It is God Himself who has called the minister to serve Him.

(1) The minister must therefore proclaim the atoning sacrifice of the Lord Jesus Christ.

"Go ye therefore, and teach all nations, baptizing them in the name of the Father, and of the Son, and of the Holy Ghost: Teaching them to observe all things whatsoever I have commanded you: and, lo, I am with you alway, even unto the end of the world. Amen" (Mt.28:19-20).

"And he said unto them, Go ye into all the world, and preach the gospel to every creature" (Mk.16:15).

"The next day John seeth Jesus coming unto him, and saith, Behold the Lamb of God, which taketh away the sin of the world" (Jn.1:29).

"Purge out therefore the old leaven, that ye may be a new lump, as ye are unleavened. For even Christ our passover is sacrificed for us" (1 Co.5:7).

"Christ hath redeemed us from the curse of the law, being made a curse for us: for it is written, Cursed is every one that hangeth on a tree" (Ga.3:13).

"But we see Jesus, who was made a little lower than the angels for the suffering of death, crowned with glory and honour; that he by the grace of God should taste death for every man" (He.2:9).

"So Christ was once offered to bear the sins of many; and unto them that look for him shall he appear the second time without sin unto salvation" (He.9:28).

"Forasmuch as ye know that ye were not redeemed with corruptible things, as silver and gold, from your vain conversation received by tradition from your fathers; But with the precious blood of Christ, as of a lamb without blemish and without spot" (1 Pe.1:18-19).

"For Christ also hath once suffered for sins, the just for the unjust, that he might bring us to God, being put to death in the flesh, but quickened by the Spirit" (1 Pe.3:18).

"But he was wounded for our transgressions, he was bruised for our iniquities: the chastisement of our peace was upon him; and with his stripes we are healed" (Is.53:5).

(2) The minister must heed God's warning: he must complete and fulfill his ministry.

"Jesus saith unto them, My meat is to do the will of him that sent me, and to finish his work" (Jn.4:34).

"I have glorified thee on the earth: I have finished the work which thou gavest me to do" (Jn.17:4).

"When Jesus therefore had received the vinegar, he said, It is finished: and he bowed his head, and gave up the ghost" (Jn.19:30).

"But none of these things move me, neither count I my life dear unto myself, so that I might finish my course with joy, and the ministry, which I have received of the Lord Jesus, to testify the gospel of the grace of God" (Ac.20:24).

"Take heed to the ministry which thou hast received in the Lord, that thou fulfil it" (Col.4:17).

"For I am now ready to be offered, and the time of my departure is at hand. I have fought a good fight, I have finished my course, I have kept the faith" (2 Ti.4:6-7).

(3) The minister—yea all persons—must know that God will not tolerate the abuse of His Son nor the trampling underfoot of His blood.

"For if we sin wilfully after that we have received the knowledge of the truth, there remaineth no more sacrifice for sins, But a certain fearful looking for of judgment and fiery indignation, which shall devour the adversaries" (He.10:26-27).

"Cry aloud, spare not, lift up thy voice like a trumpet, and show my people their transgression, and the house of Jacob their sins" (Is.58:1).

"When I say unto the wicked, Thou shalt surely die; and thou givest him not warning, nor speakest to warn the wicked from his wicked way, to save his life; the same wicked man shall die in his iniquity; but his blood will I require at thine hand" (Eze.3:18).

"Nevertheless, if thou warn the wicked of his way to turn from it; if he do not turn from his way, he shall die in his iniquity; but thou hast delivered thy soul" (Eze.33:9).

"Of how much sorer punishment, suppose ye, shall he be thought worthy, who hath trodden under foot the Son of God, and hath counted the blood of the covenant, wherewith he was sanctified, an unholy thing, and hath done despite unto the Spirit of grace?" (He.10:29).

"For we must all appear before the judgment seat of Christ; that every one may receive the things done in his body, according to that he hath done, whether it be good or bad" (2 Co.5:10).

"And if ye call on the Father, who without respect of persons judgeth according to every man's work, pass the time of your sojourning here in fear" (1 Pe.1:17).

"In the day when God shall judge the secrets of men by Jesus Christ according to my gospel" (Ro.2:16).

TYPES, SYMBOLS, AND PICTURES
Leviticus 8:1-36

Historical Term	Type or Picture (Scriptural Basis for Each)	Life Application for Today's Believer	Biblical Application
Washing in Water Le.8:6; 11:25	*Washing in water is a symbol of the need to be spiritually cleansed.* **"And Moses brought Aaron and his sons, and washed them with water" (Le.8:6).**	No person can cleanse himself, not spiritually, not from sin. Only God's mediator, Jesus Christ, can wash and cleanse a person spiritually. This He does through the blood of His cross.	***"And now why tarriest thou? arise, and be baptized, and wash away thy sins, calling on the name of the Lord" (Ac.22:16).*** ***"In whom we have redemption through his blood, the forgiveness of sins, according to the riches of his grace" (Ep.1:7).*** ***"How much more shall the blood of Christ, who through the eternal Spirit offered himself without spot to God, purge your conscience from dead works to serve the living God?" (He.9:14).***
The Putting On of the High Priest's Special Clothing Le.8:7-9	*The High Priest's Special Clothing is a symbol of Christ's righteousness and of bringing dignity and honor to the name of God. Remember: the High Priest symbolized the High Priesthood of Jesus Christ; and the clothing symbolized the righteousness of Jesus Christ.* **"And he put upon him the coat, and girded him with the girdle, and clothed him with the robe, and put the ephod upon him, and he girded him with the curious girdle of the ephod, and bound *it* unto him therewith. And he put the breastplate upon him: also he put in the breastplate the Urim and the Thummim. And he put the mitre upon his head; also upon the mitre, *even* upon his forefront, did he put the golden plate, the holy crown; as the LORD commanded Moses" (Le.8:7-9).**	A person must put on and be covered with the righteousness of Jesus Christ in order to be acceptable to God.	***"For he hath made him to be sin for us, who knew no sin; that we might be made the righteousness of God in him" (2 Co.5:21).*** ***"Even as Abraham believed God, and it was accounted to him for righteousness" (Ga.3:6).*** ***"And be found in him, not having mine own righteousness, which is of the law, but that which is through the faith of Christ, the righteousness which is of God by faith" (Ph.3:9).*** ***"And he believed in the LORD; and he counted it to him for righteousness" (Ge.15:6).***
The Linen Tunic Le.8:7	*Linen is symbolic of righteousness. The linen tunic (a long, coat-like garment that essentially covered the whole body) is symbolic of putting on God's righteousness.* **"And he put upon him the coat [tunic], and girded him with the girdle, and clothed him with the robe, and put the ephod upon him, and he girded him with the curious girdle**	What the Linen Tunic taught: If a person wishes to live in God's presence, he must put on the righteousness of Christ. A person is depraved and totally inadequate, having no righteousness of his own. Therefore, a person cannot walk before God or serve God unless he puts on the righteousness of Christ.	***"For he hath made him to be sin for us, who knew no sin; that we might be made the righteousness of God in him" (2 Co.5:21).*** ***"I put on righteousness, and it clothed me: my judgment was as a robe and a diadem" (Jb.29:14).*** ***"I will greatly rejoice in the LORD, my soul shall be joyful in my God; for he hath clothed me with the garments of salvation, he hath covered me with the***

TYPES, SYMBOLS, AND PICTURES
Leviticus 8:1-36

Historical Term	Type or Picture (Scriptural Basis for Each)	Life Application for Today's Believer	Biblical Application
	of the ephod, and bound *it* unto him therewith" (Le.8:7).		*robe of righteousness, as a bridegroom decketh himself with ornaments, and as a bride adorneth herself with her jewels"* (Is.61:10; see 1 Co.1:30).
The Sash (Le.8:7)	The multi-colored sash of fine linen is symbolic of truth, the truth of God's Word. It is comparable to the belt of truth in the armor of God that the believer is to put on (Ep.6:14). The Word of God enlightens and wraps together everything in the believer's spiritual wardrobe. **"And he put upon him the coat [tunic], and girded him with the girdle, and clothed him with the robe, and put the ephod upon him, and he girded him with the curious girdle of the ephod, and bound *it* unto him therewith"** (Le.8:7).	What the Sash taught: 1. Jesus Christ is the Truth, the Living Word of God. It is the Word of God that holds everything together. 2. A person needs help and support in life because he does not have the strength to conquer the terrible trials and temptations of life, the trials and temptations that drag him ever downward toward the grave and eternal separation from God. Only the Word of God can strengthen and hold us together as we walk through life.	*"Jesus saith unto him, I am the way, the truth, and the life: no man cometh unto the Father, but by me"* (Jn.14:6). *"Stand therefore, having your loins girt about with truth, and having on the breastplate of righteousness"* (Ep.6:14). *"Sanctify them through thy truth: thy word is truth"* (Jn.17:17). *"All scripture is given by inspiration of God, and is profitable for doctrine, for reproof, for correction, for instruction in righteousness"* (2 Ti.3:16). *"For the word of God is quick, and powerful, and sharper than any twoedged sword, piercing even to the dividing asunder of soul and spirit, and of the joints and marrow, and is a discerner of the thoughts and intents of the heart"* (He.4:12).
The Robe of the Ephod Le.8:7	The Robe of the Ephod was worn by the High Priest as he entered through the Veil and ministered to the LORD in the Sanctuary. It had small bells in the shape of pomegranates sewed to its hem. The Robe of the Ephod is symbolic of two things: 1. The Robe of the Ephod symbolized the sounding forth of the intercessory ministry of the High Priest 2. The Robe of the Ephod symbolized the sounding forth of a wonderful fact, that God accepted the offering of the High Priest, that he had not been stricken dead.	What the Robe of the Ephod taught: 1. Jesus Christ is our Great High Priest who sounds forth the glorious truth that His intercession never ends, never stops. This is a strong lesson for us: we too must pray without ceasing. We must become intercessors—great intercessors—for our loved ones and for the lost of the world. 2. We should rejoice in the fact that the sacrifice and intercessory ministry of Jesus Christ is perfectly acceptable to God the Father. Once we have been	*"But this man, because he continueth ever, hath an unchangeable priesthood. Wherefore he is able also to save them to the uttermost that come unto God by him, seeing he ever liveth to make intercession for them"* (He.7:24-25). *"The next day John seeth Jesus coming unto him, and saith, Behold the Lamb of God, which taketh away the sin of the world"* (Jn.1:29). *"Wherefore God also hath highly exalted him, and given him a name which is above every name"* (Phil. 2:9). *"Who is he that condemneth? It is Christ that died, yea rather, that is risen again, who is even at the right hand of God, who also maketh intercession for us"* (Ro.8:34). *"Therefore will I divide him a portion with the*

TYPES, SYMBOLS, AND PICTURES
Leviticus 8:1-36

Historical Term	Type or Picture (Scriptural Basis for Each)	Life Application for Today's Believer	Biblical Application
	"And he put upon him the coat [tunic], and girded him with the girdle, and clothed him with the robe, and put the ephod upon him, and he girded him with the curious girdle of the ephod, and bound *it* unto him therewith" (Le.8:7).	saved, we no longer have to worry about being condemned to death.	*great, and he shall divide the spoil with the strong; because he hath poured out his soul unto death: and he was numbered with the transgressors; and he bare the sin of many, and made intercession for the transgressors" (Is.53:12).*
The Ephod Le.8:7	*Remember, the Ephod was a linen garment worn on the chest by the High Priest. It had twelve stones sewn on it that represented God's people, the twelve tribes of Israel. The Ephod symbolized that the High Priest represented and carried the names of God's people before the LORD.* "And he put upon him the coat [tunic], and girded him with the girdle, and clothed him with the robe, and put the ephod upon him, and he girded him with the curious girdle of the ephod, and bound *it* unto him therewith" (Le.8:7).	What the Ephod taught: 1. Man cannot represent himself before God because he is a sinner. Man needs an Advocate, an Intercessor, a Mediator, a Savior who can approach God legally and perfectly. Man cannot do any of this; therefore, man needs someone who can. 2. Jesus Christ is the One who represents and carries the names of believers before the Father. No matter what our burden, no matter how terrifying, we can cast it upon Christ. He will bring us to God. He will relieve us, strengthen us, and give us rest and peace from the burden.	*"Come unto me, all ye that labour and are heavy laden, and I will give you rest. Take my yoke upon you, and learn of me; for I am meek and lowly in heart: and ye shall find rest unto your souls. For my yoke is easy, and my burden is light" (Mt.11:28-30).* *"Who is he that condemneth? It is Christ that died, yea rather, that is risen again, who is even at the right hand of God, who also maketh intercession for us" (Ro.8:34).* *"Casting all your care upon him; for he careth for you" (1 Pe.5:7).* *"Wherefore in all things it behoved him to be made like unto his brethren, that he might be a merciful and faithful high priest in things pertaining to God, to make reconciliation for the sins of the people. For in that he himself hath suffered being tempted, he is able to succour them that are tempted" (He.2:17-18).*
The Urim and Thummim Le.8:8	*The Urim and Thummim were two stones that symbolized the special revelation or guidance that God gave the High Priest. Imagine the scene as the High Priest entered into the Holy Place. The Urim and Thummim reminded him and the people that God would speak and give His direction to His people. The High Priest was there on behalf of the people of God; therefore, God would hear and answer him. God would make His will and direction known to the High Priest. How? God would speak and move upon the heart of the High Priest.*	We are to pray and seek God's face for the needs of others. The world reels under the weight of suffering and evil, of death and judgment to come. The only hope is God. God's help is needed. We must therefore seek His face, seek Him day and night for the needs of people.	*"But if from thence thou shalt seek the LORD thy God, thou shalt find him, if thou seek him with all thy heart and with all thy soul" (De.4:29).* *"Seek the LORD and his strength, seek his face continually" (1 Chr.16:11).* *"He shall call upon me, and I will answer him: I will be with him in trouble; I will deliver him, and honour him" (Ps.91:15).* *"Seek ye the LORD while he may be found, call ye upon him while he is near" (Is.55:6).* *"And it shall come to pass, that before they call, I will answer; and while*

TYPES, SYMBOLS, AND PICTURES
Leviticus 8:1-36

Historical Term	Type or Picture (Scriptural Basis for Each)	Life Application for Today's Believer	Biblical Application
	"And he put the breast-plate upon him: also he put in the breastplate the Urim and the Thummim" (Le.8:8).		*they are yet speaking, I will hear" (Is.65:24; see Je.33:3; Lu.11:9).*
The Linen Turban Le.8:9	*Linen is symbolic of righteousness. The mind and thoughts of the High Priest had to be subjected to God and His righteousness. The linen turban (a headdress cloth or cap) is symbolic of putting on God's righteousness.* "And he put the mitre [turban] upon his head; also upon the mitre [turban], *even upon his forefront,* did he put the golden plate, the holy crown; as the LORD commanded Moses" (Le.8:9).	What the Linen Headband taught: The believer must willingly submit his mind and will, his thoughts and agenda to God. He must subject every thought, every idea, every agenda to Christ.	*"Casting down imaginations, and every high thing that exalteth itself against the knowledge of God, and bringing into captivity every thought to the obedience of Christ;" (2 Co. 10:5)* *"I will greatly rejoice in the LORD, my soul shall be joyful in my God; for he hath clothed me with the garments of salvation, he hath covered me with the robe of righteousness, as a bridegroom decketh himself with ornaments, and as a bride adorneth herself with her jewels" (Is.61:10).* *"But of him are ye in Christ Jesus, who of God is made unto us wisdom, and righteousness, and sanctification, and redemption" (1 Co.1:30).*
The Gold Plate [Medallion] or Sacred Diadem Le.8:9	*The gold plate (medallion) or sacred diadem was attached with a blue ribbon to the head of the High Priest and was the crowning piece of the High Priest's wardrobe. The words "HOLINESS TO THE LORD" were written upon the medallion. The Gold Medallion...* • *symbolized that the High Priest bore the guilt for the shortcomings of the people* • *symbolized that the people must seek the acceptance of a holy God* "And he put the mitre upon his head; also upon the mitre, *even upon his fore-*	What the Gold Plate or Medallion taught: 1. We are ever so short of the glory and holiness of God. We desperately need Someone to bear the guilt for our shortcoming. That person is Jesus Christ. It is Jesus Christ who bore the shortcomings and errors of the people. A person needs a perfect sacrifice, and that Sacrifice is Jesus Christ, who died upon the cross for our sins. 2. We are guilty of sin. Our sin indicts us and places us at the mercy of a holy and righteous Judge. God beckons each person to come to Him based upon the merit of Christ and His righteousness. We must	*"Who gave himself for us, that he might redeem us from all iniquity, and purify unto himself a peculiar people, zealous of good works" (Tit.2:14).* *"For Christ also hath once suffered for sins, the just for the unjust, that he might bring us to God, being put to death in the flesh, but quickened by the Spirit" (1 Pe.3:18).* *"Jesus saith unto him, I am the way, the truth, and the life: no man cometh unto the Father, but by me" (Jn.14:6).* *"Neither is there salvation in any other: for there is none other name under heaven given among men,*

TYPES, SYMBOLS, AND PICTURES
Leviticus 8:1-36

Historical Term	Type or Picture (Scriptural Basis for Each)	Life Application for Today's Believer	Biblical Application
	front, did he put the golden plate [medallion], the holy crown; as the LORD commanded Moses" (Le.8:9).	seek the approval of God by approaching God through Christ and Christ alone.	whereby we must be saved" (Ac.4:12).
The Altar of Burnt Offering Anointed with Oil Seven Times Le.8:10-13	The altar was anointed with oil seven times to symbolize that a complete, full, and perfect sacrifice was being made for man's atonement (reconciliation) and redemption. Throughout the Bible, the number seven symbolizes the idea of completion, fullness, and perfection. "And he sprinkled thereof upon the altar seven times, and anointed the altar and all his vessels, both the laver and his foot, to sanctify them" (Le.8:11).	Why was the altar anointed seven times? Remember, the altar was where the atoning sacrifice was offered, the place where the payment or ransom for sin was made. The sacrifice or payment for sin was full and complete. It provided a perfect redemption for man.	"Wherefore he is able also to save them to the uttermost that come unto God by him, seeing he ever liveth to make intercession for them" (He.7:25). "For it became him, for whom are all things, and by whom are all things, in bringing many sons unto glory, to make the captain of their salvation perfect through sufferings" (He.2:10). "And being made perfect, he became the author of eternal salvation unto all them that obey him" (He.5:9). "But ye shall receive power, after that the Holy Ghost is come upon you: and ye shall be witnesses unto me both in Jerusalem, and in all Judaea, and in Samaria, and unto the uttermost part of the earth" (Ac.1:8).
Anointing Aaron (the High Priest) with Oil Le.8:10-13	The anointing with oil is a symbol of Aaron being dedicated or consecrated by the Holy Spirit. "And he poured of the anointing oil upon Aaron's head, and anointed him, to sanctify him" (Le.8:12).	A person being ordained to the ministry must be anointed by the Spirit of God. He must be called by God and led to the point of dedication and consecration to God. The person must be totally dedicated to the service of God through the presence and power of the Holy Spirit.	"But ye shall receive power, after that the Holy Ghost is come upon you: and ye shall be witnesses unto me both in Jerusalem, and in all Judaea, and in Samaria, and unto the uttermost part of the earth" (Ac.1:8; see Lu.9:23). "And when they had prayed, the place was shaken where they were assembled together; and they were all filled with the Holy Ghost, and they spake the word of God with boldness" (Ac.4:31; see Ac.13:2; Ro.8:14).
The Taking of Certain Parts of the Sin Offering Outside the Camp and Burning Them. This Included the Hide, the Flesh, and the Offal (Waste, Filth). Le.8:17	This is a symbol of Christ taking away the sins of the world. By this act, the sins of the priests were pictured as being removed, taken off, and taken away from them. A substitute sacrifice died for them and took away their sins. "But the bullock, and his hide, his flesh, and his dung, he burnt with fire without the camp; as the LORD commanded Moses" (Le.8:17).	When a person believes or identifies with the sacrifice of Jesus Christ, his sins… • are removed • are taken off • are taken away from him	"And now why tarriest thou? arise, and be baptized, and wash away thy sins, calling on the name of the Lord" (Ac.22:16). "Who gave himself for our sins, that he might deliver us from this present evil world, according to the will of God and our Father" (Ga.1:4; see He.9:14; 1 Jn.1:7).

TYPES, SYMBOLS, AND PICTURES
Leviticus 8:1-36

Historical Term	Type or Picture (Scriptural Basis for Each)	Life Application for Today's Believer	Biblical Application
The Ordination Offering Le.8:22-32	*The Ordination Offering symbolized the sacrifice and death of the Lord Jesus Christ. Through the Ordination Offering, God accepted a person's dedication to God through the blood of the substitute sacrifice.* **"And Moses took of the anointing oil, and of the blood which** *was* **upon the altar, and sprinkled** *it* **upon Aaron,** *and* **upon his garments, and upon his sons, and upon his sons' garments with him; and sanctified Aaron,** *and* **his garments, and his sons, and his sons' garments with him" (Le.8:30).**	It is Christ who challenges us to dedicate all that we are and do to God.	*"I beseech you therefore, brethren, by the mercies of God, that ye present your bodies a living sacrifice, holy, acceptable unto God, which is your reasonable service. And be not conformed to this world: but be ye transformed by the renewing of your mind, that ye may prove what is that good, and acceptable, and perfect, will of God"* (Ro.12:1-2). *"Therefore, my beloved brethren, be ye stedfast, unmoveable, always abounding in the work of the Lord, forasmuch as ye know that your labour is not in vain in the Lord"* (1 Co.15:58).
The Dedication or Setting Apart of One's Whole Being to God Through the Blood of the Sacrifice Le.8:23-24	*The Dedication was symbolized in two ways:* 1. *It was symbolized by placing blood on Aaron's right ear, thumb, and big toe. His hearing and the work of his hands and the direction of his feet were all sanctified, set apart, and dedicated to the service of God. His ear was set apart to listen and hear the Word of God, to hear and listen only to clean and holy conversation. His thumb or hand was set apart to touch and do only clean and holy things. His big toe or foot was set apart to walk after God and only where good, clean, and holy things were done.* 2. *It was also symbolized by placing blood on Aaron's sons, on their right ears, thumbs, and big toes.* **"And he slew** *it;* **and Moses took of the blood of it, and put** *it* **upon the tip of Aaron's right ear, and upon the thumb of his right hand, and upon the great toe of his right foot. And he brought Aaron's sons, and Moses put of the blood upon the tip of their right ear, and upon the thumbs of their right hands, and upon the great toes of their right feet: and**	The commitment of a person's right ear, thumb, and big toe is a descriptive picture of just how dedicated a believer must be. It is a lesson not only for ordained servants of God but also for every believer. 1. The believer is to dedicate and set apart his ears to God: he is to listen and hear only clean and holy conversation. 2. He is to dedicate and set apart his thumb or hand to God: he is to touch and do only that which is clean and holy. 3. He is to dedicate and set apart his feet to God: he is to walk only where good, clean, and holy things are done.	*"But blessed are your eyes, for they see: and your ears, for they hear"* (Mt.13:16). *"The heart of the prudent getteth knowledge; and the ear of the wise seeketh knowledge"* (Pr.18:15). *"And every one that heareth these sayings of mine, and doeth them not, shall be likened unto a foolish man, which built his house upon the sand"* (Mt.7:26). *"Labour not for the meat which perisheth, but for that meat which endureth unto everlasting life, which the Son of man shall give unto you: for him hath God the Father sealed"* (Jn.6:27). *"This I say then, Walk in the Spirit, and ye shall not fulfil the lust of the flesh....Now the works of the flesh are manifest, which are these; Adultery, fornication, uncleanness, lasciviousness, Idolatry, witchcraft, hatred, variance, emulations, wrath, strife, seditions, heresies, Envyings, murders, drunkenness, revellings, and such like: of the which I tell you before, as I have also told you in time past, that they which do such things shall not inherit the kingdom of God"* (Ga. 5:16, 19-21).

TYPES, SYMBOLS, AND PICTURES
Leviticus 8:1-36

Historical Term	Type or Picture (Scriptural Basis for Each)	Life Application for Today's Believer	Biblical Application
	Moses sprinkled the blood upon the altar round about" (Le.8:23-24).		
The Dedication of the Altar of Sacrifice During the Ordination Offering Le.8:24	*This is a picture of dedication. The dedication of the altar of sacrifice was symbolized by the sprinkling of blood against all sides of the altar.* **"And he brought Aaron's sons, and Moses put of the blood upon the tip of their right ear, and upon the thumbs of their right hands, and upon the great toes of their right feet: and Moses sprinkled the blood upon the altar round about" (Le.8:24).**	The minister of God, yea every believer, is to be totally dedicated to God. He is to set apart his whole being to God.	*"I beseech you therefore, brethren, by the mercies of God, that ye present your bodies a living sacrifice, holy, acceptable unto God, which is your reasonable service. And be not conformed to this world: but be ye transformed by the renewing of your mind, that ye may prove what is that good, and acceptable, and perfect, will of God" (Ro.12:1-2).* *"Therefore, my beloved brethren, be ye stedfast, unmoveable, always abounding in the work of the Lord, forasmuch as ye know that your labour is not in vain in the Lord" (1 Co.15:58).* *"And thou shalt love the LORD thy God with all thine heart, and with all thy soul, and with all thy might" (De.6:5).*
The Sweet Aroma of the Roasted Meat of the Ordination Offering Ascended Toward Heaven Le.8:28	*The sweet aroma is a symbol of pleasing the LORD. The dedication of the priest's lives to God was acceptable to Him.* **"And Moses took them from off their hands, and burnt them on the altar upon the burnt offering: they were consecrations for a sweet savour: it is an offering made by fire unto the LORD" (Le.8:28).**	It must be the goal of every believer to have a life that pleases the LORD. How does a believer please the LORD? By obeying Him, by dedicating his life to the LORD and doing everything He says.	*"My son, give me thine heart, and let thine eyes observe my ways" (Pr.23:26).* *"This book of the law shall not depart out of thy mouth; but thou shalt meditate therein day and night, that thou mayest observe to do according to all that is written therein: for then thou shalt make thy way prosperous, and then thou shalt have good success" (Jos.1:8).* *"Not every one that saith unto me, Lord, Lord, shall enter into the kingdom of heaven; but he that doeth the will of my Father which is in heaven" (Mt.7:21).*
The Ordination Service Repeated for Seven Days Le.8:33	*The ordination service repeated for seven days symbolizes that the ordained person must complete his ministry. This is the very commandment of God. Remember that seven is the number of completion, of fulfillment, of perfection.* **"And ye shall not go out of the door of the tabernacle of the congregation in seven days, until the days of your consecration be at an end: for seven days shall he consecrate you" (Le.8:33).**	Whatever we do for God, we must do our best, we must complete and finish it. Far too many people have not offered God their best nor have they completed what they started. The charge is clear: we must do our very best for God, and we must finish the task, complete it to the fullest.	*"Jesus saith unto them, My meat is to do the will of him that sent me, and to finish his work" (Jn.4:34).* *"I have glorified thee on the earth: I have finished the work which thou gavest me to do" (Jn.17:4).* *"When Jesus therefore had received the vinegar, he said, It is finished: and he bowed his head, and gave up the ghost" (Jn.19:30).* *"Take heed to the ministry which thou hast received in the Lord, that thou fulfil it" (Col.4:17).*

CHAPTER 9

B. The Work & Ministry of the Ordained Priest (Minister): Showing the People How to Become Acceptable to God, 9:1-24

And it came to pass on the eighth day, *that* Moses called Aaron and his sons, and the elders of Israel;

2 And he said unto Aaron, Take thee a young calf for a sin offering, and a ram for a burnt offering, without blemish, and offer *them* before the LORD.

3 And unto the children of Israel thou shalt speak, saying, Take ye a kid of the goats for a sin offering; and a calf and a lamb, *both* of the first year, without blemish, for a burnt offering;

4 Also a bullock and a ram for peace offerings, to sacrifice before the LORD; and a meat offering mingled with oil: for to day the LORD will appear unto you.

5 And they brought *that* which Moses commanded before the tabernacle of the congregation: and all the congregation drew near and stood before the LORD.

6 And Moses said, This *is* the thing which the LORD commanded that ye should do: and the glory of the LORD shall appear unto you.

7 And Moses said unto Aaron, Go unto the altar, and offer thy sin offering, and thy burnt offering, and make an atonement for thyself, and for the people: and offer the offering of the people, and make an atonement for them; as the LORD commanded.

8 Aaron therefore went unto the altar, and slew the calf of the sin offering, which *was* for himself.

9 And the sons of Aaron brought the blood unto him: and he dipped his finger in the blood, and put *it* upon the horns of the altar, and poured out the blood at the bottom of the altar:

10 But the fat, and the kidneys, and the caul above the liver of the sin offering, he burnt upon the altar; as the LORD commanded Moses.

11 And the flesh and the hide he burnt with fire without the camp.

12 And he slew the burnt offering; and Aaron's sons presented unto him the blood, which he sprinkled round about upon the altar.

13 And they presented the burnt offering unto him, with the pieces thereof, and the head: and he burnt *them* upon the altar.

14 And he did wash the inwards and the legs, and burnt *them* upon the burnt offering on the altar.

15 And he brought the people's offering, and took the goat, which *was* the sin offering for the people, and slew it, and offered it for sin, as the first.

16 And he brought the burnt offering, and offered it according to the manner.

17 And he brought the meat offering, and took an handful thereof, and burnt *it* upon the altar, beside the burnt sacrifice of the morning.

18 He slew also the bullock and the ram *for* a sacrifice of peace offerings, which *was* for the people: and Aaron's sons presented unto him the blood, which he sprinkled upon the altar round about,

19 And the fat of the bullock and of the ram, the rump, and that which covereth *the inwards*, and the kidneys, and the caul *above* the liver:

20 And they put the fat upon the breasts, and he burnt the fat upon the altar:

21 And the breasts and the right shoulder Aaron waved *for* a wave offering before the Lord; as Moses commanded.

22 And Aaron lifted up his hand toward the people, and blessed them, and came down from offering of the sin offering, and the burnt offering, and peace offerings.

23 And Moses and Aaron went into the tabernacle of the congregation, and came out, and blessed the people: and the glory of the LORD appeared unto all the

---

1. The challenge to the people: Prepare to meet God

a. The priests were to prepare to approach God
   1) Through the Sin Offering: Seeking forgiveness
   2) Through the Burnt Offering: Seeking atonement, reconciliation with God

b. The people were to prepare to meet God
   1) Through the Sin Offering: Seeking forgiveness
   2) Through the Burnt Offering: Seeking atonement, reconciliation
   3) Through the Fellowship Offering: Seeking to grow in fellowship with God
   4) Through the Grain Offering: Showing one's devotion

c. The purpose: That God might reveal Himself

d. The obedience of everyone
   1) They took all the items to the Tabernacle
   2) They all (3-4 million) came as near as they could & stood before the LORD

e. The preparation & purpose reemphasized: This is the command of God Himself—the people must prepare to meet God so that He might reveal His glory

2. The personal testimony: Aaron first sought God for himself

a. He was given this charge by God's mediator, Moses
   1) He was to seek God first for himself—through the sacrifice
   2) He was then to lead the people to seek God—through the sacrifice

b. He had to come for the forgiveness of sin through the sacrifice of the Sin Offering
   1) Put the sacrifice to death
   2) Put some blood on the horns of the altar
   3) Poured out the remaining blood at the base of the altar
   4) Offered the best parts of the sacrifice to the LORD:

The fat, kidneys, & liver

   5) Burned the flesh & hide outside the camp

c. He had to come for reconciliation—through the atonement, the sacrifice of the Burnt Offering
   1) Put the sacrifice to death
   2) Sprinkled blood on the altar
   3) Offered the sacrifice piece by piece, including the head

   4) Washed the inner parts & legs, then offered them

3. The proclamation to the people: They must seek God—must prepare to meet God

a. Must seek forgiveness of sin—through the Sin Offering

b. Must seek the atonement (reconciliation) through the sacrifice of the Burnt Offering

c. Must offer thanksgiving to God for the atonement & for their livelihood, dedicating their lives to God through the Grain Offering

d. Must grow in peace & fellowship with God—through the sacrifice of the Fellowship or Peace Offering
   1) Put the sacrifice to death
   2) Sprinkled blood on the altar
   3) Laid the fat, kidneys, & liver on the breasts; then he offered the fat to God

   4) Gave a wave offering of thanksgiving to the LORD: Waved the breast & right thigh

4. The blessing pronounced upon the people & the LORD's glorious presence

a. The pronouncement of the blessing
   1) He gave the blessing after leading the people to approach God through the sacrifice
   2) He then stepped down
   3) The special prayer for the people: Moses & Aaron went into the Tabernacle (to pray)

b. The blessing again pronounced

c. The result

1) The LORD appeared: Miraculous fire shot out from the presence of the LORD & consumed the sacrifices burning on the altar 2) The people worshipped the LORD: Shouted for joy & fell down upon the ground in fear	people. 24 And there came a fire out from before the LORD, and consumed upon the altar the burnt offering and the fat: *which* when all the people saw, they shouted, and fell on their faces.

DIVISION II

THE WAY TO BECOME ACCEPTABLE TO GOD (PART 2): BY THE PRIESTHOOD, A PERFECT MEDIATOR, 8:1–10:20

B. **The Work and Ministry of the Ordained Priest (Minister): Showing People How to Become Acceptable to God, 9:1-24**

(9:1-24) Introduction—Priest—Minister, Duty of—Minister, Ministry of—Minister, First Worship Service—Worship, Service of—Tabernacle, First Worship Service in: What should be the first message preached to a church? Preached by a new minister? Preached by a newly ordained minister? What should be the focus of a worship service? The theme that runs throughout the message of a minister or the lesson of a teacher? This passage tells us.

Remember what had just happened. The priests, Aaron and his four sons, had just been ordained to serve as the ministers to God's people. The ordination service had lasted for seven days. Now, the moment for which Aaron and his sons had longed was here: the ordained priests were ready to conduct their very first worship service. Imagine their apprehension. But in the midst of their apprehension, imagine their joy and expectation, their gratitude and thankfulness to God.

Picture the people also. We will see in just a moment that everyone—all two to four million of the Israelites—surrounded the Tabernacle (see note, pt.4—Ex.12:34-41). They were all eager to worship the LORD, being filled with excitement and expectation.

What a day it must have been:

⇒ The people now had priests, ministers of God, who would intercede with God for them.
⇒ The people were now to share in the very first worship service to be held in their worship center, the Tabernacle.
⇒ The priests, newly ordained, were to conduct their very first worship service for the people.

What would the priests do? What would be the focus of their message? What would be the order of service? How well would the service flow? Imagine the questions flowing through the minds of the people—all two to four million of them. This is the subject of this chapter: *The Work and Ministry of the Ordained Priest (Minister): Showing People How to Become Acceptable to God*, 9:1-24.

1. The challenge to the people: prepare to meet God (vv.1-6).
2. The personal testimony: Aaron sought God first for himself (vv.7-14).
3. The proclamation to the people: they must seek God—must prepare to meet God (vv.15-21).
4. The blessing pronounced upon the people and the LORD's glorious presence (vv.22-24).

1 **(9:1-6) Preparation—Presence of God—God, Revelation of—God, Presence of—Challenge**: there was the challenge to the people: prepare to meet God. God had promised to meet His people, to reveal Himself and give them a deep sense of His presence. But before God could reveal Himself, the people had to prepare to meet Him. God does not meet with a people until their hearts and lives are cleansed from sin. No person can experience the fullness of God's presence if there is sin in his life. God grants the fullness of God's presence only to those who are pure and clean, who have been forgiven their sins through the sacrificial substitute. The importance of being cleansed from sin is seen in this one fact: the priests had been offering sacrifice after sacrifice for seven full days during their ordination service. Yet here they were again on the very next day, during their very first worship service, being commanded to offer the substitute sacrifice for themselves. The sinfulness of man and the polluting, contaminating power of sin are seen in this command. The point is clear: the believer must walk in open confession before God. A continual cleansing from sin is needed, the cleansing that comes through the Lamb of God.

OUTLINE	SCRIPTURE	SCRIPTURE	OUTLINE

1. The challenge to the people: Prepare to meet God
a. The priests were to prepare to approach God
  1) Through the Sin Offering: Seeking forgiveness
  2) Through the Burnt Offering: Seeking atonement, reconciliation with God
b. The people were to prepare to meet God
	And it came to pass on the eighth day, *that* Moses called Aaron and his sons, and the elders of Israel;
	2 And he said unto Aaron, Take thee a young calf for a sin offering, and a ram for a burnt offering, without blemish, and offer *them* before the LORD.
	3 And unto the children of Israel thou shalt speak,
		saying, Take ye a kid of the goats for a sin offering; and a calf and a lamb, *both* of the first year, without blemish, for a burnt offering;
		4 Also a bullock and a ram for peace offerings, to sacrifice before the LORD; and a meat offering mingled with oil: for to day the LORD will appear unto you.
			1) Through the Sin Offering: Seeking forgiveness
			2) Through the Burnt Offering: Seeking atonement or reconciliation
			3) Through the Fellowship Offering: Seeking to grow in fellowship with God
			4) Through the Grain Offering: Showing one's devotion
			c. The purpose: That God might reveal Himself

OUTLINE	SCRIPTURE	SCRIPTURE	OUTLINE

d. The obedience of everyone
  1) They took all the items to the Tabernacle
  2) They all (3-4 million) came as near as they could & stood before the LORD
	5 And they brought *that* which Moses commanded before the tabernacle of the congregation: and all the congregation drew near and stood before the LORD.	6 And Moses said, This *is* the thing which the LORD commanded that ye should do: and the glory of the LORD shall appear unto you.	e. The preparation & purpose re-emphasized: This is the command of God Himself—the people must prepare to meet God so that He might reveal His glory

a. The priests were to prepare to meet God:
⇒ through the Sin Offering, seeking forgiveness of sins
⇒ through the Burnt Offering, seeking atonement or reconciliation with God

b. The people were to prepare to meet God (vv.3-4):
⇒ through the Sin Offering, seeking forgiveness of sins
⇒ through the Burnt Offering, seeking atonement or reconciliation with God
⇒ through the Fellowship and Peace Offering, seeking to grow in fellowship and peace with God
⇒ through the Grain Offering, giving thanks to God for the atonement, showing their devotion and dedication to God

c. Note that the purpose for the preparation is stressed: that God might reveal Himself to the people (v.4). God wants His people to experience His presence. He wants to reveal His glory to them. He wants them walking through life victoriously as they march toward the promised land (a symbol of heaven, eternal life). He wants them conquering all the trials and temptations of life. God wants His people to know that He cares and that He is looking after them. He will reveal and manifest Himself to them, giving them the deepest sense of His presence—if they will just prepare to meet God.

d. Note the obedience of everyone (v.5). The people secured all the items and took them to the Tabernacle. Note that they all—all two to four million—came as near as they could to the Tabernacle and stood before the LORD.

e. The preparation and purpose are re-emphasized, and note, this was the very command of God Himself: the people must prepare to meet God so that He might reveal Himself to them.

Thought 1. The minister, in his very first service, must declare this message: prepare to meet God.

"In those days came John the Baptist, preaching in the wilderness of Judaea, And saying, Repent ye: for the kingdom of heaven is at hand. For this is he that was spoken of by the prophet Esaias, saying, The voice of one crying in the wilderness, Prepare ye the way of the Lord, make his paths straight" (Mt.3:1-3).

"He said, I *am* the voice of one crying in the wilderness, Make straight the way of the Lord, as said the prophet Esaias" (Jn.1:23).

"(...behold, now *is* the accepted time; behold, now *is* the day of salvation)" (2 Co.6:2).

"O come, let us worship and bow down: let us kneel before the LORD our maker. For he *is* our God; and we *are* the people of his pasture, and the sheep of his hand. To day if ye will hear his voice" (Ps.95:6-7).

"Thus saith the LORD, the Redeemer of Israel, *and* his Holy One, to him whom man despiseth, to him whom the nation abhorreth, to a servant of rulers, Kings shall see and arise, princes also shall worship, because of the LORD that is faithful, *and* the Holy One of Israel, and he shall choose thee. Thus saith the LORD, In an acceptable time have I heard thee, and in a day of salvation have I helped thee: and I will preserve thee, and give thee for a covenant of the people, to establish the earth, to cause to inherit the desolate heritages" (Is.49:7-8).

Thought 2. The only way God will manifest Himself is for us to be prepared. The deep, intense sense of God's presence comes only from a heart cleansed from sin. Therefore, we must prepare to meet God by seeking His forgiveness and reconciliation through the Lord Jesus Christ, the Lamb of God who takes away the sin of the world.

"For every one that asketh receiveth; and he that seeketh findeth; and to him that knocketh it shall be opened" (Lu.11:10).

"The next day John seeth Jesus coming unto him, and saith, Behold the Lamb of God, which taketh away the sin of the world" (Jn.1:29).

"In whom we have redemption through his blood, the forgiveness of sins, according to the riches of his grace" (Ep.1:7).

"But if from thence thou shalt seek the LORD thy God, thou shalt find *him*, if thou seek him with all thy heart and with all thy soul" (De.4:29).

"Seek ye the LORD while he may be found, call ye upon him while he is near" (Is.55:6).

2 (9:7-14) **Testimony—Preparation, Necessary to Meet God—Sin Offering—Offering, Sin—Sacrifice of Animals—Reconciliation—Burnt Offering—Offering, Burnt:** there was the personal testimony of Aaron, the High Priest: he first had to seek God for himself. This was a public confession of sin for Aaron. He was acknowledging to the people that he himself was sinful, short of God's glory, and under the penalty of sin, which was death. He therefore had to seek God first for himself.

OUTLINE	SCRIPTURE	SCRIPTURE	OUTLINE

2. The personal testimony: Aaron first sought God for himself
a. He was given this charge by God's mediator, Moses
  1) He was to seek God first for himself—through the sacrifice
  2) He was then to lead the people to seek God—through the sacrifice
b. He had to come for the forgiveness of sin through the sacrifice of the Sin Offering
  1) Put the sacrifice to death
  2) Put some blood on the horns of the altar
  3) Poured out the remaining blood at the base of the altar
	7 And Moses said unto Aaron, Go unto the altar, and offer thy sin offering, and thy burnt offering, and make an atonement for thyself, and for the people: and offer the offering of the people, and make an atonement for them; as the LORD commanded.
	8 Aaron therefore went unto the altar, and slew the calf of the sin offering, which *was* for himself.
	9 And the sons of Aaron brought the blood unto him: and he dipped his finger in the blood, and put *it* upon the horns of the altar, and poured out the blood at the bottom of the altar:
		10 But the fat, and the kidneys, and the caul above the liver of the sin offering, he burnt upon the altar; as the LORD commanded Moses
		11 And the flesh and the hide he burnt with fire without the camp.
		12 And he slew the burnt offering; and Aaron's sons presented unto him the blood, which he sprinkled round about upon the altar.
		13 And they presented the burnt offering unto him, with the pieces thereof, and the head: and he burnt *them* upon the altar.
		14 And he did wash the inwards and the legs, and burnt *them* upon the burnt offering on the altar.
			4) Offered the best parts of the sacrifice to the LORD: The fat, kidneys, & liver
			
			5) Burned the flesh & hide outside the camp
			
			c. He had to come for reconciliation—through the atonement, the sacrifice of the Burnt Offering
			  1) Put the sacrifice to death
			  2) Sprinkled blood on the altar
			  3) Offered the sacrifice piece by piece, including the head
			
			4) Washed the inner parts & legs, then offered them

a. Note that Aaron was given this charge by God's mediator, Moses (v.7). Remember, Moses the mediator is a type of the Lord Jesus Christ, our mediator. It is Jesus Christ who charges His ministers to seek God first for themselves. Then they can lead their people to seek God. Note: this was exactly what Moses instructed Aaron to do: he was to seek God first for himself and then lead the people to seek God—all approaching God through the blood of the sacrificial substitute.

b. Aaron had to come for the forgiveness of sin—through the sacrifice of the Sin Offering (vv.8-11).

  1) He put the sacrifice to death (v.8). Note that he slew the sacrifice himself. This was a graphic confession of sin; it was he himself—his sin—that put the animal to death. He was making a public confession: he himself needed the forgiveness of God through the blood of the sacrificial substitute.

  2) He put some blood on the horns of the altar (v.9). By this act he was declaring that he needed the attention of God, that he needed the face of God looking at the blood, the sacrificial substitute, not looking at him nor his sins. Simply stated, he set the blood before the face of God, asking God to count the blood as the payment (ransom) for his sins.

  3) He poured out the remaining blood at the base of the altar. This obviously symbolized the complete and full forgiveness of sin.

  4) He offered the best parts of the sacrifice to the LORD: the fat, the kidneys, and the liver (v.10).

  5) He burned the flesh and hide outside the camp (v.11). This symbolized the taking away of sin, the complete removal of sin.

c. He had to come for reconciliation through the atonement, the sacrifice of the Burnt Offering (vv.12-14). This is a graphic confession of Aaron's personal need for reconciliation with God, a graphic picture of his need for the atonement. The atoning sacrifice was needed to pay the ransom for his life, to satisfy the justice and holiness of God.

  1) He put the sacrifice to death (v.12). By this act, he was declaring that it was his sins that were causing the death of the sacrificial substitute.

  2) He sprinkled blood on all sides of the altar (v.12). By this act, he declared that he trusted God to accept the sacrifice as his substitute, in his stead, on his behalf.

  3) He offered the sacrifice piece by piece upon the altar, including the head (v.13).

  4) He washed the inner parts and legs, then offered them on the altar (v.14). By this act, he symbolized that only a clean and pure sacrifice (sinless, perfect) could be offered to God.

Thought 1. Before a minister can lead his people, he must first of all acknowledge that he himself must seek God. He must be forgiven his sins and reconciled to God before he can ever lead his people to seek the LORD.

> "Whosoever therefore shall confess me before men, him will I confess also before my Father which is in heaven. But whosoever shall deny me before men, him will I also deny before my Father which is in heaven" (Mt.10:32-33).
>
> "Also I say unto you, Whosoever shall confess me before men, him shall the Son of man also confess before the angels of God" (Lu.12:8).
>
> "That if thou shalt confess with thy mouth the Lord Jesus, and shalt believe in thine heart that God hath raised him from the dead, thou shalt be saved. For with the heart man believeth unto righteousness; and with the mouth confession is made unto salvation" (Ro.10:9-10).
>
> "And *that* every tongue should confess that Jesus Christ *is* Lord, to the glory of God the Father" (Ph.2:11).
>
> "And hereby we do know that we know him, if we keep his commandments" (1 Jn.2:23).
>
> "Whosoever shall confess that Jesus is the Son of God, God dwelleth in him, and he in God" (1 Jn.4:15).

"And that he might reconcile both [Jew and Gentile] unto God in one body by the cross, having slain the enmity thereby; For through him we both have access by one Spirit unto the Father. Now therefore ye are no more strangers and foreigners, but fellowcitizens with the saints, and of the household of God" (Ep.2:16, 18-19).

3 (9:15-21) **Seek—Seeking, of God—Needs, Met by—Forgiveness, Spiritual—Reconciliation—Atonement—Dedication—Peace, of God—Fellowship, of God—Burnt Offering—Sin Offering—Peace or Fellowship Offering—Grain Offering—Wave Offering**: there was the proclamation to the people: they must seek God, must prepare to meet God. How? By seeking God, asking Him to meet five of their most basic needs. What are these needs?

⇒ forgiveness of sin (v.15)
⇒ redemption, reconciliation with God (v.16)
⇒ food and livelihood
⇒ purpose, meaning, and significance in life, something to which they could dedicate their lives (v.17)
⇒ peace and fellowship: with God and man

Note that all five of these basic needs are met by God when a person approaches Him through the sacrificial substitute (a symbol of Christ). Aaron, the priest and minister of God, now teaches the people one basic truth: if they want the presence and leadership of God, they must seek God through the sacrificial substitute. God reveals and manifests Himself—gives a deep, intimate sense of His presence—only if a person seeks Him through the shed blood of the sacrifice. Note that Aaron, the High Priest, represents the people before God throughout these offerings. He stands before God on behalf of the people: he stands as their mediator. This is a clear type of Jesus Christ. He represents us before God, offering the perfect sacrifice, paying the ransom price for our salvation and redemption.

OUTLINE	SCRIPTURE	SCRIPTURE	OUTLINE
3. **The proclamation to the people: They must seek God—must prepare to meet God**	15 And he brought the people's offering, and took the goat, which *was* the sin offering for the people, and slew it, and offered it for sin, as the first.	for the people: and Aaron's sons presented unto him the blood, which he sprinkled upon the altar round about,	Peace Offering 1) Put the sacrifice to death 2) Sprinkled blood on the altar
a. Must seek forgiveness of sin—through the Sin Offering		19 And the fat of the bullock and of the ram, the rump, and that which covereth *the inwards*, and the kidneys, and the caul *above* the liver:	3) Laid the fat, kidneys, & liver on the breasts; then he offered the fat to God
b. Must seek the atonement (reconciliation) through the sacrifice of the Burnt Offering	16 And he brought the burnt offering, and offered it according to the manner.		
c. Must offer thanksgiving to God for the atonement & for their livelihood, dedicating their lives to God through the Grain Offering	17 And he brought the meat offering, and took an handful thereof, and burnt *it* upon the altar, beside the burnt sacrifice of the morning.	20 And they put the fat upon the breasts, and he burnt the fat upon the altar:	
d. Must grow in peace & fellowship with God—through the sacrifice of the Fellowship or	18 He slew also the bullock and the ram *for* a sacrifice of peace offerings, which *was*	21 And the breasts and the right shoulder Aaron waved *for* a wave offering before the LORD; as Moses commanded.	4) Gave a wave offering of thanksgiving to the LORD: Waved the breast & right thigh

a. The people had to seek forgiveness of sin, seek forgiveness through the sacrifice of the Sin Offering (v.15). The sacrifice (goat) was put to death for the sins of the people. Their sins were forgiven because the sacrifice, their substitute, bore the judgment against sin for them.

Thought 1. The sacrifice was a symbol of Jesus Christ, of His dying for the sins of the world. We must prepare to meet God, prepare by seeking forgiveness of sin.

"The next day John seeth Jesus coming unto him, and saith, Behold the Lamb of God, which taketh away the sin of the world" (Jn.1:29).
"Him hath God exalted with his right hand to be a Prince and a Saviour, for to give repentance to Israel, and forgiveness of sins" (Ac.5:31).
"Be it known unto you therefore, men and brethren, that through this man is preached unto you the forgiveness of sins" (Ac.13:38).
"In whom we have redemption through his blood, the forgiveness of sins, according to the riches of his grace" (Ep.1:7).
"And that he might reconcile both unto God in one body by the cross, having slain the enmity thereby....For through him we both have access by one Spirit unto the Father. Now therefore ye are no more strangers and foreigners [Jew and Gentile], but fellowcitizens with the saints, and of the household of God" (Ep.2:16, 18-19).
"If we confess our sins, he is faithful and just to forgive us our sins, and to cleanse us from all unrighteousness" (1 Jn.1:9).

b. The people had to seek atonement or reconciliation with God through the sacrifice of the Burnt Offering. The Israelites were guilty of rebellion against God just as we are guilty of rebellion against Him. They had chosen to walk as they willed, doing their own thing, seeking the fleshly pleasures, immoralities, and possessions of this world. Their unrighteousness had separated them from God. They needed to be reconciled with God. Their sin had violated and trampled upon the holy nature of God. God's holiness and justice demanded satisfaction or else the judgment of His holy nature would have to be executed against the violator.

Only one thing could satisfy God's holy nature and justice: the offering of a perfect sacrifice for atonement. The price, the ransom, had to be paid for the sinner. This was symbolized in the offering of the atonement sacrifice. God accepted the atoning sacrifice as a substitute, as the satisfaction for sin. The people were set free from the wrath and judgment of God through the substitutionary sacrifice. They were reconciled to God.

> **Thought 1**. The atonement or reconciliation with God is now possible—through Jesus Christ. Jesus Christ has paid the price, the ransom, for us. His death satisfies the holy and just nature of God against sin. Jesus Christ is our atonement, the ransom price paid to reconcile us to God. We must prepare to meet God, prepare by seeking the atonement, by seeking to be reconciled with God.
>
> > **"To wit, that God was in Christ, reconciling the world unto himself, not imputing their trespasses unto them; and hath committed unto us the word of reconciliation" (2 Co.5:19).**
> > **"For he hath made him to be sin for us, who knew no sin; that we might be made the righteousness of God in him" (2 Co.5:21).**
> > **"And that he might reconcile both [Jew and Gentile] unto God in one body by the cross, having slain the enmity thereby:...For through him we both have access by one Spirit unto the Father. Now therefore ye are no more strangers and foreigners, but fellowcitizens with the saints, and of the household of God" (Ep.2:16, 18-19).**
> > **"And, having made peace through the blood of his cross, by him to reconcile all things unto himself; by him, I say, whether they be things in earth, or things in heaven" (Col.1:20).**
> > **"Wherefore in all things it behooved him to be made like unto his brethren, that he might be a merciful and faithful high priest in things pertaining to God, to make reconciliation for the sins of the people" (He.2:17).**

c. The people had to offer thanksgiving to God for the atonement and for their livelihood, and they had to dedicate their lives to God—through the Grain Offering (v.17). Remember: the Grain Offering was laid upon the atoning sacrifice on the altar. The odor of the burning grain along with the roasting meat ascended up toward heaven. This symbolized two things:
⇒ the offering up of thanksgiving for the atonement (for one's reconciliation) and for God's provision of one's food (crops, livelihood)
⇒ the laying of grain upon the sacrifice pictured the dedication, the laying of one's life upon God

Thought 1. The lesson is clear: we must prepare to meet God...
• prepare by giving thanks for the atonement (reconciliation with God) and for all His goodness in providing for us

> **"When thou hast eaten and art full, then thou shalt bless the LORD thy God for the good land which he hath given thee" (De.8:10).**
> **"Enter into his gates with thanksgiving, and into his courts with praise: be thankful unto him, and bless his name" (Ps.100:4).**
> **"And let them sacrifice the sacrifices of thanksgiving, and declare his works with rejoicing" (Ps.107:22).**
> **"Giving thanks unto the Father, which hath made us meet to be partakers of the inheritance of the saints in light" (Col.1:12).**

• prepare by dedicating our lives to God, by giving ourselves totally to Him

> **"And he said to them all, If any man will come after me, let him deny himself, and take up his cross daily, and follow me" (Lu.9:23).**
> **"I beseech you therefore, brethren, by the mercies of God, that ye present your bodies a living sacrifice, holy, acceptable unto God, which is your reasonable service. And be not conformed to this world: but be ye transformed by the renewing of your mind, that ye may prove what is that good, and acceptable, and perfect, will of God" (Ro.12:1-2).**
> **"And they that are Christ's have crucified the flesh with the affections and lusts" (Ga.5:24).**
> **"My son, give me thine heart, and let thine eyes observe my ways" (Pr.23:26).**

d. The people had to declare that they wanted to grow in the peace and fellowship of God. This they had to do through the sacrifice of the Peace or Fellowship Offering (vv.18-21).
1) Aaron (the High Priest) put the sacrifice to death (v.1). As the people's representative, he identified the people with the substitute. They could grow in peace and fellowship with God only through the death of the sacrificial substitute.
2) Aaron sprinkled some blood on the altar (v.2). He trusted God to see and accept the blood as the covering for the people's sin.
3) Aaron laid the fat, the kidneys, and the liver on the breasts; then he offered the fat to the LORD (vv.19-20).
4) Aaron gave a Wave Offering of thanksgiving to the LORD: he waved the breast and right thigh before the LORD (v.21).

Thought 1. The lesson is clear. We must prepare to meet God...

- prepare by seeking to grow in the peace of God

"And suddenly there was with the angel a multitude of the heavenly host praising God, and saying, Glory to God in the highest, and on earth peace, good will toward men" (Lu.2:13-14).

"For to be carnally minded is death; but to be spiritually minded is life and peace" (Ro.8:6).

"For the kingdom of God is not meat and drink; but righteousness, and peace, and joy in the Holy Ghost" (Ro.14:17).

"Peace I leave with you, my peace I give unto you: not as the world giveth, give I unto you. Let not your heart be troubled, neither let it be afraid" (Jn.14:27).

"And in that day ye shall ask me nothing. Verily, verily, I say unto you, Whatsoever ye shall ask the Father in my name, he will give *it* you" (Jn.16:23).

"Be careful for nothing; but in every thing by prayer and supplication with thanksgiving let your requests be made known unto God. And the peace of God, which passeth all understanding, shall keep your hearts and minds through Christ Jesus" (Ph.4:6-7).

"The word which *God* sent unto the children of Israel, preaching peace by Jesus Christ: (he is Lord of all" (Ac.10:36).

"Therefore being justified by faith, we have peace with God through our Lord Jesus Christ" (Ro.5:1).

"For he is our peace, who hath made both one, and hath broken down the middle wall of partition *between us*" (Ep.2:14).

"To the saints and faithful brethren in Christ which are at Colosse: Grace *be* unto you, and peace, from God our Father and the Lord Jesus Christ" (Col.1:2).

"But the fruit of the Spirit is love, joy, peace, longsuffering, gentleness, goodness, faith, Meekness, temperance: against such there is no law" (Ga.5:22-23).

"Thou wilt keep *him* in perfect peace, *whose* mind *is* stayed *on thee:* because he trusteth in thee" (Is.26:3).

"But he *was* wounded for our transgressions, *he was* bruised for our iniquities: the chastisement of our peace *was* upon him; and with his stripes we are healed" (Is.53:5).

- prepare by seeking to grow in the fellowship of God

"And it came to pass, that, while they communed together and reasoned, Jesus himself drew near, and went with them" (Lu.24:15 together [about Jesus death]).

"And they said one to another, Did not our heart burn within us, while he talked with us by the way, and while he opened to us the scriptures?" (Lu.24:32).

"God is faithful, by whom ye were called unto the fellowship of his Son Jesus Christ our Lord" (1 Co.1:9).

"That which we have seen and heard declare we unto you, that ye also may have fellowship with us: and truly our fellowship is with the Father, and with his Son Jesus Christ" (1 Jn.1:3).

"Behold, I stand at the door, and knock: if any man hear my voice, and open the door, I will come in to him, and will sup with him, and he with me" (Re.3:20).

---

4 (9:22-24) **Blessing—Presence of God—God, Presence of—Events, Miraculous—Miracles, Events of—Shekinah Glory—God, Glory of**: there was the blessing pronounced upon the people. What now happened was dramatic and spectacular, a startling, fearful experience. An encounter with God took place. God revealed and manifested His presence. As in any encounter with God, the people were stricken with awe and fear, sensing their unworthiness to be in the presence of God. Note what happened:

OUTLINE	SCRIPTURE	SCRIPTURE	OUTLINE
4. The blessing pronounced upon the people & the LORD's glorious presence	22 And Aaron lifted up his hand toward the people, and blessed them, and came down from offering of the sin offering, and the burnt offering, and peace offerings.	and the glory of the LORD appeared unto all the people.	b. The blessing again pronounced
a. The pronouncement of the blessing			b. The result
1) He gave the blessing after leading the people to approach God through the sacrifice		24 And there came a fire out from before the LORD, and consumed upon the altar the burnt offering	1) The LORD appeared: Miraculous fire shot out from the presence of the LORD & consumed the sacrifices
1) He then stepped down		and the fat: *which* when all the people saw, they shouted, and fell on their faces.	burning on the altar
1) The special prayer for the people: Moses & Aaron went into the Tabernacle (to pray)	23 And Moses and Aaron went into the tabernacle of the congregation, and came out, and blessed the people:		1) The people worshipped the LORD: Shouted for joy & fell down upon the ground in fear

a. As soon as Aaron had finished seeking God on behalf of the people, he pronounced a blessing upon them (v.22). Note that he lifted up his hands toward heaven and toward the people as he blessed them. What blessing? Most likely the blessing that God had given to Aaron, "saying...on this wise, ye shall bless the children of Israel, saying unto them..."

"The LORD bless thee, and keep thee: the LORD make his face shine upon thee, and be gracious unto thee: the LORD lift up his countenance upon thee, and give thee peace..." (Nu.6:22-26).

b. Right after pronouncing the benediction, Aaron stepped down. *Stepped down* from what? Perhaps from the altar, or some platform that had been constructed for him to stand upon as he spoke to the people. Or perhaps the Tabernacle had been erected upon a hill so that the people would be able to see the service as it was conducted.

c. Right after stepping down, Aaron and Moses went into the Tabernacle, obviously to pray. Just how long they were praying in the Tabernacle is not known. But as soon as they returned, they raised their hands toward heaven and blessed the people again (v.23).

d. Then it happened: the LORD appeared. Immediately, quicker than the eye can blink, before they could lower their arms, the Shekinah Glory fell upon them. A lightning bolt of miraculous fire shot out from the presence of the LORD and consumed the sacrifices burning upon the altar. Startled, shocked, stricken with fear—the people shouted for joy and fell face down upon the ground (vv.23-24).

The point is this: God met His people. He revealed and manifested Himself. He gave the people a deep, intense sense of His presence. Remember why: because they were prepared to meet God. They had heeded the message of the priest: they had prepared to meet God. They had sought God and God had met them...

- He had forgiven their sins (v.15)
- He had reconciled them to Himself (v.16)
- He had accepted their thanksgiving and commitment to him (v.17)
- He had seen them seeking more of His peace and fellowship (v.18)

God had met His people in a very, very special way because they had sought Him through the substitute sacrifice. A very special sense of God's presence was given to the people—all because they had prepared themselves for the presence of God.

Thought 1. The presence of God is given to those who prepare themselves. God gives a deep, intimate sense of His presence to those who do one thing: seek Him through the atoning sacrifice of His Son.

"For where two or three are gathered together in my name, there am I in the midst of them" (Mt.18:20).

"And, lo, the angel of the Lord came upon them, and the glory of the Lord shone round about them: and they were sore afraid" (Lu.2:9).

"But he [Stephen], being full of the Holy Ghost, looked up stedfastly into heaven, and saw the glory of God, and Jesus standing on the right hand of God" (Ac.7:55).

"But we all, with open face beholding as in a glass the glory of the Lord, are changed into the same image from glory to glory, *even* as by the Spirit of the Lord" (2 Co.3:18).

"That which we have seen and heard declare we unto you, that ye also may have fellowship with us: and truly our fellowship is with the Father, and with his Son Jesus Christ" (1 Jn.1:3).

"Behold, I stand at the door, and knock: if any man hear my voice, and open the door, I will come in to him, and will sup with him, and he with me" (Re.3:20).

"The LORD is nigh unto them that are of a broken heart; and saveth such as be of a contrite spirit" (Ps.34:18).

"The LORD is nigh unto all them that call upon him, to all that call upon him in truth" (Ps.145:18).

TYPES, SYMBOLS, AND PICTURES
Leviticus 9:1-24

Historical Term	Type or Picture (Scriptural Basis for Each)	Life Application for Today's Believer	Biblical Application
Pouring Out the Remaining Blood of the Sin Offering During the First Worship Service of the Priest Le.9:9; See also Le.4:7	*Pouring out the remaining blood of the substitute sacrifice symbolized the complete and full forgiveness of sin.* "And the sons of Aaron brought the blood unto him: and he dipped his finger in the blood, and put *it* upon the horns of the altar, and poured out the blood at the bottom of the altar" (Le.9:9).	It is only through the blood of Jesus Christ that our sins are forgiven—all our sins. The blood of Jesus Christ forgives us... • completely • fully • entirely • wholly • sufficiently • through and through	"If we confess our sins, he is faithful and just to forgive us our sins, and to cleanse us from all unrighteousness" (1 Jn.1:9). "Much more then, being now justified by his blood, we shall be saved from wrath through him" (Ro.5:9). "And, having made peace through the blood of his cross, by him to reconcile all things unto himself; by him, I say, whether they be things in earth, or things in heaven" (Col.1:20). "But if we walk in the light, as he is in the light, we have fellowship one with another, and the blood of Jesus Christ his Son cleanseth us from all sin" (1 Jn.1:7).

TYPES, SYMBOLS, AND PICTURES
Leviticus 9:1-24

Historical Term	Type or Picture (Scriptural Basis for Each)	Life Application for Today's Believer	Biblical Application
The Washing of the Inner Parts and Legs of the Burnt Offering During the First Worship Service of the Priest Le.9:14	*The washing of the inner parts and legs of the sacrifice symbolized that only a clean and pure sacrifice (sinless, perfect) could be offered to God.* **"And he did wash the inwards and the legs, and burnt** *them* **upon the burnt offering on the altar"** (Le.9:14).	Whatever we do for God must be offered as a clean and pure sacrifice. The best gift that we can give to God is our own personal holiness, a life that is marked with purity. Our personal witness of Christ is more authentic to the lost when our hearts have been cleansed, washed by the Word of God.	*"Having therefore these promises, dearly beloved, let us cleanse ourselves from all filthiness of the flesh and spirit, perfecting holiness in the fear of God" (2 Co.7:1).* *"That he might sanctify and cleanse it with the washing of water by the word" (Ep.5:26).* *"Draw nigh to God, and he will draw nigh to you. Cleanse your hands, ye sinners; and purify your hearts, ye double minded" (Js.4:8).* *"Wash me throughly from mine iniquity, and cleanse me from my sin" (Ps.51:2).* *"Wherewithal shall a young man cleanse his way? by taking heed thereto according to thy word" (Ps.119:9).* *"If we confess our sins, he is faithful and just to forgive us our sins, and to cleanse us from all unrighteousness" (1 Jn.1:9).*
A Goat Offered for the Sins of a Ruler: A Symbol of the Sin Offering During the First Worship Service of the Priest Le.9:15; see also Le.3:12-16	*The sacrifice of the goat is a symbol of Jesus Christ, of His dying for the sins of the world.* **"And he brought the people's offering, and took the goat, which** *was* **the sin offering for the people, and slew it, and offered it for sin, as the first" (Le.9:15).**	Jesus Christ died for the sins of the world. We must prepare to meet God, prepare by seeking forgiveness of sin.	*"The next day John seeth Jesus coming unto him, and saith, Behold the Lamb of God, which taketh away the sin of the world" (Jn.1:29).* *"Him hath God exalted with his right hand to be a Prince and a Saviour, for to give repentance to Israel, and forgiveness of sins" (Ac.5:31).* *"Be it known unto you therefore, men and brethren, that through this man is preached unto you the forgiveness of sins" (Ac.13:38).* *"In whom we have redemption through his blood, the forgiveness of sins, according to the riches of his grace" (Ep.1:7).*
The Odor of the Burning Grain and the Roasting Meat That Ascended Toward Heaven During the First Worship Service of The Priest Le.9:17	*The odor of the burning grain and the roasting meat that ascended up toward Heaven symbolizing two things:* *1. The odor symbolized the offering up of thanksgiving for the atonement (for one's reconciliation) and for God's provision of one's livelihood (food crops).*	The lesson is clear: we must prepare to meet God... • prepare by giving thanks for the atonement (reconciliation with God) and for all His goodness in providing for us • prepare by dedicating our lives to God, by giving ourselves totally to Him	*"When thou hast eaten and art full, then thou shalt bless the LORD thy God for the good land which he hath given thee" (De.8:10).* *"Enter into his gates with thanksgiving, and into his courts with praise: be thankful unto him, and bless his name" (Ps.100:4).* *"And let them sacrifice the sacrifices of thanksgiving,*

TYPES, SYMBOLS, AND PICTURES
Leviticus 9:1-24

Historical Term	Type or Picture (Scriptural Basis for Each)	Life Application for Today's Believer	Biblical Application
	2. *The laying of grain upon the sacrifice pictured the dedication, the laying of one's life upon God.* **"And he brought the meat offering, and took an handful thereof, and burnt** *it* **upon the altar, beside the burnt sacrifice of the morning" (Le.9:17).**		*and declare his works with rejoicing"* (Ps.107:22). *"Giving thanks unto the Father, which hath made us meet to be partakers of the inheritance of the saints in light"* (Col.1:12). *"And he said to them all, If any man will come after me, let him deny himself, and take up his cross daily, and follow me"* (Lu.9:23). *"And they that are Christ's have crucified the flesh with the affections and lusts"* (Ga.5:24).

CHAPTER 10

C. The Judgment of God upon Two Priests (Nadab & Abihu) for Their False Worship: Fate of All Who Approach God in a Wrong Way, 10:1-20

1. The judgment of false worshippers: Approaching God in a wrong way—contrary to His command
a. The sin of false worship: Offering unauthorized fire to the LORD
b. The judgment of false worship: Death

2. The reason why God judges false worshippers
a. They fail to approach God exactly as He says
b. They fail to acknowledge God's holiness & fail to honor Him (Ex.19:22)

3. The way to prevent the judgment of God
a. Guard against defilement
   1) Aaron, the father, was forbidden to take care of the dead bodies: Symbolized defilement—would disqualify him from serving God
   2) Two nephews were assigned the task: Removed their bodies (the defilement) outside the camp
b. Show total devotion to God
   1) The priests were to show that they did not condone sin, that they fully agreed with God's judgment: By not sharing in the rites of mourning but leaving the mourning to relatives

   2) The priests were to be steadfast, unmovable in their service for God: Because the LORD's anointing was upon them
   3) The priests obeyed

c. Avoid drunkenness
   1) Is a special commandment of God
   2) Is a permanent commandment for all generations
d. Live totally for God: Distinguish, discern between the holy & common, between the unclean & clean
e. Teach the people all the laws

And Nadab and Abihu, the sons of Aaron, took either of them his censer, and put fire therein, and put incense thereon, and offered strange fire before the LORD, which he commanded them not.
2 And there went out fire from the LORD, and devoured them, and they died before the LORD.
3 Then Moses said unto Aaron, This *is it* that the LORD spake, saying, I will be sanctified in them that come nigh me, and before all the people I will be glorified. And Aaron held his peace.
4 And Moses called Mishael and Elzaphan, the sons of Uzziel the uncle of Aaron, and said unto them, Come near, carry your brethren from before the sanctuary out of the camp.
5 So they went near, and carried them in their coats out of the camp; as Moses had said.
6 And Moses said unto Aaron, and unto Eleazar and unto Ithamar, his sons, Uncover not your heads, neither rend your clothes; lest ye die, and lest wrath come upon all the people: but let your brethren, the whole house of Israel, bewail the burning which the LORD hath kindled.
7 And ye shall not go out from the door of the tabernacle of the congregation, lest ye die: for the anointing oil of the LORD *is* upon you. And they did according to the word of Moses.
8 And the LORD spake unto Aaron, saying,
9 Do not drink wine nor strong drink, thou, nor thy sons with thee, when ye go into the tabernacle of the congregation, lest ye die: *it shall be* a statute for ever throughout your generations:
10 And that ye may put difference between holy and unholy, and between unclean and clean;
11 And that ye may teach the children of Israel all the statutes which the LORD hath spoken unto them by the hand of Moses.
12 And Moses spake unto Aaron, and unto Eleazar and unto Ithamar, his sons that were left, Take the meat offering that remaineth of the offerings of the LORD made by fire, and eat it without leaven beside the altar: for it *is* most holy:
13 And ye shall eat it in the holy place, because it *is* thy due, and thy sons' due, of the sacrifices of the LORD made by fire: for so I am commanded.
14 And the wave breast and heave shoulder shall ye eat in a clean place; thou, and thy sons, and thy daughters with thee: for *they be* thy due, and thy sons' due, *which* are given out of the sacrifices of peace offerings of the children of Israel.
15 The heave shoulder and the wave breast shall they bring with the offerings made by fire of the fat, to wave *it for* a wave offering before the LORD; and it shall be thine, and thy sons' with thee, by a statute for ever; as the LORD hath commanded.
16 And Moses diligently sought the goat of the sin offering, and, behold, it was burnt: and he was angry with Eleazar and Ithamar, the sons of Aaron *which were* left *alive*, saying,
17 Wherefore have ye not eaten the sin offering in the holy place, seeing it *is* most holy, and *God* hath given it you to bear the iniquity of the congregation, to make atonement for them before the Lord?
18 Behold, the blood of it was not brought in within the holy *place*: ye should indeed have eaten it in the holy *place*, as I commanded.
19 And Aaron said unto Moses, Behold, this day have they offered their sin offering and their burnt offering before the LORD; and such things have befallen me: and *if* I had eaten the sin offering to day, should it have been accepted in the sight of the LORD?
20 And when Moses heard *that*, he was content.

or commandments of God

4. The grace of God in the face of judgment
a. God did not forfeit the privileges of the faithful because of the sin of some
   1) The faithful priests were told to eat what was left of the Grain Offering given to the LORD:
      • It was their share, part of their support
      • It was the command of God

   2) The priests were also told to have their families join them in eating the breast & thigh of the Fellowship or Peace Offering

   3) The meat was first to be offered as a wave offering of thanksgiving

b. God set aside this part of the offering as support for the priests: Was to be given to them with each Fellowship Offering

5. The mercy & tenderness of God when dealing with people & judgment
a. A serious mistake: The goat of the Sin Offering had been burned up

   1) The goat was supposed to be eaten: It was holy, set apart to make atonement, to reconcile the people (the only time meat was not eaten was when its blood was taken into the Holy Place)
   2) The mistake: Its blood had not been taken into the Holy Place; therefore, the meat was to be eaten

b. The explanation by Aaron: The priests had approached God that day—as commanded—thru the Sin Offering & the Burnt Offering
   1) Would God have been pleased if he had eaten on the very day his sons had been stricken dead by God?
   2) God had mercy—understood Aaron's grief—despite the mistake

DIVISION II

THE WAY TO BECOME ACCEPTABLE TO GOD (PART 2): BY THE PRIESTHOOD, A PERFECT MEDIATOR, 8:1–10:20

C. The Judgment of God upon Two Priests (Nadab and Abihu) for Their False Worship: Fate of All Who Approach God in a Wrong Way, 10:1-20

(10:1-20) **Introduction**: the judgment of God is a forgotten subject. There is little fear of God in the world today. Most people deny, reject, and ignore the judgment of God. The thoughts of judgment and fear of God are considered by some to be unhealthy, even the cause of some neurosis and psychosis among sensitive-natured people. There is the feeling that what needs to be stressed among society is only the love and forgiveness of God, not the judgment of God. As the excellent commentator Gordon J. Wenham says:

> In many parts of the Church the biblical view of divine judgment is conveniently forgotten or supposed to be something that passed away with the OT. Heine's famous last words, "God will forgive me. That's his job," have become the unexpressed axiom of much modern theology. This short story is therefore an affront to liberal thinkers. It should also challenge Bible-believing Christians whose theological attitudes are influenced by prevailing trends of thought more often than they realize.[1]

This chapter covers a horrible tragedy, a tragedy that exposes man's long and sordid history of pride and self-righteousness in approaching God. Remember what had just happened. The glory of God's holy presence had just been revealed to the people. The glorious day of dedication—the dedication of the people and the Tabernacle—had just occurred. But then all of a sudden, two of Aaron's sons who had just been ordained as priests rejected God's clear commandment. They disobeyed God. They approached God in their own way, as they wished instead of as God said. They rejected the way of approach appointed by God and determined their own way. Consequently, the judgment of God struck out against them. This is the subject of this passage: *The Judgment of God upon Two Priests (Nadab and Abihu) for Their False Worship: Fate of All Who Approach God in a Wrong Way,* 10:1-20.

1. The judgment of false worshippers: Approaching God in a wrong way—contrary to His command (vv.1-2).
2. The reason why God judges false worshippers (v.3).
3. The way to prevent the judgment of God (vv.4-11).
4. The grace of God in the face of judgment (vv.12-15).
5. The mercy and tenderness of God when dealing with people and judgment (vv.16-20).

---

[1] (10:1) **Judgment—God, Approaching—Worship, False—Ministry, False**: there is the sin and judgment of false worshippers.

OUTLINE	SCRIPTURE
1. The judgment of false worshippers: Approaching God in a wrong way—contrary to His command	And Nadab and Abihu, the sons of Aaron, took either of them his censer, and put fire therein, and put incense thereon, and offered strange fire before the LORD, which he commanded them not.
a. The sin of false worship: Offering unauthorized fire to the LORD	
b. The judgment of false worship: Death	2 And there went out fire from the LORD, and devoured them, and they died before the LORD.

Note what Aaron's two sons did. They took their censors or firepans and put the hot coals of some convenient fire in them. They then laid incense on the coals and went into the Tabernacle, placing the burning incense on the Altar of Incense. What was wrong with this? What was their sin?

a. They offered strange, unauthorized fire to the LORD. Based upon Scripture, it probably means that they took the fiery coals from some fire burning nearby, some convenient fire. This was wrong, for God had insisted that the fiery coals come from the altar of Burnt Offering, never from any other source.

"And he shall take a censer full of burning coals of fire from off the altar before the LORD, and his hands full of sweet incense beaten small, and bring it within the vail:" (Le.16:12).

As stated, the live coals that were to be used to start the Alter of Incense were to come from the altar of Burnt Offering. Keep in mind that the Alter of Burnt Offering symbolized the need for atonement or reconciliation with God; whereas the Altar of Incense symbolized prayer. The sweet aroma of the incense ascending up toward heaven pictured the prayers

---

1 Gordon J. Wenham. *The Book of Leviticus.* "The New International Commentary on the Old Testament." (Grand Rapids, MI: Eerdmans Publishing Co., 1979), p.153.

of God's people ascending up to God. But prayer is based upon the atonement, upon a person's being reconciled with God through the atoning sacrifice of the Burnt Offering. If a person is not reconciled with God, his prayers are obviously not answered.

"If I regard iniquity in my heart, the LORD will not hear me" (Ps.66:18).

A person has to be cleansed from sin through the atonement (atoning sacrifice) in order for God to answer his prayers. This was the symbolism to be pictured by taking the fiery coals from the altar of Burnt Offering. Prayer is based upon the atoning sacrifice of the Burnt Offering (a symbol of Christ).

In light of this, the two sons of Aaron committed a serious, fatal sin. They approached God in a wrong way, contrary to His direct command. They confused the very meaning of worship. They twisted and distorted worship. They approached God as they desired not as God commanded. They offered a false worship to God: a will worship, a self-made worship, a worship made and created in their own minds, a worship of self-righteousness. Note other facts as well. There is the probability that the two priests went into the Most Holy Place. Remember, the Holy Place was where the holy presence of God was manifested in all the energy and light of His glory. No person was allowed to enter this hallowed and holy room except the High Priest and he only once a year. (See outline and notes—Le.16:1-2 for more discussion.)

b. Note what happened: a lightning bolt of fire from God's glory shot out from the presence of the LORD and burned them (v.2). They died before the LORD.

Thought 1. We must always remember that the true worship and religion of God are a *revealed worship* and a *revealed religion*. God has revealed through His Son and the Holy Scriptures exactly how His people are to worship Him. But these two priests ignored and rejected God's way. They created and developed their own way to approach God. How like so many today who approach God as they think and as they wish, ignoring God's way and His clear instructions.

"Jesus saith unto him, I am the way, the truth, and the life: no man cometh unto the Father, but by me" (Jn.14:6).

"Ye worship ye know not what: we know what we worship: for salvation is of the Jews. But the hour cometh, and now is, when the true worshippers shall worship the Father in spirit and in truth: for the Father seeketh such to worship him. God *is* a Spirit: and they that worship him must worship *him* in spirit and in truth" (Jn.4:22-24).

"Neither is there salvation in any other: for there is none other name under heaven given among men, whereby we must be saved" (Ac.4:12).

2 (10:3) **Judgment—False Worship**: there is the reason why God judges false worshippers. Aaron was shaken. These two priests were his sons, and the blazing holiness of God had just stricken them dead. Moses quickly explained what had happened, and in so doing, he tells us why God judges false worshippers.

OUTLINE	SCRIPTURE
2. The reason why God judges false worshippers a. They fail to approach God exactly as He says b. They fail to acknowledge God's holiness & fail to honor Him (Ex.19:22)	3 Then Moses said unto Aaron, This *is it* that the LORD spake, saying, I will be sanctified in them that come nigh me, and before all the people I will be glorified. And Aaron held his peace.

a. False worshippers fail to approach God exactly as He says and commands (v.3). God had been very clear about how the Altar of Incense was to be approached. Keep in mind that the Altar of Incense pictured exactly how God was to be approached in prayer. Prayer is based upon the atoning sacrifice. Approaching God through the atoning sacrifice is the only way God can accept a person and answer his prayers. This truth has to be taught to the people of the earth. This task belongs primarily to the priests, the ministers of God. Above everyone else, the priests were to teach people how to approach God. The two sons of Aaron, Nadab and Abihu, failed to approach God as He commanded.

Thought 1. God tells man exactly how to approach Him. God has revealed the way, the truth, and the life to us. God has revealed...

- the way of worship to us
- the truth of worship to us
- the life of worship to us

God has given us His *revealed worship*, His revealed religion. We are to worship God *exactly* as He has shown us. We are to approach God exactly as He has revealed.

"Ye worship ye know not what: we know what we worship: for salvation is of the Jews. But the hour cometh, and now is, when the true worshippers shall worship the Father in spirit and in truth: for the Father seeketh such to worship him. God is a Spirit: and they that worship him must worship him in spirit and in truth" (Jn.4:22-24).

"Jesus saith unto him, I am the way, the truth, and the life: no man cometh unto the Father, but by me" (Jn.14:6).

"Neither is there salvation in any other: for there is none other name under heaven given among men, whereby we must be saved" (Ac.4:12).

"For other foundation can no man lay than that is laid, which is Jesus Christ" (1 Co.3:11).

b. False worshippers fail to acknowledge God's holiness and fail to honor Him (v.3). Simply stated, God is so holy—so full of light, righteousness, purity, and perfection—that no person can ever stand in His presence. The blazing light of His holiness would do just what it did to Nadab and Abihu: strike them dead.

The point: any person who ever approaches God must acknowledge God's holiness and his own unworthiness. He must acknowledge how great God is in all His holy nature and being, and how sinful and short man is. When a person does this, he willingly listens to God. He willingly approaches God through the atoning sacrifice. He confesses that he is a sinner, that he has no access into God's presence—no right whatsoever to approach God—except as God dictates. The person is led by God's holiness to seek God just as God says—through the atoning sacrifice. He knows that his prayers are answered because of the atoning sacrifice.

Note how this honors God. A person honors God when he obeys God, approaches God as God commands. When a person obeys God, approaches God exactly as He says, God hears and answers the person's prayers.

The point: God judges false worshippers, any persons who fail to acknowledge God's holiness and who fail to honor Him. The judgment of God is to fall upon...

- all false worshippers
- all who approach God in a wrong way
- all who ignore and disobey the clear instructions of God's Holy Word

"For I say unto you, That except your righteousness shall exceed the righteousness of the scribes and Pharisees, ye shall in no case enter into the kingdom of heaven" (Mt.5:20).

"Whosoever therefore shall be ashamed of me and of my words in this adulterous and sinful generation; of him also shall the Son of man be ashamed, when he cometh in the glory of his Father with the holy angels" (Mk.8:38).

"And this is the condemnation, that light is come into the world, and men loved darkness rather than light, because their deeds were evil" (Jn.3:19).

"Awake to righteousness, and sin not; for some have not the knowledge of God: I speak this to your shame" (1 Co.15:34).

"And to you who are troubled rest with us, when the Lord Jesus shall be revealed from heaven with his mighty angels, In flaming fire taking vengeance on them that know not God, and that obey not the gospel of our Lord Jesus Christ" (2 Th.1:7-8).

"But we are all as an unclean thing, and all our righteousnesses are as filthy rags; and we all do fade as a leaf; and our iniquities, like the wind, have taken us away" (Is.64:6).

"I the LORD search the heart, I try the reins, even to give every man according to his ways, and according to the fruit of his doings" (Je.17:10).

3 (10:4-11) **Judgment—Drunkenness—Devotion, to God—Commitment, to the Ministry—Dedication, to the Ministry—Discernment—Believer, Life and Walk—Priest, Duty of—Minister, Duty of**: there is the way to prevent the judgment of God. God and Moses told Aaron and the people how to prevent the judgment of God, and through them, told us. There are five key essentials to prevent the judgment of God. All five essentials are applicable both to priests and ministers of God as well as to the people of God. But keep in mind, God is directing these instructions first to the priests: they must make absolutely sure that they approach and serve God exactly as He says. As stated, these are essentials that are applicable to every believer, but priests or ministers of God are more responsible to obey these instructions—more responsible because they are the teachers of the people. Simply stated, they must live what they teach. Now, note the five essentials listed before they are discussed:

OUTLINE	SCRIPTURE	SCRIPTURE	OUTLINE

3. The way to prevent the judgment of God
a. Guard against defilement
  1) Aaron, the father, was forbidden to take care of the dead bodies: Symbolized defilement—would disqualify him from serving God
  2) Two nephews are assigned the task: Removed their bodies (the defilement) outside the camp
b. Show total devotion to God
  1) The priests were to show that they did not condone sin, that they fully agreed with God's judgment: By not sharing in the rites of
	4 And Moses called Mishael and Elzaphan, the sons of Uzziel the uncle of Aaron, and said unto them, Come near, carry your brethren from before the sanctuary out of the camp.
	5 So they went near, and carried them in their coats out of the camp; as Moses had said.
	6 And Moses said unto Aaron, and unto Eleazar and unto Ithamar, his sons, Uncover not your heads, neither rend your clothes; lest ye die, and lest wrath come
		upon all the people: but let your brethren, the whole house of Israel, bewail the burning which the LORD hath kindled.
		7 And ye shall not go out from the door of the tabernacle of the congregation, lest ye die: for the anointing oil of the LORD is upon you. And they did according to the word of Moses.
		8 And the LORD spake unto Aaron, saying,
		9 Do not drink wine nor strong drink, thou, nor thy sons with thee, when ye go into the tabernacle of the
			mourning but leaving the mourning to relatives
			
			  2) The priests were to be steadfast, unmovable in their service for God: Because the LORD'S anointing was upon them
			  3) The priests obeyed
			
			c. Avoid drunkenness
			  1) Is a special commandment of God

OUTLINE	SCRIPTURE	SCRIPTURE	OUTLINE
2) Is a permanent commandment for all generations d. Live totally for God: Distinguish between the holy & common, between the unclean	congregation, lest ye die: *it shall be* a statute for ever throughout your generations: 10 And that ye may put difference between holy and unholy, and between un-	clean and clean; 11 And that ye may teach the children of Israel all the statutes which the LORD hath spoken unto them by the hand of Moses.	& clean e. Teach the people all the laws or commandments of God

a. The way to prevent the judgment of God is to guard against defilement (vv.4-5). Note that Aaron was not allowed to take care of his two dead sons. Priests were forbidden to touch or go near a corpse. Why? Because death symbolized defilement and uncleanness, corruption and decay. Defilement and corruption disqualified a priest from performing his service for God. For this reason, Aaron was forbidden to touch the two dead bodies despite the fact that they were his sons. Note that Moses had the two nephews of Aaron remove the dead bodies (the defilement) outside the camp (v.5).

b. The way to prevent the judgment of God is to show total devotion to God (vv.6-7). Note that Aaron and his two surviving sons were not even allowed to share in the rites of mourning. They had to leave the mourning and the taking care of the bodies in the hands of their relatives (v.6). Why? Because the priests had to show that they fully agreed with God's judgment against sin: they did not condone sin. The priests had to show that they were totally devoted to God, and the people had to understand their total devotion. Note that Aaron and his sons were to remain in the Tabernacle and complete their service for the LORD (v.7). They were to be steadfast, unmovable in their service for God. Note that this is exactly what Aaron and his two surviving sons did. They obeyed God: they showed that they were totally devoted to God. Think of the devotion of Aaron. His two sons had just been struck dead by the holiness of God because of a terrible sin they had committed. Yet Aaron, though gripped with a deep sense of grief and sorrow, continued on, completing his service for God. What devotion!

c. The way to prevent the judgment of God is to avoid drunkenness (vv.8-9). Note this is a very special commandment from God to the priest, Aaron. In fact, this is the only time in Leviticus that God speaks directly to Aaron. Up to this time, God had instructed Aaron through his mediator, Moses. The fact that God Himself gave this commandment to Aaron shows the importance of the commandment. But note this fact as well: the commandment is to be a permanent commandment for all generations. Every person, priest and layperson alike, is to avoid drunkenness. The commandment of God is clear: no priest or minister of God is ever to perform his service while intoxicated. Likewise, no person is ever to perform his work or duties while intoxicated. Note the severe warning of God: if anyone went into the Tabernacle intoxicated, he would die. This warning and the fact that this commandment is given in the midst of the judgment of Nadab and Abihu—all this points perhaps to the fact that the two priests had entered the Tabernacle while intoxicated. Some commentators hold this position.

d. The way to prevent the judgment of God is to live totally for God (v.10). Within the Tabernacle, there was both holy food and common food. In fact, most of the items and functions in the Tabernacle were counted holy by God. For example, the fire in the Tabernacle was counted as holy fire; whereas, all other fire was counted as common fire. The point is this: priests or ministers of God and laypersons alike were to discern between the holy and the common, between the clean and the unclean. In their lives and service for God, the priest or minister of God and the layperson must be able to discern…

- between right and wrong
- between what God has said to do and said not to do
- between how to approach God and how not to approach God
- between what is allowed and what is not allowed
- between how to serve God and how not to serve God
- between what is holy and pure and what is unholy and impure

e. The way to prevent the judgment of God is to teach the people all the laws or commandments of God (v.11). Simply stated, a person has to know the law before he can keep the law; he has to know the commandments of God before he can keep the commandments of God. The task of the priests or ministers of God is to teach the people the laws and commandments of God. Once they know the commandments of God, they can escape the judgment of God.

Thought 1. The lesson to us is clear: ministers and believers alike must do all they can to prevent the judgment of God, prevent His judgment from falling upon them or upon any other believer. The way to escape the judgment of God is the same for us is as it was for Aaron and the Israelites.

(1) We must guard against defilement and guard against all sin if we wish to escape the judgment of God.

> **"Watch and pray, that ye enter not into temptation: the spirit indeed *is* willing, but the flesh *is* weak" (Mt.26:41).**
> **"Looking diligently lest any man fail of the grace of God; lest any root of bitterness springing up trouble *you,* and thereby many be defiled" (He.12:12).**
> **"Be sober, be vigilant; because your adversary the devil, as a roaring lion, walketh about, seeking whom he may devour" (1 Pe.5:8).**

(2) We must show total devotion to God if we wish to escape the judgment of God.

> **"And thou shalt love the LORD thy God with all thine heart, and with all thy soul, and with all thy might" (De.6:5).**
> **"Blessed *are* they that keep his testimonies, *and that* seek him with the whole heart" (Ps.119:2).**

"Trust in the LORD with all thine heart; and lean not unto thine own understanding" (Pr.3:5).

"And ye shall seek me, and find *me,* when ye shall search for me with all your heart" (Je.29:13).

"Therefore also now, saith the LORD, turn ye *even* to me with all your heart, and with fasting, and with weeping, and with mourning" (Joel 2:12).

(3) We must avoid drunkenness if we wish to escape the judgment of God.

"And take heed to yourselves, lest at any time your hearts be overcharged with surfeiting, and drunkenness, and cares of this life, and so that day come upon you unawares" (Lu.21:34)

"Let us walk honestly, as in the day; not in rioting and drunkenness, not in chambering and wantonness, not in strife and envying" (Ro.13:13).

"Know ye not that the unrighteous shall not inherit the kingdom of God? Be not deceived: neither fornicators, nor idolaters, nor adulterers, nor effeminate, nor abusers of themselves with mankind, Nor thieves, nor covetous, nor drunkards, nor revilers, nor extortioners, shall inherit the kingdom of God" (1 Co.6:9-10).

(4) We must live totally for God: learn to discern between the holy and common, between the clean and unclean if we wish to escape the judgment of God.

"But the natural man receiveth not the things of the Spirit of God: for they are foolishness unto him: neither can he know *them,* because they are spiritually discerned" (1 Co.2:14).

"But strong meat belongeth to them that are of full age, *even* those who by reason of use have their senses exercised to discern both good and evil" (He.5:14).

"Give therefore thy servant an understanding heart to judge thy people, that I may discern between good and bad: for who is able to judge this thy so great a people?" (1 K.3:9).

"And the spirit of the LORD shall rest upon him, the spirit of wisdom and understanding, the spirit of counsel and might, the spirit of knowledge and of the fear of the LORD; And shall make him of quick understanding in the fear of the LORD: and he shall not judge after the sight of his eyes, neither reprove after the hearing of his ears: But with righteousness shall he judge the poor, and reprove with equity for the meek of the earth" (Is.11:2-4).

(5) We must teach the people all the laws or commandments of God if we wish to escape the judgment of God.

"Go ye therefore, and teach all nations, baptizing them in the name of the Father, and of the Son, and of the Holy Ghost: Teaching them to observe all things whatsoever I have commanded you: and, lo, I am with you alway, *even* unto the end of the world. Amen" (Mt.28:19-20).

"Go, stand and speak in the temple to the people all the words of this life" (Ac.5:20).

"For therefore we both labour and suffer reproach, because we trust in the living God, who is the Saviour of all men, specially of those that believe. These things command and teach" (1 Ti.4:10-11).

"Thou therefore, my son, be strong in the grace that is in Christ Jesus. And the things that thou hast heard of me among many witnesses, the same commit thou to faithful men, who shall be able to teach others also" (2 Ti.2:1-2).

"And the servant of the Lord must not strive; but be gentle unto all *men,* apt to teach, patient, In meekness instructing those that oppose themselves; if God peradventure will give them repentance to the acknowledging of the truth; And *that* they may recover themselves out of the snare of the devil, who are taken captive by him at his will" (2 Ti.2:24-26).

"These things speak, and exhort, and rebuke with all authority. Let no man despise thee" (Tit.2:15).

4 (10:12-15) **Grace, of God—God, Grace of—Care, of God—Priests, Support of—Ministers, Support of—Offerings, to Support Priests**: there is the grace of God in the face of judgment.

OUTLINE	SCRIPTURE	SCRIPTURE	OUTLINE
4. The grace of God in the face of judgment	12 And Moses spake unto Aaron, and unto Eleazar and unto Ithamar, his sons that were left, Take the meat offering that remaineth of the offerings of the LORD made by fire, and eat it without leaven beside the altar: for it *is* most holy:	sacrifices of the LORD made by fire: for so I am commanded.	• It was the command of God
a. God did not forfeit the privileges of the faithful because of the sin of some		14 And the wave breast and heave shoulder shall ye eat in a clean place; thou, and thy sons, and thy daughters with thee: for *they be* thy due, and thy sons' due, *which are* given out of the sacrifices of peace offerings of the children of Israel.	2) The priests were also told to have their families join them in eating the breast & thigh of the Fellowship or Peace Offering
1) The faithful priests were told to eat what was left of the Grain Offering given to the LORD:			
• It was their share, part of their support	13 And ye shall eat it in the holy place, because it *is* thy due, and thy sons' due, of the	15 The heave shoulder and the	3) The meat was first to be

OUTLINE	SCRIPTURE	SCRIPTURE	OUTLINE
offered as a wave offering of thanksgiving b. God set aside this part of the offering as support for the	wave breast shall they bring with the offerings made by fire of the fat, to wave *it for* a wave offering before the	LORD; and it shall be thine, and thy sons' with thee, by a statute for ever; as the LORD hath commanded.	priests: Was to be given to them with each Fellowship Offering

a. Note that God did not negate or cancel the privileges of the faithful because of the sin of some (vv.12-15). Aaron was obviously hurting, filled with sorrow and grief for his two dead sons. God knew this; therefore, God wanted to assure Aaron of His support, that God's hand was still upon his life and ministry. This God did by having the faithful priests, Aaron and his two surviving sons, eat what was left of the Grain Offering. This act assured Aaron and his sons that God's hand was still upon them. How? This was the regular share, the regular support, that was to go to the priests. In essence, God was telling Aaron that he was still to receive the portion belonging to the priests. He was still the priest, the minister of God. Note that God had commanded Moses to give these instructions to Aaron.

But even more than this, the priests were told to have their families join them in eating the breast and thigh of the Fellowship or Peace Offering that had been offered earlier (vv.14-15). However, the meat was first to be offered as a wave offering of thanksgiving to God (v.15).

b. Note that God made this part of their permanent support (v.15). The breast and thigh of the Fellowship or Peace Offering was to be given them every time such an offering was made.

Thought 1. God showers His grace upon the faithful. The sin of some does not cancel the privileges of the faithful. God fulfills His promises always, pouring out the abundance of His provision upon all who are faithful.

"And, behold, I *am* with thee, and will keep thee in all *places* whither thou goest, and will bring thee again into this land; for I will not leave thee, until I have done *that* which I have spoken to thee of" (Ge.28:15).

"And he said, My presence shall go *with thee,* and I will give thee rest" (Ex.33:14).

"Fear thou not; for I *am* with thee: be not dismayed; for I *am* thy God: I will strengthen thee; yea, I will help thee; yea, I will uphold thee with the right hand of my righteousness" (Is.41:10).

"When thou passest through the waters, I *will be* with thee; and through the rivers, they shall not overflow thee: when thou walkest through the fire, thou shalt not be burned; neither shall the flame kindle upon thee" (Is.43:2).

"*Let your* conversation *be* without covetousness; *and be* content with such things as ye have: for he hath said, I will never leave thee, nor forsake thee. So that we may boldly say, The Lord *is* my helper, and I will not fear what man shall do unto me" (He.13:5-6).

"For where two or three are gathered together in my name, there am I in the midst of them" (Mt.18:20).

"Teaching them to observe all things whatsoever I have commanded you: and, lo, I am with you alway, *even* unto the end of the world. Amen" (Mt.28:20).

⑤ (10:16-20) **Mercy, of God—Tenderness, of God**: there is the mercy and tenderness of God when dealing with people and judgment. What happened next is interesting. Note the Scripture and outline:

OUTLINE	SCRIPTURE	SCRIPTURE	OUTLINE
5. **The mercy & tenderness of God when dealing with people & judgment** a. A serious mistake: The goat of the Sin Offering had been burned up 1) The goat was supposed to be eaten: It was holy, set apart to make atonement, to reconcile the people (the only time meat was not eaten was when its blood was taken into the Holy Place) 2) The mistake: Its blood had not been taken into the Holy	16 And Moses diligently sought the goat of the sin offering, and, behold, it was burnt: and he was angry with Eleazar and Ithamar, the sons of Aaron *which were* left alive, saying, 17 Wherefore have ye not eaten the sin offering in the holy place, seeing it *is* most holy, and *God* hath given it you to bear the iniquity of the congregation, to make atonement for them before the LORD? 18 Behold, the blood of it was not brought in within	the holy *place:* ye should indeed have eaten it in the holy *place,* as I commanded. 19 And Aaron said unto Moses, Behold, this day have they offered their sin offering and their burnt offering before the LORD; and such things have befallen me: and *if* I had eaten the sin offering to day, should it have been accepted in the sight of the LORD? 20 And when Moses heard *that,* he was content.	Place; therefore, the meat was to be eaten b. The explanation by Aaron: The priests had approached God that day—as commanded—thru the Sin Offering & the Burnt Offering 1) Would God have been pleased if he had eaten on the very day his sons had been stricken dead by God? 2) God had mercy—understood Aaron's grief—despite the mistake

a. A serious mistake was made by Aaron. The goat of the Sin Offering had been burned up (vv.16-18). Aaron was supposed to have eaten the goat of the Sin Offering, for it was holy, set apart by God as part of the priests' support. Note what God said: the Sin Offering had been offered to make atonement, to reconcile the people to Him. Its blood had not been taken into the Holy Place; therefore, the meat was to be eaten. Keep in mind that the meat of all offerings taken into the holy place was not to be eaten. Aaron had made a serious mistake; consequently, Moses was concerned that the holiness of God would strike out in judgment against Aaron just as it had done against his two sons.

b. Note the explanation by Aaron: the priests had approached God that day as commanded, through the Sin Offering and the Burnt Offering. But now, in light of the death of his two sons, he just did not feel like eating. "Would the LORD have been pleased if I had eaten on the very day my sons had been stricken dead?" Aaron asked Moses. Note God's wonderful mercy: He understood Aaron's sorrow and grief despite the mistake.

Thought 1. God is merciful and God is tender when dealing with us in judgment. It is not God's desire to judge and condemn us but rather to save us. God is longsuffering, not willing that any should perish. True, most people deny, reject, and ignore God and His commandments in Holy Scripture. Most people choose to walk through life as they wish, doing their own thing instead of following God. Few people are willing to trust Jesus Christ as their personal Savior and do what God dictates in the Holy Scripture. Nevertheless, God loves man and wants to shower mercy and tenderness upon man. God wants to save man, make him acceptable in the atoning sacrifice of His Son, the Lord Jesus Christ.

"But God, who is rich in mercy, for his great love wherewith he loved us, Even when we were dead in sins, hath quickened us together with Christ, (by grace ye are saved)" (Ep.2:4-5).

"But after that the kindness and love of God our Saviour toward man appeared, Not by works of righteousness which we have done, but according to his mercy he saved us, by the washing of regeneration, and renewing of the Holy Ghost; Which he shed on us abundantly through Jesus Christ our Saviour; That being justified by his grace, we should be made heirs according to the hope of eternal life" (Tit.3:4-7).

"The Lord is not slack concerning his promise, as some men count slackness; but is longsuffering to usward, not willing that any should perish, but that all should come to repentance" (2 Pe.3:9).

"*It is of* the LORD'S mercies that we are not consumed, because his compassions fail not" (Lam.3:22).

"And rend your heart, and not your garments, and turn unto the LORD your God: for he *is* gracious and merciful, slow to anger, and of great kindness" (Joel 2:13).

"Who *is* a God like unto thee, that pardoneth iniquity, and passeth by the transgression of the remnant of his heritage? he retaineth not his anger for ever, because he delighteth *in* mercy" (Mi.7:18).

TYPES, SYMBOLS, AND PICTURES
Leviticus 10:1-20

Historical Term	Type or Picture (Scriptural Basis for Each)	Life Application for Today's Believer	Biblical Application
The Offering of Strange, Unauthorized Fire to the LORD Le.10:1	*The offering of strange, unauthorized fire to the LORD is a symbol of approaching God in the wrong way.* **"And Nadab and Abihu, the sons of Aaron, took either of them his censer, and put fire therein, and put incense thereon, and offered strange fire before the LORD, which he commanded them not" (Le.10:1).**	We must always remember that the true worship and religion of God are a *revealed worship* and a *revealed religion.* God has revealed through His Son and the Holy Scriptures exactly how His people are to worship Him. But these two priests (Nadab and Abihu) ignored and rejected God's way. They created and developed their own way to approach God. How like so many today who approach God as they think and as they wish, ignoring God's way and His clear instructions.	*"Jesus saith unto him, I am the way, the truth, and the life: no man cometh unto the Father, but by me" (Jn.14:6).* *"Judas saith unto him, not Iscariot, Lord, how is it that thou wilt manifest thyself unto us, and not unto the world? Jesus answered and said unto him, If a man love me, he will keep my words: and my Father will love him, and we will come unto him, and make our abode with him. He that loveth me not keepeth not my sayings: and the word which ye hear is not mine, but the Father's which sent me" (Jn.14:22-24).* *"Neither is there salvation in any other: for there is none other name under heaven given among men, whereby we must be saved" (Ac.4:12).*
Death: A Person Who Came in Contact with the Dead was Counted Unclean, Defiled Le.10:4-5	*The death of Aaron's two sons is a picture of defilement, uncleanness, corruption, and decay. Note that Aaron was not allowed to*	The lesson to us is clear: ministers and believers alike must do all they can to prevent the judgment of God, prevent His judgment from	*"All these evil things come from within, and defile the man" (Mk.7:23).* *"Having therefore these promises, dearly beloved,*

TYPES, SYMBOLS, AND PICTURES
Leviticus 10:1-20

Historical Term	Type or Picture (Scriptural Basis for Each)	Life Application for Today's Believer	Biblical Application
	take care of his two dead sons. Priests were forbidden to touch or go near dead corpses because death symbolized defilement and uncleanness, corruption and decay. Defilement and corruption disqualified a priest from performing his service for God. For this reason, Aaron was forbidden to touch the two dead bodies despite the fact that they were his sons. Note that Moses had the two nephews of Aaron remove the dead bodies (the defilement) outside the camp (v.5). "And Moses called Mishael and Elzaphan, the sons of Uzziel the uncle of Aaron, and said unto them, Come near, carry your brethren from before the sanctuary out of the camp" (Le.10:4).	falling upon them or upon any other believer. The way to escape the judgment of God is the same for us as it was for Aaron and the Israelites. We must guard against defilement if we wish to escape the judgment of God.	let us cleanse ourselves from all filthiness of the flesh and spirit, perfecting holiness in the fear of God" (2 Co. 7:1). "Looking diligently lest any man fail of the grace of God; lest any root of bitterness springing up trouble you, and thereby many be defiled" (He.12:15). "Draw nigh to God, and he will draw nigh to you. Cleanse your hands, ye sinners; and purify your hearts, ye double minded" (Js.4:8). "If a man therefore purge himself from these, he shall be a vessel unto honour, sanctified, and meet for the master's use, and prepared unto every good work" (2 Ti.2:21).

DIVISION III

THE WAY TO LIVE A HOLY LIFE BEFORE GOD (PART I): BY A CLEAN BODY (SEPARATION), 11:1–16:34

(11:1–16:34) **DIVISION OVERVIEW**: How can God's people live holy lives before God? By taking care of their bodies as well as their spirits. The body is the subject of this division. The body is to be kept clean and to be protected not only from disease and injury but from strain and stress as well (see 12:1-8). This is the purpose lying behind *The Levitical Laws of Cleansing* covered in this division.

But note this fact: God had more than health in mind when He gave the cleansing laws. God had a spiritual purpose in mind. The laws of cleanliness and defilement were symbolic of spiritual truth, of being spiritually clean and undefiled. The laws of cleanliness set God's people apart as a clean, holy people. God's people were to be distinct and different from the surrounding people and nations. The surrounding nations and people were living unholy lives, lives of immorality and lawlessness. But God's people were to be distinct and different in this very fact: they were to live holy lives. They were to bear a strong testimony that they followed God and obeyed His commandments. They ate only clean food and took care of their bodies, kept them clean and healthy—all in obedience to God's law governing cleanliness. Simply stated, holiness demands that God's people conform to the laws of God, the laws of cleanliness. (See Da.1:8, see vv.3-16.)

THE WAY TO LIVE A HOLY LIFE BEFORE GOD (PART I): BY A CLEAN BODY (SEPARATION), 11:1–16:34

A. **Laws That Govern Clean and Unclean Animals: Symbolizes Physical and Spiritual Purity—by Eating the Right Food, 11:1-47**

B. **Laws That Protect Mother and Child Right After Childbirth: Symbolizes the Need for Cleansing from the Sinful Nature, 12:1-8**

C. **Laws That Protect People from Leprosy or Other Infectious Skin Diseases: Symbolizes the Disease of Sin and the Need to Prevent the Spread of Sin, 13:1-59**

D. **Laws That Cleanse and Restore People from Leprosy, from All Forms of Infectious Skin Disease: Symbolizes the Need for Spiritual Cleansing, 14:1-57**

E. **Laws That Protect and Cleanse People from Diseases of Sexual Impurity: Symbolizes How Defiling Sin Is and the Need to Be Cleansed from Sin, 15:1-33**

F. **The Great Provision of God to Make a Person Holy, the Great Day of Atonement: Symbolizes the Only Way to Approach God—Through the Shed Blood of the Atoning Sacrifice, 16:1-34**

CHAPTER 11

III. THE WAY TO LIVE A HOLY LIFE BEFORE GOD (PART I): BY A CLEAN BODY (SEPARATION), 11:1–16:34

A. Laws That Govern Clean and Unclean Animals: Symbolizes Physical and Spiritual Purity—by Eating the Right Food, 11:1-47

1. The source of the instructions: God

2. The law governing animals that live on land

  a. The edible land creatures: Those with fully split hooves & that chew the cud

  b. The inedible land creatures: Those that either chew the cud or have split hooves
    1) The camel: Chews the cud but does not have a split hoof

    2) The coney: Chews the cud but does not have a split hoof

    3) The rabbit: Chews the cud but does not have a split hoof

    4) The pig: Has a split hoof but does not chew the cud

  c. The clear charge: Must not eat nor touch the carcasses of the inedible land creatures because they are unclean (a symbol of spiritual uncleanness)

3. The law governing animals that live in water, seas or streams

  a. The edible water creatures: Ones that have fins & scales

  b. The inedible water creatures: Ones that do not have fins & scales

    1) Are to detest: Count ceremonially, spiritually unclean

    2) Must never eat their meat nor touch their dead bodies

And the LORD spake unto Moses and to Aaron, saying unto them,

2 Speak unto the children of Israel, saying, These *are* the beasts which ye shall eat among all the beasts that *are* on the earth.

3 Whatsoever parteth the hoof, and is clovenfooted, *and* cheweth the cud, among the beasts, that shall ye eat.

4 Nevertheless these shall ye not eat of them that chew the cud, or of them that divide the hoof: as the camel, because he cheweth the cud, but divideth not the hoof; he *is* unclean unto you.

5 And the coney, because he cheweth the cud, but divideth not the hoof; he *is* unclean unto you.

6 And the hare, because he cheweth the cud, but divideth not the hoof; he *is* unclean unto you.

7 And the swine, though he divide the hoof, and be clovenfooted, yet he cheweth not the cud; he *is* unclean to you.

8 Of their flesh shall ye not eat, and their carcase shall ye not touch; they *are* unclean to you.

9 These shall ye eat of all that *are* in the waters: whatsoever hath fins and scales in the waters, in the seas, and in the rivers, them shall ye eat.

10 And all that have not fins and scales in the seas, and in the rivers, of all that move in the waters, and of any living thing which *is* in the waters, they *shall be* an abomination unto you:

11 They shall be even an abomination unto you; ye shall not eat of their flesh, but ye shall have their carcases in abomination.

12 Whatsoever hath no fins nor scales in the waters, that *shall be* an abomination unto you.

13 And these *are they which* ye shall have in abomination among the fowls; they shall not be eaten, they *are* an abomination: the eagle, and the ossifrage, and the ospray,

14 And the vulture, and the kite after his kind;

15 Every raven after his kind;

16 And the owl, and the night hawk, and the cuckow, and the hawk after his kind,

17 And the little owl, and the cormorant, and the great owl,

18 And the swan, and the pelican, and the gier eagle,

19 And the stork, the heron after her kind, and the lapwing, and the bat.

20 All fowls that creep, going upon *all* four, *shall be* an abomination unto you.

21 Yet these may ye eat of every flying creeping thing that goeth upon *all* four, which have legs above their feet, to leap withal upon the earth;

22 *Even* these of them ye may eat; the locust after his kind, and the bald locust after his kind, and the beetle after his kind, and the grasshopper after his kind.

23 But all *other* flying creeping things, which have four feet, *shall be* an abomination unto you.

24 And for these ye shall be unclean: whosoever toucheth the carcase of them shall be unclean until the even.

25 And whosoever beareth *ought* of the carcase of them shall wash his clothes, and be unclean until the even.

26 *The carcases* of every beast which divideth the hoof, and *is* not clovenfooted, nor cheweth the cud, *are* unclean unto you: every one that toucheth them shall be unclean.

27 And whatsoever goeth upon his paws, among all manner of beasts that go on *all* four, those *are* unclean unto you: whoso toucheth

---

    3) A strong re-emphasis: Are forbidden to eat any water creature that does not have fins & scales

4. The law governing birds that are inedible, that are to be detested (judged spiritually, ceremonially unclean)

  a. The eagle, the vulture, the black vulture

  b. The buzzard, kites of all kinds

  c. The ravens—of all kinds

  d. The horned owl, the nighthawk, the seagull, hawks of any kind

  e. The little owl, the cormorant, the great owl

  f. The white owl, the pelican, the vulture or eagle

  g. The stork, herons of all kinds, the hoopoe, the bat

5. The law governing insects
  a. The inedible: Swarming insects that walk on the ground
  b. The edible exceptions: Insects with jointed legs for hopping on the ground

    1) All varieties of locust, katydid, cricket, or grasshopper
    2) All others are forbidden, to be detested: Counted spiritually, ceremonially unclean

6. The way animals defiled a person & the required treatment
  a. Touching a dead insect defiled a person
    1) Counted unclean until evening
    2) The treatment: Washing one's clothes (a symbol of spiritual cleansing)
  b. Touching a dead land animal defiled a person
    1) The animals
    • Any animal with a split hoof not completely divided or that does not chew the cud
    • Any animal that has paws
    2) The ceremonial uncleanness: Unclean until evening

3) The treatment: Had to wash one's clothes (a symbol of spiritual, ceremonial cleansing)

c. Touching the carcass of a small land animal that scurries or creeps on the ground defiled a person
1) The animals listed
- The weasel, rat, lizard
- The gecko, the monitor lizard, the common lizard, the skink, the chameleon
2) The defilement: Touching the carcass made a person spiritually, ceremonially unclean

3) The treatment explained with examples
- If a dead animal fell on something, the article had to be put in water until evening—washed—to become spiritually, ceremonially clean

- If a dead animal fell into a clay pot, the clay pot was unclean, to be broken—never used again

- If any food or drink was touched by the cleaning water used to wash any defiled pot, the food & drink were spiritually, unclean—not to be eaten
- If anything was touched by a carcass, it was spiritually, ceremonially unclean: Clay ovens & cooking pots were to be broken up

- If a carcass fell into a cistern or spring, the water remained clean, but the person who removed the dead animal was counted ceremonially unclean
- If a carcass fell on seed to be planted, it remained clean

their carcase shall be unclean until the even.
28 And he that beareth the carcase of them shall wash his clothes, and be unclean until the even: they *are* unclean unto you.
29 These also *shall be* unclean unto you among the creeping things that creep upon the earth; the weasel, and the mouse, and the tortoise after his kind,
30 And the ferret, and the chameleon, and the lizard, and the snail, and the mole.
31 These *are* unclean to you among all that creep: whosoever doth touch them, when they be dead, shall be unclean until the even.
32 And upon whatsoever *any* of them, when they are dead, doth fall, it shall be unclean; whether *it be* any vessel of wood, or raiment, or skin, or sack, whatsoever vessel *it be*, wherein *any* work is done, it must be put into water, and it shall be unclean until the even; so it shall be cleansed.
33 And every earthen vessel, whereinto *any* of them falleth, whatsoever *is* in it shall be unclean; and ye shall break it.
34 Of all meat which may be eaten, *that* on which *such* water cometh shall be unclean: and all drink that may be drunk in every *such* vessel shall be unclean.
35 And every *thing* whereupon *any part* of their carcase falleth shall be unclean; *whether it be* oven, or ranges for pots, they shall be broken down: *for they are* unclean, and shall be unclean unto you.
36 Nevertheless a fountain or pit, *wherein there is* plenty of water, shall be clean: but that which toucheth their carcase shall be unclean.
37 And if *any part* of their carcase fall upon any sowing seed which is to be

sown, it *shall be* clean.
38 But if *any* water be put upon the seed, and *any part* of their carcase fall thereon, it *shall be* unclean unto you.
39 And if any beast, of which ye may eat, die; he that toucheth the carcase thereof shall be unclean until the even.
40 And he that eateth of the carcase of it shall wash his clothes, and be unclean until the even: he also that beareth the carcase of it shall wash his clothes, and be unclean until the even.
41 And every creeping thing that creepeth upon the earth *shall be* an abomination; it shall not be eaten.
42 Whatsoever goeth upon the belly, and whatsoever goeth upon *all* four, or whatsoever hath more feet among all creeping things that creep upon the earth, them ye shall not eat; for they *are* an abomination.
43 Ye shall not make yourselves abominable with any creeping thing that creepeth, neither shall ye make yourselves unclean with them, that ye should be defiled thereby.
44 For I *am* the LORD your God: ye shall therefore sanctify yourselves, and ye shall be holy; for I *am* holy: neither shall ye defile yourselves with any manner of creeping thing that creepeth upon the earth.
45 For I *am* the LORD that bringeth you up out of the land of Egypt, to be your God: ye shall therefore be holy, for I *am* holy.
46 This *is* the law of the beasts, and of the fowl, and of every living creature that moveth in the waters, and of every creature that creepeth upon the earth:
47 To make a difference between the unclean and the clean, and between the beast that may be eaten and the beast that may not be eaten.

- If water had been put on the seed & a carcass fell on it, it was unclean

d. Touching or eating the carcass of an edible animal defiled a person: Counted defiled until evening

1) The treatment for touching or eating: Washing one's clothes
2) The treatment for picking up carcasses: Washing one's clothes (a symbol of ceremonial cleansing)

7. The importance of the food laws: Summarized & re-emphasized
a. The detestable animals were never to be eaten
1) The animal that scurried along the ground
2) The animal that walked on four legs
3) The animal that walked on many legs

b. The rule: Must not defile oneself by eating or touching forbidden animals: A symbol of spiritual, ceremonial pollution, uncleanness

8. The purpose for the laws
a. To declare that Israel was God's chosen & holy people
1) Must be like God: Consecrated—set apart—holy
2) Must demonstrate by not eating & touching unclean animals
b. To declare that God is the Savior who delivered His people from Egypt (a symbol of the world): Must be their God & set them apart as holy
c. To teach His people to distinguish, discern between the unclean & clean
1) The declaration restated

2) The point clearly stated: Must distinguish, discern between the unclean & the clean

DIVISION III

THE WAY TO LIVE A HOLY LIFE BEFORE GOD (PART I):
BY A CLEAN BODY (SEPARATION), 11:1–16:34

A. Laws That Govern Clean and Unclean Animals: Symbolizes Physical and Spiritual Purity—by Eating the Right Food, 11:1-47

(11:1-47) **Introduction**: a healthy, clean body is of critical importance. For years, the media in nations all over the world have been stressing and launching programs to make people more health-conscious. Good health increases a person's quality of life as well as length of life. A person with a healthy, clean body enjoys life more and gets more out of life. Yet, many people ignore and neglect their bodies; they abuse and damage their bodies; they...

- overeat
- eat the wrong foods
- smoke, drink alcoholic beverages, or take drugs
- fail to adequately exercise
- delay medical exams

God cares for man's body. He created the human body for man; therefore, God wants man to care about and take care of his body. This is clearly seen in the food laws discussed in this chapter. Obviously God gave the laws for health reasons, to protect His people from disease, bad diets, and parasites. Medicine had not yet advanced enough for the people to fully understand the reasons for the food laws. Nevertheless, God knew, so He protected His people by giving them laws to govern what they ate. Animals that were more likely to carry parasites or disease were forbidden: they were designated as unclean food. Animals that were less likely to carry parasites or disease were edible: they were called clean animals.

The Expositor's Bible Commentary says this about the food laws:

> They are remarkably valuable in the area of public health....It would be in line with God's promised blessing that "none of these diseases" of Egypt would be visited on Israel, for "I am the LORD your Healer" (cf. Exod.15:26).
> ...In general it can be said that the laws protected Israel from bad diet, dangerous vermin, and communicable diseases....
> First, the laws protected Israel's diet. Some of the food forbidden was good some of the time, but not unless it was properly prepared. Pigs spread trichinosis; rabbits spread tularemia. Albright (Yahweh, pp.178-81) pointed out that the fish classified as clean are "normally free-swimming, whereas fish without scales and fins, such as eels, are usually mud-burrowers and therefore hosts to a great many more parasites than free-swimming fish." Cows, goats, and sheep are safe to eat under all ordinary circumstances and are economical to raise. The horse and camel were too uneconomical to use for meat....
> The Hebrew was not only to avoid eating unclean animals; he was not to touch their dead carcasses. Thus the laws automatically helped control vermin. Common unclean animals would be spiders, flies, bugs, rats, and mice. A dead rat in a Hebrew house was not overlooked. It was carefully taken out and buried. In an effort to avoid such problems, the Hebrew housewife would normally keep a clean house.[1]

In giving the hygienic interpretation of this passage, Gordon J. Wenham says this:

> ...the unclean creatures are unfit to eat because they are carriers of disease. The clean animals are those that are relatively safe to eat. This explanation is adopted by many modern writers. Pork can be a source of trichinosis. The coney and hare are carriers of tularemia. Fish without fins and scales tend to burrow into the mud and become sources of dangerous bacteria, as do the birds of prey which feed on carrion.[2]

But note this fact: God had more than health in mind when He gave the cleansing laws. God had a spiritual purpose in mind. The laws of cleanliness and defilement were symbolic of spiritual truth, of being spiritually clean and undefiled. The laws of cleanliness set God's people apart as a clean, holy people. God's people were to be distinct and different from the surrounding people and nations. The surrounding nations and people were living unholy lives, lives of immorality and lawlessness. But God's people were to be distinct and different in this very fact: they were to live holy lives. They were to bear a strong testimony that they followed God and obeyed His commandments. They ate only clean food: they took care of their bodies, kept them clean and healthy—all in obedience to God's law governing cleanliness. Simply stated, holiness demands that God's people conform to the laws of God, the laws of cleanliness. (See Daniel 1:8, see vv.3-16.)

Are these laws governing food valid for Christian believers today? The New Testament says, "No!" What, then, is their application to us? Is there meaning in the laws for us? Gordon J. Wenham gives an excellent discussion on this subject. Though lengthy, it is well worth quoting in full:

> The Levitical laws relating to food caused one of the great controversies in the NT Church, and we find references to them by most of the NT writers. The controversy was due to two factors. First, the observance of these laws had become the mark of the faithful Jew; his abstinence from certain foods and his adherence to various rituals distinguished him from the Gentiles. As a result of the dispersal of Jews throughout the ancient world and the incorporation of Judaea into foreign empires, the Jews had become acutely aware of their distinctiveness, a distinctiveness that was focused and expressed in their food laws. Those in daily contact with Gentiles were continually reminded of the differences, and not least that Israel was God's chosen people and a holy nation. These laws, therefore, occupied a central place in Jewish life and thought, and for that matter still do today. The second reason for the controversy was our LORD's insistence that the food laws did not really matter, and the apostolic decision that they need not be observed unless it gave offense to the scrupulous.
> Before discussing the theological motive underlying this radical reappraisal of the food laws, we should review the NT passages discussing the question. Matt. 15:10-20 (//Mark 7:14-23) is part of a sermon by Jesus

---

1 *The Expositor's Bible Commentary*, Vol.2. Frank E. Gaebelein, General Editor, p.569.
2 Gordon J. Wenham. *The Book of Leviticus*, p.167.

attacking the custom of the Pharisees, which allowed men who made a donation to the temple to escape the obligation imposed by the fifth commandment to look after their parents. The custom made Pharisaic tradition more important than the word of God. Then Jesus turns to another traditional practice which he said tended to be regarded as more important than moral principle. He said that it was more important to have a pure heart than to wash hands before meals. "Whatever goes into the mouth passes into the stomach, and so passes on. But what comes out of the mouth proceeds from the heart, and this defiles a man. For out of the heart come evil thoughts, murder, adultery, fornication, theft, false witness, slander. These are what defile a man; but to eat with unwashed hands does not defile a man" (Matt. 15:17-20; cf 23:25-28). Mark, commenting on Jesus' remarks, says, "Thus he declared all food clean" (7:19). In other words Jesus was abrogating the distinction between clean and unclean animals. In John's Gospel we see Jesus putting his teaching into practice by asking for a drink from a Samaritan woman. In 4:9 the woman expresses surprise that Jesus as a Jew should be prepared to accept a drink from a Samaritan, 'For Jews do not drink from the same vessels as Samaritans' (cf NEB translation). The food laws were an assertion of Israel's distinctiveness; to remove them was to put into question her special status.

This comes out more clearly in the story of Cornelius. Like the conversion of Paul, this is a story which Luke recounts three times, a clear sign of its importance in the development of the early Church. We are told that Peter had a vision in which 'he saw the heaven opened, and something descending, like a great sheet, let down by four corners upon the earth. In it were all kinds of animals and reptiles and birds of the air. And there came a voice to him, "Rise, Peter; kill and eat." But Peter said, "No, LORD; for I have never eaten anything that is common or unclean." And the voice came to him again a second time, "What God has cleansed, you must not call common." This happened three times, and the thing was taken up at once to heaven' (Ac.10:11-16). Soon afterward men come and invite Peter to go to Cornelius' house. When Peter arrives there, he explains why he has gone. 'You yourselves know how unlawful it is for a Jew to associate with or to visit anyone of another nation; but God has shown me that I should not call any man common or unclean' (Ac.10:28). Then he preaches to them, and the Spirit comes upon Cornelius and his household and they are baptized. Reporting his actions to the other apostles, Peter points to the gift of the Spirit as proof that God has removed the barriers between Jew and Gentile. What is striking about the narrative from our point of view is the way Peter links the vision abolishing the distinction between clean and unclean animals with the distinction between clean and unclean men, i.e., between Jew and Gentile.

The issue of clean and unclean foods was discussed again at the Council of Jerusalem (Ac.15), when it was debated whether it was necessary to circumcise the Gentiles and charge them to keep the law of Moses (v.5). It was decided to require from Gentile believers only that they should abstain from the pollutions of idols, from unchastity, from what is strangled, and from blood. In other words, the requirement of circumcision and the distinction between clean and unclean animals were abolished. This is sometimes seen as a compromise between the Jewish and Gentile wings of the Church. There may well have been an element of this in their decision, but it is possible to see a theological basis for their conclusion. The rite of circumcision and the distinction between clean and unclean animals were particularly associated with the special status of Israel as the covenant people, whereas the prohibition on blood (and strangled meat) went back earlier to the time of Noah (Ge.9:4). It was the laws distinguishing Israel from the other nations that were set aside, not the older moral principles that applied to all men.

In Paul's Epistles the question of food is discussed in various passages. Paul does indeed advise that the Christian should abstain from certain foods if the circumstances warrant. This is not because any foods are unclean in themselves; "the earth is the LORD's, and everything in it" (1 Co.10:26). The reason for abstaining is now different: it is the law of love. The Christian according to Paul may eat anything as long as he gives no offense in so doing. But should this freedom lead to a fellow Christian stumbling, he should avoid those foods which lead to suspicion. "If your brother is being injured by what you eat, you are no longer walking in love. Do not let what you eat cause the ruin of one for whom Christ died' (Rom. 14:15)....

The NT teaches that the OT food laws are no longer binding on the Christian. These laws symbolized God's choice of Israel. They serve as constant reminders of God's electing grace. As he had limited his choice among the nations to Israel, so they for their part had to restrict their diet to certain animals. At every turn these laws reminded them of God's grace toward Israel. In the new era when salvation was open to all men, and Israel was no longer the only object of divine grace, the laws lost their particular significance. They could only serve to divide mankind into Jew and Gentile, whereas in the age which has now begun God's further purpose is revealed "in Christ...to unite all things in him" (Ep. 1:10). The distinction between clean and unclean foods is as obsolete as the distinction between Jew and Gentile.

This is not to say that these laws have nothing to teach the Christian. As we have seen, they were constant reminders to Israel that they were chosen to be a holy people, that they were called to imitate God, and that the laws were a reminder to give thanks for this calling. The NT believer is in a very similar position. The Church is now "a chosen race, a royal priesthood, a holy nation, God's own people" (1 Pet.2:9). They are bidden to set their "minds on things that are above, not on things that are on the earth" (Col.3:2), to "give thanks in all circumstances" (1 Thess. 5:18). Though the Christian is so much more privileged than ancient Israel, it is easy to take for granted the grace that has been given him and fail to acknowledge it. The ancient food laws were designed to curb such forgetfulness.

These laws were not only reminders of Israel's redemption, they were "like signs which at every turn inspired meditation on the oneness, purity and completeness of God. By rules of avoidance, holiness was given a physical expression in every encounter with the animal kingdom and at every meal. Observance of the dietary rules would then have been a meaningful part of the great liturgical act of recognition and worship which culminated in the sacrifice of the temple." Douglas has showed that there is a connection in biblical thinking between wholeness, holiness, and integrity. God demands integrity of character and wholeness of physical form in his worshippers. These rules were symbols of a moral order. Only the normal members of each sphere of creation, e.g., fishes with fins, counted as clean. This definition, which identified 'perfect' members of the animal kingdom with purity, was a reminder that God looked for moral perfection in his people. Carrion-eating birds and carnivorous animals were unclean because they also typified a man's sinful, destructive, and murderous instincts. In a real sense, then, Jesus was drawing out the meaning of the symbolism of the Levitical laws in insisting that it was what comes out of man that defiles him, "evil thoughts, murder, adultery, etc." These rules in Leviticus served not only as reminders of redemption but of moral values. With the law of God written on his heart by the Spirit, the Christian ought not to need such tangible reminders of God's will and character. He also has ready access to the Bible, which holds up a mirror to his conduct. Let us follow James' advice to look into that perfect law, the law of liberty, and act (Js. 1:25). [3]

This is the important discussion of this passage: *Laws That Govern Clean and Unclean Animals: Symbolizes Physical and Spiritual Purity—by Eating the Right Food*, 11:1-47.

1. The source of the instructions: God (v.1).
2. The law governing animals that live on land (vv.2-8).
3. The law governing animals that live in water, seas or streams (vv.9-12).
4. The law governing birds that are inedible, that are to be detested (judged spiritually, ceremonially unclean) (vv.13-19).
5. The law governing insects (vv.20-21).
6. The way animals defiled a person and the required treatment (vv.24-40).
7. The importance of the food laws: summarized and reemphasized (vv.41-43).
8. The purpose for the laws (vv.44-47).

1 (11:1) **Commandments, Source**: the source of these laws is God. Note the Scripture and outline:

OUTLINE	SCRIPTURE
1. The source of the instructions: God	And the LORD spake unto Moses and to Aaron, saying unto them,

God cares for His people physically and spiritually; therefore, He wants them to take care of their bodies and spirits. This is the reason for these laws, that His people might have strong bodies and strong spirits. Note: this is the first detailed legal code governing food known among men. It was given to man by God Himself.

> **"For the LORD *is* our judge, the LORD *is* our lawgiver, the LORD *is* our king; he will save us"** (Is.33:22).
> **"Hearken unto me, my people; and give ear unto me, O my nation: for a law shall proceed from me, and I will make my judgment to rest for a light of the people"** (Is.51:4).
> **"There is one lawgiver, who is able to save and to destroy...?"** (Js.4:12).

2 (11:2-8) **Animals, Land—Land Animals—Animals, Clean—Animals, Unclean—Clean - Cleanliness, of Animals—Unclean - Uncleanness, of Animals—Food, Clean and Unclean—Animals, Edible and Inedible—Edible and Inedible Animals**: there was the law governing animals that live on land.

OUTLINE	SCRIPTURE	SCRIPTURE	OUTLINE
2. The law governing animals that live on land c. The edible land creatures: Those with fully split hooves & that chew the cud d. The inedible land creatures: Those that either chew the cud or have split hooves 1) The camel: Chews the cud but does not have a split hoof	2 Speak unto the children of Israel, saying, These *are* the beasts which ye shall eat among all the beasts that *are* on the earth. 3 Whatsoever parteth the hoof, and is clovenfooted, *and* cheweth the cud, among the beasts, that shall ye eat. 4 Nevertheless these shall ye not eat of them that chew the cud, or of them that divide the hoof: as the camel, because he cheweth the cud, but divideth not the hoof; he *is* unclean unto you.	5 And the coney, because he cheweth the cud, but divideth not the hoof; he *is* unclean unto you. 6 And the hare, because he cheweth the cud, but divideth not the hoof; he *is* unclean unto you. 7 And the swine, though he divide the hoof, and be clovenfooted, yet he cheweth not the cud; he *is* unclean to you. 8 Of their flesh shall ye not eat, and their carcase shall ye not touch; they *are* unclean to you.	2) The coney: Chews the cud but does not have a split hoof 3) The rabbit: Chews the cud but does not have a split hoof 4) The pig: Has a split hoof but does not chew the cud c. The clear charge: Must not eat nor touch the carcasses of the inedible land creatures because they are unclean (a symbol of spiritual uncleanness)

a. The edible land creatures were to have two specific characteristics or traits: they were to be animals with fully split hooves and that chewed the cud (vv.2-3).

b. The inedible land creatures were animals that had only one of the two above-named traits: some animals only chewed the cud and others only had split hooves. These were not to be eaten at all (v.4). Note the examples given:
⇒ The camel and the coney only chew the cud; they do not have split hooves (vv.4-5).
⇒ The rabbit only chews the cud; it does not have split hooves (v.6).
⇒ The pig has split hooves but it does not chew the cud (v.7).

---

3 Gordon J. Wenham. *The Book of Leviticus*, pp.181-185.

c. God gave a clear charge: the believer must not eat the meat of inedible land creatures nor touch their carcasses because they are unclean (v.8). However, a person could use these animals in his daily activities such as the camel for transporting goods or for riding. Note that the emphasis is upon clean and unclean animals. This law protected the health of God's people, protected them from dangerous parasites and diseases. It gave God's people a healthy diet and a healthy, clean body. But note this fact as well: the clean and unclean animals were symbols of being ceremonially, spiritually clean or unclean. This is to say that God had two purposes in giving these laws governing food:

⇒ the purpose of keeping His people physically healthy and clean
⇒ the purpose of keeping His people ceremonially, spiritually clean and healthy

Thought 1. The application for the believer is clear: the believer must keep his body clean and healthy, both physically and spiritually.

> **"Know ye not that your bodies are the members of Christ? shall I then take the members of Christ, and make *them* the members of an harlot? God forbid" (1 Co.6:15).**
> **"What? know ye not that your body is the temple of the Holy Ghost *which is* in you, which ye have of God, and ye are not your own? For ye are bought with a price: therefore glorify God in your body, and in your spirit, which are God's" (1 Co.6:19-20).**
> **"And the very God of peace sanctify you wholly; and *I pray God* your whole spirit and soul and body be preserved blameless unto the coming of our Lord Jesus Christ" (1 Th.5:23).**
> **"For bodily exercise profiteth little: but godliness is profitable unto all things, having promise of the life that now is, and of that which is to come" (1 Ti.4:8).**

3 (11:9-12) **Animals, Land—Animals, Clean—Animals, Unclean—Clean - Cleanliness, of Animals—Unclean - Uncleanness, of Animals—Food, Clean and Unclean—Animals, Edible and Inedible—Edible and Inedible Animals—Sea Animals—Animals, Sea:** there was the law governing the animals that live in water, the animals that live in the seas, lakes, rivers, and streams.

OUTLINE	SCRIPTURE	SCRIPTURE	OUTLINE
3. The law governing animals that live in water, seas or streams a. The edible water creatures: Ones that have fins & scales b. The inedible water creatures: Ones that do not have fins & scales	9 These shall ye eat of all that *are* in the waters: whatsoever hath fins and scales in the waters, in the seas, and in the rivers, them shall ye eat. 10 And all that have not fins and scales in the seas, and in the rivers, of all that move in the waters, and of any living thing which *is* in the waters: they *shall*	*be* an abomination unto you: 11 They shall be even an abomination unto you; ye shall not eat of their flesh but ye shall have their carcases in abomination. 12 Whatsoever hath no fins nor scales in the waters, that *shall be* an abomination unto you.	1) Are to detest: Count ceremonially, spiritually unclean 2) Must never eat their meat nor touch their dead bodies 3) A strong re-emphasis: Are forbidden to eat any water creature that does not have fins & scales

a. The edible water creatures were animals that had two traits or characteristics: they had to have both fins and scales (v.9).

b. The inedible water creatures had only one of the two traits or characteristics: they had only fins or only scales (v.10). Note what God says about the inedible water creatures. They were to be detested, counted ceremonially, spiritually unclean. The believer was never to eat their meat nor touch their dead bodies (v.11). Note the strong re-emphasis given to the believer: he was forbidden to eat any water creature that did not have fins and scales (v.12).

Thought 1. The believer must not damage his body or spirit. He must not reach out and partake of the things of the world, the things that damage him physically and spiritually.

(1) He must not overeat. Overeating damages the believer's body and breaks God's commandment against gluttony.

> **"(For many walk, of whom I have told you often, and now tell you even weeping, *that they are* the enemies of the cross of Christ: Whose end *is* destruction, whose God *is their* belly, and *whose* glory *is* in their shame, who mind earthly things)" (Ph.3:18-19).**
> **"All the labour of man *is* for his mouth, and yet the appetite is not filled" (Ec.6:7).**

(2) He must not partake of alcohol and drugs. Drunkenness damages the body and breaks God's commandment against drunkenness.

> **"And they shall say unto the elders of his city, This our son *is* stubborn and rebellious, he will not obey our voice; *he is* a glutton, and a drunkard" (De.21:20).**
> **"For the drunkard and the glutton shall come to poverty: and drowsiness shall clothe *a man* with rags" (Prov.23:21).**

(3) The believer must only eat and partake of the foods that will give him a clean body and spirit.

"I beseech you therefore, brethren, by the mercies of God, that ye present your bodies a living sacrifice, holy, acceptable unto God, *which is* your reasonable service. And be not conformed to this world: but be ye transformed by the renewing of your mind, that ye may prove what is that good, and acceptable, and perfect, will of God" (Ro.12:1-2).

"But put ye on the Lord Jesus Christ, and make not provision for the flesh, to *fulfil* the lusts *thereof*" (Ro.13:14).

"Whether therefore ye eat, or drink, or whatsoever ye do, do all to the glory of God" (1 Co.10:31).

"Dearly beloved, I beseech *you* as strangers and pilgrims, abstain from fleshly lusts, which war against the soul" (1 Pe.2:11).

"Love not the world, neither the things *that are* in the world. If any man love the world, the love of the Father is not in him. For all that *is* in the world, the lust of the flesh, and the lust of the eyes, and the pride of life, is not of the Father, but is of the world" (1 Jn.2:15-16).

---

4 (11:13-19) **Birds—Animals, Land—Land Animals—Animals, Clean—Animals, Unclean—Clean - Cleanliness, of Animals—Unclean - Uncleanness, of Animals—Food, Clean and Unclean—Animals, Edible and Inedible—Edible and Inedible Animals**: there was the law governing birds that are inedible, that are to be detested.

OUTLINE	SCRIPTURE	SCRIPTURE	OUTLINE
4. The law governing birds that are inedible, that are to be detested (judged spiritually, ceremonially unclean) a. The eagle, the vulture, the black vulture b. The buzzard, kites of all kinds c. The ravens—of all kinds	13 And these *are they which* ye shall have in abomination among the fowls; they shall not be eaten, they *are* an abomination: the eagle, and the ossifrage, and the ospray, 14 And the vulture, and the kite after his kind; 15 Every raven after his kind;	16 And the owl, and the night hawk, and the cuckow, and the hawk after his kind, 17 And the little owl, and the cormorant, and the great owl, 18 And the swan, and the pelican, and the gier eagle, 19 And the stork, the heron after her kind, and the lapwing, and the bat.	d. The horned owl, the nighthawk, the seagull, hawks of any kind e. The little owl, the cormorant, the great owl f. The white owl, the desert owl, the osprey g. The stork, herons of all kinds, the hoopoe, the bat

Note that this point only gives the list of inedible birds, the birds that are to be judged unclean. Keep in mind that this is a symbol of being spiritually, ceremonially unclean.

⇒ the eagle, the vulture, the black vulture
⇒ the buzzard, kites of all kinds
⇒ the ravens—of all kinds
⇒ the horned owl, the nighthawk, the seagull, hawks of any kind
⇒ the little owl, the cormorant, the great owl
⇒ the white owl, the desert owl, the osprey
⇒ the stork, herons of all kinds, the hoopoe, the bat

Thought 1. God wanted His people to live pure and clean lives, lives that were totally different from the immoral and lawless behavior of their neighbors. He wanted His people to live lives of separation and holiness, lives that were distinctive and different from the unrighteous of the earth. Obeying the food laws made God's people distinct and different from their pagan neighbors. Moreover, focusing upon the clean and unclean foods kept the believers' minds focused upon being spiritually and ceremonially clean.

---

5 (11:20-23) **Insects—Laws, of Clean and Unclean Animals—Animals, Land—Land Animals—Animals, Clean—Animals, Unclean—Clean - Cleanliness, of Animals—Unclean - Uncleanness, of Animals—Food, Clean and Unclean—Animals, Edible and Inedible—Edible and Inedible Animals**: there was the law governing insects.

OUTLINE	SCRIPTURE	SCRIPTURE	OUTLINE
5. The law governing insects a. The inedible: Swarming insects that walk on the ground b. The edible exceptions: Insects with jointed legs for hopping on the ground 1) All varieties of locust,	20 All fowls that creep, going upon *all* four, *shall be* an abomination unto you. 21 Yet these may ye eat of every flying creeping thing that goeth upon *all* four, which have legs above their feet, to leap withal upon the earth; 22 *Even* these of them ye	may eat; the locust after his kind, and the bald locust after his kind, and the beetle after his kind, and the grasshopper after his kind. 23 But all *other* flying creeping things, which have four feet, *shall be* an abomination unto you.	katydid, cricket, or grasshopper 2) All others are forbidden, to be detested: Counted spiritually, ceremonially unclean

a. The inedible insects included all flying or swarming insects that walked on the ground (v.20).

b. The edible exceptions included the insects that had jointed legs for hopping on the ground (vv.21-23). This included all varieties of locusts, katydids, crickets, or grasshoppers (v.22). Note that all other insects are forbidden, to be detested (v.23).

Thought 1. Remember, the true believers of Israel were strict in keeping these laws governing food. This means that every time a believer saw a clean or an unclean insect or any other clean or unclean animal, the thought of God entered his mind, the thought of living a holy and clean life for God. What a lesson for us today, for all believers. When we see the unclean and clean things of this earth, we should immediately think of God. We should praise Him for setting us apart to be His people, for calling us to live holy and clean lives.

"**Therefore if any man** *be* **in Christ,** *he is* **a new creature: old things are passed away; behold, all things are become new**" (2 Co.5:17).

"**Wherefore come out from among them, and be ye separate, saith the Lord, and touch not the unclean** *thing;* **and I will receive you, And will be a Father unto you, and ye shall be my sons and daughters, saith the Lord Almighty**" (2 Co.6:17-18).

"**Having therefore these promises, dearly beloved, let us cleanse ourselves from all filthiness of the flesh and spirit, perfecting holiness in the fear of God**" (2 Co.7:1).

"**And that ye put on the new man, which after God is created in righteousness and true holiness**" (Ep.4:24).

"**Draw nigh to God, and he will draw nigh to you. Cleanse** *your* **hands,** *ye* **sinners; and purify** *your* **hearts,** *ye* **double minded**" (Js.4:8).

"**For I** *am* **the Lord that bringeth you up out of the land of Egypt, to be your God: ye shall therefore be holy, for I** *am* **holy**" (Le.11:45).

6 (11:24-40) **Defilement—Uncleanness—Animals, Unclean—Animals, Clean—Clean - Cleanliness—Unclean - Uncleanness—Spiritual Cleanliness—Spiritual Uncleanness—Ceremonial Uncleanness—Ceremonial Cleanliness**: there was the way animals defiled a person and the required treatment.

OUTLINE	SCRIPTURE	SCRIPTURE	OUTLINE
6. The way animals defiled a person & the required treatment a. Touching a dead insect defiled a person 1) Counted unclean until evening 2) The treatment: Washing one's clothes (a symbol of spiritual cleansing) b. Touching a dead land animal defiled a person 1) The animals • Any animal with a split hoof not completely divided or that does not chew the cud • Any animal that has paws 2) The ceremonial uncleanness: Unclean until evening 3) The treatment: Had to wash one's clothes (a symbol of spiritual, ceremonial cleansing) c. Touching the carcass of a small land animal that scurries or creeps on the ground defiled a person 1) The animals listed • The weasel, rat, lizard • The gecko, the monitor lizard, the common lizard, the skink, the chameleon 2) The defilement: Touching the carcass made a person spiritually, ceremonially	24 And for these ye shall be unclean: whosoever toucheth the carcase of them shall be unclean until the even. 25 And whosoever beareth *ought* of the carcase of them shall wash his clothes, and be unclean until the even. 26 *The carcases* of every beast which divideth the hoof, and *is* not cloven-footed, nor cheweth the cud, *are* unclean unto you: every one that toucheth them shall be unclean. 27 And whatsoever goeth upon his paws, among all manner of beasts that go on *all* four, those *are* unclean unto you: whoso toucheth their carcase shall be unclean until the even. 28 And he that beareth the carcase of them shall wash his clothes, and be unclean until the even: they *are* unclean unto you. 29 These also *shall be* unclean unto you among the creeping things that creep upon the earth; the weasel, and the mouse, and the tortoise after his kind, 30 And the ferret, and the chameleon, and the lizard, and the snail, and the mole. 31 These *are* unclean to you among all that creep: whosoever doth touch them, when they be dead, shall be unclean until the even.	32 And upon whatsoever *any* of them, when they are dead, doth fall, it shall be unclean; whether *it be* any vessel of wood, or raiment, or skin, or sack, whatsoever vessel *it be*, wherein *any* work is done, it must be put into water, and it shall be unclean until the even; so it shall be cleansed. 33 And every earthen vessel, whereinto *any* of them falleth, whatsoever *is* in it shall be unclean; and ye shall break it. 34 Of all meat which may be eaten, *that* on which *such* water cometh shall be unclean: and all drink that may be drunk in every *such* vessel shall be unclean. 35 And every *thing* whereupon *any part* of their carcase falleth shall be unclean; *whether it be* oven, or ranges for pots, they shall be broken down: *for* they *are* unclean, and shall be unclean unto you. 36 Nevertheless a fountain or pit, *wherein there is* plenty of water, shall be clean: but that which toucheth their carcase shall be unclean. 37 And if *any part* of their carcase fall upon any sowing seed which is to be sown, it *shall be* clean. 38 But if *any* water be put	3) The treatment explained with examples • If a dead animal fell on something, the article had to be put in water until evening—washed—to become spiritually, ceremonially clean • If a dead animal fell into a clay pot, the clay pot was unclean, to be broken—never used again • If any food or drink was touched by the cleaning water used to wash any defiled pot, the food & drink were spiritually, unclean—not to be eaten • If anything was touched by a carcass, it was spiritually, ceremonially unclean: Clay ovens & cooking pots were to be broken up • If a carcass fell into a spring or cistern, the water remained clean, but the person who removed the dead animal was counted ceremonially unclean • If a carcass fell on seed to be planted, it remained clean • If water had been put on

OUTLINE	SCRIPTURE	SCRIPTURE	OUTLINE
the seed & a carcass fell on it, it was unclean d. Touching or eating the carcass of an edible animal defiled a person: Counted defiled until evening	upon the seed, and *any part* of their carcase fall thereon, it *shall be* unclean unto you. 39 And if any beast, of which ye may eat, die; he that toucheth the carcase thereof shall be unclean until the even.	40 And he that eateth of the carcase of it shall wash his clothes, and be unclean until the even: he also that beareth the carcase of it shall wash his clothes, and be unclean until the even.	1) The treatment for touching or eating: Washing one's clothes 2) The treatment for picking up carcasses: Washing one's clothes (a symbol of ceremonial cleansing)

a. Touching a dead insect defiled a person (vv.24-25). The person was counted unclean until evening. Note the treatment: he had to wash his clothes. Keep in mind that washing is a symbol of being spiritually, ceremonially cleansed.

b. Touching a dead land animal defiled a person (vv.26-27). Again, the two traits are stressed: any animal that did not have a completely split hoof or that did not chew the cud was unclean. Note also that any animal that had paws was counted unclean. The person was counted unclean until evening (v.28). Again, note that the treatment was the washing of one's clothing (a symbol of spiritual, ceremonial cleansing).

c. Touching the carcass of a small land animal that scurries or creeps on the ground defiles a person (vv.29-38).

1) Note the animals listed: the weasel, rat, lizard, the gecko, the monitor lizard, the common lizard, the skink, the chameleon (vv.29-30).

2) Note the defilement: touching the carcass made a person unclean. Again, keep in mind that this symbolizes being spiritually, ceremonially unclean.

3) Note the treatment explained with examples (vv.32-38).
- If a dead animal fell on something, the article had to be put in water until evening—washed—to become spiritually and ceremonially clean
- If a dead animal fell into a clay pot, the clay pot was unclean, to be broken—never used again
- If any food or drink was touched by the cleaning water used to wash any defiled pot, the food and drink were spiritually, unclean—not to be eaten
- If anything was touched by a carcass, it was spiritually and ceremonially unclean: clay ovens and cooking pots were to be broken up
- If a carcass fell into a spring or cistern, the water remained clean, but the person who removed the dead animal was counted ceremonially unclean
- If a carcass fell on seed to be planted, the seed remained clean
- If water had been put on the seed and a carcass fell on it, the seed was unclean

d. Touching or eating the carcass of an edible animal defiled a person. He was counted defiled, unclean until evening (vv.39-40). The treatment for touching or eating the carcass of an edible animal was, again, the washing of one's clothes (v.40). Note that the treatment for picking up a carcass was also the washing of one's clothes (v.40).

> "And now why tarriest thou? arise, and be baptized, and wash away thy sins, calling on the name of the Lord" (Ac.22:16).
> "But in a great house there are not only vessels of gold and of silver, but also of wood and of earth; and some to honour, and some to dishonour. If a man therefore purge himself from these, he shall be a vessel unto honour, sanctified, and meet for the master's use, *and* prepared unto every good work" (2 Ti.2:20-21).
> "Wash thine heart from wickedness, that thou mayest be saved. How long shall thy vain thoughts lodge within thee?" (Je.4:14).

7 (11:41-43) **Food, Laws Governing**: the importance of the food laws is summarized and re-emphasized in these three verses.

OUTLINE	SCRIPTURE	SCRIPTURE	OUTLINE
7. The importance of the food laws: Summarized & reemphasized a. The detestable animals were never to be eaten 1) The animal that scurried along the ground 2) The animal that walked on four legs 3) The animal that walked on many legs	41 And every creeping thing that creepeth upon the earth *shall be* an abomination; it shall not be eaten. 42 Whatsoever goeth upon the belly, and whatsoever goeth upon *all* four, or whatsoever hath more feet among all creeping things that creep upon the earth,	them ye shall not eat; for they *are* an abomination. 43 Ye shall not make yourselves abominable with any creeping thing that creepeth, neither shall ye make yourselves unclean with them, that ye should be defiled thereby.	b. The rule: Must not defile oneself by eating or touching forbidden animals: A symbol of spiritual, ceremonial pollution, uncleanness

a. The detestable animals were never to be eaten (vv.41-42):
⇒ not the animal that scurried along the ground
⇒ not the animal that walked on four legs
⇒ not the animal that walked on many legs

b. The law or rule was strong: a person must not defile himself by eating or touching any forbidden animal. He must not pollute nor make himself unclean by eating or touching an unclean animal. Again, this is a symbol of spiritual, ceremonial defilement, pollution, and uncleanness.

> **Thought 1**. The believer must obey God. The believer must keep the rules, the laws, and the commandments of God. He must not defile himself; he must not pollute nor contaminate himself with anything that is unclean. He must not touch the unclean thing.
>
> > "Not every one that saith unto me, Lord, Lord, shall enter into the kingdom of heaven; but he that doeth the will of my Father which is in heaven" (Mt.7:21).
> >
> > "And be not conformed to this world: but be ye transformed by the renewing of your mind, that ye may prove what is that good, and acceptable, and perfect, will of God" (Ro.12:2).
> >
> > "Wherefore come out from among them, and be ye separate, saith the Lord, and touch not the unclean *thing;* and I will receive you, And will be a Father unto you, and ye shall be my sons and daughters, saith the Lord Almighty" (2 Co.6:17-18).
> >
> > "Love not the world, neither the things *that are* in the world. If any man love the world, the love of the Father is not in him. For all that *is* in the world, the lust of the flesh, and the lust of the eyes, and the pride of life, is not of the Father, but is of the world" (1 Jn.2:15-16).
> >
> > "This day the LORD thy God hath commanded thee to do these statutes and judgments: thou shalt therefore keep and do them with all thine heart, and with all thy soul" (De.26:16).
> >
> > "And Samuel said, Hath the LORD *as great* delight in burnt offerings and sacrifices, as in obeying the voice of the LORD? Behold, to obey *is* better than sacrifice, *and* to hearken than the fat of rams" (1 S.15:22).

8 (11:44-47) **Food, Laws Governing—Law, Governing Food—Israel, Purpose of—Holy - Holiness, of God—Holy - Holiness, Duty to Be—Discernment—Salvation, Purpose for**: there were three clearly stated purposes for the food laws:

OUTLINE	SCRIPTURE	SCRIPTURE	OUTLINE
8. The purpose for the laws	44 For I *am* the LORD your God: ye shall therefore sanctify yourselves, and ye shall be holy; for I *am* holy: neither shall ye defile yourselves with any manner of creeping thing that creepeth upon the earth.	holy, for I *am* holy	God & set them apart as holy
a. To declare that Israel was God's chosen & holy people		46 This *is* the law of the beasts, and of the fowl, and of every living creature that moveth in the waters, and of every creature that creepeth upon the earth:	c. To teach His people to distinguish, discern between the unclean & clean
1) Must be like God: Consecrated—set apart—holy			1) The declaration restated
2) Must demonstrate by not eating & touching unclean animals	45 For I *am* the LORD that bringeth you up out of the land of Egypt, to be your God: ye shall therefore be	47 To make a difference between the unclean and the clean, and between the beast that may be eaten and the beast that may not be eaten.	2) The point clearly stated: Must distinguish, discern between the unclean & the clean
b. To declare that God is the Savior who delivered His people from Egypt (a symbol of the world): Must be their			

a. The first purpose for the food laws was a strong declaration: to declare that the Israelites were God's chosen and holy people (v.44). The people of the world had rejected God and were walking through life as they wished, living as they wanted. They had long ago turned away from the LORD (Jehovah, Yahweh), the only living and true God. They were living lives of selfishness and greed, hoarding and accumulating more and more while others had little or nothing and were hungry and dying. They were living lives of immorality, lawlessness, drunkenness, abuse, brutality, violence, murder, war—lives that cursed and rebelled against God, that had become so hard that they would never have anything to do with the LORD. God was in a position where He had no choice: He had to raise up a new race of people who would be set apart as the people of God, set apart as His holy and righteous people. This was the reason God had chosen Abraham. Through Abraham, God had caused the Israelites to be born. Now, Moses was formulating them into a nation. One way chosen for the Israelites to be known as the people of God was through the food laws. The Israelites were to be God's chosen and holy people. God was holy; therefore...

- they must be like God. They must consecrate themselves, set themselves apart, as holy.
- they must demonstrate their holiness, identify themselves as God's people through the food laws. They must not eat or touch any unclean animals.

b. The second purpose for the food laws was also a strong declaration: to declare that God is the Savior of the world, the Savior who delivered His people from Egypt (v.45). Remember, Egypt is a symbol of the world. God had saved His people from the slavery of the world (Egypt), from the slavery of its sin and death. Note why:

⇒ He saved them to be their God.
⇒ He saved them to set them apart as His holy people.

The point is this: God had saved Israel to be His holy people, His witnesses to a sinful, lost world. They were to give testimony that God is holy. How was Israel to bear the testimony of holiness, declare that they were the people of God? By living holy lives.

One of the ways they demonstrated holiness was through the food laws. They ate no unclean food. God wanted people to live long and healthy lives, experience the fullness and abundance of life by having healthy and strong bodies both physically and spiritually. Israel declares this to the world through the food laws. As stated, they ate no unclean food. They kept their bodies clean and holy, and they kept their spirits clean and holy by obeying the commandments of God.

c. The third purpose for the food laws was critical: it involved discernment. God gave the food laws to teach His people to discern between the unclean and clean (vv.46-47). God's people needed to keep their minds focused upon God and upon the positive and good things of life. One of the ways God led His people to do this was through the food laws. Every time a believer saw an unclean or clean animal, he was to discern between the clean and unclean.

He had a daily object lesson, a daily picture that led him to discern between obeying and disobeying God. By this, he learned to discern the more important things of life: he learned to discern between right and wrong, between justice and injustice, between morality and immorality, between the beneficial and harmful, between kindness and unkindness, between love and hate. Scripture declares this fact: through the food laws, the believer learned to discern between the unclean and clean. This he did in order…

- to have a clean, healthy body
- to have a clean, healthy spirit

Thought 1. The applications and lessons for us are clear:

(1) We must be holy because God is holy. As believers, we have no choice: the command is direct and forceful. We must be like God: consecrated—set apart—holy.

> "For I *am* the LORD that bringeth you up out of the land of Egypt, to be your God: ye shall therefore be holy, for I *am* holy" (Le.11:45).
> "That he would grant unto us, that we being delivered out of the hand of our enemies might serve him without fear, In holiness and righteousness before him, all the days of our life" (Lu.1:74-75).
> "Having therefore these promises, dearly beloved, let us cleanse ourselves from all filthiness of the flesh and spirit, perfecting holiness in the fear of God" (2 Co.7:1).
> "Because it is written, Be ye holy; for I am holy" (1 Pe.1:16).

(2) We must declare that God is the Savior of the world. He is the Savior who delivered us from the enslavement and death of the world (Egypt). We must bear testimony, strong testimony, that God is building a new race of people, a people…

- who will let Him be their God
- who will be set apart and live as the holy people of God

> "Follow peace with all men, and holiness, without which no man shall see the Lord" (He.12:14).
> "But sanctify [set apart as holy, pure] the Lord God in your hearts: and be ready always to give an answer to every man that asketh you a reason of the hope that is in you with meekness and fear" (1 Pe.3:15).
> "*Seeing* then *that* all these things shall be dissolved, what manner *of persons* ought ye to be in *all* holy conversation [behavior, conduct] and godliness, Looking for and hasting unto the coming of the day of God, wherein the heavens being on fire shall be dissolved, and the elements shall melt with fervent heat? Nevertheless we, according to his promise, look for new heavens and a new earth, wherein dwelleth righteousness. Wherefore, beloved, seeing that ye look for such things, be diligent that ye may be found of him in peace, without spot, and blameless" (2 Pe.3:11-14).

(3) We must learn to discern more and more between the clean and unclean, the holy and unholy. We must sharpen our minds and the power to discern, learning to distinguish between right and wrong, the just and the unjust, the moral and the immoral, the kind and the unkind, the selfish and the unselfish.

> "But the natural man receiveth not the things of the Spirit of God: for they are foolishness unto him: neither can he know them, because they are spiritually discerned" (1 Co.2:14).
> "But strong meat belongeth to them that are of full age, even those who by reason of use have their senses exercised to discern both good and evil" (He.5:14).
> "Give therefore thy servant an understanding heart to judge thy people, that I may discern between good and bad: for who is able to judge this thy so great a people?" (1 K.3:9).

TYPES, SYMBOLS, AND PICTURES
Leviticus 11:1-47

Historical Term	Type or Picture (Scriptural Basis for Each)	Life Application for Today's Believer	Biblical Application
The Laws of Cleanliness and Defilement Le.11:1-47	*The laws of cleanliness and defilement are symbolic of spiritual truth, of being spiritually clean and undefiled.*	God cares for His people physically and spiritually; therefore, He wants them to take care of their bodies and spirits. God had more than health in mind when He gave the food laws. God	*"Know ye not that your bodies are the members of Christ? shall I then take the members of Christ, and make them the members of an harlot? God forbid" (1 Co.6:15).*

TYPES, SYMBOLS, AND PICTURES
Leviticus 11:1-47

Historical Term	Type or Picture (Scriptural Basis for Each)	Life Application for Today's Believer	Biblical Application
	"This *is* the law of the beasts, and of the fowl, and of every living creature that moveth in the waters, and of every creature that creepeth upon the earth: To make a difference between the unclean and the clean, and between the beast that may be eaten and the beast that may not be eaten" (Le.11:46-47).	had a spiritual purpose in mind. The laws of cleanliness set God's people apart as a clean, holy people. This is the reason for these laws, that His people might have strong bodies and strong spirits.	"And the very God of peace sanctify you wholly; and I pray God your whole spirit and soul and body be preserved blameless unto the coming of our Lord Jesus Christ" (1 Th.5:23). "Know ye not that ye are the temple of God, and that the Spirit of God dwelleth in you?" (1 Co.3:16). "What? know ye not that your body is the temple of the Holy Ghost which is in you, which ye have of God, and ye are not your own?" (1 Co.6:19). "In whom ye also are builded together for an habitation of God through the Spirit" (Ep.2:22).
The Clean and Unclean Animals Le.11:2-8	*The clean and unclean animals are symbols of being ceremonially clean or unclean, of being spiritually clean or unclean. This is to say that God had two purposes in giving these laws governing food:* 1. *The purpose of keeping His people physically healthy and clean* 2. *The purpose of keeping His people ceremonially, spiritually clean and healthy* "**Speak unto the children of Israel, saying, These *are* the beasts which ye shall eat among all the beasts that *are* on the earth**" (Le.11:2).	The application and lesson for the believer is clear: 1. The believer must keep his body clean and healthy. 2. The believer must keep his spirit clean and healthy.	"What? know ye not that your body is the temple of the Holy Ghost which is in you, which ye have of God, and ye are not your own?" (1 Co.6:19). "And the very God of peace sanctify you wholly; and I pray God your whole spirit and soul and body be preserved blameless unto the coming of our Lord Jesus Christ" (1 Th.5:23). "Beloved, I wish above all things that thou mayest prosper and be in health, even as thy soul prospereth" (3 Jn.1:2).
Washing Le.11:24-40	*Washing is a symbol of being spiritually, ceremonially cleansed.* "**And whosoever beareth *ought* of the carcase of them shall wash his clothes, and be unclean until the even**" (Le.11:25).	No person can cleanse himself, not spiritually, not from sin. Only God's mediator—Jesus Christ—can wash and cleanse a person spiritually.	"And now why tarriest thou? arise, and be baptized, and wash away thy sins, calling on the name of the Lord" (Ac.22:16). "In whom we have redemption through his blood, the forgiveness of sins, according to the riches of his grace" (Ep.1:7; see Heb.9:14). Unto him that loved us, and washed us from our sins in his own blood" (Re.1:5).
Egypt Le.11:44-47. See also Le.19:33-34	*Egypt is a symbol of the world. God had saved His people from the slavery of the world (Egypt), from the slavery of its sin and death.*	The application and lesson for us is clear: 1. We must be holy because God is holy. As believers, we have no choice: the command is	"That he would grant unto us, that we being delivered out of the hand of our enemies might serve him without fear, In holiness and righteousness before him, all the days of

TYPES, SYMBOLS, AND PICTURES
Leviticus 11:1-47

Historical Term	Type or Picture (Scriptural Basis for Each)	Life Application for Today's Believer	Biblical Application
	Note why: 1. *He saved them to be their God.* 2. *He saved them to set them apart as His holy people.* **"For I *am* the LORD that bringeth you up out of the land of Egypt, to be your God: ye shall therefore be holy, for I *am* holy" (Le.11:45).**	direct and forceful. We must be like God: consecrated set apart, holy. 2. We must declare that God is the Savior of the world, the Savior who delivered us from the world (Egypt). We must bear testimony, strong testimony, that God is building a new race of people, a people... • who will let Him be their God • who will be set apart and live as the holy people of God 3. We must learn to discern more and more between the clean and unclean, the holy and unholy. We must sharpen our power to discern, learn to distinguish between right and wrong, the just and unjust, the moral and immoral, the kind and unkind, the unselfish and selfish.	*our life" (Lu.1:74-75).* *"Having therefore these promises, dearly beloved, let us cleanse ourselves from all filthiness of the flesh and spirit, perfecting holiness in the fear of God" (2 Co.7:1).* *"Follow peace with all men, and holiness, without which no man shall see the Lord" (He.12:14).* *"But sanctify [set apart as holy, pure] the Lord God in your hearts: and be ready always to give an answer to every man that asketh you a reason of the hope that is in you with meekness and fear" (1 Pe.3:15).* *"But the natural man receiveth not the things of the Spirit of God: for they are foolishness unto him: neither can he know them, because they are spiritually discerned" (1 Co.2:14).* *"But strong meat belongeth to them that are of full age, even those who by reason of use have their senses exercised to discern both good and evil" (He.5:14).* *"Give therefore thy servant an understanding heart to judge thy people, that I may discern between good and bad: for who is able to judge this thy so great a people?" (1 K.3:9).*

CHAPTER 12

B. Laws That Protect Mother & Child Right After Childbirth: Symbolizes the Need for Cleansing from the Sinful Nature, 12:1-8

1. A mother & son were protected

a. The mother was counted ceremonially unclean for 7 days
   1) Physically: Isolated to recover
   2) Spiritually: Isolated to focus upon God's grace & upon sin (how the sinful nature is passed down)
b. The son was circumcised, identified as one of God's people

c. Both needed protection through an extended semi-isolation: Had to wait 33 days more before her ritual of purification
   1) Gave time for nurturing
   2) Gave time for spiritual focus

2. A mother & daughter were protected

And the LORD spake unto Moses, saying,

2 Speak unto the children of Israel, saying, If a woman have conceived seed, and born a man child: then she shall be unclean seven days; according to the days of the separation for her infirmity shall she be unclean.

3 And in the eighth day the flesh of his foreskin shall be circumcised.

4 And she shall then continue in the blood of her purifying three and thirty days; she shall touch no hallowed thing, nor come into the sanctuary, until the days of her purifying be fulfilled.

5 But if she bear a maid child, then she shall be unclean two weeks, as in her separation: and she shall continue in the blood of her purifying threescore and six days.

6 And when the days of her purifying are fulfilled, for a son, or for a daughter, she shall bring a lamb of the first year for a burnt offering, and a young pigeon, or a turtledove, for a sin offering, unto the door of the tabernacle of the congregation, unto the priest:

7 Who shall offer it before the LORD, and make an atonement for her; and she shall be cleansed from the issue of her blood. This *is* the law for her that hath born a male or a female.

8 And if she be not able to bring a lamb, then she shall bring two turtles, or two young pigeons; the one for the burnt offering, and the other for a sin offering: and the priest shall make an atonement for her, and she shall be clean.

a. Spiritually: Counted unclean for two weeks (gave time to focus upon God and the sin nature)
b. Physically: Was to wait 66 days before her purification

3. A mother was protected by approaching God for cleansing

a. Through the Burnt Offering: Seeking reconciliation through the sacrifice (a symbol of Christ)
b. Through the Sin Offering: Seeking forgiveness through the sacrifice (a symbol of Christ)

c. The result
   1) Made atonement: Reconciliation with God, forgiveness
   2) Counted ceremonially clean: Able to participate in religious services

4. A poor mother was protected by God's mercy

a. She could offer two pigeons if she could not afford a lamb
b. The result: atonement (reconciliation) & the forgiveness of sin

---

DIVISION III

THE WAY TO LIVE A HOLY LIFE BEFORE GOD (PART I): BY A CLEAN BODY (SEPARATION), 11:1–16:34

B. Laws That Protect Mother and Child Right After Childbirth: Symbolizes the Need for Cleansing from the Sinful Nature, 12:1-8

(12:1-8) **Introduction**: this chapter concerns a mother and her newborn child right after childbirth, one of the most sensitive (delicate, tender) times for a mother. Giving birth can be a painful experience, a time of much suffering. Yet right after the travail, the sight of seeing and holding the child is one of the most joyful experiences imaginable. Realizing that she has brought a newborn life into the world is one of the most heartwarming and rich experiences in life. God has made it so because it is His chosen way for the human race to reproduce. Christ Himself described the experience:

> **"A woman when she is in travail hath sorrow, because her hour is come: but as soon as she is delivered of the child, she remembereth no more the anguish, for joy that a man is born into the world" (Jn.16:21).**

It is the time right after childbirth that is so critical for both mother and child. During these days, they need to be nurtured and bound together; they need to be protected both physically and spiritually. This is the reason God gave these laws: *Laws That Protect Mother and Child Right After Childbirth: Symbolizes the Need for Cleansing from the Sinful Nature*, 12:1-8.
1. A mother and son were protected (vv.1-4).
2. A mother and daughter were protected (v.5).
3. A mother was protected by approaching God for cleansing (vv.6-7).
4. A poor mother was protected by God's mercy (v.8).

1 (12:1-4) **Childbirth—Sons, Birth of—Cleanliness, Spiritual—Uncleanness, Spiritual—Cleanliness, Ceremonial—Uncleanness, Ceremonial—Circumcision—Mother, Needs of, Protection after Childbirth**: a mother and son need to be protected right after childbirth.

THE BASIC LAW PROTECTING MOTHER AND SON

OUTLINE	SCRIPTURE	SCRIPTURE	OUTLINE
1. A mother & son were protected a. The mother was counted ceremonially unclean for 7 days 1) Physically: Isolated to recover 2) Spiritually: Isolated to focus upon God's grace & upon sin (how the sinful nature was passed down)	And the LORD spake unto Moses, saying, 2 Speak unto the children of Israel, saying, If a woman have conceived seed, and born a man child: then she shall be unclean seven days; according to the days of the separation for her infirmity shall she be unclean.	3 And in the eighth day the flesh of his foreskin shall be circumcised. 4 And she shall then continue in the blood of her purifying three and thirty days; she shall touch no hallowed thing, nor come into the sanctuary, until the days of her purifying be fulfilled.	b. The son was circumcised, identified as one of God's people c. Both needed protection through an extended semi-isolation: Had to wait 33 days more before her ritual of purification 1) Gave time for nurturing 2) Gave time for spiritual focus

a. The mother was protected by being counted ceremonially unclean for seven days (v.2).
  1) Physically, this isolated the mother until she could gain her strength and recover. Obviously the family members or midwives who helped the mother were also counted unclean until after the seven days were up. Being unclean meant:
    ⇒ She could not do housework or any other kind of work such as cooking.
    ⇒ She could not be imposed upon by her husband.
    ⇒ She nor the baby could be disturbed by visitors such as friends and neighbors.
    ⇒ She and the baby had plenty of time to bond and grow together during the all-important first days.
    ⇒ She could focus upon nursing and nurturing the baby, conveying a sense of intimacy, peace, security, and love to the baby.

  2) Spiritually, this isolated the mother to focus upon God's grace and the terrible uncleanness of sin, in particular the fact that the sinful nature was passed down to her son and would be passed down from generation to generation.

Did the mother actually think about the uncleanness and pollution of sin? A Jewish mother obviously did. They certainly knew the law: she was considered by everyone to be religiously or ceremonially unclean. And religious uncleanness was a symbol of the pollution of sin. She also knew what we know: the Holy Scripture teaches that the suffering of childbirth is due to the first sin of mankind. The pain of childbirth was the judgment of sin pronounced upon the woman.

> **"Unto the woman he said, I will greatly multiply thy sorrow and thy conception; in sorrow thou shalt bring forth children" (Ge.3:16).**

God obviously gave this law to teach two things: God's grace and the *internal nature* of sin, the passing down of the *sinful nature*. God wanted the mother and family to have joy and rejoice in His grace through the baby; but He also wanted them to learn the awful uncleanness of sin: that sin is internal, within the very nature of man. Sin caused...
* the pain and suffering of childbirth
* the transmission or the passing down of the sinful nature
* the transmission or the passing down of death

Childbirth is one way God is able to teach the truth of human depravity. God has created man to live with Him forever in perfection, but sin has disrupted this relationship. Sin has alienated man from God and has brought about death and judgment to come. The law of ceremonial uncleanness governing childbirth taught the truth of human depravity.

Thought 1. When a child is born, God wants His people to learn more and more...
* about the joy and rejoicing of His grace in the gift of a child

> **"And he lifted up his eyes, and saw the women and the children; and said, Who are those with thee? And he said, The children which God hath graciously given thy servant" (Ge.33:5).**
> **"He maketh the barren woman to keep house, and to be a joyful mother of children. Praise ye the LORD" (Ps.113:9).**
> **"Lo, children are an heritage of the LORD: and the fruit of the womb is his reward" (Ps.127:3).**

* about the terrible uncleanness of sin in all its depraved nature

> **"By man came death" (1 Co.15:21).**
> **"Wherefore, as by one man sin entered into the world, and death by sin; and so death passed upon all men, for that all have sinned" (Ro.5:12).**
> **"For the wages of sin is death" (Ro.6:23).**
> **"Behold, I was shapen in iniquity; and in sin did my mother conceive me" (Ps.51:5).**
> **"The wicked are estranged from the womb: they go astray as soon as they be born, speaking lies" (Ps.58:3).**

Thought 2. Charles F. Pfeiffer says, "The ceremonial uncleanness following childbirth is related to the fact that man is a sinful creature. Following the fall, Eve was told that pain and suffering were to accompany motherhood. Human history has been a succession of births in which sinful man begets sinful man. In such a context the law requires ceremonial purification."[1]

Thought 3. The Bible teacher J. Vernon McGee makes several excellent statements worth quoting:
⇒ *In the preceding chapter we saw the contamination of sin by contact. The external character of sin was emphasized—we live in a world surrounded by sin.*
> *This chapter places the emphasis on the internal character of sin. Not only do we become sinners by contact, but we are sinners by birth. And this chapter is the law concerning motherhood, the transmission of sin by inheritance. The very nature that we inherit is a fallen, sinful nature. David said, 'Behold, I was shapen in iniquity, and in sin did my mother conceive me' (Ps. 51:5)."[2]*
⇒ *Obviously there were certain hygienic benefits in the practice of these God-given laws—as we saw in the matter of diet. God was caring for His people physically, and at the same time was teaching them (and us) the great spiritual truth that we are born in sin."[3]*
⇒ *Uncleanness under the law reminded her that she had brought a sinner into the world."[4]*
⇒ *Someone said, 'If my baby is born a sinner and he dies in infancy, is he lost because he is a sinner?' No. In Adam all die, and that's the reason the little one died. But the Lord Jesus said, 'Take heed that ye despise not one of these little ones; for I say unto you, That in heaven their angels [spirits] do always behold the face of my Father which is in heaven' (Matt. 18:10). The word 'angels' should be translated spirits—their spirits behold the face of the Father. In other words, when that little infant dies, his spirit goes to be with the Father. Why? Because Christ came down and died for sinners, and the little one has not reached the age of accountability. The minute he does, then he has to make a decision for Christ.*
I like the quaint epitaph that Robert Robertson placed over the graves of his four children:

> *"Bold infidelity, turn pale and die,*
> *Beneath this stone four infants' ashes lie;*
> *Say are they lost or saved,*
> *If death's by sin, they sinned for they lie here;*
> *If Heaven's by works, in Heaven they can't appear.*
> *Reason—Ah, how depraved.*
> *Reverse the Bible's sacred page, the knot's untied,*
> *They died, for Adam sinned; they live, for Jesus died."[5]*

Thought 4. The great Bible commentator Matthew Henry says this:
⇒ *This ceremonial uncleanness...was to signify the pollution of sin which we are all conceived and born in....For, if the root be impure, so is the branch, "Who can bring a clean thing out of an unclean?"[6]*

"Behold, I was shapen in iniquity; and in sin did my mother conceive me" (Ps.51:5).

⇒ *If sin had not entered, nothing but purity and honor had attended all the...blessing [of childbirth]...but now that the nature of man is degenerated...disgrace...sin and corruption that are...in remembrance of the curse upon the woman.[7]*

b. The baby son was protected by being circumcised on the eighth day (v.3). Remember, circumcision was the sign or symbol that a person was a member of God's people. Circumcision meant...
- that a baby son was to be reared as a follower of God
- that he was to be taught the covenant of God
- that he would inherit the promises of God—if he truly obeyed and followed God
- that God covered the baby under His covenant and grace until he reached the *age of accountability*

This, of course, gave great assurance to the mother during the early days of the child's life, during the early years when he was so susceptible to sickness, accident, disease, and so dependent upon others. God covered the child with His marvelous grace through the covenant of circumcision, and thereby He gave great assurance and security to the mother.

c. Both mother and child were protected through an extended isolation: the mother had to wait thirty-three days more before her purification ritual and before she could become fully active.
1) Physically, this was a semi-isolation period that allowed the mother to fully recover. She was still counted unclean, which meant that she...
- was protected from the exhaustion of travel and large crowds
- was protected from the pain of too early sexual relations
- was given the first few weeks to continue nurturing and bonding with her child
- was given time to convey the much needed sense of quietness, peace, security, and love to her child

---

[1] Charles F. Pfeiffer. *The Book of Leviticus*, p.33.
[2] J. Vernon McGee. *Thru the Bible*, Vol.1, p.374
[3] ibid., p.374.
[4] ibid., p.375.
[5] ibid., p.375.
[6] Matthew Henry. *Matthew Henry's Commentary*, Vol. 1. (Old Tappan, NJ: Fleming H. Revell Co.) p.489.
[7] ibid., p.490.

2) Spiritually, the mother was given time to grow in the joy of God's grace, in thinking and learning more about the uncleanness of sin. (See point one of this note for more discussion.)

Thought 1. What a lesson for our generation in protecting mothers and their newborn children. The one thing Scripture teaches about mothers and children is this: they are to be honored, supported, and loved by both husband and other children.

"But Jesus said, Suffer little children, and forbid them not, to come unto me: for of such is the kingdom of heaven" (Mt.19:14).

"So ought men to love their wives as their own bodies. He that loveth his wife loveth himself" (Ep.5:28).

"Husbands, love your wives, and be not bitter against them" (Col.3:19).

"And he lifted up his eyes, and saw the women and the children; and said, Who are those with thee? And he said, The children which God hath graciously given thy servant" (Ge.33:5).

"Honour thy father and thy mother: that thy days may be long upon the land which the LORD thy God giveth thee" (Ex.20:12).

"Ye shall fear every man his mother" (Le.19:3).

"He maketh the barren woman to keep house, and to be a joyful mother of children. Praise ye the LORD" (Ps.113:9).

"Lo, children are an heritage of the LORD: and the fruit of the womb is his reward" (Ps.127:3).

2 (12:5) **Daughters, Birth of—Childbirth—Cleanliness, Spiritual—Uncleanness, Spiritual—Cleanliness, Ceremonial—Uncleanness, Ceremonial—Circumcision—Mother, Needs of, Protection after Childbirth**: note the Scripture and outline of this point:

THE BASIC LAW PROTECTING MOTHER AND DAUGHTER

OUTLINE	SCRIPTURE
2. A mother & daughter were protected	5 But if she bear a maid child, then she shall be un-
a. Spiritually: Counted unclean for two weeks (gave time to focus upon God and the sin nature)	clean two weeks, as in her separation: and she shall continue in the blood of her
b. Physically: Was to wait 66 days before her purification	purifying threescore and six days.

The mother's uncleanness in having a baby girl is doubled. She is counted ceremonially unclean for two weeks; then she had to wait sixty-six days for her purification ritual. Why? Scripture does not say. Perhaps one or more of the following reasons are true:

⇒ perhaps to give extra protection to the baby daughter: more time to grow and gain strength since she was considered weaker and was being born into a harsh, cruel world.

⇒ perhaps to symbolize that the female sex was to be honored, respected, cared for and looked after in a very special way throughout life.

⇒ perhaps to stress a double lesson on God's grace and on uncleanness since the baby girl would one day suffer childbirth herself.

⇒ perhaps to give the baby daughter an extended, uninterrupted time to grow in the sense of love, nourishment, peace, and security—all of which she would someday need to convey to her own newborn children.

Whatever the case, the mother and baby daughter were both given eighty days to grow and bond together. No doubt, the last reason listed above had some bearing on the extended time for a baby daughter to be loved and nurtured. God wants strong families, and He has appointed the mother to be the focus of the love and nurturing within the family. The baby daughter was therefore given more time to *absorb* and *grow* in the uninterrupted love and nurture of her mother, given more time for the mother's nature to be absorbed, to become a part of her own little nature.

Thought 1. The lesson is clear: we must take time with our children and prepare them for their roles in life. We must take time to be with our children from the first day of their lives. Even little babies absorb, take into their nature, what we convey to them. We must, therefore, spend time in holding, loving, nurturing, feeding, playing with, and reading to our children, and on and on—all to convey a sense of love, care, peace, and security.

"Train up a child in the way he should go: and when he is old, he will not depart from it" (Pr.22:6).

"And thou shalt teach them [God's children] diligently unto thy children, and shalt talk of them when thou sittest in thine house, and when thou walkest by the way, and when thou liest down, and when thou risest up" (De.6:7).

"When I call to remembrance the unfeigned faith that is in thee, which dwelt first in thy grandmother Lois, and thy mother Eunice; and I am persuaded that in thee also" (2 Ti.1:5).

3 (12:6-7) **Mother—Childbirth—Cleanliness, Spiritual—Uncleanness, Spiritual—Cleanliness, Ceremonial—Uncleanness, Ceremonial—Circumcision—Mother, Needs of, Protection after Childbirth**: a mother was protected by approaching God for cleansing or purification.

THE BASIC LAW PROTECTING A MOTHER'S NEEDS

OUTLINE	SCRIPTURE	SCRIPTURE	OUTLINE
3. A mother was protected by approaching God for cleansing a. Through the Burnt Offering: Seeking reconciliation through the sacrifice (a symbol of Christ) b. Through the Sin Offering: Seeking forgiveness through the sacrifice (a symbol of Christ)	6 And when the days of her purifying are fulfilled, for a son, or for a daughter, she shall bring a lamb of the first year for a burnt offering, and a young pigeon, or a turtledove, for a sin offering, unto the door of the tabernacle of	the congregation, unto the priest: 7 Who shall offer it before the LORD, and make an atonement for her; and she shall be cleansed from the issue of her blood. This *is* the law for her that hath born a male or a female.	c. The result 1) Atonement, reconciliation with God, forgiveness 2) Counted ceremonially clean: Able to participate in religious services

a. She was cleansed by approaching God through the sacrifice of the Burnt Offering. Remember, this was the sacrifice that would make atonement for her, that would satisfy God's holiness and justice against sin. Through the atoning sacrifice, God reconciled the unclean person to Himself, accepted the person.

b. She was cleansed by approaching God through the sacrifice of the Sin Offering. This was the sacrifice that bought forgiveness of sins. The Bible never says that childbirth is a sin, but all who bear children are sinners just as we all are. Therefore, the mother who bore a child was to offer the sacrifice for sins because of her uncleanness: she had just brought a child into a sinful world and had passed down the sinful nature to her child.

c. Note the result of her approaching God through the sacrifice of the two offerings: atonement was made for her through the Burnt Offering. God reconciled her to Himself, accepted her. Moreover, her sins were forgiven: she was counted ceremonially clean. She was able once again to participate in religious services. She was fully acceptable to God.

Thought 1. The sacrifice of the Burnt Offering and the Sin Offering was a type, a symbol, of Jesus Christ.
(1) It is through Jesus Christ that atonement is made for us, that we are reconciled to God.

> "For all have sinned, and come short of the glory of God; Being justified freely by his grace through the redemption that is in Christ Jesus: Whom God hath set forth *to be* a propitiation through faith in his blood, to declare his righteousness for the remission of sins that are past, through the forbearance of God" (Ro.3:23-25).
> "But God commendeth his love toward us, in that, while we were yet sinners, Christ died for us. Much more then, being now justified by his blood, we shall be saved from wrath through him. For if, when we were enemies, we were reconciled to God by the death of his Son, much more, being reconciled, we shall be saved by his life. And not only *so,* but we also joy in God through our Lord Jesus Christ, by whom we have now received the atonement" (Ro.5:8-11).
> "For he hath made him *to be* sin for us, who knew no sin; that we might be made the righteousness of God in him" (2 Co.5:21).

(2) It is through Jesus Christ that our sins are forgiven.

> "For this is my blood of the new testament, which is shed for many for the remission of sins" (Mt.26:28).
> "But Peter said, Ananias, why hath Satan filled thine heart to lie to the Holy Ghost, and to keep back *part* of the price of the land?" (Ac.5:3).
> "Be it known unto you therefore, men *and* brethren, that through this man is preached unto you the forgiveness of sins" (Ac.13:38).
> "In whom we have redemption through his blood, the forgiveness of sins, according to the riches of his grace" (Ep.1:7).
> "Who his own self bare our sins in his own body on the tree, that we, being dead to sins, should live unto righteousness: by whose stripes ye were healed" (1 Pe.2:24).
> "If we confess our sins, he is faithful and just to forgive us *our* sins, and to cleanse us from all unrighteousness" (1 Jn.1:9).

4 (12:8) **Mothers, Poor—Poor, God's Mercy upon—Mercy, of God—Sacrifice, of the Poor—Sacrifice, Animal**: a poor mother was protected by God's mercy. Note the concession made for the poor by God. If a mother could not afford a lamb, she could offer the sacrifice of two pigeons, one for the Burnt Offering and the other for the Sin Offering. Note the glorious mercy of God: she was given the atonement (reconciliation with God) and the forgiveness of sin just as readily as the more advantaged mother.

THE BASIC LAW PROTECTING A POOR MOTHER

OUTLINE	SCRIPTURE

4. **A poor mother was protected by God's mercy**
  a. She could offer two pigeons if she could not afford a lamb
  b. The result: Atonement (reconciliation) & the forgiveness of sin
	8 And if she be not able to bring a lamb, then she shall bring two turtles, or two young pigeons; the one for the burnt offering, and the other for a sin offering: and the priest shall make an atonement for her, and she shall be clean.

Thought 1. God loves and cares for the poor as much as He does for the advantaged. He has made provision for the poor to be saved just as readily and easily as He has for others. Any mother can come to God for forgiveness and help: rich or poor, married or single, educated or uneducated, sick or healthy, young or old. Any person can be reconciled with God; any person can come to God for help and forgiveness of sins.

"Come unto me, all ye that labour and are heavy laden, and I will give you rest" (Mt.11:28).
"For whosoever shall call upon the name of the Lord shall be saved" (Ro.10:13).
"Ho, every one that thirsteth, come ye to the waters, and he that hath no money; come ye, buy, and eat; yea, come, buy wine and milk without money and without price" (Is.55:1).
"For God so loved the world, that he gave his only begotten Son, that whosoever believeth in him should not perish, but have everlasting life" (Jn.3:16).
"And the Spirit and the bride say, Come. And let him that heareth say, Come. And let him that is athirst come. And whosoever will, let him take the water of life freely" (Re.22:17).

TYPES, SYMBOLS, AND PICTURES
Leviticus 12:1-8

Historical Term	Type or Picture (Scriptural Basis for Each)	Life Application for Today's Believer	Biblical Application
Laws That Protect Mother And Child After Childbirth Le. 12:1-8	*Laws that protect mother and child after childbirth symbolized the need for cleansing from the sinful nature.* *"Speak unto the children of Israel, saying, If a woman have conceived seed, and born a man child: then she shall be unclean seven days; according to the days of the separation for her infirmity shall she be unclean" (Le.12:2).*	Childbirth is one way God is able to teach the truth of human depravity. God has created man to live with Him forever in perfection. But sin has disrupted this relationship, alienated man from God. Sin has brought about death, terrible separation, and judgment to come. Teaching this truth was one of the purposes for the law of ceremonial uncleanness governing childbirth.	*"By man came death" (1 Co.15:21).* *"Wherefore, as by one man sin entered into the world, and death by sin; and so death passed upon all men, for that all have sinned" (Ro.5:12).* *"For the wages of sin is death" (Ro.6:23).* *"Behold, I was shapen in iniquity; and in sin did my mother conceive me" (Ps.51:5).* *"The wicked are estranged from the womb: they go astray as soon as they be born, speaking lies" (Ps.58:3).*

Circumcision
Le. 12:1-4
	Circumcision symbolized that a person was a member of God's people. Circumcision meant...
	  • *that a baby son was to be reared as a follower of God*
	  • *that he was to be taught the covenant of God*
	  • *that he would inherit the promises of God—if he truly obeyed and*
		God covers the child of the believer with His marvelous grace through the covenant of the Lord Jesus Christ. By Christ, God gives great assurance and security to the parents: He will look after their children.	*"But Jesus said, Suffer little children, and forbid them not, to come unto me: for of such is the kingdom of heaven" (Mt.19:14).*
			"Honour thy father and thy mother, as the Lord thy God hath commanded thee; that thy days may be prolonged, and that it may go well with thee, in the land which the Lord thy God giveth thee." (De.5:16)

TYPES, SYMBOLS, AND PICTURES
Leviticus 12:1-8

Historical Term	Type or Picture (Scriptural Basis for Each)	Life Application for Today's Believer	Biblical Application
	followed God • *that God covered the baby under His covenant and grace until he reached the age of responsibility.* **"And in the eighth day the flesh of his foreskin shall be circumcised"** (Le.12:3).		*"When my father and my mother forsake me, then the Lord will take me up"* (Ps.27:10). *"He shall feed his flock like a shepherd: he shall gather the lambs with his arm, and carry them in his bosom, and shall gently lead those that are with young."* (Is.40:11) *"For the promise is unto you, and to your children, and to all that are afar off, even as many as the Lord our God shall call"* (Ac.2:39).

CHAPTER 13

C. Laws That Protect People from Leprosy or Other Infectious Skin Diseases: Symbolizes the Disease of Sin and the Need to Prevent the Spread of Sin, 13:1-59

1. The Lawgiver: God Himself

2. The examination of contagious skin disease

a. The general examination of any swelling, rash, or bright spot: The person was to be brought to the High Priest

1) Case 1: The hair in the sore has turned white & is more than skin deep
- Is an infectious disease
- Is to be pronounced unclean—ceremonially unclean

2) Case 2: The sore is only skin deep & the hair has not turned white
- To be isolated, quarantined for seven days

- To be examined on the seventh day: If clean, to be kept in isolation another seven days

- To be re-examined again on the seventh day: If sore had faded & not spread, it was only a rash
- The verdict: To be pronounced clean & to wash one's clothes

3) Case 3: A relapse—the rash spread after being pronounced clean

- To be re-examined

- To be pronounced unclean: Is an infectious disease

b. The examination of raw flesh: The person was to be brought to the priest

And the LORD spake unto Moses and Aaron, saying,
2 When a man shall have in the skin of his flesh a rising, a scab, or bright spot, and it be in the skin of his flesh *like* the plague of leprosy; then he shall be brought unto Aaron the priest, or unto one of his sons the priests:
3 And the priest shall look on the plague in the skin of the flesh: and *when* the hair in the plague is turned white, and the plague in sight *be* deeper than the skin of his flesh, it *is* a plague of leprosy: and the priest shall look on him, and pronounce him unclean.
4 If the bright spot *be* white in the skin of his flesh, and in sight *be* not deeper than the skin, and the hair thereof be not turned white; then the priest shall shut up *him that hath* the plague seven days:
5 And the priest shall look on him the seventh day: and, behold, *if* the plague in his sight be at a stay, *and* the plague spread not in the skin; then the priest shall shut him up seven days more:
6 And the priest shall look on him again the seventh day: and, behold, *if* the plague *be* somewhat dark, *and* the plague spread not in the skin, the priest shall pronounce him clean: it *is but a* scab: and he shall wash his clothes, and be clean.
7 But if the scab spread much abroad in the skin, after that he hath been seen of the priest for his cleansing, he shall be seen of the priest again:
8 And *if* the priest see that, behold, the scab spreadeth in the skin, then the priest shall pronounce him unclean: it *is* a leprosy.
9 When the plague of leprosy is in a man, then he shall be brought unto the priest;

10 And the priest shall see *him*: and, behold, *if* the rising *be* white in the skin, and it have turned the hair white, and *there be* quick raw flesh in the rising;
11 It *is* an old leprosy in the skin of his flesh, and the priest shall pronounce him unclean, and shall not shut him up: for he *is* unclean.
12 And if a leprosy break out abroad in the skin, and the leprosy cover all the skin of *him that hath* the plague from his head even to his foot, wheresoever the priest looketh;
13 Then the priest shall consider: and, behold, *if* the leprosy have covered all his flesh, he shall pronounce *him* clean *that hath* the plague: it is all turned white: he *is* clean.
14 But when raw flesh appeareth in him, he shall be unclean.
15 And the priest shall see the raw flesh, and pronounce him to be unclean: *for the* raw flesh *is* unclean: it *is* a leprosy.
16 Or if the raw flesh turn again, and be changed unto white, he shall come unto the priest;
17 And the priest shall see *him*: and, behold, *if* the plague be turned into white; then the priest shall pronounce *him* clean *that hath* the plague: he *is* clean.
18 The flesh also, in which, *even* in the skin thereof, was a boil, and is healed,
19 And in the place of the boil there be a white rising, or a bright spot, white, and somewhat reddish, and it be showed to the priest;
20 And if, when the priest seeth it, behold, it *be* in sight lower than the skin, and the hair thereof be turned white; the priest shall pronounce him unclean: it *is* a plague of leprosy broken out of the boil.
21 But if the priest look on it, and, behold, *there be* no white hairs therein, and *if* it *be* not lower than the skin, but *be* somewhat dark; then the priest shall shut him up seven days:
22 And if it spread much abroad in the skin, then the

1) Case 1: A raw sore & white hair

- Is to be pronounced unclean
- Is not to be isolated because he is already unclean

2) Case 2: A rash breaks out all over one's body

- Is to be examined & pronounced clean
- Is clean because the body turned completely white or clear

3) Case 3: Raw flesh appears
- Is unclean

- Is to be pronounced unclean: He has an infectious disease

4) Case 4: Raw flesh changed & turned white
- Is to be re-examined

- Is to be pronounced clean

c. The examination of healed boils or reappearing diseases that show up in scars
1) Case 1: A white swelling or reddish-white spot where a boil was
- Is to be examined

- If it was more than skin deep & the hair had turned white, he is to be pronounced unclean: Is an infectious disease where the boil was

2) Case 2: No white hair, not more than skin deep & has faded—is to be isolated for seven days

- If it spreads in the skin, to be pronounced

unclean: Is an infectious disease

- If the spot is unchanged & does not spread, to be pronounced clean

d. The examination of burns with a reddish-white or white spot

1) Case 1: Sore is more than skin deep & hair is white

- Is an infectious disease
- Is to be pronounced unclean

2) Case 2: Sore is no more than skin deep & there is no white hair
  - To be isolated for seven days & re-examined on the seventh day

  - To be pronounced unclean if sore is spreading

  - To be pronounced clean if sore has faded & not spread & is not swelling from the burn: Is only a scar from the burn

e. The examination of a sore on the head or chin

1) Case 1: Sore is more than skin deep & hair in it is yellow & thin

  - Is to be pronounced unclean
  - Is an itch, an infectious disease

2) Case 2: Sore is not more than skin deep & no black hair in it

  - To be isolated for seven days

  - To be examined on the seventh day: If itch has

priest shall pronounce him unclean: it *is* a plague.

23 But if the bright spot stay in his place, *and* spread not, it *is* a burning boil; and the priest shall pronounce him clean.

24 Or if there be *any* flesh, in the skin whereof *there is* a hot burning, and the quick *flesh* that burneth have a white bright spot, somewhat reddish, or white;

25 Then the priest shall look upon it: and, behold, *if* the hair in the bright spot be turned white, and it *be in* sight deeper than the skin; it *is* a leprosy broken out of the burning: wherefore the priest shall pronounce him unclean: it *is* the plague of leprosy.

26 But if the priest look on it, and, behold, *there be* no white hair in the bright spot, and it *be* no lower than the *other* skin, but *be* somewhat dark; then the priest shall shut him up seven days:

27 And the priest shall look upon him the seventh day: *and* if it be spread much abroad in the skin, then the priest shall pronounce him unclean: it *is* the plague of leprosy.

28 And if the bright spot stay in his place, *and* spread not in the skin, but it *be* somewhat dark; it *is* a rising of the burning, and the priest shall pronounce him clean: for it *is* an inflammation of the burning.

29 If a man or woman have a plague upon the head or the beard;

30 Then the priest shall see the plague: and, behold, if it *be* in sight deeper than the skin; *and there be* in it a yellow thin hair; then the priest shall pronounce him unclean: it *is* a dry scall, *even a* leprosy upon the head or beard.

31 And if the priest look on the plague of the scall, and, behold, it *be* not in sight deeper than the skin, and *that there is* no black hair in it; then the priest shall shut up *him that hath* the plague of the scall seven days:

32 And in the seventh day the priest shall look on the

plague: and, behold, *if* the scall spread not, and there be in it no yellow hair, and the scall *be* not in sight deeper than the skin;

33 He shall be shaven, but the scall shall he not shave; and the priest shall shut up *him that hath* the scall seven days more:

34 And in the seventh day the priest shall look on the scall: and, behold, *if* the scall be not spread in the skin, nor *be* in sight deeper than the skin; then the priest shall pronounce him clean: and he shall wash his clothes, and be clean.

35 But if the scall spread much in the skin after his cleansing;

36 Then the priest shall look on him: and, behold, if the scall be spread in the skin, the priest shall not seek for yellow hair; he *is* unclean.

37 But if the scall be in his sight at a stay, and *that* there is black hair grown up therein; the scall is healed, he *is* clean: and the priest shall pronounce him clean.

38 If a man also or a woman have in the skin of their flesh bright spots, *even* white bright spots;

39 Then the priest shall look: and, behold, *if* the bright spots in the skin of their flesh *be* darkish white; it *is* a freckled spot *that* groweth in the skin; he *is* clean.

40 And the man whose hair is fallen off his head, he *is* bald; *yet is* he clean.

41 And he that hath his hair fallen off from the part of his head toward his face, he *is* forehead bald: *yet is* he clean.

42 And if there be in the bald head, or bald forehead, a white reddish sore; it *is* a leprosy sprung up in his bald head, or his bald forehead.

43 Then the priest shall look upon it: and, behold, *if* the rising of the sore *be* white reddish in his bald head, or in his bald forehead, as the leprosy appeareth in the skin of the flesh;

not spread & there is no yellow hair & the sore has not spread, he is to be shaved (except for the diseased area) & kept in isolation

- To be re-examined on the seventh day: If symptoms are improving, he is to be pronounced clean & he is to wash his clothes

3) Case 3: A relapse: The itch spreads after he is pronounced clean
  - To be re-examined
  - To be pronounced unclean if the itch has spread

  - To be pronounced clean if unchanged & black hair has grown in it

f. The examination of white spots

1) Is harmless if spots are dull white

2) Is to be pronounced clean

g. The examination of baldness

1) Case 1: Total or partial baldness from natural causes—is clean

2) Case 2: A reddish-white infectious sore on the bald head

- Is to be examined

- Is to be pronounced unclean

h. The treatment of the leper or the person with skin disease
1) Must humble himself: Wear torn clothes, etc.
2) Must pronounce himself unclean (a picture of confession)
3) Must separate himself, live outside the camp (symbolized separation, alienation from God & man)

3. The examination of contaminated clothing: Caused by infectious mildew (a symbol of sin)
a. The clothing listed: Any wool or linen, any woven or knitted material, anything made of leather
b. The situation: A greenish or reddish mildew or color in the clothing spreads
c. Case 1: A spreading mildew makes the clothing unclean

1) Must be examined & isolated for seven days & then re-examined on the seventh day
2) Is a destructive mildew if the mildew has spread: The clothing is unclean & is to be burned up

44 He is a leprous man, he *is* unclean: the priest shall pronounce him utterly unclean; his plague *is* in his head.
45 And the leper in whom the plague *is*, his clothes shall be rent, and his head bare, and he shall put a covering upon his upper lip, and shall cry, Unclean, unclean.
46 All the days wherein the plague *shall be* in him he shall be defiled; he *is* unclean: he shall dwell alone; without the camp *shall* his habitation *be*.
47 The garment also that the plague of leprosy is in, *whether it be* a woollen garment, or a linen garment;
48 Whether *it be* in the warp, or woof; of linen, or of woollen; whether in a skin, or in any thing made of skin;
49 And if the plague be greenish or reddish in the garment, or in the skin, either in the warp, or in the woof, or in any thing of skin; it *is* a plague of leprosy, and shall be showed unto the priest:
50 And the priest shall look upon the plague, and shut up *it that hath* the plague seven days:
51 And he shall look on the plague on the seventh day: if the plague be spread in the garment, either in the warp, or in the woof, or in a skin, *or* in any work that is made of skin; the plague *is* a fretting leprosy; it *is* unclean.
52 He shall therefore burn that garment, whether warp or woof, in woollen or in linen, or any thing of skin, wherein the plague is: for it

is a fretting leprosy; it shall be burnt in the fire.
53 And if the priest shall look, and, behold, the plague be not spread in the garment, either in the warp, or in the woof, or in any thing of skin;
54 Then the priest shall command that they wash *the thing* wherein the plague *is*, and he shall shut it up seven days more:
55 And the priest shall look on the plague, after that it is washed: and, behold, *if* the plague have not changed his colour, and the plague be not spread; it *is* unclean; thou shalt burn it in the fire; it *is* fret inward, *whether it be* bare within or without.
56 And if the priest look, and, behold, the plague *be* somewhat dark after the washing of it; then he shall rend it out of the garment, or out of the skin, or out of the warp, or out of the woof:
57 And if it appear still in the garment, either in the warp, or in the woof, or in any thing of skin; it *is* a spreading *plague*: thou shalt burn that wherein the plague *is* with fire.
58 And the garment, either warp, or woof, or whatsoever thing of skin *it be*, which thou shalt wash, if the plague be departed from them, then it shall be washed the second time, and shall be clean.
59 This *is* the law of the plague of leprosy in a garment of woollen or linen, either in the warp, or in the woof, or any thing of skins, to pronounce it clean, or to pronounce it unclean.

d. Case 2: An unchanged color in the mildew makes the clothing unclean

1) After the seven-day wait, if the mildew has not spread, the clothing is to be washed & isolated for another seven days
2) Then the clothing is to be examined again: If the mildew has not changed its appearance, even though it has not spread, it is unclean
3) The clothing is unclean: It is to be burned

e. Case 3: A faded mildew after the clothing is washed
1) To tear out the contaminated part—can mean the clothing is either clean or unclean
2) To burn the clothing if the mold reappears after the contaminated part has been torn out

f. The treatment of mildew in clothing
1) The treatment: Must be washed
2) The result: Made clean

3) The terrible loss to mildew (a symbol of sin): Some are pronounced clean but others are pronounced unclean

DIVISION III

THE WAY TO LIVE A HOLY LIFE BEFORE GOD (PART I): BY A CLEAN BODY (SEPARATION), 11:1–16:34

C. Laws That Protect People from Leprosy or Other Infectious Skin Diseases: Symbolizes the Disease of Sin and the Need to Prevent the Spread of Sin, 13:1-59

(13:1-59) **Introduction—Leprosy, Symbol - Type of—Infectious Skin Disease, Symbol of—Sin, Symbol of—Symbol, of Sin—Disease, Symbol of**: disease is always a very serious problem. A contagious disease is especially a problem, for it can spread like wildfire and infect thousands upon thousands of people. Aids and herpes are just two examples in this day and time. But a contagious disease was a far greater problem for people prior to the 20th century. The author's own grandmother died in an epidemic in the early 1900's, leaving his mother at the age of seven to be reared by her aunt and uncle. In the words of *The Expositor's Bible Commentary*:

It is hard for moderns to imagine the severity of ancient epidemics. The black death (bubonic plague) killed a quarter of Europe's people in about 1350. Whole villages would move away from those stricken with the disease. Quarantine was the only available relief.[1]

The ancient world had no medicine or drugs—none whatsoever—to heal, control, or prevent disease from spreading. The only weapon they had to combat disease was to isolate or quarantine the person. This was the reason God gave this law, to control leprosy and infectious skin diseases.

The Hebrew word for "leprosy" means more than just leprosy as most people think of it. This is clear even in this chapter. Note verses 47-59, where mildew, fungus, or some kind of rot is discussed. The same Hebrew word is used (tsara'at). The Hebrew word obviously refers to leprosy and all other infectious, contagious skin diseases such as...

- skin rashes
- skin blemishes
- measles
- boils
- scarlet fever
- smallpox
- psoriasis
- leucoderma
- favus
- sores of all kinds

If a person had any skin disease whatsoever, he was counted unclean; he was separated and isolated from all other persons until the symptom had healed. God gave this law to His people for two reasons:

⇒ Physically, the law protected His people from contagious disease: the *law of separation* kept the disease from spreading among His people.

⇒ Spiritually, leprosy or infectious skin disease is a picture or type of sin throughout the Bible. By this law, God teaches His people *the law of separation*. His people are to guard against the infectious disease of sin and keep it from spreading. They are to obey the *law of separation* in dealing with sin.

The leprosy or infection of sin is within the very nature of man. The infectious diseases among man paint a picture of just how terrible sin is: sin is ever present with man, spreading, contaminating, arousing concern and fear within people, striking others with hopelessness and death. Sin is exceedingly vile and contagious. The picture of leprosy or infectious disease as a symbol of sin is seen throughout the Bible.

> **"And he said unto him [the leper], Arise, go thy way: thy faith hath made thee whole [saved you, sozo]" (Lu.17:19).**

> **"Then he said to him [the leper], 'Rise and go; your faith has made you well [saved you, sozo]'" (Lu.17:19, NIV).**

> **"There is no soundness in my flesh because of thine anger; neither is there any rest in my bones because of my sin....My wounds stink and are corrupt because of my foolishness....For my loins are filled with a loathsome disease: and there is no soundness in my flesh....For I will declare mine iniquity; I will be sorry for my sin" (Ps.38:3, 5, 7, 18).**

> **"Purge me with hyssop, and I shall be clean: wash me, and I shall be whiter than snow" (Ps.51:7).**

> **"Wash you, make you clean; put away the evil of your doings from before mine eyes; cease to do evil" (Is.1:16).**

Leprosy or infectious skin disease is a clear picture of sin, the sinfulness of sin. This chapter identifies the problem (13:1-59); the next chapter deals with the cleansing of the disease (14:1-5). This is the subject of this important passage: *Laws That Protect People from Leprosy or Other Infectious Skin Diseases: Symbolizes the Disease of Sin and the Need to Prevent the Spread of Sin*, 13:1-59.

1. The Lawgiver: God Himself (v.1).
2. The examination of infectious skin disease (vv.2-46).
3. The examination of contaminated clothing: caused by infectious mildew (a symbol of sin) (vv.47-59).

1 (13:1) **Leprosy, Laws Governing—Infectious Skin Disease, Laws Governing—Sin, Symbol - Type of—Law, Governing Leprosy or Infectious Skin Disease**: the Lawgiver—the person who gave these laws—was God Himself. These laws did not come from man; they came from God. God loves His people and He wants them healthy. He wants His people to be physically strong so they can live life to the fullest, worshipping and serving Him, bearing strong testimony to a world lost and dying in sin and to the hope of eternal life. This was the reason God gave this law to His people. He wanted them to protect themselves from infectious skin disease lest an epidemic break out, weakening and destroying them. He wants us declaring the glorious gospel of eternal life, of living forever with God.

OUTLINE	SCRIPTURE
1. The Lawgiver: God Himself	And the LORD spake unto Moses and Aaron, saying,

Thought 1. God loves us and cares for us; therefore He wants us healthy. He wants us experiencing the fullness of life, worshipping and serving Him. He wants us bearing strong testimony to a world lost and reeling under the weight of desperate need. This was the reason He gave Israel the law governing leprosy or infectious skin disease. This is the reason He wants all of His people throughout all generations healthy.

> **"I am come that they might have life, and that they might have *it* more abundantly" (Jn.10:10).**

---

[1] *The Expositor's Bible Commentary,* Vol.2. Frank E. Gaebelein, General Editor, p.578.

"Forasmuch then as the children are partakers of flesh and blood, he also himself likewise took part of the same; that through death he might destroy him that had the power of death, that is, the devil; And deliver them who through fear of death were all their lifetime subject to bondage. For verily he took not on *him the nature of* angels; but he took on *him* the seed of Abraham. Wherefore in all things it behooved him to be made like unto *his* brethren, that he might be a merciful and faithful high priest in things *pertaining* to God, to make reconciliation for the sins of the people. For in that he himself hath suffered being tempted, he is able to succour them that are tempted" (He.2:14-18).

"For we have not an high priest which cannot be touched with the feeling of our infirmities; but was in all points tempted like as *we are, yet* without sin. Let us therefore come boldly unto the throne of grace, that we may obtain mercy, and find grace to help in time of need" (He.4:15-16).

"My son, attend to my words; incline thine ear unto my sayings. Let them not depart from thine eyes; keep them in the midst of thine heart. For they *are* life unto those that find them, and health to all their flesh" (Pr.4:20-22).

"But he *was* wounded for our transgressions, *he was* bruised for our iniquities: the chastisement of our peace *was* upon him; and with his stripes we are healed" (Is.53:5).

"Come, and let us return unto the Lord: for he hath torn, and he will heal us; he hath smitten, and he will bind us up" (Ho.6:1).

---

2 (13:2-46) **Leprosy, Laws Governing—Infectious Skin Disease, Laws Governing—Sin, Symbol - Type of—Law, Governing Leprosy or Infectious Skin Disease**: there was the examination of infectious disease. The reader will note that this point covers forty-five verses, a long, long passage to study, preach, or teach in any given situation. But note: the passage is not complicated. It is easily outlined, making it simple to follow. The passage merely covers case after case of skin diseases that are to be examined by the priest. The best approach to studying this passage is probably to look at the outline and Scripture side by side, section by section, point by point, and then to draw personal application from the section and point.

a. There was the general examination of any swelling, rash, or bright spot that appeared on the flesh: a person had to be brought to the High Priest (vv.2-8).

OUTLINE	SCRIPTURE	SCRIPTURE	OUTLINE
2. The examination of contagious skin disease a. The general examination of any swelling, rash, or bright spot: The person was to be brought to the High Priest	2 When a man shall have in the skin of his flesh a rising, a scab, or bright spot, and it be in the skin of his flesh *like* the plague of leprosy; then he shall be brought unto Aaron the priest, or unto one of his sons the priests:	5 And the priest shall look on him the seventh day: and, behold, *if* the plague in his sight be at a stay, *and* the plague spread not in the skin; then the priest shall shut him up seven days more:	• To be examined on the seventh day: If clean, to be kept in isolation another seven days
1) Case 1: The hair in the sore had turned white & is more than skin deep • Is an infectious disease • Is to be pronounced unclean—ceremonially unclean	3 And the priest shall look on the plague in the skin of the flesh: and *when* the hair in the plague is turned white, and the plague in sight *be* deeper than the skin of his flesh, it *is* a plague of leprosy: and the priest shall look on him, and pronounce him unclean.	6 And the priest shall look on him again the seventh day: and, behold, *if* the plague *be* somewhat dark, *and* the plague spread not in the skin, the priest shall pronounce him clean: it *is but* a scab: and he shall wash his clothes, and be clean.	• To be re-examined again on the seventh day: If sore had faded & not spread, it was only a rash • The verdict: To be pronounced clean & to wash one's clothes
2) Case 2: The sore was only skin deep & the hair is not white • To be isolated, quarantined, for seven days	4 If the bright spot *be* white in the skin of his flesh, and in sight *be* not deeper than the skin, and the hair thereof be not turned white; then the priest shall shut up *him that hath* the plague seven days:	7 But if the scab spread much abroad in the skin, after that he hath been seen of the priest for his cleansing, he shall be seen of the priest again: 8 And *if* the priest see that, behold, the scab spreadeth in the skin, then the priest shall pronounce him unclean: it *is* a leprosy.	3) Case 3: A relapse—the rash spread after being pronounced clean • To be re-examined • To be pronounced unclean: Is an infectious disease

Note that this was just a general examination of any swelling, rash, or bright spot. It was not necessarily an examination of a definite disease. It was a preliminary, general examining of a potential disease. Note also that the person had to be *brought,* indicating perhaps that he was too sick to walk, that he had to be carried (v.2).

Thought 1. There is a strong lesson for us in this preliminary exam. Remember that leprosy or infectious skin disease is a symbol of sin. At the first sign of leprosy or infectious skin disease, the person was immediately brought to the priest. This is exactly what the believer should do at the first sign of sin: he should immediately go to the High Priest of God, the Lord Jesus Christ. Christ and Christ alone can deliver us from sin. He and He alone can cleanse us from sin and pronounce us clean.

"For this is my blood of the new testament, which is shed for many for the remission of sins" (Mt.26:28).

"In whom we have redemption through his blood, the forgiveness of sins, according to the riches of his grace" (Ep.1:7).

"If we confess our sins, he is faithful and just to forgive us *our* sins, and to cleanse us from all unrighteousness" (1 Jn.1:9).

"My little children, these things write I unto you, that ye sin not. And if any man sin, we have an advocate with the Father, Jesus Christ the righteous: And he is the propitiation for our sins: and not for ours only, but also for *the sins of* the whole world" (1 Jn.2:1-2).

b. There was the examination of any raw flesh that appeared on the skin of a person's body (v.9-17). Note that the person was again to be brought to the High Priest. Any possible spread of the disease was to be prevented. In this, the people were to be ever so diligent, standing on guard at all times.

OUTLINE	SCRIPTURE	SCRIPTURE	OUTLINE
b. The examination of raw flesh: The person was to be brought to the priest	9 When the plague of leprosy is in a man, then he shall be brought unto the priest;	sider: and, behold, *if* the leprosy have covered all his flesh, he shall pronounce *him* clean *that hath* the plague: it is all turned white: he *is* clean.	pronounced clean • Is clean because the body turned completely white or clear
1) Case 1: A raw sore & white hair	10 And the priest shall see *him*: and, behold, *if* the rising *be* white in the skin, and it have turned the hair white, and *there be* quick raw flesh in the rising;	14 But when raw flesh appeareth in him, he shall be unclean.	3) Case 3: Raw flesh appears • Is unclean
	11 It *is* an old leprosy in the skin of his flesh, and the priest shall pronounce him unclean, and shall not shut him up: for he *is* unclean.	15 And the priest shall see the raw flesh, and pronounce him to be unclean: *for* the raw flesh *is* unclean: it *is* a leprosy.	• Is to be pronounced unclean: He has an infectious disease
• Is to be pronounced unclean • Is not to be isolated because he is already unclean			
2) Case 2: A rash breaks out all over one's body	12 And if a leprosy break out abroad in the skin, and the leprosy cover all the skin of *him that hath* the plague from his head even to his foot, wheresoever the priest looketh;	16 Or if the raw flesh turn again, and be changed unto white, he shall come unto the priest;	4) Case 4: Raw flesh changed & turned white • Is to be re-examined
		17 And the priest shall see him: and, behold, *if* the plague be turned into white; then the priest shall pronounce *him* clean *that hath* the plague: he *is* clean.	• Is to be pronounced clean
• Is to be examined &	13 Then the priest shall con-		

Thought 1. In dealing with raw flesh, the infection is exposed. There is a raw sore that is open and easily seen. How like the behavior of so many people: sinning does not bother them, not that much. They sin openly, flagrantly, and their sin is exposed and seen by all. Their hearts have become so hardened that sin does not bother them, not any more. Even throughout society as a whole, the media and the sinful behavior of some people have so exposed society to sin that a hardness of heart has set in. Just think of the exposure of sex in the media, the use of foul, vulgar profanity, the violence, the lawlessness, the greed, the pride and arrogance, the drunkenness and so much more. There is a hardness to sin within all society, so much so that it has even affected Christian believers. But this is not so with God Himself. The raw flesh of sin is exposed, open to His piercing eyes. God sees the raw flesh of sin and declares that it is unclean. It must be isolated, separated, put out of His presence and away from His people.

"They are all gone out of the way, they are together become unprofitable; there is none that doeth good, no, not one. Their throat is an open sepulchre; with their tongues they have used deceit; the poison of asps is under their lips: Whose mouth is full of cursing and bitterness: Their feet are swift to shed blood: Destruction and misery are in their ways: And the way of peace have they not known: There is no fear of God before their eyes" (Ro.3:12-18).

"Happy is the man that feareth always: but he that hardeneth his heart shall fall into mischief" (Pr.28:14).

"He, that being often reproved hardeneth his neck, shall suddenly be destroyed, and that without remedy" (Pr.29:1).

"But after thy hardness and impenitent heart treasurest up unto thyself wrath against the day of wrath and revelation of the righteous judgment of God" (Ro.2:5).

"But exhort one another daily, while it is called To day; lest any of you be hardened through the deceitfulness of sin" (He.3:13).

c. There was the examination of healed boils or reappearing diseases that show up in healed scars (vv.18-23). Note that these cases involved reappearing diseases or spots that appear on the top of healed scars. The danger was that an old disease might be reappearing and its spread had to be prevented.

OUTLINE	SCRIPTURE	SCRIPTURE	OUTLINE
c. The examination of healed boils or reappearing diseases that show up in scars 1) Case 1: A white swelling or reddish-white spot where a boil was • Is to be examined • If it was more than skin deep & the hair had turned white, he is to be pronounced unclean: Is an infectious disease where the boil was	18 The flesh also, in which, *even* in the skin thereof, was a boil, and is healed, 19 And in the place of the boil there be a white rising, or a bright spot, white, and somewhat reddish, and it be showed to the priest; 20 And if, when the priest seeth it, behold, it *be* in sight lower than the skin, and the hair thereof be turned white; the priest shall pronounce him unclean: it *is* a plague of leprosy broken out of the boil.	21 But if the priest look on it, and, behold, *there be* no white hairs therein, and *if* it *be* not lower than the skin, but *be* somewhat dark; then the priest shall shut him up seven days: 22 And if it spread much abroad in the skin, then the priest shall pronounce him unclean: it is a plague. 23 But if the bright spot stay in his place, *and* spread not, it *is* a burning boil; and the priest shall pronounce him clean.	2) Case 2: No white hair, not more than skin deep & has faded—is to be isolated for seven days • If it spreads in the skin, to be pronounced unclean: Is an infectious disease • If the spot is unchanged & does not spread, to be pronounced clean

Thought 1. Sin can reappear. There is always the danger that old sins will raise their evil, cancerous heads again. It is not enough to be saved from sin: the habit of sin must be broken. Sin is malignant, and it can spread ever so rapidly. There is only one hope for any person to break the habit of sin: experiencing the power of the Lord Jesus Christ.

"Likewise reckon ye also yourselves to be dead indeed unto sin, but alive unto God through Jesus Christ our Lord. Let not sin therefore reign in your mortal body, that ye should obey it in the lusts thereof. Neither yield ye your members *as* instruments of unrighteousness unto sin: but yield yourselves unto God, as those that are alive from the dead, and your members *as* instruments of righteousness unto God. For sin shall not have dominion over you: for ye are not under the law, but under grace" (Ro.6:11-14).

"But God be thanked, that ye were the servants of sin, but ye have obeyed from the heart that form of doctrine which was delivered you. Being then made free from sin, ye became the servants of righteousness" (Ro.6:17-18).

"And they that are Christ's have crucified the flesh with the affections and lusts" (Ga.5:24).

"Who gave himself for our sins, that he might deliver us from this present evil world, according to the will of God and our Father" (Ga.1:4).

"Who his own self bare our sins in his own body on the tree, that we, being dead to sins, should live unto righteousness: by whose stripes ye were healed" (1 Pe.2:24).

"My little children, these things write I unto you, that ye sin not. And if any man sin, we have an advocate with the Father, Jesus Christ the righteous: And he is the propitiation for our sins: and not for ours only, but also for the sins of the whole world" (1 Jn.2:1-2).

"Can the Ethiopian change his skin, or the leopard his spots? then may ye also do good, that are accustomed to do evil" (Je.13:23).

d. There was the examination of burns with a reddish-white or white spot (v.24-28). Note that this concerns burns that have become infected. Burns had to be kept under close observation or infection could immediately set in.

OUTLINE	SCRIPTURE	SCRIPTURE	OUTLINE
d. The examination of burns with a reddish-white or white spot 1) Case 1: Sore is more than skin deep & hair is white • Is an infectious disease • Is to be pronounced unclean 2) Case 2: Sore is no more than skin deep & there is no white hair	24 Or if there be *any* flesh, in the skin whereof *there is* a hot burning, and the quick *flesh* that burneth have a white bright spot, somewhat reddish, or white; 25 Then the priest shall look upon it: and, behold, *if* the hair in the bright spot be turned white, and it *be in* sight deeper than the skin; it *is* a leprosy broken out of the burning: wherefore the priest shall pronounce him unclean: it *is* the plague of leprosy. 26 But if the priest look on it, and, behold, *there be* no white hair in the bright	spot, and it *be* no lower than the *other* skin, but *be* somewhat dark; then the priest shall shut him up seven days: 27 And the priest shall look upon him the seventh day: *and* if it be spread much abroad in the skin, then the priest shall pronounce him unclean: it *is* the plague of leprosy. 28 And if the bright spot stay in his place, *and* spread not in the skin, but it *be* somewhat dark; it *is* a rising of the burning, and the priest shall pronounce him clean: for it *is* an inflammation of the burning.	• To be isolated for seven days & re-examined on the seventh day • To be pronounced unclean if sore is spreading • To be pronounced clean if sore has faded & not spread & is not swelling from the burn: Is only a scar from the burn

Thought 1. The burn from a hot object is a descriptive picture of sin. Sin burns a person, and unless it is immediately dealt with, sin will infect the whole life of a person. In fact, the burning fire of sin can cause so much infection that it consumes a person—destroys his body and soul—it kills him.

> "For the wages of sin *is* death; but the gift of God *is* eternal life through Jesus Christ our Lord" (Ro.6:23).
> "For to be carnally minded *is* death; but to be spiritually minded *is* life and peace" (Ro.8:6).
> "But every man is tempted, when he is drawn away of his own lust, and enticed. Then when lust hath conceived, it bringeth forth sin: and sin, when it is finished, bringeth forth death" (Js.1:14-15).
> "Evil shall slay the wicked: and they that hate the righteous shall be desolate" (Ps.34:21).
> "But he that sinneth against me wrongeth his own soul: all they that hate me love death" (Pr.8:36).
> "The integrity of the upright shall guide them: but the perverseness of transgressors shall destroy them" (Pr.11:3).
> "The soul that sinneth, it shall die" (Eze.18:20).
> "O Israel, thou hast destroyed thyself; but in me is thine help" (Ho.13:9).

e. There was the examination of a sore on the head or the chin (vv.29-37). Note that this leprosy or infectious disease breaks out under the hair of the head or beard. This means that the person might not discover the disease in time because it was hidden under the hair. In such cases, the person had to shave himself and watch it ever so closely.

OUTLINE	SCRIPTURE	SCRIPTURE	OUTLINE
e. The examination of a sore on the head or chin	29 If a man or woman have a plague upon the head or the beard;	the scall shall he not shave; and the priest shall shut up *him that hath* the scall seven days more:	
1) Case 1: Sore is more than skin deep & hair in it is yellow & thin	30 Then the priest shall see the plague: and, behold, if it *be* in sight deeper than the skin; *and there be* in it a yellow thin hair; then the priest shall pronounce him unclean: it *is* a dry scall, *even a* leprosy upon the head or beard.	34 And in the seventh day the priest shall look on the scall: and, behold, *if* the scall be not spread in the skin, nor *be* in sight deeper than the skin; then the priest shall pronounce him clean: and he shall wash his clothes, and be clean.	• To be reexamined on the seventh day: If symptoms are improving, he is to be pronounced clean & he is to wash his clothes
• Is to be pronounced unclean			
• Is an itch, an infectious disease			
2) Case 2: Sore is not more than skin deep & no black hair in it	31 And if the priest look on the plague of the scall, and, behold, it *be* not in sight deeper than the skin, and *that there is* no black hair in it; then the priest shall shut up *him that hath* the plague of the scall seven days:	35 But if the scall spread much in the skin after his cleansing;	3) Case 3: A relapse: The itch spreads after he is pronounced clean
		36 Then the priest shall look on him: and, behold, if the scall be spread in the skin, the priest shall not seek for yellow hair; he *is* unclean.	• To be reexamined
• To be isolated for seven days			• To be pronounced unclean if the itch has spread
• To be examined on the seventh day: If itch has not spread & there is no yellow hair & the sore has not spread, he is to be shaved (except for the diseased area) & kept in isolation	32 And in the seventh day the priest shall look on the plague: and, behold, *if* the scall spread not, and there be in it no yellow hair, and the scall *be* not in sight deeper than the skin; 33 He shall be shaven, but	37 But if the scall be in his sight at a stay, and *that* there is black hair grown up therein; the scall is healed, he *is* clean: and the priest shall pronounce him clean.	• To be pronounced clean if unchanged & black hair has grown in it

Thought 1. This is an excellent illustration of secret or unknown sins, sins that are hidden and unknown to us. Every believer is constantly discovering sin in his life, sin that he knew nothing about. He is often discovering the secret and hidden sins lying deep down within the recesses of his heart. He is ever so aware of being short of God's glory.

(1) The believer does have secret and hidden sins in his life, sins that he knows nothing about.

> "For the wages of sin is death; but the gift of God is eternal life through Jesus Christ our Lord" (Ro.6:23).
> "For it is a shame even to speak of those things which are done of them in secret" (Ep.5:12).
> "Who can understand his errors? cleanse thou me from secret faults" (Ps.19:12).
> "Thou hast set our iniquities before thee, our secret sins in the light of thy countenance" (Ps.90:8).

(2) The believer's secret and unknown sins are seen and known by God.

> "If I sin, then thou markest me, and thou wilt not acquit me from mine iniquity" (Jb.10:14).
> "For mine eyes are upon all their ways: they are not hid from my face, neither is their iniquity hid from mine eyes" (Je.16:17).
> "Thus saith the LORD...I know the things that come into your mind, every one of them" (Eze.11:5).

f. There was the examination of white spots (vv.38-39). Note that this is the examination of harmless spots on the face such as freckles or white blotches. If found harmless, the person was pronounced clean.

OUTLINE	SCRIPTURE
f. The examination of white spots	38 If a man also or a woman have in the skin of their flesh bright spots, *even* white bright spots;
1) Is harmless if spots are dull white	39 Then the priest shall look: and, behold, *if* the bright spots in the skin of their flesh *be* darkish white;
2) Is to be pronounced clean	it *is* a freckled spot *that* groweth in the skin; he *is* clean.

Thought 1. Many believers have a sensitive conscience. They feel that they just cannot do certain things, go certain places, participate in certain activities, watch certain things, nor listen to certain things. If they did, they feel they would be sinning. Their liberty in Christ is restricted and sometimes immature. They have not yet learned to walk in the freedom and liberty of God's Spirit, being led and guided by Him. Instead, they live by the code book of do's and don'ts, rules and regulations.

"Him that is weak in the faith receive ye, but not to doubtful disputations. For one believeth that he may eat all things: another, who is weak, eateth herbs. Let not him that eateth despise him that eateth not; and let not him which eateth not judge him that eateth: for God hath received him....One man esteemeth one day above another: another esteemeth every day alike. Let every man be fully persuaded in his own mind. He that regardeth the day, regardeth it unto the Lord; and he that regardeth not the day, to the Lord he doth not regard it. He that eateth, eateth to the Lord, for he giveth God thanks; and he that eateth not, to the Lord he eateth not, and giveth God thanks" (Ro.14:1-3, 5-6).

"I know, and am persuaded by the Lord Jesus, that there is nothing unclean of itself: but to him that esteemeth any thing to be unclean, to him it is unclean. But if thy brother be grieved with thy meat, now walkest thou not charitably. Destroy not him with thy meat, for whom Christ died. Let not then your good be evil spoken of: For the kingdom of God is not meat and drink; but righteousness, and peace, and joy in the Holy Ghost....For meat destroy not the work of God. All things indeed are pure; but it is evil for that man who eateth with offence. It is good neither to eat flesh, nor to drink wine, nor any thing whereby thy brother stumbleth, or is offended, or is made weak" (Ro.14:14-17, 20-21).

"For as many as are led by the Spirit of God, they are the sons of God" (Ro.8:14).

"But take heed lest by any means this liberty of yours become a stumblingblock to them that are weak" (1 Co.8:9).

"For, brethren, ye have been called unto liberty; only use not liberty for an occasion to the flesh, but by love serve one another" (Ga.5:13).

g. There was examination of baldness (vv.40-44). Note that baldness is not necessarily due to some infectious disease. Baldness can be and usually is due to the natural loss of hair.

OUTLINE	SCRIPTURE	SCRIPTURE	OUTLINE
g. The examination of baldness 1) Case 1: Total or partial baldness from natural causes—is clean	40 And the man whose hair is fallen off his head, he *is* bald; *yet is* he clean. 41 And he that hath his hair fallen off from the part of his head toward his face, he *is* forehead bald: *yet is* he clean.	head. 43 Then the priest shall look upon it: and, behold, *if* the rising of the sore *be* white reddish in his bald head, or in his bald forehead, as the leprosy appeareth in the skin of the flesh;	• Is to be examined
2) Case 2: A reddish-white infectious sore on the bald head	42 And if there be in the bald head, or bald forehead, a white reddish sore; it *is* a leprosy sprung up in his bald head, or his bald fore-	44 He is a leprous man, he *is* unclean: the priest shall pronounce him utterly unclean; his plague *is* in his head.	• Is to be pronounced unclean

Thought 1. Note that the head can become infected with leprosy or infectious skin disease. This is a descriptive picture of the head or mind being infected by sin. A person's mind can become so infected with sin that it becomes utterly corrupted and destructive. We see this all throughout society. We see minds being polluted by a constant barrage of pornography, sex, immorality, lawlessness, violence, drunkenness—all easily seen on the television and movie screens of the world, in the magazines and books being published, in the shady and off-colored jokes being told, and in the vulgarity and profanity being used. The devastating result upon society is seen in the acts of assault, lawlessness, violence, and adulteries, in the breakup of families, and in all the other ills of society. The point is this: the infectious disease of sin has so taken over the head or mind of man that corruption is sweeping the world and

running out of control. In fact, immorality, lawlessness, and violence are running so rampant throughout the world that many feel the problems are beyond reigning in. The corruption and problems of evil are just beyond control. The only hope is Jesus Christ. He and He alone can deliver man from sin and purify the mind of man. He and He alone can take a corrupted mind that is obsessed with evil and convert it to a mind of righteousness.

(1) The disease of sin has infected the mind of man.

> "For out of the heart proceed evil thoughts, murders, adulteries, fornications, thefts, false witness, blasphemies" (Mt.15:19).
> "Because that, when they knew God, they glorified him not as God, neither were thankful; but became vain in their imaginations, and their foolish heart was darkened" (Ro.1:21).
> "And even as they did not like to retain God in their knowledge, God gave them over to a reprobate mind, to do those things which are not convenient" (Ro.1:28).
> "Because the carnal mind is enmity against God: for it is not subject to the law of God, neither indeed can be" (Ro.8:7).
> "This I say therefore, and testify in the Lord, that ye henceforth walk not as other Gentiles walk, in the vanity of their mind" (Ep.4:17).
> "Unto the pure all things are pure: but unto them that are defiled and unbelieving is nothing pure; but even their mind and conscience is defiled" (Tit.1:15).
> "And GOD saw that the wickedness of man was great in the earth, and that every imagination of the thoughts of his heart was only evil continually" (Ge.6:5).
> "An heart that deviseth wicked imaginations, feet that be swift in running to mischief" (Pr.6:18).

(2) The mind of man can be changed—changed by Christ. Man can fill his mind with righteousness through the Word of God and the power of Christ.

> "For to be carnally minded is death; but to be spiritually minded is life and peace" (Ro.8:6).
> "For who hath known the mind of the Lord, that he may instruct him? But we have the mind of Christ" (1 Co.2:16).
> "Therefore if any man be in Christ, he is a new creature: old things are passed away; behold, all things are become new" (2 Co.5:17).
> "Casting down imaginations, and every high thing that exalteth itself against the knowledge of God, and bringing into captivity every thought to the obedience of Christ" (2 Co.10:5).
> "And that ye put on the new man, which after God is created in righteousness and true holiness" (Ep.4:24).
> "Let this mind be in you, which was also in Christ Jesus" (Ph.2:5).
> "Finally, brethren, whatsoever things are true, whatsoever things are honest, whatsoever things are just, whatsoever things are pure, whatsoever things are lovely, whatsoever things are of good report; if there be any virtue, and if there be any praise, think on these things" (Ph.4:8).

h. There was the treatment of the leper or the person with an infectious skin disease (v.45-46). The disease was real; and it was infectious, contagious, and communicable. The threat was dangerous: it could possibly and easily spread, infecting and wiping out entire families or communities. God's people had to be protected from the infectious, contagious disease. Three immediate steps had to be taken in the treatment of the infected person. Note these in the Scripture and outline below.

OUTLINE	SCRIPTURE
h. The treatment of the leper or the person with skin disease	45 And the leper in whom the plague *is*, his clothes shall be rent, and his head bare, and he shall put a covering upon his upper lip, and shall cry, Unclean, unclean.
1) Must humble himself: Wear torn clothes, etc.	
2) Must pronounce himself unclean (a picture of confession)	
3) Must separate himself, live outside the camp (symbolized separation, alienation from God & man)	46 All the days wherein the plague *shall be* in him he shall be defiled; he *is* unclean: he shall dwell alone; without the camp *shall* his habitation *be*.

Thought 1. Sin is a serious matter. It is not to be taken lightly. It is infectious, contagious. Sin can spread throughout a person's life and the life of his family and community. An infected person's behavior influences people; therefore if his behavior is sinful, his sin infects (influences) the lives of others. There is only one treatment, and that treatment is found in the three steps given here.

(1) The infected person must humble himself before God and before other believers.

> "Whosoever therefore shall humble himself as this little child, the same is greatest in the kingdom of heaven" (Mt.18:4).

"For I say, through the grace given unto me, to every man that is among you, not to think of himself more highly than he ought to think; but to think soberly, according as God hath dealt to every man the measure of faith" (Ro.12:3).

"Humble yourselves in the sight of the Lord, and he shall lift you up" (Js.4:10).

"Likewise, ye younger, submit yourselves unto the elder. Yea, all of you be subject one to another, and be clothed with humility: for God resisteth the proud, and giveth grace to the humble" (1 Pe.5:5).

"If we confess our sins, he is faithful and just to forgive us *our* sins, and to cleanse us from all unrighteousness" (1 Jn.1:9).

"For thus saith the high and lofty One that inhabiteth eternity, whose name is Holy; I dwell in the high and holy place, with him also that is of a contrite and humble spirit, to revive the spirit of the humble, and to revive the heart of the contrite ones" (Is.57:15).

"He hath showed thee, O man, what is good; and what doth the LORD require of thee, but to do justly, and to love mercy, and to walk humbly with thy God?" (Mi.6:8).

(2) The infected person must pronounce himself unclean. This is a picture of confession.

"Whosoever therefore shall confess me before men, him will I confess also before my Father which is in heaven" (Mt.10:32).

"Also I say unto you, Whosoever shall confess me before men, him shall the Son of man also confess before the angels of God" (Lu.12:8).

"That if thou shalt confess with thy mouth the Lord Jesus, and shalt believe in thine heart that God hath raised him from the dead, thou shalt be saved" (Ro.10:9).

"And that every tongue should confess that Jesus Christ is Lord, to the glory of God the Father" (Ph.2:11).

"Whosoever denieth the Son, the same hath not the Father: (but) he that acknowledgeth the Son hath the Father also" (1 Jn.2:23).

"Whosoever shall confess that Jesus is the Son of God, God dwelleth in him, and he in God" (1 Jn.4:15).

(3) The infected person must separate himself and live outside the camp, that is, outside the body of Christ. He is to be separated from believers as long as he remains unclean, for he is alienated from God and his sin can influence and pull down Christian believers.

"This people draweth nigh unto me with their mouth, and honoureth me with their lips; but their heart is far from me" (Mt.15:8).

"In the name of our Lord Jesus Christ, when ye are gathered together, and my spirit, with the power of our Lord Jesus Christ, To deliver such an one unto Satan for the destruction of the flesh, that the spirit may be saved in the day of the Lord Jesus. Your glorying *is* not good. Know ye not that a little leaven leaveneth the whole lump? Purge out therefore the old leaven, that ye may be a new lump, as ye are unleavened. For even Christ our passover is sacrificed for us" (1 Co.5:4-7).

"That at that time ye were without Christ, being aliens from the commonwealth of Israel, and strangers from the covenants of promise, having no hope, and without God in the world" (Ep.2:12).

"Holding faith, and a good conscience; which some having put away concerning faith have made shipwreck: Of whom is Hymenaeus and Alexander; whom I have delivered unto Satan, that they may learn not to blaspheme" (1 Ti.1:19-20).

"A man that is an heretic after the first and second admonition reject; Knowing that he that is such is subverted, and sinneth, being condemned of himself" (Tit.3:10-11).

"If I regard iniquity in my heart, the LORD will not hear me" (Ps.66:18).

"But your iniquities have separated between you and your God, and your sins have hid his face from you, that he will not hear" (Is.59:2).

---

3 (13:47-59) **Mildew—Fungus—Rot—Clothing, Infected—Clothing, Symbol of—Unclean - Uncleanness, Spiritual—Unclean - Uncleanness, Ceremonial—Sin, Symbol of—Symbol, of Sin—Symbol, of Clothing**: there was the examination of contaminated clothing that was caused by mildew, fungus, or some rot. Note that infected clothing is also a symbol of sin and its contamination. The Hebrew word "tsara'at" is being translated infectious mildew, fungus, or rot and not leprosy because leprosy is a human disease not a disease of clothing. The symptoms given throughout the Scripture clearly picture some kind of rot caused by a mildew or fungus. Again, the best way to cover the cases is to give an overall look at the Scripture and outline and then to draw the application at the end.

OUTLINE	SCRIPTURE	SCRIPTURE	OUTLINE
3. The examination of contaminated clothing: Caused by infectious mildew (a symbol of sin) a. The clothing listed: Any	47 The garment also that the plague of leprosy is in, *whether it be* a woollen garment, or a linen garment; 48 Whether *it be* in the warp,	or woof; of linen, or of woollen; whether in a skin, or in any thing made of skin; 49 And if the plague be greenish or reddish in the	wool or linen, any woven or knitted material, anything made of leather b. The situation: A greenish or reddish mildew or color in

OUTLINE	SCRIPTURE	SCRIPTURE	OUTLINE
the clothing spreads c. Case 1: A spreading mildew makes the clothing unclean 1) Must be examined & isolated for seven days & then re-examined on the seventh day 2) Is a destructive mildew if the mildew has spread: The clothing is unclean & to be burned up	garment, or in the skin, either in the warp, or in the woof, or in any thing of skin; it *is* a plague of leprosy, and shall be showed unto the priest: 50 And the priest shall look upon the plague, and shut up *it that hath* the plague seven days: 51 And he shall look on the plague on the seventh day: if the plague be spread in the garment, either in the warp, or in the woof, or in a skin, *or* in any work that is made of skin; the plague *is* a fretting leprosy; it *is* unclean. 52 He shall therefore burn that garment, whether warp or woof, in woollen or in linen, or any thing of skin, wherein the plague is: for it *is* a fretting leprosy; it shall be burnt in the fire.	washed: and, behold, *if* the plague have not changed his colour, and the plague be not spread; it *is* unclean; thou shalt burn it in the fire; it *is* fret inward, *whether it be* bare within or without. 56 And if the priest look, and, behold, the plague *be* somewhat dark after the washing of it; then he shall rend it out of the garment, or out of the skin, or out of the warp, or out of the woof: 57 And if it appear still in the garment, either in the warp, or in the woof, or in any thing of skin; it *is* a spreading *plague*: thou shalt burn that wherein the plague *is* with fire.	the mildew has not changed its appearance, even though it has not spread, it is unclean 3) The clothing is unclean: It is to be burned e. Case 3: A faded mildew after the clothing is washed 1) To tear out the contaminated part—can mean the clothing is either clean or unclean 2) To burn the clothing if the mold reappears after the contaminated part has been torn out
d. Case 2: An unchanged color in the mildew makes the clothing unclean 1) After the seven-day exam, if the mildew has not spread, the clothing is to be washed & isolated for another seven days 2) Then the clothing is to be examined again: If	53 And if the priest shall look, and, behold, the plague be not spread in the garment, either in the warp, or in the woof, or in any thing of skin; 54 Then the priest shall command that they wash *the thing* wherein the plague *is*, and he shall shut it up seven days more: 55 And the priest shall look on the plague, after that it is	58 And the garment, either warp, or woof, or whatsoever thing of skin *it be*, which thou shalt wash, if the plague be departed from them, then it shall be washed the second time, and shall be clean. 59 This *is* the law of the plague of leprosy in a garment of woollen or linen, either in the warp, or woof, or any thing of skins, to pronounce it clean, or to pronounce it unclean.	f. The treatment of mildew in clothing 1) The treatment: Must be washed 2) The result: Made clean 3) The terrible loss to mildew (a symbol of sin): Some are pronounced clean but others are pronounced unclean

Thought 1. Throughout Scripture, clothing is either a symbol of righteousness or unrighteousness. Clean clothing is a symbol of righteousness; unclean clothing is a symbol of unrighteousness. A person must make sure, absolutely sure, that he is clothed in the righteousness of Jesus Christ. If not, the mildew of sin will rot his clothing. He will stand before God clothed in unrighteousness.

(1) The natural man is clothed in the infectious mildew of sin or unrighteousness.

> "For the wrath of God is revealed from heaven against all ungodliness and unrighteousness of men, who hold the truth in unrighteousness" (Ro.1:18).
>
> "Neither yield ye your members as instruments of unrighteousness unto sin: but yield yourselves unto God, as those that are alive from the dead, and your members as instruments of righteousness unto God" (Ro.6:13).
>
> "But these [the unrighteous], as natural brute beasts, made to be taken and destroyed, speak evil of the things that they understand not; and shall utterly perish in their own corruption; And shall receive the reward of unrighteousness, as they that count it pleasure to riot in the day time. Spots they are and blemishes, sporting themselves with their own deceivings while they feast with you" (2 Pe.2:12-13).
>
> "All unrighteousness is sin" (1 Jn.5:17).

(2) The unrighteous man must be clothed in the righteousness of Jesus Christ, clothed with the new man.

> "For Christ is the end of the law for righteousness to every one that believeth" (Ro.10:4).
>
> "But of him are ye in Christ Jesus, who of God is made unto us wisdom, and righteousness, and sanctification, and redemption" (1 Co.1:30).
>
> "Therefore if any man be in Christ, he is a new creature: old things are passed away; behold, all things are become new" (2 Co.5:17).
>
> "And that ye put on the new man, which after God is created in righteousness and true holiness" (Ep.4:24).
>
> "And be found in him, not having mine own righteousness, which is of the law, but that which is through the faith of Christ, the righteousness which is of God by faith" (Ph.3:9).
>
> "And have put on the new man, which is renewed in knowledge after the image of him that created him" (Col.3:10).

Thought 2. Note the last point in the Scripture and outline above: the treatment of infectious mildew in clothing (vv.58-59). If the clothing was washed and rid of the mildew, it was to be washed again. It was then counted clean. Scripture declares that the infectious mildew or rot of sin must be washed away by the blood of Christ. Only the blood of Christ can cleanse a person from sin and make him acceptable to God.

"And now why tarriest thou? arise, and be baptized, and wash away thy sins, calling on the name of the Lord" (Ac.22:16).

"In whom we have redemption through his blood, the forgiveness of sins, according to the riches of his grace" (Ep.1:7).

"How much more shall the blood of Christ, who through the eternal Spirit offered himself without spot to God, purge your conscience from dead works to serve the living God?" (He.9:14).

"Forasmuch as ye know that ye were not redeemed with corruptible things, as silver and gold, from your vain conversation received by tradition from your fathers; But with the precious blood of Christ, as of a lamb without blemish and without spot" (1 Pe.1:18-19).

"But if we walk in the light, as he is in the light, we have fellowship one with another, and the blood of Jesus Christ his Son cleanseth us from all sin" (1 Jn.1:7).

"If we confess our sins, he is faithful and just to forgive us our sins, and to cleanse us from all unrighteousness" (1 Jn.1:9).

"And from Jesus Christ, who is the faithful witness, and the first begotten of the dead, and the prince of the kings of the earth. Unto him that loved us, and washed us from our sins in his own blood" (Re.1:5).

TYPES, SYMBOLS, AND PICTURES
Leviticus 13:1-59

Historical Term	Type or Picture (Scriptural Basis for Each)	Life Application for Today's Believer	Biblical Application
Leprosy or Infectious Skin Disease Le. 13:1-59	*These contagious diseases symbolize the disease of sin, how contagious it is, and the need to prevent the spread of sin.* "And the leper in whom the plague *is*, his clothes shall be rent, and his head bare, and he shall put a covering upon his upper lip, and shall cry, Unclean, unclean. All the days wherein the plague *shall be* in him he shall be defiled; he *is* unclean: he shall dwell alone; without the camp *shall* his habitation *be*" (Le.13:45-46).	God gave Israel the law governing leprosy or infectious skin disease because He loves His people. God loves us and cares for us; therefore He wants us healthy. He wants us experiencing the fullness of life, worshipping and serving Him. He wants us bearing strong testimony to a world lost and reeling under the weight of desperate need. This is the reason He wants all of His people throughout all generations healthy. This was the purpose behind the laws governing leprosy or infectious skin disease.	*"The Spirit of the Lord is upon me, because he hath anointed me to preach the gospel to the poor; he hath sent me to heal the brokenhearted, to preach deliverance to the captives, and recovering of sight to the blind, to set at liberty them that are bruised"* (Lu.4:18). *"When Jesus heard it, he saith unto them, They that are whole have no need of the physician, but they that are sick: I came not to call the righteous, but sinners to repentance"* (Mk.2:17). *"Beloved, I wish above all things that thou mayest prosper and be in health, even as thy soul prospereth"* (3 Jn.1:2). *"And said, If thou wilt diligently hearken to the voice of the LORD thy God, and wilt do that which is right in his sight, and wilt give ear to his commandments, and keep all his statutes, I will put none of these diseases upon thee, which I have brought upon the Egyptians: for I am the LORD that healeth thee"* (Ex.15:26).
Clothing Le. 13:47-59	*Throughout Scripture, clothing is either a symbol of righteousness or unrighteousness.* *1. Clean clothing is a sym-*	A person must make sure, absolutely sure, that he is clothed in the righteousness of Jesus Christ. If not, then the mildew of sin will rot	*"For the wrath of God is revealed from heaven against all ungodliness and unrighteousness of men, who hold the truth in un-*

TYPES, SYMBOLS, AND PICTURES
Leviticus 13:1-59

Historical Term	Type or Picture (Scriptural Basis for Each)	Life Application for Today's Believer	Biblical Application
	bol of righteousness. 2. *Unclean clothing is a symbol of unrighteousness.* "The garment also that the plague of leprosy [infectious mildew] is in, *whether it be* a woollen garment, or a linen garment; Whether *it be* in the warp, or woof; of linen, or of woollen; whether in a skin, or in any thing made of skin; And if the plague be greenish or reddish in the garment, or in the skin, either in the warp, or in the woof, or in any thing of skin; it *is* a plague of leprosy [infectious mildew], and shall be showed unto the priest" (Le.13:47-49).	his clothing. He will stand before God clothed in unrighteousness.	*righteousness"* (Ro.1:18). *"Neither yield ye your members as instruments of unrighteousness unto sin: but yield yourselves unto God, as those that are alive from the dead, and your members as instruments of righteousness unto God"* (Ro.6:13). *"But these [the unrighteous], as natural brute beasts, made to be taken and destroyed, speak evil of the things that they understand not; and shall utterly perish in their own corruption; And shall receive the reward of unrighteousness, as they that count it pleasure to riot in the day time. Spots they are and blemishes, sporting themselves with their own deceivings while they feast with you"* (2 Pe.2:12-13). *"All unrighteousness is sin"* (1 Jn.5:17).
Infectious Mildew or a Plague of Leprosy Le. 13:47-59	*Infectious mildew or a plague of leprosy is a symbol of sin and the rot it causes in the life of a person.* "This *is* the law of the plague of leprosy [infectious mildew] in a garment of woollen or linen, either in the warp, or woof, or any thing of skins, to pronounce it clean, or to pronounce it unclean" (Le. 13:59).	Scripture declares that the infectious mildew or rot of sin must be washed away by the blood of Christ. Only the blood of Christ can cleanse a person from sin and make him acceptable to God.	*"And now why tarriest thou? arise, and be baptized, and wash away thy sins, calling on the name of the Lord"* (Ac.22:16). *"In whom we have redemption through his blood, the forgiveness of sins, according to the riches of his grace"* (Ep.1:7). *"How much more shall the blood of Christ, who through the eternal Spirit offered himself without spot to God, purge your conscience from dead works to serve the living God?"* (He.9:14). *"If we confess our sins, he is faithful and just to forgive us our sins, and to cleanse us from all unrighteousness"* (1 Jn.1:9)

1. The Lawgiver: God Himself

2. The cleansing that took place outside the camp: A symbol of being cleansed from the infectious disease of sin while one is outside, separated from God's people

a. The priest went outside the camp to examine the person wanting to be cleansed & reconciled

b. The person was to be declared clean & reconciled—through the offering of the sacrifice (a symbol of Christ)

1) The animals & materials

2) The symbolic ritual
- One bird was killed over a pot of water, letting the blood drip into the water
- The other items were dipped into the blood & water (the live bird, cedar wood, scarlet yarn, & hyssop)
- The blood was sprinkled over the person to be healed seven times; then he was pronounced clean
- The live bird was released, set free: A symbol that one's disease (sin) was gone, taken away—he was free to live with God & His people

c. The person was to declare himself clean by washing his clothes, shaving & bathing: A symbol of exposing himself, declaring that his whole being was cleansed

d. The result: A trial reconciliation
1) One could enter the camp
2) But one must stay outside one's own tent for seven days

e. The person was again to declare himself clean by the personal ritual (on the 7th day): Showing that his whole being was cleansed

CHAPTER 14

D. Laws That Cleanse & Restore People from Leprosy, from All Forms of Infectious Skin Disease: Symbolizes the Need for Spiritual Cleansing, 14:1-57

And the LORD spake unto Moses, saying,

2 This shall be the law of the leper in the day of his cleansing: He shall be brought unto the priest:

3 And the priest shall go forth out of the camp; and the priest shall look, and, behold, *if* the plague of leprosy be healed in the leper;

4 Then shall the priest command to take for him that is to be cleansed two birds alive *and* clean, and cedar wood, and scarlet, and hyssop:

5 And the priest shall command that one of the birds be killed in an earthen vessel over running water:

6 As for the living bird, he shall take it, and the cedar wood, and the scarlet, and the hyssop, and shall dip them and the living bird in the blood of the bird *that was* killed over the running water:

7 And he shall sprinkle upon him that is to be cleansed from the leprosy seven times, and shall pronounce him clean, and shall let the living bird loose into the open field.

8 And he that is to be cleansed shall wash his clothes, and shave off all his hair, and wash himself in water, that he may be clean: and after that he shall come into the camp, and shall tarry abroad out of his tent seven days.

9 But it shall be on the seventh day, that he shall shave all his hair off his head and his beard and his eyebrows, even all his hair he shall shave off: and he shall wash his clothes, also he shall wash his flesh in water, and he shall be clean.

10 And on the eighth day he shall take two he lambs without blemish, and one ewe lamb of the first year without blemish, and three tenth deals of fine flour *for* a meat offering, mingled with oil, and one log of oil.

11 And the priest that maketh *him* clean shall present the man that is to be made clean, and those things, before the LORD, *at* the door of the tabernacle of the congregation:

12 And the priest shall take one he lamb, and offer him for a trespass offering, and the log of oil, and wave them *for* a wave offering before the LORD:

13 And he shall slay the lamb in the place where he shall kill the Sin offering and the burnt offering, in the holy place: for as the Sin offering *is* the priest's, *so is* the trespass offering: it *is* most holy:

14 And the priest shall take *some* of the blood of the trespass offering, and the priest shall put *it* upon the tip of the right ear of him that is to be cleansed, and upon the thumb of his right hand, and upon the great toe of his right foot:

15 And the priest shall take *some* of the log of oil, and pour *it* into the palm of his own left hand:

16 And the priest shall dip his right finger in the oil that *is* in his left hand, and shall sprinkle of the oil with his finger seven times before the LORD:

17 And of the rest of the oil that *is* in his hand shall the priest put upon the tip of the right ear of him that is to be cleansed, and upon the thumb of his right hand, and upon the great toe of his right foot, upon the blood of the trespass offering:

18 And the remnant of the oil that *is* in the priest's hand he shall pour upon the head of him that is to be cleansed: and the priest shall make an atonement for him before the LORD.

19 And the priest shall offer

3. The cleansing that took place inside the camp: A symbol of being fully reconciled & restored through Christ

a. The person was to approach God
1) Through the sacrifice
2) Through the Grain Offering of thanksgiving & dedication

b. The priest himself presented the cleansed person & his offerings to the LORD (his offering of faith in the sacrifice to cleanse him)

c. The person was cleansed by having the priest (a symbol of Christ, the Mediator) offer the sacrifice of the Guilt Offering along with the olive oil: Symbolized being set free from guilt by Christ & being strengthened & led by God's Spirit
1) Waved them as an offering of thanksgiving (v.12)
2) Put the sacrifice to death (symbolized Christ)

3) Put some of the blood on the cleansed person's right ear, thumb, & toe: Symbolized the cleansing & dedication of one's whole being to God by the blood of the sacrifice (Christ)

4) Poured some of the olive oil into the palm of his left hand (symbolized God's Spirit, God's strength & leadership)
- Sprinkled some oil before the LORD seven times (symbolized the request for God's complete, perfect strength & guidance)

- Put some oil on the right ear, thumb, & big toe of the cleansed person (symbolized the dedication and the strengthening of the *whole person*)

- Poured the remaining oil on the head of the person cleansed (symbolized the *complete, perfect* strength & guidance of God's Spirit)
5) Result: Atonement & reconciliation

d. The person was cleansed

through the sacrifice of the Sin Offering: Made atonement or reconciliation & cleansed him (a symbol of being cleansed through Christ)

e. The person was cleansed through the sacrifice of the Burnt Offering & through the Grain Offering of commitment: Made atonement or reconciliation & cleansed him (a symbol of being cleansed through Christ)

4. The opening of the door for all to be cleansed, even the poorest of the poor: A symbol of God's grace

a. The items required
1) One male lamb, not two, for the Guilt Offering
2) One-tenth (two quarts), not three-tenths, of an ephah of fine flour with olive oil for the Grain Offering
3) Two doves or young pigeons: One for the Sin Offering & the other for the Burnt Offering

b. The poorest person had to do the same as the rich: Have the priest or mediator (a symbol of Christ) present his sacrifice to God (a symbol of Christ)

c. The poorest person was cleansed in the same way as the rich: By having the priest (a symbol of Christ) offer the sacrifice of the Guilt Offering along with the olive oil
1) The items were waved in an offering of thanksgiving
2) The sacrifice was put to death
3) Some blood was put on his right ear, thumb, & big toe (symbolized the cleansing of his whole being)

4) The olive oil was poured into the palm of the priest's left hand
• Sprinkled some oil before the LORD seven times

• Put some oil on the same places he had put the blood: The right ear, thumb, & big toe of the poorest person (who had been healed of leprosy or infectious skin disease—a symbol of sin)

the Sin offering, and make an atonement for him that is to be cleansed from his uncleanness; and afterward he shall kill the burnt offering:

20 And the priest shall offer the burnt offering and the meat offering upon the altar: and the priest shall make an atonement for him, and he shall be clean.

21 And if he *be* poor, and cannot get so much; then he shall take one lamb *for* a trespass offering to be waved, to make an atonement for him, and one tenth deal of fine flour mingled with oil for a meat offering, and a log of oil;

22 And two turtledoves, or two young pigeons, such as he is able to get; and the one shall be a Sin offering, and the other a burnt offering.

23 And he shall bring them on the eighth day for his cleansing unto the priest, unto the door of the tabernacle of the congregation, before the LORD.

24 And the priest shall take the lamb of the trespass offering, and the log of oil, and the priest shall wave them *for* a wave offering before the LORD:

25 And he shall kill the lamb of the trespass offering, and the priest shall take *some* of the blood of the trespass offering, and put *it* upon the tip of the right ear of him that is to be cleansed, and upon the thumb of his right hand, and upon the great toe of his right foot:

26 And the priest shall pour of the oil into the palm of his own left hand:

27 And the priest shall sprinkle with his right finger *some* of the oil that *is* in his left hand seven times before the LORD:

28 And the priest shall put of the oil that *is* in his hand upon the tip of the right ear of him that is to be cleansed, and upon the thumb of his right hand, and upon the great toe of his right foot, upon the place of the blood

of the trespass offering:

29 And the rest of the oil that *is* in the priest's hand he shall put upon the head of him that is to be cleansed, to make an atonement for him before the LORD.

30 And he shall offer the one of the turtledoves, or of the young pigeons, such as he can get;

31 *Even* such as he is able to get, the one *for* a Sin offering, and the other *for* a burnt offering, with the meat offering: and the priest shall make an atonement for him that is to be cleansed before the LORD.

32 This *is* the law *of him* in whom *is* the plague of leprosy, whose hand is not able to get *that which pertaineth* to his cleansing.

33 And the LORD spake unto Moses and unto Aaron, saying,

34 When ye be come into the land of Canaan, which I give to you for a possession, and I put the plague of leprosy in a house of the land of your possession;

35 And he that owneth the house shall come and tell the priest, saying, It seemeth to me *there is* as it were a plague in the house:

36 Then the priest shall command that they empty the house, before the priest go *into it* to see the plague, that all that *is* in the house be not made unclean: and afterward the priest shall go in to see the house:

37 And he shall look on the plague, and, behold, *if* the plague *be* in the walls of the house with hollow strakes, greenish or reddish, which in sight *are* lower than the wall;

38 Then the priest shall go out of the house to the door of the house, and shut up the house seven days:

39 And the priest shall come again the seventh day, and shall look: and, behold, *if* the plague be spread in the walls of the house;

40 Then the priest shall command that they take away the stones in which the

• Poured the rest of the oil on the head of the one cleansed
5) Result: Atonement or reconciliation

d. The poorest person was cleansed through the sacrifice of the other offerings: One dove or pigeon as a Sin Offering, the other as a Burnt Offering, & the Grain Offering (all symbolizing approaching God through Christ)

e. The result: The priest (a symbol of Christ) made atonement, reconciliation for the poorest person as well as the rich

5. The cleansing of mildew in houses (these laws were to apply when they entered the promised land of Canaan): A symbol of sin in houses or within one's environment

a. The head of the house must go & tell the priest about the mildew (a symbol of going to Christ about sin within one's house or environment)
b. The priest was to order the house emptied immediately
1) To keep anything else from being contaminated
2) To inspect the house

c. The mildew that was greenish or reddish & seemed to be deeper than the walls demanded immediate action

1) To close the house for seven days

2) To return & inspect the house on the seventh day
d. Case 1: The mildew had spread (a symbol of sin spreading)

1) To remove the contaminated stone: Take to an unclean place outside the

town (a place people would not go lest they be contaminated) 2) To scrape all the inside walls: Dump the scraped material in an unclean place outside the town 3) To replace the contaminated materials with new stones, new clay, & new plaster e. Case 2: A relapse—the mildew reappeared in the house 1) To be reexamined by the priest & declared to be a destructive mildew, an unclean house 2) To condemn the house: Have it torn down & all materials taken out of town to an unclean place 3) To keep people out: Anyone who entered, slept, or ate in the house was to be counted unclean till evening 4) The treatment: The contaminated person was to be washed f. Case 3: The mildew does not reappear after being replastered	plague *is*, and they shall cast them into an unclean place without the city: 41 And he shall cause the house to be scraped within round about, and they shall pour out the dust that they scrape off without the city into an unclean place: 42 And they shall take other stones, and put *them* in the place of those stones; and he shall take other morter, and shall plaister the house. 43 And if the plague come again, and break out in the house, after that he hath taken away the stones, and after he hath scraped the house, and after it is plaistered; 44 Then the priest shall come and look, and, behold, *if* the plague be spread in the house, it *is* a fretting leprosy in the house: it *is* unclean. 45 And he shall break down the house, the stones of it, and the timber thereof, and all the morter of the house; and he shall carry *them* forth out of the city into an unclean place. 46 Moreover he that goeth into the house all the while that it is shut up shall be unclean until the even. 47 And he that lieth in the house shall wash his clothes; and he that eateth in the house shall wash his clothes. 48 And if the priest shall come in, and look *upon it*,	and, behold, the plague hath not spread in the house, after the house was plaistered: then the priest shall pronounce the house clean, because the plague is healed. 49 And he shall take to cleanse the house two birds, and cedar wood, and scarlet, and hyssop: 50 And he shall kill the one of the birds in an earthen vessel over running water: 51 And he shall take the cedar wood, and the hyssop, and the scarlet, and the living bird, and dip them in the blood of the slain bird, and in the running water, and sprinkle the house seven times: 52 And he shall cleanse the house with the blood of the bird, and with the running water, and with the living bird, and with the cedar wood, and with the hyssop, and with the scarlet: 53 But he shall let go the living bird out of the city into the open fields, and make an atonement for the house: and it shall be clean. 54 This *is* the law for all manner of plague of leprosy, and scall, 55 And for the leprosy of a garment, and of a house, 56 And for a rising, and for a scab, and for a bright spot: 57 To teach when *it is* unclean, and when *it is* clean: this *is* the law of leprosy.	1) To pronounce the house clean 2) To purify the house: Through the offering of the sacrifice (see above vv.4-7) • To kill one bird over fresh water in a clay pot, mixing the blood in the water • To dip the other items into the blood & water (the cedar wood, the hyssop, the scarlet yarn, & the live bird) • To sprinkle the house seven times • To purify the house through the blood of the sacrifice • To set the live bird free, v.53 g. The purpose for cleaning houses through the sacrifice (a symbol of cleansing sin through Christ) 1) To make atonement for one's house (environment) 2) To protect cleanliness **6. The purpose for the laws governing leprosy or infectious skin disease & mildew** a. The places where disease & mildew are found: Symbolizes sin within self & within one's environment b. The purpose stated: To teach God's people to discern, distinguish between clean & unclean

DIVISION III

THE WAY TO LIVE A HOLY LIFE BEFORE GOD (PART I): BY A CLEAN BODY (SEPARATION), 11:1–16:34

D. Laws That Cleanse and Restore People from Leprosy, from All Forms of Infectious Skin Disease: Symbolizes the Need for Spiritual Cleansing, 14:1-57

(14:1-57) **Introduction**: public health is of vital concern to every community and nation, to all people everywhere. The spread of infectious disease is a constant threat. The threat is so real that thousands and in some cases millions of people have become infected with such diseases as aids, herpes, gonorrhea, syphilis, polio, hepatitis, measles, influenza, and other diseases.

The spread of disease is of vital concern to God. This is clearly seen in this chapter, just as it was in the former chapter. God had just given His people the laws that were to protect them from the spread of infectious disease (leprosy, KJV). Now, He is ready to give them the laws of cleansing and restoration. How can a person tell if he has been cured of a disease? But just as important, if he has been cured of an infectious disease that is feared, how can he go about assuring the public that he is cured? How can he be restored and reaccepted back into the community?

In studying this passage, keep in mind that God is concerned not only with man's physical health, but also with man's spiritual health. Therefore, when God speaks of leprosy or infectious disease, He applies it to the infectious disease of sin. Leprosy as an infectious disease is a symbol of sin. Sin is just as infectious, just as contagious a disease as leprosy, and it can spread just as rapidly.

Note this important fact: the laws of God dealing with disease have nothing to do with healing the disease. God is not giving the cure for the infectious disease. He is dealing with cleansing that followed the cure. He is telling a person how to be *publicly cleansed*, how to relieve the fears of the public, how to be reaccepted back into the community. The expositor Gordon J. Wenham says this:

> The procedures described in this chapter are not curative but ritual. The priests did not do anything to cure the sick person. Their duty was to diagnose when a man was unclean and when he was clean again, and to make sure that the correct rituals were carried out when the disease cleared up and the man was readmitted to the community. To use a modern analogy, the priest in ancient Israel was more like a public health inspector than a physician. He determined whether a person was infected; he did not attempt to cure him. In this respect Israel differed from her neighbors, who went in for exorcism and magical rites in attempts to cure disease. In Israel a man had to seek help directly from God in prayer, not rely on the dubious remedies of folk medicine.[1]

J. Vernon McGee also has an excellent comment on both this fact and the symbolism of infectious disease as sin:

> This chapter casts a ray of light and hope into the darkness of the leper's [diseased person's] plight. We note that no physician's prescription is given for the treatment and cure of leprosy. Rather, it shows the ceremonial cleansing which follows the cure. This alludes to the redemption of the sinner. The ritual is entirely symbolic, yet there is a therapeutic value in the washing and cleansing.
> When man sinned in the Garden of Eden, sin separated God and man. This barrier of sin moved in a twofold direction in that it affected both God and man. It moved upward toward God and made man guilty before a holy God. It moved downward toward man, and man became polluted and contaminated with sin. Leprosy [infectious disease] is a picture of sin in its pollution and contamination.[2]

This is the subject of this significant passage: *Laws That Cleanse and Restore People from Leprosy, from All Forms of Infectious Skin Disease: Symbolizes the Need for Spiritual Cleansing*, 14:1-57.

1. The Lawgiver: God Himself (v.1).
2. The cleansing that took place outside the camp: A symbol of being cleansed from the infectious disease of sin while one is outside, separated from God's people, (vv.2-9).
3. The cleansing that took place inside the camp: a symbol of being fully reconciled and restored through Christ (vv.10-20).
4. The opening of the door for all to be cleansed, even the poorest of the poor: A symbol of God's grace (vv.21-32).
5. The cleansing of mildew in houses (these laws were to apply when they entered the promised land of Canaan): A symbol of sin in houses or within one's environment (vv.33-53).
6. The purpose for the laws governing leprosy or infectious skin disease and mildew (vv.54-57).

1 (14:1) **Law, Source**: the source of the law was God Himself. Note a significant fact: the very first detailed code of laws governing health was not developed by man; it was given to man by God. God was the Lawgiver not man. God loves and cares for His people, so He naturally cares about their health. He wants His people to be healthy so they can enjoy the fullness of life, can be productive and fruitful in life. Stated simply, God wants His people strong so they can live lives that are strong in work, play, and worship. God wants His people conquering throughout all of life, being victorious over all the trials and temptations of life. He wants them physically and mentally strong so they can bear strong testimony to His glorious goodness and saving grace.

OUTLINE	SCRIPTURE
1. The Lawgiver: God Himself	And the LORD spake unto Moses, saying,

2 (14:2-9) **Cleansing, Ceremonial—Cleansing, Spiritual—Infectious Disease, Ceremonial Cleansing of—Infectious Disease, Symbol of—Symbol, of Infectious Skin Disease—Clean - Cleanness, Symbol of—Separation, Cause of—Alienation, Cause of—Reconciliation, Source of—Restoration, Source of**: there was the cleansing that took place outside the camp. This was a symbol of being cleansed from the infectious disease of sin while one is outside or separated from God's people. Infectious skin disease was a symbol of sin. Remember, the infected people were put outside the camp, quarantined and isolated from the community of God's people. This, of course, included being banned from public worship. A person who was quarantined was not allowed to attend worship services nor any other religious functions, including the sacrificial offerings through which he maintained his relationship with God. He was totally excluded from the community of God's people. This had to be, for the people feared the spread of the disease. But what happened when the person was healed? How could he be reinstated, restored, reconciled with God's people? Note the Scripture and outline:

OUTLINE	SCRIPTURE	SCRIPTURE	OUTLINE
2. The cleansing that took place outside the camp: A symbol of being cleansed from the infectious disease of sin while one is outside or separated from God's people	2 This shall be the law of the leper in the day of his cleansing: He shall be brought unto the priest: 3 And the priest shall go the priest shall look, and, be-	hold, *if* the plague of leprosy be healed in the leper; 4 Then shall the priest command to take for him that is to be cleansed two	a. The priest went outside the camp to examine the person wanting to be cleansed & reconciled b. The person was to be declared clean & reconciled—through the offering of the sacrifice

---

1 Gordon J. Wenham. *The Book of Leviticus*, p.207.
2 J. Vernon McGee. *Thru The Bible*, Vol.1, p.386.

OUTLINE	SCRIPTURE	SCRIPTURE	OUTLINE
(a symbol of Christ) 1) The animals & materials 2) The symbolic ritual • One bird was killed over a pot of water, letting the blood drip into the water • The other items were dipped into the blood & water (the live bird, cedar wood, scarlet yarn, & hyssop) • The blood was sprinkled over the person to be healed seven times; then he was pronounced clean • The live bird was released, set free: A symbol that one's disease (sin) was gone, taken away—he was free to live	birds alive *and* clean, and cedar wood, and scarlet, and hyssop: 5 And the priest shall command that one of the birds be killed in an earthen vessel over running water: 6 As for the living bird, he shall take it, and the cedar wood, and the scarlet, and the hyssop, and shall dip them and the living bird in the blood of the bird *that was* killed over the running water: 7 And he shall sprinkle upon him that is to be cleansed from the leprosy seven times, and shall pronounce him clean, and shall let the living bird	loose into the open field. 8 And he that is to be cleansed shall wash his clothes, and shave off all his hair, and wash himself in water, that he may be clean: and after that he shall come into the camp, and shall tarry abroad out of his tent seven days. 9 But it shall be on the seventh day, that he shall shave all his hair off his head and his beard and his eyebrows, even all his hair he shall shave off: and he shall wash his clothes, also he shall wash his flesh in water, and he shall be clean.	with God & His people c. The person was to declare himself clean by washing his clothes, shaving, & bathing: A symbol of exposing himself, declaring that his whole being was cleansed d. The result: A trial reconciliation 1) One could enter the camp 2) But one must stay outside one's own tent for seven days e. The person was again to declare himself clean by the personal ritual (on the 7th day): Showing that his whole being was cleansed

Thought 1. This ritual that took place outside the camp paints four descriptive lessons for the believer.

(1) The priest's going outside the camp to cleanse the diseased person is a picture of Jesus Christ (v.3). Jesus Christ left the camp of heaven to come to this sin-diseased world. He came forth from heaven's glory and freedom to cleanse all who are infected with the disease of sin. Cleansing us from our sins took place outside of heaven. He had to go outside the community of heaven with all its glory and come to where we are in order to cleanse us. This is stressed time and again throughout Scripture.

"But we see Jesus, who was made a little lower than the angels for the suffering of death, crowned with glory and honour; that he by the grace of God should taste death for every man. For it became him, for whom are all things, and by whom are all things, in bringing many sons unto glory, to make the captain of their salvation perfect through sufferings" (He.2:9-10).

"For verily he took not on him the nature of angels; but he took on him the seed of Abraham. Wherefore in all things it behooved him to be made like unto his brethren, that he might be a merciful and faithful high priest in things pertaining to God, to make reconciliation for the sins of the people" (He.2:16-17).

"But when the fulness of the time was come, God sent forth his Son, made of a woman, made under the law, To redeem them that were under the law, that we might receive the adoption of sons." (Ga.4:4-5).

(2) The person being cleansed through the sacrifice of the shed blood is a picture of the sacrifice of Jesus Christ (vv.4-7). Note that the blood of the sacrificed bird was sprinkled over a person seven times; then he was pronounced clean. The number seven symbolizes completeness, fullness. The person was completely, fully cleansed by the blood of the sacrifice. This is a picture of the believer being fully and completely cleansed through the blood of the Lord Jesus Christ. Note that the live bird was dipped into the blood and then released and set free. This was a symbol that the person's disease was gone, taken away. He was free to live with God and His people. This, of course, is a picture of the believer's sin being taken away: the believer is free of sin, free to live with God and the people of God.

"Much more then, being now justified by his blood, we shall be saved from wrath through him" (Ro.5:9).

"There is therefore now no condemnation to them which are in Christ Jesus, who walk not after the flesh, but after the Spirit. For the law of the Spirit of life in Christ Jesus hath made me free from the law of sin and death" (Ro.8:1-2).

"Who gave himself for our sins, that he might deliver us from this present evil world, according to the will of God and our Father" (Ga.1:4).

"Wherefore he is able also to save them to the uttermost that come unto God by him, seeing he ever liveth to make intercession for them. For such an high priest became us, *who is* holy, harmless, undefiled, separate from sinners, and made higher than the heavens; Who needeth not daily, as those high priests, to offer up sacrifice, first for his own sins, and then for the people's: for this he did once, when he offered up himself" (He.7:25-27).

"So Christ was once offered to bear the sins of many; and unto them that look for him shall he appear the second time without sin unto salvation" (He.9:28).

"Who his own self bare our sins in his own body on the tree, that we, being dead to sins, should live unto righteousness: by whose stripes ye were healed" (1 Pe.2:24).

(3) The person was declared clean by washing his clothes, shaving his body, and bathing (v.8). This, of course, exposed his whole body, revealing that he was completely cleansed of the contagious disease. This is a picture of the believer's being completely washed and cleansed of his sin.

"**And now why tarriest thou? arise, and be baptized, and wash away thy sins, calling on the name of the Lord**" (Ac.22:16).
"**And such were some of you: but ye are washed, but ye are sanctified, but ye are justified in the name of the Lord Jesus, and by the Spirit of our God**" (1 Co.6:11).
"**Husbands, love your wives, even as Christ also loved the church, and gave himself for it; That he might sanctify and cleanse it with the washing of water by the word**" (Ep.5:25-26).
"**How much more shall the blood of Christ, who through the eternal Spirit offered himself without spot to God, purge your conscience from dead works to serve the living God?**" (He.9:14).
"**But if we walk in the light, as he is in the light, we have fellowship one with another, and the blood of Jesus Christ his Son cleanseth us from all sin**" (1 Jn.1:7).

(4) Note that the person claiming to be cleansed had to undergo a trial period of reconciliation before he could be fully reinstated and restored to his family (v.8). He could enter the camp, but he had to stay outside his own tent, away from his family for seven days. This was to give full assurance to his family that he had been completely cleansed and could no longer infect them. How desperately needed this is within the church: to have a period of examination for those who claim to be cleansed. Often, a person is brought back too quickly into the fellowship of believers where his worldly and sinful behavior infects weaker believers. Far better to have a period of examination to make absolutely sure that a person's infectious disease of sin has been fully cleansed.

"**Examine yourselves, whether ye be in the faith; prove your own selves. Know ye not your own selves, how that Jesus Christ is in you, except ye be reprobates?**" (2 Co.13:5).
"**But let every man prove his own work, and then shall he have rejoicing in himself alone, and not in another**" (Ga.6:4).
"**Not a novice, lest being lifted up with pride he fall into the condemnation of the devil. Moreover he must have a good report of them which are without; lest he fall into reproach and the snare of the devil**" (1 Ti.3:6-7).
"**And let these also first be proved**" (1 Ti.3:10).
"**Let us search and try our ways, and turn again to the LORD**" (Lam.3:40).

3 (14:10-20) **Cleansing—Cleanness, Ritual of—Reconciliation, Source of—Reconciliation, Ritual of—Restoration, Source of—Restoration, Ritual of—Animal Sacrifice, Ritual of—Sacrifice of Animals, Ritual of—Sacrifice of Animals, Symbol of—Symbol, of Sacrificial Animals**: there was the cleansing that took place inside the camp. This was the symbol of being fully reconciled and restored through Jesus Christ. Note that this is the eighth day. Imagine how excited the healed man was. On this day, he could rejoin his family; they could be reunited and begin their life together again. But first there was another matter that had to be handled, a far more important matter. The healed person needed to make sure that he was fully reconciled to God, that he had no hidden sin in his life, that he was not suffering under the anguish of guilt. Moreover, he needed an infusion of God's strength and the assurance of God's guidance in the event some people continued to shun and fear him due to the infectious disease that had afflicted his body. All this was to be taken care of through the ritual that then took place.

OUTLINE	SCRIPTURE	SCRIPTURE	OUTLINE
3. The cleansing that took place inside the camp: A symbol of being fully reconciled & restored through Christ a. The person was to approach God 1) Through the sacrifice 2) Through the Grain Offering of thanksgiving and dedication b. The priest himself presented the cleansed person & his offerings to the LORD (his offering of faith in the sacrifice to cleanse him) c. The person was cleansed by having the priest or mediator (a symbol of Christ) offer the sacrifice of the Guilt Offering along with the olive oil: Symbolized being set free from	10 And on the eighth day he shall take two he lambs without blemish, and one ewe lamb of the first year without blemish, and three tenth deals of fine flour *for* a meat offering, mingled with oil, and one log of oil. 11 And the priest that maketh *him* clean shall present the man that is to be made clean, and those things, before the LORD, *at* the door of the tabernacle of the congregation: 12 And the priest shall take one he lamb, and offer him for a trespass offering, and the log of oil, and wave them *for* a wave offering before the LORD:	13 And he shall slay the lamb in the place where he shall kill the sin offering and the burnt offering, in the holy place: for as the sin offering *is* the priest's, *so is* the trespass offering: it *is* most holy: 14 And the priest shall take *some* of the blood of the trespass offering, and the priest shall put *it* upon the tip of the right ear of him that is to be cleansed, and upon the thumb of his right hand, and upon the great toe of his right foot: 15 And the priest shall take *some* of the log of oil, and pour *it* into the palm of his own left hand:	guilt by Christ & being strengthened & led by God's Spirit 1) Waved them as an offering of thanksgiving (v.12) 2) Put the sacrifice to death (symbolized Christ) 3) Put some of the blood on the cleansed person's right ear, thumb, & toe: Symbolized the cleansing & dedication of one's whole being to God by the blood of the sacrifice (Christ) 4) Poured some of the olive oil into the palm of his left hand (symbolized God's Spirit, God's strength & leadership)

OUTLINE	SCRIPTURE	SCRIPTURE	OUTLINE
• Sprinkled some oil before the LORD seven times (symbolized the request for God's complete, perfect strength & guidance) • Put some oil on the right ear, thumb, & big toe of the cleansed person (symbolized the dedication and the strengthening of the *whole person*) • Poured the remaining oil on the head of *the* person	16 And the priest shall dip his right finger in the oil that *is* in his left hand, and shall sprinkle of the oil with his finger seven times before the LORD: 17 And of the rest of the oil that *is* in his hand shall the priest put upon the tip of the right ear of him that is to be cleansed, and upon the thumb of his right hand, and upon the great toe of his right foot, upon the blood of the trespass offering: 18 And the *remnant* of the oil that *is* in the priest's	hand he shall pour upon the head of him that is to be cleansed: and the priest shall make an atonement for him before the LORD. 19 And the priest shall offer the sin offering, and make an atonement for him that is to be cleansed from his uncleanness; and afterward he shall kill the burnt offering: 20 And the priest shall offer the burnt offering and the meat offering upon the altar: and the priest shall make an atonement for him, and he shall be clean.	cleansed (symbolized the *complete, perfect* strength & guidance of God's Spirit) 5) Result: Atonement & reconciliation d. The person was cleansed through the sacrifice of the Sin Offering: Made atonement or reconciliation & cleansed him (a symbol of being cleansed through Christ) e. The person was cleansed through the sacrifice of the Burnt Offering & through the Grain Offering of commitment: Made atonement or reconciliation & cleansed him (a symbol of being cleansed through Christ)

Thought 1. Note that a person was fully cleansed through the substitute sacrifice. The sacrifice died in his place, in his stead, on his behalf. Remember, the person had not had the privilege of approaching God through the sacrifice since his affliction with the infectious disease. Note the three sacrifices he offered and how each one met a very special need in his life (vv.10-20).

(1) The person approached God through the sacrifice of the Guilt Offering (vv.12-18). Whatever guilt a person felt, whatever anguish weighed upon his heart—it was removed through the sacrifice of the Guilt Offering. This sacrifice is a symbol of the Lord Jesus Christ. When we approach God through Christ, He removes the anguish of guilt that afflicts our souls, that bothers and weighs ever so heavily upon our hearts. No matter how much sin has infected our bodies and no matter how condemned we feel, if we come to God through Jesus Christ, God cleanses us from the guilt of sin. And he takes away the condemnation.

> "For this is my blood of the new testament, which is shed for many for the remission of sins" (Mt.26:28).
> "Verily, verily, I say unto you, He that heareth my word, and believeth on him that sent me, hath everlasting life, and shall not come into condemnation; but is passed from death unto life" (Jn.5:24).
> "*There is* therefore now no condemnation to them which are in Christ Jesus, who walk not after the flesh, but after the Spirit. For the law of the Spirit of life in Christ Jesus hath made me free from the law of sin and death. For what the law could not do, in that it was weak through the flesh, God sending his own Son in the likeness of sinful flesh, and for sin, condemned sin in the flesh" (Ro.8:1-3).
> "Who *is* he that condemneth? *It is* Christ that died, yea rather, that is risen again, who is even at the right hand of God, who also maketh intercession for us" (Ro.8:34).
> "For if the blood of bulls and of goats, and the ashes of an heifer sprinkling the unclean, sanctifieth to the purifying of the flesh: How much more shall the blood of Christ, who through the eternal Spirit offered himself without spot to God, purge your conscience from dead works to serve the living God?" (He.9:13-14).

(2) The person approached God through the sacrifice of the Sin Offering (v.19). This symbolizes the forgiveness of sin through the Lord Jesus Christ. When we approach God through Jesus Christ, God forgives and cleanses us from sin.

> "In whom we have redemption through his blood, the forgiveness of sins, according to the riches of his grace" (Ep.1:7).
> "Who his own self bare our sins in his own body on the tree, that we, being dead to sins, should live unto righteousness: by whose stripes ye were healed" (1 Pe.2:24).
> "For Christ also hath once suffered for sins, the just for the unjust, that he might bring us to God, being put to death in the flesh, but quickened by the Spirit" (1 Pe.3:18).
> "But if we walk in the light, as he is in the light, we have fellowship one with another, and the blood of Jesus Christ his Son cleanseth us from all sin" (1 Jn.1:7).
> "If we confess our sins, he is faithful and just to forgive us *our* sins, and to cleanse us from all unrighteousness" (1 Jn.1:9).
> "But he *was* wounded for our transgressions, *he was* bruised for our iniquities: the chastisement of our peace *was* upon him; and with his stripes we are healed" (Is.53:5).

(3) The person approached God through the Burnt Offering and the Grain Offering of thanksgiving and commitment (vv.19-20). The Burnt Offering made atonement for the person, reconciling him to God, and the Grain Offering was an offering of thanksgiving and dedication to God for His wonderful goodness. The sacrifice of the Burnt

Offering was a symbol of the Lord Jesus Christ. When we approach God through Jesus Christ, God makes atonement for us, reconciles us to Himself. And because He reconciles us to God, we are filled with joy, committing our lives—all we are and have—to Him.

> "For if, when we were enemies, we were reconciled to God by the death of his Son, much more, being reconciled, we shall be saved by his life. And not only *so*, but we also joy in God through our Lord Jesus Christ, by whom we have now received the atonement" (Ro.5:10-11).
>
> "And all things *are* of God, who hath reconciled us to himself by Jesus Christ, and hath given to us the ministry of reconciliation....For he hath made him *to be* sin for us, who knew no sin; that we might be made the righteousness of God in him" (2 Co.5:18, 21).
>
> "And that he might reconcile both unto God in one body by the cross, having slain the enmity thereby" (Ep.2:16).
>
> "And, having made peace through the blood of his cross, by him to reconcile all things unto himself; by him, *I say*, whether *they be* things in earth, or things in heaven" (Col.1:20).
>
> "Wherefore in all things it behooved him to be made like unto *his* brethren, that he might be a merciful and faithful high priest in things *pertaining* to God, to make reconciliation for the sins of the people" (He.2:17).
>
> "Whom having not seen, ye love; in whom, though now ye see *him* not, yet believing, ye rejoice with joy unspeakable and full of glory: Receiving the end of your faith, *even* the salvation of *your* souls" (1 Pe.1:8-9).
>
> "I will greatly rejoice in the LORD, my soul shall be joyful in my God; for he hath clothed me with the garments of salvation, he hath covered me with the robe of righteousness, as a bridegroom decketh *himself* with ornaments, and as a bride adorneth *herself* with her jewels" (Is.61:10).

Thought 2. Note this fact about the Guilt Offering: some blood was placed on the cleansed person's right ear, thumb, and toe. This symbolized that the person's whole being was cleansed and dedicated to God through the blood of the sacrifice. He was dedicating his ear to listen to the voice of God and to allow God to guide him day by day. He was dedicating his thumb or hand to serve God as he labored day by day. He was dedicating his toe or feet to walk where God wanted him to walk, following God day by day. What a lesson for us! When we come to God through the sacrifice of the Lord Jesus Christ, we are to dedicate our whole beings to God.

(1) We are to dedicate our ears to God, listening only to the voice of God and to the things of righteousness. We are not to listen to the voices of this world, not to the foul language, immoral talk, off-colored jokes, false teachings, and worldly philosophies. We are to listen only to those things that will build up and benefit ourselves and society.

> "And every one that heareth these sayings of mine, and doeth them not, shall be likened unto a foolish man, which built his house upon the sand" (Mt.7:26).
>
> "But blessed *are* your eyes, for they see: and your ears, for they hear" (Mt.13:16).
>
> "The heart of the prudent getteth knowledge; and the ear of the wise seeketh knowledge" (Pr.18:15).
>
> "The hearing ear, and the seeing eye, the LORD hath made even both of them" (Pr.20:12).
>
> "To whom shall I speak, and give warning, that they may hear? behold, their ear *is* uncircumcised, and they cannot hearken: behold, the word of the LORD is unto them a reproach; they have no delight in it" (Je.6:10).
>
> "Son of man, thou dwellest in the midst of a rebellious house, which have eyes to see, and see not; they have ears to hear, and hear not: for they *are* a rebellious house" (Eze.12:2).

(2) We are to dedicate our thumbs and hands to serve God in our work, play, and activities throughout the day. We are only to touch and handle the things of righteousness. We are not to touch the things of unrighteousness.

> "Labour not for the meat which perisheth, but for that meat which endureth unto everlasting life, which the Son of man shall give unto you: for him hath God the Father sealed" (Jn.6:27).
>
> "Wherefore come out from among them, and be ye separate, saith the Lord, and touch not the unclean *thing;* and I will receive you, And will be a Father unto you, and ye shall be my sons and daughters, saith the Lord Almighty" (2 Co.6:17-18).
>
> "Let him that stole steal no more: but rather let him labour, working with *his* hands the thing which is good, that he may have to give to him that needeth" (Ep.4:28).
>
> "And whatsoever ye do in word or deed, *do* all in the name of the Lord Jesus, giving thanks to God and the Father by him" (Col.3:17).
>
> "And whatsoever ye do, do *it* heartily, as to the Lord, and not unto men; Knowing that of the Lord ye shall receive the reward of the inheritance: for ye serve the Lord Christ" (Col.3:23-24).
>
> "Then I looked on all the works that my hands had wrought, and on the labour that I had laboured to do: and, behold, all *was* vanity and vexation of spirit, and *there was* no profit under the sun" (Ec.2:11).
>
> "Whatsoever thy hand findeth to do, do *it* with thy might; for *there is* no work, nor device, nor knowledge, nor wisdom, in the grave, whither thou goest" (Ec.9:10).
>
> "Wherefore do ye spend money for *that which is* not bread? and your labour for *that which* satisfieth not? hearken diligently unto me, and eat ye *that which is* good, and let your soul delight itself in fatness" (Is.55:2).

(3) We are to dedicate our toes or feet to God. We are to go only where He would want us to go. We are not to walk into the bright lights and places of sinful behavior. We are to walk only into the places that will build up and benefit us and society.

> "*This* I say then, Walk in the Spirit, and ye shall not fulfil the lust of the flesh....Now the works of the flesh are manifest, which are *these;* Adultery, fornication, uncleanness, lasciviousness, Idolatry, witchcraft, hatred, variance, emulations, wrath, strife, seditions, heresies, Envyings, murders, drunkenness, revellings, and such like: of the which I tell you before, as I have also told *you* in time past, that they which do such things shall not inherit the kingdom of God" (Ga.5:16, 19-21).
>
> "I therefore, the prisoner of the Lord, beseech you that ye walk worthy of the vocation wherewith ye are called" (Ep.4:1).
>
> "And walk in love, as Christ also hath loved us, and hath given himself for us an offering and a sacrifice to God for a sweetsmelling savour" (Ep.5:2).
>
> "See then that ye walk circumspectly, not as fools, but as wise" (Ep.5:15).
>
> "But if we walk in the light, as he is in the light, we have fellowship one with another, and the blood of Jesus Christ his Son cleanseth us from all sin" (1 Jn.1:7).
>
> "He that saith he abideth in him ought himself also so to walk, even as he walked" (1 Jn.2:6).

Thought 3. Note that some oil was sprinkled before the LORD seven times; then some oil was put on the right ear, thumb, and toe of the cleansed person; then the remaining oil was poured on the head of the cleansed person (vv.16-18). Throughout the Scripture oil is a symbol of the Holy Spirit, of God's strength and guidance. The oil that was sprinkled before the LORD seven times was symbolizing the request for God's complete, perfect strength and guidance. The oil that was then placed upon the cleansed person was symbolizing that the person was being infused with the Spirit of God. He was being given the complete, perfect strength and guidance of God's Spirit as he walked day by day. He needed a special infusion of God's Spirit and strength just in case some people still rejected him because of his infectious disease. They possibly would not believe that he was fully cleansed. Only God's strength could overcome the sense of rejection and isolation that the diseased person might sense. As stated, the oil was a symbol of God's Spirit, of His strength and guidance. When a person has been infected with the disease of sin—especially for a long time—he often needs a special infusion of God's Spirit. He needs the strength and guidance of God's Spirit to combat whatever rejection and ridicule might be thrown against him by his former worldly friends. He needs God's strength and guidance to combat the onslaught of trials and temptation that will confront him day by day.

> "Who shall separate us from the love of Christ? *shall* tribulation, or distress, or persecution, or famine, or nakedness, or peril, or sword?...Nay, in all these things we are more than conquerors through him that loved us. For I am persuaded, that neither death, nor life, nor angels, nor principalities, nor powers, nor things present, nor things to come, Nor height, nor depth, nor any other creature, shall be able to separate us from the love of God, which is in Christ Jesus our Lord" (Ro.8:35, 37-39).
>
> "There hath no temptation taken you but such as is common to man: but God *is* faithful, who will not suffer you to be tempted above that ye are able; but will with the temptation also make a way to escape, that ye may be able to bear *it*" (1 Co.10:13).
>
> "And he said unto me, My grace is sufficient for thee: for my strength is made perfect in weakness. Most gladly therefore will I rather glory in my infirmities, that the power of Christ may rest upon me" (2 Co.12:9).
>
> "That he would grant you, according to the riches of his glory, to be strengthened with might by his Spirit in the inner man" (Ep.3:16).
>
> "Now unto him that is able to do exceeding abundantly above all that we ask or think, according to the power that worketh in us" (Ep.3:20).
>
> "For whatsoever is born of God overcometh the world: and this is the victory that overcometh the world, *even* our faith. Who is he that overcometh the world, but he that believeth that Jesus is the Son of God?" (1 Jn.5:4-5).
>
> "But they that wait upon the LORD shall renew *their* strength; they shall mount up with wings as eagles; they shall run, and not be weary; *and* they shall walk, and not faint" (Is.40.31).
>
> "Fear thou not; for I *am* with thee: be not dismayed; for I *am* thy God: I will strengthen thee; yea, I will help thee; yea, I will uphold thee with the right hand of my righteousness" (Is.41:10).
>
> "Fear not: for I have redeemed thee, I have called *thee* by thy name; thou *art* mine. When thou passest through the waters, I *will be* with thee; and through the rivers, they shall not overflow thee: when thou walkest through the fire, thou shalt not be burned; neither shall the flame kindle upon thee" (Is.43:1-2).

4 (14:21-32) **Poor, the—Cleansing, Ritual of—Ritual, of Cleansing—Animal Sacrifice—Sacrifice, Animal— Offering, Burnt—Offering, Sin—Offering, Guilt—Doves—Young Pigeons—Atonement:** there was the opening of the door for all to be cleansed, even the poorest of the poor. This is a symbol of God's grace. The poor are as welcomed by God as the rich, and the poor can be cleansed by God just as easily as the rich. But note, a person's poverty did not excuse him from approaching God through the sacrifice. God requires that the poor approach Him just like everyone else—through the substitute sacrifice. The only thing required by God is a willing mind and an honest heart. If a person was willing and ready to be honest and sincere in his approach to God, that was all God required. The person was allowed to substitute two doves or two young pigeons for the two male lambs. Even if a poor person did not have enough money to purchase the doves or pigeons, he could easily catch the birds, for they were plentiful throughout the land. However, the poor did have to provide one male lamb for the sacrifice of the Guilt Offering (v.21). If he was so poor that he could not purchase one male lamb, a friend or a religious benefactor or the priests themselves would have provided the lamb. The point is God's grace, His love for the poor, even the poorest of the poor. He made provision for the poor to approach Him through the substitute sacrifice. Note the Scripture and outline.

OUTLINE	SCRIPTURE	SCRIPTURE	OUTLINE

4. The opening of the door for all to be cleansed, even the poorest of the poor: A symbol of God's grace
a. The items required
  1) One male lamb, not two, for the Guilt Offering
  2) One-tenth (two quarts), not three-tenths, of an ephah of fine flour with olive oil for the Grain Offering
  3) Two doves or young pigeons: One for the Sin Offering & the other for the Burnt Offering
b. The poorest person had to do the same as the rich: Have the priest or mediator (a symbol of Christ) present his sacrifice to God (a symbol of Christ)
c. The poorest person was cleansed in the same way as the rich: By having the priest (a symbol of Christ) offer the sacrifice of the Guilt Offering along with the olive oil
  1) The items were waved in an offering of thanksgiving
  2) The sacrifice was put to death
  3) Some blood was put on his right ear, thumb, & big toe (symbolized the cleansing of his whole being)
  4) The olive oil was poured into the palm of the priest's
	21 And if he *be* poor, and cannot get so much; then he shall take one lamb *for* a trespass offering to be waved, to make an atonement for him, and one tenth deal of fine flour mingled with oil for a meat offering, and a log of oil;
	22 And two turtledoves, or two young pigeons, such as he is able to get; and the one shall be a sin offering, and the other a burnt offering.
	23 And he shall bring them on the eighth day for his cleansing unto the priest, unto the door of the tabernacle of the congregation, before the LORD.
	24 And the priest shall take the lamb of the trespass offering, and the log of oil, and the priest shall wave them *for* a wave offering before the LORD:
	25 And he shall kill the lamb of the trespass offering, and the priest shall take *some* of the blood of the trespass offering, and put *it* upon the tip of the right ear of him that is to be cleansed, and upon the thumb of his right hand, and upon the great toe of his right foot:
	26 And the priest shall pour of the oil into the palm of his
		own left hand:
		27 And the priest shall sprinkle with his right finger *some* of the oil that *is* in his left hand seven times before the LORD:
		28 And the priest shall put of the oil that *is* in his hand upon the tip of the right ear of him that is to be cleansed, and upon the thumb of his right hand, and upon the great toe of his right foot, upon the place of the blood of the trespass offering
		29 And the rest of the oil that *is* in the priest's hand he shall put upon the head of him that is to be cleansed, to make an atonement for him before the LORD.
		30 And he shall offer the one of the turtledoves, or of the young pigeons, such as he can get;
		31 *Even* such as he is able to get, the one *for* a sin offering, and the other *for* a burnt offering, with the meat offering: and the priest shall make an atonement for him that is to be cleansed before the LORD.
		32 This *is* the law *of him* in whom *is* the plague of leprosy, whose hand is not able to get *that which pertaineth* to his cleansing.
			left hand
			• Sprinkled some oil before the LORD seven times
			
			• Put some oil on the same places he had put the blood: The right ear, thumb, & big toe of the poorest person (who had been healed of leprosy or infectious skin disease—a symbol of sin)
			
			• Poured the rest of the oil on the head of the one cleansed
			  5) Result: Atonement or reconciliation
			
			d. The poorest person was cleansed through the sacrifice of the other offerings: One dove or pigeon as a Sin Offering, the other as a Burnt Offering, & the Grain Offering (all symbolizing approaching God through Christ)
			e. The result: The priest (a symbol of Christ) made atonement, reconciliation for the poorest person as well as the rich

Thought 1. God has made provision for the poor to be cleansed from the infectious disease of sin. A person is not cleansed...

- because of money or possessions
- because of position or authority
- because of social standing or status
- because of education or knowledge
- because of profession or work

A person is cleansed for one reason and one reason alone: he approaches God through the substitute sacrifice of the Lord Jesus Christ. God accepts no man's person, shows no favoritism whatsoever. The poor, the average, the rich—we are all cleansed from the infectious disease of sin by the sacrifice of Jesus Christ and by His sacrifice alone. The grace of God has opened the door for every person to be cleansed through the sacrifice of His dear Son, Jesus Christ.

> **"I love them, that love me [any person, poor or rich] and those that seek me early shall find me"** (Pr.8:17).
> **"When the poor and needy seek water, and there is none, and their tongue faileth for thirst, I the LORD will hear them, I the God of Israel will not forsake them"** (Is.41:17).
> **"Hearken, my beloved brethren, Hath not God chosen the poor of this world rich in faith, and heirs of the kingdom which he hath promised to them that love him?"** (Js.2:5).

"But we see Jesus, who was made a little lower than the angels for the suffering of death, crowned with glory and honour; that he by the grace of God should taste death for every man" (He.2:9).

"Forasmuch as ye know that ye were not redeemed with corruptible things, as silver and gold, from your vain conversation received by tradition from your fathers; But with the precious blood of Christ, as of a lamb without blemish and without spot" (1 Pe.1:18-19).

"Who his own self bare our sins in his own body on the tree, that we, being dead to sins, should live unto righteousness: by whose stripes ye were healed" (1 Pe.2:24).

"For Christ also hath once suffered for sins, the just for the unjust, that he might bring us to God, being put to death in the flesh, but quickened by the Spirit" (1 Pe.3:18).

[5] (14:33-53) **Mildew, Cleansing from—Fungus, Cleansing from—Houses, Cleansing of—Houses, Dedication of—Property, Dedication of—Environment, Clean**: there was the cleansing of mildew or fungus in houses. Mildew and fungus are symbols of sin and of the spreading power of sin. Note that these laws were to apply when God's people entered the promised land of Canaan and built houses. While out in the desert, they were naturally living in tents. Note the great hope that this law gave to God's people. Here God was giving them a law that dealt with houses made of stone and the latest building materials (v.42) and even giving them the hope of living in towns (v.45). Yet, they had never even seen the land. What hope! And what a glorious assurance God was giving His dear people: His promises would be fulfilled. His people would inherit the promised land (a symbol of heaven for the believer). Note another fact as well: houses can be infected with mildew, fungus, or rot. The Hebrew word for mildew (tsara'at) is the very same word translated as leprosy or infectious skin disease covered earlier (13:1-59). The Hebrew word obviously had a wide range of meanings: it referred to any possible infections or spreading spot found on a person's body, clothing, or house. As the Scripture and outline are studied, just keep in mind that mildew is a symbol of sin in houses or within one's environment.

OUTLINE	SCRIPTURE	SCRIPTURE	OUTLINE
5. **The cleansing of mildew in houses, a symbol of sin in houses or within one's environment (these laws were to apply when they entered the promised land of Canaan)**	33 And the LORD spake unto Moses and unto Aaron, saying, 34 When ye be come into the land of Canaan, which I give to you for a possession, and I put the plague of leprosy in a house of the land of your possession;	away the stones in which the plague is, and they shall cast them into an unclean place without the city: 41 And he shall cause the house to be scraped within round about, and they shall pour out the dust that they scrape off without the city into an unclean place:	unclean place outside the town (a place people would not go lest they be contaminated) 2) To scrape all the inside walls: Dump the scraped material in an unclean place outside the town
a. The head of the house must go & tell the priest about the mildew (a symbol of going to Christ about sin within one's house or environment)	35 And he that owneth the house shall come and tell the priest, saying, It seemeth to me there is as it were a plague in the house:	42 And they shall take other stones, and put them in the place of those stones; and he shall take other morter, and shall plaister the house.	3) To replace the contaminated materials with new stones & new clay & plaster
b. The priest was to order the house emptied immediately 1) To keep anything else from being contaminated 2) To inspect the house	36 Then the priest shall command that they empty the house, before the priest go into it to see the plague, that all that is in the house be not made unclean: and afterward the priest shall go in to see the house:	43 And if the plague come again, and break out in the house, after that he hath taken away the stones, and after he hath scraped the house, and after it is plaistered;	e. Case 2: A relapse—the mildew reappeared in the house
c. The mildew that was greenish or reddish & seemed to be deeper than the walls demanded immediate action	37 And he shall look on the plague, and, behold, if the plague be in the walls of the house with hollow strakes, greenish or reddish, which in sight are lower than the wall;	44 Then the priest shall come and look, and, behold, if the plague be spread in the house, it is a fretting leprosy in the house: it is unclean.	1) To be reexamined by the priest & declared to be a destructive mildew, an unclean house
1) To close the house for seven days	38 Then the priest shall go out of the house to the door of the house, and shut up the house seven days:	45 And he shall break down the house, the stones of it, and the timber thereof, and all the morter of the house; and he shall carry them forth out of the city into an unclean place.	2) To condemn the house: Have it torn down & all materials taken out of town to an unclean place
2) To return & inspect the house on the seventh day d. Case 1: The mildew had spread (a symbol of sin spreading)	39 And the priest shall come again the seventh day, and shall look: and, behold, if the plague be spread in the walls of the house;	46 Moreover he that goeth into the house all the while that it is shut up shall be unclean until the even.	3) To keep people out: Anyone who entered, slept, or ate in the house was to be counted unclean till evening
1) To remove the contaminated stone: Take to an	40 Then the priest shall command that they take	47 And he that lieth in the	4) The treatment: The

OUTLINE	SCRIPTURE	SCRIPTURE	OUTLINE
contaminated person was to be washed	house shall wash his clothes; and he that eateth in the house shall wash his clothes.	sop, and the scarlet, and the living bird, and dip them in the blood of the slain bird, and in	(the cedar wood, the hyssop, the scarlet yarn, & the live bird)
f. Case 3: The mildew does not reappear after being replastered	48 And if the priest shall come in, and look *upon it*	the running water, and sprinkle the house seven times:	• To sprinkle the house seven times
1) To pronounce the house clean	and, behold, the plague hath not spread in the house, after the house was plaistered: then the priest shall pronounce the house clean, because the plague is healed.	52 And he shall cleanse the house with the blood of the bird, and with the running water, and with the living bird, and with	• To purify the house through the blood of the sacrifice
2) To purify the house: Through the offering of the sacrifice (see above vv.4-7)	49 And he shall take to cleanse the house two birds, and cedar wood, and scarlet, and hyssop:	the cedar wood, and with the hyssop, and with the scarlet:	
• To kill one bird over fresh water in a clay pot, mixing the blood in the water	50 And he shall kill the one of the birds in an earthen vessel over running water:	53 But he shall let go the living bird out of the city into the open fields, and make an atonement for	• To set the live bird free, v.53
• To dip the other items into the blood & water	51 And he shall take the cedar wood, and the hys-	the house: and it shall be clean.	g. The purpose for cleansing houses through the sacrifice (a symbol of cleansing sin through Christ) 1) To make atonement for one's house (environment) 2) To protect cleanliness

Thought 1. If there has ever been a day when our homes and environment needed to be cleansed of sin and dedicated to God, it is today. Our houses and our environment must be kept clean. No believer is to allow sin nor to do sinful things within his house or environment. His house is to be dedicated to God. If sinful behavior is found within the house or environment of the believer, he needs to go before God and ask God for His cleansing power. God has the power to cleanse any of our homes; He even has the power to cleanse our environment. Just as in the day of the Israelite believers, so it is today: a cleansing power is found in the blood of the sacrifice, the sacrifice of our Lord Jesus Christ.

"**Depart ye, depart ye, go ye out from thence, touch no unclean thing; go ye out of the midst of her; be ye clean, that bear the vessels of the LORD**" (Is.52:11).

"**And with many other words did he testify and exhort, saying, Save yourselves from this untoward generation**" (Ac.2:40).

"**Be ye not unequally yoked together with unbelievers: for what fellowship hath righteousness with unrighteousness? and what communion hath light with darkness? And what concord hath Christ with Belial? or what part hath he that believeth with an infidel? And what agreement hath the temple of God with idols? for ye are the temple of the living God; as God hath said, I will dwell in them, and walk in them; and I will be their God, and they shall be my people**" (2 Co.6:14-16).

"**Wherefore come out from among them, and be ye separate, saith the Lord, and touch not the unclean thing; and I will receive you, And will be a Father unto you, and ye shall be my sons and daughters, saith the Lord Almighty**" (2 Co.6:17-18).

"**And have no fellowship with the unfruitful works of darkness, but rather reprove them**" (Ep.5:11).

"**Now we command you, brethren, in the name of our Lord Jesus Christ, that ye withdraw yourselves from every brother that walketh disorderly, and not after the tradition which he received of us**" (2 Th.3:6).

"**But speak thou the things which become sound doctrine: That the aged men be sober, grave, temperate, sound in faith, in charity, in patience. The aged women likewise, that they be in behaviour as becometh holiness, not false accusers, not given to much wine, teachers of good things; That they may teach the young women to be sober, to love their husbands, to love their children, To be discreet, chaste, keepers at home, good, obedient to their own husbands, that the word of God be not blasphemed. Young men likewise exhort to be sober minded**" (Tit.2:1-6).

6 (14:54-57) **Leprosy, Laws Governing—Infectious Skin Disease, Laws Governing—Mildew, Laws Governing—Fungus, Laws Governing—Rot, Laws Governing—Clean - Cleanliness, Laws Governing—Ritual, of Cleansing—Discernment:** there was the purpose for the laws governing leprosy or infectious skin disease and mildew. This is a summary statement covering chapters 13 and 14. Skin disease and mildew disfigured the surface of things. The disease could be easily seen. When this happened, there was danger of the infection spreading and causing a plague of destruction among human life and property. God loved His people and wanted them to be healthy so that they could enjoy the fullness of life, becoming dynamic witnesses to the surrounding people and nations of the world. This is the reason He gave them these laws, to protect them from the spread of infectious skin disease and mildew. Moreover, He gave them the laws of cleansing to assure the public that a person had really been healed. They were to openly accept the person back into the community. Note the Scripture and outline:

OUTLINE	SCRIPTURE
6. The purpose for the laws governing leprosy or infectious skin disease & mildew a. The places where disease & mildew are found: Symbolizes sin within self & within one's environment b. The purpose stated: To teach God's people to discern, distinguish between clean & unclean	54 This *is* the law for all manner of plague of leprosy, and scall, 55 And for the leprosy of a garment, and of a house, 56 And for a rising, and for a scab, and for a bright spot: 57 To teach when *it is* unclean, and when *it is* clean: this *is* the law of leprosy.

Thought 1. God's purpose was to teach His people to discern between the clean and the unclean. The Christian believer must have the power of discernment, be able to distinguish between the clean and unclean. Discernment—the ability to distinguish between what is good or bad, what is healthy or unhealthy, what to do or not to do, what is sin or not sin—is an absolute essential for the Christian believer.

"But the natural man receiveth not the things of the Spirit of God: for they are foolishness unto him: neither can he know them, because they are spiritually discerned" (1 Co.2:14).

"But strong meat belongeth to them that are of full age, even those who by reason of use have their senses exercised to discern both good and evil" (He.5:14).

"Give therefore thy servant an understanding heart to judge thy people, that I may discern between good and bad: for who is able to judge this thy so great a people?" (1 K.3:9).

"And the spirit of the LORD shall rest upon him, the spirit of wisdom and understanding, the spirit of counsel and might, the spirit of knowledge and of the fear of the LORD; And shall make him of quick understanding in the fear of the LORD: and he shall not judge after the sight of his eyes, neither reprove after the hearing of his ears: But with righteousness shall he judge" (Is.11:2-4).

TYPES, SYMBOLS, AND PICTURES
Leviticus 14:1-57

Historical Term	Type or Picture (Scriptural Basis for Each)	Life Application for Today's Believer	Biblical Application
Laws That Cleanse and Restore People from Leprosy, from All Forms of Infectious Skin Diseases Le. 14:1-57	*These laws (laws that cleanse and restore people from leprosy, from all forms of infectious skin disease) symbolize the need for spiritual cleansing.* **"This shall be the law of the leper in the day of his cleansing: He shall be brought unto the priest" (Le.14:2).**	God loves and cares for His people, so he naturally cares about their health. He wants His people to be healthy so they can enjoy the fullness of life, so they can be productive and fruitful in life. Stated simply, God wants His people strong so that they can live lives that are strong in work, play, and worship. God wants His people conquering throughout all of life, being victorious over all the trials and temptations of life. He wants them physically and mentally strong so that they can bear strong testimony to His glorious goodness and saving grace.	*"The thief cometh not, but for to steal, and to kill, and to destroy: I am come that they might have life, and that they might have it more abundantly" (Jn.10:10).* *"And God is able to make all grace abound toward you; that ye, always having all sufficiency in all things, may abound to every good work" (2 Co.9:8).* *"Now unto him that is able to do exceeding abundantly above all that we ask or think, according to the power that worketh in us" (Ep.3:20).* *"But my God shall supply all your need according to his riches in glory by Christ Jesus" (Ph.4:19).* *"They shall be abundantly satisfied with the fatness of thy house; and thou shalt make them drink of the river of thy pleasures" (Ps.36:8).*
The Cleansing That Took Place Outside the Camp Le. 14:2-9	*The cleansing that took place outside the camp is a symbol of being outside, separated from God's people, but of being healed of infectious skin disease (a symbol of sin)*	When a person walks in sin he is *outside* Christ, separated from Christ. He is living *outside the camp,* not in the camp of the righteous. If he is to be reached and cleansed, he has to be	*"The night is far spent, the day is at hand: let us therefore cast off the works of darkness, and let us put on the armour of light" (Ro.13:12).* *In the name of our Lord*

TYPES, SYMBOLS, AND PICTURES
Leviticus 14:1-57

Historical Term	Type or Picture (Scriptural Basis for Each)	Life Application for Today's Believer	Biblical Application
	"This shall be the law of the leper in the day of his cleansing: He shall be brought unto the priest: And the priest shall go forth out of the camp; and the priest shall look, and, behold, *if* the plague of leprosy be healed in the leper" (Le.14:2-3).	reached and cleansed outside the camp. Once he has been cleansed, he can then enter the camp of believers.	*Jesus Christ, when ye are gathered together, and my spirit, with the power of our Lord Jesus Christ, To deliver such an one unto Satan for the destruction of the flesh, that the spirit may be saved in the day of the Lord Jesus"* (1 Co.5:4-5). "*He that covereth his sins shall not prosper: but whoso confesseth and forsaketh them shall have mercy"* (Pr.28:13). "*For God shall bring every work into judgment, with every secret thing, whether it be good, or whether it be evil"* (Ec.12:14).
The Priest's Going Outside the Camp to Cleanse the Diseased Person Le. 14:3	*The priest's going outside the camp to cleanse the diseased person is a picture of Jesus Christ and His work. Jesus Christ left the camp and glory of heaven to come to this sin diseased world. He came to cleanse the world of sin.* "**And the priest shall go forth out of the camp; and the priest shall look, and, behold, *if* the plague of leprosy be healed in the leper**" (Le.14:3).	Jesus Christ left the camp and glory of heaven to come to this sin-diseased world. He came forth from heaven's glory to cleanse all who are infected with the disease of sin. Cleansing us from our sins took place outside of heaven. He had to go outside the community of heaven with all its glory and come to where we are in order to cleanse us.	"*But when the fulness of the time was come, God sent forth his Son, made of a woman, made under the law, To redeem them that were under the law, that we might receive the adoption of sons"* (Ga.4:4-5). "*But we see Jesus, who was made a little lower than the angels for the suffering of death, crowned with glory and honour; that he by the grace of God should taste death for every man. For it became him, for whom are all things, and by whom are all things, in bringing many sons unto glory, to make the captain of their salvation perfect through sufferings"* (He.2:9-10). "*For verily he took not on him the nature of angels; but he took on him the seed of Abraham. Wherefore in all things it behooved him to be made like unto his brethren, that he might be a merciful and faithful high priest in things pertaining to God, to make reconciliation for the sins of the people"* (He.2:16-17).
The Person Being Cleansed Through the Sacrifice of the Shed Blood— Outside the Camp Le. 14:4-7	*The person being cleansed through the sacrifice of the shed blood—outside the camp—is a symbol or picture of two things:* 1. *This is a picture of the sacrifice of Jesus Christ. Note that the*	There are two pictures that apply to the believer in this ritual: 1. There is the picture of a believer being fully and completely cleansed	"*For this is my blood of the new testament, which is shed for many for the remission of sins"* (Mt.26:28). "*Take heed therefore unto yourselves, and to all the flock, over the which the Holy Ghost hath made*"

TYPES, SYMBOLS, AND PICTURES
Leviticus 14:1-57

Historical Term	Type or Picture (Scriptural Basis for Each)	Life Application for Today's Believer	Biblical Application
	blood of the sacrificed bird was sprinkled over a person seven times; then he was pronounced clean. The number seven symbolized completeness, fullness. The person was completely, fully cleansed by the blood of the sacrifice. 2. *Note that the live bird was dipped into the blood and then released, set free. This was a symbol that the person's disease was gone, taken away. He was free to live with God and His people.* **"As for the living bird, he shall take it, and the cedar wood, and the scarlet, and the hyssop, and shall dip them and the living bird in the blood of the bird *that was* killed over the running water: And he shall sprinkle upon him that is to be cleansed from the leprosy seven times, and shall pronounce him clean, and shall let the living bird loose into the open field" (Le.14:6-7).**	through the blood of the Lord Jesus Christ. 2. The live bird, of course, is a picture of the believer's sin being taken away: the believer is free of sin, free to live with God and the people of God.	*you overseers, to feed the church of God, which he hath purchased with his own blood" (Ac.20:28).* *"Much more then, being now justified by his blood, we shall be saved from wrath through him" (Ro. 5:9).* *"How much more shall the blood of Christ, who through the eternal Spirit offered himself without spot to God, purge your conscience from dead works to serve the living God?" (He.9:14).* *"Forasmuch as ye know that ye were not redeemed with corruptible things, as silver and gold, from your vain conversation received by tradition from your fathers; But with the precious blood of Christ, as of a lamb without blemish and without spot" (1 Pe.1:18-19).*
The Washing of a Diseased Person's Clothes, Shaving His Body, and Bathing Le. 14:8	*This is a picture of being completely washed and cleansed of sin. This, of course, exposed a person's whole body, revealing that he was completely cleansed of the contagious disease.* **"And he that is to be cleansed shall wash his clothes, and shave off all his hair, and wash himself in water, that he may be clean: and after that he shall come into the camp, and shall tarry abroad out of his tent seven days" (Le.14:8).**	The person who is afflicted with the disease of sin can be completely washed and cleansed. The blood of Jesus Christ, God's son, cleanses us from sin—completely and fully.	*"But if we walk in the light, as he is in the light, we have fellowship one with another, and the blood of Jesus Christ his Son cleanseth us from all sin" (1 Jn.1:7).* *Unto him that loved us, and washed us from our sins in his own blood" (Re.1:5).* *"And I said unto him, Sir, thou knowest. And he said to me, These are they which came out of great tribulation, and have washed their robes, and made them white in the blood of the Lamb" (Re.7:14).*
The Cleansing That Took Place Inside the Camp Le. 14:10-20	*The cleansing that took place inside the camp is the symbol of being fully reconciled and restored through Jesus Christ.* **"And on the eighth day he shall take two he lambs without blemish, and one**	The believer who has sinned needs to come to Christ. Coming to Christ is the only way to make sure... • that he is fully reconciled to God • that he has no hidden sin in his life • that he is not suffering	*"And all things are of God, who hath reconciled us to himself by Jesus Christ, and hath given to us the ministry of reconciliation" (2 Co.5:18).* *"And that he might reconcile both unto God in one body by the cross, having*

TYPES, SYMBOLS, AND PICTURES
Leviticus 14:1-57

Historical Term	Type or Picture (Scriptural Basis for Each)	Life Application for Today's Believer	Biblical Application
	ewe lamb of the first year without blemish, and three tenth deals of fine flour *for a meat offering, mingled with oil, and one log of oil*" (Le.14:10).	under the weight and anguish of guilt • that he receives an infusion of God's strength, assurance and of God's guidance	*slain the enmity thereby*" (Ep.2:16). *"And, having made peace through the blood of his cross, by him to reconcile all things unto himself; by him, I say, whether they be things in earth, or things in heaven*" (Col.1:20). *"Wherefore in all things it behooved him to be made like unto his brethren, that he might be a merciful and faithful high priest in things pertaining to God, to make reconciliation for the sins of the people*" (He.2:17).
Some Blood Placed on the Cleansed Person's Right Ear, Thumb, and Toe During the Guilt Offering Le. 14:10-20	*Some blood placed on the cleansed person's right ear, thumb, and toe symbolized that the person's whole being was cleansed and dedicated to God through the blood of the sacrifice:* 1. *He was dedicating his ear to listen to the voice of God and to allow God to guide him day by day.* 2. *He was dedicating his thumb or hand to serve God as he labored day by day.* 3. *He was dedicating his toe or feet to walk where God wanted him to walk, following God day by day.* **"And the priest shall take** *some* **of the blood of the trespass offering, and the priest shall put** *it* **upon the tip of the right ear of him that is to be cleansed, and upon the thumb of his right hand, and upon the great toe of his right foot"** (Le.14:14).	When we come to God through the sacrifice of the Lord Jesus Christ, we are to dedicate our whole beings to God. • We are to dedicate our ears to God, listening only to the voice of God and to the things of righteousness. We are not to listen to the voices of this world, not to the foul language, immoral talk, off-colored jokes, false teachings, and worldly philosophies. We are to listen only to those things that will build up and benefit ourselves and society. • We are to dedicate our thumbs and hands to serve God in our work, play, and activities throughout the day. We are only to touch and handle the things of right-eousness. We are not to touch the things of unrighteousness. • We are to dedicate our toes or feet to God. We are to go only where He would want us to go. We arc not to walk into the bright lights and places of sinful behavior. We are to walk only into the places that will build up and benefit us and society.	*"I beseech you therefore, brethren, by the mercies of God, that ye present your bodies a living sacrifice, holy, acceptable unto God, which is your reasonable service*" (Ro.12:1). *"But what things were gain to me, those I counted loss for Christ. Yea doubtless, and I count all things but loss for the excellency of the knowledge of Christ Jesus my Lord: for whom I have suffered the loss of all things, and do count them but dung, that I may win Christ*" (Phil.3:7-8). *"For Moses had said, Consecrate yourselves to day to the LORD, even every man upon his son, and upon his brother; that he may bestow upon you a blessing this day*" (Ex.32:29). *"The gold for things of gold, and the silver for things of silver, and for all manner of work to be made by the hands of artificers. And who then is willing to consecrate his service this day unto the LORD?*" (1 Chr.29:5). *"My son, give me thine heart, and let thine eyes observe my ways*" (Pr.23:26).
Oil Le. 14:16-18	*Oil is a symbol of the Holy Spirit and of God's strength and guidance throughout the*	When a person has been infected with the disease of sin—especially for a long	*"For the bread of God is he which cometh down from heaven, and giveth*

TYPES, SYMBOLS, AND PICTURES
Leviticus 14:1-57

Historical Term	Type or Picture (Scriptural Basis for Each)	Life Application for Today's Believer	Biblical Application
	Scripture. This is symbolized in two ways: 1. *The oil that was sprinkled before the* LORD *seven times was symbolizing the request for God's complete, perfect strength and guidance.* 2. *The oil that was then placed upon the cleansed person was symbolizing that the person was being infused with the Spirit of God. He was being given the complete, perfect strength and guidance of God's Spirit as he walked day by day. He needed a special infusion of God's Spirit and strength just in case some people still rejected him because of his infectious disease. They possibly would not believe that he was fully cleansed. Only God's strength could overcome the sense of rejection and isolation that the diseased person might sense.* **"And the priest shall dip his right finger in the oil that *is* in his left hand, and shall sprinkle of the oil with his finger seven times before the** LORD**: And of the rest of the oil that *is* in his hand shall the priest put upon the tip of the right ear of him that is to be cleansed, and upon the thumb of his right hand, and upon the great toe of his right foot, upon the blood of the trespass offering: And the remnant of the oil that *is* in the priest's hand he shall pour upon the head of him that is to be cleansed: and the priest shall make an atonement for him before the** LORD**" (Le.14:16-18).**	time—he often needs a special infusion of God's Spirit. He needs the strength and guidance of God's Spirit to combat whatever rejection and ridicule might be thrown against him by his former worldly friends. He needs God's strength and guidance to combat the onslaught of trials and temptation that will confront him day-by-day.	*life unto the world"* (Jn.6:33). *"Even the Spirit of truth; whom the world cannot receive, because it seeth him not, neither knoweth him: but ye know him; for he dwelleth with you, and shall be in you"* (Jn.14:17). *"Howbeit when he, the Spirit of truth, is come, he will guide you into all truth: for he shall not speak of himself; but whatsoever he shall hear, that shall he speak: and he will show you things to come"* (Jn.16:13). *"But ye shall receive power, after that the Holy Ghost is come upon you: and ye shall be witnesses unto me both in Jerusalem, and in all Judaea, and in Samaria, and unto the uttermost part of the earth"* (Ac.1:8). *"But if the Spirit of him that raised up Jesus from the dead dwell in you, he that raised up Christ from the dead shall also quicken your mortal bodies by his Spirit that dwelleth in you"* (Ro.8:11). *"Who also hath made us able ministers of the new testament; not of the letter, but of the spirit: for the letter killeth, but the spirit giveth life"* (2 Co.3:6). *"Then he answered and spake unto me, saying, This is the word of the* LORD *unto Zerubbabel, saying, Not by might, nor by power, but by my spirit, saith the* LORD *of hosts"* (Zec.4:6). *"And I will put my spirit within you, and cause you to walk in my statutes, and ye shall keep my judgments, and do them"* (Eze.36:27).
The Cleansing of Mildew in Houses Le. 14:33-53	*The cleansing of mildew in houses is a symbol of sin in houses or within one's environment* **"When ye be come into the land of Canaan, which I give to you for a posses-**	Believers—in fact, every human being—should naturally keep their houses and their environment clean. No believer is to allow sin nor do sinful things within his house or environment. His	*"If ye were of the world, the world would love his own: but because ye are not of the world, but I have chosen you out of the world, therefore the world hateth you"* (Jn.15:19).

TYPES, SYMBOLS, AND PICTURES
Leviticus 14:1-57

Historical Term	Type or Picture (Scriptural Basis for Each)	Life Application for Today's Believer	Biblical Application
	sion, and I put the plague of leprosy in a house of the land of your possession" (Le.14:34).	house is to be dedicated to God. If sinful behavior is found within the house or environment of the believer, he needs to go before God and ask God for His cleansing power. God has the power to cleanse any of our homes; He even has the power to cleanse our environment.	"And with many other words did he testify and exhort, saying, Save yourselves from this untoward generation" (Ac.2:40). "Be ye not unequally yoked together with unbelievers: for what fellowship hath righteousness with unrighteousness? and what communion hath light with darkness? And what concord hath Christ with Belial? or what part hath he that believeth with an infidel? And what agreement hath the temple of God with idols? for ye are the temple of the living God; as God hath said, I will dwell in them, and walk in them; and I will be their God, and they shall be my people" (2 Co.6:14-16). "Wherefore come out from among them, and be ye separate, saith the Lord, and touch not the unclean thing; and I will receive you, And will be a Father unto you, and ye shall be my sons and daughters, saith the Lord Almighty" (2 Co.6:17-18). "Depart ye, depart ye, go ye out from thence, touch no unclean thing; go ye out of the midst of her; be ye clean, that bear the vessels of the LORD" (Is.52:11).

1. The Lawgiver: God Himself

2. The bodily discharges & cleansing of men

a. The abnormal discharge due to sickness or disease such as venereal or sexual disease: Made him & every person & thing he touched or that touched him unclean

1) Defiled his bed & chair

2) Defiled the person who touched his bed: The person had to wash his clothes & bathe in water (a symbol of Christ, the water of life)

3) Defiled the person who sat where he sat: The person had to wash his clothes & bathe with water (a symbol of Christ, the water of life)

4) Defiled the person who touched him: The person had to wash his clothes & bathe with water (a symbol of Christ, the water of life)

5) Defiled a person who was touched by his saliva: The person had to wash his clothes & bathe in water (a symbol of Christ, the water of life)

6) Defiled the person who sat on his saddle or touched anything that was under him: Had to wash his clothes & bathe with water (a symbol of Christ, the water of life)

7) Defiled anyone he touched if he did not first wash his hands: A person had to wash his clothes & bathe in water (a symbol of Christ, the water of life)

CHAPTER 15

E. Laws That Protect & Cleanse People from Diseases of Sexual Impurity: Symbolizes How Defiling Sin Is & the Need to Be Cleansed from Sin, 15:1-33

And the LORD spake unto Moses and to Aaron, saying,
2 Speak unto the children of Israel, and say unto them, When any man hath a running issue out of his flesh, *because of* his issue he *is* unclean.
3 And this shall be his uncleanness in his issue: whether his flesh run with his issue, or his flesh be stopped from his issue, it *is* his uncleanness.
4 Every bed, whereon he lieth that hath the issue, is unclean: and every thing, whereon he sitteth, shall be unclean.
5 And whosoever toucheth his bed shall wash his clothes, and bathe *himself* in water, and be unclean until the even.
6 And he that sitteth on *any* thing whereon he sat that hath the issue shall wash his clothes, and bathe *himself* in water, and be unclean until the even.
7 And he that toucheth the flesh of him that hath the issue shall wash his clothes, and bathe *himself* in water, and be unclean until the even.
8 And if he that hath the issue spit upon him that is clean; then he shall wash his clothes, and bathe *himself* in water, and be unclean until the even.
9 And what saddle soever he rideth upon that hath the issue shall be unclean.
10 And whosoever toucheth any thing that was under him shall be unclean until the even: and he that beareth *any of* those things shall wash his clothes, and bathe *himself* in water, and be unclean until the even.
11 And whomsoever he toucheth that hath the issue, and hath not rinsed his hands in water, he shall wash his clothes, and bathe *himself* in water, and be unclean until the even.

12 And the vessel of earth, that he toucheth which hath the issue, shall be broken: and every vessel of wood shall be rinsed in water.
13 And when he that hath an issue is cleansed of his issue; then he shall number to himself seven days for his cleansing, and wash his clothes, and bathe his flesh in running water, and shall be clean.
14 And on the eighth day he shall take to him two turtledoves, or two young pigeons, and come before the LORD unto the door of the tabernacle of the congregation, and give them unto the priest:
15 And the priest shall offer them, the one *for* a sin offering, and the other *for* a burnt offering; and the priest shall make an atonement for him before the LORD for his issue.
16 And if any man's seed of copulation go out from him, then he shall wash all his flesh in water, and be unclean until the even.
17 And every garment, and every skin, whereon is the seed of copulation, shall be washed with water, and be unclean until the even.
18 The woman also with whom man shall lie *with* seed of copulation, they shall *both* bathe *themselves* in water, and be unclean until the even.
19 And if a woman have an issue, *and* her issue in her flesh be blood, she shall be put apart seven days: and whosoever toucheth her shall be unclean until the even.
20 And every thing that she lieth upon in her separation shall be unclean: every thing also that she sitteth upon shall be unclean.
21 And whosoever toucheth her bed shall wash his clothes, and bathe *himself* in water, and be unclean until the even.
22 And whosoever toucheth any thing that she sat upon shall wash his clothes, and bathe *himself* in water,

8) Defiled any clay pot or wood he touched: It had to be rinsed with water (a symbol of Christ's cleansing all things)

b. The cleansing of a man from sexual impurity

1) Had to wash his clothes & self with fresh water for seven days (seven was a symbol of complete & full cleansing

2) Had to approach God for cleansing on the eighth day—through the sacrifice (a symbol of Christ)

3) Had to have the priest (a symbol of Christ) offer the sacrifice to God
   • Offer the Sin Offering: Symbolized forgiveness
   • Offer the Burnt Offering: Symbolized atonement, reconciliation

4) The result: Atonement, reconciliation with God

c. The normal bodily discharges of a man

1) Any normal excretion: Had to bathe with water (a symbol of being cleansed from disease in Christ)

2) Any clothing with semen on it: Had to be washed with water (a symbol of being clothed with purity)

3) Any sexual intercourse with discharge: Both parties had to bathe with water (a symbol of being cleansed from disease in Christ, the water of life)

3. The bodily discharges & cleansing of women

a. The discharge due to a normal menstrual period: Made her unclean for seven days & any person who touches her was unclean till evening

1) Defiled her bed & chair

2) Defiled the person who touched her bed: The person had to wash his clothes & self in water (a symbol of Christ, the living water)

3) Defiled the person who touched anything she sat on: The person had to wash his clothes & bathe in

water (a symbol of Christ, the living water)
 	
4) Defiled the person who lay or sat where she was: Made the person unclean until evening
 	
5) Defiled the person who had intercourse with her & was touched by her monthly period
  • He was unclean for seven days
  • He defiled any bed he lay on
 	
b. The discharge due to an abnormal flow or disease: Was counted unclean as long as the discharge continued
 	
1) Defiled her bed & chair
 	
2) Defiled the person who touched her bed & chair: Had to wash his clothes & bathe with water (a symbol of Christ, the living water)
 	
c. The cleansing of a woman
	and be unclean until the even.
	23 And if it *be* on *her* bed, or on any thing whereon she sitteth, when he toucheth it, he shall be unclean until the even.
	24 And if any man lie with her at all, and her flowers be upon him, he shall be unclean seven days; and all the bed whereon he lieth shall be unclean.
	25 And if a woman have an issue of her blood many days out of the time of her separation, or if it run beyond the time of her separation; all the days of the issue of her uncleanness shall be as the days of her separation: she *shall be* unclean.
	26 Every bed whereon she lieth all the days of her issue shall be unto her as the bed of her separation: and whatsoever she sitteth upon shall be unclean, as the uncleanness of her separation.
	27 And whosoever toucheth those things shall be unclean, and shall wash his clothes, and bathe *himself* in water, and be unclean until the even.
	28 But if she be cleansed of
		her issue, then she shall number to herself seven days, and after that she shall be clean.
		29 And on the eighth day she shall take unto her two turtles, or two young pigeons, and bring them unto the priest, to the door of the tabernacle of the congregation.
		30 And the priest shall offer the one *for* a sin offering, and the other *for* a burnt offering; and the priest shall make an atonement for her before the LORD for the issue of her uncleanness.
		31 Thus shall ye separate the children of Israel from their uncleanness; that they die not in their uncleanness, when they defile my tabernacle that *is* among them.
		32 This *is* the law of him that hath an issue, and *of him* whose seed goeth from him, and is defiled therewith;
		33 And of her that is sick of her flowers, and of him that hath an issue, of the man, and of the woman, and of him that lieth with her that is unclean.
			from abnormal discharges
			1) Had to do the same as the man: Wash for seven days (a symbol of total cleansing)
			2) Had to approach God for cleansing on the eighth day—through the sacrifice (a symbol of Christ)
			3) Had to have the priest (a symbol of Christ) offer the sacrifice to God
			  • Offer the Sin Offering: Symbolized forgiveness
			  • Offer the Burnt Offering: Symbolized atonement, reconciliation
			4) The result: Atonement, reconciliation with God
			
			4. **The purpose for the laws that protect people from sexual impurity**
			a. Separation: To keep God's people pure, separate from defilement
			
			b. Deliverance: To save a person from the penalty of sexual sin, death
			
			c. Protection: To guard the public & to govern the cases of sexual impurity among both men & women

DIVISION III

THE WAY TO LIVE A HOLY LIFE BEFORE GOD (PART I): BY A CLEAN BODY (SEPARATION), 11:1–16:34

E. Laws That Protect and Cleanse People from Sexual Diseases and Impurity: Symbolizes How Defiling Sexual Sin Is and the Need to Be Cleansed, 15:1-33

(15:1-33) **Introduction**: this is a sex-crazed age, an age that has gone mad over sex. Sex sells and sex buys. Society has become so sex-crazed that people are buying their most used products based on sex, such items as clothing, cars, food, and even toothpaste. The criteria for buying has become, "Does it help me look sexier?" The impact upon society is tragic and threatening: sexual sins and sexual diseases are running rampant. Divorce, illegitimacy, single parenthood, drugs, abuse, and lawlessness are largely due to society's craze over sex. Society's wrong emphasis upon sex is eating away at the very foundation of society and will lead to a collapse unless there is a change.

The wrong use of sex leads to venereal disease and to a stricken conscience for the person who has not become hardened. But regardless of what a person feels about sex outside of marriage, it is condemned by God. Illicit sex is sin, and the person stands guilty and condemned before God. But note: God loves and cares for every human being upon earth. Therefore, He cares about venereal disease and about stricken consciences and guilt over sexual sin. This is the reason He gave the laws of this chapter to Israel: to protect and cleanse them from sexual disease and impurity. This is the subject of this most important Scripture: *Laws That Protect and Cleanse People from Sexual Diseases and Impurity: Symbolizes How Defiling Sexual Sin Is and the Need to Be Cleansed*, 15:1-33.

1. The Lawgiver: God Himself (v.1).
2. The bodily discharges and cleansing of men (vv.2-18).
3. The bodily discharges and cleansing of women (vv.19-30).
4. The purpose for the laws that protect people from sexual impurity (vv.31-33).

1 (15:1) **Law, Source**: there was the Lawgiver, God Himself. These laws did not come from man but from God. God cares about the sexual behavior of His people. He wants them sexually healthy, free from venereal or sexual disease. He wants them living moral, pure, and clean lives. He wants His people to handle sex with appreciation and enjoyment but with honor and respect, always keeping sex pure within marriage. Sex is only for husband and wife, given as a gift to them and only to them. This is the reason God gave these laws to His people: to keep them sexually pure, free from sexual disease and spiritual defilement.

OUTLINE	SCRIPTURE
1. The Lawgiver: God Himself	And the LORD spake unto Moses and to Aaron, saying,

"**For ye know what commandments we gave you by the Lord Jesus. For this is the will of God, even your sanctification, that ye should abstain from fornication: That every one of you should know how to possess his vessel in sanctification and honour; Not in the lust of concupiscence, even as the Gentiles which know not God**"(1 Th.4:2-5).

2 (15:2-18) **Sexual Diseases—Disease, Sexual—Body, Discharges of—Clean - Cleanliness, Ritual of—Unclean - Uncleanness, Spiritual—Immorality, Results—Impurity, Caused by**: there was the bodily discharge and cleansing of men. Note that the abnormal discharges are dealt with first (vv.2-15), then the normal sexual discharge (vv.16-18). The abnormal discharges probably include more than just sexual discharges, discharges such as diarrhea, bleeding hemorrhoids, and blood from the colon and other internal organs. It should be noted, however, that some commentators argue against this general application. They feel that the passage refers only to abnormal discharges from the sexual organs. Whatever the case, many abnormal discharges are due to venereal or sexual disease. The disease and suffering are due to immoral, sinful behavior. For a few fleeting minutes or at most a few hours of pleasure, the person then had to bear the suffering of a diseased body and the anguish of a stricken conscience. Honor and respect were wounded; a man had defiled and corrupted himself. He was unclean. But even more than this, his disease could be contagious and infect other people. In fact, few diseases are as infectious and contagious as venereal or sexual disease. For this reason, God gave this law to His people: to prevent the spread of venereal or sexual disease. The sexually diseased person was unclean. Moreover, if there was an abnormal bodily discharge of any kind, the person was unclean. Remember, there was very little medical knowledge in that day, very little known about germs, infection, and disease. This fact alone shows the astounding wisdom of these laws, a wisdom so astounding that God alone could be the source of these laws. Note the Scripture and outline, how careful the sexually diseased person had to be. He had to make absolutely sure that he did not pass the disease on to someone else. What a contrast between God's people of that day and time and the people of today.

OUTLINE	SCRIPTURE	SCRIPTURE	OUTLINE
2. **The bodily discharges & cleansing of men** a. The abnormal discharge due to sickness or disease such as venereal or sexual disease: Made him & every person & thing he touched or that touched him unclean	2 Speak unto the children of Israel, and say unto them, When any man hath a running issue out of his flesh, *because of* his issue he *is* unclean.	clean; then he shall wash his clothes, and bathe *himself* in water, and be unclean until the even.	person had to wash his clothes & bathe in water (a symbol of Christ, the water of life)
	3 And this shall be his uncleanness in his issue: whether his flesh run with his issue, or his flesh be stopped from his issue, it *is* his uncleanness.	9 And what saddle soever he rideth upon that hath the issue shall be unclean. 10 And whosoever toucheth any thing that was under him shall be unclean until the even: and he that beareth *any of* those things shall wash his clothes, and bathe *himself* in water, and be unclean until the even.	6) Defiled the person who sat on his saddle or touched anything that was under him: Had to wash his clothes & bathe in water (a symbol of Christ, the water of life)
1) Defiled his bed & chair	4 Every bed, whereon he lieth that hath the issue, is unclean: and every thing, whereon he sitteth, shall be unclean.		
2) Defiled the person who touched his bed: The person had to wash his clothes & bathe in water (a symbol of Christ, the water of life)	5 And whosoever toucheth his bed shall wash his clothes, and bathe *himself* in water, and be unclean until the even.	11 And whomsoever he toucheth that hath the issue, and hath not rinsed his hands in water, he shall wash his clothes, and bathe *himself* in water, and be unclean until the even.	7) Defiled anyone he touched if he did not first wash his hands: A person had to wash his clothes & bathe in water (a symbol of Christ, the water of life)
3) Defiled the person who sat where he sat: The person had to wash his clothes & bathe in water (a symbol of Christ, the water of life)	6 And he that sitteth on *any* thing whereon he sat that hath the issue shall wash his clothes, and bathe *himself* in water, and be unclean until the even.	12 And the vessel of earth, that he toucheth which hath the issue, shall be broken: and every vessel of wood shall be rinsed in water.	8) Defiled any clay pot or wood he touched: It had to be rinsed with water (a symbol of Christ's cleansing all things)
4) Defiled the person who touched him: The person had to wash his clothes & bathe in water (a symbol of Christ, the water of life)	7 And he that toucheth the flesh of him that hath the issue shall wash his clothes, and bathe *himself* in water, and be unclean until the even.	13 And when he that hath an issue is cleansed of his issue; then he shall number to himself seven days for his cleansing, and wash his clothes, and bathe his flesh in running water, and shall be clean.	b. The cleansing of a man from sexual impurity 1) Had to wash his clothes & self with fresh water for seven days (seven was a symbol of complete & full cleansing
5) Defiled a person who was touched by his saliva: The	8 And if he that hath the issue spit upon him that is		

OUTLINE	SCRIPTURE	SCRIPTURE	OUTLINE
2) Had to approach God for cleansing on the eighth day—through the sacrifice (a symbol of Christ) 3) Had to have the priest offer the sacrifice to God: a symbol of Christ • Offer the sin offering: Symbolized forgiveness • Offer the burnt offering: Symbolized atonement, reconciliation 4) The result: Atonement, reconciliation with God c. The normal bodily dis-	14 And on the eighth day he shall take to him two turtledoves, or two young pigeons, and come before the LORD unto the door of the tabernacle of the congregation, and give them unto the priest: 15 And the priest shall offer them, the one *for a* sin offering, and the other *for* a burnt offering; and the priest shall make an atonement for him before the LORD for his issue. 16 And if any man's seed	of copulation go out from him, then he shall wash all his flesh in water, and be unclean until the even. 17 And every garment, and every skin, whereon is the seed of copulation, shall be washed with water, and be unclean until the even. 18 The woman also with whom man shall lie *with* seed of copulation, they shall *both* bathe *themselves* in water, and be unclean until the even.	charges of a man 1) Any normal excretion: Had to bathe with water (a symbol of being cleansed from disease in Christ) 2) Any clothing with semen on it: Had to be washed with water (a symbol of being clothed with purity) 3) Any sexual intercourse with discharge: Both parties had to bathe with water (a symbol of being cleansed from disease in Christ, the water of life)

Thought 1. Note a significant fact about the abnormal discharges or sexual diseases. They are considered far more infectious and contagious than skin diseases. The sexually diseased person could infect other people and then the secondary person could go on to infect yet even more people. The sexual disease could be passed on and on. But not only this, objects that came in contact with the infected person were considered unclean. Venereal or sexual disease was considered so contagious that a person had to be separated and isolated outside the camp. This is not specifically mentioned in this passage, but it is covered in the book of *Numbers*.

> "**Command the children of Israel, that they put out of the camp every leper, and every one that hath an issue, and whosoever is defiled by the dead: Both male and female shall ye put out, without the camp shall ye put them; that they defile not their camps, in the midst whereof I dwell**"(Nu.5:2-3).

The sexually diseased had to wait outside the camp until they were fully cleansed. How different from so many who contract venereal or sexual disease today. Many people seem to care little about infecting others. The rapid spread of sexual disease is an indication of this. The pleasure of the moment is allowed to override common sense and respect. Immorality and sexual misbehavior are severely condemned by God.

> "**Thou shalt not commit adultery**" (Ex.20:14).
> "**Know ye not that the unrighteous shall not inherit the kingdom of God? Be not deceived: neither fornicators, nor idolaters, nor adulterers, nor effeminate, nor abusers of themselves with mankind, Nor thieves, nor covetous, nor drunkards, nor revilers, nor extortioners, shall inherit the kingdom of God**" (1 Co.6:9-10).
> "**Having eyes full of adultery, and that cannot cease from sin; beguiling unstable souls**" (2 Pe.2:14).
> "**For this ye know, that no whoremonger, nor unclean person, nor covetous man, who is an idolater, hath any inheritance in the kingdom of Christ and of God**" (Ep.5:5).
> "**For ye are dead, and your life is hid with Christ in God. When Christ, who is our life, shall appear, then shall ye also appear with him in glory. Mortify therefore your members which are upon the earth; fornication, uncleanness, inordinate affection, evil concupiscence, and covetousness, which is idolatry: For which things' sake the wrath of God cometh on the children of disobedience**" (Col.3:3-6).
> "**For this is the will of God, even your sanctification, that ye should abstain from fornication: That every one of you should know how to possess his vessel in sanctification and honour; Not in the lust of concupiscence, even as the Gentiles which know not God**"(1 Th.4:3-5).

Thought 2. There is hope for the sexually impure man—there was in the day of Moses and there is today. Under the law, the sexually diseased man had to take two steps. First, he had to wash his clothes and himself with fresh water for seven days (v.13). Second, he had to approach God for cleansing on the eighth day—through the sacrifice of the Sin Offering and Burnt Offering. Remember, the Sin Offering symbolized forgiveness and the Burnt Offering symbolized atonement or reconciliation with God (vv.14-15). This is a symbol of the atonement (reconciliation) and forgiveness secured in the sacrifice of Jesus Christ.

Today, a sexually impure man must come to Jesus Christ for washing and cleansing. He needs to be cleansed from sin and to be reconciled with God. Immorality separates and alienates a person from God. A person who is sexually impure must approach God through Jesus Christ for reconciliation and forgiveness of sins.

> "**And all things are of God, who hath reconciled us to himself by Jesus Christ, and hath given to us the ministry of reconciliation; To wit, that God was in Christ, reconciling the world unto himself, not imputing their trespasses unto them; and hath committed unto us the word of reconciliation. Now then we are ambassadors for Christ, as though God did beseech you by us: we pray you in Christ's stead, be ye reconciled to God**" (2 Co.5:18-20).
> "**For God sent not his Son into the world to condemn the world; but that the world through him might be saved**" (Jn.3:17).

"In whom we have redemption through his blood, the forgiveness of sins, according to the riches of his grace" (Ep.1:7).

"Who his own self bare our sins in his own body on the tree, that we, being dead to sins, should live unto righteousness: by whose stripes ye were healed" (1 Pe.2:24).

"For Christ also hath once suffered for sins, the just for the unjust, that he might bring us to God, being put to death in the flesh, but quickened by the Spirit" (1 Pe.3:18).

"Who gave himself for our sins, that he might deliver us from this present evil world, according to the will of God and our Father" (Ga.1:4).

Thought 3. Note that the normal bodily discharges of a man were accepted as a normal function of human life (vv.16-18). The law simply governed good hygiene: a person was simply to wash after sexual relations or any other normal emission. Note that a man was considered unclean until evening, at which time he was to wash and cleanse himself. The evening was, of course, the time when most people bathed.

Hygiene is of concern and interest to God. He wants His people to take care of their bodies as well as their spirits. He wants us to keep ourselves clean and pure, both physically and spiritually.

"Let us draw near with a true heart in full assurance of faith, having our hearts sprinkled from an evil conscience, and our bodies washed with pure water" (He.10:22).

"Wash you, make you clean; put away the evil of your doings from before mine eyes; cease to do evil" (Is.1:16).

"Wash thine heart from wickedness, that thou mayest be saved. How long shall thy vain thoughts lodge within thee?" (Je.4:14).

"Having therefore these promises, dearly beloved, let us cleanse ourselves from all filthiness of the flesh and spirit, perfecting holiness in the fear of God" (2 Co.7:1).

"If a man therefore purge himself from these, he shall be a vessel unto honour, sanctified, and meet for the master's use, and prepared unto every good work" (2 Ti.2:21).

"Draw nigh to God, and he will draw nigh to you. Cleanse your hands, ye sinners; and purify your hearts, ye double minded" (Js.4:8).

---

3 (15:19-30) **Woman, Bodily Discharge of—Woman, Menstruation of—Sexual Diseases—Disease, Sexual—Body, Discharges of—Clean - Cleanliness, Ritual of—Unclean - Uncleanness, Spiritual—Immorality, Results—Impurity, Caused by**: the discharge due to a woman's normal menstrual period is now covered (vv.19-24), and then the discharge due to an abnormal flow or disease is covered (vv.25-30). (See Lu.8:43-48.) Why would a woman's menstrual period be considered unclean? The people, of course, knew that a menstrual period was not infectious or contagious. However, when a woman first began to discharge, they had no way to tell whether it was a normal or an abnormal discharge. Therefore, to protect her husband and the community from infectious disease, they counted the menstrual period as a period of uncleanness. But there was more to this law than just the protection of the community; there was the protection of the wife as well. Her menstruation is often an uncomfortable time, often causing a woman to suffer cramps, headaches, fatigue and other symptoms. By counting her unclean for seven days, the law protected her from the advances of an unfeeling husband and assured her of some help with housework and family care. Note that anyone or anything that touched her was counted unclean until evening. However, if a person had intercourse with her and was touched by her monthly period, he also was counted unclean for seven full days. He defiled any bed upon which he lay (v.24). This particular law really protected the woman during this period of uncomfortableness and, in some cases, weakness. Note the fact that a woman's period was in no sense considered to be sinful. To become ceremonially clean, she simply washed herself after her discharge. This she did on the seventh day after the beginning of the menstruation. (See note—Le.18:19 for more discussion.) Note the Scripture and outline:

OUTLINE	SCRIPTURE	SCRIPTURE	OUTLINE
3. The bodily discharges & cleansing of women a. The discharge due to a normal menstrual period: Made her unclean for seven days & any person or thing she touched or that touched her was unclean till evening 1) Defiled her bed & chair 2) Defiled a person who touched her bed: The person had to wash his clothes & self in water (a symbol of Christ, the living water) 3) Defiled the person who touched anything she sat	19 And if a woman have an issue, *and* her issue in her flesh be blood, she shall be put apart seven days: and whosoever toucheth her shall be unclean until the even. 20 And every thing that she lieth upon in her separation shall be unclean: every thing also that she sitteth upon shall be unclean. 21 And whosoever toucheth her bed shall wash his clothes, and bathe *himself* in water, and be unclean until the even. 22 And whosoever toucheth any thing that she sat upon	shall wash his clothes, and bathe *himself* in water, and be unclean until the even. 23 And if it *be* on *her* bed, or on any thing whereon she sitteth, when he toucheth it, he shall be unclean until the even. 24 And if any man lie with her at all, and her flowers be upon him, he shall be unclean seven days; and all the bed whereon he lieth shall be unclean. 25 And if a woman have an issue of her blood many days out of the time of her separation, or if it run beyond	on: The person had to wash his clothes & self in water (a symbol of Christ, the living water) 4) Defiled the person who lay or sat where she was: Made a person unclean till evening 5) Defiled the person who had intercourse with her & was touched by her monthly period • He was unclean for seven days • He defiled any bed he lay on b. The discharge due to an abnormal flow or disease: Was counted unclean as long as the discharge continued

OUTLINE	SCRIPTURE	SCRIPTURE	OUTLINE
	the time of her separation; all the days of the issue of her uncleanness shall be as the days of her separation: she *shall be* unclean.	her issue, then she shall number to herself seven days, and after that she shall be clean.	from abnormal discharges
1) Defiled her bed & chair			1) Had to do the same as the man: Wash for seven days (a symbol of total cleansing)
	26 Every bed whereon she lieth all the days of her issue shall be unto her as the bed of her separation: and whatsoever she sitteth upon shall be unclean, as the uncleanness of her separation.	29 And on the eighth day she shall take unto her two turtles, or two young pigeons, and bring them unto the priest, to the door of the tabernacle of the congregation.	2) Had to approach God for cleansing on the eighth day—through the sacrifice (a symbol of Christ)
			3) Had to have the priest (a symbol of Christ) offer the sacrifice to God
2) Defiled the person who touched her bed & chair: Had to wash his clothes & self in water (a symbol of Christ, the living water)	27 And whosoever toucheth those things shall be unclean, and shall wash his clothes, and bathe *himself* in water, and be unclean until the even.	30 And the priest shall offer the one *for* a sin offering, and the other *for* a burnt offering; and the priest shall make an atonement for her before the LORD for the issue of her uncleanness.	• Offer the Sin Offering: Symbolized forgiveness • Offer the Burnt Offering: Symbolized atonement, reconciliation
			4) The result: Atonement, reconciliation with God
c. The cleansing of a woman	28 But if she be cleansed of		

Thought 1. A woman had to be cleansed from abnormal discharges the same as a man (vv.28-30). For every man who committed sexual immorality and suffered sexual disease, there was a woman just as guilty as he was except in the case of rape and incest. Therefore, there were women who were afflicted with sexual disease and needed to be cleansed as well. They, too, needed to be cleansed from sin and reconciled with God. A woman was cleansed by washing for seven days and then approaching God for cleansing on the eighth day—through the sacrifice. She had to approach God through the Sin Offering and the Burnt Offering. They too, needed to be cleansed from sin and reconciled with God.

The immoral woman needs to be cleansed just as much as the immoral man. She is just as alienated from God and just as guilty of sin as the man. Any woman who has committed sexual sin must be cleansed and have her sins forgiven through Jesus Christ. She must come to God through Christ. Christ and Christ alone can forgive her and reconcile her with God.

> **"And the scribes and Pharisees brought unto him a woman taken in adultery; and when they had set her in the midst, They say unto him, Master, this woman was taken in adultery, in the very act". When Jesus had lifted up himself, and saw none but the woman, he said unto her, Woman, where are those thine accusers? hath no man condemned thee? She said, No man, Lord. And Jesus said unto her, Neither do I condemn thee: go, and sin no more" (Jn.8:3-4, 10-11).**

> **"If I wash thee not, thou hast no part with me" (Jn.13:8).**

> **"But God commendeth his love toward us, in that, while we were yet sinners, Christ died for us" (Ro.5:8).**

> **"This *is* a faithful saying, and worthy of all acceptation, that Christ Jesus came into the world to save sinners; of whom I am chief" (1 Ti.1:15).**

> **"I acknowledged my sin unto thee, and mine iniquity have I not hid. I said, I will confess my transgressions unto the LORD; and thou forgavest the iniquity of my sin. Selah" (Ps.32:5).**

> **"If we confess our sins, he is faithful and just to forgive us our sins, and to cleanse us from all unrighteousness" (1 Jn.1:9).**

> **"In whom we have redemption through his blood, the forgiveness of sins, according to the riches of his grace" (Ep.1:7).**

> **"To wit, that God was in Christ, reconciling the world unto himself, not imputing their trespasses unto them; and hath committed unto us the word of reconciliation. Now then we are ambassadors for Christ, as though God did beseech you by us: we pray you in Christ's stead, be ye reconciled to God" (2 Co.5:19-20).**

4 (15:31-33) **Law, Governing Sexual Impurity—Law, Governing Bodily Discharges—Separation, Purpose**: there was the purpose for the laws that protect people from sexual impurity. Note the Scripture and outline:

OUTLINE	SCRIPTURE	SCRIPTURE	OUTLINE
4. **The purpose for the laws that protect people from sexual impurity** a. Separation: To keep God's people pure, separate from defilement b. Deliverance: To save a person from the penalty of sexual	31 Thus shall ye separate the children of Israel from their uncleanness; that they die not in their uncleanness, when they defile my tabernacle that *is* among them. 32 This *is* the law of him that hath an issue, and *of him*	whose seed goeth from him, and is defiled therewith; 33 And of her that is sick of her flowers, and of him that hath an issue, of the man, and of the woman, and of him that lieth with her that is unclean.	sin, that is, death c. Protection: To guard the public & to govern the cases of sexual impurity among both men & women

180

a. There was the purpose of separation: to keep God's people pure, separate from defilement (v.31). God wanted and still wants His people to be separate from any person or thing that would make them sexually unclean. Note how serious sexual uncleanness was: if an unclean person entered the Tabernacle, he defiled the very dwelling place of God. God was teaching His people an important fact: sexual impurity defiles His very presence. Sexual impurity is against His holy nature, against His will and purpose in creating people. He created people to live together in families, fully attached to one another and learning the great virtues of...

- loyalty and faithfulness
- trust and faith
- assurance and confidence
- commitment and dedication
- love and security
- child-bearing and nurturing

On and on the great virtues of life could be listed as being learned in the family situation. The point is this: God wanted His people to learn the principle of separation, that they absolutely must keep themselves pure, separate from any sexual defilement whatsoever. In this way, the marriage bond, family life, and the great virtues of life would be kept strong.

"**Depart ye, depart ye, go ye out from thence, touch no unclean thing**" (Is.52:11).

"**And have no fellowship with the unfruitful works of darkness, but rather reprove them. For it is a shame even to speak of those things which are done of them in secret**" (Ep.5:11-12).

"**Wherefore come out from among them, and be ye separate, saith the Lord, and touch not the unclean thing; and I will receive you, And will be a Father unto you, and ye shall be my sons and daughters, saith the Lord Almighty**" (2 Co.6:17-18).

"**Love not the world, neither the things that are in the world. If any man love the world, the love of the Father is not in him. For all that is in the world, the lust of the flesh, and the lust of the eyes, and the pride of life, is not of the Father, but is of the world**" (1 Jn.2:15-16).

"**And be not conformed to this world: but be ye transformed by the renewing of your mind, that ye may prove what is that good, and acceptable, and perfect, will of God**" (Ro.12:2).

b. There was the purpose of deliverance: to save a person from the penalty of sexual sin which was, and still is, death (v.31). Remember, a person who had some venereal disease was guilty of sexual sin before God. He was unclean and could not participate in the worship of God at the Tabernacle. If he did, he defiled the Tabernacle. The penalty for this was death. The point stands as a severe warning to God's people. Sexual sin defiles God's presence. No person can stand before God, not now nor eternally, if he is guilty of sexual sin. This is exactly what Holy Scripture declares.

"**Ye have heard that it was said by them of old time, Thou shalt not commit adultery: But I say unto you, That whosoever looketh on a woman to lust after her hath committed adultery with her already in his heart**" (Mt.5:27-28).

"**Know ye not that the unrighteous shall not inherit the kingdom of God? Be not deceived: neither fornicators, nor idolaters, nor adulterers, nor effeminate, nor abusers of themselves with mankind, Nor thieves, nor covetous, nor drunkards, nor revilers, nor extortioners, shall inherit the kingdom of God**" (1 Co.6:9-10).

"**Now the works of the flesh are manifest, which are these; Adultery, fornication, uncleanness, lasciviousness, Idolatry, witchcraft, hatred, variance, emulations, wrath, strife, seditions, heresies**" (Ga.5:19-20).

"**Marriage is honourable in all, and the bed undefiled: but whoremongers and adulterers God will judge**" (He.13:4).

"**But the fearful, and unbelieving, and the abominable, and murderers, and whoremongers, and sorcerers, and idolaters, and all liars, shall have their part in the lake which burneth with fire and brimstone: which is the second death**" (Re.21:8).

c. There was the purpose of protection: to guard the public; to govern the cases of sexual sin and impurity among both men and women (v.32). God was concerned that His people learn both sexual hygiene and spiritual purity. Sexual diseases are transmittable and very contagious. Sexual diseases are also uncomfortable and cause some pain, sometimes severe pain and even death. Sexual diseases are some of the most contagious diseases on earth. Yet, they are the most ignored and overlooked diseases among people. Why? Because sex is of the very nature of man and it is one of the most intimate, enjoyable experiences of life. Moreover, it boosts the ego and esteem of a person, giving a sense of meeting someone else's need and of having one's own need met. All this is a subject for later discussion. For now, the point to see is this: God gave these laws to guard the public and to govern the cases of sexual impurity.

"**Thou shalt not commit adultery**" (Ex.20:14).

"**Ye have heard that it was said by them of old time, Thou shalt not commit adultery: But I say unto you, That whosoever looketh on a woman to lust after her hath committed adultery with her already in his heart**" (Mt.5:27-28).

"**Let not sin therefore reign in your mortal body, that ye should obey it in the lusts thereof. Neither yield ye your members as instruments of unrighteousness unto sin: but yield yourselves unto God, as those that are alive from the dead, and your members as instruments of righteousness unto God**" (Ro.6:12-13).

"I speak after the manner of men because of the infirmity of your flesh: for as ye have yielded your members servants to uncleanness and to iniquity unto iniquity; even so now yield your members servants to righteousness unto holiness" (Ro.6:19).

"For this is the will of God, even your sanctification, that ye should abstain from fornication" (1 Th.4:3).

"Now concerning the things whereof ye wrote unto me: It is good for a man not to touch a woman. Nevertheless, to avoid fornication, let every man have his own wife, and let every woman have her own husband" (1 Co.7:1-2).

"That they may teach the young women to be sober, to love their husbands, to love their children, To be discreet, chaste, keepers at home, good, obedient to their own husbands, that the word of God be not blasphemed. Young men likewise exhort to be sober minded" (Tit.2:4-6).

"And why wilt thou, my son, be ravished with a strange woman, and embrace the bosom of a stranger? For the ways of man are before the eyes of the LORD, and he pondereth all his goings" (Pr.5:20-21).

TYPES, SYMBOLS, AND PICTURES
Leviticus 15:1-33

Historical Term	Type or Picture (Scriptural Basis for Each)	Life Application for Today's Believer	Biblical Application
Laws That Protected and Cleansed People from Sexual Diseases and Impurity Le. 15:1-33	*These laws symbolize how defiling sexual sin is and the need to be cleansed.* "**Thus shall ye separate the children of Israel from their uncleanness; that they die not in their uncleanness, when they defile my tabernacle that** *is* **among them**" (Le.15:31).	God cares about the sexual behavior of His people. He wants them sexually healthy, free from venereal or sexual disease. He wants them living moral, pure, and clean lives. He wants His people to handle sex with appreciation and enjoyment, but with honor and respect, and always keeping sex pure within marriage. Sex is only for husband and wife, given as a gift to them and only to them.	"*For ye know what commandments we gave you by the Lord Jesus. For this is the will of God, even your sanctification, that ye should abstain from fornication: That every one of you should know how to possess his vessel in sanctification and honour; Not in the lust of concupiscence, even as the Gentiles which know not God*" (1 Th.4:2-5). "*Flee fornication. Every sin that a man doeth is without the body; but he that committeth fornication sinneth against his own body*" (1 Co.6:18). "*Mortify therefore your members which are upon the earth; fornication, uncleanness, inordinate affection, evil concupiscence, and covetousness, which is idolatry*" (Col.3:5).
Washing Clothes and Bathing in Water for the Bodily Discharges and Cleansing of Men and Women Le. 15:2-18; 19-30	*Washing clothes and bathing in water is a symbol of being cleansed through Christ, the water of life.* "**Speak unto the children of Israel, and say unto them, When any man hath a running issue out of his flesh, because of his issue he is unclean**" (Le.15:2). "**And if a woman have an issue,** *and* **her issue in her flesh be blood, she shall be put apart seven days: and whosoever toucheth her shall be unclean until the even**" (Le.15:19).	A sexually impure person must come to Jesus Christ for washing and cleansing. He or she needs to be cleansed from sin and reconciled with God. Immorality—sexual impurity—separates and alienates a person from God. A person who is sexually impure must approach God through Jesus Christ for reconciliation and forgiveness of sins.	"*For God sent not his Son into the world to condemn the world; but that the world through him might be saved*" (Jn.3:17). "*And all things are of God, who hath reconciled us to himself by Jesus Christ, and hath given to us the ministry of reconciliation; To wit, that God was in Christ, reconciling the world unto himself, not imputing their trespasses unto them; and hath committed unto us the word of reconciliation. Now then we are ambassadors for Christ, as though God did beseech you by us: we pray you in Christ's stead, be ye reconciled to God*" (2 Co.5:18-20).

TYPES, SYMBOLS, AND PICTURES
Leviticus 15:1-33

Historical Term	Type or Picture (Scriptural Basis for Each)	Life Application for Today's Believer	Biblical Application
			"In whom we have redemption through his blood, the forgiveness of sins, according to the riches of his grace" (Ep.1:7). *"Who his own self bare our sins in his own body on the tree, that we, being dead to sins, should live unto righteousness: by whose stripes ye were healed"* (1 Pe.2:24). *"For Christ also hath once suffered for sins, the just for the unjust, that he might bring us to God, being put to death in the flesh, but quickened by the Spirit"* (1 Pe.3:18).
The Person Who Suffered from a Sexual Disease: Defiled Any Clay Pot or Wood He Touched. The Item Had to Be Washed and Cleansed with Water Le. 15:12	*This is a symbol of the defiling, polluting nature of sin. The washing and cleansing of the pot or wood is a symbol of Christ cleansing all things. Any clay pot or wood that was defiled [touched] by an unclean person had to be rinsed with water.* **"And the vessel of earth, that he toucheth which hath the issue, shall be broken: and every vessel of wood shall be rinsed in water"** (Le.15:12).	It is the blood of Jesus Christ that cleanses us from the defilement of sin. His blood cleanses us from all things, no matter how terrible the sin—if we just repent and confess our sins.	*"For this is my blood of the new testament, which is shed for many for the remission of sins"* (Mt.26:28). *"In whom we have redemption through his blood, the forgiveness of sins, according to the riches of his grace"* (Ep.1:7). *"If we confess our sins, he is faithful and just to forgive us our sins, and to cleanse us from all unrighteousness."* (1 Jn.1:9)
The Cleansing of a Person from Sexual Impurity. He Had to Wash His Clothes and Himself with Fresh Water for Seven Days Le. 15:13	*Washing with water for seven days is a symbol of complete and full cleansing.* **"And when he that hath an issue is cleansed of his issue; then he shall number to himself seven days for his cleansing, and wash his clothes, and bathe his flesh in running water, and shall be clean"** (Le.15:13).	The believer has absolute confidence in the cleansing power of Christ. He knows that *God will* forgive Him—completely and fully. God will complete the work He began in him.	*"Jesus saith unto them, My meat is to do the will of him that sent me, and to finish his work"* (Jn.4:34). *"I have glorified thee on the earth: I have finished the work which thou gavest me to do"* (Jn.17:4). *"Be it known unto you therefore, men and brethren, that through this man is preached unto you the forgiveness of sins"* (Ac.13:38). *"Being confident of this very thing, that he which hath begun a good work in you will perform it until the day of Jesus Christ"* (Phil.1:6). *"Who forgiveth all thine iniquities; who healeth all thy diseases"* (Ps.103:3).
A Sacrifice of Two Doves or Two Young Pigeons Le. 15:14-15	*A sacrifice of two doves or two young pigeons on the eighth day is a symbol of*	There is only one way any of us can be forgiven—whether priest, minister, or	*"To whom it [righteousness] shall be imputed, if we believe on him that*

TYPES, SYMBOLS, AND PICTURES
Leviticus 15:1-33

Historical Term	Type or Picture (Scriptural Basis for Each)	Life Application for Today's Believer	Biblical Application
	Christ cleansing a man from sexual impurity. Note how clearly the sacrifice symbolizes Jesus Christ. Christ died as our substitute: on our behalf, in our stead, in our place. He died to cleanse a person from sexual impurity. **"And on the eighth day he shall take to him two turtledoves, or two young pigeons, and come before the LORD unto the door of the tabernacle of the congregation, and give them unto the priest"** (Le. 15:14).	layperson: we must present ourselves to God in the substitute sacrifice, in the Lord Jesus Christ. Christ is the only sacrifice acceptable to God. He is the only sacrifice that can cleanse a person from sexual sin. Forgiveness of sins comes only through Him: He is the one and only acceptable sacrifice.	*raised up Jesus our Lord from the dead; who was delivered for our offences, and was raised again for our justification"* (Ro.4:24-25). *"For he hath made him to be sin for us, who knew no sin; that we might be made the righteousness of God in him"* (2 Co.5:21).
The Normal Bodily Discharges (Excretion), of a Man: Had to Bathe with Water Le. 15:16	*Bathing with water is a symbol of being cleansed from disease in Christ, the water of life.* **"And if any man's seed of copulation go out from him, then he shall wash all his flesh in water, and be unclean until the even"** (Le.15:16).	It is the shed blood of Jesus Christ that washes the believer and cleanses him from the stain of sin.	*"Jesus saith to him, He that is washed needeth not save to wash his feet, but is clean every whit: and ye are clean, but not all"* (Jn. 13:10). *"Wash me throughly from mine iniquity, and cleanse me from my sin"* (Ps.51:2). *"Purge me with hyssop, and I shall be clean: wash me, and I shall be whiter than snow"* (Ps.51:7). *"There is a generation that are pure in their own eyes, and yet is not washed from their filthiness"* (Pr. 30:12).
Clothing with Semen On It: Had to Be Washed with Water (Le. 15:17)	*Washing soiled clothes with water is a symbol of being clothed with purity.* **"And every garment, and every skin, whereon is the seed of copulation, shall be washed with water, and be unclean until the even"** (Le.15:17).	God wants us to keep ourselves clean and pure, both physically and spiritually.	*"Having therefore these promises, dearly beloved, let us cleanse ourselves from all filthiness of the flesh and spirit, perfecting holiness in the fear of God"* (2 Co.7:1). *"Let us draw near with a true heart in full assurance of faith, having our hearts sprinkled from an evil conscience, and our bodies washed with pure water"* (He.10:22). *"Wash you, make you clean; put away the evil of your doings from before mine eyes; cease to do evil"* (Is.1:16).

CHAPTER 16

F. The Great Provision of God to Make a Person Holy, the Great Day of Atonement: Symbolizes the Only Way to Approach God—Through the Shed Blood of the Atoning Sacrifice, 16:1-34

And the LORD spake unto Moses after the death of the two sons of Aaron, when they offered before the LORD, and died;

2 And the LORD said unto Moses, Speak unto Aaron thy brother, that he come not at all times into the holy *place* within the vail before the mercy seat, which *is* upon the ark; that he die not: for I will appear in the cloud upon the mercy seat.

3 Thus shall Aaron come into the holy *place*: with a young bullock for a sin offering, and a ram for a burnt offering.

4 He shall put on the holy linen coat, and he shall have the linen breeches upon his flesh, and shall be girded with a linen girdle, and with the linen mitre shall he be attired: these *are* holy garments; therefore shall he wash his flesh in water, and *so* put them on.

5 And he shall take of the congregation of the children of Israel two kids of the goats for a sin offering, and one ram for a burnt offering.

6 And Aaron shall offer his bullock of the sin offering, which *is* for himself, and make an atonement for himself, and for his house.

7 And he shall take the two goats, and present them before the LORD *at* the door of the tabernacle of the congregation.

8 And Aaron shall cast lots upon the two goats; one lot for the LORD, and the other lot for the scapegoat.

9 And Aaron shall bring the goat upon which the LORD's lot fell, and offer him *for* a sin offering.

10 But the goat, on which the lot fell to be the scape-goat, shall be presented alive before the LORD, to make an atonement with him, *and* to let him go for a scapegoat into the wilderness.

11 And Aaron shall bring the bullock of the sin offering, which *is* for himself, and shall make an atonement for himself, and for his house, and shall kill the bullock of the sin offering which *is* for himself:

12 And he shall take a censer full of burning coals of fire from off the altar before the LORD, and his hands full of sweet incense beaten small, and bring *it* within the vail:

13 And he shall put the incense upon the fire before the LORD, that the cloud of the incense may cover the mercy seat that *is* upon the testimony, that he die not:

14 And he shall take of the blood of the bullock, and sprinkle *it* with his finger upon the mercy seat eastward; and before the mercy seat shall he sprinkle of the blood with his finger seven times.

15 Then shall he kill the goat of the sin offering, that *is* for the people, and bring his blood within the vail, and do with that blood as he did with the blood of the bullock, and sprinkle it upon the mercy seat, and before the mercy seat:

16 And he shall make an atonement for the holy *place*, because of the uncleanness of the children of Israel, and because of their transgressions in all their sins: and so shall he do for the tabernacle of the congregation, that remaineth among them in the midst of their uncleanness.

17 And there shall be no man in the tabernacle of the congregation when he goeth in to make an atonement in the holy *place*, until he come out, and have made an atonement for himself, and for his household, and for all the congregation of Israel.

18 And he shall go out unto the altar that *is* before the

1. There must be the correct approach to God

a. There is a wrong approach: Seen in the self-righteous approach of Aaron's sons (10:1-3)

b. There is a right approach: Acknowledging one's utter sinfulness & God's majestic holiness
   1) Man's sinfulness cannot enter God's presence (the Most Holy Place) apart from the shed blood of the sacrifice
   2) God's holiness: Man would confront the holy presence of God & die apart from the shed blood

2. There must be the correct preparation made by the High Priest (a symbol of Christ)

a. He must be prepared to present the right sacrifice before God (a Sin Offering & a Burnt Offering)

b. He must wash himself & put on the right clothing

c. He must be prepared with the right sacrifice for the people (the Sin Offering & the Burnt Offering)

d. He must be prepared to offer the sacrifice himself, to make atonement for himself & his household

e. He must immediately be ready to present the right sacrifice to the LORD for the people

   1) Must cast lots to determine which goat will be sacrificed & which will be the scapegoat
   2) Must be ready to offer the sacrifice goat as a Sin Offering
   3) Must be ready to present the scapegoat to the LORD

& send it away as atonement: Symbolizes reconciliation by the removal of sin

3. There must be the righteous, sinless standing of the High Priest before God (a symbol of Christ)

a. He had to approach God for himself thru the Sin Offering: Symbolized standing sinless & perfect before God— thru the sacrifice

b. He had to provide protection against the holy & just presence of God
   1) Symbolized by creating a smoke screen to conceal the atonement cover & to keep him from gazing upon God's Holy Presence
   2) The purpose: To keep him from being stricken dead by the blazing holiness of God

c. He had to secure mercy— forgiveness of sins—thru the shed blood of the sacrifice
   1) Sprinkled the atonement cover with the blood
   2) Sprinkled the Ark seven times (symbolizes full, perfect mercy & forgiveness)

4. There must be the atoning sacrifice—the covering & taking away of sin—for the people

a. By putting to death the sacrifice for the Sin Offering
   1) To take the blood into the Most Holy Place & sprinkle the atonement cover (Mercy Seat)
   - Secured atonement—the covering of sins—for the Most Holy Place
   - The reason: An absolute necessity because of the infectious sin & rebellion of the people
   2) To do the same for the entire Tabernacle: Because it is contaminated by their uncleanness
   3) To be acknowledged, honored as the only person who can secure atonement for people (symbolizes that Christ alone can reconcile a person to God)
   4) To make atonement for the altar of Burnt Offering

- By putting some blood on the horns of the altar

- By sprinkling blood on the altar seven times (symbolized full, perfect cleansing)
- The reason: To cleanse & consecrate the altar from the uncleanness of the people

b. By presenting the scapegoat to the LORD

1) To symbolically lay all the sins & rebellion of the people upon the scapegoat: By laying both hands on its head & confessing all their sins

2) To symbolically remove & take away the people's sin
- By sending the scapegoat away
- By letting the scapegoat carry their sins upon itself into a far, desolate land

5. There must be an acknowledgment that cleansing & sacrifice are necessary for reconciliation with God

a. The High Priest & the people acknowledged the need for cleansing & sacrifice
1) He had to put on the High Priestly clothes to offer the blood of the sacrifice
2) He had to sacrifice the Burnt Offering for himself & the people: To make atonement
3) He also had to burn the fat of the Sin Offering: Symbolized a sweet smell of acceptance by God

b. The shepherd of the scapegoat acknowledged the need for cleansing & sacrifice: By not

LORD, and make an atonement for it; and shall take of the blood of the bullock, and of the blood of the goat, and put *it* upon the horns of the altar round about.

19 And he shall sprinkle of the blood upon it with his finger seven times, and cleanse it, and hallow it from the uncleanness of the children of Israel.

20 And when he hath made an end of reconciling the holy *place*, and the tabernacle of the congregation, and the altar, he shall bring the live goat:

21 And Aaron shall lay both his hands upon the head of the live goat, and confess over him all the iniquities of the children of Israel, and all their transgressions in all their sins, putting them upon the head of the goat, and shall send *him* away by the hand of a fit man into the wilderness:

22 And the goat shall bear upon him all their iniquities unto a land not inhabited: and he shall let go the goat in the wilderness.

23 And Aaron shall come into the tabernacle of the congregation, and shall put off the linen garments, which he put on when he went into the holy *place*, and shall leave them there:

24 And he shall wash his flesh with water in the holy place, and put on his garments, and come forth, and offer his burnt offering, and the burnt offering of the people, and make an atonement for himself, and for the people.

25 And the fat of the sin offering shall he burn upon the altar.

26 And he that let go the goat for the scapegoat shall wash his clothes, and bathe his flesh in water, and

afterward come into the camp.

27 And the bullock *for* the sin offering, and the goat *for* the sin offering, whose blood was brought in to make atonement in the holy *place*, shall *one* carry forth without the camp; and they shall burn in the fire their skins, and their flesh, and their dung.

28 And he that burneth them shall wash his clothes, and bathe his flesh in water, and afterward he shall come into the camp.

29 And *this* shall be a statute for ever unto you: *that* in the seventh month, on the tenth *day* of the month, ye shall afflict your souls, and do no work at all, *whether it be* one of your own country, or a stranger that sojourneth among you:

30 For on that day shall *the priest* make an atonement for you, to cleanse you, *that* ye may be clean from all your sins before the LORD.

31 It *shall be* a sabbath of rest unto you, and ye shall afflict your souls, by a statute for ever.

32 And the priest, whom he shall anoint, and whom he shall consecrate to minister in the priest's office in his father's stead, shall make the atonement, and shall put on the linen clothes, *even* the holy garments:

33 And he shall make an atonement for the holy sanctuary, and he shall make an atonement for the tabernacle of the congregation, and for the altar, and he shall make an atonement for the priests, and for all the people of the congregation.

34 And this shall be an everlasting statute unto you, to make an atonement for the children of Israel for all their sins once a year. And he did as the LORD commanded Moses.

entering the camp until he had washed himself & his clothes
c. The people acknowledged the need for cleansing & sacrifice by having the hides, organs, & dung taken outside the camp & burned: Symbolized the judgment upon sin

d. The man who burned the waste of the sacrifice acknowledged the need for cleansing & sacrifice: By not entering the camp until he had washed himself & his clothes

6. There must be a permanent observance of this great day, the Day of Atonement
a. The specific date set: The 10th day of the seventh month
b. The duty of the people: To fast & do no work

c. The reason: Because the most important event in life was taking place—atonement, reconciliation with God, cleansing from sin was taking place
d. The importance of the day: Is to be a Sabbath day of total rest—must fast when observing the day of atonement
e. The absolute, essential requirement: The High Priest alone is to make atonement (a symbol of Christ)
1) He also puts on the sacred garments

2) He alone makes atonement

f. The limitation placed on the observance
1) To be a permanent observance
2) To be observed only once a year
g. The obedience of God's people

DIVISION III

THE WAY TO LIVE A HOLY LIFE BEFORE GOD (PART I): BY A CLEAN BODY (SEPARATION), 11:1–16:34

F.   The Great Provision of God to Make a Person Holy, the Great Day of Atonement: Symbolizes the Only Way to Approach God—Through the Shed Blood of the Atoning Sacrifice, 16:1-34

(16:1-34) Introduction—Sin, Forgiveness of—Reconciliation, Importance of—Judgment—Justice, of God: the greatest need in all the world is for forgiveness of sin and reconciliation with God. Why? How can this be said to be the greatest need of man? Because of the judgment of God. There is a day of judgment coming. This is the teaching of God throughout the Holy Scripture. We must always keep one fact in mind: there is a difference between the religious literature of religionists and Holy Scripture. The Holy Scripture is the Word of the living and true God, the Creator of the universe and the Sovereign Lord and Majesty of all. It is the only living and true God who warns: there is a day of judgment coming, a day of accounting, a day when every human being of every generation must stand before God and face the judgment of God.

"And as it is appointed unto men once to die, but after this the judgment" (He.9:27).

Some day out in the future, the terrible day of God's wrath against sin and evil is coming. Nothing—no person and no thing—can prevent God from executing justice. Justice will be executed by God. Nothing can stop the justice and judgment of God...
- not denial
- not ignorance
- not neglect
- not the best effort to escape

The justice and judgment of God are going to be executed upon the earth and throughout the whole universe. People, angels, and any other beings living anyplace throughout the universe will face the judgment of God. This is what makes forgiveness and reconciliation with God so important. Forgiveness of sins and reconciliation with God are absolute essentials in order to live with God. God accepts no person whose sins have not been forgiven, no person who has not been reconciled with Him.

The point is this: sin has separated and alienated man from God. There is a mass of sin that hangs over man's head, a mass of sin that has been committed in age after age. Sin has created a barrier of uncleanness between man and God. This barrier of sin and uncleanness has to be taken away and removed or else man has to face the judgment of God. Justice demands judgment. But this is the wonderful message of this passage: sin has been taken away and uncleanness has been removed. Justice and judgment have been executed. The penalty for sin has been paid. How? By Jesus Christ. Jesus Christ died as our *substitutionary sacrifice*. Hanging upon the cross, Jesus Christ...
- bore our sins, taking them away
- died for our uncleanness, removing it
- allowed the justice and judgment of God to be executed against Him, suffering our punishment
- paid the penalty of death, bearing the alienation and separation from God for us

This is the strong declaration of this passage: *The Great Provision of God to Make a Person Holy, the Great Day of Atonement: Symbolizes the Only Way to Approach God—Through the Shed Blood of the Atoning Sacrifice*, 16:1-34.
1. There must be the correct approach to God (vv.1-2).
2. There must be the correct preparation made by the High Priest (a symbol of Christ) (vv.3-10).
3. There must be the righteous, sinless standing of the High Priest before God (vv.11-14).
4. There must be the atoning sacrifice—the covering and taking away of sin—for the people (vv.15-22).
5. There must be an acknowledgment that cleansing and sacrifice are necessary for reconciliation with God (vv.23-28).
6. There must be a permanent observance of this great day, the Day of Atonement (vv.29-34).

1 **(16:1-2) Approach - Approaching God—Holiness, of God—Sinfulness, of Man—Man, Sinfulness of**: there must be the correct approach to God. Note the scripture and outline:

OUTLINE	SCRIPTURE
1. There must be the correct approach to God a. There is a wrong approach: Seen in the self-righteous approach of Aaron's sons (10:1-3) b. There is a right approach: Acknowledging one's utter sinfulness & God's majestic holiness 1) Man's sinfulness cannot enter God's presence (the Most Holy Place) apart from the shed blood of the sacrifice 2) God's Holiness: Man would confront the holy presence of God & die apart from the shed blood	And the LORD spake unto Moses after the death of the two sons of Aaron, when they offered before the LORD, and died; 2 And the LORD said unto Moses, Speak unto Aaron thy brother, that he come not at all times into the holy *place* within the vail before the mercy seat, which *is* upon the ark; that he die not: for I will appear in the cloud upon the mercy seat.

a. There is a wrong way to approach God. This is seen in the self-righteous approach of Aaron's two sons, Nadab and Abihu (see outline and notes—Le.10:1-3). These two sons apparently entered the Most Holy Place of the Tabernacle where the Ark of the Covenant sat. The Ark of the Covenant symbolized the very throne of God Himself, the throne upon which He sat in all of His majestic glory and holiness. Only the High Priest was allowed to enter the Most Holy Place, and he was allowed to enter only once a year—on this great day when atonement was made for the sins of the people. Consequently, when these two sons of Aaron entered the Holy Place, the pure energy and brilliance of God's holiness struck them dead. They had approached God as they wished, in their own way, totally contrary to what God had instructed. Therefore the justice and judgment of God had to be executed: they had approached Him in a wrong way, in their own self-righteousness. But note: right after their deaths, the LORD told Moses to inform Aaron how to approach Him.

b. There is a right way to approach God. This is by acknowledging one's utter sinfulness and the majestic holiness of God (v.2). Man's sinfulness cannot enter God's presence, not the Most Holy Place, not apart from the shed blood of the sacrifice. Even Aaron was not able to enter the Most Holy Place whenever he chose. He was not to go behind the curtain for the Ark of the Covenant, the very Atonement Cover or Mercy Seat and God was there. The reason is stated above: the very presence of God was symbolized as being seated upon the Mercy Seat or Atonement Cover. This was the very place of atonement, the place where atonement (reconciliation) was first brought about. Moreover, the pure, perfect energy and light of God's blazing holiness dwelt in the Most Holy Place behind the inner curtain or veil. Any person who entered God's presence would confront the blazing holiness of God and die apart from the shed blood. This is the message God wanted conveyed to Aaron, and through him to all of us, to every person down through the ages. There is a wrong approach to God, the approach of self-righteousness that will lead to death. But there is a right approach to God: the acknowledging of one's utter sinfulness and the majestic holiness of God. This is the approach that comes to God through the shed blood of the sacrifice. A person's sins must first be removed, taken away, before he can approach God and be accepted by God.

> **Thought 1**. Sin has separated and alienated man from God. Sin has created a veil, a curtain, between God and man. The curtain of sin cannot be removed by man, no matter how much he tries. No matter how righteous man seeks to be, his righteousness cannot break through the curtain of sin that separates him from God. But thank God! Jesus Christ has ripped the curtain of sin from top to bottom, opening the way into God's presence. Man now has access into the presence of God. All of us—without exception—can now enter the presence of God, all because of what Jesus Christ has done.
>
> **"But your iniquities have separated between you and your God, and your sins have hid his face from you, that he will not hear" (Is.59:2).**
>
> **"Jesus, when he had cried again with a loud voice, yielded up the ghost. And, behold, the veil of the temple [that separated man from God] was rent in twain from the top to the bottom; and the earth did quake, and the rocks rent" (Mt.27:50-51).**
>
> **"Having therefore, brethren, boldness to enter into the holiest by the blood of Jesus, By a new and living way, which he hath consecrated for us, through the veil, that is to say, his flesh; And having an high priest over the house of God; Let us draw near with a true heart in full assurance of faith, having our hearts sprinkled from an evil conscience, and our bodies washed with pure water" (He.10:19-22).**
>
> **"Therefore being justified by faith, we have peace with God through our Lord Jesus Christ: By whom also we have access by faith into this grace wherein we stand, and rejoice in hope of the glory of God" (Ro.5:1-2).**
>
> **"For through him we both have access by one Spirit unto the Father" (Ep.2:18).**

2 (16:3-10) **High Priest, Duty of—Clothing, Symbol of—Sacrifice, Animal—Animal Sacrifice—Scapegoat—Sin, Forgiveness of—Forgiveness, of Sin—Lots, Casting of—Atonement—Sin Offering—Burnt Offering**: there must be the correct preparation made by the High Priest. Note that the High Priest is a symbol of Jesus Christ. These verses are telling Aaron how he was to approach God and offer the sacrifices to God. The actual sacrifices begin with the next point. These instructions cover only the preparation the High Priest was to make to enter the sanctuary area (v.3). Note the scripture and outline.

OUTLINE	SCRIPTURE	SCRIPTURE	OUTLINE
2. There must be the correct preparation made by the High Priest (a symbol of Christ) a. He must be prepared to present the right sacrifice before God (a sin offering & a burnt offering) b. He must wash himself & put on the right clothing	3 Thus shall Aaron come into the holy *place*: with a young bullock for a sin offering, and a ram for a burnt offering. 4 He shall put on the holy linen coat, and he shall have the linen breeches upon his flesh, and shall be girded with a linen girdle, and with the linen mitre shall he be attired: these *are* holy garments; therefore shall he	wash his flesh in water, and *so* put them on. 5 And he shall take of the congregation of the children of Israel two kids of the goats for a sin offering, and one ram for a burnt offering. 6 And Aaron shall offer his bullock of the sin offering, which *is* for himself, and make an atonement for himself, and for his house 7 And he shall take the two	c. He must be prepared with the right sacrifice for the people (the sin offering & the burnt offering) d. He must be prepared to offer the sacrifice himself, to make atonement for himself & his household e. He must immediately be ready

OUTLINE	SCRIPTURE	SCRIPTURE	OUTLINE
to present the right sacrifice to the LORD for the people	goats, and present them before the LORD *at* the door of the tabernacle of the congregation.	LORD's lot fell, and offer him *for* a sin offering.	
	8 And Aaron shall cast lots upon the two goats; one lot for the LORD, and the other lot for the scapegoat.	10 But the goat, on which the lot fell to be the scapegoat, shall be presented alive before the	3) Must be ready to present the scapegoat to the LORD & send it away as atonement: Symbolizes reconciliation by the removal of sin
1) Must cast lots to determine which goat will be sacrificed & which will be the scapegoat		LORD, to make an atonement with him, *and* to let	
2) Must be ready to offer the sacrifice goat as a sin offering	9 And Aaron shall bring the goat upon which the	him go for a scapegoat into the wilderness.	

a. He must be prepared to present the right sacrifice before God. He had to secure a young bull for a Sin Offering and a ram for a Burnt Offering (v.3).

b. He must wash himself and put on the right clothing (v.4). He had to take off the beautiful and glorious clothing of the High Priest and put on a very special set of clothing in order to make the atoning sacrifice for sin. The clothing included a tunic or shirt, an undergarment, a sash, and a turban—all made of white linen. The clothing of the High Priest symbolizes righteousness. The High Priest, who was to make the sacrifice for sins, had to be clothed in the white linen of righteousness. He had to stand by God sinless, in projection.

c. He must be prepared with the right sacrifice for the people. He had to secure two male goats for a Sin Offering and a ram for the Burnt Offering (v.5).

d. He must be prepared to offer the sacrifice himself, to make atonement for himself and his household (v.6). He was to offer the bull for his own Sin Offering to make atonement for himself and his family.

e. He must immediately be ready to present the right sacrifice to the LORD for the people (v.7). He was to take the two goats and present them before the LORD at the entrance of the Tabernacle. At the entrance, he was to cast lots for the two goats to determine which goat would be sacrificed and which would be the scapegoat (v.8). He was to prepare himself and be ready to offer the sacrificed goat as a Sin Offering. He was to be ready to present the scapegoat to the LORD and send it away as atonement. The scapegoat was to symbolize that people are reconciled to God by the removal of their sins (v.10).

Thought 1. The High Priest is a symbol of Jesus Christ. The pure white linen clothing of the High Priest symbolized the clothing of righteousness, the righteousness of Jesus Christ. Jesus Christ stands before God clothed in perfect righteousness. As perfect, His righteousness is the ideal righteousness, the pattern of all righteousness. As the ideal and pattern, His righteousness can cover all men everywhere and present them righteous before God. No person stands before God in his own righteousness: he can stand before God only in the righteousness of Jesus Christ.

"For Christ is the end of the law for righteousness to every one that believeth" (Ro.10:4).

"But of him are ye in Christ Jesus, who of God is made unto us wisdom, and righteousness, and sanctification, and redemption" (1 Co.1:30).

"For he hath made him to be sin for us, who knew no sin; that we might be made the righteousness of God in him" (2 Co.5:21).

"And be found in him, not having mine own righteousness, which is of the law, but that which is through the faith of Christ, the righteousness which is of God by faith" (Ph.3:9).

"He that overcometh, the same shall be clothed in white raiment; and I will not blot his name of the book of life, but I will confess his name before my Father, and before his angels" (Re.3:5).

"I counsel thee to buy of me gold tried in the fire, that thou mayest be rich; and white raiment, that thou mayest be clothed, and that the shame of thy nakedness do not appear; and anoint thine eyes with eyesalve, that thou mayest see" (Re.3:18).

"After this I beheld, and, lo, a great multitude, which no man could number, of all nations, and kindreds, and people, and tongues, stood before the throne, and before the Lamb, clothed with white robes, and palms in their hands" (Re.7:9).

"And to her was granted that she should be arrayed in fine linen, clean and white: for the fine linen is the righteousness of saints" (Re.19:8).

Thought 2. Why were two goats used in the Sin Offering? Very simply, because no single picture can fully demonstrate what Christ has done for us by forgiving our sins.

(1) The goat that was sacrificed symbolized the sacrifice of Christ, the ransom price He paid to set us free from sin.

"Who gave himself for our sins, that he might deliver us from this present evil world, according to the will of God and our Father" (Ga.1:4).

"Who gave himself for us, that he might redeem us from all iniquity, and purify unto himself a peculiar people, zealous of good works" (Tit.2:14).

"For Christ also hath once suffered for sins, the just for the unjust, that he might bring us to God, being put to death in the flesh, but quickened by the Spirit" (1 Pe.3:18).

(2) The other goat, the scapegoat that was sent away alive bearing the sins of the people, symbolized the removal and taking away of sin—all through the sacrifice of Christ.

"So Christ was once offered to bear the sins of many; and unto them that look for him shall he appear the second time without sin unto salvation" (He.9:28).

"Who his own self bare our sins in his own body on the tree, that we, being dead to sins, should live unto righteousness: by whose stripes ye were healed" (1 Pe.2:24).

"And ye know that he was manifested to take away our sins; and in him is no sin" (1 Jn.3:5).

"But he was wounded for our transgressions, he was bruised for our iniquities: the chastisement of our peace was upon him; and with his stripes we are healed" (Is.53:5).

"Therefore will I divide him a portion with the great, and he shall divide the spoil with the strong; because he hath poured out his soul unto death: and he was numbered with the transgressors; and he bare the sin of many, and made intercession for the transgressors" (Is.53:12).

---

3 (16:11-14) **High Priest, Needs of—Holiness, of God—Atonement—Forgiveness of Sins, Need for—Sin Offering—Offering, the Sin—Sacrifice, Animal**: there must be the righteous, sinless standing of the High Priest before God. The High Priest had to prepare himself before he could make a sacrifice for the people. Note the scripture and outlines:

OUTLINE	SCRIPTURE	SCRIPTURE	OUTLINE
3. There must be the righteous, sinless standing of the High Priest before God (as symbol of Christ a. He had to approach God for himself thru the sin offering: Symbolized standing sinless & perfect before God— thru the sacrifice b. He had to provide protection against the holy & just presence of God 1) Symbolized by creating a smoke screen to conceal the atonement cover & to	11 And Aaron shall bring the bullock of the sin offering, which is for himself, and shall make an atonement for himself, and for his house, and shall kill the bullock of the sin offering which is for himself: 12 And he shall take a censer full of burning coals of fire from off the altar before the LORD, and his hands full of sweet incense beaten small, and bring it within the vail:	13 And he shall put the incense upon the fire before the LORD, that the cloud of the incense may cover the mercy seat that is upon the testimony, that he die not: 14 And he shall take of the blood of the bullock, and sprinkle it with his finger upon the mercy seat eastward; and before the mercy seat shall he sprinkle of the blood with his finger seven times.	keep him from gazing upon God's Holy Presence 2) The purpose: To keep him from being stricken dead by the blazing holiness of God c. He had to secure mercy—forgiveness of sins—thru the shed blood of the sacrifice 1) Sprinkled the atonement cover with the blood 2) Sprinkled the Ark seven times (symbolizes full, perfect mercy & forgiveness)

a. The High Priest himself had to approach God through the Sin Offering. He himself had to be cleansed from sin before he could make sacrifice for the sins of the people. Once his sins had been forgiven, he stood sinless and perfect before God: he was able to offer sacrifice for the sins of the people. This is a symbol of Jesus Christ, the High Priest of God, who stood sinless and perfect before God. As the sinless, perfect the High Priest, He sacrificed Himself for the sins of the world.

b. The High Priest had to provide protection against the holy and just presence of God (vv.12-13). Note what Aaron had to do: he had to create a smoke screen to conceal the Atonement Cover and to keep him from gazing upon God's holy presence. He took a censor full of burning coals and two handfuls of incense with him when he went behind the curtain. He put the incense on the fire before the LORD, and the smoke of the incense concealed the Atonement Cover and protected him from gazing upon the LORD's presence. It kept him safe from the blazing holiness of God.

c. The High Priest had to secure mercy, the forgiveness of sins, through the shed blood of the sacrifice (v.14). He dipped his finger in some of the bull's blood and sprinkled the Atonement Cover or Mercy Seat with the blood. He then sprinkled the Ark of the Covenant seven times. Remember that the number seven in Scripture symbolizes fullness, completion, perfection. The High Priest was symbolizing that a full, perfect mercy and forgiveness was being made for the sins of the people.

Thought 1. Note the subject of this point: there must be the righteous, sinless standing of the High Priest before God in order to make sacrifice for the sins of the people. The High Priest is a symbol of Jesus Christ. Jesus Christ lived a sinless life, securing righteousness and perfection for man. Therefore He could stand before God sinless and perfect, offering Himself as the substitute sacrifice for the sins of man. This He did.

"For he hath made him to be sin for us, who knew no sin; that we might be made the righteousness of God in him" (2 Co.5:21).

"For we have not an high priest which cannot be touched with the feeling of our infirmities; but was in all points tempted like as we are, yet without sin" (He.4:15).

"For such an high priest became us, who is holy, harmless, undefiled, separate from sinners, and made higher than the heavens" (He.7:26).

"Forasmuch as ye know that ye were not redeemed with corruptible things, as silver and gold, from your vain conversation received by tradition from your fathers; But with the precious blood of Christ, as of a lamb without blemish and without spot" (1 Pe.1:18-19).

"Who did no sin, neither was guile found in his mouth" (1 Pe.2:22).

"And he made his grave with the wicked, and with the rich in his death; because he had done no violence, neither was any deceit in his mouth" (Is.53:9).

4 (16:15-22) **Cover - Covering, of Sin—Removing, of Sin—Taking Away, of Sin—Sin, Forgiveness of—Tabernacle, Cleansing of**—Sin Offering—Burnt Offering—Sacrifice, Animal—Scapegoat: there must be the atoning sacrifice—the covering and taking away of sin—for the people. The great moment, the highlight of the day, had now arrived.

⇒ The atoning sacrifice for the sins of the people was now to be made.
⇒ The ransom price was to be paid.
⇒ The demands of God's holy nature were to be met.
⇒ The execution of God's justice was to be carried out.
⇒ The judgment of death was to be executed.

As stated, the atoning sacrifice for the people—the covering and taking away of sin—was now to take place. How? Note the Scripture and outline:

OUTLINE	SCRIPTURE	SCRIPTURE	OUTLINE
4. There must be the atoning sacrifice—the covering & taking away of sin—for the people a. By putting to death the sacrifice for the sin offering 1) To take the blood into the Most Holy Place & sprinkle the atonement cover (Mercy Seat) • Secured atonement—the covering of sins—for the Most Holy Place • The reason: An absolute necessity because of the infectious sin & rebellion of the people 2) To do the same for the entire Tabernacle: Because it is contaminated by their uncleanness 3) To be acknowledged, honored as the only person who can secure atonement for people (symbolizes that Christ alone can reconcile a person to God) 4) To make atonement for the altar of burnt offering	15 Then shall he kill the goat of the sin offering, that *is* for the people, and bring his blood within the vail, and do with that blood as he did with the blood of the bullock, and sprinkle it upon the mercy seat, and before the mercy seat: 16 And he shall make an atonement for the holy *place*, because of the uncleanness of the children of Israel, and because of their transgressions in all their sins: and so shall he do for the tabernacle of the congregation, that remaineth among them in the midst of their uncleanness. 17 And there shall be no man in the tabernacle of the congregation when he goeth in to make an atonement in the holy *place*, until he come out, and have made an atonement for himself, and for his household, and for all the congregation of Israel. 18 And he shall go out unto the altar that *is* before the LORD, and make an atonement for it; and shall take of	the blood of the bullock, and of the blood of the goat, and put *it* upon the horns of the altar round about. 19 And he shall sprinkle of the blood upon it with his finger seven times, and cleanse it, and hallow it from the uncleanness of the children of Israel. 20 And when he hath made an end of reconciling the holy *place*, and the tabernacle of the congregation, and the altar, he shall bring the live goat: 21 And Aaron shall lay both his hands upon the head of the live goat, and confess over him all the iniquities of the children of Israel, and all their transgressions in all their sins, putting them upon the head of the goat, and shall send *him* away by the hand of a fit man into the wilderness: 22 And the goat shall bear upon him all their iniquities unto a land not inhabited: and he shall let go the goat in the wilderness.	• By putting some blood on the horns of the altar • By sprinkling blood on the altar seven times (symbolized full, perfect cleansing) • The reason: To cleanse & consecrate the altar from the uncleanness of the people b. By presenting the scapegoat to the LORD 1) To symbolically lay all the sins & rebellion of the people upon the scapegoat: By laying both hands on its head & confessing all their sins 2) To symbolically remove & take away the people's sin • By sending the scapegoat away • By letting the scapegoat carry their sins upon itself into a far, desolate land

a. The sacrifice for the Sin Offering was put to death (vv.15-16). Note exactly what Scripture says: the goat was sacrificed as the Sin Offering for the people (v.15). Its blood was taken into the Most Holy Place and sprinkled on the Mercy Seat or Atonement Cover, and, apparently, on the other furnishings of the Tabernacle (vv.15-16). Note that this made atonement for the Most Holy Place and for the Tabernacle. Why was it necessary to make atonement for these? Because of the contaminating power of sin. Note this is exactly what Scripture says: the sin and rebellion of the people contaminated the Tabernacle (v.16). Therefore, before God could forgive sins and accept the people, everything contaminated by sin had to be cleansed.

Note also that the High Priest was to be acknowledged and honored as the only person who could secure atonement for the people (v.17). No person was allowed to be anyplace in the Tabernacle from the time the High Priest went in to make atonement until he came out, having made atonement. This symbolized that Christ alone can make atonement for man; He alone can approach God and reconcile a person to God. He and He alone is the Savior of man.

Note also that atonement was to be made for the Altar of Burnt Offering (vv.18-19). The High Priest was to take some blood from the bull and from the goat and put it on the horns of the altar (v.18). He was then to sprinkle blood on the altar seven times, symbolizing that a full, perfect cleansing was being made. The altar was being cleansed for the same reason that the Mercy Seat had been cleansed: the sins of the people had contaminated the entire Tabernacle and its furnishings. There were insincere, hypocritical people who approached God in that day just as there are today. Insincere, hypocritical people do not have their sins forgiven. In fact, their hypocrisy contaminates their very approach to God. The same was true of insincere, hypocritical Israelites who approached God with their sacrifices. Their hypocrisy contaminated the very Tabernacle and altar upon which they made their sacrifices. The point is obvious: everything contaminated by sin had to be cleansed by the blood of the sacrifice before God could forgive sins.

b. The momentous occasion had now arrived for the scapegoat to be presented to the LORD. As soon as the High Priest had made atonement for the Most Holy Place, the Tabernacle, and the altar, he brought forth the live goat (vv.20-22). Note what he did:

1) He symbolically laid all the sins and rebellion of the people on the scapegoat. This he symbolized by laying his hand on its head and confessing all their sins.

2) He then symbolized the removal and taking away of the people's sins (vv.21-22). This he did by sending the scapegoat away into the wilderness. The scapegoat bore the sins of the people upon itself and carried their sins away—far, far away, completely out of sights, gone forever. The picture is that sins were totally and fully removed, forgiven forever.

Thought 1. The two goats give us two descriptive symbols of the atoning death of Jesus Christ.

(1) The goat that was put to death is a symbol of the death of Christ. Jesus Christ gave Himself as an offering and a sacrifice to God so that we might be forgiven our sins. Jesus Christ died as the perfect offering for sin. His death cleanses everything contaminated by sin. But keep this fact in mind: it was the blood that made sacrifice for sin, not the Tabernacle nor any of the furnishings within the Tabernacle. Thus it is with Christ: it is Christ, His blood, that is important and that cleanses us from sin. It is not the buildings, furnishings, nor rituals of the church. Again, it is Christ, His blood alone, that cleanses us from sin.

> "Who gave himself for our sins, that he might deliver us from this present evil world, according to the will of God and our Father" (Ga.1:4).
>
> "And walk in love, as Christ also hath loved us, and hath given himself for us an offering and a sacrifice to God for a sweetsmelling savour" (Ep.5:2).
>
> "Who gave himself for us, that he might redeem us from all iniquity, and purify unto himself a peculiar people, zealous of good works" (Tit.2:14).
>
> "For Christ also hath once suffered for sins, the just for the unjust, that he might bring us to God, being put to death in the flesh, but quickened by the Spirit" (1 Pe.3:18).
>
> "But he was wounded for our transgressions, he was bruised for our iniquities: the chastisement of our peace was upon him; and with his stripes we are healed" (Is.53:5).

(2) The scapegoat that bore the sins of the people and carried them away is also a symbol of Christ. It is Jesus Christ who bore the sins of the world and who removes and takes them away.

> "For I delivered unto you first of all that which I also received, how that Christ died for our sins according to the scriptures" (1 Co.15:3).
>
> "So Christ was once offered to bear the sins of many; and unto them that look for him shall he appear the second time without sin unto salvation" (He.9:28).
>
> "Who his own self bare our sins in his own body on the tree, that we, being dead to sins, should live unto righteousness: by whose stripes ye were healed" (1 Pe.2:24).
>
> "And ye know that he was manifested to take away our sins; and in him is no sin" (1 Jn.3:5).

5 (16:23-28) **Clean - Cleansing, from Sin—Sacrifice, Animal—Sacrifice, of Jesus Christ—Burnt Offering—Atonement—Acknowledge - Acknowledgment, of Sin—Confession, of Sin—Reconciliation, with God**: there must be an acknowledgment that cleansing and sacrifice are necessary for reconciliation with God. The forgiveness of sins had just been symbolized by the substitute sacrifice of the two goats. Now reconciliation is to be symbolized by the sacrifice of the Burnt Offering. The picture of both forgiveness and reconciliation are needed in order to understand the death of Christ. The great day of atonement was to give both pictures to God's people. God's people were to see that they needed forgiveness and reconciliation with God. As stated, the taking away of their sins had just been symbolized. Now they were to acknowledge that both cleansing and sacrifice are necessary for reconciliation with God.

OUTLINE	SCRIPTURE	SCRIPTURE	OUTLINE
5. There must be an acknowledgment that cleansing & sacrifice are necessary for reconciliation with God	23 And Aaron shall come into the tabernacle of the congregation, and shall put off the linen garments, which he put on when he went into the holy *place*, and shall leave them there:	26 And he that let go the goat for the scapegoat shall wash his clothes, and bathe his flesh in water, and afterward come into the camp.	b. The shepherd of the scapegoat acknowledged the need for cleansing & sacrifice: By not entering the camp until he had washed himself & his clothes
a. The High Priest & the people acknowledged the need for cleansing & sacrifice	24 And he shall wash his flesh with water in the holy place, and put on his garments, and come forth, and offer his burnt offering, and the burnt offering of the people, and make an atonement for himself, and for the people.	27 And the bullock *for* the sin offering, and the goat *for* the sin offering, whose blood was brought in to make atonement in the holy *place*, shall *one* carry forth without the camp; and they shall burn in the fire their skins, and their flesh, and their dung.	c. The people acknowledged the need for cleansing & sacrifice by having the hides, organs, & dung taken outside the camp & burned: Symbolized the judgment upon sin
1) He had to put on the High Priestly clothes to offer the blood of the sacrifice			
2) He had to sacrifice the Burnt Offering for himself & the people: To make atonement		28 And he that burneth them shall wash his clothes, and bathe his flesh in water, and afterward he shall come into the camp.	d. The man who burned the waste of the sacrifice acknowledged the need for cleansing & sacrifice: By not entering the camp until he had washed himself & his clothes
3) He also had to burn the fat of the Sin Offering: Symbolized a sweet smell of acceptance by God	25 And the fat of the sin offering shall he burn upon the altar.		

a. The High Priest and the people acknowledged the need for cleansing and sacrifice (vv.24-25). Note that the High Priest had to wash himself and put on the High Priestly clothes before sacrificing the Burnt Offering. This was necessary because the Burnt Offering symbolized the atonement itself, reconciliation with God. In order to offer the sacrifice of the Burnt Offering—the sacrifice that makes atonement and reconciliation with God—he had to put on the clothes of the High Priest. This was a symbol of the righteousness of Jesus Christ. It is His righteousness that reconciles us with God.

Note also that the High Priest had to sacrifice one ram as a Burnt Offering for himself and the other ram as a Burnt Offering for the people. This he did to make atonement or reconciliation for himself and for the people. Note also that he had to burn the fat of the Sin Offering on the altar (v.25). The pleasing aroma of roasting meat ascending up symbolized the pleasure of God with the sacrifice. The sacrifice was accepted by God.

b. The shepherd of the scapegoat acknowledged the need for cleansing and sacrifice (v.26). This he did by not entering the camp until he had washed himself and his clothes with water.

c. The people acknowledged the need for cleansing and sacrifice by having the hides, organs, and dung taken outside the camp and burned (v.27). This symbolized that sin with all its distastefulness and repulsiveness was taken away, removed by God. The fiery judgment of God consumed sin in all its repulsive nature.

d. The man who burned the waste of the sacrifice acknowledged the need for cleansing and sacrifice (v.28). This he did by not entering the camp until he had washed himself and his clothes with water.

Thought 1. The sacrifice of the Burnt Offering is a symbol of Jesus Christ. It is Jesus Christ who reconciles us to God by His death upon the cross. Any person who approaches God through Jesus Christ will be accepted by God, reconciled with Him.

"**And all things are of God, who hath reconciled us to himself by Jesus Christ, and hath given to us the ministry of reconciliation**" (2 Co.5:18).

"**And that he might reconcile both unto God in one body by the cross, having slain the enmity thereby**" (Ep.2:16).

"**And, having made peace through the blood of his cross, by him to reconcile all things unto himself; by him, I say, whether they be things in earth, or things in heaven**" (Col.1:20).

"**Wherefore in all things it behooved him to be made like unto his brethren, that he might be a merciful and faithful high priest in things pertaining to God, to make reconciliation for the sins of the people**" (He.2:17).

Thought 2. Cleansing is necessary for reconciliation with God. A person living in sin is alienated from God, not reconciled with God. The person who approaches God must be cleansed from his sins.

"**Wash away thy sins, calling on the name of the Lord**" (Ac.22:16).

"**And such were some of you: but ye are washed, but ye are sanctified, but ye are justified in the name of the Lord Jesus, and by the Spirit of our God**" (1 Co.6:11).

"**Having therefore these promises, dearly beloved, let us cleanse ourselves from all filthiness of the flesh and spirit, perfecting holiness in the fear of God**" (2 Co.7:1).

"**Draw nigh to God, and he will draw nigh to you. Cleanse your hands, ye sinners; and purify your hearts, ye double minded**" (Js.4:8).

"**Who can understand his errors? cleanse thou me from secret faults**" (Ps.19:12).

"**Wash me thoroughly from mine iniquity, and cleanse me from my sin....Purge me with hyssop, and I shall be clean: wash me, and I shall be whiter than snow**" (Ps.51:2, 7).

"**Help us, O God of our salvation, for the glory of thy name: and deliver us, and purge away our sins, for thy name's sake**" (Ps.79:9).

"**Wash you, make you clean; put away the evil of your doings from before mine eyes; cease to do evil**" (Is.1:16).

"**Wash thine heart from wickedness, that thou mayest be saved**" (Je.4:14).

6 (16:29-34) **Atonement, Day of—Holy Days, Day of Atonement—Yom Kippur, the Jewish Day of Atonement**: there must be a permanent observance of this great day, the day of atonement. Note the Scripture and outline:

OUTLINE	SCRIPTURE	SCRIPTURE	OUTLINE
6. There must be a permanent observance of this great day, the Day of Atonement	29 And *this* shall be a statute for ever unto you: *that* in the seventh month, on the tenth *day* of the month, ye shall afflict your souls, and do no work at all, *whether it be* one of your own country, or a stranger that sojourneth among you:	31 It *shall be* a sabbath of rest unto you, and ye shall afflict your souls, by a statute for ever	d. The importance of the day: Is to be a Sabbath day of total rest—must fast when observing the day of atonement
a. The specific date set: The 10th day of the seventh month		32 And the priest, whom he shall anoint, and whom he shall consecrate to minister in the priest's office in his father's stead, shall make the atonement, and shall put on the linen clothes, *even* the holy garments:	e. The absolute, essential requirement: The High Priest alone is to make atonement (a symbol of Christ)
b. The duty of the people: To fast & do no work			1) He also puts on the sacred garments
c. The reason: Because the most important event in life was taking place—atonement, reconciliation with God, cleansing from sin was taking place	30 For on that day shall *the priest* make an atonement for you, to cleanse you, *that* ye may be clean from all your sins before the LORD.	33 And he shall make an atonement for the holy	2) He alone makes atonement

OUTLINE	SCRIPTURE	SCRIPTURE	OUTLINE
	sanctuary, and he shall make an atonement for the tabernacle of the congregation, and for the altar, and he shall make an atonement for the priests, and for all the people of the congregation.	34 And this shall be an everlasting statute unto you, to make an atonement for the children of Israel for all their sins once a year. And he did as the LORD commanded Moses.	f. The limitation placed on the observance 1) To be a permanent observance 2) To be observed only once a year g. The obedience of God's people

a. Note that the people were to observe this day on a specific date every year: the tenth day of the seventh month (approximately October).

b. This was to be a very special day for the people, a day of fasting and of no work (v.30).

c. The reason for the emphasis on this day is declared by Scripture: the most important event in life was taking place on this special day. Atonement, reconciliation with God, cleansing from sin—all this was taking place (v.30).

d. The importance of the day was to be stressed: it was to be a Sabbath day of total rest. No cooking was even to be allowed. It was to be a day of fasting (v.31).

e. Note the one, absolute essential: the High Priest alone was to make atonement (vv.32-33). He alone was to put on the sacred clothing. This symbolizes that Jesus Christ alone could make atonement for man and reconcile man to God.

f. Note the limitation placed on the observance: it was to be a permanent observance and to be observed only once a year (v.34).

g. Note the obedience of God's people: they did exactly as God commanded (v.34).

Thought 1. The High Priest alone can make atonement for the sins of the people. The High Priest was a symbol of Jesus Christ. Jesus Christ alone can make atonement for the sins of the world. Any person who comes to God must approach God through Jesus Christ.

"**Jesus saith unto him, I am the way, the truth, and the life: no man cometh unto the Father, but by me**" (Jn.14:6).

"**For God so loved the world, that he gave his only begotten Son, that whosoever believeth in him should not perish, but have everlasting life**" (Jn.3:16).

"**I said therefore unto you, that ye shall die in your sins: for if ye believe not that I am he, ye shall die in your sins**" (Jn.8:24).

"**Neither is there salvation in any other: for there is none other name under heaven given among men, whereby we must be saved**" (Ac.4:12).

"**For if, when we were enemies, we were reconciled to God by the death of his Son, much more, being reconciled, we shall be saved by his life. And not only so, but we also joy in God through our Lord Jesus Christ, by whom we have now received the atonement**" (Ro.5:10-11).

"**And he is the propitiation for our sins: and not for ours only, but also for the sins of the whole world**" (1 Jn.2:2).

Thought 2. The great day of atonement was to be celebrated until the permanent and perfect sacrifice for sin came. This permanent and perfect sacrifice for sin is Jesus Christ. He is the perfect fulfillment of the great day of atonement, the perfect fulfillment of the Sin Offering and the Burnt Offering. Jesus Christ not only secures forgiveness of sins for us, but He also gives us a consciousness, an assurance of forgiveness. The person who has fallen at the foot of the cross has risen, being fully assured of forgiveness. Moreover, Jesus Christ removes the guilt and anguish of sin. The person who falls at the foot of the cross has his sins removed, taken away, and is reconciled to God.

"**Surely he hath borne our griefs, and carried our sorrows: yet we did esteem him stricken, smitten of God, and afflicted. But he was wounded for our transgressions, he was bruised for our iniquities: the chastisement of our peace was upon him; and with his stripes we are healed. All we like sheep have gone astray; we have turned every one to his own way; and the LORD hath laid on him the iniquity of us all**" (Is.53:4-6).

"**The next day John seeth Jesus coming unto him, and saith, Behold the Lamb of God, which taketh away the sin of the world**" (Jn.1:29).

"**In whom we have redemption through his blood, the forgiveness of sins, according to the riches of his grace**" (Ep.1:7).

"**So Christ was once offered to bear the sins of many; and unto them that look for him shall he appear the second time without sin unto salvation**" (He.9:28).

"**Who his own self bare our sins in his own body on the tree, that we, being dead to sins, should live unto righteousness: by whose stripes ye were healed**" (1 Pe.2:24).

"**I know whom I have believed, and am persuaded that he is able to keep that which I have committed unto him against that day**" (2 Ti.1:12).

"**Let us draw near with a true heart in full assurance of faith, having our hearts sprinkled from an evil conscience, and our bodies washed with pure water**" (He.10:22).

"**And he is the propitiation for our sins: and not for ours only, but also for the sins of the whole world. And hereby we do know that we know him, if we keep his commandments**" (1 Jn.2:2-3).

"**Hereby know we that we dwell in him, and he in us, because he hath given us of his Spirit**" (1 Jn.4:13).

"He that believeth on the Son of God hath the witness in himself: he that believeth not God hath made him a liar; because he believeth not the record that God gave of his Son" (1 Jn.5:10).

Thought 3. The mass of sins that has hung over the heads of men age after age has now been covered or atoned for by the blood of Christ. The alienation of man—the great gulf that has separated man from God—has now been bridged. Man can now be reconciled to God.

(1) Christ is the Reconciling Power of God, the Peacemaker who reconciles man with God and man with man.

> **"For he is our peace, who hath made both one, and hath broken down the middle wall of partition between us....And that he might reconcile both [Jew and Gentile] unto God in one body by the cross, having slain the enmity thereby....For through him we both have access by one Spirit unto the Father" (Ep.2:14, 16, 18).**
>
> **"And all things are of God, who hath reconciled us to himself by Jesus Christ, and hath given to us the ministry of reconciliation" (2 Co.5:18).**
>
> **"And, having made peace through the blood of his cross, by him to reconcile all things unto himself; by him, I say, whether they be things in earth, or things in heaven" (Col.1:20).**
>
> **"Wherefore in all things it behooved him to be made like unto his brethren, that he might be a merciful and faithful high priest in things pertaining to God, to make reconciliation for the sins of the people" (He.2:17).**

(2) Jesus Christ made only one offering for sin and reconciliation. The High Priest had to make atonement annually because the blood of bulls and goats could not take away sin, not permanently, not once-for-all. When Jesus Christ stood before God offering Himself as the sacrifice for sin and reconciliation, He was the perfect, sinless Lamb of God Himself. As sinless and perfect, He stood as the Ideal and Perfect Sacrifice forever. His sacrifice was the Ideal, Perfect Pattern that could stand as the sacrifice for all people of all ages. Being perfect, He was able to make one sacrifice, once-for-all offered.

> **"Neither by the blood of goats and calves, but by his own blood he entered in once into the holy place, having obtained eternal redemption for us. For if the blood of bulls and of goats, and the ashes of an heifer sprinkling the unclean, sanctifieth to the purifying of the flesh: How much more shall the blood of Christ, who through the eternal Spirit offered himself without spot to God, purge your conscience from dead works to serve the living God?" (He.9:12-14).**
>
> **"For Christ is not entered into the holy places made with hands, which are the figures of the true; but into heaven itself, now to appear in the presence of God for us: Nor yet that he should offer himself often, as the high priest entereth into the holy place every year with blood of others; For then must he often have suffered since the foundation of the world: but now once in the end of the world hath he appeared to put away sin by the sacrifice of himself....So Christ was once offered to bear the sins of many; and unto them that look for him shall he appear the second time without sin unto salvation" (He.9:24-26, 28).**
>
> **"For it is not possible that the blood of bulls and of goats should take away sins" (He.10:4).**
>
> **"But this man, after he had offered one sacrifice for sins for ever, sat down on the right hand of God....For by one offering he hath perfected for ever them that are sanctified" (He.10:12, 14).**

Thought 4. Gordon J. Wenham has several excellent comments in discussing the day of atonement in the New Testament.

⇒ *The day of atonement prefigures the crucifixion. Christ on the cross achieved what the high priests of the Old Covenant had attempted to do on the day of atonement....*

⇒ *His atonement was demonstrated by the veil of the temple being rent in two (Matt. 27:51; Mark 15:38; Luke 23:45). For Hebrews, the tearing of the veil corresponds to the tearing of Christ's flesh. Now all believers have the right to enter into the presence of God (He. 10:19ff.)....*

⇒ *There is no longer any need for a day of atonement each year....the definitive day of atonement when man's sins were purged once and for all. Now every man who is in Christ has the right, once reserved only for the high priest, to enter into the presence of God. He could go in but once a year; we can draw near at any time.*

> *In a series of contrasts Hebrews brings out how the Christian enjoys far greater privileges than Aaron, for our high priest Christ is far superior to Aaron.*
>
> *(a) Aaron was a sinner who needed to offer sacrifice for himself before making atonement for the people. Christ is pure and sinless and needs to offer no sacrifices for himself (He. 7:26ff.).*
>
> *(b) Aaron had to repeat the sacrifices regularly. Christ secured an eternal redemption by his own death (9:6-14, 25ff.).*
>
> *(c) Aaron's rituals secured him entry into the earthly sanctuary; Christ's death led him into the heavenly (9:24).*
>
> *(d) The repetition of Aaron's sacrifices was a constant reminder of the persistence of sin. Christ's once-for-all sacrifice secured permanent forgiveness of sin (10:1-18).*
>
> *All this should give us the 'confidence to enter the sanctuary by the blood of Jesus' (10:19).*[1]

---

[1] Gordon J. Wenham. *The Book of Leviticus*, p.237, 238. First three points set apart by us for clarity.

DEEPER STUDY # 1
The Expositor's Bible Commentary gives several important facts about the day of atonement that need to be noted in our material.

The Day of Atonement is not mentioned in Exodus 23:14-17 and 34:18-23. Nor does it appear in Deuteronomy 16:1-16. These places mention only the three so-called pilgrimage festivals when the males of all Israel were to assemble before the Tabernacle. The Day of Atonement was not such a pilgrimage festival. The ordinary Israelite remained at home, and the priests carried out the ritual. It was the only day of fasting enjoined on Israel—'you must deny yourselves [NIV mg., "fast"]' (vv.29, 31)—and was to be a special Sabbath of rest and solemnity. It was a time of special contrition, special sin offerings, and atonement. It is kept to this day by the Jews and is called Yom Kippur ('Day of Atonement'). The biblical term is plural, viz., "Day of Atonements."[2]

TYPES, SYMBOLS, AND PICTURES
Leviticus 16:1-34

Historical Term	Type or Picture (Scriptural Basis for Each)	Life Application for Today's Believer	Biblical Application
The Day of Atonement Le. 16:1-34. See also Le.23:27	*The Day Of Atonement symbolizes the only way to approach God: through the shed blood of the atoning sacrifice of the Lord Jesus Christ. A person is forgiven his sins and reconciled to God only through the atoning sacrifice of Christ.* **"For on that day shall** *the priest* **make an atonement for you, to cleanse you,** *that* **ye may be clean from all your sins before the LORD" (Le.16:30).** **"Also on the tenth** *day* **of this seventh month** *there* **shall be a day of atonement: it shall be an holy convocation unto you; and ye shall afflict your souls, and offer an offering made by fire unto the LORD" (Le.23:27).**	The penalty for sin has been paid. How? By Jesus Christ. Jesus Christ died as our atoning sacrifice, reconciling us to God. Hanging upon the cross, Jesus Christ... • bore our sins, taking them away • allowed the justice and judgment of God to be executed against Him, suffering the punishment due us • paid the penalty of sin and death, bearing the alienation and separation from God for us	*"Having therefore, brethren, boldness to enter into the holiest by the blood of Jesus, By a new and living way, which he hath consecrated for us, through the veil, that is to say, his flesh; And having an high priest over the house of God; Let us draw near with a true heart in full assurance of faith, having our hearts sprinkled from an evil conscience, and our bodies washed with pure water" (He.10:19-22).* *"Therefore being justified by faith, we have peace with God through our Lord Jesus Christ: By whom also we have access by faith into this grace wherein we stand, and rejoice in hope of the glory of God" (Ro.5:1-2).*
The High Priest Le. 16:3-10; 16:11-14. See also Le. 21:10-15	*The High Priest is a symbol of Jesus Christ. The High Priest himself had to approach God through the Sin Offering and Burnt Offering. He himself had to be cleansed from sin before he could make sacrifice for the sins of the people. Once his sins had been forgiven, he stood sinless and perfect before God: he was able to offer sacrifice for the sins of the people. This is a symbol of Jesus Christ, the High Priest of God, who stood sinless and perfect before God, offering Himself as the sacrifice for sin.* **"Thus shall Aaron come into the holy** *place:* **with a young bullock for**	Sin has separated and alienated man from God. Sin has created a veil, a curtain, between God and man. The curtain of sin cannot be removed by man, no matter how much he tries. No matter how righteous man seeks to be, his righteousness cannot break through the curtain of sin that separates him and God. But thank God! Jesus Christ—our Great High Priest—has ripped the curtain of sin from top to bottom, opening the way into God's presence. Man now has access into the presence of God. All of us—without exception—can now enter the presence of God, all because of what Jesus Christ has done.	*"But your iniquities have separated between you and your God, and your sins have hid his face from you, that he will not hear" (Is.59:2).* *"Jesus, when he had cried again with a loud voice, yielded up the ghost. And, behold, the veil of the temple was rent in twain from the top to the bottom; and the earth did quake, and the rocks rent" (Mt.27:50-51).* *"Having therefore, brethren, boldness to enter into the holiest by the blood of Jesus, By a new and living way, which he hath consecrated for us, through the veil, that is to say, his flesh; And having an high*

2 *The Expositor's Bible Commentary*, Vol.2. Frank E. Gaebelein, General Editor, p.588.

196

TYPES, SYMBOLS, AND PICTURES
Leviticus 16:1-34

Historical Term	Type or Picture (Scriptural Basis for Each)	Life Application for Today's Believer	Biblical Application
	a sin offering, and a ram for a burnt offering" (Le.16:3). "And Aaron shall offer his bullock of the sin offering, which *is* for himself, and make an atonement for himself, and for his house" (Le.16:6).		*priest over the house of God; Let us draw near with a true heart in full assurance of faith, having our hearts sprinkled from an evil conscience, and our bodies washed with pure water" (He.10:19-22).*
The Pure White Linen Clothing of the High Priest Le. 16:3-10	*The pure white linen clothing of the high priest symbolized the clothing of righteousness, the righteousness of Jesus Christ.* "He shall put on the holy linen coat, and he shall have the linen breeches upon his flesh, and shall be girded with a linen girdle, and with the linen mitre shall he be attired: these *are* holy garments; therefore shall he wash his flesh in water, and *so* put them on" (Le.16:4).	Jesus Christ stands before God clothed in perfect righteousness. As perfect, His righteousness is the Ideal righteousness, the Pattern of all righteousness. As the Ideal and Pattern, His righteousness can cover all men everywhere and present them righteous before God. No person stands before God in his own righteousness: he can stand before God only in the righteousness of Jesus Christ.	*"For Christ is the end of the law for righteousness to every one that believeth" (Ro.10:4). "But of him are ye in Christ Jesus, who of God is made unto us wisdom, and righteousness, and sanctification, and redemption" (1 Co.1:30). "For he hath made him to be sin for us, who knew no sin; that we might be made the righteousness of God in him" (2 Co.5:21). "And be found in him, not having mine own righteousness, which is of the law, but that which is through the faith of Christ, the righteousness which is of God by faith" (Ph.3:9).*
The Scapegoat Le. 16:3-10; 16:20-22. See also Le. 3:12-16	*The scapegoat (the goat that was sent away alive bearing the sins of the people) symbolized the removal and taking away of sin—all through the atoning sacrifice of Christ.* "And Aaron shall bring the goat upon which the LORD's lot fell, and offer him *for* a sin offering. But the goat, on which the lot fell to be the scapegoat, shall be presented alive before the LORD, to make an atonement with him, *and* to let him go for a scapegoat into the wilderness" (Le.16:9-10).	It is Jesus Christ who has forgiven our sins. It is Jesus Christ who bore the sins of the world and who removes and takes them away—far, far away.	*"Who gave himself for our sins, that he might deliver us from this present evil world, according to the will of God and our Father" (Ga.1:4). "Who gave himself for us, that he might redeem us from all iniquity, and purify unto himself a peculiar people, zealous of good works" (Tit.2:14). "For Christ also hath once suffered for sins, the just for the unjust, that he might bring us to God, being put to death in the flesh, but quickened by the Spirit" (1 Pe.3:18). "So Christ was once offered to bear the sins of many; and unto them that look for him shall he appear the second time without sin unto salvation" (He.9:28). "Who his own self bare our sins in his own body on the tree, that we, being dead to sins, should live unto righteousness: by whose stripes ye were healed" (1 Pe.2:24).*

TYPES, SYMBOLS, AND PICTURES
Leviticus 16:1-34

Historical Term	Type or Picture (Scriptural Basis for Each)	Life Application for Today's Believer	Biblical Application
The Sprinkling of the Atone-ment Cover or Mercy Seat of the Ark Seven Times: With the Shed Blood of the Sacrifice Le. 16:11-14	*In this act, the High Priest was symbolizing that a full, perfect mercy and for-giveness was being made for the sins of the people. Re-member, the number seven in Scripture symbolizes full-ness, completion, perfection.* **"And he shall take of the blood of the bullock, and sprinkle** *it* **with his fin-ger upon the mercy seat eastward; and before the mercy seat shall he sprin-kle of the blood with his finger seven times"** (Le. 16:14).	Jesus Christ lived a sinless life, securing righteousness and perfection for man. Therefore He could stand be-fore God sinless and perfect, offering Himself as the sub-stitute sacrifice for the sins of man. This He did.	*"For he hath made him to be sin for us, who knew no sin; that we might be made the righteousness of God in him"* (2 Co.5:21). *"For we have not an high priest which cannot be touched with the feeling of our infirmities; but was in all points tempted like as we are, yet without sin"* (He. 4:15). *"For such an high priest became us, who is holy, harmless, undefiled, sepa-rate from sinners, and made higher than the heavens"* (He.7:26). *"Forasmuch as ye know that ye were not redeemed with corruptible things, as silver and gold, from your vain conversation received by tradition from your fa-thers; But with the precious blood of Christ, as of a lamb without blemish and without spot"* (1 Pe.1:18-19). *"Who did no sin, neither was guile found in his mouth"* (1 Pe.2:22).
The Only Person Who Could Secure Atonement for the People—the High Priest Le. 16:17	*The only person who could secure atonement for the people—the High Priest—symbolized that Christ alone can make atonement for man; He alone can reconcile a person to God.* **"And there shall be no man in the tabernacle of the congregation when he goeth in to make an atonement in the holy** *place,* **until he come out, and have made an atone-ment for himself, and for his household, and for all the congregation of Israel"** (Le.16:17).	Jesus Christ—our High Priest—is the only One who can make atonement for us. Christ and Christ alone can reconcile a person to God.	*"Wherefore in all things it behooved him to be made like unto his brethren, that he might be a merciful and faithful high priest in things pertaining to God, to make reconciliation for the sins of the people"* (He.2:17). *"Seeing then that we have a great high priest, that is passed into the heav-ens, Jesus the Son of God, let us hold fast our profes-sion. For we have not an high priest which cannot be touched with the feeling of our infirmities; but was in all points tempted like as we are, yet without sin"* (He.4:14-15). *"Whither the forerunner is for us entered, even Je-sus, made an high priest for ever after the order of Mel-chisedec"* (He.6:20). *"For such an high priest became us, who is holy, harmless, undefiled, sepa-rate from sinners, and made higher than the heavens"* (He.7:26).

TYPES, SYMBOLS, AND PICTURES
Leviticus 16:1-34

Historical Term	Type or Picture (Scriptural Basis for Each)	Life Application for Today's Believer	Biblical Application
			Now of the things which we have spoken this is the sum: We have such an high priest, who is set on the right hand of the throne of the Majesty in the heavens" (He.8:1).
Atonement Being Made for the Altar of Burnt Offering by Sprinkling Blood on the Altar Seven Times Le. 16:18-19	*Sprinkling blood on the altar of Burnt Offering seven times is a symbol of a full, perfect cleansing: The High Priest was to take some blood from the bull and from the goat and put it on the horns of the altar (v.18). He was then to sprinkle blood on the altar seven times, symbolizing that a full, perfect cleansing was being made. The altar was being cleansed for the same reason that the Mercy Seat had been cleansed: the sins of the people had contaminated the entire Tabernacle and its furnishings.* **"And he shall sprinkle of the blood upon it with his finger seven times, and cleanse it, and hallow it from the uncleanness of the children of Israel"** (Le. 16:19).	There were insincere, hypocritical people who approached God in that day just as there are today. Insincere, hypocritical people do not have their sins forgiven. In fact, their hypocrisy contaminates their very approach to God. The same was true of insincere, hypocritical Israelites who approached God with their sacrifices. Their hypocrisy contaminated the very Tabernacle and altar upon which they made their sacrifices. The point is obvious: everything contaminated by sin has to be cleansed by the blood of Christ before God can forgive sins.	*"Take heed therefore unto yourselves, and to all the flock, over the which the Holy Ghost hath made you overseers, to feed the church of God, which he hath purchased with his own blood"* (Ac.20:28; see Mt.26:28). *"Much more then, being now justified by his blood, we shall be saved from wrath through him"* (Ro. 5:9). *"How much more shall the blood of Christ, who through the eternal Spirit offered himself without spot to God, purge your conscience from dead works to serve the living God?"* (He.9:14). *"Forasmuch as ye know that ye were not redeemed with corruptible things, as silver and gold, from your vain conversation received by tradition from your fathers; But with the precious blood of Christ, as of a lamb without blemish and without spot"* (1 Pe.1:18-19).
The Goat That Was Slaughtered for the Sin Offering of the People Le. 16:15. See also Le. 3:12-16	*The goat that was put to death is a symbol of the death of Christ.* **"Then shall he kill the goat of the sin offering, that is for the people, and bring his blood within the vail, and do with that blood as he did with the blood of the bullock, and sprinkle it upon the mercy seat, and before the mercy seat"** (Le.16:15).	Jesus Christ gave Himself as an offering and sacrifice to God so that we might be forgiven our sins. Jesus Christ died as the perfect offering for sin. His death cleanses everything contaminated by sin. Just keep in mind, it was the blood that made sacrifice for sin; it was not the Tabernacle nor any of the furnishings within the Tabernacle. Thus it is with Christ: it is Christ, His blood, that is important and that cleanses from sin.	*"And walk in love, as Christ also hath loved us, and hath given himself for us an offering and a sacrifice to God for a sweetsmelling savour"* (Ep. 5:2). *"Who gave himself for us, that he might redeem us from all iniquity, and purify unto himself a peculiar people, zealous of good works"* (Tit.2:14). *"Who gave himself for our sins, that he might deliver us from this present evil world, according to the will of God and our Father"* (Ga.1:4). *"But he was wounded for our transgressions, he was bruised for our iniquities: the chastisement of our peace was upon him; and with his stripes we are healed"* (Is.53:5).

DIVISION IV

THE WAY TO LIVE A HOLY LIFE BEFORE GOD (PART 2): BY A PURE SPIRIT (SANCTIFICATION), 17:1–27:34

(17:1–27:34) **DIVISION OVERVIEW**: How can God's people live holy lives before God? By keeping their spirits pure—through sanctification or consecration, which means being set apart to God. This section of Scripture is sometimes called the Holiness Code.[1] It is a practical section, a record of the laws that were to govern the day-to-day lives of God's people. God spelled out exactly what to do to keep one's spirit clean, spelled out how to live a sanctified, holy life before Him.

THE WAY TO LIVE A HOLY LIFE BEFORE GOD (PART 2): BY A PURE SPIRIT (SANCTIFICATION), 17:1–27:34

A. Laws Necessary to Preserve the Atonement: Two Strong Prohibitions, One Against Idolatry and One Against Abusing the Shed Blood of the Sacrifice, 17:1-16

B. Laws That Govern Sexual Behavior: The Prohibition Against Illicit Sex and Sexual Perversion, 18:1-30

C. Laws That Govern Day-to-Day Behavior, Personal Conduct: The Duty to Live a Life of Separation, a Life of Real Devotion to God, 19:1-37

D. Laws That Spell Out the Punishment for Terrible Crimes, 20:1-27

E. Laws That Govern the Priests, the Ministers of God (Part 1): The Basic Requirement and Qualification for the Minister of God, 21:1-24

F. Laws That Govern the Priests, the Ministers of God (Part 2): The Basic Duties of the Minister of God, 22:1-33

G. Laws That Govern the Annual Feasts or Festivals of Worship: The Prophetic Picture of Salvation, 23:1-44

H. Laws That Govern the Lampstand, the Holy Bread, and the Cursing of God: The Availability of God and the Judgment Against Cursing God, 24:1-23

I. Laws That Govern the Use of Property and the Treatment of the Poor: Social Justice—Proclaim Liberty Throughout the Land, 25:1-55

J. The Exhortations to Obey God: God's Promises and Warnings to His People, 26:1-46

K. Laws That Govern Vows and Commitments Made to God: The Critical Importance of Keeping Sacred Vows, 27:1-34

---

[1] Frank E. Gaebelein, General Editor. *The Expositor's Bible Commentary*, Vol.2, p.592.

CHAPTER 17

IV. THE WAY TO LIVE A HOLY LIFE BEFORE GOD (PART 2): A PURE SPIRIT (SANCTIFICATION), 17:1–27:34)

A. Laws Necessary to Preserve the Atonement: Two Strong Prohibitions, One Against Idolatry & One Against Abusing the Shed Blood of the Sacrifice, 17:1-16

1. The Lawgiver: God Himself

a. The law is given both to the leadership & the common people

b. The law is a strong command: From the LORD Himself

2. The prohibition against idolatry

a. The prohibition clearly stated

  1) Must not offer any sacrifice to an idol (see 7)

  2) Must not offer any sacrifice any place other than the place appointed by God, at the Tabernacle

b. The guilt & judgment of idolatry

  1) The guilt: A capital offense against God—guilty as a murderer

  2) The judgment: to be cut off—rejected & condemned

c. The strong charge to idolaters

  1) Must approach the only living & true God, not idols—through the sacrifice

  2) Must approach God thru the High Priest, God's only mediator (a symbol of Christ)

  3) Must seek to grow in fellowship with God alone: Thru the Fellowship Offering

  4) Must sprinkle the blood against the Altar of Burnt Offering: Seek atonement there alone

  5) The result: God accepted, is pleased with one's obedience with the aroma of the sacrifice

d. The terrible sin being committed: Idolatry offered to idols

e. The importance of the laws against idolatry

  1) To be a permanent law

  2) The universality of the law against idolatry

And the LORD spake unto Moses, saying,

2 Speak unto Aaron, and unto his sons, and unto all the children of Israel, and say unto them; This *is* the thing which the LORD hath commanded, saying,

3 What man soever *there be* of the house of Israel, that killeth an ox, or lamb, or goat, in the camp, or that killeth *it* out of the camp,

4 And bringeth it not unto the door of the tabernacle of the congregation, to offer an offering unto the LORD before the tabernacle of the LORD; blood shall be imputed unto that man; he hath shed blood; and that man shall be cut off from among his people:

5 To the end that the children of Israel may bring their sacrifices, which they offer in the open field, even that they may bring them unto the LORD, unto the door of the tabernacle of the congregation, unto the priest, and offer them *for* peace offerings unto the LORD.

6 And the priest shall sprinkle the blood upon the altar of the LORD *at* the door of the tabernacle of the congregation, and burn the fat for a sweet savour unto the LORD.

7 And they shall no more offer their sacrifices unto devils, after whom they have gone a whoring. This shall be a statute for ever unto them throughout their generations.

8 And thou shalt say unto them, Whatsoever man *there*
be of the house of Israel, or of the strangers which sojourn among you, that offereth a burnt offering or sacrifice,

9 And bringeth it not unto the door of the tabernacle of the congregation, to offer it unto the LORD; even that man shall be cut off from among his people.

10 And whatsoever man *there be* of the house of Israel, or of the strangers that sojourn among you, that eateth any manner of blood; I will even set my face against that soul that eateth blood, and will cut him off from among his people.

11 For the life of the flesh *is* in the blood: and I have given it to you upon the altar to make an atonement for your souls: for it *is* the blood *that* maketh an atonement for the soul.

12 Therefore I said unto the children of Israel, No soul of you shall eat blood, neither shall any stranger that sojourneth among you eat blood.

13 And whatsoever man *there be* of the children of Israel, or of the strangers that sojourn among you, which hunteth and catcheth any beast or fowl that may be eaten; he shall even pour out the blood thereof, and cover it with dust.

14 For *it is* the life of all flesh; the blood of it *is* for the life thereof: therefore I said unto the children of Israel, Ye shall eat the blood of no manner of flesh: for the life of all flesh *is* the blood thereof: whosoever eateth it shall be cut off.

15 And every soul that eateth that which died *of itself,* or that which was torn *with beasts, whether it be* one of your own country, or a stranger, he shall both wash his clothes, and bathe *himself* in water, and be unclean until the even: then shall he be clean.

16 But if he wash *them* not, nor bathe his flesh; then he shall bear his iniquity.

- The law applies to all foreigners as well as to all Israelites

- The penalty applies to all foreigners: Must be cut off from God & their own people

3. The prohibition against abusing the shed blood of the sacrifice

a. The prohibition: Must not eat or drink the blood

b. The severe judgment: God's wrath

c. The reason for the prohibition: The blood is sacred; it stands for the life of man

  1) It is the blood that gives life to the body

  2) It is the blood that gives life to the spirit (atonement, reconciliation)

d. The strong charges against abusing the shed blood

  1) Must be stressed time & again: No person is to eat blood (v.10, 12, 14)

  2) Must not commit sacrilege with hunted animals: Must drain out the blood & cover it with dirt

  3) Must keep in mind the reason for the prohibition: The blood gives life to the body—the blood is to be honored

  4) Must keep in mind the judgment: Whoever violated the law was to be cut off from God & his own people

e. The rule controlling the eating of animals found dead

  1) The rule: If eat, one is counted unclean

- Must wash his clothes & himself
- Is unclean till evening

  2) The judgment: If he does not cleanse himself, he will suffer the consequences, be condemned

DIVISION IV

THE WAY TO LIVE A HOLY LIFE BEFORE GOD (PART 2):
A PURE SPIRIT (SANCTIFICATION), 17:1–27:34

A. Laws Necessary to Preserve the Atonement: Two Strong Prohibitions, One Against Idolatry and One Against Abusing the Shed Blood of the Sacrifice, 17:1-16

(17:1-16) **Introduction—Idolatry—Abuse, of Jesus Christ—Blood of Christ, Abuse of—Blood, of Sacrifice, Abuse of**: there are many dangers throughout life, dangers that are a real threat to us. Some dangers strike fear within the human heart, for they disturb the peace and security of life. There are dangers or threats such as...

- failure
- accident
- loss of promotion
- disease

- loss of job
- disability
- bankruptcy
- loss of a loved one

- financial problems
- divorce
- poverty
- abuse

As serious as these dangers are, they are not the most serious dangers facing a person. The present Scripture concerns two dangers that are even more serious, two terrifying dangers. What are they? The danger of idolatry and the danger of abusing Christ and His atoning blood. Why are these two dangers so threatening? Because idolatry and the abuse of Christ and His atoning blood lead to eternal death, to eternal separation from God, a death and separation that never ends. These two threats involve being "cut off" by God—cut off from God Himself, cut off from the promised land of heaven, cut off from all the good things of life—cut off eternally.

⇒ Listen to what Holy Scripture says about the threat and danger of idolatry.

> "For the wrath of God is revealed from heaven against all ungodliness and unrighteousness of men, who hold the truth in unrighteousness; Because that which may be known of God is manifest in them; for God hath showed it unto them. For the invisible things of him from the creation of the world are clearly seen, being understood by the things that are made, even his eternal power and Godhead; so that they are without excuse.... Who changed the truth of God into a lie, and worshipped and served the creature more than the Creator, who is blessed for ever. Amen" (Ro.1:18-20, 25).
>
> "Now the works of the flesh are manifest, which are these; Adultery, fornication, uncleanness, lasciviousness, Idolatry, witchcraft, hatred, variance, emulations, wrath, strife, seditions, heresies, Envyings, murders, drunkenness, revellings, and such like: of the which I tell you before, as I have also told you in time past, that they which do such things shall not inherit the kingdom of God" (Ga.5:19-21).
>
> "But the fearful, and unbelieving, and the abominable, and murderers, and whoremongers, and sorcerers, and idolaters, and all liars, shall have their part in the lake which burneth with fire and brimstone: which is the second death" (Re.21:8).

⇒ Listen to what Holy Scripture says about the abuse of Christ and His atoning blood.

> "Of how much sorer punishment, suppose ye, shall he be thought worthy, who hath trodden under foot the Son of God, and hath counted the blood of the covenant, wherewith he was sanctified, an unholy thing, and hath done despite unto the Spirit of grace?" (He.10:29).
>
> "For if after they have escaped the pollutions of the world through the knowledge of the Lord and Saviour Jesus Christ, they are again entangled therein, and overcome, the latter end is worse with them than the beginning. For it had been better for them not to have known the way of righteousness, than, after they have known it, to turn from the holy commandment delivered unto them" (2 Pe.2:20-21).

Idolatry and the abuse of Christ and His blood will be severely judged by God. These two threats will lead to hell and to eternal death, being cut off and separated from God and from all that is good forever. This is the warning of God. It is not what man thinks or says; it is the Word of God Himself, His warning to us. Man's denial does not void nor annul the truth. No person must ever turn to idolatry nor abuse God's Son and His atoning blood. God is the only living and true God, the Creator of the universe, the Sovereign LORD and Majesty of all. Therefore, God expects His creatures to worship Him, to live holy and righteous lives just as He is holy. The last thing God wants is for people to turn elsewhere and make gods out of their own imaginations. Such is utter foolishness.

Moreover, God loves His one and only Son, the Lord Jesus Christ. His Son willingly left the glory of heaven and came to earth to reveal the truth to man. He revealed the truth about God, man, sin, and about Himself. He is the Son of God and the Savior of the world. He revealed the truth about Himself and about heaven, hell, and the provision of salvation through His atoning death. Because of what Christ has done, God loves His Son beyond measure. Therefore, God is jealous over His Son. Any person who curses or abuses His Son and the atoning blood of His Son will face the terrible wrath and judgment of God.

Keep in mind that the great *Day of Atonement* had just been celebrated for the very first time. The atoning blood of the sacrifice had just been shed, bringing forgiveness and reconciliation to the people of God. God wanted to do all He could to preserve the atonement among His people. He wanted His people to be saved, and the only way they could be saved was to approach Him through the atonement (reconciliation) of the sacrifice. Therefore, He wanted to protect and to preserve the atonement. This He did by giving two laws to His people, one law governing idolatry and one law governing the

atoning blood of the sacrifice: *Laws Necessary to Preserve the Atonement: Two Strong Prohibitions, One Against Idolatry and One Against Abusing the Shed Blood of the Sacrifice*, 17:1-16.

1. The Lawgiver: God Himself (vv.1-2).
2. The prohibition against idolatry (vv.3-9).
3. The prohibition against abusing the shed blood of the sacrifice (vv.10-16).

1 (17:1-2) **Law - Laws, Source:** there was the Lawgiver, God Himself. God is always concerned about people's attitudes toward Him. Most people have turned away from God. They curse, ignore, neglect, reject, and deny God. Most people claim that they know God, but by this, they mean the god of their imagination. They profess to believe in a god of their own imaginations, ideas, and thoughts. However, they reject the God of revelation, the God and Father of the Lord Jesus Christ and of the Holy Scripture. This is what concerns the God and Father of the Lord Jesus Christ, for He alone is the LORD God of the universe, the great Creator and Sustainer of all that is, has been, or ever will be. The person who rejects Him is doomed, destined to an eternity separated from Him. They will have no part in the new heavens and earth. Their idolatry—turning to the gods of their own imaginations—breaks the heart of God. He created man for Himself, to live eternally in His presence and to enjoy all the glorious benefits of a perfect heaven and earth that is coming in the future (2 Pe.3:10-13). This is the reason God was giving this law to His people: to preserve their belief in Him. He wanted to do everything He could to keep His people from turning to the idolatrous practices of the world. This He did by giving them the two laws discussed in this passage.

OUTLINE	SCRIPTURE
1. The Lawgiver: God Himself	And the LORD spake unto Moses, saying,
a. The law is given both to the leadership & the common people	2 Speak unto Aaron, and unto his sons, and unto all the children of Israel, and say unto them; This *is* the
b. The law is a strong command: From the LORD Himself	thing which the LORD hath commanded, saying,

Note that the laws are given both to the leadership and the common people. The threat of idolatry and of abusing the blood of the sacrifice was a danger to all the people. They all needed the law addressed to them. Note also that the law is a direct command from God. It was a law being given from the heart of God Himself.

> "Not every one that saith unto me, Lord, Lord, shall enter into the kingdom of heaven; but he that doeth the will of my Father which is in heaven" (Mt.7:21).
>
> "For if the word spoken by angels was stedfast, and every transgression and disobedience received a just recompence of reward; How shall we escape, if we neglect so great salvation; which at the first began to be spoken by the Lord, and was confirmed unto us by them that heard him" (He.2:2-3).
>
> "Blessed are they that do his commandments, that they may have right to the tree of life, and may enter in through the gates into the city" (Re.22:14).
>
> "This day the LORD thy God hath commanded thee to do these statutes and judgments: thou shalt therefore keep and do them with all thine heart, and with all thy soul" (De.26:16).

2 (17:3-9) **Idolatry—Law, Against Idolatry—Judgment, Against Idolatry:** there was the prohibition against idolatry.

OUTLINE	SCRIPTURE	SCRIPTURE	OUTLINE
2. The prohibition against idolatry	3 What man soever *there be*	of the congregation, unto	diater (a symbol of Christ)
a. The prohibition clearly stated	of the house of Israel, that kil-	the priest, and offer them	3) Must seek to grow in fellow-
1) Must not offer any sacrifice to an idol (see 7)	leth an ox, or lamb, or goat, in the camp, or that killeth *it* out of the camp,	*for* peace offerings unto the LORD.	ship with God alone: Thru the Fellowship Offering
2) Must not offer any sacrifice any place other than the place appointed by God, at the Tabernacle	4 And bringeth it not unto the door of the tabernacle of the congregation, to offer an offering unto the LORD be-	6 And the priest shall sprinkle the blood upon the altar of the LORD *at* the door of the tabernacle of	4) Must sprinkle the blood against the Altar of Burnt Offering: Seek atonement there alone
b. The guilt & judgment of idolatry	fore the tabernacle of the LORD; blood shall be imputed	the congregation, and burn the fat for a sweet savour	5) The result: God accepted, is pleased with one's obedience
1) The guilt: A capital offense against God—guilty as a murderer	unto that man; he hath shed blood; and that man shall be	unto the LORD.	with the aroma of the sacrifice
2) The judgment: be cut off— rejected & condemned	cut off from among his peo- ple:	7 And they shall no more offer their sacrifices unto	d. The terrible sin being com- mitted: Idolatry offered to idols
c. The strong charge to idolaters	5 To the end that the children of Israel may bring their sacri-	devils, after whom they have gone a whoring. This	e. The importance of the laws against idolatry
1) Must approach the only liv- ing & true GOD, not idols— through the sacrifice	fices, which they offer in the open field, even that they may	shall be a statute for ever unto them throughout their generations.	1) To be a permanent law
2) Must approach God thru the High Priest, God's only me-	bring them unto the LORD, unto the door of the tabernacle	8 And thou shalt say unto them, Whatsoever man *there be* of the house of Israel,	2) To be a universal law against idolatry

OUTLINE	SCRIPTURE	SCRIPTURE	OUTLINE
• The law applies to all foreigners as well as to all Israelites	or of the strangers which sojourn among you, that offereth a burnt offering or sacrifice,	door of the tabernacle of the congregation, to offer it unto the LORD; even that man shall be cut off from	all foreigners: Must be cut off from God & their own people
• The penalty applies to	9 And bringeth it not unto the	among his people.	

a. Note that the prohibition was clearly stated (vv.3-4): a person must not offer any sacrifice to an idol (see v.7). No sacrifice was to be made anyplace other than the place appointed by God—and that place was the Tabernacle. This was a momentous change for God's people. Prior to this time people had built altars and offered sacrifices to God wherever they pleased. The head of each family had been a priest to his own family. This had led to tragic results. Many people had begun to build altars and to make sacrifices to the gods of their own imaginations, worshipping what they thought God was or conceived Him to be. Even some of the Israelites had worshipped the idols of Egypt while they were enslaved there. They had been surrounded by idolatry and bombarded with the worldly message and ridicule of their neighbors. Eventually, their faith in God weakened and they turned to the idols of their neighbors. No doubt, their turning away from God was by degrees. Little by little, their faith slipped away, becoming increasingly weakened due to their imaginations. They invented gods of their own thoughts and ideas. However, this was true of only some of the Israelites; not every Israelites turned away from God. Their situation would be the same as any church's is today: there are genuine believers within the church and there are hypocritical people who make false professions.

The point is this: a momentous, drastic change was now being made in man's approach to God. The family heads were no longer to serve as priests to the family. They were no longer allowed to build altars and to offer sacrifices as they willed—around their homes, in their fields, and along their journeys. Hereafter there was to be only one priesthood, and that was the Aaronic priesthood. Aaron and his descendants would thereafter serve as the priests of God's people. Moreover, every sacrifice was thereafter to be offered in the court of the Tabernacle, by the hands of the priests. The lives of God's people were to be centered around the Tabernacle. No sacrifice would be accepted by God except the sacrifice offered by the High Priest himself (a symbol of Christ). And no sacrifice would be accepted by God that was not offered in the place designated by God, in the Tabernacle.

b. Note the guilt and the judgment of idolatry (v.4): the person who worshipped and made sacrifice to an idol was guilty of committing a capital offense against God. He was as guilty as a murderer. He was to be cut off, rejected, and condemned by God.

c. Note the strong charges to God's people (vv.5-6):
1) They had to approach the only living and true God, not idols, through the sacrifice (a symbol of Christ). They were to bring to the LORD all the sacrifices that they had previously been making in the fields.
2) They had to approach God through the High Priest, God's only true mediator (a symbol of Christ). Note that this is exactly what Scripture says: the High Priest was God's representative. All sacrifices were thereafter to be brought to the entrance of the Tabernacle and presented to the LORD's representative, the priest.
3) They were to seek one thing: to grow in the fellowship and peace of God. This was to be done by bringing their Fellowship or Peace Offering to the Tabernacle and making sacrifice there and there alone (v.5).
4) They must sprinkle the blood against the altar of Burnt Offering. The Burnt Offering, of course, sat in the courtyard of the Tabernacle. They were to seek atonement at the Tabernacle and there alone (v.6).
5) Observe the result, what God promised if His people would obey Him and make sacrifice only at the Tabernacle: God would accept and be pleased with their obedience. This would be symbolized by the aroma of the roasting meat ascending up toward heaven (v.6).

d. Note the terrible sin that was being committed by some of the Israelites (v.7): they were offering sacrifices to some goat idols, or as the authorized version says, "to demons." The Hebrew word (sair) means he-goat or hairy ones which is taken to refer to goats. People in every generation have worshipped idols of various forms and wild imaginations; others have worshipped the devil and demons. God's purpose was to stop all false worship by declaring that He will accept only one worship. He must be approached through the sacrifice appointed by Him and the sacrifice must be made at the place appointed by Him: the Tabernacle itself.

Note one other fact: the people who were worshipping idols are said to have been prostituting themselves against God (v.7). The relationship between God and His people is to be close, as close as a marriage covenant between husband and wife. Consequently, when a person turns to some false god, he commits adultery against God. This is declared time and again throughout Scripture (Jud.2:17;8:27; 1 Chr.5:25; Ps.106:39; Ep.6:9; Ep.20:30; Ho.4:12;5:4;9:1).

e. The importance of the law against idolatry is clearly stated: the law was to be permanent (v.7).

f. It was also to be a universal law against idolatry (vv.8-9). The law was to apply to all foreigners as well as to all Israelites. Moreover, the penalty was to apply to all foreigners. If they disobeyed the law, they were to be cut off—expelled and banished from God's people (v.9).

Thought 1. Idolatry is forbidden by God, and the idolater is to suffer the most severe consequences imaginable.
(1) God forbids idolatry.

> **"Thou shalt not make unto thee any graven image, or any likeness of any thing that is in heaven above, or that is in the earth beneath, or that is in the water under the earth" (Ex.20:4).**
>
> **"Ye shall make you no idols nor graven image, neither rear you up a standing image, neither shall ye set up any image of stone in your land, to bow down unto it: for I am the LORD your God" (Le.26:1).**
>
> **"Take heed to yourselves, that your heart be not deceived, and ye turn aside, and serve other gods, and worship them" (De.11:16).**

"I am the LORD: that is my name: and my glory will I not give to another, neither my praise to graven images" (Is.42:8).

"Little children, keep yourselves from idols. Amen" (1 Jn.5:21).

(2) The judgment of God against idolaters will be severe.

"Now the works of the flesh are manifest, which are these; Adultery, fornication, uncleanness, lasciviousness, Idolatry, witchcraft, hatred, variance, emulations, wrath, strife, seditions, heresies, Envyings, murders, drunkenness, revellings, and such like: of the which I tell you before, as I have also told you in time past, that they which do such things shall not inherit the kingdom of God" (Ga.5:19-21).

"But the fearful, and unbelieving, and the abominable, and murderers, and whoremongers, and sorcerers, and idolaters, and all liars, shall have their part in the lake which burneth with fire and brimstone: which is the second death" (Re.21:8).

Thought 2. The High Priest is a symbol of the Lord Jesus Christ. When a person approaches God, he must come through the High Priest, the Lord Jesus Christ. The High Priesthood of Christ is the only priesthood that God accepts, and God accepts only the person who comes through Christ.

"Wherefore in all things it behooved him to be made like unto his brethren, that he might be a merciful and faithful high priest in things pertaining to God, to make reconciliation for the sins of the people" (He.2:17).

"Seeing then that we have a great high priest, that is passed into the heavens, Jesus the Son of God, let us hold fast our profession. For we have not an high priest which cannot be touched with the feeling of our infirmities; but was in all points tempted like as we are, yet without sin" (He.4:14-15).

"Wherefore he is able also to save them to the uttermost that come unto God by him, seeing he ever liveth to make intercession for them. For such an high priest became us, who is holy, harmless, undefiled, separate from sinners, and made higher than the heavens; Who needeth not daily, as those high priests, to offer up sacrifice, first for his own sins, and then for the people's: for this he did once, when he offered up himself. For the law maketh men high priests which have infirmity; but the word of the oath, which was since the law, maketh the Son, who is consecrated for evermore" (He.7:25-28).

"Now of the things which we have spoken this is the sum: We have such an high priest, who is set on the right hand of the throne of the Majesty in the heavens; A minister of the sanctuary, and of the true tabernacle, which the Lord pitched, and not man" (He.8:1-2).

Thought 3. There was only one place that God wanted people approaching Him—the place appointed by Him. For the Israelites, that place was the Tabernacle. For us, that place is the Lord Jesus Christ Himself. Jesus Christ is the fulfillment of the Tabernacle. The Tabernacle and its worship symbolized the coming of the Savior of the world and the great sacrifice He was to make upon the cross for the world. When a person approaches God, he must approach God at the designated place appointed by God: at the foot of the cross of His Son, the Lord Jesus Christ.

"For God so loved the world, that he gave his only begotten Son, that whosoever believeth in him should not perish, but have everlasting life" (Jn.3:16).

"I said therefore unto you, that ye shall die in your sins: for if ye believe not that I am he, ye shall die in your sins" (Jn.8:24).

"Jesus saith unto him, I am the way, the truth, and the life: no man cometh unto the Father, but by me" (Jn.14:6).

"Neither is there salvation in any other: for there is none other name under heaven given among men, whereby we must be saved" (Ac.4:12).

"That if thou shalt confess with thy mouth the Lord Jesus, and shalt believe in thine heart that God hath raised him from the dead, thou shalt be saved. For with the heart man believeth unto righteousness; and with the mouth confession is made unto salvation" (Ro.10:9-10).

"For other foundation can no man lay than that is laid, which is Jesus Christ" (1 Co.3:11).

"He's the door" (Jn.10:9).

"For there is one God, and one mediator between God and men, the man Christ Jesus; Who gave himself a ransom for all, to be testified in due time" (1 Ti.2:5-6).

"How much more shall the blood of Christ, who through the eternal Spirit offered himself without spot to God, purge your conscience from dead works to serve the living God? And for this cause he is the mediator of the new testament, that by means of death, for the redemption of the transgressions that were under the first testament, they which are called might receive the promise of eternal inheritance" (He.9:14-15).

"For Christ is not entered into the holy places made with hands, which are the figures of the true; but into heaven itself, now to appear in the presence of God for us" (He.9:24).

"My little children, these things write I unto you, that ye sin not. And if any man sin, we have an advocate with the Father, Jesus Christ the righteous: And he is the propitiation for our sins: and not for ours only, but also for the sins of the whole world" (1 Jn.2:1-2).

3 (17:10-16) **Blood, of Christ, Abuse of—Jesus Christ, Blood of, Abuse of—Jesus Christ, Abuse of—Abuse, of Jesus Christ—Abuse, of Christ's Blood—Law, Against Abuse of Blood**: there was the prohibition against the shed blood of the sacrifice. This law was first given to Noah as far as we know. He was given the right to eat meat but not to eat blood (Ge.9:4). The prohibition against eating blood is repeated several times throughout Scripture (Le.3:17; 7:26-27; De.12:16, 23; 15:23; 1 S.14:32-35; Eze.33:25).

OUTLINE	SCRIPTURE	SCRIPTURE	OUTLINE
3. The prohibition against abusing the shed blood of the sacrifice a. The prohibition: Must not eat or drink the blood b. The severe judgment: God's wrath c. The reason for the prohibition: The blood is sacred; it stands for the life of man 1) It is the blood that gives life to the body 2) It is the blood that gives life to the spirit (atonement, reconciliation) d. The strong charges against abusing the shed blood 1) Must be stressed time & again: No person is to eat blood (v.10, 12, 14) 2) Must not commit sacrilege with hunted animals: Must drain out the blood & cover it with dirt	10 And whatsoever man *there be* of the house of Israel, or of the strangers that sojourn among you, that eateth any manner of blood; I will even set my face against that soul that eateth blood, and will cut him off from among his people. 11 For the life of the flesh *is* in the blood: and I have given it to you upon the altar to make an atonement for your souls: for it *is* the blood *that* maketh an atonement for the soul. 12 Therefore I said unto the children of Israel, No soul of you shall eat blood, neither shall any stranger that sojourneth among you eat blood. 13 And whatsoever man *there be* of the children of Israel, or of the strangers that sojourn among you, which hunteth and catcheth	any beast or fowl that may be eaten; he shall even pour out the blood thereof, and cover it with dust. 14 For *it is* the life of all flesh; the blood of it *is* for the life thereof: therefore I said unto the children of Israel, Ye shall eat the blood of no manner of flesh: for the life of all flesh *is* the blood thereof: whosoever eateth it shall be cut off. 15 And every soul that eateth that which died *of itself*, or that which was torn *with beasts, whether it be* one of your own country, or a stranger, he shall both wash his clothes, and bathe *himself* in water, and be unclean until the even: then shall he be clean. 16 But if he wash *them* not, nor bathe his flesh; then he shall bear his iniquity.	3) Must keep in mind the reason for the prohibition: The blood gives life to the body—the blood is to be honored 4) Must keep in mind the judgment: Whoever violated the law was to be cut off from God & his own people e. The rule controlling the eating of animals found dead 1) The rule: If eat, one is counted unclean • Must wash his clothes & himself • Is unclean till evening 2) The judgment: If he does not cleanse himself, he will suffer the consequences, be condemned

a. The prohibition is strong: a person must not eat or drink the blood of the sacrifice nor any other blood (v.10). Note that this law is forcefully stated time and again in these verses (vv.10, 12, 14). A quick reading of the entire passage shows how strong the prohibition is. God is forceful: "None of you may eat blood" (v.14).

b. The importance of the prohibition is seen in the severe judgment pronounced upon the violators. God's face is set against the violator. This is a reference to His wrath. If any person eats or drinks blood, God's wrath will be set against him: the person will be cut off. And note who it is that cuts off the violator: God Himself. The person who abuses the blood of the sacrifice will be doomed, cut off, separated from God and from all other believers eternally—cut off by the hand of God Himself.

c. The reasons for this prohibition are striking. Keep in mind that the blood is sacred to God, very, very sacred (v.11).

1) First, it is the blood that gives life to the body of man. The blood stands for the life of man. This is seen in one clear fact: when an animal loses its blood, the animal dies. The animal loses its life. It is the blood that gives life to the animal. Therefore, to eat blood is to dishonor and despise life, to trample life underfoot. The purpose for the law against eating blood is, therefore, to teach the *dignity of life*. Life is to be respected and honored.

2) Second, it is the blood of the sacrifice that gives life to the spirit of man. It is the blood that makes atonement and reconciliation with God possible. This is one of the clearest statements in Scripture on the purpose of the blood. Note exactly what Scripture says: "It is the blood that maketh atonement for the soul" (v.11).

Simply stated, the blood of the sacrifice is the ransom, the price paid for atonement or reconciliation with God. God's justice demanded payment in the very same way that the justice of any honorable court demands payment for wrong done. The perfect and holy nature of God demands separation from God, that is, death—being cut off from living with God. But this is the glorious news of God: the price has been paid for man's violation of God's holy and perfect nature. The blood of the sacrifice is the payment. If a person approaches God through the blood of the sacrifice, God accepts him. The person is ransomed, reconciled with God.

Keep in mind that the blood of the sacrifice is a symbol of the blood of God's Son, the Lord Jesus Christ. Therefore, the blood is of supreme value to God, worth more than any other thing in all the universe. For this reason, no person is to eat blood; no person is to abuse the blood of the sacrifice. The blood is a symbol of the blood of God's Son; therefore, the blood is not ever to be abused.

d. Now, note the strong charges against abusing the shed blood (vv.12-14).

1) This law must be stressed time and again: no person is to eat blood (vv.10, 12, 14).

2) No person must commit sacrilege with hunted animals (v.13). The blood of wild animals must be drained and covered with earth. It must not be left upon the top of the ground where it might be eaten by other animals. This would abuse the sacredness of the blood, the sacredness of life, the life that the dead animal lived. (Note how highly God esteemed all life, even the life of animals. The dignity of life is to be respected, no matter the creature.)

3) A person must remember the reason for the prohibition: the blood gives life to the body. The blood is to be honored (v.14).

4) A person must remember the judgment: if a person violated the law—if he ate blood, abused the blood—he would be cut off (v.14).

e. Note the rule controlling the eating of animals found dead (vv.15-16): if a person found a dead animal and ate it, he was counted unclean. He had to wash his clothes and bathe himself with water. He was ceremonially unclean until evening. But note: if he did not wash his clothes and bathe himself, he was held responsible. That is, he was held accountable for violating the law against eating blood. He was to be cut off.

Thought 1. The blood is sacred to God. It is the most highly valued substance in all the universe to God, counted ever so precious. There are two reasons why God values the blood so highly:

(1) The blood is the substance of life, the very source of life that God gave to man. Blood represents, stands for, the life of man. And remember: God loves man. He created man to shower the riches of His grace and the fullness of life upon man. Therefore, God values the very substance (blood) that gives man his life.

> **"But flesh with the life thereof, which is the blood thereof, shall ye not eat" (Ge.9:4).**
> **"For the life of the flesh is in the blood" (Le.17:11).**
> **"Only be sure that thou eat not the blood: for the blood is the life; and thou mayest not eat the life with the flesh" (De.12:23).**

(2) The blood of the substitute sacrifice symbolized the blood of Christ that was shed upon the cross. The atoning blood of Christ reconciles us to God, makes us acceptable to God.

> **"For this is my blood of the new testament, which is shed for many for the remission of sins" (Mt.26:28).**
> **"Take heed therefore unto yourselves, and to all the flock, over the which the Holy Ghost hath made you overseers, to feed the church of God, which he hath purchased with his own blood" (Ac.20:28).**
> **"Much more then, being now justified by his blood, we shall be saved from wrath through him. For if, when we were enemies, we were reconciled to God by the death of his Son, much more, being reconciled, we shall be saved by his life" (Ro.5:9-10).**
> **"How much more shall the blood of Christ, who through the eternal Spirit offered himself without spot to God, purge your conscience from dead works to serve the living God?" (He.9:14).**
> **"And almost all things are by the law purged with blood; and without shedding of blood is no remission" (He.9:22).**
> **"Forasmuch as ye know that ye were not redeemed with corruptible things, as silver and gold, from your vain conversation received by tradition from your fathers; But with the precious blood of Christ, as of a lamb without blemish and without spot" (1 Pe.1:18-19).**
> **"But if we walk in the light, as he is in the light, we have fellowship one with another, and the blood of Jesus Christ his Son cleanseth us from all sin" (1 Jn.1:7).**
> **"Unto him that loved us, and washed us from our sins in his own blood" (Re.1:5).**

(3) The person who abuses God's Son and His shed blood will be judged and severely punished. No matter who the person is—the most socially acceptable, the most highly ranked, the most educated, the most wealthy, the lowest—if he abuses God's Son and the blood of God's Son, God is going to judge him and severely punish him. God loves His one and only Son too much to do any less if a person refuses to honor Him. His Son has done too much to save man.

> **"Of how much sorer punishment, suppose ye, shall he be thought worthy, who hath trodden under foot the Son of God, and hath counted the blood of the covenant, wherewith he was sanctified, an unholy thing, and hath done despite unto the Spirit of grace?" (He.10:29).**
> **"For if after they have escaped the pollutions of the world through the knowledge of the Lord and Saviour Jesus Christ, they are again entangled therein, and overcome, the latter end is worse with them than the beginning. For it had been better for them not to have known the way of righteousness, than, after they have known it, to turn from the holy commandment delivered unto them" (2 Pe.2:20-21).**

TYPES, SYMBOLS, AND PICTURES
Leviticus 17:1-16

Historical Term	Type or Picture (Scriptural Basis for Each)	Life Application for Today's Believer	Biblical Application
The Tabernacle and Its Worship Le. 17:3-9	*The Tabernacle and its worship symbolized the coming of the Savior of the world and the great sacrifice He was to make upon the cross for the world.* **"And thou shalt say unto them, Whatsoever man *there be* of the house of Israel, or of the strangers which sojourn among you, that offereth a burnt offering of sacrifice, And bringeth it not unto the door of the tabernacle of the congregation, to offer it unto the LORD; even that man shall be cut off from among his people" (Le.17:8-9).**	There was only one place that God wanted people approaching Him, the place appointed by Him. For the Israelites, that place was the Tabernacle. For us, that place is the Lord Jesus Christ Himself. Jesus Christ is the fulfillment of the Tabernacle. When a person approaches God, he must approach God at the designated place appointed by God; at the foot of the cross of His Son, the Lord Jesus Christ.	*"For God so loved the world, that he gave his only begotten Son, that whosoever believeth in him should not perish, but have everlasting life" (Jn.3:16).* *"I said therefore unto you, that ye shall die in your sins: for if ye believe not that I am he, ye shall die in your sins" (Jn.8:24).* *"Jesus saith unto him, I am the way, the truth, and the life: no man cometh unto the Father, but by me" (Jn.14:6).* *"Neither is there salvation in any other: for there is none other name under heaven given among men, whereby we must be saved" (Ac.4:12).* *"That if thou shalt confess with thy mouth the Lord Jesus, and shalt believe in thine heart that God hath raised him from the dead, thou shalt be saved. For with the heart man believeth unto righteousness; and with the mouth confession is made unto salvation" (Ro.10:9-10).*

B. Laws That Govern Sexual Behavior: The Prohibition Against Illicit Sex & Sexual Perversion, 18:1-30

1. The Lawgiver: The LORD

a. God emphatically declares: "I am the LORD your God"

1) Must live a life of separation
- Not behave as the Egyptians
- Not behave as the Canaanites
2) Must not follow their practices[DS1,2]

b. God emphatically declares: "I am the LORD your God"
1) Must obey my laws
2) Must follow my decrees

c. God emphatically declares: "I am the LORD your God"
1) Keep my decrees & laws
2) The reason: Will receive life

2. The prohibition against incest: Not to sexually approach any close family member or relative

a. The emphatic warning: "I am the LORD"
b. The sexual relations prohibited
1) Sex prohibited with mother (or father)

2) Sex prohibited with step-mothers (or step-fathers)

3) Sex prohibited with sisters or half-sisters (or brothers or half-brothers)

4) Sex prohibited with grand-children or step-grandchildren

5) Sex prohibited with step-sister (or step-brother)

6) Sex prohibited with aunt (or uncle) by birth

And the LORD spake unto Moses, saying,

2 Speak unto the children of Israel, and say unto them, I am the LORD your God.

3 After the doings of the land of Egypt, wherein ye dwelt, shall ye not do: and after the doings of the land of Canaan, whither I bring you, shall ye not do: neither shall ye walk in their ordinances.

4 Ye shall do my judgments, and keep mine ordinances, to walk therein: I *am* the LORD your God.

5 Ye shall therefore keep my statutes, and my judgments: which if a man do, he shall live in them: I *am* the LORD.

6 None of you shall approach to any that is near of kin to him, to uncover *their* nakedness: I *am* the LORD.

7 The nakedness of thy father, or the nakedness of thy mother, shalt thou not uncover: she *is* thy mother; thou shalt not uncover her nakedness.

8 The nakedness of thy father's wife shalt thou not uncover: it *is* thy father's nakedness.

9 The nakedness of thy sister, the daughter of thy father, or daughter of thy mother, *whether she be* born at home, or born abroad, *even* their nakedness thou shalt not uncover.

10 The nakedness of thy son's daughter, or of thy daughter's daughter, *even* their nakedness thou shalt not uncover: for theirs *is* thine own nakedness.

11 The nakedness of thy father's wife's daughter, begotten of thy father, she *is* thy sister, thou shalt not uncover her nakedness.

12 Thou shalt not uncover the nakedness of thy father's sister: she *is* thy father's near kinswoman.

13 Thou shalt not uncover the nakedness of thy mother's sister: for she *is* thy mother's near kinswoman.

14 Thou shalt not uncover the nakedness of thy father's brother, thou shalt not approach to his wife: she *is* thine aunt.

15 Thou shalt not uncover the nakedness of thy daughter in law: she *is* thy son's wife; thou shalt not uncover her nakedness.

16 Thou shalt not uncover the nakedness of thy brother's wife: it *is* thy brother's nakedness.

17 Thou shalt not uncover the nakedness of a woman and her daughter, neither shalt thou take her son's daughter, or her daughter's daughter, to uncover her nakedness; *for they are* her near kinswomen: it *is* wickedness.

18 Neither shalt thou take a wife to her sister, to vex *her*, to uncover her nakedness, beside the other in her life *time*.

19 Also thou shalt not approach unto a woman to uncover her nakedness, as long as she is put apart for her uncleanness.

20 Moreover thou shalt not lie carnally with thy neighbour's wife, to defile thyself with her.

21 And thou shalt not let any of thy seed pass through *the fire* to Molech, neither shalt thou profane the name of thy God: I *am* the LORD.

22 Thou shalt not lie with mankind, as with womankind: it *is* abomination.

23 Neither shalt thou lie with any beast to defile thyself therewith: neither shall any woman stand before a beast to lie down thereto: it *is* confusion.

24 Defile not ye yourselves in any of these things: for in all these the nations are defiled which I cast out before you:

25 And the land is defiled: therefore I do visit the iniquity thereof upon it, and the land itself vomiteth out her inhabitants.

26 Ye shall therefore keep my statutes and my judgments, and shall not commit *any* of these abominations;

7) Sex prohibited with aunt (or uncle) by marriage

8) Sex prohibited with daughter-in-law (or son-in-law)

9) Sex prohibited with sister-in-law (or brother-in-law)

10) Sex prohibited with a daughter (or son) or with step-grandchildren

11) Marriage prohibited with a sister-in-law while one's wife is living

3. The prohibition against having sex during a wife's period: Her time of discharge, discomfort, mood swings, sensitivity, & feelings of being unclean

4. The prohibition against illicit acts & unnatural acts (sexual deviancy)
a. The illicit act of adultery: Defiles a person
b. The illicit act of child-sacrifice to idols
1) Profaned God's name: Disgraced, dishonored God
2) The warning: "I am the LORD"
c. The unnatural, perverted act of homosexuality: Is detestable
d. The bizarre, detestable act of bestiality: Perverts & defiles a person

5. The warning of God against worldliness, against sexual impurity & deviancy
a. Warning 1: Must not defile oneself in any illicit sexual act
1) The reason: Was how the Canaanites (the worldly) defiled themselves & their land
2) The judgment: God punished them, vomited them out (rejected them)
b. Warning 2: Must keep God's decrees & laws
c. Warning 3: The citizens of a

nation—native-born or foreign—must not commit such illicit, perverted & detestable sexual acts
  1) Deviancy of this nature was done by the Canaanites (the worldly)
  2) Vulgar, uncivilized behavior defiled the land
d. Warning 4: If such acts are committed, the judgment of God will fall
  1) Will be rejected, vomited out
	neither any of your own nation, nor any stranger that sojourneth among you:
	27 (For all these abominations have the men of the land done, which *were* before you, and the land is defiled;)
	28 That the land spue not you out also, when ye defile it, as it spued out the nations that *were* before you.
		29 For whosoever shall commit any of these abominations, even the souls that commit *them* shall be cut off from among their people.
		30 Therefore shall ye keep mine ordinance, that *ye* commit not *any one* of these abominable customs, which were committed before you, and that ye defile not yourselves therein: I *am* the LORD your God.
			2) Will be cut off
			e. Warning 5: Must keep God's laws & live a life of separation—not following any detestable customs of the world
			f. Warning 6: The supreme authority standing behind the laws is "the LORD your God"

DIVISION IV

THE WAY TO LIVE A HOLY LIFE BEFORE GOD (PART 2):
A PURE SPIRIT (SANCTIFICATION), 17:1–27:34

B. Laws That Govern Sexual Behavior: The Prohibition Against Illicit Sex and Sexual Perversion, 18:1-30

(18:1-30) **Introduction—Immorality—Sex, Perversion of—Perversion, Sexual—Deviancy, Sexual**: the moral foundation of society is crumbling. People have been so bombarded with sexual exposure that few restraints against immorality remain. Illicit affairs, spouse-swapping, sexual experimentation, living together without being married—all illicit sex has contributed to the crumbling of morality. But in addition to illicit sex, the perverted forms of sex have bombarded society: homosexuality, pornography, sexual abuse of children and adults, bestiality, and incest. Immorality is hammering away at society with such force that the very foundation of society is crumbling. How can we say this? Because immorality weakens a person: it brings down a man's desires and appetites to the lowest level; it corrupts a man to live on the level of animals. Immorality causes a person to sink down until he becomes thoroughly corrupt, unable to discern between good and evil, between what is right and what is wrong. When the relationships of society crumble, society itself crumbles. Immorality destroys the relationships between people: the relationship between husband and wife, child and parent, friend and friend, neighbor and neighbor, employer and employee, boyfriend and girlfriend. Once the relationships between people are destroyed, unkindness and all forms of abuse and lawlessness become deep-rooted within society.

Note another fact about immorality: immorality affects all the great virtues and values of life. Just think how the following virtues and values are weakened by immorality:

⇒ trust and faith
⇒ love and caring
⇒ assurance and confidence
⇒ joy and enjoyment
⇒ stability and a sense of belonging
⇒ a sense of purpose and meaning

⇒ loyalty and faithfulness
⇒ child-bearing and nurturing
⇒ peace and security
⇒ self-esteem and self-worth
⇒ satisfaction and fulfillment
⇒ responsibility and accountability

If the problem of immorality is not solved, society will crumble. Immorality is eating away at the heart and foundation of society in four ways.
1) Immorality is eating away at the great virtues and values of life. Immorality is running so rampant throughout society, bombarding the minds of people so much, that *cheating* and *lying* and the abuse of the virtues listed above are becoming acceptable.
2) Immorality is leading to all forms of abuse and lawlessness. Immorality has bombarded the minds of people so much that the natural, normal act of sex is no longer satisfying. As a result, more and more people are turning to the bizarre, the perverted, the deviant, and the brutal acts of sex. People are becoming more and more lawless in order to gain or promote sex.
3) Immorality—the stimulation and excitement of illicit sex—is warping the minds of people so that they are calling evil good and good evil, refusing to be honest, denying the obvious danger and wrong of immorality.
4) Immorality has corrupted sex, corrupted one of the most precious, intimate, and enjoyable gifts of God to man and woman. Immorality has taken the holy and pure experience of sex and trampled it underfoot.

God's Holy Scripture speaks to every generation of people that become obsessed with sex. This chapter is a strong declaration of God against immorality. God tells His people exactly how to behave and live. God's people are to be marked by morality, by living holy and pure lives in the midst of worldly and immoral people. Moreover, God's people are never to compromise their witness by having illicit sex or participating in the acts of sexual perversion and deviancy. This is the subject of this most important passage of Scripture: *Laws That Govern Sexual Behavior: The Prohibition Against Illicit Sex and Sexual Perversion*, 18:1-30.
  1. The Lawgiver: the LORD (vv.1-5).
  2. The prohibition against incest: not to sexually approach any close family member or relative (vv.6-18).

3. The prohibition against having sex during a wife's period: her time of discharge, discomfort, mood swings, sensitivity, and feelings of being unclean (v.19).
4. The prohibition against illicit acts and unnatural acts (sexual deviancy) (vv.20-23).
5. The warning of God against worldliness, against sexual impurity and deviancy (vv.24-30).

1 (18:1-5) **Law, Source—Separation—Law, Meaning—Decrees, Meaning—Regulations, Meaning—Egypt, Morality of—Canaan, Morality of**: there was the Lawgiver, the LORD Himself. The importance of these laws cannot be overstated. These introductory verses show this. Note the Scripture and outline:

OUTLINE	SCRIPTURE	SCRIPTURE	OUTLINE
1. The Lawgiver: The LORD	And the LORD spake unto Moses, saying,	shall ye walk in their ordinances.	
a. God emphatically declares: "I am the LORD your God"	2 Speak unto the children of Israel, and say unto them, I am the LORD your God.	4 Ye shall do my judgments, and keep mine ordinances, to walk therein: I *am* the LORD your God.	b. God emphatically declares: "I am the LORD your God" 1) Must obey my laws 2) Must follow my decrees
1) Must live a life of separation • Not behave as the Egyptians • Not behave as the Canaanites	3 After the doings of the land of Egypt, wherein ye dwelt, shall ye not do: and after the doings of the land	5 Ye shall therefore keep my statutes, and my judgments: which if a man do, he shall live in them: I *am*	c. God emphatically declares: "I am the LORD your God" 1) Keep my decrees & laws 2) The reason: Will receive
2) Must not follow their practices	of Canaan, whither I bring you, shall ye not do: neither	the LORD.	life

There is strong authority standing behind these laws, God Himself: "I am the Lord your God." This statement of God's authority is emphatically declared three times (vv.2, 4, 5). The point is striking: God has the right to issue these laws, the right to demand sexual purity. He is holy, and He demands that His people be holy. Note a significant fact in God's threefold emphasis: the covenant is being reconfirmed with God's people. Sexual purity is so important that it is wrapped up in God's covenant with man. Simply stated, if a person will obey God's law, if a person will live a life of moral separation—a life different from the world of immorality that surrounds him—God will give him life. Again, God makes the emphatic declaration three times: "I am the LORD your God." Note that God emphasizes a different point each time.

a. God emphatically declares: "I am the LORD *your God*" (vv.2-3). The stress in this declaration is "*your God.*" This means that you must live a life of separation (v.3). God is "*your God*"; therefore live a life that is separated, set apart to Him, a life that is moral, that is different from the worldly and immoral people who live around you. God's people are not to behave as the Egyptians did nor behave as the Canaanites did. Remember, the Israelites had just come out of the land of Egypt, and they were about to enter the land of Canaan where they would be surrounded by the Canaanite people. The Egyptians and Canaanites perverted sex. They practiced the most degenerate, deviant, freakish sex imaginable. They took one of the most precious gifts God had given to man, sex within marriage, and corrupted it. The tragic and disgusting sexual behavior covered throughout this chapter had become a way of life for the Egyptians and Canaanites. History and archeological discoveries show that incest was a common practice among royal families and probably among other families as well. The horrible, distasteful sin of bestiality was practiced, and homosexuality was common, as is witnessed in Sodom and Gomorrah. The Egyptians and Canaanites stand as a warning to all generations of history, a fearful picture of the result of entrenched immorality. They sunk to a depth of unrestrained, reckless immorality. As stated, they indulged in the most horrendous, disgusting sexual acts imaginable: sodomy, bestiality, homosexuality—all forms of sexual deviancy and impurity, illicit and unnatural acts.

God had to separate His people. Holiness demanded it. If they were going to be His people—the holy people of God—they had to be separated from the influence and environment of such sexually perverted people. God's people absolutely must not follow the practices of such immoral people.

b. God emphatically declares: "I am *the LORD your God*" (v.4). This stresses that God is "*the LORD your God.*" As the Lord, God has established and given certain laws and decrees that must be kept. As the Lord, He has the right to demand that His laws and decrees be kept. By whom? He is "your God." It is you—every believer—who is to keep His laws and decrees. God emphatically declares, "I am *the LORD your God*"; therefore you must obey my laws and decrees. You must live a moral life; you must be sexually pure. You must live a life of separation, a life that is different from the immoral and sexually perverted people who surround you. You must stay away from the influence of the immoral and sexually perverted. You must not follow the immoral, perverted practices of the Egyptians, nor the immoral, perverted practices of the Canaanites. You must obey God's laws and follow His decrees because He is "*the LORD your God.*"

c. God emphatically declares: "I am *the LORD*" (v.5). This declaration stresses "the LORD" (v.5). This means that the believer will receive life if he keeps God's decrees and laws. As the Lord, God has the power and authority to give life, life abundant and life eternal. God will keep His covenant. If His people will live holy and pure lives, He will give them life—real life.

Thought 1. Three lessons are clearly seen in this point:

(1) We must live a life of separation, a life that is different from the immoral and sexually perverted people of the world. We must not follow the immoral and perverted practices of the world. We must live lives separated, set apart, to God.

> **"And take heed to yourselves, lest at any time your hearts be overcharged with surfeiting, and drunkenness, and cares of this life, and so that day come upon you unawares" (Lu.21:34).**

"If ye were of the world, the world would love his own: but because ye are not of the world, but I have chosen you out of the world, therefore the world hateth you" (Jn.15:19).

"And with many other words did he testify and exhort, saying, Save yourselves from this untoward generation" (Ac.2:40).

"And be not conformed to this world: but be ye transformed by the renewing of your mind, that ye may prove what is that good, and acceptable, and perfect, will of God" (Ro.12:2).

"Wherefore come out from among them, and be ye separate, saith the Lord, and touch not the unclean *thing;* and I will receive you, And will be a Father unto you, and ye shall be my sons and daughters, saith the Lord Almighty" (2 Co.6:17-18).

"And have no fellowship with the unfruitful works of darkness, but rather reprove *them.* For it is a shame even to speak of those things which are done of them in secret" (Ep.5:11-12).

"Thou shalt not follow a multitude to *do* evil; neither shalt thou speak in a cause to decline after many to wrest *judgment*" (Ex.23:2).

"Depart ye, depart ye, go ye out from thence, touch no unclean *thing;* go ye out of the midst of her; be ye clean, that bear the vessels of the LORD" (Is.52:11).

(2) We must obey the laws and decrees of God. We must live moral, sexually pure lives before God. We must not commit adultery nor the perversions of incest, homosexuality, and bestiality.

"Not every one that saith unto me, Lord, Lord, shall enter into the kingdom of heaven; but he that doeth the will of my Father which is in heaven" (Mt.7:21).

"For this is the love of God, that we keep his commandments: and his commandments are not grievous" (1 Jn.5:3).

"Ye shall diligently keep the commandments of the LORD your God, and his testimonies, and his statutes, which he hath commanded thee" (De.6:17).

"And now, Israel, what doth the LORD thy God require of thee, but to fear the LORD thy God, to walk in all his ways, and to love him, and to serve the LORD thy God with all thy heart and with all thy soul, To keep the commandments of the LORD, and his statutes, which I command thee this day for thy good?" (De.10:12-13).

"This day the LORD thy God hath commanded thee to do these statutes and judgments: thou shalt therefore keep and do them with all thine heart, and with all thy soul" (De.26:16).

"But take diligent heed to do the commandment and the law, which Moses the servant of the LORD charged you, to love the LORD your God, and to walk in all his ways, and to keep his commandments, and to cleave unto him, and to serve him with all your heart and with all your soul" (Jos.22:5).

(3) God keeps His promises, fulfills His covenant. If we obey God and keep His commandments, He will give us life, life abundant and life eternal. But note: we must obey God; we must live moral and pure lives.

"If thou wilt enter into life, keep the commandments" (Mt.19:17).

"Verily, verily, I say unto you, If a man keep my saying, he shall never see death" (Jn.8:51).

"Blessed *are* they that do his commandments, that they may have right to the tree of life, and may enter in through the gates into the city" (Re.22:14).

"Now therefore, if ye will obey my voice indeed, and keep my covenant, then ye shall be a peculiar treasure unto me above all people: for all the earth *is* mine: And ye shall be unto me a kingdom of priests, and an holy nation" (Ex.19:5-6).

DEEPER STUDY # 1
(18:5) **Decree** (huqqah): this word means rule, ordinance, regulation, statute. The root word means "to inscribe"; to lay down a boundary line over which no person may cross; to put some limitation on a person; to lay down and issue some rule or decree that a person must obey.

DEEPER STUDY # 2
(18:3) **Law** (mispat): this word means a judgment, a legal decision passed down by a judge (Wenham, Gordon J. *The Book of Leviticus,* p.253); a just decision that must be kept; a law or regulation of true justice; a law that has to be obeyed in order for justice to be done.

---

2 (18:6-18) **Immorality—Sexual Impurity—Incest—Family, Duty—Abuse, of Children—Abuse, of Spouse—Children, Abuse of**: there was the prohibition against incest. No person is to sexually approach any close family member or relative. This covers the human relationships established by blood or marriage. Families are usually bound together in the closest relationships, especially in the immediate family. But even more distant relatives sometimes maintain a close tie. The home and domestic situations are far too often violated sexually. God wants His people living holy and pure lives; therefore, He spells out what sexual relations are allowed. He leaves no question unanswered. Note the outline and Scripture:

OUTLINE	SCRIPTURE	SCRIPTURE	OUTLINE
2. The prohibition against Incest: Not to sexually approach any close family member or relative	6 None of you shall approach to any that is near of kin to him, to uncover *their* nakedness: I *am* the LORD.	sister: she *is* thy father's near kinswoman.	
a. The emphatic warning: "I am the LORD"	7 The nakedness of thy father, or the nakedness of thy mother, shalt thou not uncover: she *is* thy mother; thou shalt not uncover her nakedness.	13 Thou shalt not uncover the nakedness of thy mother's sister: for she *is* thy mother's near kinswoman.	
b. The sexual relations prohibited			
1) Sex prohibited with mother (or father)		14 Thou shalt not uncover the nakedness of thy father's brother, thou shalt not approach to his wife: she *is* thine aunt.	7) Sex prohibited with aunt (or uncle) by marriage
2) Sex prohibited with step-mothers (or step-fathers)	8 The nakedness of thy father's wife shalt thou not uncover: it *is* thy father's nakedness.	15 Thou shalt not uncover the nakedness of thy daughter in law: she *is* thy son's wife; thou shalt not uncover her nakedness.	8) Sex prohibited with daughter-in-law (or son-in-law)
3) Sex prohibited with sisters or half-sisters (or brothers or half-brothers)	9 The nakedness of thy sister, the daughter of thy father, or daughter of thy mother, *whether she be* born at home, or born abroad, *even* their nakedness thou shalt not uncover.	16 Thou shalt not uncover the nakedness of thy brother's wife: it *is* thy brother's nakedness.	9) Sex prohibited with sister-in-law (or brother-in-law)
4) Sex prohibited with grand-children or step-grandchildren	10 The nakedness of thy son's daughter, or of thy daughter's daughter, *even* their nakedness thou shalt not uncover: for theirs *is* thine own nakedness.	17 Thou shalt not uncover the nakedness of a woman and her daughter, neither shalt thou take her son's daughter, or her daughter's daughter, to uncover her nakedness; *for* they *are* her near kinswomen: it *is* wickedness.	10) Sex prohibited with a daughter (or son) or with step-grandchildren: This is the ultimate wickedness
5) Sex prohibited with step-sister (or step-brother)	11 The nakedness of thy father's wife's daughter, begotten of thy father, she *is* thy sister, thou shalt not uncover her nakedness.	18 Neither shalt thou take a wife to her sister, to vex *her*, to uncover her nakedness, beside the other in her life *time*.	11) Marriage prohibited with a sister-in-law while one's wife is living
6) Sex prohibited with aunt (or uncle) by birth	12 Thou shalt not uncover the nakedness of thy father's		

3 (18:19) **Women, Menstrual Period of—Menstrual Period, Sex During—Husband, Duty toward Wife—Morality, Duty of**: there was the prohibition against having sex during a wife's period. This was her time of discharge—a time of discomfort, mood swings, sensitivity, and feelings of being unclean. Very simply, God was protecting the woman against an inconsiderate husband. (See Note—Le.15:19-23 for more discussion.) Note the verse:

OUTLINE	SCRIPTURE
3. The prohibition against having sex during a wife's period: Her time of discharge, (discomfort, mood swings, sensitivity, & feelings of being unclean)	19 Also thou shalt not approach unto a woman to uncover her nakedness, as long as she is put apart for her uncleanness.

4 (18:20-23) **Deviancy, Sexual—Sex, Deviant—Homosexuality—Bestiality—Sex, Illicit—Behavior, Unnatural—Human Sacrifice—Molech, False God of—Child Sacrifice—Sacrifice, of Children**: there was the prohibition against illicit sexual acts and unnatural sexual acts (sexual deviancy). All of these were practiced by the neighbors of God's people. God's people are to protect themselves against such illicit and deviant acts of immorality. Note the Scripture and outline:

OUTLINE	SCRIPTURE	SCRIPTURE	OUTLINE
4. The prohibition against illicit acts & unnatural acts (sexual deviancy)	20 Moreover thou shalt not lie carnally with thy neighbour's wife, to defile thyself with her.	22 Thou shalt not lie with mankind, as with womankind: it *is* abomination.	c. The unnatural, perverted act of homosexuality: Is detestable
a. The illicit act of adultery: Defiles both parties		23 Neither shalt thou lie with any beast to defile thyself therewith: neither shall any woman stand before a beast to lie down thereto: it *is* confusion.	d. The bizarre, detestable act of bestiality: Perverts & defiles a person
b. The illicit act of child-sacrifice to idols	21 And thou shalt not let any of thy seed pass through *the fire* to Molech, neither shalt thou profane the name of thy God: I *am* the LORD.		
1) Profaned God's name: Disgraced, dishonored God			
2) The warning: "I am the LORD"			

Thought 1. God wants His people and their families protected against the illicit, unnatural acts of their neighbors. God is holy; therefore, the believer is to be holy. He is to live a pure and clean life, never engaging in the illicit and unnatural sexual acts of the world.

(1) God forbids the illicit act of adultery (v.20). Note that adultery defiles both parties. It makes both the man and the woman unclean before God.

"Ye have heard that it was said by them of old time, Thou shalt not commit adultery: But I say unto you, That whosoever looketh on a woman to lust after her hath committed adultery with her already in his heart" (Mt.5:27-28).
"Thou shalt not commit adultery" (Ex.20:14).
"And did not he make one? Yet had he the residue of the spirit. And wherefore one? That he might seek a godly seed. Therefore take heed to your spirit, and let none deal treacherously against the wife of his youth" (Mal.2:15).

(2) God forbids the illicit act of child-sacrifice to idols (v.21). This was a brutal and savage act. Such a brutal abuse of children is unthinkable. But note: the brutal, savage abuse of children takes place even today. Unborn and newborn children are being killed by the millions every year all over the world, thousands every day. Why? Simply because of selfishness: the child is simply not wanted. Imagine such atrocity! And just as tragic, children are beaten and battered, yelled at and screamed at by the thousands every day. There is an epidemic of child abuse sweeping the world. Note what God says: child abuse profanes the name of God Himself. God is disgraced and dishonored by the abusive behavior of parents toward their children. To state the matter a different way: to abuse a child is to abuse God Himself. This God will not tolerate from any human being. Note the warning: "I am the LORD." There is only one LORD of the universe and that LORD has the power to execute justice and judgment. And the LORD will execute justice and judgment, vengeance upon the child-abuser.

"Thou shalt not kill [murder]" (Ex.20:13).
"But Jesus said, Suffer little children, and forbid them not, to come unto me: for of such is the kingdom of heaven" (Mt.19:14).
"And, ye fathers, provoke not your children to wrath: but bring them up in the nurture and admonition of the Lord" (Ep.6:4).
"But let none of you suffer as a murderer" (1 Pe.4:15).
"No murderer hath eternal life abiding in him" (1 Jn.3:15).
"When my father and my mother forsake me, then the LORD will take me up" (Ps.27:10).
"Lo, children *are* an heritage of the LORD: *and* the fruit of the womb *is his* reward" (Ps.127:3).
"And they have built the high places of Tophet, which is in the valley of the son of Hinnom, to burn their sons and their daughters in the fire; which I commanded *them* not, neither came it into my heart. "Therefore, behold, the days come, saith the LORD, that it shall no more be called Tophet, nor the valley of the son of Hinnom, but the valley of slaughter: for they shall bury in Tophet, till there be no place. And the carcases of this people shall be meat for the fowls of the heaven, and for the beasts of the earth; and none shall fray *them* away" (Je.7:31-33; see 2 K.17:31; 23:10; Je.32:35).

(3) God forbids the unnatural, perverted act of homosexuality (v.22). Note that God declares that homosexuality is detestable: disgusting, repugnant, repulsive, an abomination. Homosexuality is a perversion of sex, an unnatural act. God gave man a sexual organ and a woman a sexual organ, each made for the other. The organ of man was not made for another man; neither was the woman's organ made for another woman. Man and woman were made to fit together and to share together. Note, the word abomination (toebah) is a word of strong disapproval. It means extreme dislike; to hate, abhor, detest; to feel contempt and nausea toward.

"For this cause God gave them up unto vile affections: for even their women did change the natural use into that which is against nature: And likewise also the men, leaving the natural use of the woman, burned in their lust one toward another; men with men working that which is unseemly, and receiving in themselves that recompence of their error which was meet. And even as they did not like to retain God in *their* knowledge, God gave them over to a reprobate mind, to do those things which are not convenient" (Ro.1:26-28).
"Know ye not that the unrighteous shall not inherit the kingdom of God? Be not deceived: neither fornicators, nor idolaters, nor adulterers, nor effeminate, nor abusers of themselves with mankind, Nor thieves, nor covetous, nor drunkards, nor revilers, nor extortioners, shall inherit the kingdom of God" (1 Co.6:9-10).
"Now the works of the flesh are manifest, which are *these*; Adultery, fornication, uncleanness, lasciviousness, Idolatry, witchcraft, hatred, variance, emulations, wrath, strife, seditions, heresies" (Ga.5:19-20).
"But the fearful, and unbelieving, and the abominable, and murderers, and whoremongers, and sorcerers, and idolaters, and all liars, shall have their part in the lake which burneth with fire and brimstone: which is the second death" (Re.21:8).

(4) God forbids the bizarre, detestable act of bestiality (v.23). Note that sexual relations with an animal perverts and defiles a person. Bestiality is a perverted, unnatural, deviant act between a man and an animal. It violates the

very God-given relationship between man and animal. Man is to live a holy life before God, and holiness involves keeping everything distinct—separated and set apart to fulfill its God-given purpose.

"Whosoever lieth with a beast shall surely be put to death" (Ex.22:19).
"And if a man lie with a beast, he shall surely be put to death: and ye shall slay the beast. And if a woman approach unto any beast, and lie down thereto, thou shalt kill the woman, and the beast: they shall surely be put to death; their blood *shall be* **upon them" (Le.20:15-16).**
"Cursed *be* **he that lieth with any manner of beast. And all the people shall say, Amen" (De.27:21).**

5 (18:24-30) **Immorality, Warning Against—Warning, Against Immorality—Worldliness, Duty Toward—Worldliness, Judgment of—Separation**: there was the warning of God against worldliness, against sexual impurity and deviancy. God gives six warnings. Note the Scripture and outline:

OUTLINE	SCRIPTURE	SCRIPTURE	OUTLINE

5. The warning of God against worldliness, against sexual impurity & deviancy
a. Warning 1: Must not defile oneself in any illicit sexual act
  1) The reason: Was how the Canaanites (the worldly) defiled themselves & their land
  2) The judgment: God punished them, vomited them out (rejected them)
b. Warning 2: Must keep God's decrees & laws
c. Warning 3: God's people to allow any person—native-born or foreign—to commit such illicit, perverted, & detestable sexual acts
  1) Deviancy of this nature was done by the Canaanites (the
	24 Defile not ye yourselves in any of these things: for in all these the nations are defiled which I cast out before you:
	25 And the land is defiled: therefore I do visit the iniquity thereof upon it, and the land itself vomiteth out her inhabitants.
	26 Ye shall therefore keep my statutes and my judgments, and shall not commit *any* of these abominations *neither* any of your own nation, nor any stranger that sojourneth among you:
	27 (For all these abominations have the men of the
		land done, which *were* before you, and the land is defiled;)
		28 That the land spue not you out also, when ye defile it, as it spued out the nations that *were* before you.
		29 For whosoever shall commit any of these abominations, even the souls that commit *them* shall be cut off from among their people.
		30 Therefore shall ye keep mine ordinance, that *ye* commit not *any one* of these abominable customs, which were committed before you, and that ye defile not yourselves therein: I *am* the LORD your God.
			worldly)
			  2) Vulgar, uncivilized behavior defiled the land
			d. Warning 4: The judgment of God will fall if such acts are committed
			  1) Will be rejected, vomited out
			  2) Will be cut off
			
			e. Warning 5: Must keep God's laws & live a life of separation—not following any detestable customs of the world
			f. Warning 6: The supreme authority standing behind the laws is "the LORD your God"

a. Warning 1: the believer must not defile himself in any illicit, perverted sexual act (vv.24-25). All sin defiles a person, but some sins cause so much corruption and dirt that God especially despises them. Sexual perversion is one of these sins.

Note what God says: sexual perversion was the terrible sin that defiled the Canaanites. Even the land was defiled by sexual perversion. How?

⇒ Immorality made the land unfit and unworthy for God's presence and Tabernacle.
⇒ Immorality made the land unfit and unwholesome for God's people lest the evil influence contaminate them and lead them astray.
⇒ Immorality made the land unfit for and repulsive to any decent, moral-minded person (see Lot, for outline and notes—Ge.19:1-38 for an example).

The land had become corrupted, defiled, despicable because of immorality and acts of illicit and perverted sex. Note what God did: He punished the land because of the sin. He vomited or removed the people from the promised land. What a descriptive picture! A people so sexually perverted that they nauseated the land itself. They just made the land unfit for God and for decent people to live within its borders.

b. Warning 2: God's people must keep God's laws and decrees. The believers must not follow the Canaanites in their immoral behavior, must not engage in illicit sex, must not commit sexual perversion (v.25). The believer must obey God: live a holy, moral, and pure life.

c. Warning 3: God's people must not allow any person—a native-born citizen or a foreigner—to commit such illicit and detestable sexual acts and perversions (vv.26-27). Why be so strict when dealing with native-born citizens and foreigners? Because sexual deviancy was a common practice among so many of the Canaanites, and their deviancy polluted and defiled the land. Sex is a normal act. If illicit sex was condoned, many would be influenced and led astray. Therefore, God's people must work to keep the whole of society morally pure and clean.

d. Warning 4: the judgment of God will fall if illicit and perverted sex is allowed to permeate and corrupt the land (vv.28-29). Note what God says:

⇒ The land will reject, vomit His people out.
⇒ All persons who engage in illicit and perverted sex must be cut off. No matter who the persons are, they will be cut off from God and from the people of God.

e. Warning 5: the believer must keep God's laws and live a life of separation. He must not follow any of the detestable customs of the worldly (v.30).

f. Warning 6: note the supreme authority standing behind the laws governing sexual behavior: "I am the LORD your God" (v.30). The point is this: God, as the Creator and Sovereign Ruler of the universe, has the power and authority to execute justice and judgment upon His people. And He will.

Thought 1. God warns both His people and the people of the world:

(1) He is going to execute justice and judgment upon the immoral...
⇒ upon all adulterers, homosexuals, and child abusers
⇒ upon all who commit incest and bestiality
⇒ upon all who defile and pervert the God-given preciousness of the sexual relationship between husband and wife

"For the wrath of God is revealed from heaven against all ungodliness and unrighteousness of men, who hold the truth in unrighteousness....For this cause God gave them up unto vile affections: for even their women did change the natural use into that which is against nature: And likewise also the men, leaving the natural use of the woman, burned in their lust one toward another; men with men working that which is unseemly, and receiving in themselves that recompence of their error which was meet. And even as they did not like to retain God in *their* knowledge, God gave them over to a reprobate mind, to do those things which are not convenient; Being filled with all unrighteousness, fornication, wickedness, covetousness, maliciousness; full of envy, murder, debate, deceit, malignity; whisperers, Backbiters, haters of God, despiteful, proud, boasters, inventors of evil things, disobedient to parents, Without understanding, covenantbreakers, without natural affection, implacable, unmerciful: Who knowing the judgment of God, that they which commit such things are worthy of death, not only do the same, but have pleasure in them that do them" (Ro.1:18, 26-32).

"Know ye not that the unrighteous shall not inherit the kingdom of God? Be not deceived: neither fornicators, nor idolaters, nor adulterers, nor effeminate, nor abusers of themselves with mankind, Nor thieves, nor covetous, nor drunkards, nor revilers, nor extortioners, shall inherit the kingdom of God" (1 Co.6:9-10).

"Now the works of the flesh are manifest, which are *these;* Adultery, fornication, uncleanness, lasciviousness, Idolatry, witchcraft, hatred, variance, emulations, wrath, strife, seditions, heresies, Envyings, murders, drunkenness, revellings, and such like: of the which I tell you before, as I have also told *you* in time past, that they which do such things shall not inherit the kingdom of God" (Ga.5:19-21).

"But the fearful, and unbelieving, and the abominable, and murderers, and whoremongers, and sorcerers, and idolaters, and all liars, shall have their part in the lake which burneth with fire and brimstone: which is the second death" (Re.21:8).

(2) He demands that the believer separate himself, have nothing to do with the sexual immorality of his neighbors and the world. The believer is to live a holy, moral, righteous, and pure life, a life that is different from the worldly, a life that is separated and set apart to God.

"And take heed to yourselves, lest at any time your hearts be overcharged with surfeiting, and drunkenness, and cares of this life, and so that day come upon you unawares" (Lu.21:34).

"I beseech you therefore, brethren, by the mercies of God, that ye present your bodies a living sacrifice, holy, acceptable unto God, *which is* your reasonable service. And be not conformed to this world: but be ye transformed by the renewing of your mind, that ye may prove what is that good, and acceptable, and perfect, will of God" (Ro.12:1-2).

"Wherefore come out from among them, and be ye separate, saith the Lord, and touch not the unclean *thing;* and I will receive you, And will be a Father unto you, and ye shall be my sons and daughters, saith the Lord Almighty" (2 Co.6:17-18).

"And have no fellowship with the unfruitful works of darkness, but rather reprove *them.* For it is a shame even to speak of those things which are done of them in secret" (Ep.5:11-12).

"Love not the world, neither the things *that are* in the world. If any man love the world, the love of the Father is not in him. For all that *is* in the world, the lust of the flesh, and the lust of the eyes, and the pride of life, is not of the Father, but is of the world" (1 Jn.2:15-16).

"Depart ye, depart ye, go ye out from thence, touch no unclean *thing;* go ye out of the midst of her; be ye clean, that bear the vessels of the LORD" (Is.52:11).

CHAPTER 19

C. Laws That Govern Day-to-Day Behavior, Personal Conduct: The Duty to Live a Life of Separation, a Life of Real Devotion to God, 19:1-37

1. Man's duty to God
 a. Must be holy: The basic, foundational duty
  1) Because God is the LORD
  2) Because God is holy
  3) Because the LORD is your God
 b. Must respect God's appointed order within the family, one's mother & father
 c. Must worship on the Sabbath
 d. Must not turn to idols or false gods

 e. Must seek the fellowship & peace of God—through the sacrifice (a symbol of Christ): Must approach God in the right way to be acceptable
  1) Must eat the sacrifice on the day it is offered or the next day: To burn any meat three days old
  2) The reason: Contamination

  3) The judgment of a violator: Held accountable, to be cut off—because he desecrated the holy sacrifice offered to God

2. Man's duty to his neighbor
 a. Must make opportunity for the poor to work & eat, even if they are foreigners or immigrants
  1) To leave enough harvest for them to feed themselves
  2) The authority of this law: God Himself

 b. Must not steal, lie, or deceive

 c. Must not swear (or use vulgarity)
  1) Profanes God's name
  2) The warning: "I am the LORD"
 d. Must not cheat or steal: Do not steal the wages of a person
 e. Must not mistreat the handicapped

And the LORD spake unto Moses, saying,
2 Speak unto all the congregation of the children of Israel, and say unto them, Ye shall be holy: for I the LORD your God *am* holy.
3 Ye shall fear every man his mother, and his father, and keep my sabbaths: I *am* the LORD your God.
4 Turn ye not unto idols, nor make to yourselves molten gods: I am the Lord your God.
5 And if ye offer a sacrifice of peace offerings unto the LORD, ye shall offer it at your own will.
6 It shall be eaten the same day ye offer it, and on the morrow: and if ought remain until the third day, it shall be burnt in the fire.
7 And if it be eaten at all on the third day, it *is* abominable; it shall not be accepted.
8 Therefore *every one* that eateth it shall bear his iniquity, because he hath profaned the hallowed thing of the LORD: and that soul shall be cut off from among his people.
9 And when ye reap the harvest of your land, thou shalt not wholly reap the corners of thy field, neither shalt thou gather the gleanings of thy harvest.
10 And thou shalt not glean thy vineyard, neither shalt thou gather *every* grape of thy vineyard; thou shalt leave them for the poor and stranger: I *am* the LORD your God.
11 Ye shall not steal, neither deal falsely, neither lie one to another.
12 And ye shall not swear by my name falsely, neither shalt thou profane the name of thy God: I *am* the LORD.
13 Thou shalt not defraud thy neighbour, neither rob *him*: the wages of him that is hired shall not abide with thee all night until the morning.
14 Thou shalt not curse the deaf, nor put a stumbling-block before the blind, but shalt fear thy God: I *am* the LORD.
15 Ye shall do no unrighteousness in judgment: thou shalt not respect the person of the poor, nor honour the person of the mighty: *but* in righteousness shalt thou judge thy neighbour.
16 Thou shalt not go up and down *as* a talebearer among thy people: neither shalt thou stand against the blood of thy neighbour: I *am* the LORD.
17 Thou shalt not hate thy brother in thine heart: thou shalt in any wise rebuke thy neighbour, and not suffer sin upon him.
18 Thou shalt not avenge, nor bear any grudge against the children of thy people, but thou shalt love thy neighbour as thyself: I *am* the LORD.
19 Ye shall keep my statutes. Thou shalt not let thy cattle gender with a diverse kind: thou shalt not sow thy field with mingled seed: neither shall a garment mingled of linen and woollen come upon thee.
20 And whosoever lieth carnally with a woman, that *is* a bondmaid, betrothed to an husband, and not at all redeemed, nor freedom given her; she shall be scourged; they shall not be put to death, because she was not free.
21 And he shall bring his trespass offering unto the LORD, unto the door of the tabernacle of the congregation, *even* a ram for a trespass offering.
22 And the priest shall make an atonement for him with the ram of the trespass offering before the LORD for his sin which he hath done: and the sin which he hath done shall be forgiven him.
23 And when ye shall come into the land, and shall have planted all manner of trees for food, then ye shall count the fruit thereof as uncircumcised: three years shall it be as uncircumcised unto you: it shall not be eaten of.
24 But in the fourth year all the fruit thereof shall be

 1) Not take advantage of
 2) The warning: Fear God

 f. Must be just & fair: Never pervert justice; never show partiality to the poor nor favoritism to the great

 g. Must love your neighbor as yourself
  1) Do not spread slander or gossip
  2) Do not do anything to endanger a neighbor
  3) Do not hate your brother
  4) Rebuke, correct your neighbor when he is doing wrong (Mt.5:23-25)

  5) Do not seek revenge or bear a grudge against anyone

 h. Must keep God's laws & live a life of total separation, a life that is distinct (symbolized by keeping all things separate in their daily lives)
  1) No cross-breeding
  2) No mixing of seed or clothes woven of different fabrics
 i. Must not sexually abuse or mistreat a slave
  1) An example: A man has intercourse with an engaged slave-girl
  2) The penalty or punishment:
   • They are not to be put to death

   • The man is to pay compensation

  3) The needed restoration with God
   • The man must seek forgiveness—through the guilt offering
   • The result: Atonement, reconciliation—his sin will be forgiven

3. Man's duty in different life situations
 a. Must be wise in all work, producing the most possible & dedicating the firstfruit to God
  1) The fruit of the first three years not to be eaten: To allow full development of a tree
  2) The offering of the firstfruit: Give all fruit in praise

to God in the fourth year	holy to praise the LORD *withal*.	defiled by them: I *am* the LORD your God.	2) The warning: "I am the LORD"
3) The blessing of God promised: An abundance of harvest was promised to God's people in the fifth year	25 And in the fifth year shall ye eat of the fruit thereof, that it may yield unto you the increase thereof: I *am* the LORD your God.	32 Thou shalt rise up before the hoary head, and honour the face of the old man, and fear thy God: I *am* the LORD.	f. Must respect the aged by rising in their presence 1) Shows one fears, reveres God 2) The warning: "I am the LORD"
b. Must reject pagan practices 1) Do not eat meat with the blood 2) Reject fortune-telling & sorcery 3) Do not disfigure the body • Not to cut one's hair on the sides or beard	26 Ye shall not eat *any thing* with the blood: neither shall ye use enchantment, nor observe times. 27 Ye shall not round the corners of your heads, neither shalt thou mar the corners of thy beard.	33 And if a stranger sojourn with thee in your land, ye shall not vex him. 34 *But* the stranger that dwelleth with you shall be unto you as one born among you, and thou shalt love	g. Must not mistreat a foreigner 1) To treat him like everyone else: To love him as yourself
• Not to cut one's body or tattoo the body	28 Ye shall not make any cuttings in your flesh for the dead, nor print any marks upon you: I *am* the LORD.	him as thyself; for ye were strangers in the land of Egypt: I *am* the LORD your God.	2) The reason: Because you were an alien in Egypt (a symbol of the world) before God freed you
c. Must not allow a daughter to become a prostitute 1) Degrades a person 2) Corrupts a land: Fills it with all kinds of evil	29 Do not prostitute thy daughter, to cause her to be a whore; lest the land fall to whoredom, and the land become full of wickedness.	35 Ye shall do no unrighteousness in judgment, in meteyard, in weight, or in measure. 36 Just balances, just weights, a just ephah, and a	h. Must be honest in business dealings 1) Do not use deceitfulness when measuring something 2) Use accurate scales & weights & containers
d. Keep the Sabbath & reverence God's sanctuary, not that of pagans—a warning from God e. Do not turn to nor rely upon mediums or psychics 1) They defile a person	30 Ye shall keep my sabbaths, and reverence my sanctuary: I *am* the LORD. 31 Regard not them that have familiar spirits, neither seek after wizards, to be	just hin, shall ye have: I *am* the LORD your God, which brought you out of the land of Egypt. 37 Therefore shall ye observe all my statutes, and all my judgments, and do them: I *am* the LORD.	3) The reason: "I am the LORD your God"—I set you free from Egypt to be a different, distinct, holy people **4. Man's duty to obey God's laws: To keep & follow all His laws**

DIVISION IV

THE WAY TO LIVE A HOLY LIFE BEFORE GOD (PART 2): A PURE SPIRIT (SANCTIFICATION), 17:1–27:34

C. Laws That Govern Day-to-Day Behavior, Personal Conduct: The Duty to Live a Life of Separation, a Life of Real Devotion to God, 19:1-37

(19:1-37) **Introduction**: the most important document ever written is *The Ten Commandments*. The influence of the Ten Commandments upon nations and societies could never be measured; indeed, the importance of the Ten Commandments could never be over-stressed (see notes and outlines—Ex.20:1-26). In this chapter, all Ten Commandments are either repeated or pointed to as the rules that are to control the day to day life of God's people. The laws of this chapter, like the Ten Commandments, cover every area and facet of human life. God wants His people to live holy and pure lives, lives that are different from the immoral and lawless lives of unbelievers. The laws discussed in this chapter tell a person how to live for God, how to live a holy life that is separated, set apart to God. These laws bring the holiness of God right down to where people live, right down into the hearts and lives of believers. This is the subject of this chapter: *Laws That Govern Day-to-Day Behavior, Personal Conduct: The Duty to Live a Life of Separation, a Life of Real Devotion to God*, 19:1-37.

1. Man's duty to God (vv.1-8).
2. Man's duty to his neighbor (vv.9-22).
3. Man's duty in different life situations (vv.23-36)
4. Man's duty to God's laws: to keep and follow all His laws (v.37).

1 (19:1-8) **Man, Duty to God—Holy, Holiness, Duty to be—God, Holiness of—Parents, Duty to—Sabbath—Idolatry—Fellowship Offering**: the first set of laws govern man's duty to God. God gave five very specific laws to govern man's behavior toward God. Note that God called His messenger to proclaim these laws to the entire assembly of people. It is important for every person to keep these laws.

OUTLINE	SCRIPTURE	SCRIPTURE	OUTLINE
1. Man's duty to God a. Must be holy: The basic, foundational duty 1) Because God is the LORD	And the LORD spake unto Moses, saying, 2 Speak unto all the congregation of the children of Isra-	el, and say unto them, Ye shall be holy: for I the LORD your God *am* holy. 3 Ye shall fear every man	2) Because God is holy 3) Because the LORD is your God b. Must respect God's appointed

OUTLINE	SCRIPTURE	SCRIPTURE	OUTLINE
order within the family, one's mother & father c. Must worship on the Sabbath d. Must not turn to idols or false gods e. Must seek the fellowship & peace of God—through the sacrifice (a symbol of Christ): Must approach God in the right way to be acceptable 1) Must eat the sacrifice on	his mother, and his father, and keep my sabbaths: I *am* the LORD your God. 4 Turn ye not unto idols, nor make to yourselves molten gods: I *am* the LORD your God. 5 And if ye offer a sacrifice of peace offerings unto the LORD, ye shall offer it at your own will. 6 It shall be eaten the same day ye offer it, and on the	morrow: and if ought remain until the third day, it shall be burnt in the fire. 7 And if it be eaten at all on the third day, it *is* abominable; it shall not be accepted. 8 Therefore *every one* that eateth it shall bear his iniquity, because he hath profaned the hallowed thing of the LORD: and that soul shall be cut off from among his people.	the day it is offered or the next day: To burn any meat three days old 2) The reason: Contamination 3) The judgment of a violator: Held accountable, to be cut off—because he desecrated the holy sacrifice offered to God

a. A person must be holy. This is the basic duty of a person to God (v.2). God gives three reasons why His people must be holy:

1) The believer must be holy because God is the LORD. He is the great Creator, the Sovereign LORD and Majesty of the universe. He demands holiness; therefore, His creatures are to do exactly what He says, "Be holy!" As the Creator and Sovereign LORD, He expects and deserves to be obeyed.
2) The believer is to be holy because God Himself, His very nature, is holy. God is distinct and different, totally set apart from all other creatures. God is perfect in righteousness and purity. He dwells in the perfection and light of righteousness and purity. Therefore God expects His people to be holy: distinct and different, righteous and pure in all that they do.
3) God's people are to be holy because the LORD is their God. Believers are to be distinct and different in this one thing: they are to be followers of God. The believer is to be distinct and different from the unbeliever and from the impure people who surround him. When the people of the world see a believer, they are to recognize that he is a follower of God. God is holy; therefore, the believer is to imitate God. The believer is to live a life that is holy, righteous, and pure—a life that is distinct and different from that of the people of the world.

b. A person must respect God's appointed order within the family, one's mother and father (v.3). This is one of the Ten Commandments (Ex.20:12). In the eyes of a small child, the parent is the ultimate authority. However, a problem often arises as a child grows older. He becomes rebellious and disrespectful of his parents. This is what God is combating in this law. Just as a young child respects his parents, so the child is to fully respect his parents as he grows older. This is God's appointed order within the family. Note this: if a parent teaches a child as he should, to obey God, then the child will grow up obeying God and reverencing his parents. Then, as an adult, he will teach his children, passing down the truth of God's commandments from generation to generation.

Tragically, so many parents within the world do not live godly and holy lives themselves. This is the reason for so much juvenile delinquency and lawlessness. Moreover, this is the reason so many young people disrespect their parents, ignoring God and His commandments. A child's behavior is learned through his contacts and through what he sees, especially through his parents. This is the reason God connects this commandment dealing with parents to the commandment to be holy. Parents are to live holy lives before their children. So much of the child's growth is determined by what the mother and father do. A mother and father must live holy, righteous, and pure lives. If they do, the likelihood is that the child will respect his parents.

But note this striking fact: even if the parents do not follow God, a child is to respect his mother and father. Of course, a child is not to respect the evil deeds and behavior of his parents. This is not what God means by the commandment. God does not want any person respecting and following unrighteous or evil behavior. What God means is that a child is to respect the authority and the good things that a mother and father do. A child is to have within his heart an inward reverence and respect for his parents. In fact, a child is to grow up with an inward reverence and esteem for every human being. A child—in truth all of us—is to be a follower of God; and in following God, he is to respect his father and mother.

Thought 1. Jewish scholars explained this commandment as follows: "What is this fear that is owing to a father?...It is not to stand in his way nor to sit in his place, not to contradict what he says nor to carp at it, not to call him by his name, either living or dead, but 'My Father,' or 'Sir;' it is to provide for him if he be poor, and the like."[1]

c. A person must worship God on the Sabbath (v.3). This, too, is one of the Ten Commandments (see outline and notes—Ex.20:8). There is a close connection between this commandment and the two commandments already discussed. The believer—a true believer—will worship God on the Sabbath because he wants to live a holy life before God, because he wants to set an example for his family.

d. A person must not turn to idols or false gods created by the imaginations of people (v.4). The Hebrew word for *idols* (eliyl) means an object that is empty, meaningless, weak, without power, without value; a false object that is no god. The believer must not turn from the true God to false gods, from the Mighty God to impotent gods, from the God of holiness to the god of deception and ruin.[2] Simply stated, the believer is not to turn to false gods that are meaningless and powerless. The believer is to worship and serve the only living and true God.

---

1 *Matthew Henry's Commentary*, Vol.1, p.518.
2 *ibid.*, p.518.

e. The believer must seek the fellowship and peace of God—through the sacrifice: he must approach God in the right way for God to accept him (vv.5-8). Remember, the sacrifice is a symbol of the death of Christ. Note that the focus of this law is the eating of the fellowship offering. When a person brought the fellowship or peace offering to the LORD, he was to eat a portion of the meat. This law stresses that the sacrifice must be eaten on the day it is offered or at the latest on the next day. No meat was to be eaten on the third day: it was impure and would not be accepted by God. It had to be burned. Obviously, the reason for this was spoilage and contamination, and God wanted His people protected. Note that the violator was to be judged and held accountable by God: he was to be cut off from God's presence and from other believers. Why so severe a judgment? Because he had desecrated the holy sacrifice offered to God. Keep in mind that the sacrifice was a symbol of Christ and His sacrifice upon the cross. No person must ever desecrate the sacrifice.

Thought 1. The believer has a relationship with God. He has turned away from the world and trusted the Lord Jesus Christ, His sacrifice, to reconcile him to God. Furthermore God has accepted his trust and adopted the believer to become a part of the family of God. God has become the Father of the believer and the believer has become an adopted son or daughter of God. As stated, the believer now has a relationship with God; therefore, the believer is to obey the Father just as any son or daughter obeys his or her earthly father. The believer is to obey the five rules or laws spelled out in this passage.

(1) The believer is to live a holy life, a life that is set apart to God, that is righteous and pure. God is holy; therefore the believer is to be holy.

"That he would grant unto us, that we being delivered out of the hand of our enemies might serve him without fear, In holiness and righteousness before him, all the days of our life" (Lu.1:74-75).

"Having therefore these promises, dearly beloved, let us cleanse ourselves from all filthiness of the flesh and spirit, perfecting holiness in the fear of God" (2 Co.7:1).

"Follow peace with all *men*, and holiness, without which no man shall see the Lord" (He.12:14).

"Because it is written, Be ye holy; for I am holy" (1 Pe.1:16).

"*Seeing* then *that* all these things shall be dissolved, what manner *of persons* ought ye to be in *all* holy conversation and godliness" (2 Pe.3:11).

"Exalt the LORD our God, and worship at his holy hill; for the LORD our God *is* holy" (Ps.99:9).

(2) The believer is to respect his mother and father.

"Children, obey your parents in the Lord: for this is right. Honour thy father and mother; (which is the first commandment with promise;) That it may be well with thee, and thou mayest live long on the earth" (Ep.6:1-3).

"Children, obey *your* parents in all things: for this is well pleasing unto the Lord" (Col.3:20).

"My son, hear the instruction of thy father, and forsake not the law of thy mother" (Pr.1:8).

"My son, keep thy father's commandment, and forsake not the law of thy mother" (Pr.6:20).

(3) The believer is to worship God on the Sabbath: he is to keep the day of worship holy.

"Remember the sabbath day, to keep it holy" (Ex.20:8).

"Six days thou shalt work, but on the seventh day thou shalt rest: in earing time and in harvest thou shalt rest" (Ex.34:21).

"And upon the first *day* of the week, when the disciples came together to break bread, Paul preached unto them, ready to depart on the morrow; and continued his speech until midnight" (Ac.20:7).

"Upon the first *day* of the week let every one of you lay by him in store, as *God* hath prospered him, that there be no gatherings when I come" (1 Co.16:2).

"Not forsaking the assembling of ourselves together, as the manner of some *is*; but exhorting *one another*: and so much the more, as ye see the day approaching" (He.10:25).

"Blessed *is* the man *that* doeth this, and the son of man *that* layeth hold on it; that keepeth the sabbath from polluting it, and keepeth his hand from doing any evil" (Is.56:2).

"If thou turn away thy foot from the sabbath, *from* doing thy pleasure on my holy day; and call the sabbath a delight, the holy of the LORD, honourable; and shalt honour him, not doing thine own ways, nor finding thine own pleasure, nor speaking *thine own* words: Then shalt thou delight thyself in the LORD; and I will cause thee to ride upon the high places of the earth, and feed thee with the heritage of Jacob thy father: for the mouth of the LORD hath spoken *it*" (Is.58:13-14).

(4) The believer must never turn to idols or false gods.

"Thou shalt not make unto thee any graven image, or any likeness *of any thing* that *is* in heaven above, or that *is* in the earth beneath, or that *is* in the water under the earth" (Ex.20:4).

"Know ye not that the unrighteous shall not inherit the kingdom of God? Be not deceived: neither fornicators, nor idolaters, nor adulterers, nor effeminate, nor abusers of themselves with mankind, Nor thieves, nor covetous, nor drunkards, nor revilers, nor extortioners, shall inherit the kingdom of God" (1 Co.6:9-10).

"Little children, keep yourselves from idols. Amen" (1 Jn.5:21).

"But the fearful, and unbelieving, and the abominable, and murderers, and whoremongers, and sorcerers, and idolaters, and all liars, shall have their part in the lake which burneth with fire and brimstone: which is the second death" (Re.21:8).

"Take heed to yourselves, that your heart be not deceived, and ye turn aside, and serve other gods, and worship them" (De.11:16).

"I *am* the LORD: that *is* my name: and my glory will I not give to another, neither my praise to graven images" (Is.42:8).

(5) The believer must seek to grow in the fellowship and peace of God through the sacrifice of the Lord Jesus Christ.

"Therefore being justified by faith, we have peace with God through our Lord Jesus Christ: By whom also we have access by faith into this grace wherein we stand, and rejoice in hope of the glory of God" (Ro.5:1-2).

"Let us draw near with a true heart in full assurance of faith, having our hearts sprinkled from an evil conscience, and our bodies washed with pure water" (He.10:22).

"Draw nigh to God, and he will draw nigh to you. Cleanse *your* hands, *ye* sinners; and purify *your* hearts, *ye* double minded" (Js.4:8).

"That which we have seen and heard declare we unto you, that ye also may have fellowship with us: and truly our fellowship *is* with the Father, and with his Son Jesus Christ" (1 Jn.1:3).

"Behold, I stand at the door, and knock: if any man hear my voice, and open the door, I will come in to him, and will sup with him, and he with me" (Re.3:20).

"The LORD *is* nigh unto them that are of a broken heart; and saveth such as be of a contrite spirit" (Ps.34:18).

"The LORD *is* nigh unto all them that call upon him, to all that call upon him in truth" (Ps.145:18).

2 (19:9-22) **Neighbor, Duty to—Stealing—Lying—Deceiving—Swearing—Profanity—Vulgarity—Cheating—Handi-capped, The—Justice—Partiality—Favoritism—Love, Duty—Separation—Slave, Sexual Abuse of—Sex, Abuse of**: the second set of laws govern man's duty to his neighbor.

OUTLINE	SCRIPTURE	SCRIPTURE	OUTLINE
2. Man's duty to his neighbor	9 And when ye reap the harvest of your land, thou shalt not wholly reap the corners of thy field, neither shalt thou gather the gleanings of thy harvest.	the person of the mighty: *but* in righteousness shalt thou judge thy neighbour.	
a. Must make opportunity for the poor to work & eat, even if they are foreigners or immigrants			g. Must love your neighbor as yourself
1) To leave enough harvest for them to feed themselves		16 Thou shalt not go up and down *as* a talebearer among thy people: neither shalt thou stand against the blood of thy neighbour: I *am* the LORD.	1) Do not spread slander or gossip
2) The authority of this law: God Himself	10 And thou shalt not glean thy vineyard, neither shalt thou gather *every* grape of thy vineyard; thou shalt leave them for the poor and stranger: I *am* the LORD your God.		2) Do not do anything to endanger a neighbor
		17 Thou shalt not hate thy brother in thine heart: thou shalt in any wise rebuke thy neighbour, and not suffer sin upon him.	3) Do not hate your brother
			4) Rebuke, correct your neighbor when he is doing wrong (Mt.5:23-25)
b. Must not steal, lie, or deceive	11 Ye shall not steal, neither deal falsely, neither lie one to another.		
		18 Thou shalt not avenge, nor bear any grudge against the children of thy people, but thou shalt love thy neighbour as thyself: I *am* the LORD.	5) Do not seek revenge or bear a grudge against anyone
c. Must not swear (or use vulgarity)	12 And ye shall not swear by my name falsely, neither shalt thou profane the name of thy God: I *am* the LORD.		
1) Profanes God's name			
2) The warning: "I am the LORD"			
d. Must not cheat or steal: Do not steal the wages of a person	13 Thou shalt not defraud thy neighbour, neither rob *him*: the wages of him that is hired shall not abide with thee all night until the morning.	19 Ye shall keep my statutes. Thou shalt not let thy cattle gender with a diverse kind: thou shalt not sow thy field with mingled seed: neither shall a garment mingled of linen and woollen come upon thee.	h. Must keep God's laws & live a life of total separation, a life that is distinct (symbolized by keeping all things separate in their daily lives)
			1) No cross-breeding
e. Must not mistreat the handicapped	14 Thou shalt not curse the deaf, nor put a stumblingblock before the blind, but shalt fear thy God: I *am* the LORD		2) No mixing of seed or clothes woven of different fabrics
1) Not take advantage of			
2) The warning: Fear God		20 And whosoever lieth carnally with a woman, that *is* a bondmaid, betrothed to an husband, and not at all redeemed, nor freedom given her; she shall be scourged;	i. Must not sexually abuse or mistreat a slave
f. Must be just & fair: Never pervert justice; never show partiality to the poor nor favoritism to the great	15 Ye shall do no unrighteousness in judgment: thou shalt not respect the person of the poor, nor honour		1) An example: A man has intercourse with an engaged slave-girl
			2) The penalty or

OUTLINE	SCRIPTURE	SCRIPTURE	OUTLINE
punishment: • They are not to be put to death • The man is to pay compensation	they shall not be put to death, because she was not free. 21 And he shall bring his trespass offering unto the LORD, unto the door of the tabernacle of the congregation, *even* a ram for a trespass offering.	22 And the priest shall make an atonement for him with the ram of the trespass offering before the LORD for his sin which he hath done: and the sin which he hath done shall be forgiven him.	3) The needed restoration with God • The man must seek forgiveness—through the guilt offering • The result: Atonement, reconciliation—his sin will be forgiven

a. The believer must make opportunity for the poor to work and eat, even if they are foreigners or immigrants (vv.9-10; see Le.23:22; De.24:19-22). This was known as the law of gleaning. Note that the poor were not fed by handouts nor fed by the crops that had been harvested by the property owners. During harvest, the property owners were to reap their crops and vineyards only one time. The gleanings that were left belonged to the poor. The poor were allowed to go out into the fields and vineyards to glean or harvest whatever was left. But note: they had to harvest their own food. Also note that this law applied to the foreigners or immigrants as well. God loves the poor, and God insists that the property owners and wealthy of this world give opportunity to the poor to work and provide for themselves (see Ruth 2).

> "Jesus said unto him, If thou wilt be perfect, go *and* sell that thou hast, and give to the poor, and thou shalt have treasure in heaven: and come *and* follow me" (Mt.19:21).
> "Only *they would* that we should remember the poor; the same which I also was forward to do" (Ga.2:10).
> "If there be among you a poor man of one of thy brethren within any of thy gates in thy land which the LORD thy God giveth thee, thou shalt not harden thine heart, nor shut thine hand from thy poor brother" (De.15:7).
> "Blessed *is* he that considereth the poor: the LORD will deliver him in time of trouble" (Ps.41:1).
> "Defend the poor and fatherless: do justice to the afflicted and needy" (Ps.82:3).

b. The believer must not steal, lie, or deceive (v.11). This law is taken from two of the Ten Commandments (see outline and notes—Ex.20:15; 20:16). Believers must be fair and honest in all their dealings. They must always be truthful, never lying or deceiving.

> "Thou shalt not steal" (Ex.20:15).
> "Let him that stole steal no more: but rather let him labour, working with *his* hands the thing which is good, that he may have to give to him that needeth" (Ep.4:28).
> "Lie not one to another, seeing that ye have put off the old man with his deeds" (Col.3:9).
> "Not purloining [stealing], but showing all good fidelity; that they may adorn the doctrine of God our Saviour in all things" (Tit.2:10).
> "But the fearful, and unbelieving, and the abominable, and murderers, and whoremongers, and sorcerers, and idolaters, and all liars, shall have their part in the lake which burneth with fire and brimstone: which is the second death" (Re.21:8).
> "Thou shalt destroy them that speak leasing [lying]: the LORD will abhor the bloody and deceitful man" (Ps.5:6).
> "He that worketh deceit shall not dwell within my house: he that telleth lies shall not tarry in my sight" (Ps.101:7).
> "Lying lips *are* abomination to the LORD: but they that deal truly *are* his delight" (Pr.12:22).
> "A false witness shall not be unpunished, and *he that* speaketh lies shall not escape" (Pr.19:5).

c. The believer must not swear nor use profanity or vulgarity (v.12). This law has to do with one of the Ten Commandments as well (see outline and notes—Ex.20:7 for more discussion). Note the words *swear falsely*. This law refers to using God's name in business dealings, taking oaths in court trials or other situations, and making vows—using God's name in such situations when one knows he is lying. This law also refers to profanity and vulgarity, using God's name to curse or using it in some profane way. Note the warning: "I am the LORD." As the LORD, God's name deserves respect and honor. Moreover, as the LORD, God has the power and the authority to defend His name, to execute the most severe judgment upon those who profane and curse His name.

> "Thou shalt not take the name of the LORD thy God in vain; for the LORD will not hold him guiltless that taketh his name in vain" (Ex.20:7).
> "And ye shall not swear by my name falsely, neither shalt thou profane the name of thy God: I *am* the LORD" (Le.19:12).
> "But above all things, my brethren, swear not, neither by heaven, neither by the earth, neither by any other oath: but let your yea be yea; and *your* nay, nay; lest ye fall into condemnation" (Js.5:12).
> "As he loved cursing, so let it come unto him: as he delighted not in blessing, so let it be far from him" (Ps.109:17).

d. The believer must not cheat or steal. This includes stealing the wages of a person who works for him (v.13). This law is also taken from two of the commandments (see outline and notes, *Commandments*—Ex. 20:15; 20:17 for more discussion). Note that in antiquity a person was paid daily. The employer was not allowed to keep his wages overnight. An employer is to pay his workers and pay them on time. No employer is ever to shortchange his workers, neither his hours nor his wages. The employer must pay a fair wage.

> "At his day thou shalt give *him* his hire, neither shall the sun go down upon it; for he *is* poor, and setteth his heart upon it: lest he cry against thee unto the LORD, and it be sin unto thee" (De.24:15).
> "Woe unto him that buildeth his house by unrighteousness, and his chambers by wrong; *that* useth his neighbour's service without wages, and giveth him not for his work" (Je.22:13).
> "And I will come near to you to judgment; and I will be a swift witness against the sorcerers, and against the adulterers, and against false swearers, and against those that oppress the hireling in *his* wages, the widow, and the fatherless, and that turn aside the stranger *from his right,* and fear not me, saith the LORD of hosts" (Mal.3:5).
> "Masters, give unto *your* servants that which is just and equal; knowing that ye also have a Master in heaven" (Col.4:1).
> "Behold, the hire of the labourers who have reaped down your fields, which is of you kept back by fraud, crieth: and the cries of them which have reaped are entered into the ears of the LORD of sabaoth" (Js.5:4).

e. The believer must not mistreat the handicapped (v.14). A deaf person could not hear someone cursing him; therefore, he did not know that he needed to defend his name or position. A blind person, of course, could not see a stumblingblock placed in his path. The point is this: no person is to take advantage of the handicapped, neither by ridicule nor in business dealings. The believer must show compassion and care for the handicap person. Note that God is the protector and avenger of the handicapped. The person who mistreats the handicapped had better fear God. He is the LORD who will execute judgment upon those who take advantage of and mistreat handicapped people.

> "And fear not them which kill the body, but are not able to kill the soul: but rather fear him which is able to destroy both soul and body in hell" (Mt.10:28).
> "For I was an hungered, and ye gave me meat: I was thirsty, and ye gave me drink: I was a stranger, and ye took me in: Naked, and ye clothed me: I was sick, and ye visited me: I was in prison, and ye came unto me" (Mt.25:35-36).
> "I have showed you all things, how that so labouring ye ought to support the weak, and to remember the words of the Lord Jesus, how he said, It is more blessed to give than to receive" (Ac.20:35).
> "We then that are strong ought to bear the infirmities of the weak, and not to please ourselves" (Ro.15:1).
> "Now we exhort you, brethren, warn them that are unruly, comfort the feebleminded, support the weak, be patient toward all *men*" (1 Th.5:14).
> "Honour all *men.* Love the brotherhood. Fear God. Honour the king" (1 Pe.2:17).

f. The believer must be just and fair: he must never pervert justice, never show partiality to the poor nor favoritism to the great (v.15). Justice is to be administered impartially without any regard whatsoever being shown to any person. False information and rumors are not to be spread about a person in order to damage a person's reputation. People are to be treated fairly and justly in all situations. Partiality is not to be shown to the poor because of their poverty; neither is favoritism to be shown to the great because of their wealth and position. Justice and fair treatment are to be equally executed upon both the poor and the great. No partiality or favoritism is to be shown to any person—no matter who the person is.

> "Ye shall do no unrighteousness in judgment: thou shalt not respect the person of the poor, nor honour the person of the mighty: *but* in righteousness shalt thou judge thy neighbour" (Le.19:15).
> "That which is altogether just shalt thou follow, that thou mayest live, and inherit the land which the LORD thy God giveth thee" (De.16:20).
> "He will surely reprove you, if ye do secretly accept persons" (Jb.13:10).
> "Defend the poor and fatherless: do justice to the afflicted and needy" (Ps.82:3).
> "To do justice and judgment *is* more acceptable to the LORD than sacrifice" (Pr.21:3).
> "Therefore have I also made you contemptible and base before all the people, according as ye have not kept my ways, but have been partial in the law" (Mal.2:9).
> "Render therefore to all their dues: tribute to whom tribute *is due;* custom to whom custom; fear to whom fear; honour to whom honour" (Ro.13:7).
> "Masters, give unto *your* servants that which is just and equal; knowing that ye also have a Master in heaven" (Col.4:1).
> "I charge *thee* before God, and the Lord Jesus Christ, and the elect angels, that thou observe these things without preferring one before another, doing nothing by partiality" (1 Ti.5:21).

g. The believer must love his neighbor as himself (vv.16-18). Note the five things said here:
1) The believer must not spread slander or gossip about his neighbor.
2) The believer must not do anything that endangers his neighbor's life.
3) The believer must not hate his brother in his heart for any cause (v.17).
4) The believer must rebuke and correct his neighbor when the neighbor is doing wrong (v.17). Very simply, if a person is doing something wrong or offends a believer personally, the believer is to go to the person and discuss the matter with him. If the person is allowed to continue in his wrong or sinful behavior, he may become so entrenched that he can never recover himself. He may become enslaved to some sinful behavior and be lost to God forever. For this reason, the believer must go to his friend or neighbor—go in love—and correct him.

"Therefore if thou bring thy gift to the altar, and there rememberest that thy brother hath ought against thee; Leave there thy gift before the altar, and go thy way; first be reconciled to thy brother, and then come and offer thy gift. Agree with thine adversary quickly, whiles thou art in the way with him; lest at any time the adversary deliver thee to the judge, and the judge deliver thee to the officer, and thou be cast into prison" (Mt.5:23-25).

5) The believer must not seek revenge or bear a grudge against anyone (v.18). The believer is to love his neighbor as himself.

"And the second *is* like, *namely* this, Thou shalt love thy neighbour as thyself. There is none other commandment greater than these" (Mk.12:31).

"Love worketh no ill to his neighbour: therefore love *is* the fulfilling of the law" (Ro.13:10).

"We then that are strong ought to bear the infirmities of the weak, and not to please ourselves. Let every one of us please *his* neighbour for *his* good to edification" (Ro.15:1-2).

"For all the law is fulfilled in one word, *even* in this; Thou shalt love thy neighbour as thyself" (Ga.5:14).

"If ye fulfil the royal law according to the scripture, Thou shalt love thy neighbour as thyself, ye do well" (Js.2:8).

h. The believer must keep God's laws and live a life of total separation, a life that is distinct—totally separated to God (v.19). Note that this commandment was symbolized by keeping all things separate in their daily lives. The truth of *spiritual separation* was driven into their minds and hearts through everything they did. God wanted His people separated, set apart to Him, not to the world and its sinful ways. Therefore God commanded...

• that there be no crossbreeding of animals
• that there be no mixing of seed when sowing a field
• that no person wear any clothing woven of two kinds of material

These items were not to be mixed; each item was to maintain its difference and distinctiveness. Each item was to maintain its own identity and be separate from all other items. Again, this was to teach the great spiritual truth of separation. There was to be no mixture of truth and error; no mixture of godliness and ungodliness; no mixture of morality and immorality. This law was to protect God's people from becoming mixed with the worldly people of this world. God's people were to remain distinct and different, totally separated and set apart to God. When the world looked at God's people, they were to see a people who were totally separated to God *in all they did*. God's people were to be set apart to God in *every area of life*.

"I beseech you therefore, brethren, by the mercies of God, that ye present your bodies a living sacrifice, holy, acceptable unto God, *which is* your reasonable service. And be not conformed to this world: but be ye transformed by the renewing of your mind, that ye may prove what is that good, and acceptable, and perfect, will of God" (Ro.12:1-2).

"Wherefore come out from among them, and be ye separate, saith the Lord, and touch not the unclean *thing;* and I will receive you, And will be a Father unto you, and ye shall be my sons and daughters, saith the Lord Almighty" (2 Co.6:17-18).

"And have no fellowship with the unfruitful works of darkness, but rather reprove *them*" (Ep.5:11).

"Love not the world, neither the things *that are* in the world. If any man love the world, the love of the Father is not in him. For all that *is* in the world, the lust of the flesh, and the lust of the eyes, and the pride of life, is not of the Father, but is of the world" (1 Jn.2:15-16).

i. The believer must not sexually abuse nor mistreat a slave (v.20-22). When a person enslaves another person, the slave is often tragically abused, especially sexually. This law is not condoning slavery; it is dealing with the sexual abuse of a slave. In antiquity, the slave-owner had full rights to the slave. He could do what he wanted without any fear of retribution. He could sexually abuse, beat, or mistreat the slave—and even kill the slave if he wished. This law corrects the sexual abuse; other laws corrected the abuse of slavery. But for now, note the example given: a man had intercourse with an engaged slave-girl (v.2). He was to be punished. Note that they were not to be put to death, which was the penalty in most adultery cases. In this particular situation, the man and woman were not to be put to death because she had not yet been freed. But the man was to pay compensation, that is, the bride money, to the girl's father. Moreover, the man had to make a public confession of his sin and seek the forgiveness of God through the Guilt Offering. Once he had done this, he was reconciled to God; his sin was forgiven. (See note—Ex.21:2-6; see outline and notes, pts.8 and 10, *Laws to Protect the Slave*—Ex.21:12-27.)

"Thou shalt not commit adultery" (Ex.20:14).

"And the man that committeth adultery with *another* man's wife, *even he* that committeth adultery with his neighbour's wife, the adulterer and the adulteress shall surely be put to death" (Le.20:10).

"Ye have heard that it was said by them of old time, Thou shalt not commit adultery: But I say unto you, That whosoever looketh on a woman to lust after her hath committed adultery with her already in his heart" (Mt.5:27-28).

"Know ye not that the unrighteous shall not inherit the kingdom of God? Be not deceived: neither fornicators, nor idolaters, nor adulterers, nor effeminate, nor abusers of themselves with mankind,

Nor thieves, nor covetous, nor drunkards, nor revilers, nor extortioners, shall inherit the kingdom of God" (1 Co.6:9-10).

"But the fearful, and unbelieving, and the abominable, and murderers, and whoremongers, and sorcerers, and idolaters, and all liars, shall have their part in the lake which burneth with fire and brimstone: which is the second death" (Re.21:8).

3 (19:23-36) **Giving—Firstfruits—Pagan, Practices of—Unbelievers, Practices of—Prostitution—Sanctuary, Reverence for—Sabbath—Psychics—Fortune-telling—Sorcery—Elderly—Foreigners—Business—Honesty**: the third set of laws govern man's duty in different life situations.

OUTLINE	SCRIPTURE	SCRIPTURE	OUTLINE
3. Man's duty in different life situations	23 And when ye shall come into the land, and shall have planted all manner of trees for food, then ye shall count the fruit thereof as uncircumcised: three years shall it be as uncircumcised unto you: it shall not be eaten of.	30 Ye shall keep my sabbaths, and reverence my sanctuary: I *am* the LORD	d. Keep the Sabbath & reverence God's sanctuary, not that of pagans—a warning from God
a. Must be wise in all work, producing the most possible & dedicating the firstfruit to God		31 Regard not them that have familiar spirits, neither seek after wizards, to be defiled by them: I *am* the LORD your God.	e. Do not turn to nor rely upon mediums or psychics
1) The fruit of the first three years not to be eaten: To allow full development of a tree			1) They defile a person
			2) The person: "I am the LORD"
2) The offering of the firstfruit: Give all fruit in praise to God in the fourth year	24 But in the fourth year all the fruit thereof shall be holy to praise the LORD *withal*.	32 Thou shalt rise up before the hoary head, and honour the face of the old man, and fear thy God: I *am* the LORD.	f. Must respect the aged by arising in their presence
3) The blessing of God promised: An abundance of harvest was promised to God's people in the fifth year	25 And in the fifth year shall ye eat of the fruit thereof, that it may yield unto you the increase thereof: I *am* the LORD your God.		1) Shows one fears, reveres God
			2) The warning: "I am the LORD"
		33 And if a stranger sojourn with thee in your land, ye shall not vex him.	g. Must not mistreat a foreigner
b. Must reject pagan practices	26 Ye shall not eat *any thing* with the blood: neither shall ye use enchantment, nor observe times.	34 *But* the stranger that dwelleth with you shall be unto you as one born among you, and thou shalt love him as thyself; for ye were strangers in the land of Egypt: I *am* the LORD your God.	1) To treat him like everyone else: To love him as yourself
1) Do not eat meat with the blood			
2) Reject fortune-telling & sorcery			2) The reason: Because you were an alien in Egypt (a symbol of the world) before God freed you
3) Do not disfigure the body	27 Ye shall not round the corners of your heads, neither shalt thou mar the corners of thy beard.		
• Not to cut one's hair on the sides or beard			
• Not to cut one's body or tattoo the body	28 Ye shall not make any cuttings in your flesh for the dead, nor print any marks upon you: I *am* the LORD.	35 Ye shall do no unrighteousness in judgment, in meteyard, in weight, or in measure.	h. Must be honest in business dealings
			1) Do not use deceitfulness when measuring something
c. Must not allow a daughter to become a prostitute	29 Do not prostitute thy daughter, to cause her to be a whore; lest the land fall to whoredom, and the land become full of wickedness.	36 Just balances, just weights, a just ephah, and a just hin, shall ye have: I *am* the LORD your God, which brought you out of the land of Egypt.	2) Use accurate scales & weights & containers
1) Degrades a person			3) The reason: "I am the LORD your God"—I set you free from Egypt to be a different, distinct, holy people
2) Corrupts a land: Fills it with all kinds of evil			

a. The believer must be wise in all work, producing the most possible and dedicating the firstfruit to God (vv.23-25). The Israelites were to be wise in planting their vineyards. They were to let a newly planted fruit tree develop for three years before harvesting its crop. Even today, some horticulturists say that a fruit tree will grow much faster and produce better fruit if its buds are pinched off for the first few years. Note that the fruit from the fourth year was to be the offering of the firstfruit to God. The people were to give all their fruit and praise to God in the fourth year. If they were faithful in offering the firstfruit to God, the blessing of God was promised: they would receive an abundance of harvest in the fifth year.

The lesson behind this law was to teach God's people to be wise in all their work, producing the most possible, and dedicating their firstfruit to God. If a person puts God first, God promises to bless him richly.

> "But seek ye first the kingdom of God, and his righteousness; and all these things shall be added unto you" (Mt.6:33).
>
> "Not slothful in business; fervent in spirit; serving the Lord" (Ro.12:11).
>
> "Upon the first *day* of the week let every one of you lay by him in store, as *God* hath prospered him, that there be no gatherings when I come" (1 Co.16:2).
>
> "Every man *shall give* as he is able, according to the blessing of the LORD thy God which he hath given thee" (De.16:17).
>
> "He becometh poor that dealeth *with* a slack hand: but the hand of the diligent maketh rich" (Pr.10:4).
>
> "Go to the ant, thou sluggard; consider her ways, and be wise" (Pr.6:6).

"He that tilleth his land shall be satisfied with bread: but he that followeth vain *persons is* void of understanding" (Pr.12:11).

"Whatsoever thy hand findeth to do, do *it* with thy might; for *there is* no work, nor device, nor knowledge, nor wisdom, in the grave, whither thou goest" (Ec.9:10).

"Bring ye all the tithes into the storehouse, that there may be meat in mine house, and prove me now herewith, saith the LORD of hosts, if I will not open you the windows of heaven, and pour you out a blessing, that *there shall* not *be room* enough *to receive it*" (Mal.3:10).

b. The believer must reject pagan practices (vv.26-28). Three common pagan practices are mentioned here. The believer was forbidden to participate in any of these.
⇒ The believer must not eat meat with blood still in it.
⇒ The believer must reject fortune-telling and sorcery (witchcraft).
⇒ The believer must not disfigure his body in pagan-like rituals. It was a common practice for a pagan to cut his hair on the sides or to clip off the edges of his beard during certain rituals. It was also a common practice for a pagan to cut or tattoo his body during certain rituals. God forbids His people from disfiguring their bodies. God's people are to be different, distinct, separated and set apart unto Him, living lives that are totally different from their worldly and immoral neighbors. They were not to engage in the practices and superstitions of the pagans.

"Take heed to yourselves, that your heart be not deceived, and ye turn aside, and serve other gods, and worship them" (De.11:16).

"Ye *are* the children of the LORD your God: ye shall not cut yourselves, nor make any baldness between your eyes for the dead. for thou *art* an holy people unto the LORD thy God, and the LORD hath chosen thee to be a peculiar people unto himself, above all the nations that *are* upon the earth" (De.14:1-2).

"What? know ye not that your body is the temple of the Holy Ghost *which is* in you, which ye have of God, and ye are not your own? For ye are bought with a price: therefore glorify God in your body, and in your spirit, which are God's" (1 Co.6:19-20).

"Little children, keep yourselves from idols. Amen" (1 Jn.5:21).

c. The believer must not allow a daughter to become a prostitute (v.29). Sexual immorality was and still is a common practice in the rituals of some religions. Immorality is condemned by God in any situation, but to think that prostitution has anything to do with pleasing God is the height of corrupt thinking. Note what God says: the land that turns to prostitution will be filled with wickedness. The idea is that the land will be corrupted: all kinds of evil—wickedness and lawlessness—will run rampant throughout the land. Prostitution and all forms of immorality are forbidden and condemned by God.

"That they have committed adultery, and blood is in their hands, and with their idols have they committed adultery, and have also caused their sons, whom they bare unto me, to pass for them through *the fire,* to devour *them*" (Eze.23:37).

"Know ye not that the unrighteous shall not inherit the kingdom of God? Be not deceived: neither fornicators, nor idolaters, nor adulterers, nor effeminate, nor abusers of themselves with mankind, Nor thieves, nor covetous, nor drunkards, nor revilers, nor extortioners, shall inherit the kingdom of God" (1 Co.6:9-10).

"For this is the will of God, *even* your sanctification, that ye should abstain from fornication: That every one of you should know how to possess his vessel in sanctification and honour; Not in the lust of concupiscence, even as the Gentiles which know not God" (1 Th.4:3-5).

"But the fearful, and unbelieving, and the abominable, and murderers, and whoremongers, and sorcerers, and idolaters, and all liars, shall have their part in the lake which burneth with fire and brimstone: which is the second death" (Re.21:8).

d. The believer must keep the Sabbath and reverence God's sanctuary (v.30). Man must not abuse the Sabbath nor the sanctuary. God warns man: "I am the LORD."

"Remember the sabbath day, to keep it holy" (Ex.20:8).

"Ye shall keep the sabbath therefore; for it *is* holy unto you: every one that defileth it shall surely be put to death: for whosoever doeth *any* work therein, that soul shall be cut off from among his people" (Ex.31:14).

"Six days thou shalt work, but on the seventh day thou shalt rest: in earing time and in harvest thou shalt rest" (Ex.34:21).

"Thou hast despised mine holy things, and hast profaned my sabbaths. And I will scatter thee among the heathen, and disperse thee in the countries, and will consume thy filthiness out of thee" (Eze.22:8, 15).

"Moreover this they have done unto me: they have defiled my sanctuary in the same day, and have profaned my sabbaths" (Eze.23:38).

"How much then is a man better than a sheep? Wherefore it is lawful to do well on the sabbath days" (Mt.12:12).

e. The believer must not turn to nor rely upon mediums and psychics (v.31). God alone can help a person; therefore, no person is seek the false help of mediums and spiritists. These false helpers only defile a person and keep the person away from God, the only One who can really help him. Note what God claims: "I am the LORD *your God*." It is "the LORD your God" alone who can help a person. People must always remember this one fact: within the spiritual world or dimension of being, there is a demonic power that tries to deceive and mislead people. These demonic powers try to keep people away from God, trying to block them from gaining the saving knowledge of Jesus Christ our LORD. Therefore a person must protect himself against the mediums and spiritists who are, no doubt, used by these demonic powers.

> "There shall not be found among you *any one* that maketh his son or his daughter to pass through the fire, or that useth divination, *or* an observer of times, or an enchanter, or a witch, Or a charmer, or a consulter with familiar spirits, or a wizard, or a necromancer. For all that do these things *are* an abomination unto the LORD: and because of these abominations the LORD thy God doth drive them out from before thee" (De.18:10-12).
> "And to him they had regard, because that of long time he had bewitched them with sorceries. But when they believed Philip preaching the things concerning the kingdom of God, and the name of Jesus Christ, they were baptized, both men and women. Then Simon himself believed also: and when he was baptized, he continued with Philip, and wondered, beholding the miracles and signs which were done" (Ac.8:11-13).
> "But the fearful, and unbelieving, and the abominable, and murderers, and whoremongers, and sorcerers, and idolaters, and all liars, shall have their part in the lake which burneth with fire and brimstone: which is the second death" (Re.21:8).

f. The believer must respect the aged by arising in their presence (v.32). Age is to be honored because age brings experience and wisdom, in particular if a person has lived a godly and responsible life. Note that the person who respects the elderly shows that he reveres and honors God. Note also the warning: "I am the LORD." He is the *Ancient of days* and He has a special feeling for the elderly. Therefore God expects His people to respect and honor the aged.

> "Cast me not off in the time of old age; forsake me not when my strength faileth" (Ps.71:9).
> "With long life will I satisfy him, and show him my salvation" (Ps.91:16).
> "The fear of the LORD prolongeth days: but the years of the wicked shall be shortened" (Pr.10:27).
> "The hoary [gray] head *is* a crown of glory, *if* it be found in the way of righteousness" (Pr.16:31).
> "And *even* to *your* old age I *am* he; and *even* to hoar hairs will I carry *you:* I have made, and I will bear; even I will carry, and will deliver *you*" (Is.46:4).
> "That the aged men be sober, grave, temperate, sound in faith, in charity, in patience. The aged women likewise, that *they be* in behaviour as becometh holiness, not false accusers, not given to much wine, teachers of good things" (Tit.2:2-3).

g. The believer must not mistreat foreigners (vv.33-34). Foreigners are to be treated just like everyone else, just like the native-born person. Note exactly what God says about the foreigner: the believer is to love him as himself. The reason is clearly stated: because the believer was an alien in Egypt before God freed him. Remember that Egypt is a symbol of the world; therefore the symbolism teaches a strong lesson for all believers. Believers of all generations are to love foreigners, never mistreating them. The love is to be as strong as the love for oneself.

> "Love ye therefore the stranger: for ye were strangers in the land of Egypt" (De.10:19).
> "And the second *is* like unto it, Thou shalt love thy neighbour as thyself" (Mt.22:39).
> "By this shall all *men* know that ye are my disciples, if ye have love one to another" (Jn.13:35).
> "This is my commandment, That ye love one another, as I have loved you" (Jn.15:12).
> "*Let* love be without dissimulation [hypocrisy]. Abhor that which is evil; cleave to that which is good" (Ro.12:9).
> "And the Lord make you to increase and abound in love one toward another, and toward all *men,* even as we *do* toward you" (1 Th.3:12).

h. The believer must be honest in all business dealings (vv.35-36). The believer must not use dishonest standards when measuring something. On the contrary, he is to use accurate scales, weights, and containers. Note the reason: "I am the LORD your God." God has set His people free from Egypt (a symbol of the world). He did this so that His people would be a distinct and holy people, a people totally different from the dishonest and unjust people of the world. God's people are to be honest in all their business dealings. God's people represent God in their day to day labor and business dealings.

> "Thou shalt not steal" (Ex.20:15).
> "Thou shalt not have in thy bag divers weights, a great and a small" (De.25:13).
> "*But* thou shalt have a perfect and just weight, a perfect and just measure shalt thou have: that thy days may be lengthened in the land which the LORD thy God giveth thee" (De.25:15).
> "A false balance *is* abomination to the LORD: but a just weight *is* his delight" (Pr.11:1).
> "*It is* naught, *it is* naught, saith the buyer: but when he is gone his way, then he boasteth" (Pr.20:14).
> "The getting of treasures by a lying tongue *is* a vanity tossed to and fro of them that seek death" (Pr.21:6).
> "Woe unto you, scribes and Pharisees, hypocrites! for ye make clean the outside of the cup and of the platter, but within they are full of extortion and excess" (Mt.23:25).

"And he said unto them, Exact no more than that which is appointed you" (Lu.3:13).

"Recompense to no man evil for evil. Provide things honest in the sight of all men" (Ro.12:17).

"Owe no man any thing, but to love one another: for he that loveth another hath fulfilled the law" (Ro.13:8).

4 (19:37) **Laws, Duty—Decrees, Duty—Obedience**: there was man's duty to obey God's laws, to keep and follow all of His laws. This is the final command of God, an emphatic command. The idea is that believers are to be careful, to be on constant guard and watch, making absolutely sure that they obey God. Believers must keep all the decrees and laws of God: they must follow them all, omitting none. No person is allowed to pick and choose which laws he is to obey. Note the warning: "I am the LORD." The idea is that God will judge the disobedient, judge any person who fails to keep His decrees and laws.

OUTLINE	SCRIPTURE
4. **Man's duty to obey God's laws: To keep & follow all His laws**	37 Therefore shall ye observe all my statutes, and all my judgments, and do them: I *am* the LORD

"This day the LORD thy God hath commanded thee to do these statutes and judgments: thou shalt therefore keep and do them with all thine heart, and with all thy soul" (De.26:16).

"This book of the law shall not depart out of thy mouth; but thou shalt meditate therein day and night, that thou mayest observe to do according to all that is written therein: for then thou shalt make thy way prosperous, and then thou shalt have good success" (Jos.1:8).

"But if ye will not obey the voice of the LORD, but rebel against the commandment of the LORD, then shall the hand of the LORD be against you, as *it was* against your fathers" (1 S.12:15).

"Not every one that saith unto me, Lord, Lord, shall enter into the kingdom of heaven; but he that doeth the will of my Father which is in heaven" (Mt.7:21).

"Jesus answered and said unto him, If a man love me, he will keep my words: and my Father will love him, and we will come unto him, and make our abode with him" (Jn.14:23).

"If ye keep my commandments, ye shall abide in my love; even as I have kept my Father's commandments, and abide in his love" (Jn.15:10).

"Let no man deceive you with vain words: for because of these things cometh the wrath of God upon the children of disobedience" (Ep.5:6).

"Blessed *are* they that do his commandments, that they may have right to the tree of life, and may enter in through the gates into the city" (Re.22:14).

TYPES, SYMBOLS, AND PICTURES
Leviticus 19:1-37

Historical Term	Type or Picture (Scriptural Basis for Each)	Life Application for Today's Believer	Biblical Application
The Sacrifice of the Fellowship and Peace Offering Le. 19:5	*The sacrifice of the Fellowship or Peace Offering is a symbol of Christ and His sacrifice upon the cross. By His sacrifice a believer is able to grow in the peace and fellowship of God.* "And if ye offer a sacrifice of peace offerings unto the LORD, ye shall offer it at your own will" (Le. 19:5).	The believer must seek to grow in the peace and fellowship of God thru the sacrifice of the Lord Jesus Christ.	*"That which we have seen and heard declare we unto you, that ye also may have fellowship with us: and truly our fellowship is with the Father, and with his Son Jesus Christ"* (1 Jn.1:3). *"The LORD is nigh unto them that are of a broken heart; and saveth such as be of a contrite spirit"* (Ps. 34:18). *"The LORD is nigh unto all them that call upon him, to all that call upon him in truth"* (Ps.145:18). *"Therefore being justified by faith, we have peace with God through our Lord Jesus Christ: By whom also we have access by faith into this grace wherein we stand, and rejoice in hope of the glory of God"* (Ro.5:1-2).

TYPES, SYMBOLS, AND PICTURES
Leviticus 19:1-37

Historical Term	Type or Picture (Scriptural Basis for Each)	Life Application for Today's Believer	Biblical Application
Keeping God's Laws and Living a Life of Total Separation, a Life That Is Distinct and Different from the Immoral and Lawless of This World Le. 19:19	*Keeping God's laws and living a life of total separation is a symbol of not being mixed with the things of the world. This commandment was symbolized by keeping all things separate in the daily lives of God's people. The truth of spiritual separation was driven into their hearts and minds through everything they did. God wanted His people separated, set apart to Him and not to the world and its sinful ways. Therefore God commanded…* • *that there be no cross-breeding of animals* • *that there be no mixing of seed when sowing a field* • *that no person wear any clothing woven of two kinds of material* **"Ye shall keep my statutes. Thou shalt not let thy cattle gender with a diverse kind: thou shalt not sow thy field with mingled seed: neither shall a garment mingled of linen and woollen come upon thee"** (Le.19:19).	Note the great lessons of this symbol: There was to be… • no mixture of truth and error • no mixture of godliness and ungodliness • no mixture of morality and immorality This law was to protect God's people from becoming mixed with the immoral and lawless people of this world. God's people were to remain distinct and different, totally separated and set apart to God.	*"Wherefore come out from among them, and be ye separate, saith the Lord, and touch not the unclean thing; and I will receive you"* (2 Co.6:17). *"And have no fellowship with the unfruitful works of darkness, but rather reprove them"* (Ep.5:11). *"I beseech you therefore, brethren, by the mercies of God, that ye present your bodies a living sacrifice, holy, acceptable unto God, which is your reasonable service. And be not conformed to this world: but be ye transformed by the renewing of your mind, that ye may prove what is that good, and acceptable, and perfect, will of God"* (Ro.12:1-2). *"Love not the world, neither the things that are in the world. If any man love the world, the love of the Father is not in him. For all that is in the world, the lust of the flesh, and the lust of the eyes, and the pride of life, is not of the Father, but is of the world"* (1 Jn.2:15-16).
Foreigners or Strangers in Egypt Le. 19:33-34; see also Le. 11:44-47; Le. 22:33	*Foreigners or strangers in Egypt is a picture of how God's people are to treat those who are different. They are to love people…* • *who are from another culture* • *who are of another race or color* • *who speak another language* • *who are of a different social status* **"But the stranger that dwelleth with you shall be unto you as one born among you, and thou shalt love him as thyself; for ye were strangers in the land of Egypt: I am the LORD your God"** (Le.19:34).	The picture teaches a strong lesson for all believers. Believers of all generations are to love those who are different, including foreigners. Believers are never to mistreat those who are different. Their love is to be as strong as the love for oneself. Why? Because the believer was an alien in Egypt (the world) before God freed him.	*"Love ye therefore the stranger: for ye were strangers in the land of Egypt"* (De.10:19). *"And the second is like unto it, Thou shalt love thy neighbour as thyself"* (Mt.22:39). *"By this shall all men know that ye are my disciples, if ye have love one to another"* (Jn.13:35). *"This is my commandment, That ye love one another, as I have loved you"* (Jn.15:12). *"Let love be without dissimulation. Abhor that which is evil; cleave to that which is good"* (Ro.12:9). *"And the Lord make you to increase and abound in love one toward another, and toward all men, even as we do toward you"* (1 Th.3:12).

1. The Judge: The LORD

2. The justice executed upon the person who commits human sacrifice
   a. Civil justice: To be executed

   b. God's justice: He will set, lock His face against the person & cut him off (eternally)
      1) Bc. he defiles God's sanctuary (worship)
      2) Bc. he profanes God's holy name, shames God by such a horrible practice
   c. God's warning: He will judge the community—any man & his family—if they fail to execute justice upon such a horrible crime
      1) God will set or lock his face against them & all who follow their silence or softness & cut them all off (eternally[1])
      2) The reason: They are as guilty as the offender

3. The justice executed upon the person who turns to mediums or psychics
   a. He prostitutes himself: Turns to false helps, false gods
   b. God's justice: Will set His face against & cut off (forever)

4. The justice of God demands sanctification, being set apart to holiness
   a. The reason: Because the LORD is your God
   b. The way to live holy lives: Keep God's laws
   c. The source of holiness: The LORD

5. The justice executed upon the person who abuses parents
   a. Civil justice: To be executed
   b. God's justice: Is blamable, guilty, to be held accountable

6. The justice executed upon the person who commits various sexual sins & crimes
   a. Committing adultery: Death

CHAPTER 20

D. Laws That Spell Out the Punishment for Terrible Crimes, 20:1-27

And the LORD spake unto Moses, saying,

2 Again, thou shalt say to the children of Israel, Whosoever he be of the children of Israel, or of the strangers that sojourn in Israel, that giveth *any* of his seed unto Molech; he shall surely be put to death: the people of the land shall stone him with stones.

3 And I will set my face against that man, and will cut him off from among his people; because he hath given of his seed unto Molech, to defile my sanctuary, and to profane my holy name.

4 And if the people of the land do any ways hide their eyes from the man, when he giveth of his seed unto Molech, and kill him not:

5 Then I will set my face against that man, and against his family, and will cut him off, and all that go a whoring after him, to commit whoredom with Molech, from among their people.

6 And the soul that turneth after such as have familiar spirits, and after wizards, to go a whoring after them, I will even set my face against that soul, and will cut him off from among his people.

7 Sanctify yourselves therefore, and be ye holy: for I *am* the LORD your God.

8 And ye shall keep my statutes, and do them: I *am* the LORD which sanctify you.

9 For every one that curseth his father or his mother shall be surely put to death: he hath cursed his father or his mother; his blood *shall be* upon him.

10 And the man that committeth adultery with *another* man's wife, *even he* that committeth adultery with his neighbour's wife, the adulterer and the adulteress shall surely be put to death.

11 And the man that lieth with his father's wife hath uncovered his father's nakedness: both of them shall surely be put to death; their blood *shall be* upon them.

12 And if a man lie with his daughter in law, both of them shall surely be put to death: they have wrought confusion; their blood *shall be* upon them.

13 If a man also lie with mankind, as he lieth with a woman, both of them have committed an abomination: they shall surely be put to death; their blood *shall be* upon them.

14 And if a man take a wife and her mother, it *is* wickedness: they shall be burnt with fire, both he and they; that there be no wickedness among you.

15 And if a man lie with a beast, he shall surely be put to death: and ye shall slay the beast.

16 And if a woman approach unto any beast, and lie down thereto, thou shalt kill the woman, and the beast: they shall surely be put to death; their blood *shall be* upon them.

17 And if a man shall take his sister, his father's daughter, or his mother's daughter, and see her nakedness, and she see his nakedness; it *is* a wicked thing; and they shall be cut off in the sight of their people: he hath uncovered his sister's nakedness; he shall bear his iniquity.

18 And if a man shall lie with a woman having her sickness, and shall uncover her nakedness; he hath discovered her fountain, and she hath uncovered the fountain of her blood: and both of them shall be cut off from among their people.

19 And thou shalt not uncover the nakedness of thy mother's sister, nor of thy father's sister: for he uncovereth his near kin: they shall bear their iniquity.

20 And if a man shall lie with his uncle's wife, he hath uncovered his uncle's nakedness: they shall bear

   b. Committing incest with one's step-mother (or step-father)
      1) Civil justice: Death
      2) God's justice: Is blamable, guilty, to be held accountable
   c. Committing incest with one's daughter-in-law (or son-in-law)
      1) Civil justice: Death
      2) God's justice: Is blamable, guilty, to be held accountable
   d. Committing the unnatural, perverted act against human nature, that of homosexuality
      1) Civil justice: Death
      2) God's justice: Is blamable, guilty, to be held accountable
   e. Committing incest by marrying both a woman & her mother (or a man & his father): To be executed & the dead bodies burned in fire—demonstrating the horrible wickedness
   f. Committing the bizarre, detestable act of bestiality
      1) Civil justice
         • Death for the man & the animal
         • Death for the woman & the animal

      2) God's justice: Is blamable, guilty, to be held accountable
   g. Committing incest by marrying a sister or step-sister (a brother or step-brother)
      1) Civil justice: Is a disgrace—to be cut off

      2) God's justice: Is accountable, without excuse

   h. Committing the unclean act of having sex during a woman's monthly period
      1) Exposes, uncovers her flow: Lacks a spirit of caring, of consideration, at such a sensitive time
      2) Civil & godly judgment: To be cut off, excommunicated
   i. Committing incest by having sex with a blood aunt (or blood uncle): Dishonors a close relative—accountable, without excuse

   j. Committing incest by having sex with an aunt (or uncle) by marriage: Is accountable & will die childless

---

1   Gordon J. Wenham. *The Book of Leviticus*, p.242.

k. Committing incest by marrying a sister-in-law: Is impure & dishonors one's brother—to be childless
 	
7. The way to escape judgment
a. A person must obey God
  1) Must keep all His laws & rules
  2) The reason: To keep from being vomited out of the promised land
b. A person must live a life of separation, different from the world
  1) Not to follow worldly customs
  2) The reasons
    • God abhors, detests worldliness: Worldliness disgusts, repulses God
    • God has promised to give an inheritance to the obedient: The land of the worldly nations that flows with milk & honey
	their sin; they shall die childless.
	21 And if a man shall take his brother's wife, it *is* an unclean thing: he hath uncovered his brother's nakedness; they shall be childless.
	22 Ye shall therefore keep all my statutes, and all my judgments, and do them: that the land, whither I bring you to dwell therein, spue you not out.
	23 And ye shall not walk in the manners of the nation, which I cast out before you: for they committed all these things, and therefore I abhorred them.
	24 But I have said unto you, Ye shall inherit their land, and I will give it unto you to possess it, a land that floweth with milk
	
	milk and honey: I *am* the LORD your God, which have separated you from *other* people.
	25 Ye shall therefore put difference between clean beasts and unclean, and between unclean fowls and clean: and ye shall not make your souls abominable by beast, or by fowl, or by any manner of living thing that creepeth on the ground, which I have separated from you as unclean.
	26 And ye shall be holy unto me: for I the LORD *am* holy, and have severed you from *other* people, that ye should be mine.
	27 A man also or woman that hath a familiar spirit, or that is a wizard, shall surely be put to death: they shall stone them with stones: their blood *shall be* upon them.
		(a symbol of the new heavens & earth)
		• God has set apart the obedient to be His people
		c. A person must discern between the clean & unclean in day-to-day behavior
		  1) By obeying God's laws that govern clean & unclean animals for food (see 11:1-47)
		  2) By not defiling oneself through disobedience
		
		d. A person must live a holy life
		  1) Bc. God is holy
		  2) Bc. God has set His people apart from all others: to be His own special possession
		e. A person must execute justice upon mediums & psychics
		  1) Civil justice: Death
		  2) God's justice: Is blamable, guilty, to be held accountable

DIVISION IV

THE WAY TO LIVE A HOLY LIFE BEFORE GOD (PART 2): A PURE SPIRIT (SANCTIFICATION), 17:1–27:34

D. Laws That Spell Out the Punishment for Terrible Crimes, 20:1-27

(20:1-27) **Introduction—Justice**: justice must be executed upon the earth. Without justice, all forms of lawlessness, violence, and sexual perversion would run wild throughout the earth. There would be no peace or security within society, no safety whatsoever. Selfishness and immorality would rip homes and families apart. Every form of adultery and sexual perversion would sweep the earth, destroying the human body and all the great virtues and qualities of life. Without justice being executed, drug and alcohol abuse would be unbridled. Robbery, theft, assault, murder—all forms of lawlessness and violence—would be unleashed upon the earth. Selfishness would reign supreme and society would slowly but surely disintegrate. (See outline and notes—Gen.6:1-8 for more discussion.)

This is the reason God wants justice executed upon the earth. God knows that society will collapse unless justice is executed fairly and evenly. But note: before man can execute justice, laws must be established, laws that will build a strong society and give man a fruitful life. Remember, this is exactly what God had been doing, spelling out the laws that were to govern His people. Keep in mind that Israel, God's people, was camped out at the foot of Mt. Sinai. In the book of Exodus, God had given His people the Ten Commandments and other laws that were to govern their day-by-day lives. And now throughout Leviticus, He has continued to give His people law after law to help them govern themselves, to help them build a strong society. The present passage spells out the punishment for breaking certain laws. The laws themselves were discussed earlier (see outline and notes—Le.18:1-30). This chapter discusses: *Laws That Spell Out the Punishment for Terrible Crimes*, 20:1-27.

1. The Judge: the LORD (v.1).
2. The justice executed upon the person who commits human sacrifice (vv.2-5).
3. The justice executed upon the person who turns to mediums or psychics (v.6).
4. The justice of God demands sanctification, being set apart to holiness (vv.7-8).
5. The justice executed upon the person who abuses parents (v.9).
6. The justice executed upon the person who commits various sexual sins and crimes (vv.10-21).
7. The way to escape judgment (vv.22-27).

1 (20:1) **Judgment—Justice—Judges**: the judge who pronounces the punishments in this chapter is God Himself. Note how clearly this is stated in the Scripture and outline. God executes perfect justice: no person is ever punished beyond what he deserves. A person receives exactly what is due him. God does not want sadistic, psychotic criminals turned loose in society, nor does He want any form of lawlessness or immorality running rampant throughout society. He wants the foundation of society to be strong, firmly based upon the great laws of morality and justice. God wants His people experiencing the fullness of life within a society of peace and righteousness. God wants a society in which neighbor loves neighbor and together they experience the fullness of life, bearing a strong witness to the only living and true God.

"Before the LORD: for he cometh, for he cometh to judge the earth: he shall judge the world with righteousness, and the people with his truth" (Ps.96:13).

"I said in mine heart, God shall judge the righteous and the wicked: for *there is* a time there for every purpose and for every work" (Ec.3:17).

"The Lord knoweth how to deliver the godly out of temptations, and to reserve the unjust unto the day of judgment to be punished" (2 Pe.2:9).

"But the heavens and the earth, which are now, by the same word are kept in store, reserved unto fire against the day of judgment and perdition of ungodly men" (2 Pe.3:7).

"And Enoch also, the seventh from Adam, prophesied of these, saying, Behold, the Lord cometh with ten thousands of his saints, To execute judgment upon all, and to convince all that are ungodly among them of all their ungodly deeds which they have ungodly committed, and of all their hard *speeches* which ungodly sinners have spoken against him" (Jude 1:14-15).

2 (20:2-5) **Justice—Human Sacrifice—Molech—Judgment—Sacrifice, Human**: justice was to be executed upon the person who committed human sacrifice. Note how terrible this practice is, how utterly it shames and disgraces the name of God.

OUTLINE	SCRIPTURE	SCRIPTURE	OUTLINE
2. The justice executed upon the person who commits human sacrifice a. Civil justice: To be executed	2 Again, thou shalt say to the children of Israel, Whosoever *he be* of the children of Israel, or of the strangers that sojourn in Israel, that giveth *any* of his seed unto Molech; he shall surely be put to death: the people of the land shall stone him with stones. 3 And I will set my face against that man, and will cut him off from among his people; because he hath given of his seed unto Molech, to defile my sanctu-	ary, and to profane my holy name 4 And if the people of the land do any ways hide their eyes from the man, when he giveth of his seed unto Molech, and kill him not: 5 Then I will set my face against that man, and against his family, and will cut him off, and all that go a whoring after him, to commit whoredom with Molech, from among their people	Name, shames God by such a horrible practice c. God's warning: He will judge the community—any man & his family—if they fail to execute justice upon such a horrible crime 1) God will set, lock his face against them & all who follow their silence or softness & cut them all off (eternally) 2) The reason: They are as guilty as the offender
b. God's justice: He will set, lock His face against the person & cut him off (eternally) 1) Bc he defiles God's sanctuary (worship) 2) Bc he profanes God's holy			

The sacrifice of human beings demanded by some religions is a monstrous practice. It exposes a warped, twisted mind and reason. It tramples underfoot the sanctity and dignity of life. It points to a people stripped of all sound reason and affection. Seeking the approval of some so-called god by sacrificing a human being is savage and brutal. It is the height of ignorance, the depravity of a warped mind. It is satanic and demonic—a terrible, horrible tragedy. This was a common sin among the Canaanites, in particular the people of Tyre. They worshipped a false god called Molech (or Melkar). In their warped thinking and corrupt reasoning, the people offered the best gift they had, their children, in order to secure the greatest acceptance and blessings of the god Molech.

a. Note the civil justice demanded by God against human sacrifice (v.2). The person who offers human sacrifice to a god was to be executed. There was danger that the Israelites could be influenced by this ungodly practice and false religion when they entered the land of Canaan. Therefore, God warns His people: if any of them ever participated in the ritual of human sacrifice, that person was to be executed. The form of execution was to be by stoning. Note that the whole community was to be involved in the stoning. This was, no doubt, to be an object lesson and warning to everyone against this horrible crime.

b. Note God's justice (v.3). The person who commits the crime of human sacrifice is not only to be executed by a civil court, he is to face the eternal justice and judgment of God. God says that He will set or lock His face against the person and cut him off. The idea is that the person will be condemned eternally. He will be cut off, separated from the people of God forever and ever. By human sacrifice—putting a human to death in the worship of some so-called false god—the people defiled God's sanctuary and worship. Moreover, the people profaned God's holy name: they disgraced, trashed, shamed God by such a horrible practice. The people had sought the approval and blessing of God by approaching a false god in the form of an idol, engaging in a savage and demonic ritual: the people had sacrificed a human being, putting the person to death—all in the name of God and worship. The very name of God was defiled. This demonic practice and ritual was and is condemned by God, condemned by His holy wrath.

c. Note God's warning: He will judge the community—any man and his family—if they fail to execute justice upon such a horrible crime. God expects justice and judgment to be executed against such a demonic, fiendish crime. If a neighbor failed to report such a crime, or if a community failed to execute justice against such a crime, God said that He would set or lock His face against the community, against all who follow their silence or softness. Again, the idea is that He will cut off any and all who remain silent or show softness against such a criminal. Note the reason: they are as guilty as the offender. They all prostitute themselves to Molech, the god of human sacrifice.

"Thou shalt not kill [murder]" (Ex.20:13).

"But let none of you suffer as a murderer" (1 Pe.4:15).

"No murderer hath eternal life abiding in him" (1 Jn.3:15).

"Lo, children *are* an heritage of the LORD: *and* the fruit of the womb *is his* reward" (Ps.127:3).

"But Jesus said, Suffer little children, and forbid them not, to come unto me: for of such is the kingdom of heaven" (Mt.19:14).

"When my father and my mother forsake me, then the LORD will take me up" (Ps.27:10).

"And, ye fathers, provoke not your children to wrath: but bring them up in the nurture and admonition of the Lord" (Ep.6:4).

"And they have built the high places of Tophet, which is in the valley of the son of Hinnom, to burn their sons and their daughters in the fire; which I commanded *them* not, neither came it into my heart. "Therefore, behold, the days come, saith the LORD, that it shall no more be called Tophet, nor the valley of the son of Hinnom, but the valley of slaughter: for they shall bury in Tophet, till there be no place. And the carcases of this people shall be meat for the fowls of the heaven, and for the beasts of the earth; and none shall fray *them* away" (Je.7:31-33; see 2 K.17:31; 23:10; Je.32:35).

3 (20:6) **Justice—Mediums—Psychics**: justice was to be executed upon the person who turned to mediums or psychics (see Le.19:31; 20:27). This a serious offense against God, an evil that deserves and will result in eternal separation from God.

OUTLINE	SCRIPTURE
3. The justice executed upon the person who turns to mediums or psychics a. He prostitutes himself: Turns to false helps, false gods b. God's justice: Will set His face against & cut off (forever)	6 And the soul that turneth after such as have familiar spirits, and after wizards, to go a whoring after them, I will even set my face against that soul, and will cut him off from among his people.

Note that this person prostitutes himself by following after mediums and spiritists. He simply turns away from God to others just as a man turns away from his wife to another woman. There is such a thing as infidelity to God, spiritual adultery. The believer has entered a covenant with God, promised to love and cherish God, to be loyal to Him. If a person turns and places his confidence in a medium or psychic, he prostitutes himself. He places his confidence and trust in another person or spirit instead of in God. He seeks understanding, leadership, and guidance or to know the future—his faith and destiny—from some person or spirit instead of from God. This is spiritual prostitution in the eyes of God: it is turning one's faith and affection away from God and placing it into the hands of spiritists and mediums. Note what God says: He will execute His justice and judgment. He will cut the person off eternally. The person will be cut off from God's people forever and ever, never allowed to live with them in the promised land (a symbol of heaven).

"Now the works of the flesh are manifest, which are *these;* Adultery, fornication, uncleanness, lasciviousness, Idolatry, witchcraft, hatred, variance, emulations, wrath, strife, seditions, heresies, Envyings, murders, drunkenness, revellings, and such like: of the which I tell you before, as I have also told *you* in time past, that they which do such things shall not inherit the kingdom of God" (Ga.5:19-21).

"Thou shalt not suffer a witch to live" (Ex.22:18).

"Regard not them that have familiar spirits, neither seek after wizards, to be defiled by them: I *am* the LORD your God" (Le.19:31).

"So Saul died for his transgression which he committed against the LORD, *even* against the word of the LORD, which he kept not, and also for asking *counsel* of *one that had* a familiar spirit, to enquire *of it;* And enquired not of the LORD: therefore he slew him, and turned the kingdom unto David the son of Jesse" (1 Chr.10:13-14; see 1 S.28:7).

"And when they shall say unto you, Seek unto them that have familiar spirits, and unto wizards that peep, and that mutter: should not a people seek unto their God? for the living to the dead? To the law and to the testimony: if they speak not according to this word, *it is* because *there is* no light in them" (Is.8:19-20).

"And I will cut off witchcrafts out of thine hand; and thou shalt have no *more* soothsayers: Thy graven images also will I cut off, and thy standing images out of the midst of thee; and thou shalt no more worship the work of thine hands. And I will pluck up thy groves out of the midst of thee: so will I destroy thy cities. And I will execute vengeance in anger and fury upon the heathen, such as they have not heard" (Mi.5:12-15).

4 (20:7-8) **Sanctification—Consecration—Holiness—Obedience**: the justice of God demands sanctification or consecration, being set apart to holiness. In simpler terms, the justice of God demands one thing of people: holiness. People, in particular believers, are to live holy lives because God Himself is holy. Any deviation from the standard of God's holiness is a serious breach of conduct.[2] Thus the wickedness, immorality, and corruption of man compared to the holiness of God is sufficient reason for the death penalty.

OUTLINE	SCRIPTURE	SCRIPTURE	OUTLINE
4. The justice of God demands sanctification, being set apart to holiness a. The reason: Because the LORD is your God	7 Sanctify yourselves therefore, and be ye holy: for I *am* the LORD your God.	8 And ye shall keep my statutes, and do them: I *am* the LORD which sanctify you.	b. The way to live holy lives: Keep God's laws c. The source of holiness: The LORD

---

2 J. Vernon McGee. *Thru The Bible,* Vol.1, p.417.

Sanctify, consecrate, set yourselves apart, be holy—this is the command of God. People are to live sanctified lives, lives that are consecrated to God, totally set apart to Him. This is particularly true with believers, those who truly believe and follow God.

a. Note what God says: "I am the LORD *your God*." The LORD is the God of believers; therefore the believer is to set his life apart to God, to live a holy and pure life. The believer is to cleanse himself from all the defilement of sin and be totally consecrated to God, living a holy life before God and the world.

b. Note how a person lives a holy life: he keeps the decrees of God and follows them

> "If ye keep my commandments, ye shall abide in my love; even as I have kept my Father's commandments, and abide in his love" (Jn.15:10).
> "Blessed *are* they that do his commandments, that they may have right to the tree of life, and may enter in through the gates into the city" (Re.22:14).
> "This day the LORD thy God hath commanded thee to do these statutes and judgments: thou shalt therefore keep and do them with all thine heart, and with all thy soul" (De.26:16).
> "This book of the law shall not depart out of thy mouth; but thou shalt meditate therein day and night, that thou mayest observe to do according to all that is written therein: for then thou shalt make thy way prosperous, and then thou shalt have good success" (Jos.1:8).

c. Also note the source of holiness: the LORD Himself. The energy, strength, and power to live a holy life comes only from God. It is the spirit of God that injects and infuses the energy to live a holy life. The believer is to seek the LORD for the strength to live a holy life, and then he is to arise and march forth, living a life that is set apart to God. As he marches forth, the spirit of God infuses the strength to live a holy and righteous life before the world—all as a strong witness to the living and true God, the LORD God Himself. The believer becomes a dynamic witness to the immoral and lawless people of the world, to those who turn to mediums, psychics and the false gods of this world.

> "Having therefore these promises, dearly beloved, let us cleanse ourselves from all filthiness of the flesh and spirit, perfecting holiness in the fear of God" (2 Co.7:1).
> "Follow peace with all *men,* and holiness, without which no man shall see the Lord" (He.12:14).
> "But as he which hath called you is holy, so be ye holy in all manner of conversation; Because it is written, Be ye holy; for I am holy" (1 Pe.1:15-16).
> "*Seeing* then *that* all these things shall be dissolved, what manner *of persons* ought ye to be in *all* holy conversation and godliness" (2 Pe.3:11)

5 (20:9) **Justice—Parents, Abuse of—Children, Abuse of Parents**: justice was to be executed upon the person who abused his parents. The honor of parents is a constant theme of the Scripture. In fact, the honor of father and mother is so important in the eyes of God that He has made it one of the Ten Commandments (Ex.20:12). Cursing and abusing one's parents was a capital offense, subject to execution. Note the Scripture and Outline:

OUTLINE	SCRIPTURE
5. The justice executed upon the person who abuses parents a. Civil justice: To be executed b. God's justice: Is blamable, guilty, to be held accountable	9 For every one that curseth his father or his mother shall be surely put to death: he hath cursed his father or his mother; his blood *shall be* upon him.

This Scripture is not speaking about the occasional angry word that may be uttered against a parent. Cursing and abusing a parent involves deep-seated feelings that are full of poisonous venom and bitterness. Deep-seated anger, hate, and hostility—a hard and harsh spirit—would be involved. The person who so cursed and abused his parents was to be put to death. And note God's judgment: the blood of the abusive child is upon his own head. That is, he is blamable, guilty, to be held accountable by God Himself. The idea is that of judgment and condemnation: the guilty child will be condemned and separated from God forever.

> "And he that curseth his father, or his mother, shall surely be put to death" (Ex.21:17).
> "Cursed *be* he that setteth light by his father or his mother. And all the people shall say, Amen. (De.27:16).
> "Whoso curseth his father or his mother, his lamp shall be put out in obscure darkness" (Pr.20:20).
> "This know also, that in the last days perilous times shall come. For men shall be lovers of their own selves, covetous, boasters, proud, blasphemers, disobedient to parents, unthankful, unholy" (2 Ti.3:1-2).

6 (20:10-21) **Justice—Immorality—Adultery—Incest—Homosexuality—Bestiality**: justice was to be executed upon the person who committed various sexual sins and crimes. All the sexual sins known among men are forbidden by the seventh commandment: a person must not commit adultery (Ex.20:14). All forms of illicit sex are covered in the present passage. Unbelievable and unspeakable acts are covered, such illicit acts as incest with the closest of family members, homosexuality, bestiality, and adultery. Such sins tear down the very nature of man, man who is the summit of God's creation. Moreover, such terrible acts of immorality cause great pain and suffering: they destroy wives, husbands, and children, and eventually society itself. The sins of immorality destroy the family, the very foundation of society, the institution God ordained to give purpose and meaning, form and structure to society. The laws governing these terrible sins of immorality were discussed earlier (Le.18:1-30). Now, God spells out the punishment for these terrible sexual sins and crimes. Note the Scripture and outline.

OUTLINE	SCRIPTURE	SCRIPTURE	OUTLINE
6. The justice executed upon the person who commits various sexual sins & crimes a. Committing adultery: Death	10 And the man that committeth adultery with *another* man's wife, *even he* that committeth adultery with his neighbour's wife, the adulterer and the adulteress shall surely be put to death.	beast: they shall surely be put to death; their blood *shall be* upon them. 17 And if a man shall take his sister, his father's daughter, or his mother's daughter, and see her nakedness, and she see his nakedness; it *is* a wicked thing; and they	2) God's justice: Is blamable, guilty, to be held accountable g. Committing incest by marrying a sister or step-sister (a brother or step-brother) 1) Civil justice: Is a disgrace—to be cut off
b. Committing incest with one's step-mother (or step-father) 1) Civil justice: Death 2) God's justice: Is blamable, guilty, to be held accountable	11 And the man that lieth with his father's wife hath uncovered his father's nakedness: both of them shall surely be put to death; their blood *shall be* upon them.	shall be cut off in the sight of their people: he hath uncovered his sister's nakedness; he shall bear his iniquity.	2) God's justice: Is accountable, without excuse
c. Committing incest with one's daughter-in-law (or son-in-law) 1) Civil justice: Death 2) God's justice: Is blamable, guilty, to be held accountable	12 And if a man lie with his daughter in law, both of them shall surely be put to death: they have wrought confusion; their blood *shall be* upon them.	18 And if a man shall lie with a woman having her sickness, and shall uncover her nakedness; he hath discovered her fountain, and she hath uncovered the fountain of her blood: and	h. Committing the unclean act of having sex during a woman's monthly period 1) Exposes, uncovers her flow: Lacks a spirit of caring, of consideration, at such a sensitive time
d. Committing the unnatural, perverted act against human nature, that of homosexuality 1) Civil justice: Death 2) God's justice: Is blamable, guilty, to be held accountable	13 If a man also lie with mankind, as he lieth with a woman, both of them have committed an abomination: they shall surely be put to death; their blood *shall be* upon them.	both of them shall be cut off from among their people. 19 And thou shalt not uncover the nakedness of thy mother's sister, nor of thy father's sister: for he uncovereth his near kin: they shall bear their iniquity.	2) Civil & godly judgment: To be cut off, excommunicated i. Committing incest by having sex with a blood aunt (or blood uncle): Dishonors a close relative—accountable, without excuse
e. Committing incest by marrying both a woman & her mother (or a man & his father): To be executed & the dead bodies burned in fire—demonstrating the horrible wickedness	14 And if a man take a wife and her mother, it *is* wickedness: they shall be burnt with fire, both he and they; that there be no wickedness among you.	20 And if a man shall lie with his uncle's wife, he hath uncovered his uncle's nakedness: they shall bear their sin; they shall die childless.	j. Committing incest by having sex with an aunt (or uncle) by marriage: Is accountable & will die childless
f. Committing the bizarre, detestable act of bestiality 1) Civil justice • Death for the man & the animal • Death for the woman & the animal	15 And if a man lie with a beast, he shall surely be put to death: and ye shall slay the beast. 16 And if a woman approach unto any beast, and lie down thereto, thou shalt kill the woman, and the	21 And if a man shall take his brother's wife, it *is* an unclean thing: he hath uncovered his brother's nakedness; they shall be childless.	k. Committing incest by marrying a sister-in-law: Is impure & dishonors one's brother—to be childless

Thought 1. Immorality does irreparable harm to all parties involved. Adultery causes great pain and injury to husbands and wives and children. It can break up families and destroy homes. When immorality breaks up homes, it causes a part of society to crumble. Moreover, immorality corrupts the mind and conscience of the offender, enslaving him to unbridled lust. When a mind becomes enslaved by unbridled lust, it is subject—far more subject—to committing all forms of lawlessness and corrupt behavior. (See outlines and notes—Ge.6:1-8; Ro.1:24-32 for more discussion.)

Lax morals are sweeping the world today. It was lax morals, in particular the sin of homosexuality, that caused the judgment of God's fire and brimstone to fall upon Sodom and Gomorrah. A people or society can become so immoral that God is forced to give up on them, turning them over to their unbridled lusts. They refuse to repent of their sin and immorality; therefore, God has to give them up to the burning of their passion and lust. They are to bear the judicial judgment of God: what they sow they will reap. They sow lust and immorality; therefore they burn in their lust and immorality as long as they live upon the earth. But then, once they die, they face the eternal judgment and condemnation of God.

"For the wrath of God is revealed from heaven against all ungodliness and unrighteousness of men, who hold the truth in unrighteousness; Wherefore God also gave them up to uncleanness through the lusts of their own hearts, to dishonour their own bodies between themselves: Who changed the truth of God into a lie, and worshipped and served the creature more than the Creator, who is blessed for ever. Amen. For this cause God gave them up unto vile affections: for even their women did change

the natural use into that which is against nature: And likewise also the men, leaving the natural use of the woman, burned in their lust one toward another; men with men working that which is unseemly, and receiving in themselves that recompence of their error which was meet. And even as they did not like to retain God in *their* knowledge, God gave them over to a reprobate mind, to do those things which are not convenient; Being filled with all unrighteousness, fornication, wickedness, covetousness, maliciousness; full of envy, murder, debate, deceit, malignity; whisperers, Backbiters, haters of God, despiteful, proud, boasters, inventors of evil things, disobedient to parents, Without understanding, covenantbreakers, without natural affection, implacable, unmerciful: Who knowing the judgment of God, that they which commit such things are worthy of death, not only do the same, but have pleasure in them that do them" (Ro.1:18, 24-32).

"Know ye not that the unrighteous shall not inherit the kingdom of God? Be not deceived: neither fornicators, nor idolaters, nor adulterers, nor effeminate, nor abusers of themselves with mankind, Nor thieves, nor covetous, nor drunkards, nor revilers, nor extortioners, shall inherit the kingdom of God" (1 Co.6:9-10).

"Now the works of the flesh are manifest, which are *these;* Adultery, fornication, uncleanness, lasciviousness, Idolatry, witchcraft, hatred, variance, emulations, wrath, strife, seditions, heresies, Envyings, murders, drunkenness, revellings, and such like: of the which I tell you before, as I have also told *you* in time past, that they which do such things shall not inherit the kingdom of God" (Ga.5:19-21).

"But the fearful, and unbelieving, and the abominable, and murderers, and whoremongers, and sorcerers, and idolaters, and all liars, shall have their part in the lake which burneth with fire and brimstone: which is the second death" (Re.21:8)

---

7 (20:22-27) **Exhortation, to Obey God—Obedience—Holiness—Separation, Spiritual—Spiritual Separation—Discernment—Clean - Cleanliness, Duty—Mediums—Spiritists—Justice—Judgment**: the way to escape the justice and judgment of God is clearly spelled out. God's people live in an immoral age, in a world of false religion. The appeal of sex, the bright lights of the world, and the good feelings of religion all appeal to the flesh of people—even to God's people. God knows this; therefore He warns His people just as He warns the people of the world. This is a strong exhortation for His people to escape the coming judgment upon the immorality and terrible lawlessness of people—or else face His judgment. Note that God gives five charges in order to escape His judgment.

OUTLINE	SCRIPTURE	SCRIPTURE	OUTLINE
7. The way to escape judgment	22 Ye shall therefore keep all my statutes, and all my judgments, and do them: that the land, whither I bring you to dwell therein, spue you not out.	difference between clean beasts and unclean, and between unclean fowls and clean: and ye shall not make your souls abominable by beast, or by fowl, or by any manner of living thing that creepeth on the ground, which I have separated from you as unclean.	tween the clean & unclean in day-to-day behavior
a. A person must obey God			1) By obeying God's laws that govern clean & unclean animals for food (see 11:1-47)
1) Must keep all His laws & rules			
2) The reason: To keep from being vomited out of the promised land			2) By not defiling oneself through disobedience
b. A person must live a life of separation, different from the world	23 And ye shall not walk in the manners of the nation, which I cast out before you: for they committed all these things, and therefore I abhorred them.		
1) Not to follow worldly customs			
2) The reasons			d. A person must live a holy life
• God abhors, detests worldliness: Worldliness disgusts, repulses God		26 And ye shall be holy unto me: for I the LORD *am* holy, and have severed you from *other* people, that ye should be mine.	1) Bc. God is holy
			2) Bc. God has set His people apart from all others to be His very own special possession
• God has promised to give an inheritance to the obedient: The land of the worldly nations that flows with milk & honey (a symbol of the new heavens & earth)	24 But I have said unto you, Ye shall inherit their land, and I will give it unto you to possess it, a land that floweth with milk and honey: I *am* the LORD your God, which have separated you from *other* people.	27 A man also or woman that hath a familiar spirit, or that is a wizard, shall surely be put to death: they shall stone them with stones: their blood *shall be* upon them.	e. A person must execute justice upon mediums & psychics
• God has set apart the obedient to be His people			1) Civil justice: Death
c. A person must discern be-	25 Ye shall therefore put		2) God's justice: Is blamable, guilty, to be held accountable

a. *A person must obey God* in order to escape His judgment (v.22). God's people must keep all His laws and rules. They must diligently follow God with whole hearts. If they fail to obey Him, note what happens: the promised land itself will vomit them out. They will be judged and condemned. They will be expelled, thrown out of the promised land, not allowed to live with the people of God. Remember, it was these very sins that caused God to judge the Canaanites. The land vomited them out; that is, God put them out of the land. God was warning His people: He is no respecter of persons. A person must obey Him, keep all His laws and rules, if he is to escape His judgment.

"Not every one that saith unto me, Lord, Lord, shall enter into the kingdom of heaven; but he that doeth the will of my Father which is in heaven" (Mt.7:21).

"But whoso looketh into the perfect law of liberty, and continueth *therein,* he being not a forgetful hearer, but a doer of the work, this man shall be blessed in his deed" (Js.1:25).

"Blessed *are* they that do his commandments, that they may have right to the tree of life, and may enter in through the gates into the city" (Re.22:14).

b. *A person must live a life of separation,* a life that is different from the world, if he is to escape the justice and judgment of God (vv.23-24). Note what God says: believers must not live according to the worldly customs of their neighbors. Their neighbors were so immoral and lawless that He was going to drive them out of the land. God abhors immorality and lawlessness. The worldliness of people and nations disgusts, repulses God. Therefore, God had promised to give the land of the immoral and lawless to His people. They were to inherit the land of the worldly nations, a land that flowed with milk and honey. Keep in mind that the promised land is a symbol of the new heavens and earth. God has set apart the *obedient* to be His people and to inherit the promised land, the land that flows with milk and honey. But note this self-evident truth: only the person who obeys God is obedient. The *obedient* is the person who lives a life of separation, a life that is entirely different from the immoral and lawless people of the earth. It is the obedient who will receive the inheritance of God, the promised land that flows with milk and honey. This is what God was saying to the Israelites, to the people He was choosing to be His followers. If they obeyed Him, they would inherit the land; but if they disobeyed Him, the land would spew them out. God's people must live lives of separation, lives that are totally set apart to God, lives that are different from the immoral and lawless of the world.

"And take heed to yourselves, lest at any time your hearts be overcharged with surfeiting, and drunkenness, and cares of this life, and so that day come upon you unawares" (Lu.21:34).

"And with many other words did he testify and exhort, saying, Save yourselves from this untoward generation" (Ac.2:40).

"I beseech you therefore, brethren, by the mercies of God, that ye present your bodies a living sacrifice, holy, acceptable unto God, *which is* your reasonable service. And be not conformed to this world: but be ye transformed by the renewing of your mind, that ye may prove what is that good, and acceptable, and perfect, will of God" (Ro.12:1-2).

"Wherefore come out from among them, and be ye separate, saith the Lord, and touch not the unclean *thing;* and I will receive you, And will be a Father unto you, and ye shall be my sons and daughters, saith the Lord Almighty" (2 Co.6:17-18).

"And have no fellowship with the unfruitful works of darkness, but rather reprove *them*" (Ep.5:11).

"If any man see his brother sin a sin *which is* not unto death, he shall ask, and he shall give him life for them that sin not unto death. There is a sin unto death: I do not say that he shall pray for it" (1 Jn.5:16).

c. *A person must discern between the clean and unclean* in day-to-day behavior (v.25). This is the way to escape the judgment of God. Remember, God had spelled out the laws governing clean and unclean animals. God wanted His people to develop physical purity by eating the right food. Food laws protected His people from disease and from unhealthy bodies. Moreover, by obeying the food laws, a person became identified as a follower of God. He developed a strong testimony for obeying the commandments of God. (See outline and notes—Lev.11:1-47.) The charge in this verse in strong: the believer is not to defile himself by eating anything that would make him unclean. His disobedience would defile him in the eyes of God. The believer must discern or distinguish between clean and unclean food. He must obey all of God's laws, even the food laws. By such, he becomes identified as a strong, obedient follower of God.

"But the natural man receiveth not the things of the Spirit of God: for they are foolishness unto him: neither can he know *them,* because they are spiritually discerned" (1 Co.2:14).

"But strong meat belongeth to them that are of full age, *even* those who by reason of use have their senses exercised to discern both good and evil" (He.5:14).

"Give therefore thy servant an understanding heart to judge thy people, that I may discern between good and bad: for who is able to judge this thy so great a people?" (1 K.3:9).

"And shall make him of quick understanding in the fear of the LORD: and he shall not judge after the sight of his eyes, neither reprove after the hearing of his ears" (Is.11:3).

d. *A person must live a holy life* if he is to escape the justice and judgment of God (v.26). The believer is to be holy for two reasons:
⇒ because God is holy
⇒ because God has set His people apart from all other people, set them apart to be His, His very special possession. The believer belongs to God; the believer is an adopted son or daughter of God, a member of God's household, a member of His very own family. Therefore the believer must not disgrace or bring shame to the family of God nor to the name of God. The believer must live a holy life before the immoral and lawless of the world.

"That he would grant unto us, that we being delivered out of the hand of our enemies might serve him without fear, In holiness and righteousness before him, all the days of our life" (Lu.1:74-75).

"Having therefore these promises, dearly beloved, let us cleanse ourselves from all filthiness of the flesh and spirit, perfecting holiness in the fear of God" (2 Co.7:1).

"Follow peace with all *men,* and holiness, without which no man shall see the Lord" (He.12:14).

"But as he which hath called you is holy, so be ye holy in all *manner of* conversation [behavior, conduct]; Because it is written, Be ye holy; for I am holy. And if ye call on the Father, who without respect of persons judgeth according to every man's work, pass the time of your sojourning *here* in fear" (1 Pe.1:15-17).

"*Seeing* then *that* all these things shall be dissolved, what manner *of persons* ought ye to be in *all* holy conversation and godliness, Looking for and hasting unto the coming of the day of God, wherein the heavens being on fire shall be dissolved, and the elements shall melt with fervent heat? Nevertheless we, according to his promise, look for new heavens and a new earth, wherein dwelleth righteousness. Wherefore, beloved, seeing that ye look for such things, be diligent that ye may be found of him in peace, without spot, and blameless" (2 Pe.3:11-14).

e. *A person must reject mediums and psychics and execute justice upon mediums and psychics* (v.27). Seeking counsel or one's fate and destiny through mediums or spiritists is the same as pagan worship. The penalty of all pagan worship is execution. But note God's justice and judgment: the blood of all mediums and spiritists will be on their own heads. They are responsible and held accountable for their false worship, for seeking counsel and the counsel fate and destiny of people someplace other than in God. The idea is that they will be judged and condemned to eternal separation from God.

> "Now the works of the flesh are manifest, which are *these;* Adultery, fornication, uncleanness, lasciviousness, Idolatry, witchcraft, hatred, variance, emulations, wrath, strife, seditions, heresies, Envyings, murders, drunkenness, revellings, and such like: of the which I tell you before, as I have also told *you* in time past, that they which do such things shall not inherit the kingdom of God" (Ga.5:19-21).
>
> "Thou shalt not suffer a witch to live" (Ex.22:18).
>
> "Regard not them that have familiar spirits, neither seek after wizards, to be defiled by them: I *am* the LORD your God" (Le.19:31).
>
> "So Saul died for his transgression which he committed against the LORD, *even* against the word of the LORD, which he kept not, and also for asking *counsel* of *one that had* a familiar spirit, to enquire *of it;* And enquired not of the LORD: therefore he slew him, and turned the kingdom unto David the son of Jesse" (1 Chr.10:13-14; see 1 S.28:7).
>
> "And when they shall say unto you, Seek unto them that have familiar spirits, and unto wizards that peep, and that mutter: should not a people seek unto their God? for the living to the dead? To the law and to the testimony: if they speak not according to this word, *it is* because *there is* no light in them" (Is.8:19-20).
>
> "And I will cut off witchcrafts out of thine hand; and thou shalt have no *more* soothsayers: Thy graven images also will I cut off, and thy standing images out of the midst of thee; and thou shalt no more worship the work of thine hands. And I will pluck up thy groves out of the midst of thee: so will I destroy thy cities. And I will execute vengeance in anger and fury upon the heathen, such as they have not heard" (Mi.5:12-15).

TYPES, SYMBOLS, AND PICTURES
Leviticus 20:1-27

Historical Term	Type or Picture (Scriptural Basis for Each)	Life Application for Today's Believer	Biblical Application
The Promised Land Le. 20:24	*The promised land is a symbol of heaven, of the new heavens and earth. God has set apart the obedient to be His people and to inherit the promised land, the land that flows with milk and honey, the land that once belonged to the immoral and lawless of the world.* "But I have said unto you, Ye shall inherit their land, and I will give it unto you to possess it, a land that floweth with milk and honey: I *am* the LORD your God, which have separated you from *other* people" (Le.20:24).	The obedient person is the person who lives a life of separation, a life that is entirely different from the immoral and lawless people of the earth. It is the obedient who will receive the inheritance of God, the promised land that flows with milk and honey.	*"In my Father's house are many mansions: if it were not so, I would have told you. I go to prepare a place for you. And if I go and prepare a place for you, I will come again, and receive you unto myself; that where I am, there ye may be also."* (Jn.14:2-3) *"For our conversation [citizenship] is in heaven; from whence also we look for the Saviour, the Lord Jesus Christ:"* (Ph.3:20; see 2 Co.5:1; 1 Pe.1:3-4; 2 Pe.3:10-13)

CHAPTER 21

E. Laws That Govern the Priests, the Ministers of God (Part 1): The Basic Requirements & Qualifications for the Minister of God, 21:1-24

1. **The basic requirement for the priest, the minister of God: To be holy, totally set apart to God**
   a. Must not defile himself by overly mourning for the dead: Symbolizes the need to focus upon life not death
      1) To show the utmost love, comfort, & hope by mourning for his immediate family & a sister (or brother) who is dependent upon him

      2) Not to defile himself by overly mourning or by interrupting his service too much for other relatives who face death
   b. Must not follow pagan practices such as disfiguring his body (see 19:27-28)

   c. Must live a holy, pure life for God
      1) Must never profane, dishonor God's name
      2) The reason: He is set apart for the service of God—to present the offerings to the LORD, pleasing the LORD
   d. Must marry a pure woman
      1) Not a woman sexually defiled by prostitution or divorce
      2) The reason: Holiness
   e. Must have a strong testimony of holiness, of being totally set apart to God
      1) Because he serves God
      2) Because God is holy

   f. Must have godly, children
      1) An example: A daughter (or son) who becomes a prostitute must be judged
      2) Because she disgraces her father & God
2. **The basic requirement for the High Priest (a type of Christ, the High Priest): Must be totally dedicated to the service of God**
   a. Must have the special anointing & priestly clothing
   b. Must never be defiled by

And the LORD said unto Moses, Speak unto the priests the sons of Aaron, and say unto them, There shall none be defiled for the dead among his people:
2 But for his kin, that is near unto him, *that is*, for his mother, and for his father, and for his son, and for his daughter, and for his brother,
3 And for his sister a virgin, that is nigh unto him, which hath had no husband; for her may he be defiled.
4 *But* he shall not defile himself, *being* a chief man among his people, to profane himself.
5 They shall not make baldness upon their head, neither shall they shave off the corner of their beard, nor make any cuttings in their flesh.
6 They shall be holy unto their God, and not profane the name of their God: for the offerings of the LORD made by fire, *and* the bread of their God, they do offer: therefore they shall be holy.
7 They shall not take a wife *that is* a whore, or profane; neither shall they take a woman put away from her husband: for he *is* holy unto his God.
8 Thou shalt sanctify him therefore; for he offereth the bread of thy God: he shall be holy unto thee: for I the LORD, which sanctify you, *am* holy.
9 And the daughter of any priest, if she profane herself by playing the whore, she profaneth her father: she shall be burnt with fire.
10 And *he that is* the high priest among his brethren, upon whose head the anointing oil was poured, and that is consecrated to put on the garments, shall not uncover his head, nor

rend his clothes;
11 Neither shall he go in to any dead body, nor defile himself for his father, or for his mother;
12 Neither shall he go out of the sanctuary, nor profane the sanctuary of his God; for the crown of the anointing oil of his God *is* upon him: I *am* the LORD.
13 And he shall take a wife in her virginity.
14 A widow, or a divorced woman, or profane, *or* an harlot, these shall he not take: but he shall take a virgin of his own people to wife.
15 Neither shall he profane his seed among his people: for I the LORD do sanctify him.
16 And the LORD spake unto Moses, saying,
17 Speak unto Aaron, saying, Whosoever *he be* of thy seed in their generations that hath *any* blemish, let him not approach to offer the bread of his God.
18 For whatsoever man *he be* that hath a blemish, he shall not approach: a blind man, or a lame, or he that hath a flat nose, or any thing superfluous,
19 Or a man that is brokenfooted, or brokenhanded,
20 Or crookbackt, or a dwarf, or that hath a blemish in his eye, or be scurvy, or scabbed, or hath his stones broken;
21 No man that hath a blemish of the seed of Aaron the priest shall come nigh to offer the offerings of the LORD made by fire: he hath a blemish; he shall not come nigh to offer the bread of his God.
22 He shall eat the bread of his God, *both* of the most holy, and of the holy.
23 Only he shall not go in unto the vail, nor come nigh unto the altar, because he hath a blemish; that he profane not my sanctuaries: for I the LORD do sanctify them.
24 And Moses told *it* unto Aaron, and to his sons, and unto all the children of Israel.

death
   1) Must not grieve over death, showing the marks of mourning over death

   2) Must not put aside his service for God even to bury the dead (see Mt.8:21-22)
      • Bc. he has been chosen, dedicated to serve God
      • Bc. the LORD Himself is commanding him
   c. Must marry a pure woman, a virgin: Not a widow, a divorcee, a prostitute

      1) To marry a woman from his own people
      2) The reason: To guarantee holy, godly children above reproach & a successor to the family of priests
3. **The basic qualification for the priest: Must be physically perfect, having no blemish, no defect (a symbol of Christ, the perfect Priest)**

   a. The blemishes, defects listed
      1) A man who is blind, lame, disfigured, or deformed

      2) A man with a crippled foot or hand
      3) A man with a humpback, a dwarf, one with an eye defect, festering or oozing sores, or damaged testicles

   b. The reason: An imperfect (blemished, defective) priest would paint the picture of an imperfect priesthood & sacrifice being made to God

   c. The provision for the person with a defect: Can eat the food of God, share & fellowship with God
   d. The qualification emphasized: Must be perfect—no defect
      1) Is essential to go near the curtain, to approach God
      2) Is essential to go near the altar to offer the sacrifice

DIVISION IV

THE WAY TO LIVE A HOLY LIFE BEFORE GOD (PART 2): A PURE SPIRIT (SANCTIFICATION), 17:1–27:34

E. Laws That Govern the Priests, the Ministers of God (Part 1): The Basic Requirements and Qualifications for the Minister of God, 21:1-24

(21:2-24) **Introduction—Minister of God, Duty of—Priest, Duty of**: the minister of God is to be holy, totally set apart to God. There are two reasons why: first, the office of the minister is holy. God has ordained the office to be holy, an office that is distinct and different because it is totally set apart to God. Second, God has called the minister to serve in the holy office. Therefore, the person is to honor the office by living a holy life.

Simply stated, the minister is the ambassador or representative of God who is called to serve God's people. As the representative of God, the minister is to be totally dedicated and consecrated to God. That is, he is to be holy, totally set apart to God and to the ministry of God's people. The minister is to live a righteous life, a life that will bring honor, not shame, to God.

Note this fact: in chapters 11–20, God had given the laws that were to govern His people, the laws that showed His people how to live holy lives and build a strong society. Now, in chapters 21–22, God gives the laws that were to govern His priests or ministers, laws that would bring honor to God and to the office of the priesthood. The office of the priest was an official office, an office ordained by God to be holy. Therefore, the priest was to live a holy and pure life before God and the people. His office—the office of the priest—demanded a higher standard. The priest was to be more holy, more set apart to God, than other believers. He was to be more holy in word and behavior and in his witness for God. There was a very special reason for this: his holiness pointed to the perfect priesthood of the Lord Jesus Christ. The holy character and behavior of the priest was a symbol or type of Christ, the coming Messiah and Savior of the world. This will be seen throughout the discussion of this Scripture:[1] *Laws That Govern the Priests, the Ministers of God (Part 1): The Basic Requirements and Qualifications for the Minister of God,* 21:1-24.

1. The basic requirement for the priest, the minister of God: to be holy, totally set apart to God (vv.1-9).
2. The basic requirement for the High Priest (a type of Christ, the High Priest): must be totally dedicated to the service of God (vv.10-15).
3. The basic qualification for the priest: must be physically perfect, having no blemish, no defect (a symbol of Christ, the perfect Priest) (vv.16-24).

1 (21:1-9) **Minister, Duty of—Priest, Duty of—Holiness—Commitment—Mourning, Over the Dead—Paganism, Practices of—Minister, Marriage of—Priest, Marriage of—Children, of Ministers—Ministers, Children of**: the basic requirement for the priest or minister of God was an absolute essential: he was to be holy, totally set apart to God. Six specific laws are given to assure the holiness of God's servant. Note the Scripture and outline:

OUTLINE	SCRIPTURE	SCRIPTURE	OUTLINE
1. The basic requirement for the priest, the minister of God: To be holy, totally set apart to God a. Must not defile himself by overly mourning for the dead: Symbolizes the need to focus upon life not death 　1) To show the utmost love, comfort, & hope by mourning for his immediate family & a sister (or brother) who is dependent upon him	And the LORD said unto Moses, Speak unto the priests the sons of Aaron, and say unto them, There shall none be defiled for the dead among his people: 2 But for his kin, that is near unto him, *that is,* for his mother, and for his father, and for his son, and for his daughter, and for his brother, 3 And for his sister a virgin, that is nigh unto him, which hath had no husband; for her may he be defiled.	6 They shall be holy unto their God, and not profane the name of their God: for the offerings of the LORD made by fire, *and* the bread of their God, they do offer: therefore they shall be holy. 7 They shall not take a wife *that is* a whore, or profane; neither shall they take a woman put away from her husband: for he *is* holy unto his God.	c. Must live a holy, pure life for God 　1) Must never profane, dishonor God's name 　2) The reason: He is set apart for the service of God—to present the offerings to the LORD, pleasing the LORD d. Must marry a pure woman 　1) Not a woman sexually defiled by prostitution or divorce 　2) The reason: Holiness
2) Not to defile himself by overly mourning or by interrupting his service too much for other relatives who face death b. Must not follow pagan practices such as disfiguring his body (see 19:27-28)	4 *But* he shall not defile himself, *being* a chief man among his people, to profane himself. 5 They shall not make baldness upon their head, neither shall they shave off the corner of their beard, nor make any cuttings in their flesh.	8 Thou shalt sanctify him therefore; for he offereth the bread of thy God: he shall be holy unto thee: for I the LORD, which sanctify you, *am* holy. 9 And the daughter of any priest, if she profane herself by playing the whore, she profaneth her father: she shall be burnt with fire.	e. Must have a strong testimony of holiness, of being totally set apart to God 　1) Because he serves God 　2) Because God is holy f. Must have godly, children 　1) An example: A daughter (or son) who be-comes a prostitute must be judged 　2) Because. she disgraces her father & God

---

[1] Ideas for this introduction were stirred by *The Expositor's Bible Commentary*, p.616.

a. The priest or minister of God must not defile himself by mourning excessively for the dead (vv.1-4). This law symbolized the need to focus upon life not death. The priest was allowed to show the utmost love, comfort, and hope by mourning for his immediate family, including a sister or brother who was dependent upon him. But he was not to defile himself by overly mourning other relatives who faced death. This would interrupt his service for God, and this he was not allowed to do. Remember, death was a symbol of defilement, and death was the penalty for sin pronounced by God. Therefore, a person was counted ceremonially unclean if he touched a dead body or stood around in the room where a dead body lay (Nu.19:14). The person defiled by death was counted unclean for seven days. In fact, all the mourners at any funeral were considered defiled by death and not allowed to enter the sanctuary for seven full days. For this reason, the priest was not allowed to excessively mourn for anyone other than his immediate family. His service for God would be interrupted for too long a time. His call was to focus upon holiness and life not death. Death symbolized corruption and the penalty for sin; therefore, he was to have as little to do with it as possible. He was to live a life of holiness before the people, a life totally set apart to God. He was to demonstrate holiness in every conceivable way he could. One clear way was just this: not mourning excessively for the dead—focusing upon life not death.

> "But Jesus said unto him, Follow me; and let the dead bury their dead" (Mt.8:22).
>
> "For whether we live, we live unto the LORD; and whether we die, we die unto the LORD: whether we live therefore, or die, we are the LORD's. For to this end Christ both died, and rose, and revived, that he might be LORD both of the dead and living" (Ro.14:8-9).
>
> "Take heed therefore unto yourselves, and to all the flock, over the which the Holy Ghost hath made you overseers, to feed the church of God, which he hath purchased with his own blood" (Ac.20:28).
>
> "Therefore, my beloved brethren, be ye stedfast, unmovable, always abounding in the work of the LORD, forasmuch as ye know that your labour is not in vain in the LORD" (1 Co.15:58).
>
> "Be thou an example of the believers, in word, in conversation, in charity, in spirit, in faith, in purity" (1 Ti.4:12).

b. The priest or minister of God must not follow pagan practices (v.5). It was a common practice of pagans to disfigure their bodies when mourning for the dead. Some of their rituals of mourning involved shaving their heads, shaving off the edges of their beards, and shedding blood by cutting their bodies—all in order to appease the anger of their false gods against the dead. God's servant was not to engage in these superstitious practices. The priest or minister was to present a holy body to the LORD, a body that was complete and whole, free from any disfigurement whatsoever.

> "I beseech you therefore, brethren, by the mercies of God, that ye present your bodies a living sacrifice, holy, acceptable unto God, *which is* your reasonable service. And be not conformed to this world: but be ye transformed by the renewing of your mind, that ye may prove what is that good, and acceptable, and perfect, will of God" (Ro.12:1-2).
>
> "Know ye not that your bodies are the members of Christ? shall I then take the members of Christ, and make *them* the members of an harlot? God forbid" (1 Co.6:15).
>
> "What? know ye not that your body is the temple of the Holy Ghost *which is* in you, which ye have of God, and ye are not your own? For ye are bought with a price: therefore glorify God in your body, and in your spirit, which are God's" (1 Co.6:19-20).
>
> "And what agreement hath the temple of God with idols? for ye are the temple of the living God; as God hath said, I will dwell in them, and walk in *them;* and I will be their God, and they shall be my people" (2 Co.6:16).
>
> "And the very God of peace sanctify you wholly; and *I pray God* your whole spirit and soul and body be preserved blameless unto the coming of our Lord Jesus Christ" (1 Th.5:23).

c. The priest or minister of God must live a holy, pure life for God (v.6). He must never profane nor dishonor the name of God. He must never pollute himself with any sin, never give in to the passions of the flesh. He must not put a stain upon the name of God by engaging in any form of sin. Because of his position as priest or minister of God, he represents God. Therefore, what he does is a reflection upon the name of God. He has been set apart for the service of God, to present the offerings and sacrifices to the LORD. Therefore, he must live a holy, pure life for God and for the sake of the people of God.

> "That he would grant unto us, that we being delivered out of the hand of our enemies might serve him without fear, In holiness and righteousness before him, all the days of our life" (Lu.1:74-75).
>
> "Thou therefore which teachest another, teachest thou not thyself? thou that preachest a man should not steal, dost thou steal? Thou that sayest a man should not commit adultery, dost thou commit adultery? thou that abhorrest idols, dost thou commit sacrilege? Thou that makest thy boast of the law, through breaking the law dishonourest thou God? For the name of God is blasphemed among the Gentiles through you, as it is written" (Ro.2:21-24).
>
> "Having therefore these promises, dearly beloved, let us cleanse ourselves from all filthiness of the flesh and spirit, perfecting holiness in the fear of God" (2 Co.7:1).
>
> "*Seeing* then *that* all these things shall be dissolved, what manner *of persons* ought ye to be in *all* holy conversation and godliness, Looking for and hasting unto the coming of the day of God, wherein the heavens being on fire shall be dissolved, and the elements shall melt with fervent heat? Nevertheless we, according to his promise, look for new heavens and a new earth, wherein dwelleth righteousness. Wherefore, beloved, seeing that ye look for such things, be diligent that ye may be found of him in peace, without spot, and blameless" (2 Pe.3:11-14).

d. The priest or minister of God must marry a pure woman (v.7). The priest or minister held a high position, an official position before the LORD and the people. Therefore, he was not to marry a woman who had been sexually defiled by prostitution or divorce. The priest or minister was counted holy by God, totally set apart to the service of God; therefore, his wife was to be a virgin, a woman of excellent character. The reason is clearly seen: her character reflected on her husband. The personal and private life of the priest was to be a life of holiness, a life above reproach. Both the priest and his wife were responsible to live lives of holiness, lives that were distinct and different, totally set apart to God. Remember, the priest was a type of Christ who was perfect in righteousness and holiness. Therefore, the priest was to be holy and godly in every area of life. One area that he could control was the area of marriage. Therefore, he was to marry a virgin, a pure woman, a woman completely free from sexual impurity.

> "A bishop then must be blameless, the husband of one wife, vigilant, sober, of good behaviour, given to hospitality, apt to teach" (1 Ti.3:2).
> "If any be blameless, the husband of one wife, having faithful children not accused of riot or unruly" (Tit.1:6).

e. The priest or minister of God must have a *strong testimony* of holiness, of being totally set apart to God (v.8). He serves God; therefore he must be holy because God is holy. Note that it is God who makes the priest or minister holy, who sets him apart to serve the people of God. The priest or minister is to be regarded and considered holy by God's people. He is to be highly esteemed, honored and respected, for God has put honor upon him by setting him apart for the ministry.

> "For thou shalt be his witness unto all men of what thou hast seen and heard" (Ac.22:15).
> "Not because we have not power, but to make ourselves an example unto you to follow us" (2 Th.3:9).
> "Let no man despise thy youth; but be thou an example of the believers, in word, in conversation, in charity, in spirit, in faith, in purity" (1 Ti.4:12).
> "In all things showing thyself a pattern [example] of good works: in doctrine *showing* uncorruptness, gravity, sincerity" (Tit.2:7).

f. The priest or minister of God must have godly, disciplined children (v.9). Note the example given: a daughter (or son) who becomes a prostitute must be severely judged. She was to be burned in the fire. Why so severe a judgment? Because she disgraced God and she disgraced her father who was a representative of God before the people. The daughter (or son) of a priest had the most honorable privilege in all the world for children, that of being a part of a godly family, of a family that had been set apart in a special way by God. Therefore, the daughter was not to give herself to prostitution. This sinful act would reflect upon her father and God. Her sinful behavior would dishonor not only her father and family but also the office of the priesthood. This God would not tolerate; therefore, the punishment for this sin was to serve as a deterrent to keep other children from sinning. Note another fact as well: sex was practiced as a ceremonial ritual in many of the false religions of that day. Consequently, it was an honor for a young girl to become a religious prostitute in order to lead men into a deeper experience with their false gods. There was the possibility that God's people would be contaminated by this horrible, pagan practice. Therefore, this severe punishment was given partly to prevent the prostitution of the daughter of a priest. The point is strong: the children of a priest or minister must live godly, disciplined lives before God.

> "One [a minister] that ruleth well his own house, having his children in subjection with all gravity; (For if a man know not how to rule his own house, how shall he take care of the church of God?)" (1 Ti. 3:4-5).
> "If any be blameless, the husband of one wife, having faithful children not accused of riot or unruly. For a bishop [minister] must be blameless, as the steward of God; not selfwilled, not soon angry, not given to wine, no striker, not given to filthy lucre" (Tit.1:6-7).
> "For I say unto you, That except your righteousness shall exceed *the righteousness* of the scribes and Pharisees, ye shall in no case enter into the kingdom of heaven" (Mt.5:20).
> "Awake to righteousness, and sin not; for some have not the knowledge of God: I speak *this* to your shame" (1 Co.15:34).
> "That ye may approve things that are excellent; that ye may be sincere and without offence till the day of Christ; Being filled with the fruits of righteousness, which are by Jesus Christ, unto the glory and praise of God" (Ph.1:10-11).
> "Lay hands suddenly on no man, neither be partaker of other men's sins: keep thyself pure" (1 Ti.5:22).
> "Follow peace with all *men,* and holiness, without which no man shall see the LORD" (He.12:14).
> "Pure religion and undefiled before God and the Father is this, To visit the fatherless and widows in their affliction, *and* to keep himself unspotted from the world" (Js.1:27).
> "*Seeing* then *that* all these things shall be dissolved, what manner *of persons* ought ye to be in *all* holy conversation and godliness, Looking for and hasting unto the coming of the day of God, wherein the heavens being on fire shall be dissolved, and the elements shall melt with fervent heat? Nevertheless we, according to his promise, look for new heavens and a new earth, wherein dwelleth righteousness. Wherefore, beloved, seeing that ye look for such things, be diligent that ye may be found of him in peace, without spot, and blameless" (2 Pe.3:11-14).

Thought 1. The minister of God must live a holy life, a life totally set apart to God. The office of the minister is held to a higher standard than other professions. The person who occupies the office of a minister must therefore live a far more strict life than other people. He must live a life of holiness, a life of separation, a life that is totally set apart from the immoral and lawless ways of the world. He must be holy, totally set apart to God.

2 (21:10-15) **High Priest, Duty of—Dedication—Commitment—Minister, Duty—Minister, Marriage**: the basic requirement for the High Priest was an absolute essential: he must be totally dedicated to the service of God. Remember, the High Priest was a type of Christ the High Priest. The High Priest held a very special position before God and man. He was the *supreme mediator* who represented the case of man before God; therefore, more strict requirements were placed upon him.

OUTLINE	SCRIPTURE	SCRIPTURE	OUTLINE

2. The basic requirement for the High Priest (a type of Christ, the High Priest): Must be totally dedicated to the service of God
a. Must have the special anointing & priestly clothing.
b. Must never be defiled by death
  1) Must not grieve over death, showing the marks of mourning over death
 	
  2) Must not put aside his service for God even to bury the dead (see Mt.8:21-22)
	10 And *he that is* the high priest among his brethren, upon whose head the anointing oil was poured, and that is consecrated to put on the garments, shall not uncover his head, nor rend his clothes;
	11 Neither shall he go in to any dead body, nor defile himself for his father, or for his mother;
	12 Neither shall he go out of the sanctuary, nor profane the sanctuary of his
		God; for the crown of the anointing oil of his God *is* upon him: I *am* the LORD.
		13 And he shall take a wife in her virginity.
		14 A widow, or a divorced woman, or profane, *or* an harlot, these shall he not take: but he shall take a virgin of his own people to wife.
		15 Neither shall he profane his seed among his people: for I the LORD do sanctify him.
			• Bc. he has been chosen, dedicated to serve God
			• Bc. the LORD Himself is commanding him
			c. Must marry a pure woman, a virgin: Not a widow, a divorcee, a prostitute
			
			  1) To marry a woman from his own people
			  2) The reason: To guarantee holy, godly children above reproach & a successor to the family of priests

a. The High Priest was set apart by being ordained with a very special anointing oil and by wearing the High Priestly garments. It was the anointing oil and the clothing that set the office apart from all others, that symbolized his position as a mediator between God and man. Again, keep in mind that this is a symbol of Christ, the Supreme Mediator, who brings people to God.

b. The High Priest must never be defiled by death (vv.10-12). He was never to show the marks of mourning over death, marks such as disheveling his hair or tearing his clothes. He was not to enter a place where a dead body lay. He was forbidden to attend the funeral of close relatives, even of his father and mother. Why? Because he was not to put aside his service for God under any circumstances. His heart and his time were to be totally devoted to God—to God and God alone. His ministry for God even took precedence over the death of a close relative. Keep in mind that death was a symbol of corruption and of the penalty for sin. The High Priest—the supreme mediator standing between God and man—was to have nothing, absolutely nothing, to do with death. He was the minister of life, not of death. Note God's authoritative words: "I am the LORD." The LORD Himself gave this law and commanded that it be obeyed. It had to be obeyed because it pointed toward the High Priesthood of Jesus Christ, the Supreme Mediator between God and man.

c. The High Priest had to marry a pure woman, a virgin. He was not allowed to marry a widow, a divorcee, or a prostitute (vv.13-15). Note that the woman had to be from his own people, that is, an Israelite. This guaranteed offspring from Israel who could carry on the succession of the High Priesthood. This also helped to guarantee the likelihood of holy, godly children who would live lives above reproach. If the High Priest had ever married a woman from another nationality, the High Priesthood would have been corrupted. This was never to be. Note what God declares: "I am the LORD, who makes him [the High Priest] holy." The High Priesthood was to be of pure lineage—all pointing toward the pure lineage of Jesus Christ, the coming Mediator and Savior of the world.

Thought 1. The High Priest was a symbol of Jesus Christ, the supreme High Priest and Mediator who stands between God and man.

"For *there is* one God, and one mediator between God and men, the man Christ Jesus; Who gave himself a ransom for all, to be testified in due time" (1 Ti.2:5-6).

"Now of the things which we have spoken *this is* the sum: We have such an high priest, who is set on the right hand of the throne of the Majesty in the heavens" (He.8:1).

"How much more shall the blood of Christ, who through the eternal Spirit offered himself without spot to God, purge your conscience from dead works to serve the living God? And for this cause he is the mediator of the new testament, that by means of death, for the redemption of the transgressions *that were* under the first testament, they which are called might receive the promise of eternal inheritance" (He.9:14-15).

"For Christ is not entered into the holy places made with hands, *which are* the figures of the true; but into heaven itself, now to appear in the presence of God for us" (He.9:24).

"Jesus [is] the mediator of the new covenant" (He.12:24).

"My little children, these things write I unto you, that ye sin not. And if any man sin, we have an advocate with the Father, Jesus Christ the righteous: And he is the propitiation for our sins: and not for ours only, but also for *the sins of* the whole world" (1 Jn.2:1-2).

3 (21:16-24) **Priest, Qualification of—Minister, Qualification of—Symbol, of Christ—Jesus Christ, Symbol of**: the basic qualification for the priest was an absolute essential: he had to be physically perfect, having no blemish or defect whatsoever. This was a symbol of Christ, the *perfect* High Priest. Because the priest was to represent the perfection of the coming Savior of the world, he was not allowed to serve as a priest if he had any deformity or physical defect whatsoever.

OUTLINE	SCRIPTURE	SCRIPTURE	OUTLINE
3. **The basic qualification for the priest: Must be physically perfect, having no blemish, no defect (a symbol of Christ, the perfect Priest)**	16 And the LORD spake unto Moses, saying, 17 Speak unto Aaron, saying, Whosoever *he be* of thy seed in their generations that hath *any* blemish, let him not approach to offer the bread of his God.	21 No man that hath a blemish of the seed of Aaron the priest shall come nigh to offer the offerings of the LORD made by fire: he hath a blemish; he shall not come nigh to offer the bread of his God.	b. The reason: An imperfect (blemished, defective) priest would paint the picture of an imperfect priesthood & sacrifice being made to God
a. The blemishes, defects listed 1) A man who is blind, lame, disfigured, or deformed	18 For whatsoever man *he be* that hath a blemish, he shall not approach: a blind man, or a lame, or he that hath a flat nose, or any thing superfluous,	22 He shall eat the bread of his God, *both* of the most holy, and of the holy. 23 Only he shall not go in unto the vail, nor come nigh	c. The provision for the person with a defect: Can eat the food of God, share & fellowship with God

2) A man with a crippled foot or hand
  3) A man with a humpback, a dwarf, one with an eye defect, festering or oozing sores, or damaged testicles
	19 Or a man that is brokenfooted, or brokenhanded, 20 Or crookbackt, or a dwarf, or that hath a blemish in his eye, or be scurvy, or scabbed, or hath his stones broken;	unto the altar, because he hath a blemish; that he profane not my sanctuaries: for I the LORD do sanctify them. 24 And Moses told *it* unto Aaron, and to his sons, and unto all the children of Israel.	d. The qualification emphasized: Must be perfect—no defect
			  1) Is essential to go near the curtain, to approach God
			  2) Is essential to go near the altar to offer the sacrifice

a. Note the defects and blemishes that are listed (vv.18-20): a man was not allowed to serve as priest if he was blind, lame, disfigured, or deformed. Neither was he allowed to serve if he had a crippled foot or hand (v.19). If he was a humpback, dwarf, had an eye defect, festering or oozing sores, or damaged testicles, he was not allowed to serve in the ministry of God.

b. Note the reason: an imperfect—blemished or defective—priest would paint the picture of an imperfect priesthood and sacrifice being made to God (v.21). God can accept only a perfect priest and sacrifice; therefore, the appearance of the priest had to paint the picture of a perfect priesthood and sacrifice being offered to God.

c. But note the provision of God for the person with a defect: the person with a defect born into the family or line of the priesthood could eat the food of God, share and fellowship with God (v.22). He had perfect access into the presence of God, being accepted by God; he just was not allowed to serve in the ministry of the priesthood. Keep in mind the reason: the priest and the sacrifice he was offering to God had to paint the picture of a perfect priesthood and sacrifice. All this was pointing to the perfect priesthood and sacrifice of the Lord Jesus Christ who was yet to come.

d. Note that the qualification was again emphasized, which stresses its importance. The priest must be perfect, having no defect whatsoever (vv.23-24). Only a perfect priest was to go near the altar of God. No person with a defect was to be allowed to go near the curtain or to approach the altar of God. A defective or deformed person would desecrate God's sanctuary. Again, remember that the priest was symbolizing the perfect priesthood and sacrifice of the coming Savior and Messiah (Christ) of the world. Note that Moses gave these instructions to Aaron and his sons and to all the people.

Thought 1. The priest with no defect and no blemish was a symbol of the perfection of the Lord Jesus Christ and His sacrifice. The Lord Jesus Christ had to stand before God as the perfect priest and sacrifice in order for God to accept His priesthood and offering. Christ—His person and sacrifice—had to be perfect in order to represent man before God. His perfection had to stand as the *ideal perfection* for all men in order for God to accept man. Any person who comes to God through the Lord Jesus Christ is accepted by God because Jesus Christ intercedes in behalf of the person. God accepts the person *in Christ*. Jesus Christ is the perfect, sinless High Priest and sacrifice who stands before God. He stands before God as the mediator for the human race.

"Who *is* he that condemneth? *It is* Christ that died, yea rather, that is risen again, who is even at the right hand of God, who also maketh intercession for us" (Ro.8:34).

"For he hath made him *to be* sin for us, who knew no sin; that we might be made the righteousness of God in him" (2 Co.5:21).

"Wherefore in all things it behooved him to be made like unto *his* brethren, that he might be a merciful and faithful high priest in things *pertaining* to God, to make reconciliation for the sins of the people" (He.2:17).

"Seeing then that we have a great high priest, that is passed into the heavens, Jesus the Son of God, let us hold fast *our* profession. For we have not an high priest which cannot be touched with the feeling of our infirmities; but was in all points tempted like as *we are, yet* without sin" (He.4:14-15).

"But this *man,* because he continueth ever, hath an unchangeable priesthood. Wherefore he is able also to save them to the uttermost that come unto God by him, seeing he ever liveth to make intercession for them. For such an high priest became us, *who is* holy, harmless, undefiled, separate from sinners, and made higher than the heavens; Who needeth not daily, as those high priests, to offer up sacrifice, first for his own sins, and then for the people's: for this he did once, when he offered up himself" (He.7:24-27).

"Forasmuch as ye know that ye were not redeemed with corruptible things, *as* silver and gold, from your vain conversation *received* by tradition from your fathers; But with the precious blood of Christ, as of a lamb without blemish and without spot" (1 Pe.1:18-19).

TYPES, SYMBOLS, AND PICTURES
Leviticus 21:1-24

Historical Term	Type or Picture (Scriptural Basis for Each)	Life Application for Today's Believer	Biblical Application
The Dead, Overly Mourning for the Dead Le.21:1-4	*This law symbolized the need to focus upon life not death. The priest was allowed to show the utmost love, comfort, and hope by mourning for his immediate family and for a sister or brother who was dependent upon him. But he was not to defile himself by overly mourning for other relatives who died. This would interrupt his service for God, and this he was not allowed to do.* **"And the LORD said unto Moses, Speak unto the priests the sons of Aaron, and say unto them, There shall none be defiled for the dead among his people:" (Le.21:1).**	The believer is not to set his attention upon death but upon the One who gives life, the Lord Jesus Christ.	*"Verily, verily, I say unto you, He that heareth my word, and believeth on him that sent me, hath everlasting life, and shall not come into condemnation; but is passed from death unto life" (Jn.5:24).* *"The thief cometh not, but for to steal, and to kill, and to destroy: I am come that they might have life, and that they might have it more abundantly" (Jn.10:10).* *"Jesus saith unto him, I am the way, the truth, and the life: no man cometh unto the Father, but by me" (Jn.14:6).* *"He that hath the Son hath life; and he that hath not the Son of God hath not life" (1 Jn.5:12).*
The Perfect Priest, the Priest Without Any Deformity or Defect Le. 21:16-24	*The Priest is a symbol of Jesus Christ, the perfect High Priest. Because the priest was to represent the perfection of the coming Savior, he was not allowed to serve as a priest if he had any deformity or physical defect whatsoever.* **"No man that hath a blemish of the seed of Aaron the priest shall come nigh to offer the offerings of the LORD made by fire: he hath a blemish; he shall not come nigh to offer the bread of his God" (Le.21:21).**	Any person who comes to God through the Lord Jesus Christ is accepted by God. The person is accepted by God because Jesus Christ stands before God as the perfect High Priest, interceding in behalf of the person. God accepts the person in Christ. Jesus Christ is the perfect, sinless High Priest and sacrifice who stands before God for the human race.	*"For he hath made him to be sin for us, who knew no sin; that we might be made the righteousness of God in him" (2 Co.5:21).* *"Seeing then that we have a great high priest, that is passed into the heavens, Jesus the Son of God, let us hold fast our profession. For we have not an high priest which cannot be touched with the feeling of our infirmities; but was in all points tempted like as we are, yet without sin" (He. 4:14-15; see He.7:24-27).*

CHAPTER 22

F. Laws That Govern the Priests, the Ministers of God (Part 2): The Basic Duties of the Minister of God, 22:1-33

1. **Duty 1: Must treat the ministry, the sacred offerings, with great respect—must not profane nor shame God's name nor His ministry**

   a. The emphatic charge: One must be disqualified in the service of God if one is unclean
      1) The fact: One must not be leading people to make their offerings & put their trust in the substitute sacrifice if one is unclean
      2) The warning: Will be cut off from God's presence
      3) The things that defile & disqualify a person from serving God (symbolizes sin)
         • Infectious skin diseases & bodily discharges
         • Touching a corpse or anything defiled by a discharge of semen
         • Touching any crawling thing that was counted unclean
         • Touching any person who was counted unclean
   b. The way to restoration: Must follow God's clear instruction to be restored
      1) Must be counted unclean till evening
      2) Must wash, be cleansed
      3) Must undergo a waiting period: Till sundown
      4) Result: May then eat, share in the sacred offering
   c. The clear prohibition one must obey in eating: Must not eat anything found dead or torn by animals
   d. The warning: Must keep God's laws
      1) If disobey, are guilty of treating them with contempt
      2) The penalty: Death (eternal)
      3) The authority: The LORD
2. **Duty 2: Must protect the holy food of God (a symbol of Christ, the holy Sacrifice or Food)**
   a. No outsider could eat holy food
      1) Guests or hired workers

And the LORD spake unto Moses, saying,
2 Speak unto Aaron and to his sons, that they separate themselves from the holy things of the children of Israel, and that they profane not my holy name *in those things* which they hallow unto me: I *am* the LORD.
3 Say unto them, Whosoever *he be* of all your seed among your generations, that goeth unto the holy things, which the children of Israel hallow unto the LORD, having his uncleanness upon him, that soul shall be cut off from my presence: I *am* the LORD.
4 What man soever of the seed of Aaron *is* a leper, or hath a running issue; he shall not eat of the holy things, until he be clean. And whoso toucheth any thing *that is* unclean by the dead, or a man whose seed goeth from him;
5 Or whosoever toucheth any creeping thing, whereby he may be made unclean, or a man of whom he may take uncleanness, whatsoever uncleanness he hath;
6 The soul which hath touched any such shall be unclean until even, and shall not eat of the holy things, unless he wash his flesh with water.
7 And when the sun is down, he shall be clean, and shall afterward eat of the holy things; because it is his food.
8 That which dieth of itself, or is torn *with beasts*, he shall not eat to defile himself therewith: I *am* the LORD.
9 They shall therefore keep mine ordinance, lest they bear sin for it, and die therefore, if they profane it: I the LORD do sanctify them.
10 There shall no stranger eat *of* the holy thing: a sojourner of the priest, or an hired servant, shall not eat *of* the holy thing.
11 But if the priest buy *any* soul with his money, he shall eat of it, and he that is born in his house: they shall eat of his meat.
12 If the priest's daughter also be *married* unto a stranger, she may not eat of an offering of the holy things.
13 But if the priest's daughter be a widow, or divorced, and have no child, and is returned unto her father's house, as in her youth, she shall eat of her father's meat: but there shall no stranger eat thereof.
14 And if a man eat *of* the holy thing unwittingly, then he shall put the fifth *part* thereof unto it, and shall give *it* unto the priest with the holy thing.
15 And they shall not profane the holy things of the children of Israel, which they offer unto the LORD;
16 Or suffer them to bear the iniquity of trespass, when they eat their holy things: for I the LORD do sanctify them.
17 And the LORD spake unto Moses, saying,
18 Speak unto Aaron, and to his sons, and unto all the children of Israel, and say unto them, Whatsoever *he be* of the house of Israel, or of the strangers in Israel, that will offer his oblation for all his vows, and for all his freewill offerings, which they will offer unto the LORD for a burnt offering;
19 *Ye shall offer* at your own will a male without blemish, of the beeves, of the sheep, or of the goats.
20 *But* whatsoever hath a blemish, *that* shall ye not offer: for it shall not be acceptable for you.
21 And whosoever offereth a sacrifice of peace offerings unto the LORD to accomplish *his* vow, or a freewill offering in beeves or sheep, it shall be perfect to be accepted; there shall be no blemish therein.
22 Blind, or broken, or maimed, or having a wen, or scurvy, or scabbed, ye shall not offer these unto the LORD, nor make an offering by fire of them upon the altar unto the

could not eat the holy food
      2) Slaves were counted as family members & were allowed to eat

      3) A daughter who married an outsider was not allowed to eat the holy food

      4) A daughter who was widowed or divorced & had no children could eat the holy food

   b. The mercy upon an offender who ate the holy food by mistake: Was allowed to make restitution plus 20% for the holy food he ate

   c. The warning & the restriction re-emphasized
      1) Must not defile the holy food by allowing unauthorized persons to eat it
      2) The warning & the authority standing behind the restriction: "I am the LORD"

3. **Duty 3: Must approach God exactly as He dictates—must present the perfect sacrifice to the LORD (a symbol of Christ)**
   a. Must present a perfect sacrifice when approaching God for reconciliation—through the Burnt Offering (a symbol of Christ)

      1) Must present a male without defect: A calf, sheep, or goat
      2) The reason: That one may be accepted
      3) The emphatic rule re-stressed: A defective sacrifice will be rejected
   b. Must present a perfect sacrifice when seeking peace or fellowship with God—through the Fellowship or Peace Offering (a symbol of Christ)
      1) Must present a sacrifice without defect or blemish
      2) The reason: Is acceptable
      3) The emphatic rule spelled out: Must not offer defective sacrifices—must never be placed on the altar
         • Not if blind, injured, or maimed
         • Not anything with warts,

festering or oozing sores

c. May present an optional sacrifice with minor blemishes: As a sign of one's imperfection, humility, & unworthiness— through a freewill Thanksgiving or Peace Offering

d. Must not offer a sacrifice that had been castrated: Castration was a forbidden practice in the land (the necessity of reproduction: a symbol of reproducing believers through Christ)

e. Must never accept a defective animal from foreigners and present it as a sacrifice to the LORD

f. Must leave a newborn animal with its mother for at least seven days to be acceptable (symbolized timing, the full-

the LORD.

23 Either a bullock or a lamb that hath any thing superfluous or lacking in his parts, that mayest thou offer *for* a freewill offering; but for a vow it shall not be accepted.

24 Ye shall not offer unto the LORD that which is bruised, or crushed, or broken, or cut; neither shall ye make *any offering thereof* in your land.

25 Neither from a stranger's hand shall ye offer the bread of your God of any of these; because their corruption *is* in them, *and* blemishes *be* in them: they shall not be accepted for you.

26 And the LORD spake unto Moses, saying,

27 When a bullock, or a sheep, or a goat, is brought forth, then it shall be seven days under the dam; and

from the eighth day and thenceforth it shall be accepted for an offering made by fire unto the LORD.

28 And *whether it be* cow or ewe, ye shall not kill it and her young both in one day.

29 And when ye will offer a sacrifice of thanksgiving unto the LORD, offer *it* at your own will.

30 On the same day it shall be eaten up; ye shall leave none of it until the morrow: I *am* the LORD.

31 Therefore shall ye keep my commandments, and do them: I *am* the LORD.

32 Neither shall ye profane my holy name; but I will be hallowed among the children of Israel: I *am* the LORD which hallow you,

33 That brought you out of the land of Egypt, to be your God: I *am* the LORD.

ness of time for Christ to be sacrificed, Ga.4:4-5)

g. Must not sacrifice both a mother & her young on the same day (symbolized the respect for life)

h. The warning
1) Must offer a Thanksgiving Offering exactly as God dictates for it to be acceptable
2) Must eat the sacrifice that same day

4. **Duty 4: Must keep God's commands & follow them**

a. Must not profane (defile, shame, abuse) His holy name

b. Must acknowledge God & acknowledge Him as holy

c. The reasons: God is the LORD
1) He is holy
2) He alone makes people holy
3) He delivers people: Saved His people from Egypt (a symbol of the world)

DIVISION IV

THE WAY TO LIVE A HOLY LIFE BEFORE GOD (PART 2): A PURE SPIRIT (SANCTIFICATION), 17:1–27:34

F. Laws That Govern the Priests, the Ministers of God (Part 2): The Basic Duties of the Minister of God, 22:1-33

(22:1-33) **Introduction—Minister, Duty of**: when God calls a person to serve Him in the ministry, there are some very basic qualifications demanded by God. A person must be holy, totally dedicated and set apart to God. Once the minister is set apart to God, God then expects the minister to walk in the righteousness of Christ, to stand perfect before God in the righteousness of Jesus Christ. This means that the minister will be victorious over all the defects of human nature and the temptations of this world. These two very basic requirements or qualifications were covered in the former outline and study. Now, God covers the basic duties of the minister. There are some very basic duties that God demands of the minister, and those duties have to be done for the minister to be counted faithful. This is the subject of this important passage: *Laws That Govern the Priests, the Ministers of God (Part 2): The Basic Duties of the Minister of God*, 22:1-33.

1. Duty 1: must treat the ministry, the sacred offerings, with great respect—must not profane nor shame God's name nor His ministry (vv.1-9).
2. Duty 2: must protect the holy food of God (a symbol of Christ, the holy Sacrifice or Food) (vv.10-16).
3. Duty 3: must approach God exactly as He dictates—must present the perfect sacrifice to the LORD (a symbol of Christ) (vv.17-30).
4. Duty 4: must keep God's commands and follow them (vv.31-34).

1 (22:1-9) **Priest, Duty of—Ministry, Duty to—Ministry, Respect of—Offerings, the Sacred—Law, Penalty for Breaking—Sin, Profaning and Shaming God's Name**: the priest or minister must treat the ministry, the sacred offerings, with great respect. He must not profane nor shame God's name in the ministry. When a believer approached God through one of the sacred offerings—when he brought a substitute sacrifice to be presented to God in his behalf—the priest was to treat the offering and sacrifice with utmost respect. He was to take his call, his responsibility and charge, very, very seriously. God had given the priest or minister of God one of the greatest calls in all the world, that of approaching God with the sacred offerings of God's people. Therefore, the priest was to treat his call with the greatest respect. He was to treat the ministry, the sacred offerings, with the greatest care.

OUTLINE	SCRIPTURE	SCRIPTURE	OUTLINE
1. Duty 1: Must treat the ministry, the sacred offerings, with great respect—must not profane nor shame God's name nor His ministry	And the LORD spake unto Moses, saying, 2 Speak unto Aaron and to his sons, that they separate themselves from the holy things of the children of Israel, and that they profane not my holy name *in those things* which they hallow unto me: I *am* the LORD.	5 Or whosoever toucheth any creeping thing, whereby he may be made unclean, or a man of whom he may take uncleanness, whatsoever uncleanness he hath;	• Touching any crawling thing that was counted unclean • Touching any person who was counted unclean
a. The emphatic charge: One must be disqualified in the service of God if one is unclean 1) The fact: One must not be leading people to make their offerings & put their trust in the substitute sacrifice if one is unclean 2) The warning: Will be cut off from God's presence 3) The things that defile & disqualify a person from serving God (symbolizes sin) • Infectious skin diseases & bodily discharges • Touching a corpse or having a discharge of semen	3 Say unto them, Whosoever *he be* of all your seed among your generations, that goeth unto the holy things, which the children of Israel hallow unto the LORD, having his uncleanness upon him, that soul shall be cut off from my presence: I *am* the LORD. 4 What man soever of the seed of Aaron *is* a leper, or hath a running issue; he shall not eat of the holy things, until he be clean. And whoso toucheth any thing *that is* unclean *by the* dead, or a man whose seed goeth from him;	6 The soul which hath touched any such shall be unclean until even, and shall not eat of the holy things, unless he wash his flesh with water. 7 And when the sun is down, he shall be clean, and shall afterward eat of the holy things; because it *is* his food. 8 That which dieth of itself, or is torn *with beasts*, he shall not eat to defile himself therewith: I *am* the LORD. 9 They shall therefore keep mine ordinance, lest they bear sin for it, and die therefore, if they profane it: I the LORD do sanctify them.	b. The way to restoration: Must follow God's clear instruction to be restored 1) Must be counted unclean till evening 2) Must wash, be cleansed 3) Must undergo a waiting period: Till sundown 4) Result: May then eat, share in the sacred offering c. The clear prohibition one must obey in eating: Must not eat anything found dead or torn by animals d. The warning: Must keep God's laws 1) If disobey, are guilty of treating them with contempt 2) The penalty: Death (eternal) 3) The authority: The LORD

a. Note the emphatic charge given by God (vv.3-5): the priest or minister was to be disqualified in the service of God if he was defiled or unclean. He was not to be leading God's people to make their offerings and put their trust in the substitute sacrifice if he was unclean. He was not fit to be serving in the ministry of God, not fit to be leading God's people to put their trust in God.

Note the warning: if he was unclean and still ministering, he was to be cut off from God's presence (v.3). He was to be removed from the service of God, removed so long as he remained unclean. Note the things that defiled and disqualified the priest or minister from serving God:

⇒ infectious skin diseases and bodily discharges
⇒ touching a corpse or anything defiled by a discharge of semen
⇒ touching any crawling thing that was counted unclean
⇒ touching any person who was counted unclean (vv.4-5)

Remember, all these causes of defilement have been covered before (chapters 13–15; 11:39-40). These defilements are a symbol of sin, a symbol of being ceremonially and spiritually unclean. The picture is this: if a priest or minister sins, he becomes unclean, unfit to carry out the ministry of God.

b. Note that there was a way to be restored: if a person followed God's clear instructions, he could be restored (vv.6-7). He was counted unclean until evening; then he had to wash himself in order to be cleansed. The point is clearly stated: he was not to eat his portion of the sacred offerings until he had been washed with water. After washing himself, he had to undergo a waiting period, waiting until sundown. Note the result: he could then eat and share in the sacred offering. He had followed God's clear instructions, taken the steps God had laid out; therefore he was restored to the ministry.

c. Note the clear prohibition that the priest or minister had to obey in eating: he must not eat anything found dead or torn by animals (v.8).

d. Note the strong warning: the priest or minister must keep God's laws (v.9). If he disobeyed God's laws, he was guilty of treating them (the laws) with contempt. The penalty was severe: death—the idea is eternal death. God would cut off or separate the sinful priest or minister from His presence—eternally. Who has the right, the authority, to make such a pronouncement and judgment? The LORD. Note what God says: "I am the LORD, who makes them [the priest, minister] holy."

> **Thought 1**. The application is forceful: the minister of God must treat the ministry with great respect. He must not abuse the ministry nor profane or shame God's name.

> > "Take heed therefore unto yourselves, and to all the flock, over the which the Holy Ghost hath made you overseers, to feed the church of God, which he hath purchased with his own blood" (Ac.20:28).
> > "But I keep under my body, and bring *it* into subjection: lest that by any means, when I have preached to others, I myself should be a castaway" (1 Co.9:27).

"Obey them that have the rule over you, and submit yourselves: for they watch for your souls, as they that must give account, that they may do it with joy, and not with grief: for that *is* unprofitable for you" (He.13:17).

"Feed the flock of God which is among you, taking the oversight *thereof,* not by constraint, but willingly; not for filthy lucre, but of a ready mind" (1 Pe.5:2).

"And I will give you pastors according to mine heart, which shall feed you with knowledge and understanding" (Je.3:15).

"Therefore thus saith the LORD God of Israel against the pastors that feed my people; Ye have scattered my flock, and driven them away, and have not visited them: behold, I will visit upon you the evil of your doings, saith the LORD" (Je.23:2).

"My people hath been lost sheep: their shepherds have caused them to go astray, they have turned them away *on* the mountains: they have gone from mountain to hill, they have forgotten their resting-place" (Je.50:6).

"Son of man, prophesy against the shepherds of Israel, prophesy, and say unto them, Thus saith the LORD GOD unto the shepherds; Woe *be* to the shepherds of Israel that do feed themselves! should not the shepherds feed the flocks? Ye eat the fat, and ye clothe you with the wool, ye kill them that are fed: *but* ye feed not the flock" (Eze.34:2-3).

2 (22:10-16) **Offering, the Sacred—Food, the Holy—Priest, Duty of—Minister, Duty of**: the priest or minister must protect the *holy food* of God. Remember that the *holy food* is a symbol of Christ, the *holy sacrifice* or *holy food* of God. In certain offerings, a portion of the sacrificial animal was to be given to the priest. The whole sacrificial animal was considered to be a holy offering; consequently, the portion given to the priest was considered *holy food*. This holy food is the subject of this particular discussion. The point is this: the portion given to the priest was no less holy than the portions sacrificed upon the altar. There was danger that some might consider it less important and less holy. But it was just as important and just as holy in the sight of God. For this reason, the portion given to the priest was to be treated as holy, just as holy as the rest of the sacrifice offered upon the alter. The portion given to the priest was the holy food of God.

OUTLINE	SCRIPTURE	SCRIPTURE	OUTLINE
2. Duty 2: Must protect the holy food of God (a symbol of Christ, the holy Sacrifice or Food)	10 There shall no stranger eat *of* the holy thing: a sojourner of the priest, or an hired servant, shall not eat *of* the holy thing	ther's house, as in her youth, she shall eat of her father's meat: but there shall no stranger eat thereof.	
a. No outsider could eat holy food			
1) Guests or hired workers could not eat the holy food			
2) Slaves were counted as family members & were allowed to eat	11 But if the priest buy *any* soul with his money, he shall eat of it, and he that is born in his house: they shall eat of his meat.	14 And if a man eat *of* the holy thing unwittingly, then he shall put the fifth *part* thereof unto it, and shall give *it* unto the priest with the holy thing.	b. The mercy upon an offender who ate the holy food by mistake: Was allowed to make restitution plus 20% for the holy food he ate
3) Not even a daughter who married an outsider was allowed to eat the holy food	12 If the priest's daughter also be *married* unto a stranger, she may not eat of an offering of the holy things.	15 And they shall not profane the holy things of the children of Israel, which they offer unto the LORD;	c. The warning & the restriction re-emphasized
			1) Must not defile the holy food by allowing unauthorized persons to eat it
4) A daughter who was widowed or divorced & had no children could eat the holy food	13 But if the priest's daughter be a widow, or divorced, and have no child, and is returned unto her fa-	16 Or suffer them to bear the iniquity of trespass, when they eat their holy things: for I the LORD do sanctify them.	2) The warning & the authority standing behind the restriction: "I am the LORD"

a. Note that no outsider was allowed to eat the "holy food" (vv.10-13). Not even a guest or a hired worker could eat it. But slaves were counted as family members and were allowed to eat the holy food (v.11). A daughter who married an outsider, that is, a person who was not a priest, was not allowed to eat the holy food (v.12). On the other hand, a daughter who was widowed or divorced and had no children could eat it (v.13). This was probably because the only family attachment she had would have been her father and mother who were of the priestly family.

b. Note the mercy upon an offender who ate the holy food by mistake: he was allowed to make restitution plus 20 percent for the holy food he ate (v.14). Remember, there were some two to four million Israelites during this period of history; consequently, there was bound to be a constant flow of sacrifices being made. In the midst of so much activity, there was the chance of some holy food getting mixed in with other food. This law made allowance for any offender who ate the holy food by mistake.

c. Note the warning and the restriction re-emphasized (vv.15-16): the priests or ministers must not defile the holy food by allowing unauthorized persons to eat it. If they did, they would bring guilt upon themselves which would require payment.

Thought 1. The sacrifice was holy in the sight of God—all of it, including the portion given to the priest as holy food. The sacrifice is a symbol of Christ, of His sacrifice. The sacrifice of Jesus Christ was presented to God as the holy, perfect sacrifice on behalf of man. The minister of God must protect this message, that Jesus Christ is the holy, perfect sacrifice offered to God for the sins of the world.

"The next day John seeth Jesus coming unto him, and saith, Behold the Lamb of God, which taketh away the sin of the world" (Jn.1:29).

"Take heed therefore unto yourselves, and to all the flock, over the which the Holy Ghost hath made you overseers, to feed the church of God, which he hath purchased with his own blood" (Ac.20:28).

"And I, brethren, when I came to you, came not with excellency of speech or of wisdom, declaring unto you the testimony of God. For I determined not to know any thing among you, save Jesus Christ, and him crucified" (1 Co.2:1-2).

"Moreover, brethren, I declare unto you the gospel which I preached unto you, which also ye have received, and wherein ye stand; By which also ye are saved, if ye keep in memory what I preached unto you, unless ye have believed in vain. For I delivered unto you first of all that which I also received, how that Christ died for our sins according to the scriptures; And that he was buried, and that he rose again the third day according to the scriptures" (1 Co.15:1-4).

"Who gave himself for us, that he might redeem us from all iniquity, and purify unto himself a peculiar people, zealous of good works" (Tit.2:14).

"Who his own self bare our sins in his own body on the tree, that we, being dead to sins, should live unto righteousness: by whose stripes ye were healed" (1 Pe.2:24).

"And ye know that he was manifested to take away our sins; and in him is no sin" (1 Jn.3:5).

3 **(22:17-30) Sacrifice, Animal—Animal Sacrifice—Humility—Life, Respect for—Burnt Offering—Fellowship or Peace Offering—Freewill Offering**: the priest or minister must approach God exactly as God dictates. He must present the perfect sacrifice to the LORD. The sacrifice could have no defect whatsoever. Remember, this is a symbol of Christ, of the perfect sacrifice He made on behalf of man. This is the strong thrust of this point. Note the Scripture and outline:

OUTLINE	SCRIPTURE	SCRIPTURE	OUTLINE
3. Duty 3: Must approach God exactly as He dictates—must present the perfect sacrifice to the LORD (a symbol of Christ)	17 And the LORD spake unto Moses, saying,	parts, that mayest thou offer *for* a freewill offering; but for a vow it shall not be accepted.	humility & unworthiness—through a freewill thanksgiving or peace offering
a. Must present a perfect sacrifice when approaching God for reconciliation—through the burnt offering (a symbol of Christ)	18 Speak unto Aaron, and to his sons, and unto all the children of Israel, and say unto them, Whatsoever *he be* of the house of Israel, or of the strangers in Israel, that will offer his oblation for all his vows, and for all his freewill offerings, which they will offer unto the LORD for a burnt offering;	24 Ye shall not offer unto the LORD that which is bruised, or crushed, or broken, or cut; neither shall ye make *any offering thereof* in your land.	d. Must not offer a sacrifice that had been castrated: Castration was a forbidden practice in the land (the necessity of reproduction: a symbol of reproducing believers through Christ)
		25 Neither from a stranger's hand shall ye offer the bread of your God of any of these; because their corruption *is* in them, *and* blemishes *be* in them: they shall not be accepted for you.	e. Must never accept a defective animal from foreigners and present it as a sacrifice to the LORD
1) Must present a male without defect: A calf, sheep, or goat	19 *Ye shall offer* at your own will a male without blemish, of the beeves, of the sheep, or of the goats.		
2) The reason: That one may be accepted	20 *But* whatsoever hath a blemish, *that* shall ye not offer: for it shall not be acceptable for you.	26 And the LORD spake unto Moses, saying,	
3) The emphatic rule re-stressed: A defective sacrifice will be rejected		27 When a bullock, or a sheep, or a goat, is brought forth, then it shall be seven days under the dam; and from the eighth day and thenceforth it shall be accepted for an offering made by fire unto the LORD.	f. Must leave a newborn animal with its mother for at least seven days to be acceptable (symbolized timing, the fullness of time for Christ to be sacrificed, Ga.4:4-5)
b. Must present a perfect sacrifice when seeking peace or fellowship with God—through the fellowship or peace offering (a symbol of Christ)	21 And whosoever offereth a sacrifice of peace offerings unto the LORD to accomplish *his* vow, or a freewill offering in beeves or sheep, it shall be perfect to be accepted; there shall be no blemish therein.		
1) Must present a sacrifice without defect or blemish		28 And *whether it be* cow or ewe, ye shall not kill it and her young both in one day.	g. Must not sacrifice both a mother & its young on the same day (symbolized the respect for life)
2) The reason: Is acceptable	22 Blind, or broken, or maimed, or having a wen, or scurvy, or scabbed, ye shall not offer these unto the LORD, nor make an offering by fire of them upon the altar unto the LORD.	29 And when ye will offer a sacrifice of thanksgiving unto the LORD, offer *it* at your own will.	h. The warning
3) The emphatic rule spelled out: Must not offer defective sacrifices—must never be placed on the altar • Not if blind, injured, or maimed • Not anything with warts, festering or oozing sores			1) Must offer a thanksgiving offering exactly as God dictates for it to be acceptable
c. May present an optional sacrifice with minor blemishes: As a sign of one's imperfection,	23 Either a bullock or a lamb that hath any thing superfluous or lacking in his	30 On the same day it shall be eaten up; ye shall leave none of it until the morrow: I *am* the LORD.	2) Must eat the sacrifice that same day

Thought 1. The sacrifice offered to the LORD had to be without defect, a perfect sacrifice. This was an absolute necessity, for it was a symbol of the perfect sacrifice of the coming Savior of the world, the Lord Jesus Christ. His sacrifice stands before God as the *Perfect and Ideal sacrifice*, the sacrifice that can stand for and cover all men. It is the perfect sacrifice of Christ that paid the penalty for the sins of the world. Jesus Christ is the perfect Lamb of God who takes away the sins of the world.

> **"The next day John seeth Jesus coming unto him, and saith, Behold the Lamb of God, which taketh away the sin of the world" (Jn.1:29).**
> **"So Christ was once offered to bear the sins of many; and unto them that look for him shall he appear the second time without sin unto salvation" (He.9:28).**
> **"Forasmuch as ye know that ye were not redeemed with corruptible things, *as* silver and gold, from your vain conversation *received* by tradition from your fathers; But with the precious blood of Christ, as of a lamb without blemish and without spot" (1 Pe.1:18-19).**
> **"For Christ also hath once suffered for sins, the just for the unjust, that he might bring us to God, being put to death in the flesh, but quickened by the Spirit" (1 Pe.3:18).**
> **"He was oppressed, and he was afflicted, yet he opened not his mouth: he is brought as a lamb to the slaughter, and as a sheep before her shearers is dumb, so he openeth not his mouth" (Is.53:7).**

Thought 2. There are two clear lessons here for the minister:
(1) The minister himself much approach God exactly as God dictates: he must approach God through the perfect sacrifice of the Lord Jesus Christ upon the cross. The minister is no different than any other believer: he approaches God in the very same way, through the sacrificial death of the Son of God, the Lord Jesus Christ.

> **"For when we were yet without strength, in due time Christ died for the ungodly. But God commendeth his love toward us, in that, while we were yet sinners, Christ died for us. Much more then, being now justified by his blood, we shall be saved from wrath through him" (Ro.5:6, 8-9).**
> **"Purge out therefore the old leaven, that ye may be a new lump, as ye are unleavened. For even Christ our passover is sacrificed for us" (1 Co.5:7).**
> **"For I delivered unto you first of all that which I also received, how that Christ died for our sins according to the scriptures" (1 Co.15:3).**
> **"And *that* he died for all, that they which live should not henceforth live unto themselves, but unto him which died for them, and rose again" (2 Co.5:15).**
> **"And walk in love, as Christ also hath loved us, and hath given himself for us an offering and a sacrifice to God for a sweetsmelling savour" (Ep.5:2).**
> **"Hereby perceive we the love *of God*, because he laid down his life for us: and we ought to lay down *our* lives for the brethren" (1 Jn.3:16).**

(2) The minister of God must perform and carry out his ministry exactly as God dictates. He must fulfill his ministry in obedience to the call and dictates of God.

> **"Go ye therefore, and teach all nations, baptizing them in the name of the Father, and of the Son, and of the Holy Ghost: Teaching them to observe all things whatsoever I have commanded you: and, lo, I am with you alway, *even* unto the end of the world. Amen" (Mt.28:19-20).**
> **"And he said unto them, Go ye into all the world, and preach the gospel to every creature" (Mk.16:15).**
> **"Then said Jesus to them again, Peace *be* unto you: as *my* Father hath sent me, even so send I you" (Jn.20:21).**
> **"He saith unto him the third time, Simon, *son* of Jonas, lovest thou me? Peter was grieved because he said unto him the third time, Lovest thou me? And he said unto him, Lord, thou knowest all things; thou knowest that I love thee. Jesus saith unto him, Feed my sheep" (Jn.21:17).**
> **"Take heed therefore unto yourselves, and to all the flock, over the which the Holy Ghost hath made you overseers, to feed the church of God, which he hath purchased with his own blood" (Ac.20:28).**
> **"Take heed" and say to Archippus, Take heed to the ministry which thou hast received in the Lord, that thou fulfil it" (Col.4:17).**
> **"Feed the flock of God which is among you, taking the oversight *thereof,* not by constraint, but willingly; not for filthy lucre, but of a ready mind; Neither as being lords over *God's* heritage, but being examples to the flock. And when the chief Shepherd shall appear, ye shall receive a crown of glory that fadeth not away" (1 Pe.5:2-4).**
> **"I have set watchmen upon thy walls, O Jerusalem, *which* shall never hold their peace day nor night: ye that make mention of the LORD, keep not silence" (Is.62:6).**
> **"Son of man, I have made thee a watchman unto the house of Israel: therefore hear the word at my mouth, and give them warning from me" (Eze.3:17).**
> **"But if the watchman see the sword come, and blow not the trumpet, and the people be not warned; if the sword come, and take *any* person from among them, he is taken away in his iniquity; but his blood will I require at the watchman's hand" (Eze.33:6).**

4 (22:31-33) **Commandments, of God—Obedience—Name, of God—God, Name of—Holiness, of God—Confession, of God**: the priest or minister must keep God's commandments and follow them. Note the Scripture and outline:

OUTLINE	SCRIPTURE
4. Duty 4: Must keep God's commands & follow them	31 Therefore shall ye keep my commandments, and do them: I *am* the LORD.
a. Must not profane (defile, shame, abuse) His holy name	32 Neither shall ye profane my holy name; but I will be hallowed among the
b. Must acknowledge God & acknowledge Him as holy	children of Israel: I *am* the LORD which hallow
c. The reasons: God is the LORD	you,
1) He is holy	33 That brought you out of
2) He alone makes people holy	the land of Egypt, to be your
3) He delivers people: Saved His people from Egypt (a symbol of the world)	God: I *am* the LORD

a. The priest or minister must not profane God's holy name. He must not defile, shame, or abuse God's holy name. How does the priest or minister protect the name of God? By keeping God's commandments and following them. The priest has been called to serve God's people in the ministry; consequently he is to fulfill God's calling. He is to be faithful in the ministry. He is to do exactly what God has dictated and called him to do. By being obedient, he will not profane or shame the holy name of God.

"Not every one that saith unto me, Lord, Lord, shall enter into the kingdom of heaven; but he that doeth the will of my Father which is in heaven" (Mt.7:21).

"I beseech you therefore, brethren, by the mercies of God, that ye present your bodies a living sacrifice, holy, acceptable unto God, *which is* your reasonable service. And be not conformed to this world: but be ye transformed by the renewing of your mind, that ye may prove what is that good, and acceptable, and perfect, will of God" (Ro.12:1-2).

"Let a man so account of us, as of the ministers of Christ, and stewards of the mysteries of God. Moreover it is required in stewards, that a man be found faithful" (1 Co.4:1-2).

"Therefore, my beloved brethren, be ye stedfast, unmovable, always abounding in the work of the Lord, forasmuch as ye know that your labour is not in vain in the Lord" (1 Co.15:58).

"Blessed *are* they that do his commandments, that they may have right to the tree of life, and may enter in through the gates into the city" (Re.22:14).

"This day the LORD thy God hath commanded thee to do these statutes and judgments: thou shalt therefore keep and do them with all thine heart, and with all thy soul" (De.26:16).

b. The priest or minister must acknowledge God and acknowledge Him as holy (v.32). There is only one living and true God, only one Creator of the universe. He is the LORD (YAHWEH, JEHOVAH). Consequently, the LORD demands that His creatures acknowledge Him as God, as being holy, totally set apart, distinct and different from all other creatures. He is the sovereign LORD and Majesty of the universe; therefore He expects to be treated and honored as the LORD. For a priest or minister not to acknowledge God and His holiness is a paradox, for he represents God. How can a person represent the LORD in the ministry and refuse to acknowledge the LORD and His holiness? This person profanes, defiles, and abuses the holy name of God. Such should never be. This is the declaration of God in this verse, and the priest or minister is far more responsible and to be held far more accountable than anyone else for acknowledging and confessing the LORD and His holiness.

"Whosoever therefore shall confess me before men, him will I confess also before my Father which is in heaven. But whosoever shall deny me before men, him will I also deny before my Father which is in heaven" (Mt.10:32-33).

"Whosoever therefore shall be ashamed of me and of my words in this adulterous and sinful generation; of him also shall the Son of man be ashamed, when he cometh in the glory of his Father with the holy angels" (Mk.8:38).

"Also I say unto you, Whosoever shall confess me before men, him shall the Son of man also confess before the angels of God" (Lu.12:8).

"That if thou shalt confess with thy mouth the Lord Jesus, and shalt believe in thine heart that God hath raised him from the dead, thou shalt be saved. For with the heart man believeth unto righteousness; and with the mouth confession is made unto salvation" (Ro.10:9-10).

"Wherefore God also hath highly exalted him, and given him a name which is above every name: That at the name of Jesus every knee should bow, of *things* in heaven, and *things* in earth, and *things* under the earth; And *that* every tongue should confess that Jesus Christ *is* Lord, to the glory of God the Father" (Ph.2:9-11).

"But there were false prophets also among the people, even as there shall be false teachers among you, who privily [secretly] shall bring in damnable heresies, even denying the Lord that bought them, and bring upon themselves swift destruction" (2 Pe.2:1).

"Who is a liar but he that denieth that Jesus is the Christ? He is antichrist, that denieth the Father and the Son. Whosoever denieth the Son, the same hath not the Father: *(but) he that acknowledgeth the Son hath the Father also*" (1 Jn.2:22-23).

"Whosoever shall confess that Jesus is the Son of God, God dwelleth in him, and he in God" (1 Jn.4:15).

c. Note why the priest or minister must keep God's commandments and follow them. God gives three reasons:
   1) Because God is holy (v. 32).

   "Exalt the LORD our God, and worship at his holy hill; for the LORD our God *is* holy" (Ps.99:9).

   "And one cried unto another, and said, Holy, holy, holy, *is* the LORD of hosts: the whole earth *is* full of his glory" (Is.6:3).

   "So will I make my holy name known in the midst of my people Israel; and I will not *let them* pollute my holy name any more: and the heathen shall know that I *am* the LORD, the Holy One in Israel" (Eze.39:7).

   "And the four beasts had each of them six wings about *him;* and *they were* full of eyes within: and they rest not day and night, saying, Holy, holy, holy, Lord God Almighty, which was, and is, and is to come. And when those beasts give glory and honour and thanks to him that sat on the throne, who liveth for ever and ever" (Re.4:8-9).

   "Who shall not fear thee, O Lord, and glorify thy name? for *thou* only *art* holy: for all nations shall come and worship before thee; for thy judgments are made manifest" (Re.15:4).

   2) Because God alone makes people holy (v.32).

   "Having therefore these promises, dearly beloved, let us cleanse ourselves from all filthiness of the flesh and spirit, perfecting holiness in the fear of God" (2 Co.7:1).

   "Follow peace with all *men,* and holiness, without which no man shall see the Lord" (He.12:14).

   "But as he which hath called you is holy, so be ye holy in all manner of conversation; Because it is written, Be ye holy; for I am holy" (1 Pe.1:15-16).

   "*Seeing* then *that* all these things shall be dissolved, what manner *of persons* ought ye to be in *all* holy conversation and godliness, Looking for and hasting unto the coming of the day of God, wherein the heavens being on fire shall be dissolved, and the elements shall melt with fervent heat? Nevertheless we, according to his promise, look for new heavens and a new earth, wherein dwelleth righteousness. Wherefore, beloved, seeing that ye look for such things, be diligent that ye may be found of him in peace, without spot, and blameless" (2 Pe.3:11-14).

   3) Because God delivers His people: He saves His people from Egypt (v.33). Remember, Egypt is a symbol of the world.

   "And it shall come to pass, *that* whosoever shall call on the name of the Lord shall be saved" (Ac.2:21).

   "That if thou shalt confess with thy mouth the Lord Jesus, and shalt believe in thine heart that God hath raised him from the dead, thou shalt be saved. For with the heart man believeth unto righteousness; and with the mouth confession is made unto salvation" (Ro.10:9-10).

   "Who gave himself for our sins, that he might deliver us from this present evil world, according to the will of God and our Father" (Ga.1:4).

   "For this *is* good and acceptable in the sight of God our Saviour; Who will have all men to be saved, and to come unto the knowledge of the truth. For *there is* one God, and one mediator between God and men, the man Christ Jesus; Who gave himself a ransom for all, to be testified in due time" (1 Ti.2:3-6).

   "For the grace of God that bringeth salvation hath appeared to all men, Teaching us that, denying ungodliness and worldly lusts, we should live soberly, righteously, and godly, in this present world" (Tit.2:11-12).

   "Forasmuch then as the children are partakers of flesh and blood, he also himself likewise took part of the same; that through death he might destroy him that had the power of death, that is, the devil; And deliver them who through fear of death were all their lifetime subject to bondage" (He.2:14-15).

   "The Lord is not slack concerning his promise, as some men count slackness; but is longsuffering to us-ward, not willing that any should perish, but that all should come to repentance" (2 Pe.3:9).

TYPES, SYMBOLS, AND PICTURES
Leviticus 22:1-33

Historical Term	Type or Picture (Scriptural Basis for Each)	Life Application for Today's Believer	Biblical Application
Defilement Le. 22:1-9	*Defilement is a symbol of sin, a symbol of being ceremonially and spiritually unclean. The picture is this: if a priest or minister sins, he becomes unclean, that is unfit to carry out the ministry of God.* **"Say unto them, Whosoever** *he be* **of all your seed among your generations, that goeth unto the holy things, which the children of Israel hallow unto the LORD, having his uncleanness upon him, that soul shall be cut off from my presence: I** *am* **the LORD"** (Le.22:3).	The application is clear: the minister of God must treat the ministry with great respect. He must not abuse the ministry nor profane or shame God's name in the ministry.	*"But I keep under my body, and bring it into subjection: lest that by any means, when I have preached to others, I myself should be a castaway"* (1 Co.9:27). *"Take heed therefore unto yourselves, and to all the flock, over the which the Holy Ghost hath made you overseers, to feed the church of God, which he hath purchased with his own blood"* (Ac.20:28). *"Be thou diligent to know the state of thy flocks, and look well to thy herds"* (Pr.27:23). *"Feed the flock of God which is among you, taking the oversight thereof, not by constraint, but willingly; not for filthy lucre, but of a ready mind"* (1 Pe.5:2; see Pr.27:23; Je.3:15).
The Holy Food of God Le. 22:10-16	*The holy food is a symbol of Christ the holy sacrifice or holy food of God. The sacrifice was holy in the sight of God—all of it, including the portion given to the priest as holy food.* **"There shall no stranger eat** *of* **the holy thing: a sojourner of the priest, or an hired servant, shall not eat** *of* **the holy thing"** (Le.22:10).	The sacrifice of Jesus Christ was presented to God as the holy, perfect sacrifice. This sacrifice is the perfect sacrifice offered to God on behalf of man. The minister of God must protect this message, that Jesus Christ is the holy, perfect sacrifice offered to God for the sins of the world.	*"The next day John seeth Jesus coming unto him, and saith, Behold the Lamb of God, which taketh away the sin of the world"* (Jn.1:29; see Mt.28:19-20; Mk.16:15). *"And straightway he preached Christ in the synagogues, that he is the Son of God"* (Ac.9:20). *"And ye know that he was manifested to take away our sins; and in him is no sin"* (1 Jn.3:5).

CHAPTER 23

G. Laws That Govern the Annual Feasts or Festivals of Worship: The Prophetic Picture of Salvation, 23:1-44

1. The festivals were appointed or set by God: They were sacred assemblies or festivals not secular, a time when the people came together for worship & joyful celebration

2. The Sabbath Day of rest: The 1st & most basic appointed day
a. To work 6 days; rest on the 7th day
b. The purpose: Is the LORD'S day, a day set aside for His people to rest & worship

3. The three spring festivals were closely connected

a. The Passover: To remember God's deliverance from Egypt (a symbol of Christ, our Passover who was sacrificed for us)
b. The Festival of Unleavened Bread: To recall the need & urgency to leave Egypt (a symbol of the urgency to be freed from the world)
   1) The date: Day after Passover—to eat no yeast bread for 7 days
   2) To come together on the 1st day for worship
   3) To approach God for atonement each day—for reconciliation & forgiveness—through the Burnt Offering & the Sin Offering
   4) To gather on the 7th day for worship

c. The Festival of Firstfruits: To thank God for the crops, the harvest of life (a symbol of Christ's resurrection: He is the first of the harvest, first to arise from the dead)
   1) To celebrate after entering the promised land
   2) To give the first of the harvest
   3) To have the priest wave it as an offering before the LORD—on the day after the Sabbath, on Sunday

   4) To approach God for atonement (reconciliation) on the same day—through the Burnt Offering

And the LORD spake unto Moses, saying,

2 Speak unto the children of Israel, and say unto them, *Concerning* the feasts of the LORD, which ye shall proclaim *to be* holy convocations, *even* these *are* my feasts.

3 Six days shall work be done: but the seventh day *is* the sabbath of rest, an holy convocation; ye shall do no work *therein*: it *is* the sabbath of the LORD in all your dwellings.

4 These *are* the feasts of the LORD, *even* holy convocations, which ye shall proclaim in their seasons.

5 In the fourteenth *day* of the first month at even *is* the LORD'S passover.

6 And on the fifteenth day of the same month *is* the feast of unleavened bread unto the LORD: seven days ye must eat unleavened bread.

7 In the first day ye shall have an holy convocation: ye shall do no servile work therein.

8 But ye shall offer an offering made by fire unto the LORD seven days: in the seventh day *is* an holy convocation: ye shall do no servile work *therein*.

9 And the LORD spake unto Moses, saying,

10 Speak unto the children of Israel, and say unto them, When ye be come into the land which I give unto you, and shall reap the harvest thereof, then ye shall bring a sheaf of the firstfruits of your harvest unto the priest:

11 And he shall wave the sheaf before the LORD, to be accepted for you: on the morrow after the sabbath the priest shall wave it.

12 And ye shall offer that day when ye wave the sheaf an he lamb without blemish of the first year for a burnt offering unto the LORD.

13 And the meat offering thereof *shall be* two tenth deals of fine flour mingled with oil, an offering made by fire unto the LORD *for* a sweet savour: and the drink offering thereof *shall be* of wine, the fourth *part* of an hin.

14 And ye shall eat neither bread, nor parched corn, nor green ears, until the selfsame day that ye have brought an offering unto your God: *it shall be* a statute for ever throughout your generations in all your dwellings.

15 And ye shall count unto you from the morrow after the sabbath, from the day that ye brought the sheaf of the wave offering; seven sabbaths shall be complete:

16 Even unto the morrow after the seventh sabbath shall ye number fifty days; and ye shall offer a new meat offering unto the LORD.

17 Ye shall bring out of your habitations two wave loaves of two tenth deals: they shall be of fine flour; they shall be baken with leaven; *they* *are* the firstfruits unto the LORD.

18 And ye shall offer with the bread seven lambs without blemish of the first year, and one young bullock, and two rams: they shall be *for* a burnt offering unto the LORD, with their meat offering, and their drink offerings, *even* an offering made by fire, of sweet savour unto the LORD.

19 Then ye shall sacrifice one kid of the goats for a sin offering, and two lambs of the first year for a sacrifice of peace offerings.

20 And the priest shall wave them with the bread of the firstfruits *for* a wave offering before the LORD, with the two lambs: they shall be holy to the LORD for the priest.

21 And ye shall proclaim on the selfsame day, *that* it may be an holy convocation unto you: ye shall do no servile work *therein: it shall be* a statute for ever in all your dwellings throughout your generations.

5) To offer a Grain Offering also, two times larger than usual—three quarts of fine flour mixed with oil, & the usual drink offering, one quart of wine
6) The result: The aroma symbolized God's acceptance
7) The one clear prohibition: To put God first; not to eat any of the harvest until the Firstfruit Offering was given to God

4. The Festival of Harvest or Pentecost: To give thanks for the harvest & to dedicate one's life anew to God (a symbol of Pentecost, of the great harvest of souls, & of people giving their lives to God)
a. To celebrate fifty days after the Festival of Firstfruits

b. To make a wave offering of firstfruits to the LORD, using two fresh loaves of bread

c. To approach God for atonement (reconciliation, acceptance) through the Burnt Offering
   1) To sacrifice seven male lambs, one young bull, & two rams—with no defect (a symbol of Christ, His perfect, sinless sacrifice)
   2) To offer the necessary Grain & Drink Offering
   3) The result: Acceptance; pleases God
d. To approach God for forgiveness of sins & a deeper fellowship—through the Sin Offering & the Fellowship Offering

e. To lift up all these offerings as a wave offering before the LORD: Are holy offerings belonging to the priests

f. To declare a sacred assembly on that day: To take a day of rest & call the people out for worship
g. To make a permanent, lasting law for all generations

h. To help & to protect the poor: Leave enough harvest for them to reap & eat

5. The Festival of Trumpets: To arouse the people to trust God more & more, proclaiming the message of joy for the atonement (reconciliation)

a. The date: 7th month, 1st day

b. The features: To rest & approach God for atonement—through the Burnt Offering

6. The Day of Atonement: To cleanse the people from their sins (a symbol of sins' being cleansed through the shed blood)

a. The date: 7th month, 10th day

b. The features
   1) To deny self (a fast)
   2) To approach God for atonement (reconciliation)—through the Burnt Offering
   3) To be a day of rest

c. The warning: Will be cut off or destroyed if refuse to observe the Day of Atonement (reconciliation)

d. The day set forever, permanently

e. The hours to be observed: To begin the evening before the Day of Atonement till the following evening

7. The Festival of Tabernacles: To celebrate the wilderness wanderings when the people lived in tents on their way to the promised land, & to thank God for the harvest (a symbol of the believer's march through this world to heaven)

22 And when ye reap the harvest of your land, thou shalt not make clean riddance of the corners of thy field when thou reapest, neither shalt thou gather any gleaning of thy harvest: thou shalt leave them unto the poor, and to the stranger: I *am* the LORD your God.

23 And the LORD spake unto Moses, saying,

24 Speak unto the children of Israel, saying, In the seventh month, in the first *day* of the month, shall ye have a sabbath, a memorial of blowing of trumpets, an holy convocation.

25 Ye shall do no servile work *therein*: but ye shall offer an offering made by fire unto the LORD.

26 And the LORD spake unto Moses, saying,

27 Also on the tenth *day* of this seventh month *there shall be* a day of atonement: it shall be an holy convocation unto you; and ye shall afflict your souls, and offer an offering made by fire unto the LORD.

28 And ye shall do no work in that same day: for it *is* a day of atonement, to make an atonement for you before the LORD your God.

29 For whatsoever soul *it be* that shall not be afflicted in that same day, he shall be cut off from among his people.

30 And whatsoever soul *it be* that doeth any work in that same day, the same soul will I destroy from among his people.

31 Ye shall do no manner of work: *it shall be* a statute for ever throughout your generations in all your dwellings.

32 It *shall be* unto you a sabbath of rest, and ye shall afflict your souls: in the ninth *day* of the month at even, from even unto even, shall ye celebrate your sabbath.

33 And the LORD spake unto Moses, saying,

34 Speak unto the children of Israel, saying, The fifteenth day of this seventh month *shall be* the feast of tabernacles *for* seven days unto the LORD.

35 On the first day *shall be* an holy convocation: ye shall do no servile work *therein*.

36 Seven days ye shall offer an offering made by fire unto the LORD: on the eighth day shall be an holy convocation unto you; and ye shall offer an offering made by fire unto the LORD: it *is* a solemn assembly; *and* ye shall do no servile work *therein*.

37 These *are* the feasts of the LORD, which ye shall proclaim *to be* holy convocations, to offer an offering made by fire unto the LORD, a burnt offering, and a meat offering, a sacrifice, and drink offerings, every thing upon his day:

38 Beside the sabbaths of the LORD, and beside your gifts, and beside all your vows, and beside all your freewill offerings, which ye give unto the LORD.

39 Also in the fifteenth day of the seventh month, when ye have gathered in the fruit of the land, ye shall keep a feast unto the LORD seven days: on the first day *shall be* a sabbath, and on the eighth day *shall be* a sabbath.

40 And ye shall take you on the first day the boughs of goodly trees, branches of palm trees, and the boughs of thick trees, and willows of the brook; and ye shall rejoice before the LORD your God seven days.

41 And ye shall keep it a feast unto the LORD seven days in the year. *It shall be* a statute for ever in your generations: ye shall celebrate it in the seventh month.

42 Ye shall dwell in booths seven days; all that are Israelites born shall dwell in booths:

43 That your generations may know that I made the children of Israel to dwell in booths, when I brought them out of the land of Egypt: I *am* the LORD your God.

44 And Moses declared unto the children of Israel the feasts of the LORD.

a. The date: 7th month, 15th day

b. The features
   1) To stop all work on the 1st day for a sacred assembly
   2) To approach God for seven days, seeking atonement each of the seven days—through the Burnt Offering
   3) To hold another sacred assembly to close the festival: Approach God for atonement (reconciliation)—thru another Burnt Offering

c. The importance of the Feast of Tabernacles & of the other feasts
   1) Are annual, sacred assemblies for worship
   2) Are for the purpose of approaching God for atonement (reconciliation)—through the sacrifices & offerings
   3) Are in addition to all other approaches to God, all other offerings & gifts

d. The importance of the Feast of Tabernacles re-emphasized
   1) The date: 7th month, 15th day, lasting for seven days after crops are harvested
   2) The 1st day is a day of rest & the 8th day is a day of rest
   3) To build booths or shelters from tree leaves on the 1st day
   4) To make the festival a celebration of great joy & rejoicing before the LORD

e. The festival is to be a lasting, permanent law

f. The purpose of the festival: To live in booths or shelters for seven days—to teach all descendants that God's people had to live in booths when God delivered them out of Egypt (a symbol of how temporary this world is)

DIVISION IV

THE WAY TO LIVE A HOLY LIFE BEFORE GOD (PART 2): A PURE SPIRIT (SANCTIFICATION), 17:1-27:34

G. Laws That Govern the Annual Feasts or Festivals of Worship: The Prophetic Picture of Salvation, 23:1-44

(23:1-44) **Introduction—Festivals of Worship, Annual—Feast of Worship, Annual**: in human history, God has one primary focus, that of salvation—the saving of people and their worship of Him. Holy Scripture tells us that God created man to live with Him, that God's great purpose is to reveal the riches of His grace to man throughout all eternity (Ep.2:7). To get this point across to the people of ancient history, God set aside several religious holidays. Note two striking points about the annual feasts or festivals:

First, these holidays focused upon the salvation and redemption of man and the worship of God.

Second, the holidays painted the prophetic picture of salvation, the salvation that God was to bring to man through His Son, the Lord Jesus Christ.

God used the annual festivals to show a believer how he was to walk day by day throughout life. This will be clearly seen as the feasts or festivals are studied. This is the subject of this chapter: *Laws that Govern the Annual Feasts or Festivals of Worship: The Prophetic Picture of Salvation*, 23:1-44.

1. The festivals were appointed or set by God: they were sacred assemblies or festivals not secular, a time when the people came together for worship and joyful celebration (vv.1-2).
2. The Sabbath Day of rest: the first and most basic appointed day (v.3).
3. The three spring festivals were closely connected (vv.4-14).
4. The Festival of Harvest or Pentecost: to give thanks for the harvest and to dedicate one's life anew to God (a symbol of Pentecost, of the great harvest of souls, and of people giving their lives to God) (vv.15-22).
5. The Festival of Trumpets: to arouse the people to trust God more and more and to heed the message of joy and atonement (reconciliation) (vv.23-25).
6. The Day of Atonement: to cleanse the people from their sins (a symbol of sins' being cleansed through the shed blood) (vv.26-32).
7. The Festival of Tabernacles: to celebrate the wilderness wanderings when the people lived in tents on their way to the promised land, and to thank God for the harvest (a symbol of the believer's march through this world to heaven) (vv.33-44).

1 (23:1-2) **Feasts of the LORD, the—Sacred Assemblies—Holidays—Festivals of the LORD**: the festivals were appointed or set by God; they were sacred or holy assemblies that were held on very special holidays. The festivals were a time when the people came together for worship and the celebration of significant events. They were religious holidays that celebrated holy events. Consequently, the holidays included a time for worship as well as a time for great joy and festivity. Only one festival involved mourning; that was the Day of Atonement. Note the Scripture and outline:

OUTLINE	SCRIPTURE
1. The festivals were appointed or set by God: They were sacred assemblies or festivals not secular, a time when the people came together for worship & joyful celebration	And the LORD spake unto Moses, saying, 2 Speak unto the children of Israel, and say unto them, *Concerning* the feasts of the LORD, which ye shall proclaim *to be* holy convocations, *even* these *are* my feasts.

Man may set aside a day for celebration, but only God can make a day holy. Note the term "my appointed feasts." These were feasts that were appointed or set by God. They were God's feasts, the appointed and set feasts of the LORD. Again, only God can make a time truly holy, for God is the sovereign LORD of time. God alone can take a period of time and make it holy, a time set aside for true worship and joyful celebration in the Spirit of God. This is what God did with the annual feast or festivals of worship. He appointed a block of time to be a very special time for His people, a time for special worship and joyful celebration of significant events (Ac.17:24-27).

2 (23:3) **Sabbath, Purpose of—Worship, Purpose of—Rest, Spiritual—Spiritual Rest—Salvation, Remembrance of**: there was the Sabbath day of rest, the very first day appointed and set aside by God. The Sabbath day of rest is actually the most important day set aside by God. It is pre-Mosaic, stretching all the way back to the beginning of creation. Right after creating the universe, God blessed the Sabbath day and set it apart for rest and worship (Ge.2:3).

OUTLINE	SCRIPTURE
2. The Sabbath Day of rest: The 1st & most basic appointed day a. To work 6 days; rest on the 7th day b. The purpose: Is the LORD's day, a day set aside for His people to rest & worship	3 Six days shall work be done: but the seventh day *is* the sabbath of rest, an holy convocation; ye shall do no work *therein*: it *is* the sabbath of the LORD in all your dwellings.

Note this Scripture: God tells man to work six days, then he is to rest on the seventh day. The seventh day is the LORD's day, a day that God has set aside to be His day, a day in which man is to focus entirely upon the LORD. There are two purposes for the Sabbath day:

a. The Sabbath day is for complete rest. It is to be a day of physical restoration, a day when the human body is allowed to restore itself. Man's mind and body need to relax and rest; to be free from the duties, responsibilities, pressure and tensions of day to day work. For this purpose, God set aside the Sabbath day for complete rest and relaxation. But note this fact as well: the Sabbath rest is a symbol of the spiritual rest that God promises to those who believe and follow Him. The Sabbath rest is a symbol of redemption, of God's deliverance from the heavy burdens and trials of this life.

"**Come unto me, all *ye* that labour and are heavy laden, and I will give you rest**" (Mt.11:28).

"**There remaineth therefore a rest to the people of God. For he that is entered into his rest, he also hath ceased from his own works, as God *did* from his. Let us labour therefore to enter into that rest, lest any man fall after the same example of unbelief**" (He.4:9-11).

"**Remember the sabbath day, to keep it holy. For *in* six days the LORD made heaven and earth, the sea, and all that in them *is*, and rested the seventh day: wherefore the LORD blessed the sabbath day, and hallowed it**" (Ex.20:8, 11).

b. The Sabbath day is a day set aside for worship. Note exactly what this verse says: the Sabbath day is a day of holy convocation, a day of sacred assembly, a day when God's people are to come together and assemble for worship. In another Scripture, God even told His people what the focus of their worship was to be: they were to focus upon their redemption from Egypt. Remember: for the Christian believer, Egypt is a symbol of the world. Therefore, the focus of worship is to be upon God's redemption, His salvation and deliverance from the world and its enslavements.

"**Who delivered us from so great a death, and doth deliver: in whom we trust that he will yet deliver *us*** " (2 Co.1:10).

"**Forasmuch then as the children are partakers of flesh and blood, he also himself likewise took part of the same; that through death he might destroy him that had the power of death, that is, the devil; And deliver them who through fear of death were all their lifetime subject to bondage**" (He.2:14-15).

"**And remember that thou wast a servant in the land of Egypt, and *that* the LORD thy God brought thee out thence through a mighty hand and by a stretched out arm: therefore the LORD thy God commanded thee to keep the sabbath day**" (De.5:15).

3 (23:4-14) **Passover—Feast, of Passover—Feast, of Unleavened Bread—Feast, of Firstfruits—Firstfruits, Feast of**: there were the three spring feasts or festivals. These three feasts were closely connected, taking place during an eight-day holiday period. Simply stated:

⇒ The Passover took place on the first day (the fourteenth day of the first month).
⇒ Then on the very next day the Festival of Unleavened Bread began and lasted for seven days.
⇒ The Festival of Firstfruits was celebrated on the day after the Sabbath which is Sunday.

OUTLINE	SCRIPTURE	SCRIPTURE	OUTLINE
3. The three spring Festivals were closely connected a. The Passover: To remember God's deliverance from Egypt (a symbol of Christ, our Passover who was sacrificed for us) b. The Festival of Unleavened Bread: To recall the need & urgency to leave Egypt (a symbol of the urgency to be freed from the world) 1) The date: Day after Passover—to eat no yeast bread	4 These *are* the feasts of the LORD, *even* holy convocations, which ye shall proclaim in their seasons. 5 In the fourteenth *day* of the first month at even *is* the LORD'S passover. 6 And on the fifteenth day of the same month *is* the feast of unleavened bread unto the LORD: seven days ye must eat unleavened bread. 7 In the first day ye shall	have an holy convocation: ye shall do no servile work therein. 8 But ye shall offer an offering made by fire unto the LORD seven days: in the seventh day *is* an holy convocation: ye shall do no servile work *therein*. 9 And the LORD spake unto Moses, saying, 10 Speak unto the children of Israel, and say unto them, When ye be come into the	for 7 days 2) To come together on the 1st day for worship 3) To approach God for atonement each day—for reconciliation & forgiveness—through the burnt offering & the sin offering 4) To gather on the 7th day for worship c. The Festival of Firstfruits: To thank God for the crops, the harvest of life (a symbol of

OUTLINE	SCRIPTURE	SCRIPTURE	OUTLINE
Christ's resurrection: He is the first of the harvest, first to arise from the dead) 1) To celebrate after entering the promised land 2) To give the first of the harvest 3) To have the priest wave it as an offering before the LORD—on the day after the Sabbath, on Sunday 4) To approach God for atonement (reconciliation) on the same day—through the Burnt Offering 5) To also offer a Grain Offer-	land which I give unto you, and shall reap the harvest thereof, then ye shall bring a sheaf of the firstfruits of your harvest unto the priest: 11 And he shall wave the sheaf before the LORD, to be accepted for you: on the morrow after the sabbath the priest shall wave it. 12 And ye shall offer that day when ye wave the sheaf an he lamb without blemish of the first year for a burnt offering unto the LORD. 13 And the meat offering	thereof *shall be* two tenth deals of fine flour mingled with oil, an offering made by fire unto the LORD *for* a sweet savour: and the drink offering thereof *shall be* of wine, the fourth *part* of an hin. 14 And ye shall eat neither bread, nor parched corn, nor green ears, until the self-same day that ye have brought an offering unto your God: *it shall be* a stat-ute for ever throughout your generations in all your dwellings.	ing two times larger than usual—three quarts of fine flour mixed with oil, & the usual drink offering, one quart of wine 6) The result: The aroma sym-bolized God's acceptance 7) The one clear prohibition: To put God first; not to eat any of the harvest until the Firstfruit Offering was given to God

a. There was the Festival of the Passover (v.5). The Passover celebrated God's great deliverance of His people from Egyptian slavery (see outline and notes—Ex.12:21-51 for more discussion). God had told His people that the Egyptians had gone too far, well beyond repentance, that they had become so evil, brutal and savage that He was going to execute severe judgment upon them. He was going to send the angel of death throughout the land and execute the firstborn son of every Egyptian family. Then and only then would Pharaoh release God's people from their four-hundred years of en-slavement. But God's people could escape the judgments. How? By believing God and trusting the blood of the sacrificial substitute.

God instructed His people to take a Lamb without defect, put it to death, and smear its blood on the doorposts of their homes. By so doing, God would know that the family trusted Him and trusted the blood of the substitute sacrifice to take their place in bearing the judgment of God. Therefore, the judgment of God would pass over the believers. This is exactly what happened on the night that God's terrifying judgment fell. On the very next day, the Egyptians began to set God's people free after four-hundred years of savage, brutal enslavement. As a result, the Passover celebrates the most impor-tant event in Israel's history.

Thought 1. The Passover is a symbol of Jesus Christ our Passover who was sacrificed for us. Jesus Christ is the perfect fulfillment of the Passover Lamb that was slain on behalf of God's people. Through the blood of Jesus Christ, a person escapes the judgment of God. God accepts the blood of the substitute sacrifice as full payment for the sins committed by a person. Note that the Passover is His sign or prophetic picture of the coming Savior, of His salvation and redemption.

"**The next day John seeth Jesus coming unto him, and saith, Behold the Lamb of God, which ta-keth away the sin of the world**" (**Jn.1:29**).

"**Purge out therefore the old leaven, that ye may be a new lump, as ye are unleavened. For even Christ our passover is sacrificed for us**" (**1 Co.5:7**).

"**Who gave himself for our sins, that he might deliver us from this present evil world, according to the will of God and our Father**" (**Ga.1:4**).

"**And walk in love, as Christ also hath loved us, and hath given himself for us an offering and a sacrifice to God for a sweetsmelling savour**" (**Ep.5:2**).

"**Who gave himself for us, that he might redeem us from all iniquity, and purify unto himself a pe-culiar people, zealous of good works**" (**Tit.2:14**).

"**Forasmuch as ye know that ye were not redeemed with corruptible things,** *as* **silver and gold, from your vain conversation** *received* **by tradition from your fathers; But with the precious blood of Christ, as of a lamb without blemish and without spot**" (**1 Pe.1:18-19**).

"**But he** *was* **wounded for our transgressions,** *he was* **bruised for our iniquities: the chastisement of our peace** *was* **upon him; and with his stripes we are healed. All we like sheep have gone astray; we have turned every one to his own way; and the LORD hath laid on him the iniquity of us all. He was oppressed, and he was afflicted, yet he opened not his mouth: he is brought as a lamb to the slaughter, and as a sheep before her shearers is dumb, so he openeth not his mouth**" (**Is.53:5-7**).

b. There was the Festival of Unleavened Bread (vv.6-8). This festival recalled the need and urgency of God's people to leave Egypt. After God's hand of judgment fell, events moved rapidly. The Egyptians were desperate for Pharaoh to re-lease the Israelites and get rid of the them. In fact, the Israelites were forced to leave so quickly that they had no time to adequately prepare. They did not even have time to let their dough rise; they had no time to put yeast or leaven in their bread. They were forced to take unleavened bread. There was the need and the urgency to get out of Egypt immediately. This is a symbol of a believer's need and urgency to be freed from the world. Note the facts given in this passage con-cerning the Feast or Festival of Unleavened Bread.

1) The festival was to begin on the day after Passover. For seven days the people were to eat unleavened bread, bread made without any yeast whatsoever (v.6).
2) The were to assemble or gather together on the first day for worship. They were to do no regular work on that day (v.7).

3) The people were to approach God for atonement on each of the seven days, for reconciliation and forgiveness of sins (v.8). Scripture tells us elsewhere that the offerings were to be a Burnt Offering and a Sin Offering.

"And in the fourteenth day of the first month *is* the passover of the LORD. And in the fifteenth day of this month *is* the feast: seven days shall unleavened bread be eaten. In the first day *shall be* an holy convocation; ye shall do no manner of servile work *therein:* But ye shall offer a sacrifice made by fire *for* a burnt offering unto the LORD; two young bullocks, and one ram, and seven lambs of the first year: they shall be unto you without blemish: And their meat offering *shall be of* flour mingled with oil: three tenth deals shall ye offer for a bullock, and two tenth deals for a ram; A several tenth deal shalt thou offer for every lamb, throughout the seven lambs: And one goat *for* a sin offering, to make an atonement for you. Ye shall offer these beside the burnt offering in the morning, which *is* for a continual burnt offering. After this manner ye shall offer daily, throughout the seven days, the meat of the sacrifice made by fire, of a sweet savour unto the LORD: it shall be offered beside the continual burnt offering, and his drink offering. And on the seventh day ye shall have an holy convocation; ye shall do no servile work" (Nu.28:16-25).

4) The people were then to assemble on the seventh day for worship (v.8).

Thought 1. The Feast or Festival of Unleavened Bread paints a clear picture for the believer. It symbolizes the need and urgency for the believer to be freed from the world and its enslavement to sin and death. There is a need—an urgent, desperate need—to be delivered from all the oppressions and pollutions of this world, from all the sin and evil, immorality and lawlessness, corruption and death of this world. There is a need and urgency to be set free and liberated to live for God. There is a desperate need and urgency to begin the march to the promised land of heaven. Note the prophetic picture:
⇒ The Passover pictures salvation, deliverance, and redemption.
⇒ The Festival of Unleavened Bread pictures the immediate need and urgency to begin the march to the promised land.

"Seek ye the LORD while he may be found, call ye upon him while he is near" (Is.55:6).
"...Behold, now *is* the accepted time; behold, now *is* the day of salvation" (2 Co. 6:2).
"But this I say, brethren, the time *is* short" (1 Co.7:29).
"See then that ye walk circumspectly, not as fools, but as wise, Redeeming the time, because the days are evil" (Ep.5:15-16).
"For our conversation [citizenship] is in heaven; from whence also we look for the Saviour, the Lord Jesus Christ" (Ph.3:20).
"Henceforth there is laid up for me a crown of righteousness, which the Lord, the righteous judge, shall give me at that day: and not to me only, but unto all them also that love his appearing" (2 Ti. 4:8).
"Blessed *be* the God and Father of our Lord Jesus Christ, which according to his abundant mercy hath begotten us again unto a lively hope by the resurrection of Jesus Christ from the dead, To an inheritance incorruptible, and undefiled, and that fadeth not away, reserved in heaven for you" (1 Pe.1:3-4).
"But the day of the Lord will come as a thief in the night; in the which the heavens shall pass away with a great noise, and the elements shall melt with fervent heat, the earth also and the works that are therein shall be burned up. *Seeing* then *that* all these things shall be dissolved, what manner *of persons* ought ye to be in all holy conversation and godliness, Looking for and hasting unto the coming of the day of God, wherein the heavens being on fire shall be dissolved, and the elements shall melt with fervent heat?" (2 Pe.3:10-12).

c. There was the Festival of Firstfruits (vv.9-14). This was a festival to thank God for the crops, for the harvest of food that gave people life. This was a symbol of Christ's resurrection: He is the first of the harvest, the first to arise from the dead. Note that this festival could not begin until the people had entered the promised land (v.10). They, of course, could not plant crops out in the desert while they were marching to the promised land. Once they arrived and began planting crops, they were to give the first of their harvest to the LORD during this festival. They were to take a sheaf, that is, a stalk, here and there, bundle it together, and bring it to the priest. He was then to take the sheaf and wave it as an offering before the LORD. This was to be done on the day after the Sabbath, which would be Sunday. After giving the wave offering to the LORD, the priest was to approach God for atonement through a special Burnt Offering. Note also that a special Grain Offering was to be offered to the LORD, a Grain Offering two times larger than usual.

Note the result: the aroma of the burning sacrifice and Grain Offering ascended up, symbolizing God's acceptance. He was pleased with the aroma of the sacrifice, the obedience of the people. However, there was one clear prohibition: the people had to put God first. They were not to eat any of the harvest until the Firstfruit Offering was given to God. This was to be a permanent law for all the generations to come, no matter where the Israelites lived.

Thought 1. The believer is to give God the first of his harvest, the first of his income. He is to tithe, for the tithe belongs to the LORD. The tithe should be an expression of appreciation and thanksgiving to God, for God is the One who has given us all that we have. Our crops and jobs are due to Him; so is our health that enables us to work and earn a living. We are to give the firstfruit to support the church and the messengers of the gospel around the world, give so that they can reach the world for Christ.

"Upon the first *day* of the week let every one of you lay by him in store, as *God* hath prospered him, that there be no gatherings when I come" (1 Co.16:2).
"But this *I say,* He which soweth sparingly shall reap also sparingly; and he which soweth bountifully shall reap also bountifully. Every man according as he purposeth in his heart, *so let him give;* not grudgingly, or of necessity: for God loveth a cheerful giver" (2 Co.9:6-7).

"And all the tithe of the land, *whether* of the seed of the land, *or* of the fruit of the tree, *is* the LORD'S: *it is* holy unto the LORD" (Le.27:30).

"Every man *shall give* as he is able, according to the blessing of the LORD thy God which he hath given thee" (De.16:17).

"Bring ye all the tithes into the storehouse, that there may be meat in mine house, and prove me now herewith, saith the LORD of hosts, if I will not open you the windows of heaven, and pour you out a blessing, that *there shall* not *be room* enough *to receive it*" (Mal.3:10).

Thought 2. The Festival of Firstfruits is also a symbol of the LORD's resurrection. Christ is the first of the harvest, the first to arise from the dead. It is Jesus Christ and His resurrection that give the believer hope of arising from the dead to live eternally with God. The prophetic picture of salvation is this:

(1) The Passover symbolized the believer's deliverance or redemption from the world.

(2) The Festival of Unleavened Bread symbolized the urgency of the believer to leave the world to begin his march to the promised land.

(3) The Festival of Firstfruits symbolizes the glorious hope the believer has as he marches toward the promise land, the hope of being raised from the dead to live eternally with God—all because of the resurrection of Christ.

"That Christ should suffer, *and* that he should be the first that should rise from the dead, and should show light unto the people, and to the Gentiles" (Ac.26:23).

"But now is Christ risen from the dead, *and* become the firstfruits of them that slept. For since by man *came* death, by man *came* also the resurrection of the dead. For as in Adam all die, even so in Christ shall all be made alive. But every man in his own order: Christ the firstfruits; afterward they that are Christ's at his coming" (1 Co.15:20-23).

"Knowing that he which raised up the Lord Jesus shall raise up us also by Jesus, and shall present *us* with you" (2 Co.4:14).

"Blessed *be* the God and Father of our Lord Jesus Christ, which according to his abundant mercy hath begotten us again unto a lively hope by the resurrection of Jesus Christ from the dead, To an inheritance incorruptible, and undefiled, and that fadeth not away, reserved in heaven for you" (1 Pe.1:3-4).

4 (23:15-22) **Harvest, Festival of—Feast of Harvest or Pentecost—Pentecost, Feast of—Dedication—Witnessing—Soul Winning, Harvest of—Salvation, Harvest of—Festival, of Weeks—Weeks, Festival of**: there was the Festival of Harvest or Pentecost. The purpose of this festival was to give thanksgiving to God for the harvest and to dedicate one's life anew to God. The Festival of Harvest (Ex.23:16) is sometimes called "The Feast of Weeks" or "The Firstfruits of the Wheat Harvest" (Ex.34:22). The festival is a strong symbol of Pentecost, of the great harvest of souls that took place when the Holy Spirit came upon the disciples in the upper room (Ac.2:1f). It was a joyful occasion celebrating the end of the harvest season and dedicating one's life anew to God.

OUTLINE	SCRIPTURE	SCRIPTURE	OUTLINE
4. **The Festival of Harvest or Pentecost: To give thanks for the harvest & to dedicate one's life anew to God (a symbol of Pentecost, of the great harvest of souls, & of people giving their lives to God)**	15 And ye shall count unto you from the morrow after the sabbath, from the day that ye brought the sheaf of the wave offering; seven sabbaths shall be complete:	19 Then ye shall sacrifice one kid of the goats for a sin offering, and two lambs of the first year for a sacrifice of peace offerings.	d. To approach God for forgiveness of sins & a deeper fellowship—through the Sin Offering & the Fellowship Offering
a. To celebrate fifty days after the Festival of Firstfruits	16 Even unto the morrow after the seventh sabbath shall ye number fifty days; and ye shall offer a new meat offering unto the LORD.	20 And the priest shall wave them with the bread of the firstfruits *for* a wave offering before the LORD, with the two lambs: they shall be holy to the LORD for the priest.	e. To lift up all these offerings as a wave Offering before the LORD: Are holy offerings belonging to the priests
b. To make a wave offering of firstfruits to the LORD, using two fresh loaves of bread	17 Ye shall bring out of your habitations two wave loaves of two tenth deals: they shall be of fine flour; they shall be baken with leaven; *they are* the firstfruits unto the LORD.	21 And ye shall proclaim on the selfsame day, *that* it may be an holy convocation unto you: ye shall do no servile work *therein: it shall be* a statute for ever in all your dwellings throughout your generations.	f. To declare a sacred assembly on that day: To take a day of rest & call the people out for worship
			g. To make a permanent, lasting law for all generations
c. To approach God for atonement (reconciliation, acceptance) through the Burnt Offering 1) To sacrifice seven male lambs, one young bull, & two rams—with no defect (a symbol of Christ, His perfect, sinless sacrifice) 2) To offer the necessary Grain & Drink Offering 3) The result: Acceptance, pleases God	18 And ye shall offer with the bread seven lambs without blemish of the first year, and one young bullock, and two rams: they shall be *for* a burnt offering unto the LORD, with their meat offering, and their drink offerings, *even* an offering made by fire, of sweet savour unto the LORD.	22 And when ye reap the harvest of your land, thou shalt not make clean riddance of the corners of thy field when thou reapest, neither shalt thou gather any gleaning of thy harvest: thou shalt leave them unto the poor, and to the stranger: I *am* the LORD your God.	h. To help & to protect the poor: Leave enough harvest for them to reap & eat

a. Historically, the day of Pentecost actually took place fifty days after the resurrection of the Lord Jesus Christ (v.16). Remember, the Festival of Firstfruits symbolized the resurrection of Jesus Christ; now the Festival of Harvest symbolizes Pentecost. These two festivals were celebrated fifty days apart. God's people were to celebrate the Festival of Harvest fifty days after the Festival of Firstfruits. In God's sovereignty, centuries before Christ ever came, God appointed these festivals to paint the prophetic picture of salvation for men. What strong evidence for the sovereignty and the truthfulness of Holy Scripture!

b. The people were to give a wave offering of Firstfruits to the LORD, using two fresh loaves of bread (v.17). In this particular offering, leavened bread (bread with yeast) had to be brought (Le.2:11; see 7:13).

c. The people were to approach God for atonement, seeking God's reconciliation and acceptance through the Burnt Offering (v.18). Note that they were to sacrifice seven male lambs, one young bull and two rams—all with no defect. Remember that the number seven symbolizes completion, fulfillment, and perfection. This was a symbol of Christ, His perfect and sinless sacrifice. After offering the perfect sacrifice to God, the people were then to offer the necessary Grain and Drink Offerings. The result was just what God had promised: the aroma of the sacrifice pleased God and He accepted the sacrifice on behalf of the people. Atonement was made for them: they were reconciled to God.

d. The people had to approach God for forgiveness of sins and for a deeper fellowship with Him. This was done through the sacrifice of the Sin Offering and another sacrifice for the Fellowship and Peace Offering (v.19).

e. The people were to have the priest take the animal sacrifices and wave them before the LORD as a wave offering, together with the bread of the Firstfruits. Note that these were holy offerings belonging to the priest (v.20).

f. The people were to declare a sacred assembly on that day: they were to take a day of rest and gather together for worship (v.21).

g. The people were to make this a permanent, lasting law for all generations (v.21).

h. The people were to help and to protect the poor. How? When they reaped the harvest, they were to leave enough for the poor to enter the fields to gather food for survival (v.22).

Thought 1. The Festival of Harvest is also known as the Festival of Pentecost. The Festival of Pentecost is a clear prophetic picture of salvation. Fifty days after the resurrection of Christ, the dramatic day of Pentecost took place. The disciples were filled with the Holy Spirit, filled with so much power that they went forth immediately witnessing to everyone walking along the streets or standing in the doorways of their homes. This scene was so dramatic that several thousand people gathered and Peter preached to them. The result: three thousand people were saved and became followers of the Lord Jesus Christ. As stated, the Festival of Harvest or Pentecost was a strong prophetic picture of salvation. It symbolized the great harvest of souls, of people giving their lives to God on the great Day of Pentecost when the Holy Spirit was to come upon men.

In looking at the prophetic picture of salvation, this is what we have seen this far:
⇒ The Passover symbolized God's salvation, the deliverance and redemption from the world by God.
⇒ The Festival of Unleavened Bread symbolized the need and urgency of the believer to be freed from the world, freed from the enslavement of sin and death.
⇒ The Festival of Firstfruits symbolized the great hope for the believer as he marched toward the promised land, the great hope of being raised from the dead by the power of the resurrection of Jesus Christ.
⇒ The Festival of Harvest symbolized the great day of Pentecost that took place fifty days after the resurrection of Christ, the great day when the Holy Spirit came upon the disciples giving a great harvest of souls. As the believer marches to the promised land, he is to be filled with God's Spirit and bear strong testimony, seeking a great harvest of souls.

5 (23:23-25) **Trumpets, Festival of—Festival, of Trumpets—Trust, Growing in—Maturity, Growing in**: there was the Festival of Trumpets. This was a one-day festival that apparently had a single purpose: to arouse the people to trust God more and more, proclaiming the message of joy for the atonement or reconciliation. The Festival of Trumpets was a picture or symbol of salvation and of the rapture, the glorious day when Christ will return and take all believers to live with Him forever. The Israelites had two silver trumpets that were used to call the people together and to signal directions as they journeyed to the promised land. Trumpeters were apparently stationed at regular intervals to pass the signal through the entire camp. Remember, there were two to four million Israelites camped around the Tabernacle. Note the Scripture and outline:

OUTLINE	SCRIPTURE	SCRIPTURE	OUTLINE
5. The Festival of Trumpets: To arouse the people to trust God more & more proclaiming the message of joy for the atonement(reconciliation) a. The date: 7th month, 1st day	23 And the LORD spake unto Moses, saying, 24 Speak unto the children of Israel, saying, the seventh month, in the first *day* of the month, shall ye have a sabbath,	a memorial of blowing of trumpets, an holy convocation. 25 Ye shall do no servile work *therein*: but ye shall offer an offering made by fire unto the LORD.	b. The features: To rest & approach God for atonement—through the Burnt Offering

a. The date of the Festival of Trumpets was the first day of the seventh month (v.24). Actually the seventh month was a busy time for festivals, a month of great celebration and worship before the LORD. Both the Day of Atonement and the Festival of Tabernacles also took place during this month. Note that the Festival of Trumpets was a sacred assembly that began with a loud trumpet blast all throughout the camp. When the people heard the blowing of the trumpets echoing throughout the camp, it was a signal for the Festival of Trumpets to begin.

b. The people were to rest and approach God for atonement and reconciliation through the Burnt Offering (v.25; see 29:1-6). This day was set aside so the people could focus upon God, learning to trust Him more and more, proclaiming the message of joy for the atonement or reconciliation provided by God.

Thought 1. The prophetic picture of salvation and deliverance is seen in the Festival of Trumpets. As the believer marches to the promised land, he is to focus upon God, ever learning to trust God more and more, proclaiming the message of joy for the atonement or reconciliation with God. God has saved him; consequently, the believer is to take joy in his salvation, joy in the atonement and reconciliation with God. Moreover, the Festival of Trumpets pictures the rapture, the great salvation of God's people when Christ returns. Christ will sound the trumpet; the dead in Christ will be raised, and then all who are alive and remain will be caught up together with Him in the clouds to meet the LORD in the air—to be with Him forever (I Th.4:16-17). Simply stated, the believer is to grow in his trust and joy; he is to be ever maturing, learning to focus more and more upon the LORD.

"Hitherto have ye asked nothing in my name: ask, and ye shall receive, that your joy may be full" (Jn.16:24).

"Now he that ministereth seed to the sower both minister bread for *your* food, and multiply your seed sown, and increase the fruits of your righteousness" (2 Co.9:10).

"But speaking the truth in love, may grow up into him in all things, which is the head, *even* Christ" (Ep.4:15).

"Rejoice in the Lord always: *and* again I say, Rejoice" (Ph.4:4).

"For the Lord himself shall descend from heaven with a shout, with the voice of the archangel, and with the trump of God: and the dead in Christ shall rise first: Then we which are alive *and* remain shall be caught up together with them in the clouds, to meet the Lord in the air: and so shall we ever be with the Lord" (1 Th.4:16-17).

"As newborn babes, desire the sincere milk of the word, that ye may grow thereby: If so be ye have tasted that the Lord *is* gracious" (1 Pe.2:2-3).

"But grow in grace, and *in* the knowledge of our Lord and Saviour Jesus Christ. To him *be* glory both now and for ever. Amen" (2 Pe.3:18).

"The LORD *is* my light and my salvation; whom shall I fear? the LORD *is* the strength of my life; of whom shall I be afraid?" (Ps.27:1).

"*Oh* how great *is* thy goodness, which thou hast laid up for them that fear thee; *which* thou hast wrought for them that trust in thee before the sons of men!" (Ps.31:19).

"Trust in the LORD, and do good; *so* shalt thou dwell in the land, and verily thou shalt be fed" (Ps.37:3).

"Trust in the LORD with all thine heart; and lean not unto thine own understanding" (Pr.3:5).

"Behold, God *is* my salvation; I will trust, and not be afraid: for the LORD JEHOVAH *is* my strength and *my* song; he also is become my salvation" (Is.12:2).

"And it shall be said in that day, Lo, this *is* our God; we have waited for him, and he will save us: this *is* the LORD; we have waited for him, we will be glad and rejoice in his salvation" (Is.25:9).

"Thou wilt keep *him* in perfect peace, *whose* mind *is* stayed *on thee:* because he trusteth in thee" (Is.26:3).

6 (23:26-32) **Atonement, Day of—Day of Atonement—Cleansing, from Sin—Sin, Cleansing of**: there was the great Day of Atonement. This day had one purpose and one purpose only: to focus upon the necessity for the substitute sacrifice in order to make atonement or reconciliation with God. A person had to be cleansed from sin through the substitute sacrifice before he could be reconciled or made acceptable to God. A detailed discussion on the Day of Atonement has already been given (see outline and notes—Le.16:1-34 for more discussion).

OUTLINE	SCRIPTURE	SCRIPTURE	OUTLINE
6. The Day of Atonement: To cleanse the people from their sins (a symbol of sins' being cleansed through the shed blood)	26 And the LORD spake unto Moses, saying,	cut off from among his people	
a. The date: 7th month, 10th day	27 Also on the tenth *day* of this seventh month *there shall be* a day of atonement:	30 And whatsoever soul *it be* that doeth any work in that same day, the same soul will I destroy from among his people.	
b. The features	it shall be an holy convocation unto you; and ye shall		
1) To deny self (a fast)	afflict your souls, and offer	31 Ye shall do no manner of work: *it shall be* a statute for ever throughout your generations in all your dwellings.	d. The day set forever, permanently
2) To approach God for atonement (reconciliation)—through the Burnt Offering	an offering made by fire unto the LORD.		
3) To be a day of rest	28 And ye shall do no work in that same day: for it *is* a day of atonement, to make an atonement for you before the LORD your God.	32 It *shall be* unto you a sabbath of rest, and ye shall afflict your souls: in the ninth *day* of the month at even, from even unto even, shall ye celebrate your sabbath.	e. The hours to be observed: To begin the evening before the Day of Atonement till the following evening
c. The warning: Will be cut off, destroyed if refuse to observe the Day of Atonement	29 For whatsoever soul *it be* that shall not be afflicted in that same day, he shall be		

a. The Day of Atonement was to be observed on the tenth day of the seventh month (v.27).

b. The Day of Atonement was to be a day of self-denial, a day of fasting (vv.22-28). The people were to focus upon their approach to God as the priest sought atonement or reconciliation through the sacrifice of the Burnt Offering. Moreover, the day was to be a day of complete rest. No work whatsoever was to be done. Note why: because this was the great Day of Atonement, the day when atonement was made for the people before the LORD their God.

c. Note the warning: if a person refused to observe the Day of Atonement, he was to be cut off, destroyed (vv.29-30). He was to be exiled from the people of God, forbidden to live with them. There was also the idea that God would cut him off from His presence—eternally. The sacrifice of the Burnt Offering made atonement for the souls of God's people. The atoning sacrifice was a symbol of the Lord Jesus Christ. If a person refused to approach God through the atoning sacrifice, he was unacceptable to God. He was alienated and separated from God. Reconciliation had to take place before God could accept him, and reconciliation took place only through the atoning sacrifice. The person who refused to so approach God was eternally doomed.

d. The day was set as a permanent observance (v.31).

e. Note the hours that the day was to be observed: a person was to fast and do no work from the evening of the ninth day of the month until the following evening (v.32).

> **Thought 1**. The Day of Atonement paints the prophetic picture of salvation. As the believer walks toward the promised land of heaven, he is to keep before his mind the atoning sacrifice of the Lord Jesus Christ. He is never to forget that it is Christ who has cleansed him from sin and delivered him from the penalty of sin, which is death. He is to walk day by day in open confession before the LORD, confessing his sins throughout the day and striving to captivate every thought, bringing them into subjection to Christ. The cross of Christ is always to be before the face of the believer. The cross of Christ is to be the focus of the believer's mind and thoughts. The believer stands reconciled to God only through the shed blood of Christ.
>
> > "For this is my blood of the new testament, which is shed for many for the remission of sins" (Mt.26:28).
> >
> > "Much more then, being now justified by his blood, we shall be saved from wrath through him" (Ro.5:9).
> >
> > "And not only *so*, but we also joy in God through our Lord Jesus Christ, by whom we have now received the atonement" (Ro.5:11).
> >
> > "For he hath made him *to be* sin for us, who knew no sin; that we might be made the righteousness of God in him" (2 Co.5:21).
> >
> > "How much more shall the blood of Christ, who through the eternal Spirit offered himself without spot to God, purge your conscience from dead works to serve the living God?" (He.9:14).
> >
> > "In whom we have redemption through his blood, the forgiveness of sins, according to the riches of his grace" (Ep.1:7).
> >
> > "Forasmuch as ye know that ye were not redeemed with corruptible things, *as* silver and gold, from your vain conversation *received* by tradition from your fathers; But with the precious blood of Christ, as of a lamb without blemish and without spot" (1 Pe.1:18-19).
> >
> > "Who his own self bare our sins in his own body on the tree, that we, being dead to sins, should live unto righteousness: by whose stripes ye were healed" (1 Pe.2:24).
> >
> > "But if we walk in the light, as he is in the light, we have fellowship one with another, and the blood of Jesus Christ his Son cleanseth us from all sin" (1 Jn.1:7).
> >
> > "If we confess our sins, he is faithful and just to forgive us *our* sins, and to cleanse us from all unrighteousness" (1 Jn.1:9).

7 (23:33-44) **Festival of Tabernacles—Tabernacles, Festival of—Wilderness Wanderings—Wanderings, Wilderness—Journeys, Wilderness—Heaven, Journey** to: there was the Festival of Tabernacles. This festival celebrated the wilderness wanderings when the people of God had to live in tents on their way to the promised land. It also celebrated a gathering of the harvest at the end of the year; therefore it was to be a period of thanksgiving to God for the harvest (Ex.23:16). The Festival of Tabernacles is a symbol of the believer's march through this world to heaven. On their march to the promised land, the people of God had to live in tents. It was going to take God forty years to teach the people to follow Him and to obey His commandments through trial after trial. Therefore, the people had to be able to pitch camp and to break camp on the spur of the moment when the need to escape some trial arose. Moreover, the desert or wilderness was not to be their permanent home; consequently, they were not allowed to build any kind of permanent housing. They were to live in tents until they reached the promised land, at which time they would be allowed to build houses and to settle down. Because they were forced to wander about so long in the wilderness, their journey is referred to as the *Wilderness Wanderings* or *Wilderness Journeys*. During this period of time while they were marching to the promised land, they lived in temporary tents. As stated, the Festival of Tabernacles was to celebrate the wilderness wanderings when they lived in tents on their way to the promised land. They were to be forever thankful to God and to keep their minds focused upon the promised land. Note the Scripture and outline:

OUTLINE	SCRIPTURE	SCRIPTURE	OUTLINE
7. The Festival of Tabernacles: To celebrate the wilderness wanderings when the people lived in tents on their way to the promised land, & to thank God for the harvest	33 And the LORD spake unto Moses, saying, 34 Speak unto the children of Israel, saying, The fifteenth day of this	seventh month *shall be* the feast of tabernacles *for* seven days unto the LORD 35 On the first day *shall be*	**(a symbol of the believer's march through this world to heaven)** a. The date: 7th month, 15th day

OUTLINE	SCRIPTURE	SCRIPTURE	OUTLINE
b. The features 1) To stop all work on the 1st day for a sacred assembly 2) To approach God for seven days, seeking atonement each of the seven days—through the Burnt Offering 3) To hold another sacred assembly to close the festival: Approach God for atonement (reconciliation)—through another Burnt Offering c. The importance of the Feast of Tabernacles & of the other feasts 1) Are annual, sacred assemblies for worship 2) Are for the purpose of approaching God for atonement (reconciliation)—through the sacrifices & offerings 3) Are in addition to all other approaches to God, all other offerings & gifts d. The importance of the Feast of Tabernacles reemphasized 1) The date: 7th month, 15th day, lasting for seven days,	an holy convocation: ye shall do no servile work *therein*. 36 Seven days ye shall offer an offering made by fire unto the LORD: on the eighth day shall be an holy convocation unto you; and ye shall offer an offering made by fire unto the LORD: it *is* a solemn assembly; *and* ye shall do no servile work *therein*. 37 These *are* the feasts of the LORD, which ye shall proclaim *to* be holy convocations, to offer an offering made by fire unto the LORD, a burnt offering, and a meat offering, a sacrifice, and drink offerings, every thing upon his day: 38 Beside the sabbaths of the LORD, and beside your gifts, and beside all your vows, and beside all your freewill offerings, which ye give unto the LORD. 39 Also in the fifteenth day of the seventh month, when ye have gathered in the fruit of the land, ye shall keep a	feast unto the LORD seven days: on the first day *shall be* a sabbath, and on the eighth day *shall be* a sabbath. 40 And ye shall take you on the first day the boughs of goodly trees, branches of palm trees, and the boughs of thick trees, and willows of the brook; and ye shall rejoice before the LORD your God seven days. 41 And ye shall keep it a feast unto the LORD seven days in the year. *It shall be* a statute for ever in your generations: ye shall celebrate it in the seventh month. 42 Ye shall dwell in booths seven days; all that are Israelites born shall dwell in booths: 43 That your generations may know that I made the children of Israel to dwell in booths, when I brought them out of the land of Egypt: I *am* the LORD your God. 44 And Moses declared unto the children of Israel the feasts of the LORD	after crops are harvested 2) The 1st day is a day of rest & the 8th day is a day of rest 3) To build booths or shelters from tree leaves on the 1st day 4) To make the festival a celebration of great joy & rejoicing before the LORD e. The festival is to be a lasting, permanent law f. The purpose of the festival: To live in booths or shelters for seven days—to teach all descendants that God's people had to live in booths when God delivered them out of Egypt (a symbol of how temporary this world is)

a. The people were to celebrate the Festival of Tabernacles on the fifteenth day of the seventh month (v.34). It was to last for seven days, a full week of festivities and worship.

b. The people were to begin with a sacred assembly on the first day, doing no work whatsoever (v.35). They were to approach God for atonement (reconciliation) during each of the seven days, approach God through the Burnt Offering (v.36). On the eighth day, they were to hold another sacred assembly to close the festival. The body of the whole nation was called together to approach God for atonement or reconciliation—through another Burnt Offering (v.36).

c. Note that the importance of the Feast of Tabernacles and the other feasts was stressed (vv.37-38):
⇒ They were all annual sacred assemblies for worship, a time when the whole nation was to assemble together to approach God (v.37).
⇒ They were for the purpose of approaching God for atonement or reconciliation—through the sacrifices and offerings (v.37).
⇒ They were to be additional celebrations, not to replace a person's regular approach to God. They were to be in addition to all other approaches to God.
⇒ They were not to replace the Freewill Offerings, nor the regular Sabbath day worship, nor any other gift or offerings that the people brought to God. They were, as stated, to be an additional period of worship or celebration of the LORD (v.38).

d. Note that the importance of the Feast of Tabernacles is re-emphasized (vv.39-40). It was to be celebrated on the fifteenth day of the seventh month and last for seven days. It was to be celebrated after the crops had been harvested. Both the first day and the eighth day were to be days of rest.

Note that the people were to build booths or shelters from tree leaves on the first day (v.40) They were to live in these booths or shelters for seven days (vv.40, 42). The festival was to be a celebration of great joy and rejoicing before the LORD (vv.40-41).

e. The festival was to be a lasting, permanent law (v.41).

f. Note the purpose for the festival: it was to teach all descendants that their ancestors had to live in booths when God delivered them out of Egypt. Note that this was a symbol of how temporary this world is. Also note the warning of God: "I am the LORD your God" (v.43). God expected His people to celebrate the Festival of Tabernacles. If they failed, His judgment would fall upon them. He is the LORD their God, able to execute judgment.

Thought 1. As the believer marches to heaven, his dwelling upon this earth is only temporary. No matter what kind of house he lives in, it is temporary. It is made out of decaying, corruptible materials. It will waste away, and some day, perhaps decades or even centuries out in the future, it will cease to be. Earthly homes are only temporary structures. Moreover, the believer is living in a temporary body, a body that the Bible describes as a temporary tent or tabernacle (2 Co.5:1-4). The body is corruptible and will decay and cease to exist. The believer's journey or pilgrimage through this world is only a temporary journey. He is marching to his permanent and eternal home in heaven, where he will live forever in the presence of God.

"Lay not up for yourselves treasures upon earth, where moth and rust doth corrupt, and where thieves break through and steal: But lay up for yourselves treasures in heaven, where neither moth nor rust doth corrupt, and where thieves do not break through nor steal: For where your treasure is, there will your heart be also" (Mt.6:19-21).

"For we know that if our earthly house of *this* tabernacle were dissolved [our body], we have a building of God, an house not made with hands, eternal in the heavens. For in this we groan, earnestly desiring to be clothed upon with our house which is from heaven: If so be that being clothed we shall not be found naked. For we that are in *this* tabernacle do groan, being burdened: not for that we would be unclothed, but clothed upon, that mortality might be swallowed up of life" (2 Co.5:1-4).

"For our conversation [citizenship] is in heaven; from whence also we look for the Saviour, the Lord Jesus Christ: Who shall change our vile body, that it may be fashioned like unto his glorious body, according to the working whereby he is able even to subdue all things unto himself" (Ph.3:20-21).

"For the hope which is laid up for you in heaven, whereof ye heard before in the word of the truth of the gospel" (Col.1:5)

"Teaching us that, denying ungodliness and worldly lusts, we should live soberly, righteously, and godly, in this present world; Looking for that blessed hope, and the glorious appearing of the great God and our Saviour Jesus Christ" (Tit.2:12-13).

"Blessed *be* the God and Father of our Lord Jesus Christ, which according to his abundant mercy hath begotten us again unto a lively hope by the resurrection of Jesus Christ from the dead, To an inheritance incorruptible, and undefiled, and that fadeth not away, reserved in heaven for you" (1 Pe.1:3-4).

"For all flesh *is* as grass, and all the glory of man as the flower of grass. The grass withereth, and the flower thereof falleth away" (1 Pe.1:24).

"Blessed *are* they that do his commandments, that they may have right to the tree of life, and may enter in through the gates into the city" (Re.22:14).

"Remember, I beseech thee, that thou hast made me as the clay; and wilt thou bring me into dust again?" (Jb.10:9).

"What man *is he that* liveth, and shall not see death? shall he deliver his soul from the hand of the grave? Selah" (Ps.89:48).

"*As for* man, his days *are* as grass: as a flower of the field, so he flourisheth" (Ps.103:15).

"The voice said, Cry. And he said, What shall I cry? All flesh *is* grass, and all the goodliness thereof *is* as the flower of the field: The grass withereth, the flower fadeth: because the spirit of the LORD bloweth upon it: surely the people *is* grass" (Is.40:6-7).

TYPES, SYMBOLS, AND PICTURES
Leviticus 23:1-44

Historical Term	Type or Picture (Scriptural Basis for Each)	Life Application for Today's Believer	Biblical Application
The Sabbath Le. 23:3	*The Sabbath is a symbol of the spiritual rest that God promises to those who believe and follow him. The Sabbath rest is a symbol of redemption, of God's deliverance from the heavy burdens and trials of this life.* **"Six days shall work be done: but the seventh day *is* the sabbath of rest, an holy convocation; ye shall do no work *therein*: it *is* the sabbath of the LORD in all your dwellings" (Le.23:3).**	The Sabbath is a picture of the perfect rest that Jesus Christ brings to a person. The Sabbath gives a person a day to rest and worship, but... • Jesus Christ gives a person rest itself, a complete rest, a perfect rest of mind and soul. • Jesus Christ gives a person the perfect assurance that we are acceptable to God. A person is to be faithful to worship and rest on the Sabbath, as God has ordained. It is only through obedience to God's command that we are able to receive the perfect rest that only God can give.	*"There remaineth therefore a rest to the people of God. For he that is entered into his rest, he also hath ceased from his own works, as God did from his. Let us labour therefore to enter into that rest, lest any man fall after the same example of unbelief" (He.4:9-11).* *"Come unto me, all ye that labour and are heavy laden, and I will give you rest" (Mt.11:28).* *"But they that wait upon the LORD shall renew their strength; they shall mount up with wings as eagles; they shall run, and not be weary; and they shall walk, and not faint" (Is.40:31).* *"For the Son of man is Lord even of the sabbath day" (Mt.12:8).*

TYPES, SYMBOLS, AND PICTURES
Leviticus 23:1-44

Historical Term	Type or Picture (Scriptural Basis for Each)	Life Application for Today's Believer	Biblical Application
The Passover Le. 23:5	*The Passover is a symbol of Christ our Passover who was sacrificed for us.* "**In the fourteenth** *day* **of the first month at even** *is* **the LORD'S passover**" (Le. 23:5).	Jesus Christ is the perfect fulfillment of the Passover Lamb that was slain on behalf of God's people. Through the blood of Jesus Christ, a person escapes the judgment of God. God accepts the blood of His Son—the blood of the substitute sacrifice—as full payment for a person's sin and rebellion against God.	"*The next day John seeth Jesus coming unto him, and saith, Behold the Lamb of God, which taketh away the sin of the world*" *(Jn.1:29).* "*...For even Christ our passover is sacrificed for us*" *(1 Co.5:7).* "*He was oppressed, and he was afflicted, yet he opened not his mouth: he is brought as a lamb to the slaughter, and as a sheep before her shearers is dumb, so he openeth not his mouth*" *(Is.53:7).* "*Who gave himself for our sins, that he might deliver us from this present evil world, according to the will of God and our Father*" *(Ga.1:4).*
The Festival of Unleavened Bread Le. 23:6	*The Feast or Festival of Unleavened Bread symbolizes the need for a person to be free from the world and its enslavement to sin and death, the urgency for a person to begin the march to the promised land.* "**And on the fifteenth day of the same month** *is* **the feast of unleavened bread unto the LORD: seven days ye must eat unleavened bread**" (Le. 23:6).	There is a need—an urgent, desperate need— to be delivered from all the oppression and pollution of this world, from all the sin and evil, immorality and lawlessness, corruption and death of this world. There is a need and urgency to be set free and liberated to live for God, a desperate need and urgency to begin the march to the promise land of heaven.	"*...behold, now is the day of salvation* (2 Co.6:2). "*Seek ye the LORD while he may be found, call ye upon him while he is near*" *(Is.55:6).* "*But this I say, brethren, the time is short: it remaineth, that both they that have wives be as though they had none*" *(1 Co.7:29).* "*For our conversation [citizenship] is in heaven; from whence also we look for the Saviour, the Lord Jesus Christ*" *(Phil.3:20; see 2 Ti.4:8).*
The Festival of First-fruits Le. 23:9-14	*The Festival Of Firstfruits is a symbol of Christ's resurrection: He is the first of the harvest, the first to arise from the dead.* "**Speak unto the children of Israel, and say unto them, When ye be come into the land which I give unto you, and shall reap the harvest thereof, then ye shall bring a sheaf of the firstfruits of your harvest unto the priest**" (Le. 23:10).	Christ is the first of the harvest, the first to arise from the dead. It is Jesus Christ and His resurrection that gives the believer hope of arising from the dead and living eternally with God. The prophetic picture of salvation is this: the Passover symbolized the believers deliverance or redemption from the world; the Festival of Unleavened Bread symbolized the urgency of the believer to leave the world and begin his march to the promise land; and now, the Festival of Firstfruits symbolizes the glorious hope the believer has as he marches toward the promise land, the hope of being raised from	"*That Christ should suffer, and that he should be the first that should rise from the dead, and should show light unto the people, and to the Gentiles*" *(Ac.26:23).* "*But now is Christ risen from the dead, and become the firstfruits of them that slept. For since by man came death, by man came also the resurrection of the dead. For as in Adam all die, even so in Christ shall all be made alive. But every man in his own order: Christ the firstfruits; afterward they that are Christ's at his coming*" *(1 Co. 15:20-23).* "*Knowing that he which*

TYPES, SYMBOLS, AND PICTURES
Leviticus 23:1-44

Historical Term	Type or Picture (Scriptural Basis for Each)	Life Application for Today's Believer	Biblical Application
		the dead and living eternally with God—all because of the resurrection of Christ.	*raised up the Lord Jesus shall raise up us also by Jesus, and shall present us with you" (2 Co.4:14).* *"Blessed be the God and Father of our Lord Jesus Christ, which according to his abundant mercy hath begotten us again unto a lively hope by the resurrection of Jesus Christ from the dead, To an inheritance incorruptible, and undefiled, and that fadeth not away, reserved in heaven for you" (1 Pe.1:3-4).*
The Aroma of the Burning Sacrifice and Grain Offering That Ascended: During the Festival of Firstfruits Le. 23:13	*The aroma of the burning sacrifice and Grain Offering symbolized God's acceptance. He was pleased with the aroma of the sacrifice, the obedience of the people.* **"And the meat offering thereof** *shall be* **two tenth deals of fine flour mingled with oil, an offering made by fire unto the LORD** *for* **a sweet savour: and the drink offering thereof** *shall be* **of wine, the fourth part of an hin" (Le.23:13).**	What can we do to please God? We must… ⇒ approach God as He says, approach Him through the sacrifice of the Lord Jesus Christ ⇒ commit ourselves to God, thanking Him for the atoning sacrifice of Christ, for so great a salvation	*"This day the LORD thy God hath commanded thee to do these statutes and judgments: thou shalt therefore keep and do them with all thine heart, and with all thy soul" (De.26:16).* *"And Samuel said, Hath the LORD as great delight in burnt offerings and sacrifices, as in obeying the voice of the LORD? Behold, to obey is better than sacrifice, and to hearken than the fat of rams" (1 S. 15:22).* *"Not every one that saith unto me, Lord, Lord, shall enter into the kingdom of heaven; but he that doeth the will of my Father which is in heaven" (Mt.7:21).*
The Festival of Harvest or Pentecost Le. 23:15-22	*The Festival of Harvest or Pentecost is a symbol of Pentecost, of the great harvest of souls and of people giving their lives to God. The Festival of Harvest symbolized the great day of Pentecost that took place fifty days after the resurrection of Christ, the great day when the Holy Spirit came upon the disciples and gave a great harvest of souls.* **"Even unto the morrow after the seventh sabbath shall ye number fifty days; and ye shall offer a new meat offering unto the LORD" (Le.23:16).**	As the believer marches to the Promised Land, he is to be filled with God's Spirit and bear strong testimony, seeking a great harvest of souls.	*"And when the day of Pentecost was fully come, they were all with one accord in one place. And suddenly there came a sound from heaven as of a rushing mighty wind, and it filled all the house where they were sitting. And there appeared unto them cloven tongues like as of fire, and it sat upon each of them. And they were all filled with the Holy Ghost, and began to speak with other tongues, as the Spirit gave them utterance" (Ac.2:1-4).* *"Now when they heard this, they were pricked in their heart, and said unto Peter and to the rest of the apostles, Men and brethren, what shall we do? Then Peter said unto them,*

TYPES, SYMBOLS, AND PICTURES
Leviticus 23:1-44

Historical Term	Type or Picture (Scriptural Basis for Each)	Life Application for Today's Believer	Biblical Application
			Repent, and be baptized every one of you in the name of Jesus Christ for the remission of sins, and ye shall receive the gift of the Holy Ghost" (Ac.2:37-38). *"Then they that gladly received his word were baptized: and the same day there were added unto them about three thousand souls" (Ac.2:41).*
The Sacrifice of Seven Male Lambs, One Young Bull and Two Rams— All with No Defect—in the Festival of Harvest Le. 23:18	*The sacrifice of seven male lambs, one young bull and two rams—all with no defect—in the Festival of Harvest is a symbol of Christ, His perfect and sinless sacrifice. Remember that the number seven symbolizes completion, fulfillment and perfection.* **"And ye shall offer with the bread seven lambs without blemish of the first year, and one young bullock, and two rams: they shall be** *for* **a burnt offering unto the LORD, with their meat offering, and their drink offerings,** *even* **an offering made by fire, of sweet savour unto the LORD" (Le.23:18).**	Jesus Christ is the perfect and sinless sacrifice. His death upon the cross was the perfect solution to the problem of sin: The finished work of a perfect and sinless Man has secured our salvation	*"And being made perfect, he became the author of eternal salvation unto all them that obey him" (He.5:9).* *"And he made his grave with the wicked, and with the rich in his death; because he had done no violence, neither was any deceit in his mouth" (Is.53:9).* *"For he hath made him to be sin for us, who knew no sin; that we might be made the righteousness of God in him" (2 Co.5:21).* *"For we have not an high priest which cannot be touched with the feeling of our infirmities; but was in all points tempted like as we are, yet without sin" (He.4:15).* *"For such an high priest became us, who is holy, harmless, undefiled, separate from sinners, and made higher than the heavens" (He.7:26).*
The Festival of Trumpets Le. 23:23-25	*The Feast of Trumpets is a picture of salvation and of the rapture, the glorious day when Christ will return and take believers—both the living and the dead—to live with Him forever.* **"Speak unto the children of Israel, saying, In the seventh month, in the first** *day* **of the month, shall ye have a sabbath, a memorial of blowing of trumpets, an holy convocation" (Le.23:24).**	As the believer marches to the promised land, he is to focus upon God, learning to trust God more and more and to heed the message of joy over the atonement or reconciliation with God. God has saved him; consequently, the believer is to take joy in his salvation, joy in the atonement and reconciliation with God. Moreover, he is to focus upon God more and more and learn to trust God more and more. Simply stated, the believer is to grow in his trust and joy; he is to be ever maturing, learning to focus upon the Lord.	*"But I would not have you to be ignorant, brethren, concerning them which are asleep, that ye sorrow not, even as others which have no hope. For if we believe that Jesus died and rose again, even so them also which sleep in Jesus will God bring with him. For this we say unto you by the word of the Lord, that we which are alive and remain unto the coming of the Lord shall not prevent them which are asleep. For the Lord himself shall descend from heaven with a shout, with the voice of the archangel, and with the trump [the*

TYPES, SYMBOLS, AND PICTURES
Leviticus 23:1-44

Historical Term	Type or Picture (Scriptural Basis for Each)	Life Application for Today's Believer	Biblical Application
			be caught up together with them in the clouds, to meet the Lord in the air: and so shall we ever be with the Lord. Wherefore comfort one another with these words" (1 Th.4:13-18).
The Festival of Tabernacles or Booths or Shelters Le. 23:33-34	*The Festival Of Tabernacles is a symbol of the believer's short, temporary life and march through this world to the promised land of heaven.* **"Speak unto the children of Israel, saying, The fifteenth day of this seventh month** *shall be* **the feast of tabernacles** *for* **seven days unto the LORD"** (Le. 23:34). **"Ye shall dwell in booths seven days; all that are Israelites born shall dwell in booths: That your generations may know that I made the children of Israel to dwell in booths, when I brought them out of the land of Egypt: I** *am* **the LORD your God"** (Le. 23:42-43).	As the believer marches through this world to the promised land of heaven, his dwelling is only temporary. No matter what kind of house he lives in, it is temporary. It is made out of decaying, corruptible materials. It will waste away and some day, perhaps decades or even a few centuries, it will cease to be. Earthly homes are only temporary structures. Moreover, the believer is living in a temporary body, a body that the Bible describes as a temporary tent or tabernacle. The body is corruptible and will decay and cease to exist. The believer's journey or pilgrimage through this world is only temporary. He is marching to his permanent and eternal home in heaven where he will live forever in the presence of God.	*"For we know that if our earthly house of this tabernacle were dissolved, we have a building of God, an house not made with hands, eternal in the heavens" (2 Co.5:1).* *"Of old hast thou laid the foundation of the earth: and the heavens are the work of thy hands. They shall perish, but thou shalt endure: yea, all of them shall wax old like a garment; as a vesture shalt thou change them, and they shall be changed" (Ps. 102:25-26).* *"And they that use this world, as not abusing it: for the fashion of this world passeth away" (1 Co.7:31).* *"While we look not at the things which are seen, but at the things which are not seen: for the things which are seen are temporal; but the things which are not seen are eternal" (2 Co.4:18; see 2 Pe.3:10; Re.21:1).*

THE FEASTS OR FESTIVALS OF WORSHIP:
THE PROPHETIC PICTURE OF SALVATION,
Leviticus 23:1-44

THE FEAST OR FESTIVAL	PURPOSE FOR THE FEAST	PROPHETIC SYMBOL OF THE FEAST
The Passover SCRIPTURE REFERENCES: Le. 23:6; Nu.9:5; Jos.5:10; 2 K.23:22; 2 Chr. 35:1; Mt.26:17; Lu. 2:41; 22:15; He.11:28	To remember God's judgment and deliverance from the enslavement of Egypt (a symbol of being enslaved by the world). God's judgment forced the Egyptians to set God's people free after four hundred years of savage, brutal enslavement. As a result, the Passover celebrates the most important event in Israel's history, that of being set free from Egyptian slavery.	A symbol of Christ, our Passover who was sacrificed for us. Jesus Christ is the perfect fulfillment of the Passover Lamb that was slain on behalf of God's people. Through His sacrifice we are delivered from the judgment of God and from being enslaved to the sin and death of this world. Note that the Passover is a picture, a prophetic picture of salvation and redemption through the sacrifice of Christ. **"Purge out therefore the old leaven, that ye may be a new lump, as ye are unleavened. For even Christ our passover is sacrificed for us" (1 Co.5:7).**
The Feast of Unleavened Bread SCRIPTURE REFERENCES: Ex. 12:17-18; 13:6-7; 23:15; 34:18; Le.23:6; Nu. 28:17; De.16:3; 16:16; 2 Chr.8:13; 2 Chr. 30:13; Mt.26:17; Mk. 14:1	To recall the need and urgency to leave Egypt and to begin the march to the promised land. The Egyptians were desperate for Pharaoh to release and get rid of the Israelites. In fact, the Israelites were forced to leave so quickly that they had no time to adequately prepare. They did not even have time to let their dough rise, no time to put yeast or leaven in their bread. They were forced to take unleavened bread. There was the need, the urgency to get out of Egypt (the world) immediately.	A symbol of the urgency to be freed from the world and to begin one's march to the promised land of heaven. There is a need—an urgent, desperate need—to be delivered from all the oppression and pollution of this world, from all the sin and evil, immorality and lawlessness, corruption and death of this world. There is an urgent need to be set free and liberated to live for God and to begin the march to the promised land of heaven. **"For our conversation [citizenship] is in heaven; from whence also we look for the Saviour, the Lord Jesus Christ" (Ph.3:20).**
The Festival of Firstfruits SCRIPTURE REFERENCES: Ex. 34:22; Le.23:10; Nu. 28:26	To thank God for the crops, for the harvest of food that sustains people and gives them life. Note that this festival could not begin until the people had entered the promised land. They, of course, could not plant crops out in the desert while they were marching to the promised land. Once they arrived and began planting crops, they were to give the first of their harvest to the LORD during this festival.	A symbol of Christ's resurrection and of the great hope the believer has as he marches to the promised land. Christ is the first of the harvest, the first to arise from the dead. The prophetic picture of salvation is just this: As the believer marches to the promised land, he has the great hope of being raised from the dead and of living eternally with God—all because of the resurrection of Christ Jesus. **"But now is Christ risen from the dead, *and* become the firstfruits of them that slept. For since by man *came* death, by man *came* also the resurrection of the dead. For as in Adam all die, even so in Christ shall all be made alive. But every man in his own order: Christ the firstfruits; afterward they that are Christ's at his coming" (1 Co.15:20-23).**
The Festival of Harvest or Pentecost SCRIPTURE REFERENCES: Ex. 23:16; 34:22; Le.23:16; Nu.28:26; De.16:10; Ac.2:1-47	To give thanks for the harvest and to dedicate one's life anew to God. God's people were to celebrate the Festival of Harvest fifty days after of the Festival of Firstfruits.	A symbol of Pentecost, of the great harvest of souls and of people giving their lives to God. The Festival of Harvest symbolized the great day of Pentecost that took place fifty days after the resurrection of Christ, the great day when the Holy Spirit came upon the disciples and gave a great harvest of souls. As the believer marches to the promised land, he is to be filled with God's Spirit and bear strong testimony, seeking a great harvest of souls. **"But ye shall receive power, after that the Holy Ghost is come upon you: and ye shall be witnesses unto me both in Jerusalem, and in all Judaea, and in Samaria, and unto the uttermost part of the earth" (Ac.1:8).** **"And when the day of Pentecost was fully come, they were all with one accord in one place....And they were all filled with the Holy Ghost, and began to speak with other**

THE FEAST OR FESTIVAL	PURPOSE FOR THE FEAST	PROPHETIC SYMBOL OF THE FEAST
		tongues, as the Spirit gave them utterance" (Ac.2:1, 4).
The Festival of Trumpets SCRIPTURE REFERENCES: Le. 23:24; Nu.29:1; Ne.8:2	To focus upon God, learning to trust God more and more and to proclaim the message of joy for the atonement or reconciliation with God. The Israelites had two silver trumpets that were used to call the people together and to signal directions as they journeyed to the promised land. Trumpeters were obviously stationed ever so far to pass the signal through the entire camp.	A symbol of salvation and of the rapture, the glorious day when Christ will return and take believers to be with Him forever. As the believer marches to the promised land of heaven, he is to grow in his trust and joy; he is to be ever maturing, learning to focus and to bear a stronger witness to the atonement of Christ. He is to focus upon the LORD and His glorious return. **"For the LORD himself shall descend from heaven with a shout, with the voice of the archangel, and with the trump of God: and the dead in Christ shall rise first: Then we which are alive and remain shall be caught up together with them in the clouds, to meet the LORD in the air: and so shall we ever be with the LORD" (1 Th.4:16-17).**
The Day of Atonement SCRIPTURE REFERENCES: Ex. 30:10; Le.16:30; 23:27; Nu.29:7; He.9:7	To focus upon the atonement and reconciliation with God through the substitute sacrifice, the only way to become acceptable to God. The Day of Atonement was to be a day of self-denial or fasting. The people were to approach God for atonement or reconciliation through the sacrifice of the Burnt Offering. Moreover, the day was to be a day of complete rest. No work whatsoever was to be done. Note why: because this was the Day of Atonement, the Day when atonement was made for the people before the LORD their God.	A symbol of being reconciled with God through the atonement, through the substitute sacrifice of Christ. The Day of Atonement paints the prophetic picture of salvation. As the believer walks toward the promised land of heaven, he is to keep before his mind the atoning sacrifice of the Lord Jesus Christ. He is never to forget that it is Christ who has cleansed him from sin and delivered him from the penalty of death. **"For if, when we were enemies, we were reconciled to God by the death of his Son, much more, being reconciled, we shall be saved by his life. And not only *so*, but we also joy in God through our Lord Jesus Christ, by whom we have now received the atonement" (Ro.5:10-11).**
The Festival of Tabernacles SCRIPTURE REFERENCES: Le. 23:34, 39; Nu.29:12; De.16:13; 2 Chr.8:13; Ezr.3:4; Ne.8:14; Zec. 14:16; Jn.7:2	To celebrate the wilderness wanderings when the people lived in tents on their way to the promised land and to thank God for the harvest. During this period of time, they lived in temporary tents. Despite the harsh conditions of their lives, as they marched forward, they were to be forever thankful to God and to keep their minds focused upon the promised land.	A symbol of the believer's march through this world to heaven, a symbol of how temporary the believer's march through this world is. As the believer marches to heaven, his dwelling is only temporary. No matter what kind of house he lives in, it is temporary. It is made out of decaying, corruptible materials. It will waste away and some day, perhaps decades or even a few centuries, it will cease to be. Earthly homes are only temporary structures. Moreover, the believer is living in a temporary body, a body that the Bible describes as a temporary tent or tabernacle. The body is corruptible and will decay and cease to exist. The believer's journey through this world is only a temporary pilgrimage. He is marching to his permanent and eternal home in heaven, marching forth to live forever in the presence of God. **"For we know that if our earthly house of this tabernacle were dissolved, we have a building of God, an house not made with hands, eternal in the heavens" (2 Co.5:1).** **"Blessed *be* the God and Father of our Lord Jesus Christ, which according to his abundant mercy hath begotten us again unto a lively hope by the resurrection of Jesus Christ from the dead, To an inheritance incorruptible, and undefiled, and that fadeth not away, reserved in heaven for you" (1 Pe.1:3-4).**

CHAPTER 24

H. Laws That Govern the Lampstand, the Holy Bread, & the Cursing of God: The Availability of God & the Judgment Against Cursing God, 24:1-23

1. **The lampstand: A symbol that the way into God's presence must always shine brightly—is always open for people to approach God**
   a. Must provide pure olive oil to keep the light burning continually: A symbol of the Holy Spirit
   b. Must keep the lamp right outside the inner curtain of the Most Holy Place (where God's presence was enthroned)
   c. Must keep the lamp burning in the LORD's presence day & night
   d. Must make this a permanent law
   e. Must be tended continually, giving clear access into God's presence (a symbol of Christ, the Light of the world)
2. **The Holy Bread: A symbol of Christ as the Bread of Life— God fulfills His covenant, satisfies man's hunger**
   a. To bake 12 loaves of bread
   b. To place the bread on the table in two rows of six each: A symbol of the twelve tribes (God's people) before the LORD's face
   c. To sprinkle some pure incense near each row: To be burned in place of the bread as an offering to the LORD
   d. To be replaced every Sabbath as a regular offering to the LORD
   e. To be a lasting covenant: A symbol of God's people continually offering themselves to God
   f. To be eaten by the priests— once removed from the table—in a holy place: Is a part of their share of the offerings (a symbol of feeding upon Christ, the Bread of Life)
3. **The judgment of a man who failed to approach God but instead cursed & blasphemed God**
   a. The cause of the offense
      1) He was of mixed blood
      2) He was mocked & began to fight
      3) He was so angered that he cursed God's name

And the LORD spake unto Moses, saying,
2 Command the children of Israel, that they bring unto thee pure oil olive beaten for the light, to cause the lamps to burn continually.
3 Without the vail of the testimony, in the tabernacle of the congregation, shall Aaron order it from the evening unto the morning before the LORD continually: *it shall be* a statute for ever in your generations.
4 He shall order the lamps upon the pure candlestick before the LORD continually.
5 And thou shalt take fine flour, and bake twelve cakes thereof: two tenth deals shall be in one cake.
6 And thou shalt set them in two rows, six on a row, upon the pure table before the LORD.
7 And thou shalt put pure frankincense upon *each* row, that it may be on the bread for a memorial, *even* an offering made by fire unto the LORD.
8 Every sabbath he shall set it in order before the LORD continually, *being taken* from the children of Israel by an everlasting covenant.
9 And it shall be Aaron's and his sons'; and they shall eat it in the holy place: for it is most holy unto him of the offerings of the LORD made by fire by a perpetual statute.
10 And the son of an Israelitish woman, whose father *was* an Egyptian, went out among the children of Israel: and this son of the Israelitish *woman* and a man of Israel strove together in the camp;
11 And the Israelitish woman's son blasphemed

the name *of the LORD*, and cursed. And they brought him unto Moses: (and his mother's name *was* Shelomith, the daughter of Dibri, of the tribe of Dan:)
12 And they put him in ward, that the mind of the LORD might be showed them.
13 And the LORD spake unto Moses, saying,
14 Bring forth him that hath cursed without the camp; and let all that heard *him* lay their hands upon his head, and let all the congregation stone him.
15 And thou shalt speak unto the children of Israel, saying, Whosoever curseth his God shall bear his sin.
16 And he that blasphemeth the name of the LORD, he shall surely be put to death, *and* all the congregation shall certainly stone him: as well the stranger, as he that is born in the land, when he blasphemeth the name *of the LORD*, shall be put to death.
17 And he that killeth any man shall surely be put to death.
18 And he that killeth a beast shall make it good; beast for beast.
19 And if a man cause a blemish in his neighbour; as he hath done, so shall it be done to him;
20 Breach for breach, eye for eye, tooth for tooth: as he hath caused a blemish in a man, so shall it be done to him *again*.
21 And he that killeth a beast, he shall restore it: and he that killeth a man, he shall be put to death.
22 Ye shall have one manner of law, as well for the stranger, as for one of your own country: for I *am* the LORD your God.
23 And Moses spake to the children of Israel, that they should bring forth him that had cursed out of the camp, and stone him with stones. And the children of Israel did as the LORD commanded Moses.

(LORD—Jehovah, Yahweh)
   b. The accounting
      1) He was brought to Moses

      2) He was put in custody until the LORD's will was clearly known

   c. The judgment of God
      1) To be taken outside the camp
      2) To have all who heard him cursing lay their hands on his head: Symbolized the removal of guilt from the hearers
      3) To execute him
   d. The warning to one who curses & blasphemes God's name
      1) He will be held accountable

      2) He must be put to death, no matter who he is, foreigner or native-born

   e. The principle of exact, perfect justice (lex talionis)

      1) To execute exact justice for murder: Revenge forbidden

      2) To execute exact justice for animals willfully or carelessly killed: Make restitution, life for life
      3) To execute exact justice for injuries: Fracture for fracture, eye for eye, tooth for tooth

      4) To execute exact justice for a death:
         • restitution for an animal's life
         • execution for a person's life
      5) To execute exact justice for the foreigner as well as for the native-born
   f. The execution of the blasphemer carried out
      1) Taken outside the camp & executed

      2) The people obeyed the LORD

DIVISION IV

THE WAY TO LIVE A HOLY LIFE BEFORE GOD (PART 2): A PURE SPIRIT (SANCTIFICATION), 17:1–27:34

H. Laws that Govern the Lampstand, the Holy Bread, and the Cursing of God: The Availability of God and the Judgment Against Cursing God, 24:1-23

(24:1-23) **Introduction**: God is not far off in another universe someplace, unreachable, unapproachable. However, many people feel a great distance between themselves and God. They feel that God is far, far off, completely out of reach. Within their hearts there is no sense of God, no closeness, no assurance, no confidence that God is looking after them and taking care of them. Prayer seems useless, for their prayers go unanswered. Finding God and knowing God—being assured of His presence and care—seem to be hopeless pursuits. God just seems far, far away—completely out of reach.

This is a false notion and an unnecessary feeling. God, the living and true God, is available to every human being. There is a light surrounding God, a bright light, that leads a person into the very presence of God. This is the message of the Lampstand that is covered in this passage. Moreover, there is a bread, a holy bread, that can satisfy the deep hunger of the human heart—if a person will just partake of the bread. God wants people to know that He can be reached, that there is a light that shines ever so brightly to lead people into His presence. There is a bread that will satisfy the deep emptiness of a person. But note: a person must approach God by following the light, and he must partake of the bread offered by God. The one thing a person must not do is react against God, reject, curse and blaspheme God. This is the subject of this important Scripture, Scripture that must be heeded by all: *Laws that Govern the Lampstand, the Holy Bread, and the Cursing of God: The Availability of God and the Judgment Against Cursing God*, 24:1-23.

1. The lampstand: a symbol that the way into God's presence must always shine brightly—is always open for people to approach God (vv.1-4).
2. The Holy Bread: a symbol of Christ as the Bread of Life—God fulfills His covenant, satisfies man's hunger (vv.5-9).
3. The judgment of a man who failed to approach God but instead who cursed and blasphemed God (vv.10-23).

---

1 (24:1-4) **Lampstand—Access, into God's Presence—God, Access to—Jesus Christ, Light of the World—Light, Symbol of—Symbols, of Light**: there was the law governing the lampstand. The lampstand is a symbol that the way into God's presence must always shine brightly, that it is always open for people to approach God. Scripture has already discussed the lampstand in detail: its design (Ex.25:31-40), the instructions governing it (Ex.27:20-21), and its placement in the Tabernacle (Ex.40:24-25). A person should refer to these Scriptures as well as the outlines and notes for a full discussion of the lampstand. The lampstand was made of solid gold that was formed into the shape of seven beautiful almond branches extending out from one main stem.

OUTLINE	SCRIPTURE	SCRIPTURE	OUTLINE
1. **The lampstand: A symbol that the way into God's presence must always shine brightly—is always open for people to approach God**	And the LORD spake unto Moses, saying,	Aaron order it from the evening unto the morning before the LORD continu-	God's presence was enthroned)
a. Must provide pure olive oil to keep the light burning continually: A symbol of the Holy Spirit	2 Command the children of Israel, that they bring unto thee pure oil olive beaten for the light, to cause the lamps to burn continually.	ally: *it shall be* a statute for ever in your generations.	c. Must keep the lamp burning in the LORD's presence day & night
b. Must keep the lamp right outside the inner curtain of the Most Holy Place (where	3 Without the vail of the testimony, in the tabernacle of the congregation, shall	4 He shall order the lamps upon the pure candlestick before the LORD continually.	d. Must make a permanent law
			e. Must be tended continually, giving clear access into God's presence (a symbol of Christ, the Light of the world)

a. The people had to provide pure olive oil to keep the light burning continually (v.2). The oil was to be free from all impurities. Why? Because the oil throughout Scripture is a symbol of the Holy Spirit. The oil had to be pure, a representation of perfection, in order to symbolize the Holy Spirit of God. Note that the people had a part in keeping the light burning in the Tabernacle. The people were just as responsible as the priests or ministers for keeping the way into God's presence shining brightly.

b. The lampstand was to be placed right outside the inner curtain of the Most Holy Place (v.3). This was the Most Holy Place where the Ark of the Covenant sat. The presence of God was manifested in a very special way right above the Ark. In fact, the Ark symbolized the very throne and presence of God (see outline and notes—Ex 25:10-22 for more discussion).

c. The lamps were to burn continually in the LORD's presence, day and night (v.3). The way into God's presence was to be brightly lit, to be open always.

d. This was to be a permanent, lasting law (v.3). The lamps were never to go out. There was, of course, one exception to this: when the Tabernacle was being moved from campsite to campsite. This was understandable and obviously did not affect the meaning or symbolism of the lampstand. The people clearly understood the symbolism, that the way into God's presence was brightly lit, always open. They had open access into His presence at anytime and anyplace, from evening until morning.

e. The lamps on the lampstand had to be tended continually (v.4).

Thought 1. There are two strong lessons seen in the lampstand.

(1) The Lampstand is a symbol of Christ, the light of the world. Jesus Christ gives a clear light and open access into the presence of God. The way into God's presence can be seen clearly through Jesus Christ. In fact, the brightest light ever lit is the light of Christ into God's presence. Through Christ, the way into God's presence has been lit so brightly that it is wide open. There is not a single barrier, not even the slightest shadow, between man and God. Again, the brightest light ever lit has been set ablaze by Christ Jesus, the Son of God Himself. He is the light of the universe, giving light into God's presence for every person to enter.

"In him was life; and the life was the light of men" (Jn.1:4).

"Then spake Jesus again unto them, saying, I am the light of the world: he that followeth me shall not walk in darkness, but shall have the light of life" (Jn.8:12).

"I am come a light into the world, that whosoever believeth on me should not abide in darkness" (Jn.12:46).

"For God, who commanded the light to shine out of darkness, hath shined in our hearts, to *give* the light of the knowledge of the glory of God in the face of Jesus Christ" (2 Co.4:6).

"Wherefore he saith, Awake thou that sleepest, and arise from the dead, and Christ shall give thee light" (Ep.5:14).

"And the city had no need of the sun, neither of the moon, to shine in it: for the glory of God did lighten it, and the Lamb *is* the light thereof" (Re.21:23).

"The people that walked in darkness have seen a great light: they that dwell in the land of the shadow of death, upon them hath the light shined" (Is.9:2).

(2) The people were responsible for the oil that kept the light burning. Remember, the oil is a symbol of the Holy Spirit. Believers are responsible for keeping the light of Christ burning ever so brightly before the eyes of people. Believers are to bring the oil, the power of the Holy Spirit, to the worship of God. They are to proclaim the message of Christ, the light of the world. Scripture declares that believers themselves are the light of the world. Ever since Jesus Christ ascended into heaven, they are the representatives of Christ upon the earth. They are now the lights of the world, proclaiming the saving Light of Jesus Christ.

"Ye are the light of the world. A city that is set on an hill cannot be hid" (Mt.5:14).

"For so hath the Lord commanded us, *saying,* I have set thee to be a light of the Gentiles, that thou shouldest be for salvation unto the ends of the earth" (Ac.13:47).

"For ye were sometimes darkness, but now *are ye* light in the Lord: walk as children of light" (Ep.5:8).

"That ye may be blameless and harmless, the sons of God, without rebuke, in the midst of a crooked and perverse nation, among whom ye shine as lights in the world" (Ph.2:15).

2 (24:5-9) **Bread, Holy—Holy Bread—Bread of the Presence—Showbread—Spiritual Hunger, of Man—Bread, of Life—Symbol, of Bread—Bread, Symbol of**: there was the law governing the Holy Bread or the Showbread. The Holy Bread was also called the Presence, referring to the Presence of God. The Holy Bread set upon a small table known as the table of Showbread or the table of the Holy Bread. The table and the bread are discussed elsewhere (see outline and notes—Ex.25:23-30; 37:10-16; 40:22-23). For a complete understanding of the Holy Bread, these passages should be studied. But note, this is the only passage that covers the actual offering of the Holy Bread to the LORD. It served as an offering to the LORD for one week, then it became part of the tithe or provision for the livelihood of the priest.

OUTLINE	SCRIPTURE	SCRIPTURE	OUTLINE
2. The Holy Bread: A symbol of Christ as the Bread of Life— God fulfills His covenant, satisfies man's hunger	5 And thou shalt take fine flour, and bake twelve cakes thereof: two tenth deals shall be in one cake.	the LORD. 8 Every sabbath he shall set it in order before the LORD continually, *being taken* from the children of	d. To be replaced every Sabbath as a regular offering to the LORD
a. To bake 12 loaves of bread		Israel by an everlasting	e. To be a lasting covenant: A symbol of God's people continually offering themselves to God
b. To place the bread on the table in two rows of six each: A symbol of the twelve tribes (God's people) before the LORD's face	6 And thou shalt set them in two rows, six on a row, upon the pure table before the LORD.	covenant. 9 And it shall be Aaron's and his sons'; and they	
c. To sprinkle some pure incense near each row: To be burned in place of the bread as an offering to the LORD	7 And thou shalt put pure frankincense upon *each* row, that it may be on the bread for a memorial, *even* an offering made by fire unto	shall eat it in the holy place: for it *is* most holy unto him of the offerings of the LORD made by fire by a perpetual statute.	f. To be eaten by the priests—once removed from the table—in a holy place: Is a part of their share of the offerings (a symbol of feeding upon Christ, the Bread of Life)

a. The people were to bake 12 loaves of bread (v.5). The bread was to be baked out of fine flour, using about three quarts of flour for each loaf. Note that the people had a part in keeping the bread before the LORD, being responsible for baking it and bringing it to the Tabernacle.

b. The bread was to be placed on the table of pure gold in two rows of six each (v.6). The twelve loaves represented the twelve tribes of Israel. This was a symbol of God's people always being before the face of God.

c. The priests were to sprinkle some pure incense near each row (v.7). This incense was to be burned in place of the bread as an offering to the LORD. As the aroma of the incense ascended upward, it pleased the LORD and was acceptable to Him. The twelve tribes were offering themselves up to God, being represented by the twelve loaves sitting before His face. When the aroma ascended up, it symbolized that God was accepting the offering of their lives to Him.

d. The Holy Bread was to be replaced every Sabbath as a regular offering to the LORD (v.8).

e. The offering of the Holy Bread was to be a lasting covenant between God and His people (v.8). This is a symbol of God's people continually offering themselves to God. Each of the twelve tribes was represented in one of the loaves that set before God's face. So long as God's people remained faithful in committing their lives to Him, He would fulfill His part of the covenant. God would look after and care for His people, fulfilling His promise to lead them to the promised land.

f. The Holy Bread was to be eaten by the priests once it was removed from the table (v.9). But note, they had to eat the bread in a holy place, that is, within the Tabernacle precinct. The point is this: once the bread had served its purpose as an offering to God, it was to be eaten by the priest. None of it was to be wasted. This is a symbol of feeding upon Christ, the Bread of Life.

Thought 1. The Holy Bread paints two strong lessons for us.

(1) The Holy Bread symbolized God's people—the twelve tribes of Israel—setting their lives before the face of God, offering and placing themselves under the care of God. The believer is likewise offer himself to God, setting himself before the face of God and trusting God to take care of him. If a person will so offer himself to God, God promises that He will enter a covenant with that person. God will look after and take care of the person who trusts him; moreover, God will lead him to the promised land of heaven.

"And he said to *them* all, If any *man* will come after me, let him deny himself, and take up his cross daily, and follow me" (Lu.9:23).

"I beseech you therefore, brethren, by the mercies of God, that ye present your bodies a living sacrifice, holy, acceptable unto God, *which is* your reasonable service. And be not conformed to this world: but be ye transformed by the renewing of your mind, that ye may prove what is that good, and acceptable, and perfect, will of God" (Ro.12:1-2).

"For Moses had said, Consecrate yourselves to day to the LORD, even every man upon his son, and upon his brother; that he may bestow upon you a blessing this day" (Ex.32:29).

"Trust in the LORD with all thine heart; and lean not unto thine own understanding" (Pr.3:5).

"My son, give me thine heart, and let thine eyes observe my ways" (Pr.23:26).

(2) The Holy Bread is a symbol of Christ, the Bread of Life. The bread sitting before the face of God is a symbol that God fulfills His covenant; He satisfies man's hunger. The person who sets his life before God will be given the Bread of Life: his spiritual hunger will be met. God gave His Son, the Lord Jesus Christ, to be the Bread of Life who will satisfy the spiritual hunger of man.

"Blessed *are* they which do hunger and thirst after righteousness: for they shall be filled" (Mt.5:6).

"For the bread of God is he which cometh down from heaven, and giveth life unto the world" (Jn.6:33).

"And Jesus said unto them, I am the bread of life: he that cometh to me shall never hunger; and he that believeth on me shall never thirst" (Jn.6:35).

"I am that bread of life" (Jn.6:48).

"This is the bread which cometh down from heaven, that a man may eat thereof, and not die. I am the living bread which came down from heaven: if any man eat of this bread, he shall live for ever: and the bread that I will give is my flesh, which I will give for the life of the world" (Jn.6:50-51).

"This is that bread which came down from heaven: not as your fathers did eat manna, and are dead: he that eateth of this bread shall live for ever" (Jn.6:58).

---

3 (24:10-23) **Blasphemy—Profanity—Cursing—Vulgarity—Judgment—Rejection, of God**: there was the law governing the judgment of a man who failed to approach God but instead cursed and blasphemed God. What happened next is interesting: a man got into a fist fight, and while fighting, he cursed God, blaspheming the name of God. As a result, he was brought to Moses who held him in custody or jail until the will of God about the matter was revealed. As the incident is studied, note that God Himself pronounced the judgment, not Moses. Moreover, God used the incident to establish a permanent law concerning the cursing and blaspheming of His name. The major lesson to glean from this incident is this: the cursing and blaspheming of God's name is a serious offense. God considers it a serious offense and will execute severe judgment upon the offender. Remember, not taking the name of the LORD God in vain is one of the Ten Commandments (Ex.20:7). This is often ignored and, tragically, violated. Nevertheless, the judgment of God stands sure. His judgment upon the curser will be executed—sometimes in this life, but always in the great day of judgment.

OUTLINE	SCRIPTURE	SCRIPTURE	OUTLINE
3. The judgment of a man who failed to approach God, but instead cursed & blasphemed God	10 And the son of an Israelitish woman, whose father *was* an Egyptian, went out among the children of Israel: and this son of the Israelitish *woman* and a man of Israel strove together in the camp;	the name *of the LORD*, and cursed. And they brought him unto Moses: (and his mother's name *was* Shelomith, the daughter of Dibri, of the tribe of Dan:)	Jehovah, Yahweh)
a. The cause of the offense			b. The accounting
1) He was of mixed blood			1) He was brought to Moses
2) He was mocked & began to fight		12 And they put him in ward, that the mind of the LORD might be showed them.	
3) He was so angered that he cursed God's name (LORD—	11 And the Israelitish woman's son blasphemed		2) He was put in custody until the LORD's will was clearly known

OUTLINE	SCRIPTURE	SCRIPTURE	OUTLINE

c. The judgment of God
  1) To be taken outside the camp
  2) To have all who heard him cursing lay their hands on his head: Symbolized the removal of guilt from the hearers
  3) To execute him
 	
d. The warning to all who curses & blasphemes God's name
  1) He will be held accountable
 	
  2) He must be put to death, no matter who he is, foreigner or native-born
e. The principle of exact, perfect justice (lex talionis)
 	
  1) To execute exact justice for murder: Revenge forbidden
  2) To execute exact justice for animals willfully or
	13 And the LORD spake unto Moses, saying,
	14 Bring forth him that hath cursed without the camp; and let all that heard *him* lay their hands upon his head, and let all the congregation stone him.
	15 And thou shalt speak unto the children of Israel, saying, Whosoever curseth his God shall bear his sin.
	16 And he that blasphemeth the name of the LORD, he shall surely be put to death, *and* all the congregation shall certainly stone him: as well the stranger, as he that is born in the land, when he blasphemeth the name *of the* LORD, shall be put to death.
	17 And he that killeth any man shall surely be put to death.
	18 And he that killeth a beast shall make it good;
		beast for beast.
		19 And if a man cause a blemish in his neighbour; as he hath done, so shall it be done to him;
		20 Breach for breach, eye for eye, tooth for tooth: as he hath caused a blemish in a man, so shall it be done to him *again*.
		21 And he that killeth a beast, he shall restore it: and he that killeth a man, he shall be put to death.
		22 Ye shall have one manner of law, as well for the stranger, as for one of your own country: for I *am* the LORD your God.
		23 And Moses spake to the children of Israel, that they should bring forth him that had cursed out of the camp, and stone him with stones. And the children of Israel did as the LORD commanded Moses.
			carelessly killed: Make restitution, life for life
			  3) To execute exact justice for injuries: fracture for fracture, eye for eye, tooth for tooth
			
			  4) To execute exact justice for a death:
			  • restitution for an animal's life
			  • execution for a person's life
			  5) To execute exact justice for the foreigner as well as for the native-born
			f. The execution of the blasphemer carried out
			  1) Taken outside the camp & executed
			
			  2) The people obeyed the LORD

a. There was the cause of the offense (vv.10-11). The man was of mixed blood: his mother was an Israelite, but his father was an Egyptian who had fled Egypt with the Israelites. Obviously, the young man was mocked, and he began to fight in retaliation. During the heat of the battle he became so angered that he cursed the sacred Name of God (LORD—Jehovah, Yahweh). Some commentators hold that he did more than just use God's name profanely, that he most likely used God's name to pronounce some curse upon his opponent. However this is most unlikely. Cursing God's name is one of the most severe offenses that can be committed again, not taking His name in vain is one of the Ten Commandments. Just because cursing and vulgarity become a common practice in some societies does not lessen God's hatred of the offense. Just think about the matter for a moment: a person is cursing the name of the LORD God Himself, the very Being who created the universe, who is so holy that the bright and glorious light of His holiness consumes anything that stands illegally in His presence. On and on the person and nature of God could be described, but the point is well taken: the name of God is to be honored, not cursed, by His creatures. Cursing God is a serious matter, and the indication of Holy Scripture is that it will be severely judged.

b. There was the accounting (vv.11-12). The young man was brought to Moses and put in custody (jail) until Moses could learn God's will concerning the matter.

c. Note that God Himself pronounced the judgment not Moses (vv.13-14). God instructed Moses to have the man taken outside the camp. Then all who had heard the man cursing were to lay their hands on his head. This symbolized the removal of guilt from the hearers. This is critical to note: in God's eyes, the people who hear His name taken in vain are just as guilty as the curser until they correct him. This is how serious the cursing of God's name is. The hearers had to have their guilt removed: this was done by laying their hands on the offender's head. The offender was then executed.

d. Note the warning to all who curse and blaspheme God's name (vv.15-16): the person is to be held accountable by being put to death—no matter who he is, whether foreigner or native-born.

e. There was the principle of exact, perfect justice. Throughout the legal system of the Bible and some of the near Eastern Nations there is this fundamental principal: the punishment must match the crime. This is known as the principal of *lex talionis*. It is sometimes called the principal of retaliation or of retribution. In the Bible, however, it should be noted that the principal was seldom carried out literally. The basic principal in the Holy Scripture is that of restitution, except in the case of deliberate murder. Premeditated murder and serious sins against the family and God's holy name did merit the death penalty. But in most if not all other cases of crime, restitution that equaled the crime had to be paid. This fact is seen throughout the present list of laws governing crimes.

  1) God's people were to execute exact justice for murder: the murderer was to be put to death. Note that revenge was forbidden. Execution was to be carried out by the courts.
  2) God's people were to execute exact justice for animals that were willfully or carelessly killed. They were to make restitution equal to a life for a life (v.18).
  3) God's people were to execute exact justice for injuries (vv.19-20). They were to make restitution equal to a fracture for a fracture, an eye for an eye, a tooth for a tooth.
  4) God's people were to execute exact justice by making restitution for animal deaths and by executing murderers (v.21). Note this is the second time that the law governing murder is covered. Murder is a serious offense to God. All murderers whose crime was premeditated were to be executed.
  5) God's people were to execute exact justice for the foreigner as well as for the native-born (v.22).

f. There was the execution of the blasphemer carried out (v.23). The young man who had cursed the sacred name of God was taken outside the camp and executed. God's people obeyed the LORD.

Thought 1. Profanity, vulgarity, and cursing God are serious matters in the eyes of God. Taking the name of the LORD God in vain is even one of the Ten Commandments. The person who curses God and uses profanity of any sort will face the judgment of God (see outline and notes—Ex.20:7 for more discussion).

"Again, ye have heard that it hath been said by them of old time, Thou shalt not forswear thyself, but shalt perform unto the Lord thine oaths: But I say unto you, Swear not at all; neither by heaven; for it is God's throne: Nor by the earth; for it is his footstool: neither by Jerusalem; for it is the city of the great King. Neither shalt thou swear by thy head, because thou canst not make one hair white or black. But let your communication be, Yea, yea; Nay, nay: for whatsoever is more than these cometh of evil" (Mt.5:33-37).

"Their throat *is* an open sepulchre; with their tongues they have used deceit; the poison of asps *is* under their lips: Whose mouth *is* full of cursing and bitterness: Their feet *are* swift to shed blood: Destruction and misery *are* in their ways: And the way of peace have they not known: There is no fear of God before their eyes" (Ro.3:13-18).

"Let all bitterness, and wrath, and anger, and clamour, and evil speaking, be put away from you, with all malice" (Ep.4:31).

"Of whom is Hymenaeus and Alexander; whom I have delivered unto Satan, that they may learn not to blaspheme" (1 Ti.1:20).

"If any man among you seem to be religious, and bridleth not his tongue, but deceiveth his own heart, this man's religion *is* vain" (Js.1:26).

"Do not they blaspheme that worthy name by the which ye are called?" (Js.2:7).

"And the tongue *is* a fire, a world of iniquity: so is the tongue among our members, that it defileth the whole body, and setteth on fire the course of nature; and it is set on fire of hell" (Js.3:6).

"Therewith bless we God, even the Father; and therewith curse we men, which are made after the similitude of God. Out of the same mouth proceedeth blessing and cursing. My brethren, these things ought not so to be" (Js.3:9-10).

"But above all things, my brethren, swear not, neither by heaven, neither by the earth, neither by any other oath: but let your yea be yea; and *your* nay, nay; lest ye fall into condemnation" (Js.5:12).

"Wherefore laying aside all malice, and all guile, and hypocrisies, and envies, and all evil speakings" (1 Pe.2:1).

"For he that will love life, and see good days, let him refrain his tongue from evil, and his lips that they speak no guile" (1 Pe.3:10).

"Thou shalt not take the name of the LORD thy God in vain; for the LORD will not hold him guiltless that taketh his name in vain" (Ex.20:7).

"And ye shall not swear by my name falsely, neither shalt thou profane the name of thy God: I *am* the LORD" (Le.19:12).

"And all people of the earth shall see that thou art called by the name of the LORD; and they shall be afraid of thee" (De.28:10).

"His mouth is full of cursing and deceit and fraud: under his tongue *is* mischief and vanity. He sitteth in the lurking places of the villages: in the secret places doth he murder the innocent: his eyes are privily set against the poor....He hath said in his heart, God hath forgotten: he hideth his face; he will never see *it*" (Ps.10:7-8, 11).

"Thou givest thy mouth to evil, and thy tongue frameth deceit" (Ps.50:19).

"As he loved cursing, so let it come unto him: as he delighted not in blessing, so let it be far from him" (Ps.109:17).

"Sanctify the LORD of hosts himself; and *let* him *be* your fear, and *let* him *be* your dread" (Is.8:13).

"And I will come near to you to judgment; and I will be a swift witness against the sorcerers, and against the adulterers, and against false swearers, and against those that oppress the hireling in *his* wages, the widow, and the fatherless, and that turn aside the stranger *from his right*, and fear not me, saith the LORD of hosts" (Mal.3:5).

TYPES, SYMBOLS, AND PICTURES
Leviticus 24:1-23

Historical Term	Type or Picture (Scriptural Basis for Each)	Life Application for Today's Believer	Biblical Application
The Lampstand Le. 24:1-4	*The Lampstand is a symbol that the way into God's presence always shines brightly—is always open for people to approach God. The Lampstand is a symbol of Christ, the light of the world. Jesus Christ gives a clear light, and open access into the presence of God.*	The way into God's presence can be clearly seen through Jesus Christ. In fact, the brightest light ever lived is the light of Christ that shows the way into God's presence. Through Christ, the way into God's presence has been lit so brightly that it is wide open. There is not a single barrier,	*"In him was life; and the life was the light of men" (Jn.1:4).* *"Then spake Jesus again unto them, saying, I am the light of the world: he that followeth me shall not walk in darkness, but shall have the light of life" (Jn.8:12).* *"I am come a light into the world, that whosoever*

TYPES, SYMBOLS, AND PICTURES
Leviticus 24:1-23

Historical Term	Type or Picture (Scriptural Basis for Each)	Life Application for Today's Believer	Biblical Application
	"Command the children of Israel, that they bring unto thee pure oil olive beaten for the light, to cause the lamps to burn continually" (Le.24:2).	not even the slightest shadow of a barrier, between man and God. Again, the most brightly lit light every created has been set ablaze by Christ Jesus, the Son of God himself. He is the light of the universe, giving light into God's presence.	believeth on me should not abide in darkness" (Jn. 12:46). "For God, who commanded the light to shine out of darkness, hath shined in our hearts, to give the light of the knowledge of the glory of God in the face of Jesus Christ" (2 Co.4:6). "And the city had no need of the sun, neither of the moon, to shine in it: for the glory of God did lighten it, and the Lamb is the light thereof" (Re.21:23).
Pure Olive Oil That Kept the Lampstand Burning Continually Le. 24:2	Pure olive oil that kept the Lampstand burning continually is a symbol of the Holy Spirit. The oil had to be pure, a representation of perfection in order to symbolize the Holy Spirit of God. Note that the people had a part in keeping the light burning in the Tabernacle. The people were just as responsible as the priest or ministers for keeping the way into God's presence shining brightly. "Command the children of Israel, that they bring unto thee pure oil olive beaten for the light, to cause the lamps to burn continually" (Le.24:2).	Believers are responsible for keeping the light of Christ burning ever so brightly before the eyes of people. Believers are to bring the oil, the power of the Holy Spirit, to the worship of God, proclaiming the message of Christ the light of the world. Scripture declares that believers themselves are the light of the world. Ever since Jesus Christ ascended into heaven, they are the representatives of Christ upon the earth. They are now the lights of the world proclaiming the saving light of Jesus Christ.	"Ye are the light of the world. A city that is set on an hill cannot be hid" (Mt.5:14). "For so hath the Lord commanded us, saying, I have set thee to be a light of the Gentiles, that thou shouldest be for salvation unto the ends of the earth" (Ac.13:47). "For ye were sometimes darkness, but now are ye light in the Lord: walk as children of light" (Ep.5:8). "That ye may be blameless and harmless, the sons of God, without rebuke, in the midst of a crooked and perverse nation, among whom ye shine as lights in the world" (Ph.2:15).
The High Priest Tending the Lampstand Continually Le. 24:4	The High Priest tending the Lampstand continually is a symbol of Christ, the Light of the World. "He [Aaron, the High Priest] shall order the lamps upon the pure candlestick before the LORD continually" (Le.24:4).	Believers are now the light of the world. Jesus said, "As long as I am in the world, I am the light of the world" (John 9:5). Jesus is no longer in the world, not bodily. His light is now in the lives of believers. Believers are reflections of Him.	"For ye were sometimes darkness, but now are ye light in the Lord: walk as children of light" (Ep.5:8). "The night is far spent, the day is at hand: let us therefore cast off the works of darkness, and let us put on the armour of light" (Ro.13:12). "That ye may be blameless and harmless, the sons of God, without rebuke, in the midst of a crooked and perverse nation, among whom ye shine as lights in the world" (Ph.2:15).
The Holy Bread Le. 24:5-9	There are three symbols associated with the Holy Bread: 1. The Holy Bread is a symbol of Christ as the Bread of Life—God	The Holy Bread paints two strong lessons for us: 1. The believer is to offer himself to God, setting himself before the face	"And he said to them all, If any man will come after me, let him deny himself, and take up his cross daily, and follow me" (Lu.9:23).

TYPES, SYMBOLS, AND PICTURES
Leviticus 24:1-23

Historical Term	Type or Picture (Scriptural Basis for Each)	Life Application for Today's Believer	Biblical Application
	fulfills His covenant, satisfies man's hunger. 2. *The Holy Bread is a symbol of God's people (the twelve tribes of Israel)—setting their lives before the face of God, offering and placing themselves under the care of God.* 3. *The aroma of the burning incense that ascended up symbolizes that God was accepting the offering of their lives to Him.* **"Every sabbath he shall set it [the holy bread] in order before the LORD continually,** *being taken* **from the children of Israel by an everlasting covenant"** **(Le.24:8).**	of God and trusting God to take care of him. If a person so offers himself to God, God promises that he will enter a covenant with the person. God will take care and look after the person who trusts him; moreover, God will lead him to the promise land of heaven. 2. The person who sets his life before God will be given the Bread of Life: his spiritual hunger will be met. God gave his Son, the Lord Jesus Christ, to be the Bread who will satisfy the spiritual hunger of man.	*"I beseech you therefore, brethren, by the mercies of God, that ye present your bodies a living sacrifice, holy, acceptable unto God, which is your reasonable service. And be not conformed to this world: but be ye transformed by the renewing of your mind, that ye may prove what is that good, and acceptable, and perfect, will of God"* *(Ro.12:1-2).* *"Blessed are they which do hunger and thirst after righteousness: for they shall be filled"* *(Mt.5:6).* *"For the bread of God is he which cometh down from heaven, and giveth life unto the world"* *(Jn.6:33).* *"And Jesus said unto them, I am the bread of life: he that cometh to me shall never hunger; and he that believeth on me shall never thirst"* *(Jn.6:35; see Jn.6:58).*
The Laying of Hands on the Person Who Cursed God Le. 24:10-23	*The laying of hands on the person who cursed God symbolized the removal of guilt from the hearers. This is critical to note: in God's eyes, the cursing of His name is so serious that the people who hear His name taken in vain are just as guilty as the curser until they correct him. The hearers had to have their guilt removed: this was done by laying their hands on the offender who was to be executed.* **"Bring forth him that hath cursed without the camp; and let all that heard** *him* **lay their hands upon his head, and let all the congregation stone him"** **(Le.24:14).**	Profanity, vulgarity, and cursing God are serious matters in the eyes of God. Taking the name of the Lord God in vain is even one of the Ten Commandments. The person who curses God and uses profanity of any sort will face the judgment of God.	*"Thou shalt not take the name of the LORD thy God in vain; for the LORD will not hold him guiltless that taketh his name in vain"* *(Ex.20:7).* *"But above all things, my brethren, swear not, neither by heaven, neither by the earth, neither by any other oath: but let your yea be yea; and your nay, nay; lest ye fall into condemnation"* *(Js.5:12).* *"And all people of the earth shall see that thou art called by the name of the LORD; and they shall be afraid of thee"* *(De.28:10).* *"As he loved cursing, so let it come unto him: as he delighted not in blessing, so let it be far from him"* *(Ps.109:17).* *"Wherefore laying aside all malice, and all guile, and hypocrisies, and envies, and all evil speakings"* *(1 Pe.2:1; see 1 Ti.1:20).*

CHAPTER 25

I. Laws That Govern the Use of Property & the Treatment of the Poor: Social Justice—Proclaim Liberty Throughout the Land, 25:1-55

1. The Lawgiver: God Himself

2. The Sabbatical Year
a. The law: Must give the land a "Sabbath of rest"—dedicated to the LORD
  1) To plant & reap for six years
  2) To give the land a "Sabbath of rest" during the seventh year—dedicated to the LORD
    • Not to sow the fields nor prune the vineyards
    • Not to reap what grows
    • To give the land a year of rest
b. The provisions of food: Are to gather from the land only what naturally grows & is needed
  1) For oneself (family)
  2) For one's servants
  3) For one's employees
  4) For any temporary resident
  5) For livestock
  6) For wild animals

3. The Year of Jubilee—the rules for observing
a. The law
  1) To keep count of seven Sabbatical Years: To equal 49 years
  2) To then sound forth the trumpet on the Day of Atonement—all across the land
  3) To sanctify, set apart, the 50th year as the Jubilee: Proclaim liberty throughout all the land
    • Release all people to return to their families' property & clan
    • Release all property to the original family

And the LORD spake unto Moses in mount Sinai, saying,
2 Speak unto the children of Israel, and say unto them, When ye come into the land which I give you, then shall the land keep a sabbath unto the LORD.
3 Six years thou shalt sow thy field, and six years thou shalt prune thy vineyard, and gather in the fruit thereof;
4 But in the seventh year shall be a sabbath of rest unto the land, a sabbath for the LORD: thou shalt neither sow thy field, nor prune thy vineyard.
5 That which groweth of its own accord of thy harvest thou shalt not reap, neither gather the grapes of thy vine undressed: *for* it is a year of rest unto the land.
6 And the sabbath of the land shall be meat for you; for thee, and for thy servant, and for thy maid, and for thy hired servant, and for thy stranger that sojourneth with thee,
7 And for thy cattle, and for the beast that *are* in thy land, shall all the increase thereof be meat.
8 And thou shalt number seven sabbaths of years unto thee, seven times seven years; and the space of the seven sabbaths of years shall be unto thee forty and nine years.
9 Then shalt thou cause the trumpet of the jubile to sound on the tenth *day* of the seventh month, in the day of atonement shall ye make the trumpet sound throughout all your land.
10 And ye shall hallow the fiftieth year, and proclaim liberty throughout *all* the land unto all the inhabitants thereof: it shall be a jubile unto you; and ye shall return every man unto his possession, and ye shall return every man unto his family.
11 A jubile shall that fiftieth year be unto you: ye shall not sow, neither reap that which groweth of itself in it, nor gather *the grapes* in it of thy vine undressed.
12 For it *is* the jubile; it shall be holy unto you: ye shall eat the increase thereof out of the field.
13 In the year of this jubile ye shall return every man unto his possession.
14 And if thou sell ought unto thy neighbour, or buyest *ought* of thy neighbour's hand, ye shall not oppress one another:
15 According to the number of years after the jubile thou shalt buy of thy neighbour, *and* according unto the number of years of the fruits he shall sell unto thee:
16 According to the multitude of years thou shalt increase the price thereof, and according to the fewness of years thou shalt diminish the price of it: for *according* to the number *of the years* of the fruits doth he sell unto thee.
17 Ye shall not therefore oppress one another; but thou shalt fear thy God: for I *am* the LORD your God.
18 Wherefore ye shall do my statutes, and keep my judgments, and do them; and ye shall dwell in the land in safety.
19 And the land shall yield her fruit, and ye shall eat your fill, and dwell therein in safety.
20 And if ye shall say, What shall we eat the seventh year? behold, we shall not sow, nor gather in our increase:
21 Then I will command my blessing upon you in the sixth year, and it shall bring forth fruit for three years.
22 And ye shall sow the eighth year, and eat *yet* of old fruit until the ninth year; until her fruits come in ye shall eat *of* the old *store*.
23 The land shall not be sold for ever: for the land *is* mine; for ye *are* strangers and sojourners with me.
24 And in all the land of your possession ye shall grant a redemption for the land.

b. The rules to govern the Jubilee
  1) To make the 50th year a Jubilee
  2) To let the land rest
  3) To make the Jubilee a holy year
  4) To eat only what grows naturally
  5) To return to one's own property
  6) To be fair & just in business dealings: Not to take advantage of one another in buying & selling
    • To buy on the basis of the Jubilee Year: Setting the price in proportion to the years since the Jubilee
    • To sell based on the number or years of crops left before the Jubilee

c. The warning: Must fear God & not take advantage of people

d. The promise of God: Will provide for His people
  1) The promise is conditional: Must obey God's laws
  2) The promise: Will live in safety & have plenty to eat
  3) The natural, expected question: What can we eat if we do not plant crops?
  4) The promise of God reemphasized & explained: He will bless the crops of the sixth year; they will yield enough for three years

4. The Year of Jubilee: The redemption of property
a. The law: The land must be leased, never permanently sold
  1) Because it belongs to God
  2) The law: Must provide for the land to be redeemed, bought back

281

b. Case 1—a person is forced to sell some property: The nearest relative is to buy it back for him, if possible (a symbol of Christ our Kinsman-Redeemer)

c. Case 2—the person prospers & is able to redeem his own property
 1) He is to have the right to buy it back
 2) He is to pay a fair market price for the property: To be based on the number of crops left until the next Jubilee
 3) He can then return

d. Case 3—the original owner is never able to redeem or buy back his property
 1) The buyer keeps the property until the Jubilee
 2) The buyer returns the property in the Year of Jubilee (a symbol of free grace)

e. Case 4—a person sells a house in a walled city
 1) The right of repurchase is to be set for one year
 2) The house, after one year, belongs to the buyer & his descendants permanently
 3) The house is not returned in the Jubilee

f. Case 5—a house in a village without walls
 1) The house is to be treated like property in open fields
 2) The house can be bought back & is to be returned in the Jubilee

g. Case 6—the houses of the Levites, the priests, in the Levitical towns belonging to them
 1) Their houses are always redeemable
 2) Their houses are to be returned in the Jubilee

 3) Their pasture land must never be sold: It is their permanent ancestral property

5. The Year of Jubilee: The protection & treatment of the poor
 a. Case 1: A person becomes poor & cannot support himself

25 If thy brother be waxen poor, and hath sold away *some* of his possession, and if any of his kin come to redeem it, then shall he redeem that which his brother sold. 26 And if the man have none to redeem it, and himself be able to redeem it; 27 Then let him count the years of the sale thereof, and restore the overplus unto the man to whom he sold it; that he may return unto his possession. 28 But if he be not able to restore *it* to him, then that which is sold shall remain in the hand of him that hath bought it until the year of jubile: and in the jubile it shall go out, and he shall return unto his possession. 29 And if a man sell a dwelling house in a walled city, then he may redeem it within a whole year after it is sold; *within* a full year may he redeem it. 30 And if it be not redeemed within the space of a full year, then the house that *is* in the walled city shall be established for ever to him that bought it throughout his generations: it shall not go out in the jubile. 31 But the houses of the villages which have no wall round about them shall be counted as the fields of the country: they may be redeemed, and they shall go out in the jubile. 32 Notwithstanding the cities of the Levites, *and* the houses of the cities of their possession, may the Levites redeem at any time. 33 And if a man purchase of the Levites, then the house that was sold, and the city of his possession, shall go out in *the year of* jubile: for the houses of the cities of the Levites *are* their possession among the children of Israel. 34 But the field of the suburbs of their cities may not be sold; for it *is* their perpetual possession. 35 And if thy brother be waxen poor, and fallen in decay with thee; then thou shalt relieve him: *yea,*

though he be a stranger, or a sojourner; that he may live with thee. 36 Take thou no usury of him, or increase: but fear thy God; that thy brother may live with thee. 37 Thou shalt not give him thy money upon usury, nor lend him thy victuals for increase. 38 I *am* the LORD your God, which brought you forth out of the land of Egypt, to give you the land of Canaan, *and* to be your God. 39 And if thy brother *that dwelleth* by thee be waxen poor, and be sold unto thee; thou shalt not compel him to serve as a bondservant: 40 *But* as an hired servant, *and* as a sojourner, he shall be with thee, *and* shall serve thee unto the year of jubile: 41 And *then* shall he depart from thee, *both* he and his children with him, and shall return unto his own family, and unto the possession of his fathers shall he return. 42 For they *are* my servants, which I brought forth out of the land of Egypt: they shall not be sold as bondmen. 43 Thou shalt not rule over him with rigour; but shalt fear thy God. 44 Both thy bondmen, and thy bondmaids, which thou shalt have, *shall be* of the heathen that are round about you; of them shall ye buy bondmen and bondmaids. 45 Moreover of the children of the strangers that do sojourn among you, of them shall ye buy, and of their families that *are* with you, which they begat in your land: and they shall be your possession. 46 And ye shall take them as an inheritance for your children after you, to inherit *them for* a possession; they shall be your bondmen for ever: but over your brethren the children of Israel, ye shall not rule one over another with rigour. 47 And if a sojourner or stranger wax rich by thee, and thy brother *that dwelleth* by him wax poor, and sell himself unto the stranger *or*

1) Are to help him

2) Are not to charge interest on loans to him, but rather fear God

3) The point restressed: Are not to charge interest nor sell food at a profit

4) The warning: "I am the LORD your God" who helped you
 • Delivered you out of Egypt
 • Am giving you the promised land

b. Case 2: A person becomes poor & has to sell his labor
 1) Not to be treated as a slave

 2) To be treated as an employee or temporary resident
 3) To be employed until the Year of Jubilee
 4) To be released & returned to his own property & clan

 5) The reason: Because God delivered the Israelites to be His servants

 • No person is to rule over them ruthlessly
 • A person must fear God

 6) The exception
 • Foreigners who were poor & had to sell themselves just to have shelter & food could be held as slaves

 • Temporary residents who needed shelter & food could sell themselves and be held as slaves
 • A person could will the poor to his children as inherited property, as slaves for life, but could never mistreat the poor

c. Case 3: A person becomes bankrupt & sells himself to a resident foreigner

1) He retains the right of redemption, of being bought back	sojourner by thee, or to the stock of the stranger's family:	the price of his redemption out of the money that he was bought for.	
• A relative—called a "kinsman redeemer," a type of Christ—may buy him: An uncle, cousin, or blood relative	48 After that he is sold he may be redeemed again; one of his brethren may redeem him:	52 And if there remain but few years unto the year of jubile, then he shall count with him, *and* according unto his years shall he give him again the price of his redemption.	• If few years remain until the Jubilee Year, he is to compute the price & pay accordingly
• He may buy himself back	49 Either his uncle, or his uncle's son, may redeem him, or *any* that is nigh of kin unto him of his family may redeem him; or if he be able, he may redeem himself.		3) He is to be treated as a servant hired from year-to-year: He is not to be treated ruthlessly
2) He is to pay the buyer a fair market value based on the Jubilee Year: To pay the rate it would cost to hire a servant for that number of years	50 And he shall reckon with him that bought him from the year that he was sold to him unto the year of jubile: and the price of his sale shall be according unto the number of years, according to the time of an hired servant shall it be with him.	53 *And* as a yearly hired servant shall he be with him: *and the other* shall not rule with rigour over him in thy sight.	4) He is to be released, set free, in the Year of Jubilee
		54 And if he be not redeemed in these *years*, then he shall go out in the year of jubile, *both* he, and his children with him.	
	51 If *there be* yet many years *behind*, according unto them he shall give again	55 For unto me the children of Israel *are* servants; they *are* my servants whom I brought forth out of the land of Egypt: I *am* the LORD your God.	5) The reason • He is God's servant • He was freed from Egypt (the world) to serve God
• If many years remain, he is to pay most of what the buyer paid him, if any			

DIVISION IV

THE WAY TO LIVE A HOLY LIFE BEFORE GOD (PART 2): A PURE SPIRIT (SANCTIFICATION) 17:1–27:34)

I. Laws That Govern the Use of Property and the Treatment of the Poor: Social Justice—Proclaim Liberty Throughout the Land, 25:1-55

(25:1-55) **Introduction—Property, Land**: most people either own or want to own some land, a home they can call their own. Most societies have laws that govern the purchase, the sale and the use of land within its borders. When God's people reached the promised land of Canaan, they were going to need laws that would govern the use of their land. The land was going to actually be divided among the twelve tribes of Israel, and then within the twelve tribes, every family was going to receive the gift of some land. Therefore, laws had to be established to govern the buying and selling of the land and the use to which it could be put. In dealing with the promised land, God wanted His people to understand one clear truth: the land belonged to God. "The land is mine," He forcefully declared (Le.25:23).

God was giving the land to his people as a sacred, holy gift. Therefore, the people were never allowed to sell their land. The farms were to belong to the ancestral families down through the generations. How could such a system of land ownership ever work within any society? There is always a tendency for the rich to increase their holdings at the expense of the poor. This is the subject of the present Scripture: *Laws That Govern the Use of Property and the Treatment of the Poor: Social Justice—Proclaim Liberty Throughout the Land*, 25:1-55.

1. The Lawgiver: God Himself (v.1).
2. The Sabbatical Year (vv.2-7).
3. The Year of Jubilee—the rules for observing (vv.8-22).
4. The Year of Jubilee: the redemption of property (vv.23-34).
5. The Year of Jubilee: the protection and treatment of the poor (vv.35-55).

1 (25:1) **Law, Source of—Lawgiver, The**: there was the lawgiver, God Himself. Note the Scripture and Outline:

OUTLINE	SCRIPTURE
1. The Lawgiver: God Himself	And the LORD spake unto Moses in mount Sinai, saying,

Concern for the poor lays heavily upon Gods heart, for the poor are so often mistreated and abused. Some people, of course, are poor because of being lazy, slothful, and irresponsible. Scripture never encourages nor even suggests that the lazy and slothful be fed and housed. The message to these people is clear and forceful: be responsible and go to work. On the other hand there are many people who are poor due to circumstances beyond their control. It is these that God expects His people to help. This is the reason God is addressing these laws governing the use of property and the treatment of the poor. Social justice is a concern to God, a vital concern. When it comes to the distribution of wealth and the care of the poor, God wants His people to be fair and compassionate. God wants liberty to be proclaimed throughout all the land, liberty for all people.

2 (25:2-7) **Sabbatical Year—Year, Sabbatical—Land, Law Governing—Law, Governing Land**: there was the law governing the Sabbatical Year. One of the earliest institutions established by God was the Sabbath Day. Right after creating the universe, God rested on the seventh day. On that very day, He declared that the seventh day was to be set apart in a very special way: it was to be remembered as the Day of the LORD, a day to be kept holy. Man was to use the day only for rest and worship. Now God established an additional institution for His people, the seventh year. Note the Scripture and outline:

OUTLINE	SCRIPTURE	SCRIPTURE	OUTLINE
2. The Sabbatical Year a. The law: Must give the land a "Sabbath of rest"—dedicated to the LORD 1) To plant & reap for six years 2) To give the land a "Sabbath of rest" during the seventh year—dedicated to the LORD • Not to sow the fields nor prune the vineyards	2 Speak unto the children of Israel, and say unto them, When ye come into the land which I give you, then shall the land keep a sabbath unto the LORD. 3 Six years thou shalt sow thy field, and six years thou shalt prune thy vineyard, and gather in the fruit thereof; 4 But in the seventh year shall be a sabbath of rest unto the land, a sabbath for the LORD: thou shalt neither sow thy field, nor prune thy vineyard.	5 That which groweth of its own accord of thy harvest thou shalt not reap, neither gather the grapes of thy vine undressed: *for* it is a year of rest unto the land. 6 And the sabbath of the land shall be meat for you; for thee, and for thy servant, and for thy maid, and for thy hired servant, and for thy stranger that sojourneth with thee, 7 And for thy cattle, and for the beast that *are* in thy land, shall all the increase thereof be meat.	• Not to reap what grows • To give the land a year of rest b. The provisions of food: Are to gather from the land only what naturally grows & is needed 1) For oneself (family) 2) For one's servants 3) For one's employees 4) For any temporary resident 5) For livestock 6) For wild animals

The Sabbatical year was to be a year when the land was to lie fallow, untilled and undisturbed. This is astounding. To think that God set aside a seventh day of rest for His people and a seventh year of rest for the land. This was long before farmers knew the wisdom of rotating crops in order to preserve the soil, long before they knew the benefits of letting fields lie fallow for a year. But God knew, and He had promised to take care of His people. Therefore, He gave this law of the Sabbatical Year.

Thought 1. The Sabbatical Year taught God's people to trust and depend upon Him. They had to trust God during the sixth year...
- that He would give enough rain and good seed
- that He would control the insects and disease of crops
- that He would give a long season and a fruitful harvest

Thought 2. The Sabbatical Year speaks strongly against covetousness. By keeping the Sabbatical Year, God's people were being taught to obey the commandment of God: "You shall not covet" (Ex.20:17). But God's people failed to keep the Sabbatical Year. During a 490 year period, they failed to keep the required 70 Sabbatical Years. As a result, God's judgment fell upon them, and they were conquered and taken into captivity by the Babylonians (2 Chr.36:21).[1]

> "**Study to show thyself approved unto God, a workman that needeth not to be ashamed, rightly dividing the word of truth**" (2 Ti.2:15).
> "**All scripture** *is* **given by inspiration of God, and** *is* **profitable for doctrine, for reproof, for correction, for instruction in righteousness**" (2 Ti.3:16).

Thought 3. The basic idea behind the Sabbath or seventh day is rest and worship. The Sabbatical Year gave God's people additional time to learn more about God, drawing ever closer to Him. They had more time to study God's law and to pray. The lesson for us is clear: God wants us to take time to learn more about Him, time to draw closer to Him. He wants us to live in His Word and in prayer.

Thought 4. The Sabbath or seventh day refers back to the perfect creation of God, the day of God's perfect rest. This is a symbol of the rest of redemption, of the spiritual rest that God promises the believer.

> "**There remaineth therefore a rest to the people of God. For he that is entered into his rest, he also hath ceased from his own works, as God** *did* **from his. Let us labour therefore to enter into that rest, lest any man fall after the same example of unbelief**" (He.4:9-11).

The lesson is graphic: we are to trust God for our livelihood. We are to trust Him for food, clothing, and housing. God makes this striking promise: If we will seek Him first, He will give us the necessities of life.

> "**But seek ye first the kingdom of God, and his righteousness; and all these things shall be added unto you**" (Mt.6:33).
> "**But my God shall supply all your need according to his riches in glory by Christ Jesus**" (Ph.4:19).
> "**And ye shall serve the LORD your God, and he shall bless thy bread, and thy water; and I will take sickness away from the midst of thee**" (Ex.23:25).

---

[1] J. Vernon McGee, *Thru The Bible*, Vol.1, p.437.

"And thou shalt gird them with girdles, Aaron and his sons, and put the bonnets on them: and the priest's office shall be theirs for a perpetual statute: and thou shalt consecrate Aaron and his sons" (Ex.29:9).

"And the LORD thy God will make thee plenteous in every work of thine hand, in the fruit of thy body, and in the fruit of thy cattle, and in the fruit of thy land, for good: for the LORD will again rejoice over thee for good, as he rejoiced over thy fathers" (De.30:9).

"*Oh* how great *is* thy goodness, which thou hast laid up for them that fear thee; *which* thou hast wrought for them that trust in thee before the sons of men!" (Ps.31:19).

"Blessed *be* the LORD, *who* daily loadeth us *with benefits, even* the God of our salvation. Selah" (Ps.68:19).

"I will abundantly bless her provision: I will satisfy her poor with bread" (Ps.132:15).

---

3 (25:8-22) **Jubilee, Year of—Year, of Jubilee—Law, Governing the Jubilee**: there was the law governing the Year of Jubilee. The Sabbatical Year of rest was not all that God set aside for His people. He also established the *Year of Jubilee. Jubilee* refers to a fifty-year celebration of liberty, freedom, and redemption. The Year of Jubilee proclaimed one of the greatest messages God ever gave His people: the message of freedom and redemption. It is the message inscribed on the Liberty Bell of the United States of America: "Proclaim liberty throughout all the land to all its inhabitants" (v.10).

In the Year of Jubilee everyone and everything was set free. If a person had sold or mortgaged his land, it was set free and returned to the original owner. If a person had sold himself or his labor as a slave in order to eat and live, he was set free. All debts and financial obligations were written off as well as all labor obligations. All obligations and enslavements due to debt were wiped out. All land was returned to the family of the original owner and every owner and family member returned to his family homestead (see Is.61:1; Je.34:8-17; Eze.46:17).

The word *Jubilee* (Yobel) means a ram's horn or the blowing of a ram's horn. The year was apparently to be announced by various horn-blowers stationed within each city and tribe throughout the land. A clear understanding of the Jubilee year can be gained by glancing at the Scripture and outline:

OUTLINE	SCRIPTURE	SCRIPTURE	OUTLINE
3. The Year of Jubilee—the rules for observing a. The law 1) To keep count of seven Sabbatical Years: To equal 49 years	8 And thou shalt number seven sabbaths of years unto thee, seven times seven years; and the space of the seven sabbaths of years shall be unto thee forty and nine years.	15 According to the number of years after the jubile thou shalt buy of thy neighbour, *and* according unto the number of years of the fruits he shall sell unto thee:	• To buy on the basis of the Jubilee Year: Setting the price in proportion to the years left before the Jubilee
2) To then sound forth the trumpet on the Day of Atonement—all across the land	9 Then shalt thou cause the trumpet of the jubile to sound on the tenth *day* of the seventh month, in the day of atonement shall ye make the trumpet sound throughout all your land.	16 According to the multitude of years thou shalt increase the price thereof, and according to the fewness of years thou shalt diminish the price of it: for *according* to the number *of the years* of the fruits doth he sell unto thee.	• To set the price based on the number or years of crops left

3) To sanctify, set apart, the 50th year as the Jubilee: Proclaim liberty throughout all the land
  • Release all people to return to their families' property & clan
  • Release all property to the original family
	10 And ye shall hallow the fiftieth year, and proclaim liberty throughout *all* the land unto all the inhabitants thereof: it shall be a jubile unto you; and ye shall return every man unto his possession, and ye shall return every man unto his family	17 Ye shall not therefore oppress one another; but thou shalt fear thy God: for I *am* the LORD your God.
		18 Wherefore ye shall do my statutes, and keep my judgments, and do them; and ye shall dwell in the land in safety.
			c. The warning: Must fear God & not take advantage of people
			d. The promise of God
			  1) The promise is conditional: Must obey God's laws

b. To return to one's family property & clan
  1) The rules to govern the Jubilee
  2) To let the land rest
 	
  3) To make the Jubilee a holy year
  4) To eat only what grows naturally
  5) To return to one's own property
  6) To be fair & just in business dealings: Not to take advantage of one another in buying & selling
	11 A jubile shall that fiftieth year be unto you: ye shall not sow, neither reap that which groweth of itself in it, nor gather *the grapes* in it of thy vine undressed.
	12 For it *is* the jubile; it shall be holy unto you: ye shall eat the increase thereof out of the field.
	13 In the year of this jubile ye shall return every man unto his possession.
	14 And if thou sell ought unto thy neighbour, or buyest *ought* of thy neighbour's hand, ye shall not oppress one another:
		19 And the land shall yield her fruit, and ye shall eat your fill, and dwell therein in safety.
		20 And if ye shall say, What shall we eat the seventh year? behold, we shall not sow, nor gather in our increase:
		21 Then I will command my blessing upon you in the sixth year, and it shall bring forth fruit for three years.
		22 And ye shall sow the eighth year, and eat *yet* of old fruit until the ninth year; until her fruits come in ye shall eat *of* the old *store*.
			2) The promise: Will live in safety & have plenty to eat
			
			3) The natural, expected question: What can we eat if we do not plant crops?
			
			4) The promise of God reemphasized & explained: He will bless the crops of the sixth year; they will yield enough for three years

Thought 1. In the Year of Jubilee every person returned to the land—the promised land—originally given him. When a person receives Jesus Christ, he is reconciled to God and the hope of the promised land becomes his. God promises the hope of heaven to every person who comes to Him through the Lord Jesus Christ.

> "For the hope which is laid up for you in heaven, whereof ye heard before in the word of the truth of the gospel" (Col.1:5).
> "Teaching us that, denying ungodliness and worldly lusts, we should live soberly, righteously, and godly, in this present world; Looking for that blessed hope, and the glorious appearing of the great God and our Saviour Jesus Christ" (Tit.2:12-13).
> "Blessed *be* the God and Father of our Lord Jesus Christ, which according to his abundant mercy hath begotten us again unto a lively hope by the resurrection of Jesus Christ from the dead, To an inheritance incorruptible, and undefiled, and that fadeth not away, reserved in heaven for you" (1 Pe.1:3-4).

Thought 2. In the Year of Jubilee every debt was paid: every person was set free to return home. So it is with the day of salvation. Jesus Christ paid the debt of sin for the believer: the note of debt against the believer is canceled by Christ and the believer is set free by Christ. He canceled the note of debt. Jesus Christ sets the true believer free.

> "But God be thanked, that ye were the servants of sin, but ye have obeyed from the heart that form of doctrine which was delivered you. Being then made free from sin, ye became the servants of righteousness. For the wages of sin *is* death; but the gift of God *is* eternal life through Jesus Christ our Lord" (Ro.6:17-18, 23).
> "But now being made free from sin, and become servants to God, ye have your fruit unto holiness, and the end everlasting life" (Ro.6:22).
> "For the law of the Spirit of life in Christ Jesus hath made me free from the law of sin and death. (Ro.8:2).
> "Now the Lord is that Spirit: and where the Spirit of the Lord *is,* there *is* liberty" (2 Co.3:17).
> "For he hath made him *to be* sin for us, who knew no sin; that we might be made the righteousness of God in him" (2 Co.5:21).
> "Who gave himself for our sins, that he might deliver us from this present evil world, according to the will of God and our Father" (Ga.1:4).
> "Stand fast therefore in the liberty wherewith Christ hath made us free, and be not entangled again with the yoke of bondage" (Ga.5:1).
> "The Spirit of the LORD GOD *is* upon me; because the LORD hath anointed me to preach good tidings unto the meek; he hath sent me to bind up the brokenhearted, to proclaim liberty to the captives, and the opening of the prison to *them that are* bound" (Is.61:1).

Thought 3. Note that the trumpet announcing the Year of Jubilee was blown on the Day of Atonement (v.9). Sacrifice for sin had to be made before a person was set free. A person has to approach God through the sacrifice of the Lord Jesus Christ before he can be reconciled to God and set free. Through Christ he is set free to live in peace and victory over all the trials and temptations of life.

> "That it might be fulfilled which was spoken by Esaias the prophet, saying, Himself took our infirmities, and bare *our* sicknesses" (Mt.8:17).
> "Therefore being justified by faith, we have peace with God through our Lord Jesus Christ: By whom also we have access by faith into this grace wherein we stand, and rejoice in hope of the glory of God" (Ro.5:1-2).
> "Who shall separate us from the love of Christ? *shall* tribulation, or distress, or persecution, or famine, or nakedness, or peril, or sword?" (Ro.8:35).
> "Nay, in all these things we are more than conquerors through him that loved us" (Ro.8:37).
> "Now thanks *be* unto God, which always causeth us to triumph in Christ, and maketh manifest the savour of his knowledge by us in every place" (2 Co.2:14).
> "Who his own self bare our sins in his own body on the tree, that we, being dead to sins, should live unto righteousness: by whose stripes ye were healed" (1 Pe.2:24).
> "For Christ also hath once suffered for sins, the just for the unjust, that he might bring us to God, being put to death in the flesh, but quickened by the Spirit" (1 Pe.3:18).
> "For whatsoever is born of God overcometh the world: and this is the victory that overcometh the world, *even* our faith. Who is he that overcometh the world, but he that believeth that Jesus is the Son of God?" (1 Jn.5:4-5).
> "But he *was* wounded for our transgressions, *he was* bruised for our iniquities: the chastisement of our peace *was* upon him; and with his stripes we are healed" (Is.53:5).

Thought 4. *This civil legislation was good and proper for Israel in her situation, but it was no longer applicable to Israel after she became mingled among the nations. Christians can, however, gather from these laws principles of good government that we can strive to have adopted today. Good laws are based on good principles of ethics and morality that are ingrained in the human heart but are found more completely in the Word of God.*
"For instance, cities today usually require fences to be built around swimming pools. Also today governments have a duty toward the poor. It is a duty of mercy and justice both. The poor need more than land in Central America or money in a city ghetto. They need care, advice, support, and also restraint and punishment for crime. A good government should deal effectively with these problems. Christian citizens should also be concerned in these areas as

city missions have been for years in a small way. Christians can add, in addition to physical help, the basic ingredient of God's saving grace, which the government cannot directly offer.[2]

Thought 5. *This was the communal sharing that works well in a family where all have the strongest ties of love and interest. Even in families the system breaks down if the common bond is not there. Israel, like the early church, was a community of people united in worship of the true God and sanctified in him. In times of revival, at least, the bulk of Israel's citizens would have been God-fearing men and women earnest in obeying God's law.*

During the present age of puriformity, with the church a separated body gathered out of the world, there is no exact parallel to the nation of Israel. No rule of the saints, such as the Puritans envisaged, long endures today. Even Israel's land reforms probably would not be tolerated today by a self-seeking citizenry. These land laws cannot be duplicated in our day, but they can teach us the importance of curbing the tendency to increase wealth in the hands of the few. The poor had better be protected in any society, or revolts will follow as wealth accumulates and people decay.[3]

Thought 6. *The success of laws such as these depended on the people's obedience, but the system still would not work except for the special blessing of God, who owned the land and also the people and had his sovereign purposes for both (vv.18-19). Verse 21 underlines the importance of the providential blessing of God. It was doubtless good for the land to lie fallow one year. God would bless an obedient nation with rains, and pests would cease under his hand. Unfortunately the nation turned to other gods, and God vacated the land until it had 'enjoyed its sabbath rests" (2 Chron 36:21).*[4]

---

4 (25:23-34) **Property, Laws Governing—Property—Year of Jubilee—Jubilee, Year of—Kinsman-Redeemer—Jesus Christ, Symbolized by**: there was the law governing the redemption of property during the Year of Jubilee. Remember, the Jubilee took place every 50 years. A large number of people would be forced to mortgage or lease their land out during such a long period of time. Moreover, a large number of people would die and never be able to return to their property if they had to wait a decade or more before the Jubilee came back around. God knew this. Furthermore, God was giving the land for the enjoyment of His people...

* that they might provide a livelihood for themselves, living in peace and security
* that they might learn to trust Him more and more
* that they might have a base from which to bear a strong witness to the surrounding people

Simply stated, God wanted His people living on the land that He was giving them. Therefore, if a person lost his land due to some debt, God made provision for the land to be recovered by the family. By law, a family member who had the money was allowed to pay the debt off allowing his relative to return to the land, reimbursing him when possible. Of course, the relative who paid the note off could just tear up the note and allow the owner to return to his property free and clear. This particular law is called the *Kinsman-Redeemer* Law. This, of course, is a symbol of Christ, our *Kinsman-Redeemer*. There is an excellent example of the Kinsman-Redeemer Law being worked out in the Book of Ruth. Because of either debt or poverty, Naomi's family had to sell their land. A close relative was apparently willing to redeem the land for her, thinking that she had no heirs and that he would eventually inherit the land himself. However, when he found out that he had to marry Ruth, who was a widow, in order to raise up an heir who would inherit the land, he backed out of the deal and refused to redeem the land. (See the Book of *Ruth*.)

Note one other significant fact: the land is God's. God clearly says, "The land is mine" (v.23). The land really belongs to God. He was giving the land to His people, but it was only a temporary gift. His people were, so to speak, only foreigners and tenants on the land. The fact to keep in mind is that the land was a gift from God (Ge.15:7, 17:8, 24:7; Ex.6:4; Le.20:24; 25:2, 23, 38; De.5:16). God was going to give some land to each tribe and to each family within each tribe (Nu.32; Jos.13-22). If a person faced financial difficulty, his land could be leased but never permanently sold. He had no right to sell the land because it belonged to God not him. Therefore, in business dealings involving land, provision had to be made for the land to be redeemed or bought back. This is what God is doing in the present Scripture, spelling out how land is to be handled from a business perspective. How land can be sold, leased, redeemed, or bought back—all this is discussed. Note the cases considered in the scripture and outline:

OUTLINE	SCRIPTURE	SCRIPTURE	OUTLINE
4. The Year of Jubilee: The redemption of property a. The law: The land must be leased, never permanently sold 1) Because it belongs to God 2) The law: Must provide for the land to be redeemed, bought back b. Case 1—a person is forced to sell some property: The nearest relative is to buy it back for him, if possible (a symbol	23 The land shall not be sold for ever: for the land *is* mine; for ye *are* strangers and sojourners with me. 24 And in all the land of your possession ye shall grant a redemption for the land. 25 If thy brother be waxen poor, and hath sold a and if any of his kin come to redeem it, then shall he	redeem that which his brother sold. 26 And if the man have none to redeem it, and himself be able to redeem it; 27 Then let him count the years of the sale thereof, and restore the overplus unto the man to whom he sold it; that he may return unto his possession.	of Christ our Kinsman-Redeemer) c. Case 2—the person prospers & is able to redeem his own property 1) He is to have the right to buy it back 2) He is to pay a fair market price for the property: To be based on the number of crops left until the next Jubilee 3) He can then return

---

2 Frank E. Gaebelein, General Editor. *The Expositor's Bible Commentary*, Vol.2, p.637.
3 ibid., p.636.
4 ibid., p.636.

OUTLINE	SCRIPTURE	SCRIPTURE	OUTLINE

d. Case 3—the original owner is never able to redeem or buy back his property
  1) The buyer keeps the property until the Jubilee
  2) The buyer returns the property in the Year of Jubilee (a symbol of free grace)
 	
e. Case 4—a person sells a house in a walled city
  1) The right of repurchase is to be set for one year
 	
  2) The house, after one year, belongs to the buyer & his descendants permanently
  3) The house is not returned in the Jubilee
 	
f. Case 5—a house in a village
	28 But if he be not able to restore *it* to him, then that which is sold shall remain in the hand of him that hath bought it until the year of jubile: and in the jubile it shall go out, and he shall return unto his possession.
	29 And if a man sell a dwelling house in a walled city, then he may redeem it within a whole year after it is sold; *within* a full year may he redeem it.
	30 And if it be not redeemed within the space of a full year, then the house that *is* in the walled city shall be established for ever to him that bought it throughout his generations: it shall not go out in the jubile.
	31 But the houses of the vil-
		lages which have no wall round about them shall be counted as the fields of the country: they may be redeemed, and they shall go out in the jubile.
		32 Notwithstanding the cities of the Levites, *and* the houses of the cities of their possession, may the Levites redeem at any time.
		33 And if a man purchase of the Levites, then the house that was sold, and the city of his possession, shall go out in *the year of* jubile: for the houses of the cities of the Levites *are* their possession among the children of Israel.
		34 But the field of the suburbs of their cities may not be sold; for it *is* their perpetual possession.
			without walls
			  1) The house is to be treated like property in open fields
			  2) The house can be bought back & is to be returned in the Jubilee
			g. Case 6—the houses of the Levites, the priests, in the Levitical towns belonging to them
			  1) Their houses are always redeemable
			  2) Their houses are to be returned in the Jubilee
			
			  3) Their pasture land must never be sold: It is their permanent ancestral property

Thought 1. Note two striking lessons:

(1) The Kinsman-Redeemer is a symbol of the Lord Jesus Christ. (v.25) Christ is our Kinsman in that he took our nature upon Himself and came to earth as a man. Jesus Christ shared in our humanity, became flesh and blood, in order to redeem us.

> **"For all have sinned, and come short of the glory of God; Being justified freely by his grace through the redemption that is in Christ Jesus" (Ro.3:23-24).**
> **"Christ hath redeemed us from the curse of the law, being made a curse for us: for it is written, Cursed *is* every one that hangeth on a tree" (Ga.3:13).**
> **"In whom we have redemption through his blood, *even* the forgiveness of sins" (Col.1:14).**
> **"For the grace of God that bringeth salvation hath appeared to all men, Teaching us that, denying ungodliness and worldly lusts, we should live soberly, righteously, and godly, in this present world; Looking for that blessed hope, and the glorious appearing of the great God and our Saviour Jesus Christ; Who gave himself for us, that he might redeem us from all iniquity, and purify unto himself a peculiar people, zealous of good works" (Tit.2:11-14).**
> **"Neither by the blood of goats and calves, but by his own blood he entered in once into the holy place, having obtained eternal redemption *for us*" (He.9:12).**
> **"Forasmuch as ye know that ye were not redeemed with corruptible things, *as* silver and gold, from your vain conversation *received* by tradition from your fathers; But with the precious blood of Christ, as of a lamb without blemish and without spot" (1 Pe.1:18-19).**
> **"And they sung a new song, saying, Thou art worthy to take the book, and to open the seals thereof: for thou wast slain, and hast redeemed us to God by thy blood out of every kindred, and tongue, and people, and nation; And hast made us unto our God kings and priests: and we shall reign on the earth" (Re.5:9-10).**

(2) The Kinsman-Redeemer bought back the land that his relatives had forfeited or lost because of debt (v.25). This is what Jesus Christ has done for us. Through sin we have forfeited and lost our possession and the promised land of heaven. But Jesus Christ has paid the debt for our sin: He has redeemed or bought back our inheritance or possession in the promised land of heaven.

> **"Let not your heart be troubled: ye believe in God, believe also in me. In my Father's house are many mansions: if *it were* not so, I would have told you. I go to prepare a place for you. And if I go and prepare a place for you, I will come again, and receive you unto myself; that where I am, *there* ye may be also" (Jn.14:1-3).**
> **"And there shall in no wise enter into it any thing that defileth, neither *whatsoever* worketh abomination, or *maketh* a lie: but they which are written in the Lamb's book of life" (Re.21:27).**
> **"And now, brethren, I commend you to God, and to the word of his grace, which is able to build you up, and to give you an inheritance [heaven] among all them which are sanctified" (Ac.20:32).**
> **"To open their eyes, *and* to turn *them* from darkness to light, and *from* the power of Satan unto God, that they may receive forgiveness of sins, and inheritance [heaven] among them which are sanctified by faith that is in me" (Ac.26:18).**

"For our conversation is in heaven; from whence also we look for the Saviour, the Lord Jesus Christ: Who shall change our vile body, that it may be fashioned like unto his glorious body, according to the working whereby he is able even to subdue all things unto himself" (Ph.3:20-21).

"Giving thanks unto the Father, which hath made us meet to be partakers of the inheritance of the saints in light: Who hath delivered us from the power of darkness, and hath translated *us* into the kingdom of his dear Son" (Col.1:12-13).

"Blessed *be* the God and Father of our Lord Jesus Christ, which according to his abundant mercy hath begotten us again unto a lively hope by the resurrection of Jesus Christ from the dead, To an inheritance incorruptible, and undefiled, and that fadeth not away, reserved in heaven for you" (1 Pe.1:3-4).

5 (25:35-55) **Jubilee, Year of—Year of Jubilee—Poor, The—Slavery—Foreigners, Laws Governing—Servant, Laws Governing—Laws, Governing Poverty**: the Year of Jubilee established laws that protected the poor, laws that governed the protection and treatment of the poor. God's people are to take care of the poor, never mistreating nor taking advantage of them. Throughout ancient history in serious cases of debt, a person might be forced to sell himself into slavery in order to survive. The pagan and ungodly nations and the wealthy of the world often mistreated and abused slaves. Such brutal, savage mistreatment of the poor is strongly forbidden by God. In the midst of a savage and brutal world, God spells out how His people are to treat the poor and the slaves of the earth. He takes the despicable practice of slavery and demands that the poor and enslaved of the earth be treated as hired servants not as slaves.

This fact is of such importance that it needs to be repeated and emphasized time and again. God demands that the poor and enslaved of the earth be treated as hired servants or employees not as slaves. God's people were to be compassionate and caring. The poor were to be responsible in working and paying off their debts, and the rich were to be compassionate and understanding. As these laws are studied, note what a leap forward they are in the midst of a world built upon the economy of slavery. (See outline and notes—Ex.21:2-6 for more discussion on the subject of slavery.)

OUTLINE	SCRIPTURE	SCRIPTURE	OUTLINE
5. The Year of Jubilee: The protection & treatment of the poor a. Case 1: A person becomes poor & cannot support himself 1) Are to help him	35 And if thy brother be waxen poor, and fallen in decay with thee; then thou shalt relieve him: *yea though he be* a stranger, or a sojourner; that he may live with thee.	him with rigour; but shalt fear thy God. 44 Both thy bondmen, and thy bondmaids, which thou shalt have, *shall be* of the heathen that are round about you; of them shall ye buy bondmen and bondmaids.	them ruthlessly • A person must fear God
2) Are not to charge interest on loans to him, but rather fear God	36 Take thou no usury of him, or increase: but fear thy God; that thy brother may live with thee.	45 Moreover of the children of the strangers that do sojourn among you, of them shall ye buy, and of their families that *are* with you, which they begat in your land: and they shall be your possession.	6) The exception • Foreigners who were poor & had to sell themselves just to have shelter & food could be held as slaves
3) The point restressed: Are not to charge interest nor sell food at a profit	37 Thou shalt not give him thy money upon usury, nor lend him thy victuals for increase.		
4) The warning: "I am the LORD your God" who helped you • Delivered you out of Egypt • Am giving you the promised land	38 I *am* the LORD your God, which brought you forth out of the land of Egypt, to give you the land of Canaan, *and* to be your God.	46 And ye shall take them as an inheritance for your children after you, to inherit *them for* a possession; they shall be your bondmen for ever: but over your brethren the children of Israel, ye	• Temporary residents who needed shelter & food could sell themselves and be held as slaves • A person could will the poor to his children as inherited property, as
b. Case 2: A person becomes poor & has to sell his labor 1) Not to be treated as a slave	39 And if thy brother *that dwelleth* by thee be waxen poor, and be sold unto thee; thou shalt not compel him to serve as a bondservant:	shall not rule one over another with rigour.	slaves for life, but could never mistreat the poor
2) To be treated as an employee or temporary resident	40 *But* as an hired servant, *and* as a sojourner, he shall be with thee, *and* shall	47 And if a sojourner or stranger wax rich by thee, and thy brother *that dwelleth*	c. Case 3: A person becomes bankrupt & sells himself to a resident foreigner
3) To be employed until the Year of Jubilee	serve thee unto the year of jubile:	by him wax poor, and sell himself unto the stranger *or* sojourner by thee, or to the	
4) To be released & returned to his own property & clan	41 And *then* shall he depart from thee, *both* he and his children with him, and shall return unto his own family, and unto the possession of his fathers shall he return.	stock of the stranger's family: 48 After that he is sold he may be redeemed again; one of his brethren may redeem him:	1) He retains the right of redemption, of being bought back
5) The reason: Because God delivered the Israelites to be His servants	42 For they *are* my servants, which I brought forth out of the land of Egypt: they shall not be sold as bondmen.	49 Either his uncle, or his uncle's son, may redeem him, or *any* that is nigh of kin unto him of his family may	• A relative—called a "kinsman redeemer," a type of Christ—may buy him: An uncle, cousin,
• No person is to rule over	43 Thou shalt not rule over	redeem him; or if he be able,	or blood relative

OUTLINE	SCRIPTURE	SCRIPTURE	OUTLINE
• He may buy himself back	he may redeem himself.	count with him, *and* according unto his years shall he give him again the price of his redemption.	accordingly
2) He is to pay the buyer a fair market value based on the Jubilee Year: To pay the rate it would cost to hire a servant for that number of years	50 And he shall reckon with him that bought him from the year that he was sold to him unto the year of jubile: and the price of his sale shall be according unto the number of years, according to the time of an hired servant shall it be with him.	53 *And* as a yearly hired servant shall he be with him: *and the other* shall not rule with rigour over him in thy sight.	3) He is to be treated as a servant hired from year-to-year: He is not to be treated ruthlessly
• If many years remain, he is to pay most of what the buyer paid him, if any	51 If *there be* yet many years *behind*, according unto them he shall give again the price of his redemption out of the money that he was bought for.	54 And if he be not redeemed in these *years*, then he shall go out in the year of jubile, *both* he, and his children with him.	4) He is to be released, set free, in the Year of Jubilee
• If few years remain until the Jubilee Year, he is to compute the price & pay	52 And if there remain but few years unto the year of jubile, then he shall count	55 For unto me the children of Israel *are* servants; they *are* my servants whom I brought forth out of the land of Egypt: I *am* the LORD your God.	5) The reason • He is God's servant • He was freed from Egypt (the world) to serve God

Thought 1. Jesus Christ is our Kinsman-Redeemer (v.48). In fact, Jesus Christ became poor in order to redeem and make us rich. He left the glory and riches of heaven to come to this sinful, poverty-stricken earth to redeem us for the glory and riches of heaven.

"For ye know the grace of our Lord Jesus Christ, that, though he was rich, yet for your sakes he became poor, that ye through his poverty might be rich' (2 Co.8:9).

Who gave himself for our sins, that he might deliver us from this present evil world, according to the will of God and our Father" (Ga.1:4).

"The eyes of your understanding being enlightened; that ye may know what is the hope of his calling, and what the riches of the glory of his inheritance in the saints" (Ep.1:18).

"Unto me, who am less than the least of all saints, is this grace given, that I should preach among the Gentiles the unsearchable riches of Christ; (Ep.3:8).

"By faith Moses, when he was come to years, refused to be called the son of Pharaoh's daughter; Choosing rather to suffer affliction with the people of God, than to enjoy the pleasures of sin for a season; Esteeming the reproach of Christ greater riches than the treasures in Egypt: for he had respect unto the recompence of the reward. (He.11:24-26).

"Hearken, my beloved brethren, Hath not God chosen the poor of this world rich in faith, and heirs of the kingdom which he hath promised to them that love him?" (Js.2:5).

"The blessing of the LORD, it maketh rich, and he addeth no sorrow with it" (Pr.10:22).

Thought 2. No human being is to be enslaved, especially one of God's followers. Note why: because the believer belongs to God. God had freed the Israelites from Egyptian slavery for one purpose and one purpose alone: that they might be His servants, the servants of God Himself. Keep in mind that Egypt is a symbol of the world. The picture is this: believers have been freed from the slavery of the world in order to be the servants of God. Therefore, any person who has been enslaved is to be set free so that he can serve God not serve man.

"Thou shalt love thy neighbour as thyself" (Mt.22:39).

"If I then, *your* Lord and Master, have washed your feet; ye also ought to wash one another's feet" (Jn.13:14).

"A new commandment I give unto you, That ye love one another; as I have loved you, that ye also love one another. By this shall all *men* know that ye are my disciples, if ye have love one to another" (Jn.13:34-35).

"This is my commandment, That ye love one another, as I have loved you" (Jn.15:12).

"*Let* love be without dissimulation. Abhor that which is evil; cleave to that which is good" (Ro.12:9).

"Wherefore we receiving a kingdom which cannot be moved, let us have grace, whereby we may serve God acceptably with reverence and godly fear" (He.12:28).

"Bear ye one another's burdens, and so fulfil the law of Christ" (Ga.6:2).

"As we have therefore opportunity, let us do good unto all *men,* especially unto them who are of the household of faith" (Ga.6:10).

"With good will doing service, as to the Lord, and not to men" (Ep.6:7).

"If a brother or sister be naked, and destitute of daily food, And one of you say unto them, Depart in peace, be ye warmed and filled; notwithstanding ye give them not those things which are needful to the body; what *doth it* profit? Even so faith, if it hath not works, is dead, being alone. Yea, a man may say, Thou hast faith, and I have works: show me thy faith without thy works, and I will show thee my faith by my works" (Js.2:15-18).

"But whoso hath this world's good, and seeth his brother have need, and shutteth up his bowels *of compassion* from him, how dwelleth the love of God in him?" (1 Jn.3:17).

"And ye shall serve the LORD your God, and he shall bless thy bread, and thy water; and I will take sickness away from the midst of thee" (Ex.23:25).

"And now, Israel, what doth the LORD thy God require of thee, but to fear the LORD thy God, to walk in all his ways, and to love him, and to serve the LORD thy God with all thy heart and with all thy soul" (De.10:12).

"Serve the LORD with fear, and rejoice with trembling" (Ps.2:11).

Thought 3. The believer is to treat the poor with compassion and care, helping the poor all that he can. In fact, Scripture teaches that the believer is to work so diligently that he has enough to help those who are in need (Ep.4:28).

"Jesus said unto him, If thou wilt be perfect, go *and* sell that thou hast, and give to the poor, and thou shalt have treasure in heaven: and come *and* follow me" (Mt.19:21).

"Only *they would* that we should remember the poor; the same which I also was forward to do" (Ga.2:10).

"Let him that stole steal no more: but rather let him labour, working with *his* hands the thing which is good, that he may have to give to him that needeth" (Ep.4:28).

"If there be among you a poor man of one of thy brethren within any of thy gates in thy land which the LORD thy God giveth thee, thou shalt not harden thine heart, nor shut thine hand from thy poor brother" (De.15:7).

"Blessed *is* he that considereth the poor: the LORD will deliver him in time of trouble" (Ps.41:1).

"Defend the poor and fatherless: do justice to the afflicted and needy" (Ps.82:3).

"He that hath pity upon the poor lendeth unto the LORD; and that which he hath given will he pay him again" (Pr.19:17).

"Whoso stoppeth his ears at the cry of the poor, he also shall cry himself, but shall not be heard" (Pr.21:13).

TYPES, SYMBOLS, AND PICTURES
Leviticus 25:1-55

Historical Term	Type or Picture (Scriptural Basis for Each)	Life Application for Today's Believer	Biblical Application
The Kinsman-Redeemer Law Le. 25:23-34	*The Kinsman-Redeemer Law is a symbol of Christ, our Kinsman-Redeemer.* "If thy brother be waxen poor, and hath sold away *some* of his possession, and if any of his kin come to redeem it, then shall he redeem that which his brother sold" (Le. 25:25).	Note two striking lessons: 1. The Kinsman—Redeemer is a symbol of the Lord Jesus Christ. Christ is our Kinsman in that he took our nature upon himself and came to earth as a man. Jesus Christ shared in our humanity, became flesh and blood, in order to redeem us. 2. The Kinsman-Redeemer bought back the land that his relative had forfeited or lost because of debt. This is what Jesus Christ has done for us. This is a symbol of free grace. Through sin we have forfeited and lost our possession and the promised land of heaven. But Jesus Christ has paid the debt for our sin; He has redeemed or bought back our inheritance or possession in the Promised Land of heaven.	*"For all have sinned, and come short of the glory of God; Being justified freely by his grace through the redemption that is in Christ Jesus" (Ro.3:23-24).* *"Christ hath redeemed us from the curse of the law, being made a curse for us: for it is written, Cursed is every one that hangeth on a tree" (Ga.3:13).* *"In whom we have redemption through his blood, the forgiveness of sins, according to the riches of his grace" (Ep.1:7; Col.1:14).* *"Blessed be the God and Father of our Lord Jesus Christ, which according to his abundant mercy hath begotten us again unto a lively hope by the resurrection of Jesus Christ from the dead, To an inheritance incorruptible, and undefiled, and that fadeth not away, reserved in heaven for you" (1 Pe.1:3-4).* *"For our conversation [citizenship] is in heaven; from whence also we look for the Saviour, the Lord Jesus Christ: Who shall*

TYPES, SYMBOLS, AND PICTURES
Leviticus 25:1-55

Historical Term	Type or Picture (Scriptural Basis for Each)	Life Application for Today's Believer	Biblical Application
			change our vile body, that it may be fashioned like unto his glorious body, according to the working whereby he is able even to subdue all things unto himself" (Ph.3:20-21).

CHAPTER 26

J. The Exhortations to Obey God: God's Promises & Warnings to His People, 26:1-46

Ye shall make you no idols nor graven image, neither rear you up a standing image, neither shall ye set up *any* image of stone in your land, to bow down unto it: for I *am* the LORD your God.

2 Ye shall keep my sabbaths, and reverence my sanctuary: I *am* the LORD.

3 If ye walk in my statutes, and keep my commandments, and do them;

4 Then I will give you rain in due season, and the land shall yield her increase, and the trees of the field shall yield their fruit.

5 And your threshing shall reach unto the vintage, and the vintage shall reach unto the sowing time: and ye shall eat your bread to the full, and dwell in your land safely.

6 And I will give peace in the land, and ye shall lie down, and none shall make *you* afraid: and I will rid evil beasts out of the land, neither shall the sword go through your land.

7 And ye shall chase your enemies, and they shall fall before you by the sword.

8 And five of you shall chase an hundred, and an hundred of you shall put ten thousand to flight: and your enemies shall fall before you by the sword.

9 For I will have respect unto you, and make you fruitful, and multiply you, and establish my covenant with you.

10 And ye shall eat old store, and bring forth the old because of the new.

11 And I will set my tabernacle among you: and my soul shall not abhor you.

12 And I will walk among you, and will be your God, and ye shall be my people.

13 I *am* the LORD your God, which brought you forth out of the land of Egypt, that ye should not be their bondmen; and I have broken the bands of your yoke, and made you go upright.

14 But if ye will not hearken unto me, and will not do all these commandments;

15 And if ye shall despise my statutes, or if your soul abhor my judgments, so that ye will not do all my commandments, *but* that ye break my covenant:

16 I also will do this unto you; I will even appoint over you terror, consumption, and the burning ague, that shall consume the eyes, and cause sorrow of heart: and ye shall sow your seed in vain, for your enemies shall eat it.

17 And I will set my face against you, and ye shall be slain before your enemies: they that hate you shall reign over you; and ye shall flee when none pursueth you.

18 And if ye will not yet for all this hearken unto me, then I will punish you seven times more for your sins.

19 And I will break the pride of your power; and I will make your heaven as iron, and your earth as brass:

20 And your strength shall be spent in vain: for your land shall not yield her increase, neither shall the trees of the land yield their fruits.

21 And if ye walk contrary unto me, and will not hearken unto me; I will bring seven times more plagues upon you according to your sins.

22 I will also send wild beasts among you, which shall rob you of your children, and destroy your cattle, and make you few in number; and your *high* ways shall be desolate.

23 And if ye will not be reformed by me by these things, but will walk contrary unto me;

24 Then will I also walk contrary unto you, and will punish you yet seven times for your sins.

25 And I will bring a sword upon you, that shall avenge the quarrel of *my* covenant: and when ye are gathered together within your cities, I will send the pestilence

---

OUTLINE

1. The conditions for receiving the promises of God
 a. Must not worship idols or false gods
  1) No idol of any kind
  2) The warning: Is only one true God—"I am the LORD..."
 b. Must keep God's Sabbaths
 c. Must reverence God's sanctuary
 d. Must keep God's laws & obey His commands

2. The promises of God to the obedient
 a. The blessing of food & plenty, even an abundance
  1) A full season of rain, crops, & fruit
  2) A full harvest season
  3) An abundance of food
  4) An assurance of safety: God will provide, take care of, & look after
 b. The blessing of peace & security
  1) From lawless attacks at night
  2) From savage animals
  3) From hostile people & war
 c. The blessing of victory
  1) The obedient will defeat the enemy & cause him to fall
  2) The obedient will be filled with courage
 d. The blessing of children, of being fruitful: Was a promise of the covenant with Abraham (Ge.12:1-3)
 e. The blessing of having more than enough: Will have enough to give & help others (see Ep.4:28)
 f. The blessing of God's presence
  1) He will dwell among—not despise—the obedient
  2) He will walk among the obedient: Be their God & make them His people
 g. The guarantee that God can fulfill His promises & His blessings
  1) He is the LORD, the true God
  2) He is the One who delivered His people from Egypt
  3) He is the One who enabled His people to walk with their heads held high

3. The causes that stir God's discipline or punishment
 a. Failing to listen & obey God
 b. Breaking the covenant of God
  1) By rejecting & abhorring His laws
  2) By disobeying God's commands

4. The warning of judgment & punishment to the disobedient
 a. The first warning of punishment: Mental & physical suffering (see Jud.2:14; 3:8; 4:2)
  1) Will suffer mental terror & problems
  2) Will suffer physical disease
  3) Will have crops (food) stolen & ravaged (Je.5:17)
  4) Will be defeated & ruled over by one's enemies
  5) Will be stricken with fear of one's enemies
 b. The second warning of punishment: Drought & poor harvests
  1) Will suffer multiple, repeated punishments if continue to disobey God
  2) Will have one's stubborn pride broken (see De.8:11-20)
  3) Will cause a harsh drought & hard, unproductive ground
  4) Will cause crops to fail: A food shortage, hunger, thirst
 c. The third warning of punishment: Wild animals (snakes, scorpions)
  1) Will suffer because "your sins" deserve judgment
  2) Will suffer the loss of livestock, crops, & even human life by attacks of wild animals
  3) Will have so few people remaining that roads will be deserted
 d. The fourth warning of punishment: War
  1) The reason: Because of continued rejection & hostility toward God
  2) Will suffer God's rejection & hostility, suffer multiple & repeated corrections: Because of sins
  3) Will suffer attacks, war
  4) Will suffer a disease, some plague, while fighting (see Eze.5:12)
  5) Will be defeated

6) Will suffer a shortage of food, face starvation

e. The fifth warning of punishment: Desolation & exile
1) The reason: Because of continued rejection & hostility toward God
2) Will suffer God's continued rejection: Suffer multiple disciplines & corrections because of sins
3) Will suffer cannibalism (2 K.6:28-29; La.2:20; 4:10)
4) Will suffer a terrible, savage slaughter or holocaust (Am. 8:3; Eze.6:5)

5) Will suffer the utter destruction of one's cities & sanctuaries (Eze.6:3f)
6) Will suffer the rejection of one's cry & plea to God (Is.1:11-15)
7) Will suffer the total devastation of one's land (Je.9:11; Eze.5:15)
8) Will suffer the deportation & scattering of one's people (Je.9:16)
9) Will suffer the terrible ruin of both land & cities
• The land will lie so desolate that it will rest & enjoy the Sabbaths

• The land will gain the rest denied it by the disobedient (cp. the Babylonian captivity, 2 Chr.36:21)
10) Will suffer a terrifying fear in the lands of their enemies (Eze.21:7)

11) Will suffer so terrifying a fear that they will flee even

among you; and ye shall be delivered into the hand of the enemy.
26 *And* when I have broken the staff of your bread, ten women shall bake your bread in one oven, and they shall deliver *you* your bread again by weight: and ye shall eat, and not be satisfied.
27 And if ye will not for all this hearken unto me, but walk contrary unto me;
28 Then I will walk contrary unto you also in fury; and I, even I, will chastise you seven times for your sins.
29 And ye shall eat the flesh of your sons, and the flesh of your daughters shall ye eat.
30 And I will destroy your high places, and cut down your images, and cast your carcases upon the carcases of your idols, and my soul shall abhor you.
31 And I will make your cities waste, and bring your sanctuaries unto desolation, and I will not smell the savour of your sweet odours.
32 And I will bring the land into desolation: and your enemies which dwell therein shall be astonished at it.
33 And I will scatter you among the heathen, and will draw out a sword after you: and your land shall be desolate, and your cities waste.
34 Then shall the land enjoy her sabbaths, as long as it lieth desolate, and ye *be* in your enemies' land; *even* then shall the land rest, and enjoy her sabbaths.
35 As long as it lieth desolate it shall rest; because it did not rest in your sabbaths, when ye dwelt upon it.
36 And upon them that are left *alive* of you I will send a faintness into their hearts in the lands of their enemies; and the sound of a shaken leaf shall chase them; and they shall flee, as fleeing from a sword; and they shall fall when none pursueth.
37 And they shall fall one upon another, as it were be-

fore a sword, when none pursueth: and ye shall have no power to stand before your enemies.
38 And ye shall perish among the heathen, and the land of your enemies shall eat you up.
39 And they that are left of you shall pine away in their iniquity in your enemies' lands; and also in the iniquities of their fathers shall they pine away with them.
40 If they shall confess their iniquity, and the iniquity of their fathers, with their trespass which they trespassed against me, and that also they have walked contrary unto me;
41 And *that* I also have walked contrary unto them, and have brought them into the land of their enemies; if then their uncircumcised hearts be humbled, and they then accept of the punishment of their iniquity:
42 Then will I remember my covenant with Jacob, and also my covenant with Isaac, and also my covenant with Abraham will I remember; and I will remember the land.
43 The land also shall be left of them, and shall enjoy her sabbaths, while she lieth desolate without them: and they shall accept of the punishment of their iniquity: because, even because they despised my judgments, and because their soul abhorred my statutes.
44 And yet for all that, when they be in the land of their enemies, I will not cast them away, neither will I abhor them, to destroy them utterly, and to break my covenant with them: for I *am* the LORD their God.
45 But I will for their sakes remember the covenant of their ancestors, whom I brought forth out of the land of Egypt in the sight of the heathen, that I might be their God: I *am* the LORD.
46 These *are* the statutes and judgments and laws, which the LORD made between him and the children of Israel in mount Sinai by the hand of Moses.

when there is no reason to flee

12) Will perish, die in foreign lands: Be devoured & waste away in the lands of their enemies (Je.31:10; 49:32; Eze.5:12; 12:14)
13) The reason: Because of their sins (see the Roman siege in A.D. 70 foretold by Christ, Mt.24:1f)

5. **The faithfulness of God to His promises: The promise of restoration**
a. The conditions for being restored
1) One must confess his sins

2) One must humble his hard heart
3) One must repent

b. The faithfulness of God to restore
1) He will renew His covenant

2) He will remember the land: Will see that it rests & recovers (enjoys Sabbaths)

3) He will fulfill His Word & warning: Will judge & condemn the disobedient

4) He will not reject nor destroy them completely, will not break His covenant with them

5) He is the LORD their God, able to fulfill all His promises, able to restore them
6) He will remember His covenant with their ancestors: The ancestors who believed God & accepted His power to deliver them: Will restore them

7) He is the source of all the laws given to His people: He will fulfill all the promises

DIVISION IV

THE WAY TO LIVE A HOLY LIFE BEFORE GOD (PART 2): A PURE SPIRIT (SANCTIFICATION), 17:1–27:34

J. The Exhortations to Obey God: God's Promises and Warnings to His People, 26:1-46

(26:1-46) **Introduction—Prophecy, of Israel—Israel, Prophecy of—Promises, of God—Warnings, of Judgment**: this chapter covers the great promises and warnings of God to the world. The promises and warnings are directed to Israel, but they are applicable to all nations and people. First, God spells out the promises, then He spells out the warnings. God warns any nation or people who reject Him: they will face the judgment and punishment of God, both in this world and in the world to come. If they live immoral and lawless lives, they will bring punishment down upon their heads now but they will also bring the eternal judgment of God upon themselves at the end of the world, at the great day of judgment. J. Vernon McGee has an excellent introduction to this chapter showing how this chapter applies to Israel as a nation and to the believers of today.

> *This is a marvelous chapter. It is a prophetic history that covers Israel's entire tenure of the Promised Land until the present hour and gives the conditions in the future on which they will occupy the land....this is the direct word of Jehovah to the nation Israel concerning their future. This is history prewritten and reveals the basis on which Israel entered the land of Canaan and their tenancy there.*
>
> *This is an "iffy" chapter. "If" occurs nine times and it has to do with the conditions on which they occupy the land. God says "I will" twenty-four times. God will act and react according to their response to the "if." God gave them the land, but their occupancy of it is determined by their answer to the "if." Obedience is the ground of blessing in the land. This chapter is not only the calendar of their history, but it serves as the barometer of their blessings. Their presence in the land, rainfall, and bountiful crops denote the favor of God. Their absence from the land, famine, and drought denote the judgment of God because of their disobedience.*
>
> *You and I are blessed with all spiritual blessings in the heavenlies in Christ Jesus. However there are some "ifs" connected to that also. God loves you and wants to shower you with His blessings. But you can put up an umbrella of indifference, you can put up an umbrella of sin, you can put up an umbrella of stepping out of the will of God. When you do that, the sunshine of His love won't get through to you. You must put down your umbrella to experience His spiritual blessings.* [1]

This is: *The Exhortations to Obey God: God's Promises and Warnings to His People*, 26:1-46.
1. The conditions for receiving the promises of God (vv.1-3).
2. The promises of God to the obedient (vv.4-13).
3. The causes that stir God's discipline or punishment (vv.14-15).
4. The warning of judgment and punishment to the disobedient (vv.16-39).
5. The faithfulness of God to His promises: the promise of restoration (vv.40-46).

1 (26:1-3) **Believers, Duty of—Promises, of God, Conditions for Receiving—Idolatry, Commandment Against—Sabbath—Sanctuary—Reverence—Commandments—Law, of God**: there are the conditions for receiving the promises of God. God spelled the conditions out for His people.

OUTLINE	SCRIPTURE	SCRIPTURE	OUTLINE
1. The conditions for receiving the promises of God a. Must not worship idols or false gods 1) No idol of any kind 2) The warning: Is only one true God— "I am	Ye shall make you no idols nor graven image, neither rear you up a standing image, neither shall ye set up *any* image of stone in your land, to bow down unto it: for I *am* the LORD	your God. 2 Ye shall keep my sabbaths, and reverence my sanctuary: I *am* the LORD. 3 If ye walk in my statutes, and keep my commandments, and do them;	the LORD..." b. Must keep God's Sabbaths c. Must reverence God's sanctuary d. Must keep God's laws & obey His commands

a. A person must not worship idols or false gods (v.1). The word for *idols* (eliyl) means something that is good for nothing, empty, of no value, vain. An idol is nothing more than physical materials that have been formed or constructed into some image. The image is nothing more than physical materials: it has no meaning, no value whatsoever for worship. It is a worthless, useless thing for worship. False gods are nothing more than the wild and corrupt imaginations of people. Note the warning from God: there is only one true and living God, "I am the LORD Your God." The *LORD* (Jehovah, Yahweh) and the *LORD* alone is to be worshipped. Scripture declares that God is Spirit; no form or image nor anything else within creation—neither the sun, moon, or stars—nothing can represent God. He is beyond anything that exists or ever could exist. There is only one Creator and Sovereign LORD of the universe, the *LORD* God Himself. It is He and He alone who is to be worshipped and served.

> **"God *is* a Spirit: and they that worship him must worship *him* in spirit and in truth" (Jn.4:24).**
> **"Little children, keep yourselves from idols. Amen" (1 Jn.5:21).**

---

[1] J. Vernon McGee. *Thru the Bible*, Vol.1, p.442.

"Take ye therefore good heed unto yourselves; for ye saw no manner of similitude on the day *that* the LORD spake unto you in Horeb out of the midst of the fire: Lest ye corrupt *yourselves,* and make you a graven image, the similitude of any figure, the likeness of male or female, The likeness of any beast that *is* on the earth, the likeness of any winged fowl that flieth in the air, The likeness of any thing that creepeth on the ground, the likeness of any fish that *is* in the waters beneath the earth: And lest thou lift up thine eyes unto heaven, and when thou seest the sun, and the moon, and the stars, *even* all the host of heaven, shouldest be driven to worship them, and serve them, which the LORD thy God hath divided unto all nations under the whole heaven" (De.4:15-19).

"Take heed to yourselves, that your heart be not deceived, and ye turn aside, and serve other gods, and worship them" (De.11:16).

b. A person must keep God's Sabbaths (v.2). The Sabbaths included not only the weekly worship of the Sabbath day, but also the Sabbatical week that was observed every seven years and the Sabbatical Jubilee that was observed every forty-nine or fifty-years (see outline and notes—Le.25:1-55 for more discussion). God expects His people to worship. He has set aside one day out of every week for worship, the Sabbath or Sunday. Physically and spiritually, man needs one day a week for rest and worship; therefore it is man's responsibility to obey God by maintaining a healthy body and spirit. But man needs more than just a Sabbath day of rest and worship: he needs other times throughout the year when work stops and he is allowed to rest and worship. This is the reason God set aside special holidays and festivals. God demands that His people observe these special holidays or festivals throughout the year. In fact, keep the major point in mind: these are the conditions for receiving the promises of God. Man must keep God's Sabbaths in order to receive the promises of God.

"Upon the first *day* of the week let every one of you lay by him in store, as *God* hath prospered him, that there be no gatherings when I come" (1 Co.16:2).

"Not forsaking the assembling of ourselves together, as the manner of some *is;* but exhorting *one another:* and so much the more, as ye see the day approaching" (He.10:25).

"Remember the sabbath day, to keep it holy" (Ex.20:8).

"Six days thou shalt work, but on the seventh day thou shalt rest: in earing time and in harvest thou shalt rest" (Ex.34:21).

c. A person must reverence God's sanctuary (v.2). The sanctuary is the holy place of God. It is the place where God's presence dwells in a very special way. The sanctuary is a place that has been sanctified, set apart for God, set apart for the worship of God. Therefore God's sanctuary must be reverenced, kept holy. God's people are to guard and watch their behavior within the sanctuary. Only holy behavior and holy conversation are to take place within the sanctuary. The sanctuary is God's: it is the very place where God's holy presence dwells in a most special way.

"Then said the Lord to him, Put off thy shoes from thy feet: for the place where thou standest is holy ground" (Ac.7:33).

"Know ye not that ye are the temple of God, and *that* the Spirit of God dwelleth in you [plural, the church]? If any man defile the temple of God, him shall God destroy; for the temple of God is holy, which *temple* ye are" (1 Co.3:16-17).

"And he said, Draw not nigh hither: put off thy shoes from off thy feet, for the place whereon thou standest is holy ground" (Ex.3:5).

"And the captain of the LORD'S host said unto Joshua, Loose thy shoe from off thy foot; for the place whereon thou standest *is* holy. And Joshua did so" (Jos.5:15).

"Let all the earth fear the LORD: let all the inhabitants of the world stand in awe of him" (Ps.33:8).

"God is greatly to be feared in the assembly of the saints, and to be had in reverence of all *them that are* about him. (Ps.89:7).

"But the LORD *is* in his holy temple: let all the earth keep silence before him" (Hab.2:20).

d. A person must keep God's laws and obey His commandments (v.3). The one thing God wants above anything else is obedience. This is the declaration of God throughout all of scripture. The person who truly loves God will obey God.

"Not every one that saith unto me, Lord, Lord, shall enter into the kingdom of heaven; but he that doeth the will of my Father which is in heaven" (Mt.7:21).

"Therefore whosoever heareth these sayings of mine, and doeth them, I will liken him unto a wise man, which built his house upon a rock" (Mt.7:24).

"He that hath my commandments, and keepeth them, he it is that loveth me: and he that loveth me shall be loved of my Father, and I will love him, and will manifest myself to him" (Jn.14:21).

"Jesus answered and said unto him, If a man love me, he will keep my words: and my Father will love him, and we will come unto him, and make our abode with him" (Jn.14:23).

"This day the LORD thy God hath commanded thee to do these statutes and judgments: thou shalt therefore keep and do them with all thine heart, and with all thy soul" (De.26:16).

"And Samuel said, Hath the LORD *as great* delight in burnt offerings and sacrifices, as in obeying the voice of the LORD? Behold, to obey *is* better than sacrifice, *and* to hearken than the fat of rams" (1 S.15:22).

2 (26:4-13) **Promises, of God—Obedience—Israel, Promises to—Promises, List of**: there are the promises of God to the obedient. As these promises are studied, a person must remember that they are conditional. The promises of God are given to the obedient and only to the obedient. If a person obeys God, then he receives some great and precious promises from God.

OUTLINE	SCRIPTURE	SCRIPTURE	OUTLINE
2. The promises of God to the obedient	4 Then I will give you rain in due season, and the land shall yield her increase, and the trees of the field shall yield their fruit.	hundred of you shall put ten thousand to flight: and your enemies shall fall before you by the sword.	
a. The blessing of food & plenty, even an abundance		9 For I will have respect unto you, and make you fruitful, and multiply you, and establish my covenant with you.	d. The blessing of children, of being fruitful: Was a promise of the covenant with Abraham (Ge.12:1-3)
1) A full season of rain, crops, & fruit			
2) A full harvest season	5 And your threshing shall reach unto the vintage, and the vintage shall reach unto the sowing time: and ye shall eat your bread to the full, and dwell in your land safely.	10 And ye shall eat old store, and bring forth the old because of the new.	e. The blessing of having more than enough: Will have enough to give & help others (see Ep.4:28)
3) An abundance of food			
4) An assurance of safety: God will provide, take care of, & look after		11 And I will set my tabernacle among you: and my soul shall not abhor you.	f. The blessing of God's presence
			1) He will dwell among—not despise—the obedient
b. The blessing of peace & security	6 And I will give peace in the land, and ye shall lie down, and none shall make *you* afraid: and I will rid evil beasts out of the land, neither shall the sword go through your land.	12 And I will walk among you, and will be your God, and ye shall be my people.	2) He will walk among the obedient: Be their God & make them His people
1) From lawless attacks at night			
2) From savage animals		13 I *am* the LORD your God, which brought you forth out of the land of Egypt, that ye should not be their bondmen; and I have broken the bands of your yoke, and made you go upright.	g. The guarantee that God can fulfill His promises & His blessings
3) From hostile people & war			1) He is the LORD, the true God
c. The blessing of victory	7 And ye shall chase your enemies, and they shall fall before you by the sword.		2) He is the One who delivered His people from Egypt
1) The obedient will defeat the enemy & cause him to fall			3) He is the One who enabled His people to walk with their heads held high
2) The obedient will be filled with courage	8 And five of you shall chase an hundred, and an		

a. There was the blessing of food and plenty, of even having an abundance (vv.4-5). If a person obeyed God, God promised a full season of rain, crops, and fruit—a full season of harvest. There would be an abundance of food; moreover, God would provide safety from any enemy who might steal or ravage the crops. Note: when armies march across land, they are often forced to live off the land. Moreover, what they do not need, they often destroy to keep the food out of the hands of their enemies. God was promising His people safety from thieves and from armies of war. He would provide and take care of them, making sure that they had plenty of food, even an abundance of food.

> **"But seek ye first the kingdom of God, and his righteousness; and all these things shall be added unto you [food, shelter, clothing]" (Mt.6:33).**
> **"But my God shall supply all your need according to his riches in glory by Christ Jesus" (Ph.4:19).**
> **"And ye shall serve the LORD your God, and he shall bless thy bread, and thy water; and I will take sickness away from the midst of thee" (Ex.23:25).**

b. There was the blessing of peace and security (v.6) This is an interesting promise because it mentions lawless attacks at night and attacks from savage animals. Thieves and rapists are usually the lawless who attack at night. The dangerous or savage animals would include snakes and scorpions, and lions and bears who roamed the land of Canaan during the days of Moses. Security was also promised against hostile people and war. The person who obeys God will have a blessing of peace and security even during the night while he is sleeping.

> **"But even the very hairs of your head are all numbered. Fear not therefore: ye are of more value than many sparrows" (Lu.12:7).**
> **"So that we may boldly say, The Lord *is* my helper, and I will not fear what man shall do unto me" (He.13:6).**
> **"And who *is* he that will harm you, if ye be followers of that which is good?" (1 Pe.3:13).**
> **"Casting all your care upon him; for he careth for you" (1 Pe.5:7).**
> **"For the eyes of the LORD run to and fro throughout the whole earth, to show himself strong in the behalf of *them* whose heart *is* perfect toward him. Herein thou hast done foolishly: therefore from henceforth thou shalt have wars" (2 Ch.16:9).**
> **"He shall cover thee with his feathers, and under his wings shalt thou trust: his truth *shall be thy* shield and buckler" (Ps.91:4).**
> **"Thou shalt not be afraid for the terror by night; *nor* for the arrow *that* flieth by day" (Ps.91:5).**
> **"He shall not be afraid of evil tidings: his heart is fixed, trusting in the LORD" (Ps.112:7).**
> **"Behold, he that keepeth Israel shall neither slumber nor sleep (Ps.121:4).**
> **"When thou liest down, thou shalt not be afraid: yea, thou shalt lie down, and thy sleep shall be sweet" (Pr.3:24).**

c. There was the blessing of victory (vv.7-8). If an enemy—a nation, mob, or individual—attacked any or all of God's people, God promised that they would be defeated. The believer would strike with the sword and the enemy would fall before the believer. Note a striking fact: the obedient believer will be filled with courage. It takes just a few obedient believers to defeat a mob or army of unbelievers. Note the example given: five obedient believers will have so much courage that they will chase a hundred, and a hundred obedient believers so much courage that they will chase ten thousand. What a wonderful promise! Victory over all enemies is guaranteed to the obedient believer.

Thought 1. God promises victory to the believer, even victory over the terrible enemy of death and hell.

"Who shall separate us from the love of Christ? *shall* tribulation, or distress, or persecution, or famine, or nakedness, or peril, or sword? Nay, in all these things we are more than conquerors through him that loved us" (Ro.8:35, 37).

"There hath no temptation taken you but such as is common to man: but God *is* faithful, who will not suffer you to be tempted above that ye are able; but will with the temptation also make a way to escape, that ye may be able to bear *it*" (1 Co.10:13).

"Now thanks *be* unto God, which always causeth us to triumph in Christ, and maketh manifest the savour of his knowledge by us in every place" (2 Co.2:14).

"Forasmuch then as the children are partakers of flesh and blood, he also himself likewise took part of the same; that through death he might destroy him that had the power of death, that is, the devil; And deliver them who through fear of death were all their lifetime subject to bondage" (He.2:14-15).

"For whatsoever is born of God overcometh the world: and this is the victory that overcometh the world, *even* our faith" (1 Jn.5:4)

"He that overcometh shall inherit all things; and I will be his God, and he shall be my son" (Re.21:7).

d. There was the blessing of children, of being fruitful. This was a promise to fulfill the covenant with Abraham (v.9). (See outline and notes—Ge.12:1-3 for more discussion.) If God's people obeyed Him, He promised that the population would dramatically increase.

e. There was the blessing of having more than enough, of having enough to give and help others (v.10). The believer who obeys God will never face a food shortage. He will always have enough to eat and to give to help others. Note the picture God uses to describe the abundance of harvest: the believer will still be eating last year's harvest when he has to make room for the new harvest.

f. There was the blessing of God's presence (vv.11-12). God promised to dwell among His people and not despise them if they obeyed Him. He would walk among them and be their God and make them His people. This is a great promise: that God would live among and fellowship with His people if they would just obey Him. What an amazing thought! That the God of the universe—the great Creator and Sustainer of all—would allow a personal relationship with Himself. He would actually live and fellowship with an obedient believer. He would take the believer and make him a member of God's family—an astounding truth!

"For where two or three are gathered together in my name, there am I in the midst of them" (Mt.18:20).

"Lo, I am with you alway, *even* unto the end of the world. Amen" (Mt.28:20).

"God *is* faithful, by whom ye were called unto the fellowship of his Son Jesus Christ our Lord" (1 Co.1:9).

"That which we have seen and heard declare we unto you, that ye also may have fellowship with us: and truly our fellowship *is* with the Father, and with his Son Jesus Christ" (1 Jn.1:3).

"Behold, I stand at the door, and knock: if any man hear my voice, and open the door, I will come in to him, and will sup with him, and he with me" (Re.3:20).

"And he said, My presence shall go *with thee,* and I will give thee rest" (Ex.33:14).

"The LORD *is* nigh unto them that are of a broken heart; and saveth such as be of a contrite spirit" (Ps.34:18).

"The LORD *is* nigh unto all them that call upon him, to all that call upon him in truth" (Ps.145:18).

When thou passest through the waters, I *will be* with thee; and through the rivers, they shall not overflow thee: when thou walkest through the fire, thou shalt not be burned; neither shall the flame kindle upon thee" (Is.43:2).

g. There was the guarantee that God could fulfill His promises and His blessings (v.13). Note the forceful declaration: "I am the LORD your God." It is He who has delivered His people from the slavery of Egypt. Remember, Egypt is a symbol of the world. God is the One who enables His people to walk with their heads held high. God is declaring that He has the power to fulfill His promises and His blessings. He has proven His power by delivering His people from the enslavement of Egypt. Because of His power, His people can walk with their heads held high. His promises will be fulfilled.

"For the which cause I also suffer these things: nevertheless I am not ashamed: for I know whom I have believed, and am persuaded that he is able to keep that which I have committed unto him against that day" (2 Ti.1:12).

3 (26:14-15) **Discipline—Judgment—Punishment—Disobedience—Covenant, Violation of—Commandment, Breaking**: there are two major causes that stir God's discipline or punishment, that arouse His judgment: note the Scripture and outline:

OUTLINE	SCRIPTURE	SCRIPTURE	OUTLINE
3. The causes that stir God's discipline or punishment a. Failing to listen & obey God b. Breaking the covenant of God	14 But if ye will not hearken unto me, and will not do all these commandments; 15 And if ye shall despise my	statutes, or if your soul abhor my judgments, so that ye will not do all my commandments, *but* that ye break my covenant:	1) By rejecting & abhorring His laws 2) By disobeying God's commands

a. There is failing to listen to God and failing to obey God. God had spoken; He had given His commandments and His promises to the people. Their first obligation was to listen, to pay attention to what He said. They needed to study His commandments and His promises, make sure they grasped and understood exactly what He was saying. Then they needed to obey God, do exactly what He said. God's promises were conditional; therefore, understanding the promises and the conditions was an absolute essential. Listening to God and obeying God were necessary in order to inherit the promised land and experience the promises of God.

b. There is violating or breaking the covenant of God. Rejecting and despising the laws of God will arouse the discipline of God. Disobeying any of God's laws will stir the discipline or punishment of God. This is understandable, logical. If a person obeys God, God is bound to bless the person. But the opposite is also true: if a person refuses to do what God says, God is bound—even forced—to discipline the person. Why? Because God loves His people and wants only the best for them. Therefore, when a person goes astray, God is bound to correct His loved one, bound to discipline him—all in the hope that the loved one will be saved from some serious or fatal harm.

Thought 1. A person will fail to stir the judgment of God, fail His discipline or judgment for two reasons.
(1) A person fails to listen to and obey God.

"*Ye* hypocrites, ye can discern the face of the sky and of the earth; but how is it that ye do not discern this time?" (Lu.12:56).

"Why do ye not understand my speech? *even* because ye cannot hear my word" (Jn.8:43).

"For the heart of this people is waxed gross, and their ears are dull of hearing, and their eyes have they closed; lest they should see with *their* eyes, and hear with *their* ears, and understand with *their* heart, and should be converted, and I should heal them" (Ac.28:27).

"And they shall turn away *their* ears from the truth, and shall be turned unto fables" (2 Ti.4:4).

"To whom shall I speak, and give warning, that they may hear? behold, their ear *is* uncircumcised, and they cannot hearken: behold, the word of the LORD is unto them a reproach; they have no delight in it" (Je.6:10).

"Son of man, thou dwellest in the midst of a rebellious house, which have eyes to see, and see not; they have ears to hear, and hear not: for they *are* a rebellious house" (Eze.12:2).

"But they refused to hearken, and pulled away the shoulder, and stopped their ears, that they should not hear" (Zec.7:11).

(2) A person violates the covenant of God, rejects and despises His laws and disobeys His commandments.

"Let no man deceive you with vain words: for because of these things cometh the wrath of God upon the children of disobedience" (Ep.5:6).

"In flaming fire taking vengeance on them that know not God, and that obey not the gospel of our Lord Jesus Christ" (2 Th.1:8).

"For if the word spoken by angels was stedfast, and every transgression and disobedience received a just recompence of reward; How shall we escape, if we neglect so great salvation; which at the first began to be spoken by the LORD, and was confirmed unto us by them that heard *him*" (He.2:2-3).

"And a curse, if ye will not obey the commandments of the LORD your God, but turn aside out of the way which I command you this day, to go after other gods, which ye have not known" (De.11:28).

"But if ye will not obey the voice of the LORD, but rebel against the commandment of the LORD, then shall the hand of the LORD be against you, as *it was* against your fathers" (1 S.12:15).

4 (26:16-39) **Warning, of Judgment—Judgment, Described—Punishment, Described—Judgment, of Israel—Israel, Judgment of—Israel, Warning of Judgment—Nations, Warning to:** God warned that the disobedient would face judgment and be punished. Keep in mind that this warning was given to Israel while they were being formed into a nation. God was telling His people what would happen to them if they rejected Him and His laws. This was just a list of the judgments and punishments that would fall upon them, but they would become a living reality if His people rejected Him.

Tragically, Israel did reject God and did suffer the punishments pronounced here. Note the scripture and outline, in particular the five warnings or kinds of punishment that are given.

a. There is the first warning or kind of punishment: mental and physical suffering (vv.16-17).

OUTLINE	SCRIPTURE	SCRIPTURE	OUTLINE

4. The warning of judgment & punishment to the disobedient
a. The first warning of punishment: Mental & physical suffering (see Jud.2:14; 3:8; 4:2)
  1) Will suffer mental terror & problems
  2) Will suffer physical disease
	16 I also will do this unto you; I will even appoint over you terror, consumption, and the burning ague, that shall consume the eyes, and cause sorrow of heart: and ye shall sow your seed in vain, for your enemies	shall eat it.
		17 And I will set my face against you, and ye shall be slain before your enemies: they that hate you shall reign over you; and ye shall flee when none pursueth you.
			3) Will have crops (food) stolen & ravaged (Je.5:17)
			4) Will be defeated & ruled over by one's enemies
			5) Will be stricken with fear of one's enemies

Note that mental anguish will be brought about by disease, epidemics, and fevers that will destroy a person's eyesight, sapping his life away. But not only this, mental anguish will be caused by the attack of enemies and famine due to their ravaging of the crops and food supply. The attacks and assaults will be so severe and strike so much fear in the hearts that people will be fleeing even when the enemy is not pursuing. The picture being painted is graphic: a terrible period of mental anguish and physical suffering.

> "And the children of Israel did evil in the sight of the LORD, and served Baalim: And they forsook the LORD God of their fathers, which brought them out of the land of Egypt, and followed other gods, of the gods of the people that *were* round about them, and bowed themselves unto them, and provoked the LORD to anger. And they forsook the LORD, and served Baal and Ashtaroth. And the anger of the LORD was hot against Israel, and he delivered them into the hands of spoilers that spoiled them, and he sold them into the hands of their enemies round about, so that they could not any longer stand before their enemies. Whithersoever they went out, the hand of the LORD was against them for evil, as the LORD had said, and as the LORD had sworn unto them: and they were greatly distressed" (Jud.2:11-15).

> "And the children of Israel dwelt among the Canaanites, Hittites, and Amorites, and Perizzites, and Hivites, and Jebusites: And they took their daughters to be their wives, and gave their daughters to their sons, and served their gods. And the children of Israel did evil in the sight of the LORD, and forgat the LORD their God, and served Baalim and the groves. Therefore the anger of the LORD was hot against Israel, and he sold them into the hand of Chushan-rishathaim king of Mesopotamia: and the children of Israel served Chushan-rishathaim eight years (Jud.3:5-8).

> "And the children of Israel again did evil in the sight of the LORD, when Ehud was dead. And the LORD sold them into the hand of Jabin king of Canaan, that reigned in Hazor; the captain of whose host *was* Sisera, which dwelt in Harosheth of the Gentiles" (Jud.4:1-2).

> "And they shall eat up thine harvest, and thy bread, *which* thy sons and thy daughters should eat: they shall eat up thy flocks and thine herds: they shall eat up thy vines and thy fig trees: they shall impoverish thy fenced cities, wherein thou trustedst, with the sword" (Je.5:17).

b. There was the second warning or kind of punishment: drought and poor harvest (vv.18-20).

OUTLINE	SCRIPTURE	SCRIPTURE	OUTLINE
b. The second warning of punishment: Drought & poor harvests 1) Will suffer multiple, repeated punishments if continue to disobey God 2) Will have one's stubborn pride broken (see De.8:11-20)	18 And if ye will not yet for all this hearken unto me, then I will punish you seven times more for your sins. 19 And I will break the pride of your power; and I	will make your heaven as iron, and your earth as brass: 20 And your strength shall be spent in vain: for your land shall not yield her increase, neither shall the trees of the land yield their fruits.	3) Will cause a harsh drought & hard, unproductive ground 4) Will cause crops to fail: A food shortage, hunger, thirst

Note that the purpose for the drought and poor harvest is to break the stubborn pride of people. Success and having plenty (prosperity) often make a person self-sufficient and prideful. Whereas the judgment of God cuts a person down to size and often arouses him to seek after God.[2]

> "He hath showed strength with his arm; he hath scattered the proud in the imagination of their hearts" (Lu.1:51).

> "Now Jacob's well was there. Jesus therefore, being wearied with *his* journey, sat thus on the well: *and* it was about the sixth hour" (Jn.4:6).

> "They are exalted for a little while, but are gone and brought low; they are taken out of the way as all *other,* and cut off as the tops of the ears of corn" (Jb.24:24).

> "Pride *goeth* before destruction, and an haughty spirit before a fall" (Pr.16:18).

> "And I will punish the world for *their* evil, and the wicked for their iniquity; and I will cause the arrogancy of the proud to cease, and will lay low the haughtiness of the terrible" (Is.13:11).

c. There was the third warning or kind of punishment: wild animals such as snakes, scorpions, lions, bears, wolves, and perhaps tigers and other ferocious animals (vv.21-22).

OUTLINE	SCRIPTURE	SCRIPTURE	OUTLINE
c. The third warning of punishment: Wild animals (snakes, scorpions) 1) Will suffer because "your sins deserve" judgment 2) Will suffer the loss of	21 And if ye walk contrary unto me, and will not hearken unto me; I will bring seven times more plagues upon you according to your sins. 22 I will also send wild	beasts among you, which shall rob you of your children, and destroy your cattle, and make you few in number; and your *high* ways shall be desolate.	livestock, crops, & even human life by attacks of wild animals 3) Will have so few people remaining that roads will be deserted

Note that such judgment falls upon a people because of sin and hostility toward God. People became stiff-necked, refusing to listen to God. Note also that the population of the people would be so decimated that only a few people would be traveling along the highways.

---

2 Gordon J. Wenham. *The Book of Leviticus,* p.331.

"In the days of Shamgar the son of Anath, in the days of Jael, the highways were unoccupied, and the travelers walked through byways" (Jud.5:6).

"And *so* it was at the beginning of their dwelling there, *that* they feared not the LORD: therefore the LORD sent lions among them, which slew *some* of them" (2 K.17:25).

"So will I send upon you famine and evil beasts, and they shall bereave thee; and pestilence and blood shall pass through thee; and I will bring the sword upon thee. I the LORD have spoken *it*" (Eze.5:17).

"If I cause noisome beasts to pass through the land, and they spoil it, so that it be desolate, that no man may pass through because of the beasts" (Eze.14:15).

"For thus saith the LORD GOD; How much more when I send my four sore judgments upon Jerusalem, the sword, and the famine, and the noisome beast, and the pestilence, to cut off from it man and beast?" (Eze.14:21).

d. There was the fourth warning or kind of punishment: war (vv.23-26).

OUTLINE	SCRIPTURE	SCRIPTURE	OUTLINE
d. The fourth warning of punishment: War 1) The reason: Because of continued rejection & hostility toward God 2) Will suffer God's rejection & hostility: Suffer multiple & repeated corrections: Because of sins 3) Will suffer attacks, war 4) Will suffer a disease, some plague, while fighting (see Eze.5:12)	23 And if ye will not be reformed by me by these things, but will walk contrary unto me; 24 Then will I also walk contrary unto you, and will punish you yet seven times for your sins. 25 And I will bring a sword upon you, that shall avenge the quarrel of *my* covenant: and when ye are gathered together within your cities, I	will send the pestilence among you; and ye shall be delivered into the hand of the enemy. 26 *And* when I have broken the staff of your bread, ten women shall bake your bread in one oven, and they shall deliver *you* your bread again by weight: and ye shall eat, and not be satisfied.	5) Will be defeated 6) Will suffer a shortage of food, face starvation

What causes war? Selfishness and hostility toward God. When a people are selfish and hostile toward God, conflict within the national borders and war soon follow. This is seen time and again throughout the Bible and human history. Canaanite nations were to be driven out because of their lawlessness, immorality, and hostility toward God. Moreover, Israel itself was to suffer internal conflict and war because of the people's selfishness and hostility toward God. A people who become basically selfish and hostile toward God cannot escape internal conflict and war. Conflict among the people themselves and attack from other nations of people are inevitable. People—whether nations or individuals—will tolerate selfish behavior only so long before retaliating. Thus, this fact is certainly true of God: He will tolerate selfish behavior and hostility only so long before He executes justice and judgment.

"And there was a great famine in Samaria: and, behold, they besieged it, until an ass's head was *sold* for fourscore *pieces* of silver, and the fourth part of a cab of dove's dung for five *pieces* of silver" (2 K.6:25).

"For, behold, the LORD, the LORD of hosts, doth take away from Jerusalem and from Judah the stay and the staff, the whole stay of bread, and the whole stay of water" (Is.3:1).

"If I go forth into the field, then behold the slain with the sword! and if I enter into the city, then behold them that are sick with famine! yea, both the prophet and the priest go about into a land that they know not" (Je.14:18).

"Moreover he said unto me, Son of man, behold, I will break the staff of bread in Jerusalem: and they shall eat bread by weight, and with care; and they shall drink water by measure, and with astonishment" (Eze.4:16).

"A third part of thee shall die with the pestilence, and with famine shall they be consumed in the midst of thee: and a third part shall fall by the sword round about thee and I will scatter a third part into all the winds, and I will draw out a sword after them" (Eze.5:12).

e. There was the fifth warning or kind of punishment: desolation and exile (vv.27-39).

OUTLINE	SCRIPTURE	SCRIPTURE	OUTLINE
e. The fifth warning of punishment: Desolation & exile 1) The reason: Because of continued rejection & hostility toward God 2) Will suffer God's continued rejection: Suffer multiple disciplines & corrections because of sins 3) Will suffer cannibalism (2 K.6:28-29; La.2:20; 4:10)	27 And if ye will not for all this hearken unto me, but walk contrary unto me; 28 Then I will walk contrary unto you also in fury; and I, even I, will chastise you seven times for your sins. 29 And ye shall eat the flesh of your sons, and the flesh	of your daughters shall ye eat. 30 And I will destroy your high places, and cut down your images, and cast your carcases upon the carcases of your idols, and my soul shall abhor you. 31 And I will make your cities waste, and bring your sanctuaries unto desolation,	4) Will suffer a terrible, savage slaughter or holocaust (Am.8:3; Eze.6:5) 5) Will suffer the utter destruction of one's cities & sanctuaries (Eze.6:3f)

OUTLINE	SCRIPTURE	SCRIPTURE	OUTLINE
6) Will suffer the rejection of one's cry & plea to God (Is.1:11-15) 7) Will suffer the total devastation of one's land (Je.9:11; Eze.5:15) 8) Will suffer the deportation & scattering of one's people (Je.9:16) 9) Will suffer the terrible ruin of both land & cities • The land will lie so desolate that it will rest & enjoy the Sabbaths • The land will gain the rest denied it by the disobedient (see the Babylonian captivity, 2 Chr.36:21) 10) Will suffer a terrifying fear	and I will not smell the savour of your sweet odours. 32 And I will bring the land into desolation: and your enemies which dwell therein shall be astonished at it. 33 And I will scatter you among the heathen, and will draw out a sword after you: and your land shall be desolate, and your cities waste. 34 Then shall the land enjoy her sabbaths, as long as it lieth desolate, and ye *be* in your enemies' land; *even* then shall the land rest, and enjoy her sabbaths. 35 As long as it lieth desolate it shall rest; because it did not rest in your sabbaths, when ye dwelt upon it. 36 And upon them that are	left *alive* of you I will send a faintness into their hearts in the lands of their enemies; and the sound of a shaken leaf shall chase them; and they shall flee, as fleeing from a sword; and they shall fall when none pursueth. 37 And they shall fall one upon another, as it were before a sword, when none pursueth: and ye shall have no power to stand before your enemies. 38 And ye shall perish among the heathen, and the land of your enemies shall eat you up. 39 And they that are left of you shall pine away in their iniquity in your enemies' lands; and also in the iniquities of their fathers shall they pine away with them.	in the lands of their enemies (Eze.21:7) 11) Will suffer so terrifying a fear that they will flee even 12) Will perish, die in foreign lands: Be devoured & waste away in the lands of their enemies (Je.31:10; 49:32; Eze.5:12; 12:14) 13) The reason: Because of their sins (cp. the Roman siege in A.D. 70 foretold by Christ, Mt.24:1f)

What is described here are the atrocities and horrors of war. The terrible picture being painted shows just how savage man can be. In fact, one of the most tragic themes that runs throughout human history is that of war, the hellish brutality and savagery of the human heart that is seen in atrocity after atrocity. Rape, murder, dismemberment, torture, medical experimentation, enslavement, starvation, cannibalism, destruction, deportation—monstrous, barbaric atrocities are the terrifying results of war.

Thought 1. Standing at this point in history, a person can look back and see how these judgments fell upon Israel. For example, the Israelites or Jewish people were scattered throughout the nations of the world from the Babylonian captivity until right after the second world war. But close observation of human history reveals a startling fact: any nation or people who have become basically selfish and hostile toward God have brought these same kinds of judgments and punishments upon themselves. Holy Scripture declares time and again that God will execute justice and judgment upon the nations and the peoples of this earth. The people who become basically selfish—immoral and lawless—rejecting, living in hostility toward God, will face the terrible judgment of God. They bring the judgment and punishment of God upon themselves, both in this life and in the life to come. God will judge us, every human being who has ever lived, both the leaders and the citizens of every nation.

"For the Son of man shall come in the glory of his Father with his angels; and then he shall reward every man according to his works. (Mt.16:27).

"And then shall appear the sign of the Son of man in heaven: and then shall all the tribes of the earth mourn, and they shall see the Son of man coming in the clouds of heaven with power and great glory" (Mt.24:30).

"When the Son of man shall come in his glory, and all the holy angels with him, then shall he sit upon the throne of his glory: And before him shall be gathered all nations: and he shall separate them one from another, as a shepherd divideth *his* sheep from the goats: And he shall set the sheep on his right hand, but the goats on the left" (Mt.25:31-33).

"For we must all appear before the judgment seat of Christ; that every one may receive the things *done* in *his* body, according to that he hath done, whether *it be* good or bad" (2 Co.5:10).

"And to you who are troubled rest with us, when the Lord Jesus shall be revealed from heaven with his mighty angels, In flaming fire taking vengeance on them that know not God, and that obey not the gospel of our Lord Jesus Christ" (2 Th.1:7-8).

"And as it is appointed unto men once to die, but after this the judgment" (He.9:27).

"And if ye call on the Father, who without respect of persons judgeth according to every man's work, pass the time of your sojourning *here* in fear" (1 Pe.1:17).

"The Lord knoweth how to deliver the godly out of temptations, and to reserve the unjust unto the day of judgment to be punished" (2 Pe.2:9).

"But the heavens and the earth, which are now, by the same word are kept in store, reserved unto fire against the day of judgment and perdition of ungodly men" (2 Pe.3:7).

"And Enoch also, the seventh from Adam, prophesied of these, saying, Behold, the Lord cometh with ten thousands of his saints, To execute judgment upon all, and to convince all that are ungodly among them of all their ungodly deeds which they have ungodly committed, and of all their hard *speeches* which ungodly sinners have spoken against him" (Jude 1:14-15).

"Behold, he cometh with clouds; and every eye shall see him, and they *also* which pierced him: and all kindreds of the earth shall wail because of him. Even so, Amen" (Re.1:7).

"And I saw the dead, small and great, stand before God; and the books were opened: and another book was opened, which is *the book* of life: and the dead were judged out of those things which were written in the books, according to their works" (Re.20:12).

"And, behold, I come quickly; and my reward *is* with me, to give every man according as his work shall be" (Re.22:12).

"Also unto thee, O LORD, *belongeth* mercy: for thou renderest to every man according to his work" (Ps.62:12).

"I the LORD search the heart, *I* try the reins, even to give every man according to his ways, *and* according to the fruit of his doings" (Je.17:10).

5 (26:40-46) **Faithfulness, of God—Restoration—Repentance—Return—Returning, to God**: there was the faithfulness of God to His promises: the promise of restoration. There is hope for any person or people upon earth, even for the most sinful and evil. God loves every human being upon the earth, and He wants every human being to know the fullness of life, both now and eternally.

OUTLINE	SCRIPTURE	SCRIPTURE	OUTLINE
5. The faithfulness of God to His promises: The promise of restoration a. The conditions for being restored 1) One must confess his sins	40 If they shall confess their iniquity, and the iniquity of their fathers, with their trespass which they trespassed against me, and that also they have walked contrary unto me;	punishment of their iniquity: because, even because they despised my judgments, and because their soul abhorred my statutes.	3) He will fulfill His Word & warning: Will judge & condemn the disobedient
2) One must humble his hard heart 3) One must repent	41 And *that* I also have walked contrary unto them, and have brought them into the land of their enemies; if then their uncircumcised hearts be humbled, and they then accept of the punishment of their iniquity:	44 And yet for all that, when they be in the land of their enemies, I will not cast them away, neither will I abhor them, to destroy them utterly, and to break my covenant with them: for I *am* the LORD their God.	4) He will not reject nor destroy them completely, will not break His covenant with them 5) He is the LORD their God, able to fulfill all His promises, able to restore them
b. The faithfulness of God to restore 1) He will renew His covenant	42 Then will I remember my covenant with Jacob, and also my covenant with Isaac, and also my covenant with Abraham will I remember; and I will remember the land.	45 But I will for their sakes remember the covenant of their ancestors, whom I brought forth out of the land of Egypt in the sight of the heathen, that I might be their God: I *am* the LORD.	6) He will remember His covenant with their ancestors: The ancestors who believed God & accepted His power to deliver them: Will restore them
2) He will remember the land: Will see that it rests & recovers (enjoys Sabbaths)	43 The land also shall be left of them, and shall enjoy her sabbaths, while she lieth desolate without them: and they shall accept of the	46 These *are* the statutes and judgments and laws, which the LORD made between him and the children of Israel in mount Sinai by the hand of Moses.	7) He is the source of all the laws given to His people: He will fulfill all the promises

a. This scripture tells the sinful and evil person what he must do to be saved and restored, what he must do to become acceptable to God. The conditions for salvation and restoration are simply stated: a person must confess his sins, humble his hard heart, and repent. These conditions stand true both for individuals and for nations. This is exactly what God declared to Israel after Israel had fallen and suffered the above judgments and punishments:

"Then Peter said unto them, Repent, and be baptized every one of you in the name of Jesus Christ for the remission of sins, and ye shall receive the gift of the Holy Ghost" (Ac.2:38).

"Repent therefore of this thy wickedness, and pray God, if perhaps the thought of thine heart may be forgiven thee" (Ac.8:22).

"If we confess our sins, he is faithful and just to forgive us *our* sins, and to cleanse us from all unrighteousness" (1 Jn.1:9).

"If my people, which are called by my name, shall humble themselves, and pray, and seek my face, and turn from their wicked ways; then will I hear from heaven, and will forgive their sin, and will heal their land" (2 Ch.7:14).

"The LORD *is* nigh unto them that are of a broken heart; and saveth such as be of a contrite spirit" (Ps.34:18).

"The sacrifices of God *are* a broken spirit: a broken and a contrite heart, O God, thou wilt not despise" (Ps.51:17).

"He that covereth his sins shall not prosper: but whoso confesseth and forsaketh *them* shall have mercy" (Pr.28:13).

"Let the wicked forsake his way, and the unrighteous man his thoughts: and let him return unto the LORD, and he will have mercy upon him; and to our God, for he will abundantly pardon" (Is.55:7).

"For all those *things* hath mine hand made, and all those *things* have been, saith the LORD: but to this *man* will I look, *even to him that is* poor and of a contrite spirit, and trembleth at my word" (Is.66:2).

"Only acknowledge thine iniquity, that thou hast transgressed against the LORD thy God, and hast scattered thy ways to the strangers under every green tree, and ye have not obeyed my voice, saith the LORD" (Je.3:13).

"But if the wicked will turn from all his sins that he hath committed, and keep all my statutes, and do that which is lawful and right, he shall surely live, he shall not die" (Eze.18:21).

b. Note that God is faithful to save and restore any person or nation who turns to Him. Although this passage is speaking directly to Israel, it is applicable to all other nations and peoples of the earth. Note the promises God makes to the person or people who return to Him:

1) God will renew His covenant with them (v.42). God will make sure that the land rests and recovers, that it enjoys its Sabbaths (see outline and notes, *The Sabbatical Year*—Le.25:1-7 for more discussion).

2) God will fulfill His word and warning: He will judge and condemn the disobedient (v.43).

3) God will not reject nor destroy His people completely; He will not break His covenant with them (v.44).

4) God is the LORD their God (v.44). God is able to fulfill all His promises, able to restore them when they return to Him (v.44).

5) God will remember His covenant with their ancestors, the ancestors who believed God and accepted His power to deliver them (v.45). God will restore them to Himself.

6) God is the Source of all the laws given to His people. He will fulfill all the promises He has made to them (v.46).

Thought 1. J. Vernon McGee has an excellent exposition dealing with this particular passage that is well worth quoting in full:

> All of their past iniquity does not destroy the fact that Israel holds the title deed to that land. This is a remarkable prophecy and one that God says He will fulfill when the time has come. God will not utterly destroy them because of His covenant with Abraham and the other patriarchs. We found in the book of Exodus that when Israel was in slavery in Egypt, God heard their groaning, God remembered His covenant with Abraham, Isaac, and Jacob, and so God delivered them out of Egypt (Exod. 2:24-25).
>
> Now God tells them they can stay in the land if they will obey Him. If not, they must leave the land. But if they will repent and turn to God when they are out of the land, then He will bring them back into the land. So we find that Daniel turned to God in prayer when he was down in Babylon. He turned his face toward Jerusalem, he confessed his sins and the sins of his people, and when he did that, God heard. God sent a messenger to him to tell him they would return to the land. And they did return back to the land!
>
> God still has a future purpose for the nation which the judgment of the past cannot nullify. Read Romans 11:1-25 and Jeremiah 31:31-34 in this connection....This is a remarkable passage of Scripture. Can you say that God is through with the nation Israel after you have read this passage? If you believe that God means what He says, then He is not through with them at all....[The Israelites] brought judgment upon Palestine just as Adam brought judgment upon the whole earth by his sin. Because of God's covenant with their fathers, He will return them to the land and restore all that He had promised to them.
>
> We have come to the end of the giving of these laws here in Leviticus, God confirms the Pentateuch here as given through Moses. This verse seems to end the book, but it doesn't.
>
> God looks down through the ages to their repeated failures and His faithfulness and final victory. Moses could not bring them eternal blessings, although he was a mediator. The world must look to Another. John gives us the answer: 'For the law was given by Moses, but grace and truth came by Jesus Christ' (John 1:17). [3]

Thought 2. *The Expositors Bible Commentary* also makes an excellent statement concerning this passage:

> In 25:23 God said, "The land is mine," and he would remember his promises to the patriarchs to give them that land. Incidentally, the promises given here to Israel are not limited to the time of the judges or the Babylonian captivity. Paul declares that the promises to Israel and the fathers are "irrevocable: (Rom 11:28-29). But the Jews will not reinherit Palestine in peace and blessing until they return to the Lord.
>
> Verse 36 stated that only some of the people of the Captivity will be left. But God will spare some (v.44) and use their punishments to bring them back to him. A sad commentary on human nature is that in prosperity men tend to forget God from whom all blessings flow, and God must often punish them to bring them back to him. The wise child of God will stay close to God in the first place and rejoice in the blessings without having to get the punishments. [4]

Thought 3. In comparing Leviticus 26 and the New Testament teaching concerning it, Gordon J. Wenham asks a question that needs to be considered: "Does (this passage) apply only to Israel, to the church, or to the whole world?" He then proceeds to show how this passage and the teaching of the New Testament apply to all three. What he has to say is an excellent exposition that needs to be considered by all biblical students. For this reason, his statement is being quoted in full:

> The blessings and curses of this chapter are addressed to the elect nation of Israel. The prophets saw the curses fulfilled in the tribulations that culminated in the exile, while Ezekiel (Ezek. 34-37) looked forward to the

---

3 J. Vernon McGee. *Thru the Bible*, Vol.1, p.446
4 Frank E. Gaebelein, General Editor. *The Expositor's Bible Commentary*, Vol.2, p.648.

fulfillment of the blessings in the messianic age. But the dawning of that age brings new complications to the interpretation of this chapter. The elect are not to be found now in Israel alone, but among all nations. The kingdom promised to the Church is a spiritual one, not an earthly one (cf. John 18:36). How does the NT see the relevance of this chapter? Does it apply only to Israel, to the Church, or to the whole world? Are the blessings and curses to be understood entirely spiritually or are they experienced in this life as well? Some of these questions seem to receive no clear answer, but in some cases we can be more definite.

1) *First the NT does consider that the nation of Israel is still God's covenant people and subject, therefore, to the blessings and curses entailed in this chapter. Christ's warnings to his fellow countrymen presuppose that they are God's covenant people, liable to God's judgment if they do not listen to his word. Some of the curses in Lev.26 have their counterparts in Christ's teaching about wars and famines and the destruction of the temple (Mark 13//Luke 19-21).*

2) *The NT also seems to regard the principle of blessing and curse as applying to the Church, individually and corporately. In both testaments salvation is brought by the grace of God, whether that grace is to be seen in the promises to Abraham or in the death of Christ; but those who accept that grace will enjoy its privileges in doing God's will but will suffer if they do not. Thus Jesus speaks of rewards for the faithful disciples and warns shirkers that their laxity will not pass unnoticed in the last judgment (e.g., Matt. 5:19; 6:25ff.; Luke 11:41ff.). Paul expects all to appear before God's judgment seat to receive the reward for the things done on earth (1 Co.3:10-15; 2 Co.5:10).*

   Though the NT seems to expect that it will only be at the last judgment that the blessings and curses will finally be seen to be fairly distributed, the Gospels and Epistles also envisage a partial and provisional fulfilment in this life. Jesus promised, 'seek first his kingdom and his righteousness, and all these things (i.e., food and clothing) shall be yours as well' (Matt. 6:33). Paul ascribed the illness and death of Corinthian believers to their misbehavior at the Lord's supper (1 Co.11:30; cf. Lev.26:16). But the NT does not look for an exact correspondence between the present lot of the believer and his final glory. In some societies in deed "all who desire to live a godly life in Christ Jesus will be persecuted." (2 Ti.3:12).

3) *Finally, the NT points out that as the whole word enjoys God's bounty (Matt 5:45; Acts 17:25) and should believe in the gospel, so all men should fear his curse (Ac.17:30-31). What this means in detail is spelled out in the book of Revelation: many of the horrifying judgments described in Rev. 6:ff. find their original setting in the covenant curses of Lev. 26 and Deut. 28.*[5]

---

5   Gordon J. Wenham. *The Book of Leviticus*, pp.333-334. Points set apart by us for clarity.

CHAPTER 27

K. Laws That Govern Vows & Commitments Made to God: The Critical Importance of Keeping Sacred Vows, 27:1-34

1. The vow to dedicate oneself or some other person to God

a. Are to pay the monetary value of that person to the sanctuary

b. Are to use this scale: Based upon the labor value of a person

　1) A male 20-60 years old: Fifty shekels or pieces of silver

　2) A female 20-60 years old: Thirty shekels or pieces of silver

　3) A person 5-20 years old:
　　• Male: 20 shekels or pieces of silver
　　• Female: 10 shekels or pieces of silver

　4) A person one month-five years old
　　• A male: Five shekels or pieces of silver
　　• A female: Three shekels or pieces of silver

　5) A person 60 plus years old
　　• A male: Fifteen shekels or pieces of silver
　　• A female: Ten shekels or pieces of silver

　6) A poor person
　　• To present his vow to the priest
　　• To have a value set based upon what he can pay

2. The vow to dedicate an animal to God

a. The clean animal: One that is acceptable as an offering to God
　1) Is counted holy or set apart for that very purpose
　2) Is not ever to be exchanged or replaced by another: If it is, both the original animal & the substitute are counted holy (to be set apart & given to God)

b. The unclean animal: One not acceptable as an offering
　1) Is to be presented to the Priest

And the LORD spake unto Moses, saying,

2 Speak unto the children of Israel, and say unto them, When a man shall make a singular vow, the persons *shall be* for the LORD by thy estimation.

3 And thy estimation shall be of the male from twenty years old even unto sixty years old, even thy estimation shall be fifty shekels of silver, after the shekel of the sanctuary.

4 And if it *be* a female, then thy estimation shall be thirty shekels.

5 And if *it be* from five years old even unto twenty years old, then thy estimation shall be of the male twenty shekels, and for the female ten shekels.

6 And if *it be* from a month old even unto five years old, then thy estimation shall be of the male five shekels of silver, and for the female thy estimation *shall be* three shekels of silver.

7 And if *it be* from sixty years old and above; if *it be* a male, then thy estimation shall be fifteen shekels, and for the female ten shekels.

8 But if he be poorer than thy estimation, then he shall present himself before the priest, and the priest shall value him; according to his ability that vowed shall the priest value him.

9 And if *it be* a beast, whereof men bring an offering unto the LORD, all that *any man* giveth of such unto the LORD shall be holy.

10 He shall not alter it, nor change it, a good for a bad, or a bad for a good: and if he shall at all change beast for beast, then it and the exchange thereof shall be holy.

11 And if *it be* any unclean beast, of which they do not offer a sacrifice unto the LORD, then he shall present the beast before the priest:

12 And the priest shall value it, whether it be good or bad: as thou valuest it, *who art* the priest, so shall it be.

13 But if he will at all redeem it, then he shall add a fifth *part* thereof unto thy estimation.

14 And when a man shall sanctify his house *to be* holy unto the LORD, then the priest shall estimate it, whether it be good or bad: as the priest shall estimate it, so shall it stand.

15 And if he that sanctified it will redeem his house, then he shall add the fifth *part* of the money of thy estimation unto it, and it shall be his.

16 And if a man shall sanctify unto the LORD *some part* of a field of his possession, then thy estimation shall be according to the seed thereof: an homer of barley seed *shall be* valued at fifty shekels of silver.

17 If he sanctify his field from the year of jubile, according to thy estimation it shall stand.

18 But if he sanctify his field after the jubile, then the priest shall reckon unto him the money according to the years that remain, even unto the year of the jubile, and it shall be abated from thy estimation.

19 And if he that sanctified the field will in any wise redeem it, then he shall add the fifth *part* of the money of thy estimation unto it, and it shall be assured to him.

20 And if he will not redeem the field, or if he have sold the field to another man, it shall not be redeemed any more.

21 But the field, when it goeth out in the jubile, shall be holy unto the LORD, as a field devoted; the possession thereof shall be the priest's.

22 And if *a man* sanctify unto the LORD a field which he hath bought, which *is* not of the fields of his possession;

23 Then the priest shall reckon unto him the worth of thy estimation, *even* unto

　2) Is to have its value determined by the priest

　3) Is to have a 20% interest charge added if the original owner ever wished to redeem, buy back the animal

3. The vow to dedicate a house or land to the LORD

a. The vow to dedicate a house
　1) The value is set when the house is dedicated

　2) The owner wishes to redeem or buy back the house from the sanctuary or priests: Must add 20% interest to its value

b. The vow to dedicate land
　1) The value is to be set: To be based upon the amount of seed needed to plant the land—50 shekels or pieces of silver to a homer of barley seed (about 5 bushels)

　2) The full value applies if the land is dedicated during the Year of Jubilee

　3) The value is adjusted, or reduced if the land is dedicated after the Jubilee: Based on the number of years or crops remaining

　4) The 1st case: The person who dedicated his land wishes to redeem it—must pay 20% interest

　5) The 2nd case: The dedicated field is not redeemed or it is sold to someone else
　　• It can never be redeemed

　　• The land is released in the Jubilee & becomes holy, devoted to the LORD: It becomes the permanent property of the priests

　6) The 3rd case: A person dedicates some land he has bought that is not a part of his family land

　　• The value is determined or based upon the years or crops left until Jubilee:

The man pays its value on the day of dedication	the year of the jubile: and he shall give thine estimation in that day, *as* a holy thing unto the LORD.	of his possession, shall be sold or redeemed: every devoted thing *is* most holy unto the LORD.	apart) to the LORD
• The land will revert to the original owner in the Year of Jubilee	24 In the year of the jubile the field shall return unto him of whom it was bought, *even* to him to whom the possession of the land *did belong.*	29 None devoted, which shall be devoted of men, shall be redeemed; *but* shall surely be put to death.	2) Not a person condemned to death: Must be executed
c. The basis for seeking the value of property: The Tabernacle shekel (about ½ ounce)	25 And all thy estimations shall be according to the shekel of the sanctuary: twenty gerahs shall be the shekel.	30 And all the tithe of the land, *whether* of the seed of the land, *or* of the fruit of the tree, *is* the LORD's: it is holy unto the LORD.	c. Are not to pledge the tithe in a vow: It already belongs to the LORD—it is holy to the LORD
4. The three things that already belong to the LORD by law & cannot be vowed or dedicated	26 Only the firstling of the beasts, which should be the LORD'S firstling, no man shall sanctify it; whether *it be* ox, or sheep: it *is* the LORD'S.	31 And if a man will at all redeem *ought* of his tithes, he shall add thereto the fifth *part* thereof.	1) Must pay 20% more if the tithe is redeemed or used by the person
a. Are not allowed to dedicate the firstborn animal			
1) It is the LORD's by law		32 And concerning the tithe of the herd, or of the flock, *even* of whatsoever passeth under the rod, the tenth shall be holy unto the LORD.	2) Must tithe a tenth of everything; every tenth animal born is to be tithed: It is holy (set apart) to the LORD
2) It can be bought back if the animal is defective	27 And if *it be* of an unclean beast, then he shall redeem *it* according to thine estimation, and shall add a fifth *part* of it thereto: or if it be not redeemed, then it shall be sold according to thy estimation.	33 He shall not search whether it be good or bad, neither shall he change it: and if he change it at all, then both it and the change thereof shall be holy; it shall not be redeemed.	• Must not pick out the good from the bad to tithe
• Must add 20% interest if redeemed			• The penalty: Must give both the good & bad to the LORD
• Must be sold at its value if sold by the priests			
b. Are never to sell or redeem anything already pledged or devoted to the LORD	28 Notwithstanding no devoted thing, that a man shall devote unto the LORD of all that he hath, *both* of man and beast, and of the field	34 These *are* the commandments, which the LORD commanded Moses for the children of Israel in mount Sinai.	**5. The conclusion to the great book of Leviticus: These are the commands of the LORD for His people**
1) Not man, animal, or land: Because it is most holy (set			

DIVISION IV

THE WAY TO LIVE A HOLY LIFE BEFORE GOD (PART 2): A PURE SPIRIT (SANCTIFICATION), 17:1–27:34

K. Laws That Govern Vows and Commitments Made to God: The Critical Importance of Keeping Sacred Vows, 27:1-34

(27:1-34) **Introduction**: death, disease, accident, war and other desperate circumstances often stir people to pray and pray intensely. They want help and deliverance. Often they cry out to God, begging God for help. If God will deliver them, they make promises to God, vows such as...

* serving God
* dedicating their families to God
* giving money, houses, or property to God
* changing sinful habits, reckless lifestyles, destructive behavior
* being more faithful to the church
* seeking to restore some damaged relationship

In some cases, the promises or vows are sincere and heartfelt; in other cases, they are shallow and hastily made with no forethought. There is sometimes no plan and far too often no real intention of following through with the vow. Once a crisis has passed, a person sometimes feels...

* that he made the vow too hastily, in the heat of the moment
* that the vow was really not necessary, perhaps even foolish
* that he can forget the vow
* that he is not obligated to carry out the vow
* that he can only partially fulfill the vow
* that he is not accountable to anyone to keep the vow
* that his deliverance or recovery was not really due to God but to his own sufficiency or to the technology and ability of man

Vows and promises are very serious to God. Once a vow is made, it is sacred: it must be kept. Vows made before God are not to be taken lightly. A just society even declares the truth: that "a man is only as good as his word." Time and time again, Scripture warns:

> "When thou shalt vow a vow unto the LORD thy God, thou shalt not slack to pay it: for the LORD thy God will surely require it of thee; and it would be sin in thee. But if thou shalt forbear to vow, it shall be no sin in thee. That which is gone out of thy lips thou shalt keep and perform; *even* a freewill offering, according as thou hast vowed unto the LORD thy God, which thou hast promised with thy mouth" (De.23:21-23).
>
> "*It is* a snare to the man *who* devoureth *that which is* holy, and after vows to make enquiry" (Pr.20:25).
>
> "When thou vowest a vow unto God, defer not to pay it; for *he hath* no pleasure in fools: pay that which thou hast vowed. Better *is it* that thou shouldest not vow, than that thou shouldest vow and not pay. Suffer not thy mouth to cause thy flesh to sin; neither say thou before the angel, that it *was* an error: wherefore should God be angry at thy voice, and destroy the work of thine hands?" (Ec.5:4-6).

One other fact needs to be noted about vows or promises made to God. A genuine believer is sometimes driven to make a vow or promise to God. Why? Because he is deeply thankful for all that God has done for him, so thankful that he is constantly wanting to give more and more of himself—all he is and has—to God. Therefore, the genuine believer dedicates more and more to God: he is forever growing by dedicating himself to serve more. It is his love for Christ and his desire to grow in Christ that drives him to make vows, to follow through with his commitment.

> "I beseech you therefore, brethren, by the mercies of God, that ye present your bodies a living sacrifice, holy, acceptable unto God, *which is* your reasonable service. And be not conformed to this world: but be ye transformed by the renewing of your mind, that ye may prove what is that good, and acceptable, and perfect, will of God" (Ro.12:1-2).
>
> "What shall I render unto the LORD *for* all his benefits toward me?" (Ps.116:12).

Vows—the promises we make—are of profound importance to God. This is the subject of this last passage in the great book of *Leviticus*: *Laws That Govern Vows and Commitments Made to God: The Critical Importance of Keeping Sacred Vows*, 27:1-34.

1. The vow to dedicate oneself or some other person to God (vv.1-8).
2. The vow to dedicate an animal to God (vv.9-13).
3. The vow to dedicate a house or land to the LORD (vv.14-25).
4. The three things that already belong to the LORD by law and cannot be vowed or dedicated (vv.26-33).
5. The conclusion to the great book of Leviticus: these are the commands of the LORD for His people (v.34).

1 (27:1-8) **Vows—Dedication—Pledge, of Vows:** there was the vow to dedicate oneself or some other person to God. The most common vow ever made is the dedication of one's life to God. The second most common vow is probably the dedication of one's child or family to God. In the eyes of God, the dedication of a human life to God is the most important vow ever made. Note the Scripture and outline.

OUTLINE	SCRIPTURE	SCRIPTURE	OUTLINE
1. The vow to dedicate oneself or some other person to God	And the LORD spake unto Moses, saying,	twenty shekels, and for the female ten shekels.	pieces of silver
a. Are to pay the monetary value of that person to the sanctuary	2 Speak unto the children of Israel, and say unto them, When a man shall make a singular vow, the persons *shall be* for the LORD by thy estimation.	6 And if *it be* from a month old even unto five years old, then thy estimation shall be of the male five shekels of silver, and for the female thy esti-	4) A person one month-five years old • A male: Five shekels or pieces of silver • A female: Three shekels or pieces of silver
b. Are to use this scale: Based upon the labor value of a person		mation *shall be* three shekels of silver.	
1) A male 20-60 years old: Fifty shekels or pieces of silver	3 And thy estimation shall be of the male from twenty years old even unto sixty years old, even thy estimation shall be fifty shekels of silver, after the shekel of the sanctuary.	7 And if *it be* from sixty years old and above; if *it be* a male, then thy estimation shall be fifteen shekels, and for the female ten shekels.	5) A person 60 plus years old • A male: Fifteen shekels or pieces of silver • A female: Ten shekels or pieces of silver
2) A female 20-60 years old: Thirty shekels or pieces of silver	4 And if it *be* a female, then thy estimation shall be thirty shekels.	8 But if he be poorer than thy estimation, then he shall present himself before the priest, and the priest shall value him; according to his ability that vowed shall the priest value him.	6) A poor person • To present his vow to the priest • To have a value set based upon what he can pay
3) A person 5-20 years old: • Male: 20 shekels or pieces of silver • Female: 10 shekels or	5 And if *it be* from five years old even unto twenty years old, then thy estimation shall be of the male		

Note the word *singular* (KJV) or *special* (NIV, NLT) (v.2). The Hebrew word (pala) means special, wonderful, marvelous, amazing, astounding, and even miraculous. In relation to vows, the idea is that a very special—wonderful, marvelous—vow is made to God. A person has been moved by the goodness of God to dedicate himself or some other person to God. The dedication of a human life is the most special vow or gift that can be made to God: it is a miraculous, amazing gift or vow.

In the days of Moses, a lay person could not dedicate himself or his children to the ministry. That task belonged only to the Levitical priesthood, only to Aaron and his sons and their descendants. Therefore, a person who dedicated himself or some other person to God was required to pay the monetary value of that person to the sanctuary. Note that the monetary value was based upon the labor value of a person, based upon the ability of a person to work. The idea was that a person was committing some life to become a servant of God; therefore, the value of a servant or slave—the ability to work—was used as the monetary scale.

The Monetary Value of Persons Dedicating Their Lives to God			
Verses	**Age**	**Value of Male**	**Value of Female**
vv.3-4	20–60 years	50 shekels or pieces of silver	30 shekels or pieces of silver
v.5	5–20 years	20 shekels or pieces of silver	10 shekels or pieces of silver
v.6	1 month-5 years	5 shekels or pieces of silver	3 shekels or pieces of silver
v.7	60 years plus	15 shekels or pieces of silver	10 shekels or pieces of silver
v.8	poor person	set by the priest: based upon what he could pay	set by the priest: based upon what she could pay

Thought 1. There is a striking lesson here for the believer. The monetary value of a person was based upon the value of a person's entire life, based upon the value of a temple slave, who was to serve in the temple for life. A genuine believer does just this: he dedicates himself to become God's servant. He is God's bond-slave, bound to God for all of life, both now and eternally. This is also true in the dedication of one's child and family to God. The believer dedicates them to serve God as His bond-servants, to serve God throughout all of life.

"And he said to *them* all, If any *man* will come after me, let him deny himself, and take up his cross daily, and follow me" (Lu.9:23).

"So likewise, whosoever he be of you that forsaketh not all that he hath, he cannot be my disciple" (Lu.14:33).

"If any man serve me, let him follow me; and where I am, there shall also my servant be: if any man serve me, him will *my* Father honour" (Jn.12:26).

"I beseech you therefore, brethren, by the mercies of God, that ye present your bodies a living sacrifice, holy, acceptable unto God, *which is* your reasonable service" (Ro.12:1).

"And the very God of peace sanctify you wholly; and *I pray God* your whole spirit and soul and body be preserved blameless unto the coming of our Lord Jesus Christ" (1 Th.5:23).

"For this child [Samuel] I prayed; and the LORD hath given me my petition which I asked of him: Therefore also I have lent him to the LORD; as long as he liveth he shall be lent to the LORD" (1 S.1:27-28)

"Train up a child in the way he should go: and when he is old, he will not depart from it" (Pr.22:6).

2 (27:9-13) **Vows, Dedicating Animals to God—Dedication, of Animals to God—Animals, Dedicated to God:** there was the vow to dedicate an animal to God. Note the Scripture and outline.

OUTLINE	SCRIPTURE	SCRIPTURE	OUTLINE
2. The vow to dedicate an animal to God a. The clean animal: One that is acceptable as an offering to God 1) Is counted holy or set apart for that very purpose 2) Is not ever to be exchanged or replaced by another: If it is, both the original animal & the substitute are counted holy (to be set apart & given to God)	9 And if *it be* a beast, whereof men bring an offering unto the LORD, all that *any man* giveth of such unto the LORD shall be holy. 10 He shall not alter it, nor change it, a good for a bad, or a bad for a good: and if he shall at all change beast for beast, then it and the exchange thereof shall be holy.	11 And if *it be* any unclean beast, of which they do not offer a sacrifice unto the LORD, then he shall present the beast before the priest 12 And the priest shall value it, whether it be good or bad: as thou valuest it, *who art* the priest, so shall it be. 13 But if he will at all redeem it, then he shall add a fifth *part* thereof unto thy estimation.	b. The unclean animal: One not acceptable as an offering 1) Is to be presented to the Priest 2) Is to have its value determined by the priest 3) Is to have a 20% interest charge added if the original owner ever wished to redeem or buy back the animal

Remember, the way people approached God was through the *sacrifice* of a clean animal. Therefore, people were constantly vowing or dedicating an animal to God. Once an animal had been dedicated to God, it could never be exchanged or replaced by another animal. After an animal had been vowed to God and the time for sacrifice came, there was always the possibility that a person might want to substitute a cheaper or less valuable animal to the LORD. This law prohibited such an act. Moreover, the sacrifice made to God had to be a pure, clean sacrifice, a sacrifice without any defect whatsoever. This was an absolute necessity, for the sacrifice symbolized the sacrifice of the Lord Jesus Christ. Consequently, God had to institute a law that would forbid the offering of a less expensive sacrifice. In fact, note what God says: If a person attempted this, both animals became holy and were to be set apart to God.

Note that unclean or defective animals were also vowed and given to God (vv.11-13). These animals were not sacrificed to God but rather given to be used in the service of God. For example, the priest needed animals for food, farming, and transportation. The unclean or defective animals were used for these purposes. However, note that a person could redeem or buy back the defective animal by paying the value plus twenty percent interest.

> **Thought 1**. No person should attempt to cheat God nor to give God less than the best. God is the Supreme Being of the universe; therefore, only the supreme and best gifts are to be offered to God. God will accept no substitutes and nothing less than the best.

> > "But rather give alms of such things as ye have; and, behold, all things are clean unto you" (Lu.11:41).
> > "But a certain man named Ananias, with Sapphira his wife, sold a possession, And kept back *part* of the price, his wife also being privy *to it,* and brought a certain part, and laid *it* at the apostles' feet" (Ac.5:1-2).
> > "Every man according as he purposeth in his heart, *so let him give;* not grudgingly, or of necessity: for God loveth a cheerful giver" (2 Co.9:7).
> > "Honour the LORD with thy substance, and with the firstfruits of all thine increase" (Pr.3:9).
> > "Will a man rob God? Yet ye have robbed me. But ye say, Wherein have we robbed thee? In tithes and offerings" (Mal.3:8).

3 (27:14-25) **Vows, of Gifts to God—Dedication, of Property—Giving, of Property**: there was the vow to dedicate a house or land to God. Some believers are so committed to God that they want to see His witness carried forth as strongly and quickly as possible. Because of their love and fervor for God, they give their estates to God, estates that sometimes include houses and lands. This scripture deals with the subject:

OUTLINE	SCRIPTURE	SCRIPTURE	OUTLINE

3. The vow to dedicate a house or land to the LORD
  a. The vow to dedicate a house
    1) The value is set when the house is dedicated
	14 And when a man shall sanctify his house *to be* holy unto the LORD, then the priest shall estimate it, whether it be good or bad: as the priest shall estimate it, so shall it stand.	the fifth *part* of the money of thy estimation unto it, and it shall be assured to him.
		20 And if he will not redeem the field, or if he have sold the field to another man, it shall not be redeemed any more.
			wishes to redeem it—must pay 20% interest
			
			5) The 2nd case: The dedicated field is not redeemed or it is sold to someone else
			  • It can never be redeemed

2) The owner wishes to redeem or buy back the house from the sanctuary or priests: Must add 20% interest to its value b. The vow to dedicate land	15 And if he that sanctified it will redeem his house, then he shall add the fifth *part* of the money of thy estimation unto it, and it shall be his.	21 But the field, when it goeth out in the jubile, shall be holy unto the LORD, as a field devoted; the possession thereof shall be the priest's.	• The land is released in the Jubilee & becomes holy, devoted to the LORD: It becomes the permanent property of the priests
1) The value is to be set: To be based upon the amount of seed needed to plant the land—50 shekels or pieces of silver to a homer of barley seed (about 5 bushels)	16 And if a man shall sanctify unto the LORD *some part* of a field of his possession, then thy estimation shall be according to the seed thereof: an homer of barley seed *shall be valued* at fifty shekels of silver.	22 And if *a man* sanctify unto the LORD a field which he hath bought, which *is* not of the fields of his possession; 23 Then the priest shall reckon unto him the worth of thy estimation, *even* unto the year of the jubile: and he	6) The 3rd case: A person dedicates some land he has bought that is not a part of his family land • The value is determined or based upon the years or crops left until Jubilee: The man pays its
2) The full value applies if the land is dedicated during the Year of Jubilee	17 If he sanctify his field from the year of jubile, according to thy estimation it shall stand.	shall give thine estimation in that day, *as* a holy thing unto the LORD.	value on the day of dedication
3) The value is adjusted or reduced if the land is dedicated after the Jubilee: Based on the number of years or crops remaining	18 But if he sanctify his field after the jubile, then the priest shall reckon unto him the money according to the years that remain, even unto the year of the jubile, and it shall be abated from thy estimation.	24 In the year of the jubile the field shall return unto him of whom it was bought, *even* to him to whom the possession of the land *did belong.*	• The land will revert to the original owner in the Year of Jubilee
4) The 1st case: The person who dedicated his land	19 And if he that sanctified the field will in any wise redeem it, then he shall add	25 And all thy estimations shall be according to the shekel of the sanctuary: twenty gerahs shall be the shekel.	c. The basis for seeking the value of property: The Tabernacle shekel (about ½ ounce)

a. Note the law governing the vow to dedicate or pledge a house to God (vv.14-15). The value of a house was set when the house was dedicated to God. If a person ever wanted to redeem or buy back his house, he was to pay the value plus 20 percent more. The deed to the house was then returned.

b. Note that the law governing the vow to give land is more complicated than any other gift. This was because of the Jubilee, the fifty-year celebration of liberty when all land reverted back to the original owner (see outline and notes—Le.25:8-55 for more discussion). Taken step by step, the law governing the gift of land is clearly seen:

1) The value of the land was set based upon the amount of seed needed to plant the land. The value was fifty shekels or pieces of silver for an area that produced five bushels of barley seed (v.16). This obviously means that the value of land was equal to the value of the crops it would produce.

2) The full value of the land applied if it was dedicated during the Year of Jubilee (v.17).

3) The value of the land however was adjusted and reduced if the land was dedicated after the Jubilee (v.18). The land was then based on the number of years or crops remaining until the Jubilee. This was only fair because the property reverted back to the original owner during the Year of the Jubilee.

4) The first case given is that of a person who dedicated his land but wished to redeem or buy it back (v.19). He had to pay the value of the land plus twenty percent more as interest.

5) The second case given is that of a field dedicated by a person who never redeemed it; instead he sold it to someone else before the Jubilee. (vv.20-21). Once a person sold the land, the land could never be redeemed. However, when the land was released in the Jubilee, it became holy and devoted to the LORD. That is, it became the permanent property of the priest.

6) Case three involved a person who dedicated some land he had bought that was not part of his family land (vv.22-24). The value of the land was based upon the years or crops left until Jubilee. The man paid its value on the day of dedication. This land was to revert to the original owner in the Year of Jubilee.

c. Note that the basis for setting the value of property was to be the Tabernacle shekel (v.25). A shekel measured one-half ounce or 11 grams in weight.

Thought 1. Believers must give generously to meet the desperate needs of the world and to carry the gospel to the world. God demands that we give all we are and have. Giving what we have is just as important as giving who we are. We must give our work estates to God: our houses, lands, and money—all to meet the desperate needs of the world and to get the gospel out.

"Jesus said unto him, If thou wilt be perfect, go *and* sell that thou hast, and give to the poor, and thou shalt have treasure in heaven: and come *and* follow me" (Mt.19:21).

"Sell that ye have, and give alms; provide yourselves bags which wax not old, a treasure in the heavens that faileth not, where no thief approacheth, neither moth corrupteth" (Lu.12:33).

"I have *showed* you all things, how that so labouring ye ought to support the weak, and to remember the words of the Lord Jesus, how he said, It is more blessed to give than to receive" (Ac.20:35).

"Upon the first *day* of the week let every one of you lay by him in store, as *God* hath prospered him, that there be no gatherings when I come" (1 Co.16:2).

"But this *I say,* He which soweth sparingly shall reap also sparingly; and he which soweth bountifully shall reap also bountifully. Every man according as he purposeth in his heart, *so let him give;* not grudgingly, or of necessity: for God loveth a cheerful giver" (2 Co.9:6-7).

"Every man *shall give* as he is able, according to the blessing of the LORD thy God which he hath given thee" (De.16:17).

[4] (27:26-33) **Vows, Laws Governing—Law, Governing Vows—Dedication, Laws Governing—Tithe—Firstborn—Ban, Under the**: there were three things that already belonged to the LORD and could not be vowed or dedicated. By His authority, God has demanded that some things be dedicated to Him. These things are an obligation laid upon man; they are not voluntary gifts. Another way to say the same thing is this: there are "required gifts" and "voluntary gifts." Required gifts of dedication are demanded by God; whereas voluntary gifts are given from a free and willing heart. Required gifts cannot be vowed or pledged to God simply because they are already required and demanded. What are the required gifts, the three things that already belong to the LORD that cannot be vowed or pledged?

OUTLINE	SCRIPTURE	SCRIPTURE	
4. The three things that already belong to the LORD by law & cannot be vowed or dedicated	26 Only the firstling of the beasts, which should be the LORD'S firstling, no man shall sanctify it; whether *it be* ox, or sheep: it *is* the LORD'S .	28 Notwithstanding no devoted thing, that a man shall devote unto the LORD of all that he hath, *both* of man and beast, and of the field of his possession, shall be sold or redeemed: every devoted thing *is* most holy unto the LORD.	b. Are never to sell or redeem anything already pledged or devoted to the LORD
a. Are not allowed to dedicate the firstborn animal			1) Not man, animal, or land: Because it is most holy (set apart) to the LORD
1) It is the LORD's by law			
2) It can be bought back if the animal is defective	27 And if *it be* of an unclean beast, then he shall redeem *it* according to thine estimation, and shall add a fifth *part* of it thereto: or if it be not redeemed, then it shall be sold according to thy estimation.	28 None devoted, which shall be devoted of men, shall be redeemed; *but* shall surely be put to death.	2) Not a person condemned to death: Must be executed
• Must add 20% interest if redeemed			
• Must be sold at its value if sold by the priests		29 And all the tithe of the	c. Are not to pledge the tithe in a

OUTLINE	SCRIPTURE	SCRIPTURE	OUTLINE
vow: It already belongs to the LORD—it is holy to the LORD	land, *whether* of the seed of the land, *or* of the fruit of the tree, *is* the LORD's : *it is* holy unto the LORD.	*even* of whatsoever passeth under the rod, the tenth shall be holy unto the LORD.	born is to be tithed: It is holy (set apart) to the LORD
1) Must pay 20% more if the tithe is redeemed or used by the person	31 And if a man will at all redeem *ought* of his tithes, he shall add thereto the fifth *part* thereof.	33 He shall not search whether it be good or bad, neither shall he change it: and if he change it at all, then both it and the change thereof shall be holy; it shall not be redeemed.	• Must not pick out the good from the bad to tithe
2) Must tithe a tenth of everything; every tenth animal	32 And concerning the tithe of the herd, or of the flock,		• The penalty: Must give both the good & bad to the LORD

a. A person was not allowed to vow or dedicate the firstborn animal to the LORD (vv.26-27). The firstborn of both man and animal already belonged to the LORD: it was the LORD's by law (see outlines and notes—Ex.13:1-2; 34:19-20 for more discussion). But note, if the animal was unclean or defective, it could be redeemed or bought back (v.27). However a person had to add twenty percent more if it was to be redeemed. If the owner did not redeem the animal, the priests were to sell it at its value.

b. A person was never allowed to sell or redeem anything already pledged or devoted to the LORD (vv.28-29). No man, animal, or land could be sold if it had already been devoted to the LORD. Once devoted, it was most holy or set apart to the LORD. Things devoted to the LORD were considered *under the ban*. Note that the Hebrew word for *devoted thing* (herem) has a double meaning: some things are devoted to God for holy purposes. Other things are devoted to God for judgment. Note in verse 29 where some evil people are said to be devoted to destruction. Once a person has been devoted to destruction, he is placed under the ban and can never be ransomed: he must be put to death. For example, Jericho was devoted to God for destruction (Jos.6:1f). Other evil cities and people who stood against God were also said to be devoted to the LORD, condemned and set under the ban of destruction (Ex.22:20; Nu.21:2; De.7:2; De.13:15; 1 S.15:1-35).

c. A person was not to pledge the tithe in a vow (vv.30-33). The tithe already belonged to the LORD; it was already holy to the LORD. Note what happened if a person used the tithe, whether money, grain, or fruit: the person had to pay the tithe and add twenty percent more. Under the law of God, a person had to pay a tithe, a tenth of everything. He even had to give every tenth animal to the LORD. And note, he could not pick out the good animal from the bad to tithe. If he did, the penalty was costly; he had to give both the good and bad to the LORD.

Thought 1. Note two strong lessons for the believer.

(1) The believer is to tithe, give at least one tenth of his income to the LORD. In the Old Testament God demanded that His people tithe. In the New Testament tithing is expected. It is assumed that a believer tithes and even does more. The attitude of the New Testament is this: since God has done so much for the believer through His Son, the Lord Jesus Christ, the believer is compelled to give all he is and has. The believer is driven to get the glorious message of the gospel out to the whole world, meeting the desperate needs of the world. How could a person do any less considering how much God has done for him? Studying and understanding the teachings of Christ is not enough. Honesty is demanded: a person has to be honest in facing the teachings of Christ and honest in declaring what those teachings say. Jesus Christ demands everything a person is and has to carry forth the gospel of His saving grace and to meet the desperate needs of the world.

"Heal the sick, cleanse the lepers, raise the dead, cast out devils: freely ye have received, freely give" (Mt.10:8).

"And, behold, one came and said unto him, Good Master, what good thing shall I do, that I may have eternal life? Jesus said unto him, If thou wilt be perfect, go *and* sell that thou hast, and give to the poor, and thou shalt have treasure in heaven: and come *and* follow me" (Mt.19:16, 21).

"Woe unto you, scribes and Pharisees, hypocrites! for ye pay tithe of mint and anise and cummin, and have omitted the weightier *matters* of the law, judgment, mercy, and faith: these ought ye to have done, and not to leave the other undone" (Mt.23:23).

"Give, and it shall be given unto you; good measure, pressed down, and shaken together, and running over, shall men give into your bosom. For with the same measure that ye mete withal it shall be measured to you again" (Lu.6:38).

"Then the disciples, every man according to his ability, determined to send relief unto the brethren which dwelt in Judaea" (Ac.11:29).

"Upon the first *day* of the week let every one of you lay by him in store, as *God* hath prospered him, that there be no gatherings when I come" (1 Co.16:2).

"For if there be first a willing mind, *it is* accepted according to that a man hath, *and* not according to that he hath not" (2 Co.8:12).

"But this *I say*, He which soweth sparingly shall reap also sparingly; and he which soweth bountifully shall reap also bountifully" (2 Co.9:6).

"Every man according as he purposeth in his heart, *so let him give;* not grudgingly, or of necessity: for God loveth a cheerful giver" (2 Co.9:7).

(2) The believer is to keep his vows and pledges. When a believer dedicates himself or something else to God, the gift is to be given to God. God expects a person to keep his word, the vows he makes.

"If a man vow a vow unto the LORD, or swear an oath to bind his soul with a bond; he shall not break his word, he shall do according to all that proceedeth out of his mouth" (Nu.30:2).

"When thou shalt vow a vow unto the LORD thy God, thou shalt not slack to pay it: for the LORD thy God will surely require it of thee; and it would be sin in thee" (De.23:21).

"Keep thy tongue from evil, and thy lips from speaking guile [deception]" (Ps.34:13).

"When thou vowest a vow unto God, defer not to pay it; for *he hath* no pleasure in fools: pay that which thou hast vowed" (Ec.5:4).

5 (27:34) **Commandments, of God—Leviticus, Conclusion of—Conclusion, of Leviticus**: the conclusion to the great book of *Leviticus* is brief and straightforward:

OUTLINE	SCRIPTURE
5. The conclusion to the great book of Leviticus: These are the commands of the LORD for His people	34 These *are* the commandments, which the Lord commanded Moses for the children of Israel in mount Sinai.

Gordon J. Wenham gives an excellent conclusion to the great book of Leviticus that is well worth quoting in full:

With these laws on vows and tithes Leviticus closes. On first reading it seems a strange point at which to end. But the theme of vowing is in fact closely related to the principal concerns of the whole book. Men who dedicate themselves to God become as it were God's slaves, holy to the LORD. Some men, the priests, can indeed serve God in the sanctuary. Chs. 8–10 tell of the ordination of Aaron and his sons to the priesthood. Chs. 21–22 expound the qualities looked for in priests, qualities which symbolize the perfection and holiness of God. Those not of priestly stock can still serve God, indeed they must be holy for God is holy (11:44-45; 19:2; 20:7, 26). This theme runs through chs. 11–20; the elect people of God must visibly embody the character of God. In their choice of food, in sickness and in health, in their family life, in their honest and upright dealing, and in their love of neighbor, they show the world what God is like.

Vowed animals are intended for sacrifice; they too become holy when vowed. Sacrifice was the heart of OT worship, and Leviticus gives more precise direction about sacrificial procedures than any other part of Scripture, and also lists the occasions when animals had to be offered (chs. 1–7, 12–17, 22–23). Finally a man can dedicate land or property to God, recalling the jubilee legislation (ch. 25).

Thus this chapter in effect recapitulates and reminds us of the great themes that have engaged our attention in the rest of the book. Lev. 27 points out that holiness is more than a matter of divine call and correct ritual. Its attainment requires the total consecration of a man's life to God's service. It involves giving yourself, your family, and all your possessions to God.

"Be holy, for I the LORD your God am holy." [1]

---

1 Gordon J. Wenham. *The Book of Leviticus*. pp.342-343.

PRACTICAL BIBLE HELPS & RESOURCES

THE SACRIFICES OR OFFERINGS OF THE OLD TESTAMENT
SYMBOLS POINTING TO JESUS CHRIST AS THE SUBSTITUTE SACRIFICE[1]

THE OFFERING & ITS PURPOSE	THE ELEMENTS & HOW ONE SECURED THE PROMISE OF THE OFFERING	THE SYMBOLISM: HOW THE OFFERING POINTS TO JESUS CHRIST
The Burnt Offering: *To provide the atonement or reconciliation with God. The Burnt Offering was the only way to approach God, to become reconciled, acceptable to God,* Le.1:1-17 OTHER SCRIPTURE REFERENCES: Le.6:8-13; 8:18-21; 9:2; 16:24; Ex.29:18; Nu.28:3-15; 29:6; De.33:8-10; Jos.8:31; 1 S.6:15; 7:9; 2 S.24:25; 1 K.3:4; 1 Chr.16:40; 2 Chr.13:11; Ezr.3:3; Ps.40:6; Ep.5:2	A person secured atonement or reconciliation with God through the substitute sacrifice: ⇒ The rich person by offering the sacrifice of a male bull without defect ⇒ The average person by offering the sacrifice of a male sheep or goat without defect ⇒ The poor person by offering the sacrifice of a dove or young pigeon Note: The sacrifice was totally consumed by fire. This is a symbol that the sacrifice paid the full ransom to free the believer from sin and death; the sacrifice bore the full punishment of God's justice and judgment that was due the sinner.	The Burnt Offering is a type of Christ, a picture of Christ dying as the substitute sacrifice for us. By dying for us: ⇒ Christ bore the full justice and judgment of God against sin—paid the ransom price to deliver us from sin and death. ⇒ Christ secured the atonement or reconciliation with God for us **"...by whom [Christ] we have now received the atonement" (Ro.5:11).**
The Grain or Meal Offering: *To provide the way to express thanksgiving and the dedication of one's life to God,* Le.2:1-15 OTHER SCRIPTURE REFERENCES: Le.6:14-23; 9:17; 10:12; 23:18; Nu.15:4; 28:5	A person expressed his thanks and the dedication of his life to God by giving the best of his grain. The offering... • was to be of fine flour mixed with olive oil and some incense and without yeast or honey • could be cooked in an oven, a griddle, or a pan • was seasoned with salt Note: the Grain Offering was offered on top of the Burnt Offering of the daily sacrifice. This was... • a declaration of thanksgiving to God for the atonement (reconciliation) and for all else God had done • a declaration of laying one's life upon God—all one was and had—and dedicating oneself totally to God	The Grain or Meal Offering is a type of Christ, a picture of Christ as the Bread of Life. Jesus Christ is the Bread of Life... • Who satisfies the hunger of our souls for God and for purpose, meaning, and significance • Who satisfies us so much that we break out in joy, giving thanks to God for the atonement (reconciliation) and for all else God has done • Who satisfies us to the point of dedication, committing all we are and have to God **"I am the bread of life: he that cometh to me shall never hunger; and he that believeth on me shall never thirst" (Jn.6:35).**
The Fellowship or Peace Offering: *To provide the way to grow in the peace and fellowship of God—seeking a deeper life with God,* Le.3:1-17 OTHER SCRIPTURE REFERENCES: Le.7:11-34; 9:4; 9:18; 17:1-9; 19:5-8; Ex.20:24; 24:5; 29:28; Nu.6:14; 7:17; 10:10	The believer sought to grow in the peace and fellowship of God through the substitute sacrifice.[1] He had... • the option of offering a bull or cow without defect. The bull (an animal of service) focused his attention upon service, the dedication of his life to God. • the option of offering a lamb without defect. The lamb (the animal most used in sacrifice) focused a person's attention upon the sacrifice, dying to self and following God totally. • the option of offering a goat. The goat (the animal that bore away the judgment of sin) focused his attention upon God's judgment. Note: the sacrifice was burned on top of the Burnt Offering. This symbolizes that the peace and fellowship of God is based upon the atonement, based upon being reconciled with God. A person has to experience the atonement, be reconciled with God before he can know the peace and fellowship of God.	The Fellowship or Peace Offering is a type of Christ... ⇒ A picture of Christ as the Perfect Servant of God **"Even as the Son of man came not to be ministered unto, but to minister, and to give his life a ransom for many" (Mt.20:28).** ⇒ A picture of Christ as the Lamb of God **"The next day John seeth Jesus coming unto him, and saith, Behold the Lamb of God, which taketh away the sin of the world" (Jn.1:29).** ⇒ A picture of Christ as the Substitute Sacrifice who died on the cross bearing the judgment of sin for us, as the Sacrifice who removed and took away our sin **"Who his own self bare our sins in his own body on the tree, that we, being dead to sins, should live unto righteousness: by whose stripes ye were healed" (1 Pe.2:24).**

---

[1] **Substitute Sacrifice:** Note how clearly the sacrifice symbolizes Jesus Christ. Jesus Christ died as our substitute: in our behalf, in our stead, in our place. He died for us. There is only one way any of us can be delivered from sin and death and escape the judgment to come. We must approach God through the substitute sacrifice which is the Lord Jesus Christ. He is the only Perfect Sacrifice, the one and only sacrifice acceptable to God. Forgiveness of sins comes only through Him: He is the one and only acceptable sacrifice.

THE SACRIFICES OR OFFERINGS OF THE OLD TESTAMENT

THE OFFERING & ITS PURPOSE	THE ELEMENTS & HOW ONE SECURED THE PROMISE OF THE OFFERING	THE SYMBOLISM: HOW THE OFFERING POINTS TO JESUS CHRIST
The Sin Offering: To secure the way to receive continual forgiveness of sins, Le.4:1-5:13 OTHER SCRIPTURE REFERENCES: Le.6:24-30; 8:14-17; 9:2; 9:15; 10:17; 16:3-22; Ex.29:14; 30:10; Nu.6:11; 8:8; 15:27; 2 K. 12:16; He.9:13; 10:11	God provided the way for every person to secure forgiveness of sins through the substitute sacrifice of a sin offering: ⇒ The anointed priest had to offer a young bull without defect. ⇒ The community or society had to offer a young bull without defect. ⇒ A leader had to offer a male goat without defect. ⇒ An individual person had to offer a female goat or lamb without defect. ⇒ The poor person had to offer two doves or two young pigeons. ⇒ The poorest of the poor had to offer a tenth of an ephah (two quarts; two liters) of fine flour. The substitute sacrifice paid the penalty of sin that was due the sinner; the substitute sacrifice set the believer free from the condemnation and judgment of sin.	The Sin Offering is a type of Christ, a picture of Christ. It is through Jesus Christ—through His blood, His death upon the cross—that we receive forgiveness of sins. By walking throughout the day in *open confession,* Christ continually forgives us and cleanses us from all unrighteousness. **"In whom we have redemption through his blood, the forgiveness of sins, according to the riches of his grace" (Ep.1:7).** **"If we confess our sins, he is faithful and just to forgive us *our* sins, and to cleanse us from all unrighteousness" (1 Jn.1:9).**
The Guilt Offering: To provide the way to be set free from the weight and anguish of guilt, the pricking of conscience, Le.5:14-6:7 OTHER SCRIPTURE REFERENCES: Le.7:1-6; 14:12; 19:21; 1 S.6:3; 2 K.12:16; Ezr.10:19	The believer secured freedom from the weight and anguish of guilt, the pricking of conscience through the substitute sacrifice. This he did... • by offering a ram without defect and of true value • by making restitution plus 20% Note the result: the sacrifice made atonement, reconciliation with God—the guilty person was forgiven and the weight and anguish of guilt was removed.	The Guilt Offering is a type of Christ, a picture of Christ. Jesus Christ bore our guilt, bore the judgment and condemnation of our guilt when He died upon the cross. Through the death of Christ, we are set free from the guilt of our sin. We are able to stand before God free from all condemnation and accusation. **"*There is* therefore now no condemnation to them which are in Christ Jesus" (Ro.8:1).** **"Who shall lay any thing to the charge of God's elect? It is God that justifieth. Who is he that condemneth? It is Christ that died, yea rather, that is risen again, who is even at the right hand of God, who also maketh intercession for us" (Ro.8:33-34).**
The Ordination Offering:[2] To provide the way for a person to be set apart to the priesthood, set apart to God and His service, Le.8:22-32	A person was ordained, set apart to the ministry of God, by offering a ram as a substitute sacrifice. The person identified with the substitute sacrifice in the following ways: ⇒ by laying his hands on the sacrifice's head ⇒ by placing the shed blood of the sacrifice on the priests right ears, thumbs, and big toes, symbolizing the dedication of one's whole being to God ⇒ by sprinkling all sides of the altar with blood, symbolizing the dedication of the altar ⇒ by offering certain parts of the sacrifice as a wave offering to the Lord Note: the ordination ceremony was consummated with the sprinkling of oil and blood upon the priests. This symbolized that God's anointing (the giving of His Spirit) was based upon the blood, based upon being cleansed from sin.	The Ordination Offering is a type of Christ, a picture of the sacrifice and death of the Lord Jesus Christ. ⇒ It is Christ who died so that we might become acceptable to serve God. ⇒ It is the death of Christ—the demonstration of God's love—that compels us to serve God, that compels us to dedicate all we are and do to God. **"For the love of Christ constraineth us; because we thus judge, that if one died for all, then were all dead" (2 Co.5:14).** **"I beseech you therefore, brethren, by the mercies of God, that ye present your bodies a living sacrifice, holy, acceptable unto God, *which is* your reasonable service" (Ro.12:1).**

---

2 **The Ordination Offering:** The Ordination Offering is being included in this chart because of its importance to the ministers of God, those who are set apart for the special service of God.

THE FEASTS OR FESTIVALS OF WORSHIP:
THE PROPHETIC PICTURE OF SALVATION,
Leviticus 23:1-44

THE FEAST OR FESTIVAL	PURPOSE FOR THE FEAST	PROPHETIC SYMBOL OF THE FEAST
The Passover SCRIPTURE REFERENCES: Le. 23:6; Nu.9:5; Jos.5:10; 2 K.23:22; 2 Chr. 35:1; Mt.26:17; Lu. 2:41; 22:15; He.11:28	To remember God's judgment and deliverance from the enslavement of Egypt (a symbol of being enslaved by the world). God's judgment forced the Egyptians to set God's people free after four hundred years of savage, brutal enslavement. As a result, the Passover celebrates the most important event in Israel's history, that of being set free from Egyptian slavery.	A symbol of Christ, our Passover who was sacrificed for us. Jesus Christ is the perfect fulfillment of the Passover Lamb that was slain on behalf of God's people. Through His sacrifice we are delivered from the judgment of God and from being enslaved to the sin and death of this world. Note that the Passover is a picture, a prophetic picture of salvation and redemption through the sacrifice of Christ. **"Purge out therefore the old leaven, that ye may be a new lump, as ye are unleavened. For even Christ our passover is sacrificed for us" (1 Co.5:7).**
The Feast of Unleavened Bread SCRIPTURE REFERENCES: Ex. 12:17-18; 13:6-7; 23:15; 34:18; Le.23:6; Nu. 28:17; De.16:3; 16:16; 2 Chr.8:13; 2 Chr. 30:13; Mt.26:17; Mk. 14:1	To recall the need and urgency to leave Egypt and to begin the march to the promised land. The Egyptians were desperate for Pharaoh to release and get rid of the Israelites. In fact, the Israelites were forced to leave so quickly that they had no time to adequately prepare. They did not even have time to let their dough rise, no time to put yeast or leaven in their bread. They were forced to take unleavened bread. There was the need, the urgency to get out of Egypt (the world) immediately.	A symbol of the urgency to be freed from the world and to begin one's march to the promised land of heaven. There is a need—an urgent, desperate need—to be delivered from all the oppression and pollution of this world, from all the sin and evil, immorality and lawlessness, corruption and death of this world. There is an urgent need to be set free and liberated to live for God and to begin the march to the promised land of heaven. **"For our conversation [citizenship] is in heaven; from whence also we look for the Saviour, the Lord Jesus Christ" (Ph.3:20).**
The Festival of Firstfruits SCRIPTURE REFERENCES: Ex. 34:22; Le.23:10; Nu. 28:26	To thank God for the crops, for the harvest of food that sustains people and gives them life. Note that this festival could not begin until the people had entered the promised land. They, of course, could not plant crops out in the desert while they were marching to the promised land. Once they arrived and began planting crops, they were to give the first of their harvest to the LORD during this festival.	A symbol of Christ's resurrection and of the great hope the believer has as he marches to the promised land. Christ is the first of the harvest, the first to arise from the dead. The prophetic picture of salvation is just this: As the believer marches to the promised land, he has the great hope of being raised from the dead and of living eternally with God—all because of the resurrection of Christ Jesus. **"But now is Christ risen from the dead, *and* become the firstfruits of them that slept. For since by man *came* death, by man *came* also the resurrection of the dead. For as in Adam all die, even so in Christ shall all be made alive. But every man in his own order: Christ the firstfruits; afterward they that are Christ's at his coming" (1 Co.15:20-23).**
The Festival of Harvest or Pentecost SCRIPTURE REFERENCES: Ex. 23:16; 34:22; Le.23:16; Nu.28:26; De.16:10; Ac.2:1-47	To give thanks for the harvest and to dedicate one's life anew to God. God's people were to celebrate the Festival of Harvest fifty days after of the Festival of Firstfruits.	A symbol of Pentecost, of the great harvest of souls and of people giving their lives to God. The Festival of Harvest symbolized the great day of Pentecost that took place fifty days after the resurrection of Christ, the great day when the Holy Spirit came upon the disciples and gave a great harvest of souls. As the believer marches to the promised land, he is to be filled with God's Spirit and bear strong testimony, seeking a great harvest of souls. **"But ye shall receive power, after that the Holy Ghost is come upon you: and ye shall be witnesses unto me both in Jerusalem, and in all Judaea, and in Samaria, and unto the uttermost part of the earth" (Ac.1:8).** **"And when the day of Pentecost was fully come, they were all with one accord in one place....And they were all filled with the Holy Ghost, and began to speak with other**

THE FEAST OR FESTIVAL	PURPOSE FOR THE FEAST	PROPHETIC SYMBOL OF THE FEAST
		tongues, as the Spirit gave them utterance" (Ac.2:1, 4).
The Festival of Trumpets SCRIPTURE REFERENCES: Le. 23:24; Nu.29:1; Ne.8:2	To focus upon God, learning to trust God more and more and to proclaim the message of joy for the atonement or reconciliation with God. The Israelites had two silver trumpets that were used to call the people together and to signal directions as they journeyed to the promised land. Trumpeters were obviously stationed ever so far to pass the signal through the entire camp.	A symbol of salvation and of the rapture, the glorious day when Christ will return and take believers to be with Him forever. As the believer marches to the promised land of heaven, he is to grow in his trust and joy; he is to be ever maturing, learning to focus and to bear a stronger witness to the atonement of Christ. He is to focus upon the LORD and His glorious return. **"For the LORD himself shall descend from heaven with a shout, with the voice of the archangel, and with the trump of God: and the dead in Christ shall rise first: Then we which are alive and remain shall be caught up together with them in the clouds, to meet the LORD in the air: and so shall we ever be with the LORD" (1 Th.4:16-17).**
The Day of Atonement SCRIPTURE REFERENCES: Ex. 30:10; Le.16:30; 23:27; Nu.29:7; He.9:7	To focus upon the atonement and reconciliation with God through the substitute sacrifice, the only way to become acceptable to God. The Day of Atonement was to be a day of self-denial or fasting. The people were to approach God for atonement or reconciliation through the sacrifice of the Burnt Offering. Moreover, the day was to be a day of complete rest. No work whatsoever was to be done. Note why: because this was the Day of Atonement, the Day when atonement was made for the people before the LORD their God.	A symbol of being reconciled with God through the atonement, through the substitute sacrifice of Christ. The Day of Atonement paints the prophetic picture of salvation. As the believer walks toward the promised land of heaven, he is to keep before his mind the atoning sacrifice of the Lord Jesus Christ. He is never to forget that it is Christ who has cleansed him from sin and delivered him from the penalty of death. **"For if, when we were enemies, we were reconciled to God by the death of his Son, much more, being reconciled, we shall be saved by his life. And not only *so*, but we also joy in God through our Lord Jesus Christ, by whom we have now received the atonement" (Ro.5:10-11).**
The Festival of Tabernacles SCRIPTURE REFERENCES: Le. 23:34, 39; Nu.29:12; De.16:13; 2 Chr.8:13; Ezr.3:4; Ne.8:14; Zec. 14:16; Jn.7:2	To celebrate the wilderness wanderings when the people lived in tents on their way to the promised land and to thank God for the harvest. During this period of time, they lived in temporary tents. Despite the harsh conditions of their lives, as they marched forward, they were to be forever thankful to God and to keep their minds focused upon the promised land.	A symbol of the believer's march through this world to heaven, a symbol of how temporary the believer's march through this world is. As the believer marches to heaven, his dwelling is only temporary. No matter what kind of house he lives in, it is temporary. It is made out of decaying, corruptible materials. It will waste away and some day, perhaps decades or even a few centuries, it will cease to be. Earthly homes are only temporary structures. Moreover, the believer is living in a temporary body, a body that the Bible describes as a temporary tent or tabernacle. The body is corruptible and will decay and cease to exist. The believer's journey through this world is only a temporary pilgrimage. He is marching to his permanent and eternal home in heaven, marching forth to live forever in the presence of God. **"For we know that if our earthly house of this tabernacle were dissolved, we have a building of God, an house not made with hands, eternal in the heavens" (2 Co.5:1).** **"Blessed *be* the God and Father of our Lord Jesus Christ, which according to his abundant mercy hath begotten us again unto a lively hope by the resurrection of Jesus Christ from the dead, To an inheritance incorruptible, and undefiled, and that fadeth not away, reserved in heaven for you" (1 Pe.1:3-4).**

SACRED DAYS IN THE HEBREW CALENDAR
AND THEIR PROPHETIC SYMBOLISM

NAME OF FEAST OR EVENT	OLD TESTAMENT PURPOSE	NEW TESTAMENT SYMBOLISM	CALENDAR TIME	FARM SEASON (Crops/ Weather)
The Festival of Passover	To remember God's judgment and deliverance from Egyptian bondage. (Le.23:6; Nu.9:5; Jos.5:10; 2 K.23:22; 2 Chr.35:1)	A symbol of Christ our Passover who was sacrificed to deliver us from the judgment of God. (Mt.26:17; Lu.2:41; Lu.22:15; He.11:28)	*Hebrew Time*: The 1st Month [Abib or Nisan], 14th Day *Secular Equivalent*: March - April	Harvesting barley & flax; Later Spring rains.***
The Festival of Unleavened Bread	To recall the need and urgency to leave Egypt (a symbol of the world). (Ex.12:17-18; Ex.13:6-7; Ex.23:15; Ex.34:18; Le.23:6; Nu.28:17; De.16:3; De.16:16; 2 Chr.8:13; 2 Chr.30:13)	A symbol of the urgency for God's people to escape the enslavement of the world and immediately begin their march to the promised land of heaven. (Mt.26:17; Mk.14:1)	*Hebrew Time*: The 1st Month [Abib or Nisan], 15th thru the 21st Day *Secular Equivalent*: March - April	Harvesting barley & flax; Later Spring rains.
The Festival of Firstfruits	To thank God for the crops, the first harvest of the season that sustained life. (Ex.34:22; Le.23:10; Nu.28:26)	A symbol of Christ's resurrection and of the believers hope: Christ is the first of the harvest, the first to arise from the dead. (Ro.8:23; 1 Co.15:23)	*Hebrew Time*: The 1st Month [Abib or Nisan], 16th Day *Secular Equivalent*: March - April	Harvesting barley & flax; Later Spring rains
The Festival of Pentecost or Harvest or Weeks	To give thanks for the harvest and to dedicate one's life anew to God This festival took place fifty days after the Festival of Firstfruits. (Ex.23:16; Ex.34:22; Le.23:16; Nu.28:26; De.16:10)	A symbol of Pentecost... • of the great harvest of souls • of people giving their lives to God • of the coming of the Holy Spirit & the birth of the church (Ac.2:1-47; Ac.20:16; 1 Co.16:8)	*Hebrew Time*: The 3rd Month [Sivan], the 6th Day *Secular Equivalent*: May - June	Wheat harvest; other crops—grapes and almonds begin to open.
The Festival of Trumpets	To focus upon God, learning to trust God more and more and to proclaim the message of joy over the atonement or reconciliation with God. (Le.23:24; Nu.29:1; Ne.8:2)	A symbol of salvation and of the rapture, the glorious day when Christ will return and take believers—both the living and the dead—to with Him forever.	*Hebrew Time*: 7th Month, [Ethanim or Tishri **], the 1st Day *Secular Equivalent* September - October	Plowing of the fields: Early autumn rains.
The Day of Atonement	To focus upon the only way to approach God and be forgiven—through the shed blood of the atoning sacrifice. Celebrated yearly, it was a national day of repentance. (Ex.30:10; Le.16:30; Le.23:27; Nu.29:7)	A symbol of being reconciled with God through the atonement, through the substitute sacrifice of Christ. (He.9:7)	*Hebrew Time*: 7th Month, [Ethanim or Tishri **], the 10th Day *Secular Equivalent*: September - October	Plowing of the fields: Early autumn rains.
The Feast of Tabernacles or Booths	To celebrate the wilderness wanderings when the people lived in tents on their way to the promised land and to thank God for the harvest. (Le.23:34, 39; Nu.29:12; De.16:13; 2 Chr.8:13; Ezr.3:4; Ne.8:14; Zec.14:16)	A symbol of the believer's march through this world to heaven, a symbol of how temporary our world is as believers march to heaven. (Jn.7:2)	*Hebrew Time*: 7th Month, [Ethanim or Tishri **], the 15th thru the 21st Day *Secular Equivalent*: September - October	Plowing of the fields: Early autumn rains.
The Feast of Purim	To remember God's deliverance from Israel's enemies during the time of Esther. Purim was a time of sharing with one's neighbor and with the poor. (Est.9:18-32)	Not mentioned in the New Testament.	*Hebrew Time*: The 12th Month [Adar *], the 14th & 15th Day *Secular Equivalent*: February - March	Blooming of almond trees; Harvesting of citrus fruit; the later rains begin.

*   Note: An additional month (Second Adar or Adar Sheni or Veadar) was added to the Hebrew calendar about every three years. This was how the lunar calendar corresponded to the solar year.

**   Hebrew names of the month that are not in the Bible are marked with two stars (**). These are known as "Post-exilic" names, from the period of history known as "The Babylonian Exile."

***   The idea for listing the Farm Seasons was stirred by *The NIV Study Bible*, Grand Rapids, MI: Zondervan Bible Publishers, 1985, pp.102-103.

OTHER SACRED DAYS IN THE HEBREW CALENDAR

NAME OF FEAST OR EVENT	OLD TESTAMENT PURPOSE	NEW TESTAMENT SYMBOLISM	CALENDAR TIME	FARM SEASON (Crops/ Weather)
The Sabbath Day	To have a day of rest and worship (Ex.20:8-11; Ex.31:12-17; Le.23:3; De.5:12-15)	The Sabbath is a symbol of the spiritual rest that God promises to those who believe and follow him. The Sabbath rest is a symbol of redemption, of God's deliverance from the heavy burdens and trials of this life. (Mt.12:1-14; Mt.28:1; Lu. 4:16; Jn.5:9; Ac.13:42; Col.2:16; He.4:1-11)	*Hebrew Time*: Celebrated on the seventh day of each week *Secular Equivalent*: Same as above	Not Applicable.
The Sabbatical Year	The Sabbatical Year was celebrated every seven years. During the seventh year the land was given rest from agricultural use and debts were forgiven (Ex.23:10-11; Le. 25:1-7; De.15:1)	Not mentioned in the New Testament.	*Hebrew Time*: Celebrated every seven years *Secular Equivalent*: Same as above	Not Applicable.
The Year of Jubilee	The Year of Jubilee was celebrated at the end of every forty-ninth year on the Day of Atonement. On this special day, the trumpet would sound out the message of freedom to all the inhabitants of the land who had been held in bondage. In addition, all property was to be returned to the original owners who had been forced to sell because of poverty. This meant that all prices in the economy throughout the forty-nine years were to be fairly adjusted according to the closeness to The Year of Jubilee. (Le.25:8-17; Le. 27:17-24; Nu.36:4)	Not mentioned in the New Testament.	*Hebrew Time*: Celebrated at the end of every forty-ninth year on the Day of Atonement. *Secular Equivalent*: Same as above	Not Applicable.
The Sacred Assembly	To celebrate the end of the final feast. The sacred assembly was a day of sacrifice and then rest. (Le.23:36; Nu.29:35-38)	Not mentioned in the New Testament.	*Hebrew Time:* The 7th Month [Ethanim or Tishri **], on the 22nd Day. *Secular Equivalent:* September – October	Plowing of the fields; early autumn rains.

Types, Symbols, and Pictures
The Book of Leviticus

Alphabetical Outline

What is a *biblical type* or *symbol*? Simply put, a biblical type is a *foreshadowing* of what was to come at a later time in history. Through a person, place, or thing, a biblical type or symbol points toward a New Testament fulfillment.

In addition to biblical types, there are what we may call *biblical pictures*. A biblical picture is a lesson that we can see in the Scriptures *without distorting the truth*. The study of biblical types and pictures is a valuable tool in that it helps us apply the truth of Scripture to our lives. Scripture itself tells us this:

> **"Now all these things happened unto them for examples: and they are written for our admonition, upon whom the ends of the world are come"** (1 Co.10:11).
> **"For whatsoever things were written aforetime were written for our learning, that we through patience and comfort of the scriptures might have hope"** (Ro.15:4).

INSTRUCTIONS FOR BEST USE: for quick and easy reference, every type, symbol, and picture in *Leviticus* has been alphabetized and cross-referenced with similar subjects. A key number, in bold, has been assigned to each type or picture. To further assist one's study, page numbers and Scripture references are also included.

PERSON/PLACE/THING	KEY NUMBER	SCRIPTURE, OUTLINE AND DISCUSSION
Aaron (See Anointing...)	45	Le.8:10-13
Altar of Burnt Offering (See Poured-out...)	22	Le.4:7
Altar of Burnt Offering Anointed with Oil Seven Times	44	Le.8:10-13
Altar of Incense (See Blood put upon...)	21	Le.4:7
Animal Sacrifice that Had to Be a Male	3	Le.1:3
Animal Sacrifice that Had to Be Perfect, Without Defect or Blemish	4	Le.1:3; 4:3-12
Animal Sacrifice, Laying Hands On (See Laying of one's...)	5	Le.1:4; 8:14
Animals, Clean and Unclean (See Clean...)	59	Le.11:2-8
Anointed Priest (See Blood put upon...)	21	Le.4:7
Anointed Priest (See Blood sprinkled...)	20	Le.4:5-12
Anointing Aaron (The High Priest) with Oil	45	Le.8:10-13
Aroma Ascending Upward (See Sweet...)	8	Le.1:9; 8:21; 16:27-28
Aroma of the Burning Sacrifice and Grain Offering Ascended Up in the Festival of Firstfruits	104	Le.23:13
Aroma of the Grain Offering Laid upon the Burnt Offering	32	Le.6:14-18; 6:19-23
Ash Heap	23	Le.4:12; 9:11
Atonement (See High Priest: the only person...)	88	Le.16:17
Atonement Was to Be Made for the Altar of Burnt Offering by Sprinkling Blood on the Altar *Seven Times*	89	Le.16:18-19
Atonement, Day of (See Day of...)	83	Le.16:1-34. See also Le.23:27
Bathe with Water (See Normal bodily...)	81	Le.15:16
Blood of the Sacrifice (See Dedication...)	48	Le.8:23-24
Blood of the Sacrifice (See High Priest sprinkled...)	87	Le.16:11-14
Blood of the Substitute Sacrifice (See Pouring out...)	52	Le.9:9. See also Le.4:7
Blood Placed on the Cleansed Person's Right Ear, Thumb, and Toe During the Guilt Offering	73	Le.14:10-20

PERSON/PLACE/THING	KEY NUMBER	SCRIPTURE, OUTLINE AND DISCUSSION
Blood Put upon the Altar of Incense During the Sin Offering for the Anointed Priest or Minister	21	Le.4:7
Blood Sprinkled Seven Times in Front of the Inner Curtain of the Most Holy Place During the Sin Offering for the Anointed Priest or Minister	20	Le.4:5-12
Blood, Poured Out (See Poured-out...)	22	Le.4:7
Blood, Sprinkling of (See Atonement was...)	89	Le.16:18-19
Bread (See Holy Bread)	112	Le.24:5-9
Bull or Cow Sacrificed in the Fellowship or Peace Offering	14	Le.3:1-5
Bull Sacrificed for Society During the Sin Offering	24	Le.4:21
Bull, Young Bull Without Defect (See Young bull...)	19	Le.4:3-12. See also Le.1:3
Burning And Consuming of the Entire Sacrifice on the Altar of Burnt Offering	7	Le.1:6-9
Burning of the Lord's Portion on the Altar As Food Being Offered to God	16	Le.3:6-11; 7:18
Burnt Offering	1	Le.1:1-17; 6:8-13; 8:18-21; 16:24
Burnt Offering (See Burning and consuming of...)	7	Le.1:6-9
Burnt Offering, Altar of (See Atonement was...)	89	Le.16:18-19
Burnt Offering, Aroma of (See Aroma of...)	32	Le.6:14-18; 6:19-23
Burnt Offering, Laying the Grain upon (See Laying...)	30	Le.6:14-18
Burnt Offering, Perpetual Fire of (See Perpetual...)	27	Le.6:8-13
Burnt Offering, Sweet Aroma of (See Sweet...)	8	Le.1:9; 8:21; 16:27-28
Camp, Outside the (See Person being cleansed...)	70	Le.14:4-7
Childbirth, Laws that Protect Mother and Child (See Laws that protect...)	62	Le.12:1-8
Circumcision	63	Le.12:1-4
Clean and Unclean Animals	59	Le.11:2-8
Cleanliness, Laws of (See Laws of...)	58	Le.11:1-47
Cleanse, Laws that (See Laws that cleanse...)	67	Le.14:1-57
Cleansed (See Person being cleansed...)	70	Le.14:4-7
Cleansing of a Man from Sexual Impurity: Had to Wash His Clothes and Self with Fresh Water for *Seven Days*	79	Le.15:13
Cleansing of Mildew in Houses	75	Le.14:33-53
Cleansing that Took Place Inside the Camp	72	Le.14:10-20
Cleansing that Took Place Outside the Camp	68	Le.14:2-9
Cleansing the Diseased Person (See Priest's going outside...)	69	Le.14:3
Clothing	65	Le.13:47-59
Clothing of the High Priest (See Pure white...)	85	Le.16:3-10
Clothing with Semen on It: Had to Be Washed with Water	82	Le.15:17
Clothing, Priestly (See Priestly clothing)	28	Le.6:8-13

PERSON/PLACE/THING	KEY NUMBER	SCRIPTURE, OUTLINE AND DISCUSSION
Clothing, Putting on of the High Priest's Special (See Special...)	36	Le.8:7-9
Clothing, Regular (See Priest's regular...)	29	Le.6:8-13
Consuming of the Entire Sacrifice (See Burning and...)	7	Le.1:6-9
Cursing God (See Laying on of hands...)	113	Le.24:10-23
Day of Atonement	83	Le.16:1-34. See also Le.23:27
Dead, Overly Mourning for the	97	Le.21:1-4
Death (The Defilement of Aaron's Two Sons)	57	Le.10:4-5
Dedication of the Altar of Sacrifice During the Ordination Offering	49	Le.8:24
Dedication or Setting Apart of One's Whole Being to God Through the Blood of the Sacrifice	48	Le.8:23-24
Defilement	98	Le.22:1-9
Defilement of Aaron's Two Sons (See Death...)	57	Le.10:4-5
Defilement, Laws of (See Laws of...)	58	Le.11:1-47
Discharges, Normal Bodily of a Man (See normal bodily...)	81	Le.15:16
Doves, Sacrifice of Two (See Sacrifice of...)	80	Le.15:14-15
Egypt	61	Le.11:44-47. See also Le.19:33-34
Ephod	40	Le.8:7
Fellowship And Peace of God Offering, Sacrifice of (See Sacrifice of...)	92	Le.19:5
Fellowship or Peace Offering	13	Le.3:1-17
Fellowship or Peace Offering, Sacrifice of (See Bull or cow sacrificed...)	14	Le.3:1-5
Festival of Firstfruits	103	Le.23:9-14
Festival of Firstfruits, Aroma of Burning and Grain Offerings (See Aroma of...)	104	Le.23:13
Feast or Festival of Harvest or Pentecost	105	Le.23:15-22
Feast or Festival of Harvest, Sacrifice of (See Sacrifice of seven...)	106	Le.23:18
Feast or Festival of Tabernacles	108	Le.23:33-34
Feast or Festival of Trumpets	107	Le.23:23-25
Feast or Festival of Unleavened Bread	102	Le.23:6
Fire, Perpetual of the Burnt Offering (See Perpetual...)	27	Le.6:8-13
Fire, Unauthorized (See Offering of strange...)	56	Le.10:1
First Worship Service of the Priest, the Sin Offering (See Pouring out...)	52	Le.9:9. See also Le.4:7
Firstfruits, Festival of (See Festival...)	103	Le.23:9-14
Food (See Holy food...)	99	Le.22:10-16
Food Offered to God (See Burning of the Lord's...)	16	Le.3:6-11; 7:18

PERSON/PLACE/THING	KEY NUMBER	SCRIPTURE, OUTLINE AND DISCUSSION
Foreigners or Strangers in Egypt	94	Le.19:33-34. See also Le.11:44-47; Le.22:33
Goat: The Sacrifice Used in... a. The Fellowship or Peace Offering b. The First Worship Service of the Priest c. The Removal of Sins d. The Death of Christ	17	a. Le.3:12-16 b. Le.9:15 c. Le.16:3-10 d. Le.16:15
Goat Offered for the Sins of a Ruler During the First Worship Service of the Priest	54	Le.9:15. See also Le.3:12-16
Goat that Was Slaughtered for the Sin Offering for the People	90	Le.16:15. See also Le.3:12-16
Gold Plate (Medallion) or Sacred Diadem	43	Le.8:9
Grain Offering	11	Le.2:3
Grain Offering, Aroma of (See Aroma of...)	32	Le.6:14-18; 6:19-23
Grain Offering, Incense Used in (See Incensed used...)	10	Le.2:1
Grain Offering, Oil Used in (See Oil used...)	9	Le.2:1
Guilt Offering	25	Le.5:14-6:7
Guilt Offering During The Special Duties of the Priests in Conducting the Offerings	34	Le.7:1-10. See also Le.5:14–6:7
Guilt Offering, Blood Placed On (See Blood placed on...)	73	Le.14:10-20
High Priest	84	Le.16:3-10; 16:11-14. See also Le.21:10-15
High Priest Sprinkled the Atonement Cover or Mercy Seat on the Ark of the Covenant Seven Times with the Shed Blood of the Sacrifice	87	Le.16:11-14
High Priest Tended the Lampstand Continually	111	Le.24:4
High Priest: The Only Person Who Could Secure Atonement for the People	88	Le.16:17
Holy Bread	112	Le.24:5-9
Holy Food of God	99	Le.22:10-16
Honey and Yeast	12	Le.2:11-12
Impurity, Cleansing of (See Cleansing of a man...)	79	Le.15:13
Incense Used in the Grain Offering	10	Le.2:1
Infectious Mildew or Plague of Leprosy	66	Le.13:47-59
Infectious Skin Disease (See Leprosy...)	64	Le.13:1-59
Infectious Skin Disease, Laws that Cleanse and Restore People from (See Laws that cleanse...)	67	Le.14:1-57
Inner Curtain (See Blood sprinkled...)	20	Le.4:5-12
Keeping God's Laws and Living a Life of Total Separation, Distinction	93	Le.19:19
Kinsman-Redeemer Law	114	Le.25:23-34
Lamb: The Sacrifice Used in... a. The Fellowship or Peace Offering b. The Sin Offering	15	a. Le.3:6-11 b. Le.4:32, 35; 5:6

PERSON/PLACE/THING	KEY NUMBER	SCRIPTURE, OUTLINE AND DISCUSSION
c. The First Worship Service of the Priest		c. Le.9:3
d. The Burnt Offering for a Mother's Protection Right After Childbirth		d. Le.12:6
e. The Cleansing that Took Place Inside the Camp		e. Le.14:10, 13
f. The Guilt Offering for the Poorest of the Poor		f. Le.14:21, 24-25
g. The Festival of Firstfruits, of the Burnt Offering		g. Le.23:12
Lampstand	109	Le.24:1-4
Lampstand (See High Priest tended...)	111	Le.24:4
Lampstand (See Pure olive oil...)	111	Le.24:2
Laws of Cleanliness and Defilement	58	Le.11:1-47
Laws that Cleanse and Restore People from Leprosy, from All Forms of Infectious Skin Disease	67	Le.14:1-57
Laws that Protect and Cleanse People from Sexual Diseases and Impurity	76	Le.15:1-33
Laws That Protect Mother And Child After Childbirth	62	Le.12:1-8
Laws, Keeping God's (See Keeping God's laws...)	93	Le.19:19
Laying of Hands on the Head of the Animal Sacrifice	5	Le.1:4; 8:14
Laying of Hands on the Person Who Cursed God	113	Le.24:10-23
Laying the Grain upon the Burnt Offering	30	Le.6:14-18
Leprosy or Infectious Skin Disease	64	Le.13:1-59
Leprosy, Laws that Cleanse and Restore People from (See Laws that cleanse...)	67	Le.14:1-57
Leprosy, Plague of (See Infectious mildew...)	66	Le.13:47-59
Linen Tunic	37	Le.8:7
Linen Turban	42	Le.8:9
Mildew, Cleansing of (See Cleansing of...)	75	Le.14:33-53
Mildew, Infectious (See Infectious mildew...)	66	Le.13:47-59
Moses	2	Le.1:1; 8:1-5
Mourning, for the Dead (See Dead...)	97	Le.21:1-4
Normal Bodily Discharges (Excretion) of a Man: Had to Bathe with Water	81	Le.15:16
Odor of the Burning Grain Along with the Roasting Meat Ascended Up Toward Heaven During the First Worship Service of the Priest	55	Le.9:17
Offering of Strange, Unauthorized Fire to the LORD	56	Le.10:1
Oil	74	Le.14:16-18
Oil Used in the Grain Offering	9	Le.2:1
Oil, Anointed with Seven Times (See Altar of...)	44	Le.8:10-13
Oil, Anointing Aaron with (See Anointing...)	45	Le.8:10-13
Olive Oil, Pure (See Pure olive oil...)	110	Le.24:2

TYPES, SYMBOLS, AND PICTURES
Alphabetical Outline

PERSON/PLACE/THING	KEY NUMBER	SCRIPTURE, OUTLINE AND DISCUSSION
Ordination Offering	47	Le.8:22-32
Ordination Offering, Dedication of (See Dedication...)	49	Le.8:24
Ordination Service Repeated for Seven Days	51	Le.8:33
Passover	101	Le.23:5
Peace Offering (See Fellowship...)	13	Le.3:1-17
Pentecost (See Festival of...)	105	Le.23:15-22
Perpetual Fire of the Burnt Offering	27	Le.6:8-13
Person Being Cleansed Through the Sacrifice of the Shed Blood—Outside the Camp	70	Le.14:4-7
Person Who Suffered from a Sexual Disease Defiled Any Clay Pot or Wood He Touched	78	Le.15:12
Physically Perfect Priest	96	Le.21:16-24
Pigeons, Sacrifice of Two Young (See Sacrifice of...)	80	Le.15:14-15
Poured-Out Blood at the Bottom of the Altar of Burnt Offering	22	Le.4:7
Pouring Out the Remaining Blood of the Substitute Sacrifice of the Sin Offering During the First Worship Service of the Priest	52	Le.9:9. See also Le.4:7
Priest's Going Outside the Camp to Cleanse the Diseased Person	69	Le.14:3
Priest's Regular Clothing Worn When Taking the Ashes of The Sacrifice Outside the Camp	29	Le.6:8-13
Priest, First Worship Service of (See Odor of...)	55	Le.9:17
Priest, Physically Perfect (See Physically...)	96	Le.21:16-24
Priestly Clothing	28	Le.6:8-13
Promised Land	95	Le.20:24
Pure Olive Oil that Kept the Lampstand Burning Continually	110	Le.24:2
Pure White Linen Clothing of the High Priest	85	Le.16:3-10
Ram Without Defect and of Proper Value: the Sacrifice Used in the Guilt Offering	26	Le.5:15, 18; 6:6
Roasted Meat of the Ordination Offering, Sweet Aroma of (See Sweet...)	50	Le.8:28
Robe of the Ephod	39	Le.8:7
Sabbath	100	Le.23:3
Sacrifice of Seven Male Lambs, One Young Bull and Two Rams—All with No Defect in the Festival of Harvest	106	Le.23:18
Sacrifice of The Fellowship and Peace of God Offering	92	Le.19:5
Sacrifice of Two Doves or Two Young Pigeons	80	Le.15:14-15
Sacrifice, Animal; Sacrifice, Male (See Animal sacrifice...)	3	Le.1:3
Sacrifice, Bull (See Bull sacrificed...)	24	Le.4:21
Sacrifice, Perfect (See Animal sacrifice...)	4	Le.1:3; 4:3-12

PERSON/PLACE/THING	KEY NUMBER	SCRIPTURE, OUTLINE AND DISCUSSION
Sacrifice, the Taking of Certain Parts (See Taking of...)	46	Le.8:17
Sash	38	Le.8:7
Scapegoat: the Sacrifice of the Sin Offering During the Atonement	86	Le.16:3-10; 16:20-22. See also Le.3:12-16
Separation, Living a Life of (See Keeping God's laws...)	93	Le.19:19
Setting Apart of One's Whole Being to God (See Dedication...)	48	Le.8:23-24
Seven (See Blood sprinkled...)	20	Le.4:5-12
Seven Days (See Cleansing of a man...)	79	Le.15:13
Seven Days (See Ordination service...)	51	Le.8:33
Seven Times (See High Priest sprinkled...)	87	Le.16:11-14
Sexual Disease (See Person who suffered...)	78	Le.15:12
Sexual Diseases, Laws That Protect and Cleanse People (See Laws that protect...)	76	Le.15:1-33
Shed Blood of the Sacrifice	6	Le.1:5; 8:19; 17:10-16
Sin Offering	18	Le.4:1-5:13. See also Le.6:24-30; 8:14-17; 9:2; 9:15; 10:17; 16:3-22
Sin Offering (See Bull sacrificed...)	24	Le.4:21
Sin Offering During the Special Duties of the Priests in Conducting the Offerings	33	Le.6:24-30. See also Le.4:1-5:13
Sin Offering for the People (See Goat that was...)	90	Le.16:15. See also Le.3:12-16
Sins of a Ruler (See Goat offered...)	54	Le.9:15. See also Le.3:12-16
Special Clothing, Putting On of the High Priest's	36	Le.8:7-9
Sweet Aroma Ascending Upward in the Burnt Offering	8	Le.1:9; 8:21; 16:27-28
Sweet Aroma of the Roasted Meat of the Ordination Offering Ascended Up Toward Heaven	50	Le.8:28
Tabernacle and It's Worship	91	Le.17:3-9
Tabernacles (See Festival...)	108	Le.23:33-34
Taking of Certain Parts of the Sacrifice (The Sin Offering) Outside the Camp and Burning Them	46	Le.8:17
Trumpets (See Festival...)	107	Le.23:23-25
Tunic (See Linen...)	37	Le.8:7
Turban (See Linen...)	42	Le.8:9
Unleavened Bread (See Festival...)	102	Le.23:6
Urim and Thummim	41	Le.8:8
Washed with Water (See Clothing with...)	82	Le.15:17
Washing	60	Le.11:24-40
Washing Clothes and Bathing in Water for the Bodily Discharges and Cleansing of Men and Women	77	Le.15:2-18; 19-30

PERSON/PLACE/THING	KEY NUMBER	SCRIPTURE, OUTLINE AND DISCUSSION
Washing in Water	35	Le.8:6; 11:25
Washing of the Inner Parts and Legs of the Substitute Sacrifice of the Burnt Offering During the First Worship Service of the Priest	53	Le.9:14
Washing of the Person's Clothes, Shaving His Body, and Bathing	71	Le.14:8
Worship (See Tabernacle...)	91	Le.17:3-9
Yeast And Honey	12	Le.2:11-12
Yeast or Leaven Withheld from the Grain Offering	31	Le.6:14-18
Young Bull Without Defect: The Sacrifice Used in the Sin Offering for the Anointed Priest or Minister	19	Le.4:3-12. See also Le.1:3

TYPES, SYMBOLS, AND PICTURES
THE BOOK OF LEVITICUS

CHRONOLOGICAL OUTLINE

What is a *biblical type* or *symbol*? Simply put, a biblical type is a *foreshadowing* of what was to come at a later time in history. Through a person, place, or thing, a biblical type or symbol points toward a New Testament fulfillment.

In addition to biblical types, there are what we may call *biblical pictures*. A biblical picture is a lesson that we can see in the Scriptures *without distorting the truth*. The study of biblical types and pictures is a valuable tool in that it helps us apply the truth of Scripture to our lives. Scripture itself tells us this:

> **"Now all these things happened unto them for examples: and they are written for our admonition, upon whom the ends of the world are come" (1 Co.10:11).**
> **"For whatsoever things were written aforetime were written for our learning, that we through patience and comfort of the scriptures might have hope" (Ro.15:4).**

PERSON/PLACE/THING	SCRIPTURE, OUTLINE AND DISCUSSION
1. *The Burnt Offering*	Le.1:1-17; 6:8-13; 8:18-21; 16:24
2. *Moses*	Le.1:1; 8:1-5
3. *The Animal Sacrifice that Had to Be a Male*	Le.1:3
4. *The Animal Sacrifice that Had to Be Perfect, Without Defect or Blemish*	Le.1:3; 4:3-12
5. *The Laying of One's Hands on the Head of the Animal Sacrifice*	Le.1:4; 8:14
6. *The Shed Blood of the Sacrifice*	Le.1:5; 8:19; 17:10-16
7. *The Burning and Consuming of the Entire Sacrifice on the Altar of Burnt Offering*	Le.1:6-9
8. *The Sweet Aroma Ascending Up in the Burnt Offering*	Le.1:9; 8:21; 16:27-28
9. *Oil Used in the Grain Offering*	Le.2:1
10. *Incense Used in the Grain Offering*	Le.2:1
11. *Grain Offering*	Le.2:3
12. *Yeast and Honey*	Le.2:11-12
13. *The Fellowship or Peace Offering*	Le.3:1-17
14. *Bull or Cow Sacrificed in the Fellowship or Peace Offering*	Le.3:1-5

15. *Lamb: the Sacrifice Used in...*
   a. *The Fellowship or Peace Offering*
   b. *The Sin Offering*
   c. *The First Worship Service of the Priest*
   d. *The Burnt Offering for a Mother's Protection Right After Childbirth*
   e. *The Cleansing that Took Place Inside the Camp*
   f. *The Guilt Offering for the Poorest of the Poor*
   g. *The Festival of Firstfruits, of the Burnt Offering*
	a. Le.3:6-11
	b. Le.4:32, 35; 5:6
	c. Le.9:3
	d. Le.12:6
	e. Le.14:10, 13
	f. Le.14:21, 24-25
	g. Le.23:12

17. *The Burning of the Lord's Portion on the Altar As Food Being Offered to God*	Le.3:6-11; 7:18

18. *The Goat: The Sacrifice Used in...*
   a. *The Fellowship or Peace Offering*
   b. *The First Worship Service of the Priest*
   c. *The Removal of Sins*
   d. *The Death of Christ*
	a. Le.3:12-16
	b. Le.9:15
	c. Le.16:3-10
	d. Le.16:15

19. *The Sin Offering*	Le.4:1-5:13. See also Le.6:24-30; 8:14-17; 9:2; 9:15; 10:17; 16:3-22
20. *Young Bull Without Defect: the Sacrifice Used in the Sin Offering for the Anointed Priest or Minister*	Le.4:3-12; See also Le.1:3
21. *Blood Sprinkled Seven Times in Front of the Inner Curtain of the Most Holy Place: During the Sin Offering for the Anointed Priest or Minister*	Le.4:5-12

PERSON/PLACE/THING	SCRIPTURE, OUTLINE AND DISCUSSION
22. *Blood Put upon the Altar of Incense: During the Sin Offering for the Anointed Priest or Minister*	Le.4:7
23. *The Poured-Out Blood at the Bottom of the Altar of Burnt Offering*	Le.4:7
24. *The Ash Heap*	Le.4:12; 9:11
25. *The Bull Sacrificed for Society: During the Sin Offering*	Le.4:21
26. *The Guilt Offering*	Le.5:14-6:7
27. *Ram Without Defect and of True Value: the Sacrifice Used in the Guilt Offering*	Le.5:15, 18; 6:6
28. *The Perpetual Fire of the Burnt Offering*	Le.6:8-13
29. *The Priestly Clothing*	Le.6:8-13
30. *The Priest's Regular Clothing Worn When Taking the Ashes of the Sacrifice Outside the Camp*	Le.6:8-13
31. *Laying the Grain upon the Burnt Offering*	Le.6:14-18
32. *Yeast or Leaven Withheld from the Grain Offering*	Le.6:14-18
33. *The Aroma of the Grain Offering Laid upon the Burnt Offering*	Le.6:14-18; 6:19-23
34. *The Sin Offering: During the Special Duties of the Priests in Conducting the Offerings*	Le.6:24-30. See also Le.4:1-5:13
35. *The Guilt Offering: During the Special Duties of the Priests in Conducting The Offerings*	Le.7:1-10. See also Le.5:14-6:7
36. *Washing in Water*	Le.8:6; 11:25
37. *The Putting on of the High Priest's Special Clothing*	Le.8:7-9
38. *The Linen Tunic*	Le.8:7
39. *The Sash*	Le.8:7
40. *The Robe of the Ephod*	Le.8:7
41. *The Ephod*	Le.8:7
42. *The Urim and Thummim*	Le.8:8
43. *The Linen Turban*	Le.8:9
44. *The Gold Plate Medallion or Sacred Diadem*	Le.8:9
45. *The Altar of Burnt Offering Anointed with Oil Seven Times*	Le.8:10-13
46. *Anointing Aaron the High Priest with Oil*	Le.8:10-13
47. *Taking of Certain Parts of the Sacrifice the Sin Offering Outside the Camp and Burning Them*	Le.8:17
48. *The Ordination Offering*	Le.8:22-32
49. *The Dedication or Setting Apart of One's Whole Being to God Through the Blood of the Sacrifice*	Le.8:23-24
50. *The Dedication of the Altar of Sacrifice: During the Ordination Offering*	Le.8:24
51. *The Sweet Aroma of the Roasted Meat Ascending Up Toward Heaven: During the Ordination Offering*	Le.8:28
52. *The Ordination Service Repeated for Seven Days*	Le.8:33
53. *Pouring Out the Remaining Blood of the Substitute Sacrifice of the Sin Offering: During the First Worship Service of the Priest*	Le.9:9; See also Le.4:7
54. *The Washing of the Inner Parts and Legs of the Burnt Offering: During the First Worship Service of the Priest*	Le.9:14
55. *A Goat Offered for the Sins of a Ruler the Sin Offering: During the First Worship Service of the Priest*	Le.9:15. See also Le.3:12-16

PERSON/PLACE/THING	SCRIPTURE, OUTLINE AND DISCUSSION
56. *The Odor of the Burning Grain Along with the Roasting Meat Ascended Up Toward Heaven During the First Worship Service of the Priest*	Le.9:17
57. *The Offering of Strange, Unauthorized Fire to the LORD.*	Le.10:1
58. *Death The Defilement of Aaron's Two Sons*	Le.10:4-5
59. *The Laws of Cleanliness and Defilement*	Le.11:1-47
60. *The Clean and Unclean Animals*	Le.11:2-8
61. *Washing*	Le.11:24-40
62. *Egypt*	Le.11:44-47. See also Le.19:33-34
63. *Laws that Protect Mother and Child After Childbirth*	Le.12:1-8
64. *Circumcision*	Le.12:1-4
65. *Leprosy or Infectious Skin Disease*	Le.13:1-59
66. *Clothing*	Le.13:47-59
67. *Infectious Mildew or Plague of Leprosy*	Le.13:47-59
68. *Laws that Cleanse and Restore People from Leprosy, from All Forms of Infectious Skin Disease*	Le.14:1-57
69. *The Cleansing that Took Place Outside the Camp*	Le.14:2-9
70. *The Priest's Going Outside the Camp to Cleanse the Diseased Person*	Le.14:3
71. *The Person Being Cleansed Through the Sacrifice of the Shed Blood—Outside the Camp*	Le.14:4-7
72. *The Washing of the Person's Clothes, Shaving His Body, and Bathing*	Le.14:8
73. *The Cleansing that Took Place Inside the Camp*	Le.14:10-20
74. *Some Blood Placed on the Cleansed Person's Right Ear, Thumb, and Toe During the Guilt Offering*	Le.14:10-20
75. *Oil*	Le.14:16-18
76. *The Cleansing of Mildew in Houses*	Le.14:33-53
77. *Laws that Protect and Cleanse People from Sexual Diseases and Impurity*	Le.15:1-33
78. *Washing Clothes and Bathing in Water for the Bodily Discharges and Cleansing of Men and Women*	Le.15:2-18; 19-30
79. *The Person Who Suffered from a Sexual Disease: Defiled Any Clay Pot or Wood He Touched*	Le.15:12
80. *The Cleansing of a Man from Sexual Impurity: Had to Wash His Clothes and Self with Fresh Water for Seven Days*	Le.15:13
81. *A Sacrifice of Two Doves or Two Young Pigeons*	Le.15:14-15
82. *The Normal Bodily Discharges [Excretion] of a Man: Had to Bathe with Water*	Le.15:16
83. *Clothing with Semen On It: Had to Be Washed with Water*	Le.15:17
84. *The Day of Atonement*	Le.16:1-34. See also Le.23:27
85. *The High Priest*	Le.16:3-10; 16:11-14. See also Le.21:10-15
86. *The Pure White Linen Clothing of the High Priest*	Le.16:3-10
87. *The Scapegoat: Symbolized the Removal and Taking Away of Sin*	Le.16:3-10; 16:20-22. See also Le.3:12-16
88. *The High Priest Sprinkling the Atonement Cover or Mercy Seat on the Ark: Seven Times with the Shed Blood of the Sacrifice*	Le.16:11-14
89. *The Only Person [the High Priest] Who Could Secure Atonement for the People*	Le.16:17

PERSON/PLACE/THING	SCRIPTURE, OUTLINE AND DISCUSSION
90. *Atonement Being Made for the Altar of Burnt Offering by Sprinkling Blood on the Altar Seven Times*	Le.16:18-19
91. *The Goat that Was Slaughtered for the Sin Offering for the People*	Le.16:15. See also Le. 3:12-16
92. *The Tabernacle and It's Worship*	Le.17:3-9
93. *The Sacrifice of the Fellowship and Peace Offering*	Le.19:5
94. *Keeping God's Laws and Living a Life of Total Separation, a Life that Is Distinct*	Le.19:19
95. *Foreigners or Strangers in Egypt*	Le.19:33-34; See also Le. 11:44-47; Le. 22:33
96. *The Promised Land*	Le.20:24
97. *The Physically Perfect Priest*	Le.21:16-24
98. *Dead, Overly Mourning for the*	Le.21:1-4
99. *Defilement*	Le.22:1-9
100. *The Holy Food of God*	Le.22:10-16
101. *The Sabbath*	Le.23:3
102. *The Passover*	Le.23:5
103. *The Festival of Unleavened Bread*	Le.23:6
104. *The Festival of Firstfruits*	Le.23:9-14
105. *The Aroma of the Burning Sacrifice and Grain Offering Ascending Up: During the Festival of Firstfruits*	Le.23:13
106. *The Festival of Harvest or Pentecost*	Le.23:15-22
107. *The Sacrifice of Seven Male Lambs, One Young Bull and Two Rams—All with No Defect in the Festival of Harvest*	Le.23:18
108. *The Festival of Trumpets*	Le.23:23-25
109. *The Festival of Tabernacles or Booths or Shelters*	Le.23:33-43
110. *The Lampstand*	Le.24:1-4
111. *Pure Olive Oil that Kept the Lampstand Burning Continually*	Le.24:2
112. *The High Priest Tending the Lampstand Continually*	Le.24:4
113. *The Holy Bread*	Le.24:5-9
114. *The Laying of Hands on the Person Who Cursed God*	Le.24:10-23
115. *The Kinsman-Redeemer Law*	Le.25:23-34

Historical Term	Type or Picture (Scriptural Basis for Each)	Life Application for Today's Believer	Biblical Application
1. *The Burnt Offering* (Le.1:1-17; 6:8-13; 8:18-21; 16:24)	*A symbol of atonement, reconciliation with God.* The Burnt Offering is a type of Christ, a symbol or picture of Christ dying as the substitute sacrifice for us. By dying for us: ⇒ Christ bore the full justice and judgment of God against sin—paid the ransom price to deliver us from sin and death ⇒ Christ secured the atonement for us, reconciling us to God **"And he shall put his hand upon the head of the burnt offering; and it shall be accepted for him to make atonement for him"** (Le.1:4). **"...by whom [Christ] we have now received the atonement"** (Ro.5:11).	Jesus Christ died for us as our substitute sacrifice. He died to secure the atonement or reconciliation with God for us. A person can now approach God and be reconciled with God; a person can now become acceptable to God. How? By approaching God through the sacrifice of Christ.	*"But God commendeth his love toward us, in that, while we were yet sinners, Christ died for us. Much more then, being now justified by his blood, we shall be saved from wrath through him. For if, when we were enemies, we were reconciled to God by the death of his Son, much more, being reconciled, we shall be saved by his life. And not only so, but we also joy in God through our Lord Jesus Christ, by whom we have now received the atonement."* (Ro.5:8-11). *"Wherefore he is able also to save them to the uttermost that come unto God by him, seeing he ever liveth to make intercession for them. For such an high priest became us, who is holy, harmless, undefiled, separate from sinners, and made higher than the heavens; Who needeth not daily, as those high priests, to offer up sacrifice, first for his own sins, and then for the people's: for this he did once, when he offered up himself"* (He.7:25-27; see 2 Co.5:21).
2. *Moses* (Le.1:1; 8:1-5)	*A clear type of Jesus Christ, the appointed Mediator, who stood between man and God, revealing and declaring the way to God. Moses was the mediator appointed by God to stand between the Israelites and God, revealing and declaring the way to God.* **"And the LORD called unto Moses, and spake unto him out of the tabernacle of the congregation..."** (Le.1:1).	It is Jesus Christ who is the appointed Mediator. It is Christ, and Christ alone. • who stands in the gap between God and man. • who proclaims the way to God • who opens the way into God's presence	*"For there is one God, and one mediator between God and men, the man Christ Jesus"* (1 Ti.2:5). *"God, who at sundry times and in divers manners spake in time past unto the fathers by the prophets, Hath in these last days spoken unto us by his Son, whom he hath appointed heir of all things, by whom also he made the worlds; Who being the brightness of his glory, and the express image of his person, and upholding all things by the word of his power, when he had by himself purged our sins, sat down on the right hand of the Majesty on high"* (He.1:1-3). *"My little children, these things write I unto you, that ye sin not. And if any man*

Historical Term	Type or Picture (Scriptural Basis for Each)	Life Application for Today's Believer	Biblical Application
Moses (continued) (Le.1:1; 8:1-5)			sin, we have an advocate with the Father, Jesus Christ the righteous" (1 Jn.2:1; see Jn.14:6).
3. *The Animal Sacrifice That Had To Be A Male* (Le.1:3)	*The fact that the animal sacrifice had to be a male symbolized strength, the strength of our LORD to save.* **"If his offering be a burnt sacrifice of the herd, let him offer a male without blemish: he shall offer it of his own voluntary will at the door of the tabernacle of the congregation before the LORD" (Le.1:3).**	Jesus Christ is mighty to save and able to save completely, to the utmost.	*"Who needeth not daily, as those high priests, to offer up sacrifice, first for his own sins, and then for the people's: for this he did once, when he offered up himself" (He.7:27).* *"Wherefore he is able also to save them to the uttermost that come unto God by him, seeing he ever liveth to make intercession for them" (He.7:25).*
4. *The Animal Sacrifice That Had To Be Perfect, Without Defect Or Blemish* (Le.1:3; 4:3-12)	*The fact that the sacrifice had to be perfect—without defect or blemish—symbolized the sinlessness, the perfect righteousness of the Lord Jesus Christ.* **"If his offering be a burnt sacrifice of the herd, let him offer a male without blemish: he shall offer it of his own voluntary will at the door of the tabernacle of the congregation before the LORD" (Le.1:3).**	By living a perfect, sinless life, Jesus Christ secured righteousness for man—the *Ideal Righteousness*. As the Ideal Righteousness, His righteousness can cover or stand for every person of all generations. When a person believes in Jesus Christ, the *Ideal Righteousness* of Christ covers the person, makes him acceptable to God.	*"And ye know that he was manifested to take away our sins; and in him is no sin" (1 Jn.3:5).* *"For he hath made him to be sin for us, who knew no sin; that we might be made the righteousness of God in him." (2 Co.5:21)* *"Forasmuch as ye know that ye were not redeemed with corruptible things, as silver and gold, from your vain conversation received by tradition from your fathers; But with the precious blood of Christ, as of a lamb without blemish and without spot" (1 Pe.1:18-19).*
5. *The Laying Of One's Hands On The Head Of The Animal Sacrifice* (Le.1:4; 8:14)	*This is a symbol of identifying with the sacrifice. To the person who truly believed, God did a wonderful thing: God counted his faith in the symbol as righteousness. The person believed God; therefore he obeyed God: he offered a male sacrifice that was perfect, and he laid his hands on its head…* • *identifying himself with the sacrifice* • *believing that God would do just what He said: accept the animal sacrifice as atonement, as a ransom, as a substitute for him. He believed that God accepted the sacrifice as the substitute for him, to bear his sins and punishment. And because he believed God, God did accept the sacrifice on his behalf, in his stead, in his place—as his substitute.*	Note how identification with the substitute sacrifice symbolizes exactly what Jesus Christ did for us: Jesus Christ… • took our place • became our substitute • became our righteousness • became the perfect sacrifice for us In order to be counted righteous, we must identify with the sacrifice of Jesus Christ. We must believe that God will do just what He says: accept the sacrifice of Christ as the atonement, the ransom, the substitute for us.	*"But he was wounded for our transgressions, he was bruised for our iniquities: the chastisement of our peace was upon him; and with his stripes we are healed" (Is.53:5).* *"For he hath made him to be sin for us, who knew no sin; that we might be made the righteousness of God in him" (2 Co.5:21).* *"Christ hath redeemed us from the curse of the law, being made a curse for us: for it is written, Cursed is every one that hangeth on a tree" (Ga.3:13).* *"But we see Jesus, who was made a little lower than the angels for the suffering of death, crowned with glory and honour; that he by the grace of God should taste death for every man" (He.2:9).* *"Who his own self bare our sins in his own body on the tree, that we, being*

Historical Term	Type or Picture (Scriptural Basis for Each)	Life Application for Today's Believer	Biblical Application
The Laying Of One's Hands On The Head Of The Animal Sacrifice (continued) (Le.1:4; 8:14)	"And he shall put his hand upon the head of the burnt offering; and it shall be accepted for him to make atonement for him" (Le.1:4).		*dead to sins, should live unto righteousness: by whose stripes ye were healed" (1 Pe.2:24).* *"For Christ also hath once suffered for sins, the just for the unjust, that he might bring us to God, being put to death in the flesh, but quickened by the Spirit" (1 Pe.3:18).*
6. *The Shed Blood Of The Sacrifice* (Le.1:5; 8:19; 17:10-16)	*A picture of deliverance from God's judgment upon the sinner. The shed blood of the sacrifice covered the altar of sacrifice. Keep in mind that the altar was the place of judgment, the place where the animal sacrifice died bearing the judgment that was due the sinner. The sacrifice shed its blood on behalf of the believer, delivering the believer from judgment and making him acceptable to God.* "And he shall kill the bullock before the LORD: and the priests, Aaron's sons, shall bring the blood, and sprinkle the blood round about upon the altar that *is* by the door of the tabernacle of the congregation" (Le.1:5).	The blood of Jesus Christ redeems us, delivers us from the consuming judgment and wrath of God.	*"Much more then, being now justified by his blood, we shall be saved from wrath through him" (Ro.5:9).* *"How much more shall the blood of Christ, who through the eternal Spirit offered himself without spot to God, purge your conscience from dead works to serve the living God?" (He.9:14).* *"Forasmuch as ye know that ye were not redeemed with corruptible things, as silver and gold, from your vain conversation received by tradition from your fathers; But with the precious blood of Christ, as of a lamb without blemish and without spot" (1 Pe. 1:18-19).*
7. *The Burning And Consuming Of The Entire Sacrifice On The Altar Of Burnt Offering* (Le.1:6-9)	*The fire that burns and consumes the entire sacrifice is a picture of two things:* 1. *A picture of the sharp, painful sufferings of Christ, a picture of His awful death on the cross.* 2. *A picture of the full justice and judgment of God that was borne by the substitute sacrifice.* "And he shall flay the burnt offering, and cut it into his pieces. And the sons of Aaron the priest shall put fire upon the altar, and lay the wood in order upon the fire: And the priests, Aaron's sons, shall lay the parts, the head, and the fat, in order upon the wood that *is* on the fire which *is* upon the altar: But his inwards and his legs shall he wash in water: and the priest shall burn all on the altar, *to be* a burnt sacrifice, an offering made by fire, of a sweet savour unto the LORD" (Le.1:6-9).	Jesus Christ did two things for us: 1. Jesus Christ suffered for us, bore the painful suffering that was due the sinner. 2. Jesus Christ gave Himself fully, totally, entirely to be *the Sacrifice* for man. The animal was sacrificed and suffered in man's place—totally. The animal bore the full judgment of God against sin. So it was with Christ. Jesus Christ sacrificed Himself and suffered for man. He gave Himself totally—in the entirety of His Being—to bear the judgment of God against sin.	*"He was oppressed, and he was afflicted, yet he opened not his mouth: he is brought as a lamb to the slaughter, and as a sheep before her shearers is dumb, so he openeth not his mouth" (Is.53:7).* *"But God commendeth his love toward us, in that, while we were yet sinners, Christ died for us" (Ro.5:8).* *"Much more then, being now justified by his blood, we shall be saved from wrath through him" (Ro.5:9).* *"Christ hath redeemed us from the curse of the law, being made a curse for us: for it is written, Cursed is every one that hangeth on a tree" (Ga.3:13).*

	Historical Term	Type or Picture (Scriptural Basis for Each)	Life Application for Today's Believer	Biblical Application
8.	*The Sweet Aroma Ascending Up In The Burnt Offering* (Le.1:9; 8:21; 16:27-28)	*A symbol of the persons faith (obedience) in the sacrifice ascending up like a sweet aroma to the LORD.* *Note this fact: the Hebrew word for the burnt sacrifice (olah) means that which ascends, that which goes up. Again, this is most likely a symbol of the person's faith in the sacrifice ascending up like a sweet aroma to the LORD. The LORD accepts the person's faith in the sacrifice as atonement, as reconciliation—as righteousness by which he becomes reconciled to God (see Ge.15:6; Ro.4:9; 2 Co.5:21)* **"But his inwards and his legs shall he wash in water: and the priest shall burn all on the altar, *to be* a burnt sacrifice, an offering made by fire, of a sweet savour unto the LORD"** (Le.1:9).	What can we do to please the LORD? We must have faith in the sacrifice of Christ—obey God, do exactly what God says: approach Him through the sacrifice of Christ. When we approach God through the sacrifice of Christ, God is pleased and He accepts us. God reconciles us to Him.	*"And walk in love, as Christ also hath loved us, and hath given himself for us an offering and a sacrifice to God for a sweetsmelling savour"* (Ep.5:2). *"For God so loved the world, that he gave his only begotten Son, that whosoever believeth in him should not perish, but have everlasting life."* (John 3:16)
9.	*Oil Used In The Grain Offering* (Le.2:1)	*A picture of anointing and joy: The Grain Offering was an act of joy and thanksgiving to God as well as an act of dedication and commitment.* **"And when any will offer a meat offering unto the LORD, his offering shall be *of* fine flour; and he shall pour oil upon it, and put frankincense thereon"** (Le.2:1).	We are to offer the joy and thanksgiving of our hearts to God for everything: 1. For the joy of the atonement: salvation, redemption, reconciliation 2. For our livelihood: the harvest food, crops, rain, sunshine, housing, clothing	*"Enter into his gates with thanksgiving, and into his courts with praise: be thankful unto him, and bless his name"* (Ps.100:4). *"And let them sacrifice the sacrifices of thanksgiving, and declare his works with rejoicing"* (Ps.107:22). *"Giving thanks always for all things unto God and the Father in the name of our Lord Jesus Christ"* (Ep.5:20). *"In every thing give thanks: for this is the will of God in Christ Jesus concerning you"* (1 Th.5:18).
10.	*Incense Used In The Grain Offering* (Le.2:1)	*A symbol of the believer's praise and prayer ascending up to God and being accepted like the smell of a sweet aroma.* **"And when any will offer a meat offering unto the LORD, his offering shall be *of* fine flour; and he shall pour oil upon it, and put frankincense thereon"** (Le.2:1).	The most pleasing aroma a believer can offer up to God is that of his prayers and that of placing his trust and hope in the saving grace of God, in the sacrifice of Jesus Christ. Like the incense that drifted continually up to God, our prayers should be constantly ascending up and pleasing God.	*"He shall call upon me, and I will answer him: I will be with him in trouble; I will deliver him, and honour him"* (Ps.91:15) *"And I say unto you, Ask, and it shall be given you; seek, and ye shall find; knock, and it shall be opened unto you"* (Lu.11:9). *"If ye abide in me, and my words abide in you, ye shall ask what ye will, and it shall be done unto you"* (Jn.15:7). *"By him therefore let us offer the sacrifice of praise to God continually, that is, the fruit of our lips giving thanks to his name"* (He.13:15).

LEVITICUS - TYPES, SYMBOLS, AND PICTURES

Historical Term	Type or Picture (Scriptural Basis for Each)	Life Application for Today's Believer	Biblical Application
11. *Grain Offering* (Le.2:3)	*The Grain Offering is a symbol of three things:* *1. A symbol of joy and thanksgiving to God...* • *for the joy of atonement: salvation, redemption, reconciliation* • *for one's livelihood: the harvest, crops, rain, sunshine, housing, clothing* *2. A symbol of an act of dedication and dependence upon God* *3. In addition, the Grain Offering was also a symbol of Christ, the Bread of Life.* **"And the remnant of the meat offerings** *shall be* **Aaron's and his sons':** *it is* **a thing most holy of the offerings of the LORD made by fire"** (Le.2:3).	The symbol of the Grain Offering teaches us three things: 1. We are to offer the joy and thanksgiving of our hearts to God for everything: • for the joy of the atonement: salvation, redemption, reconciliation • for our livelihood: the harvest food, crops, rain, sunshine, housing, clothing 2. It is God who has given us life: air, water, sun, moon, stars, crops, food, clothing, housing—all the necessities of life. God created the materials of the universe, everything that sustains our lives and keeps us going. We owe God everything we are and have: we must, therefore, give the offering of dedication to God and declare our dependence upon Him. 3. Jesus Christ is the Bread of Life... • who feeds us • who nourishes us • who sustains us with Himself	*"For the bread of God is he which cometh down from heaven, and giveth life unto the world. Then said they unto him, LORD, evermore give us this bread. And Jesus said unto them, I am the bread of life: he that cometh to me shall never hunger; and he that believeth on me shall never thirst"* (Jn.6:33-35). *"Verily, verily, I say unto you, He that believeth on me hath everlasting life. I am that bread of life"* (Jn.6:47-48). *"I am the living bread which came down from heaven: if any man eat of this bread, he shall live for ever: and the bread that I will give is my flesh, which I will give for the life of the world"* (Jn.6:51). *"This is that bread which came down from heaven: not as your fathers did eat manna, and are dead: he that eateth of this bread shall live for ever"* (Jn.6:58). *"And as they did eat, Jesus took bread, and blessed, and brake it, and gave to them, and said, Take, eat: this is my body"* (Mk.14:22).
12. *Yeast And Honey* (Le.2:11-12)	*Yeast and honey are symbols of corruption, evil, and worldliness. Yeast or leaven sours the bread. Honey is a natural sweetener, but it too will eventually ferment and turn sour. Honey represents natural sweetness or worldliness that eventually ruins the bread or life of a person.* **"No meat offering, which ye shall bring unto the LORD, shall be made with leaven: for ye shall burn no leaven, nor any honey, in any offering of the LORD made by fire"** (Le.2:11).	Jesus Christ delivers us and gives us victory over the world. Note the strong contrasts: 1. The world offers corruption. Christ delivers us from corruption and offers us eternity. 2. The world is the source of evil. Christ—the source of all goodness—gives us victory over evil. 3. The world's consuming passion is the frenzied pursuit of the sinful nature, the flesh. Jesus Christ delivers us from worldliness and fills us with the deep yearning... • to love Him more intimately • to walk with Him more closely • to count all things as loss in order to know Him and to make Him known to the world.	*"Then Jesus said unto them, Take heed and beware of the leaven [false teaching] of the Pharisees and of the Sadducees"* (Mt.16:6). *"A little leaven leaveneth [corrupts] the whole lump"* (Ga.5:9). *"Your glorying is not good. Know ye not that a little leaven leaveneth the whole lump? Purge out therefore the old leaven, that ye may be a new lump, as ye are unleavened. For even Christ our passover is sacrificed for us: Therefore let us keep the feast, not with old leaven, neither with the leaven of malice and wickedness; but with the unleavened bread of sincerity and truth"* (1 Co.5:6-8). *"Hast thou found honey? eat so much as is sufficient for thee, lest thou be filled therewith, and vomit it"* (Pr.25:16).

LEVITICUS - TYPES, SYMBOLS, AND PICTURES

Historical Term	Type or Picture (Scriptural Basis for Each)	Life Application for Today's Believer	Biblical Application
Yeast And Honey (continued) (Le.2:11-12)			*"It is not good to eat much honey: so for men to search their own glory is not glory"* (Pr.25:27)
13. *The Fellowship Or Peace Offering* (Le.3:1-17)	*The Fellowship Or Peace Offering is a type of Christ, a symbol or picture of Christ, the One who died on the cross bearing the judgment of God for man. The sacrifice of Christ made peace between a holy God and an alienated, fallen, depraved people. The sacrifice of Christ and Christ alone brings peace and fellowship between man and God.* **"And if his oblation** *be* **a sacrifice of peace offering, if he offer** *it* **of the herd; whether** *it be* **a male or female, he shall offer it without blemish before the LORD"** (Le.3:1).	How do we grow in the fellowship and peace of God? Very simply, by seeking more of the fellowship and peace of God. We must stand upon the completed work of Christ's sacrifice on the cross. Because of Christ... • we can enjoy the fellowship of the Lord • we can experience the peace of God	*"Yea doubtless, and I count all things but loss for the excellency of the knowledge of Christ Jesus my LORD: for whom I have suffered the loss of all things, and do count them but dung, that I may win Christ"* (Ph.3:8) *"That I may know him, and the power of his resurrection, and the fellowship of his sufferings, being made conformable unto his death"* (Ph.3:10). *"That which we have seen and heard declare we unto you, that ye also may have fellowship with us: and truly our fellowship is with the Father, and with his Son Jesus Christ"* (1 Jn.1:3).
14. *Bull Or Cow Sacrificed In The Fellowship Or Peace Offering* (Le.3:1-5)	*The bull or cow is an animal of service, therefore, this animal would be a picture of the sacrifice of service. This particular sacrifice would focus a person's attention upon...* • *sacrificing more and more service to God* • *serving God more and more* **"And if his oblation** *be* **a sacrifice of peace offering, if he offer** *it* **of the herd; whether** *it be* **a male or female, he shall offer it without blemish before the LORD"** (Le.3:1).	How do we grow in the peace and fellowship of God? By looking to the Person symbolized by the sacrifice of the bull or cow, the Lord Jesus Christ. Jesus Christ is the Perfect Servant of God. We must therefore focus upon Christ, upon His sacrifice of service. His sacrifice stirs us to sacrifice more and more of our service to God.	*"I beseech you therefore, brethren, by the mercies of God, that ye present your bodies a living sacrifice, holy, acceptable unto God, which is your reasonable service. And be not conformed to this world: but be ye transformed by the renewing of your mind, that ye may prove what is that good, and acceptable, and perfect, will of God"* (Ro.12:1-2). *"Then said Jesus to them again, Peace be unto you: as my Father hath sent me, even so send I you"* (Jn.20:21; see Mt.20:28). *"We then that are strong ought to bear the infirmities of the weak, and not to please ourselves"* (Ro.15:1).
15. *Lamb: The Sacrifice Used In...* ⇒ *The Fellowship Or Peace Offering,* (Le.3:6-11) ⇒ *The Sin Offering,* (Le.4:32, 35; 5:6) ⇒ *The First Worship Service Of The Priest,* (Le.9:3) ⇒ *The Burnt Offering For A Mother's Protection Right After Childbirth,* (Le.12:6) ⇒ *The Cleansing That Took Place Inside The*	*A symbol of sacrifice. In fact, the animal most used in sacrifice was the lamb. The sacrifice of a lamb would focus a person's attention...* • *upon the sacrificing of oneself more and more to God* • *upon dedication, the giving up, of oneself to God* • *upon the sacrifice of one's life completely to God*	How do we grow in the peace and fellowship of God? By looking to the Person symbolized in the sacrifice of the lamb, the Lord Jesus Christ. Jesus Christ is the Lamb of God, the Lamb who so willingly submitted and dedicated Himself, to die for us. We must focus upon the *sacrifice of dedication...* • sacrificing ourselves more and more to God	*"For whosoever will save his life shall lose it: and whosoever will lose his life for my sake shall find it"* (Mt.16:25). *"And he said to them all, If any man will come after me, let him deny hiself, and take up his cross daily, and follow me"* (Lu.9:23). *"And whosoever doth not bear his cross, and come after me, cannot be my disciple"* (Lu.14:27).

LEVITICUS - TYPES, SYMBOLS, AND PICTURES

Historical Term	Type or Picture (Scriptural Basis for Each)	Life Application for Today's Believer	Biblical Application
Camp, (Le.14:10, 13) ⇒ The Guilt Offering For The Poorest Of The Poor, (Le.14:21, 24-25) ⇒ The Burnt Offering celebrated during the Festival Of Firstfruits, (Le.23:12)	• upon dying to self and living totally for God **"If he offer a lamb for his offering, then shall he offer it before the LORD" (Le.3:7).**	• dedicating ourselves, willingly submitting ourselves more and more to God	*"Likewise reckon ye also yourselves to be dead indeed unto sin, but alive unto God through Jesus Christ our LORD" (Ro.6:11).*
16. The Burning Of The Lord's Portion On The Altar As Food Being Offered To God (Le.3:6-11; 7:18)	This food is a picture of having a fellowship meal with God. Having a fellowship meal with God, symbolized a very special time with God... • a time of peace: comfort, calm, rest, assurance, agreement, satisfaction, fulfillment • a time of fellowship: communion, companionship, caring, closeness **"And the priest shall burn it upon the altar: it is the food of the offering made by fire unto the LORD" (Le.3:11).**	Jesus Christ is the Bread of God who alone can satisfy the hunger of man. Jesus Christ invites His people to fellowship, eat, and commune with Him.	*"Behold, I stand at the door, and knock: if any man hear my voice, and open the door, I will come in to him, and will sup with him, and he with me" (Re.3:20).* *"That which we have seen and heard declare we unto you, that ye also may have fellowship with us: and truly our fellowship is with the Father, and with his Son Jesus Christ" (1 Jn.1:3; see Is.55:2; Jn.6:51; Ph.3:10).*
17. The Goat: The Sacrifice Used In... ⇒ The Fellowship Or Peace Offering, (Le.3:12-16) ⇒ The First Worship Service Of The Priest, (Le.9:15) ⇒ The Day of Atonement, (Le.16:3-10; 15)	The goat most symbolized the bearing of God's judgment against sin. (Note that this sacrifice is a symbol of Christ on the cross, bearing the judgment of God.) The sacrifice of a goat would focus a person's attention upon... • the justice and judgment of God against sin • the atonement, the ransom price demanded by God's anger and wrath against sin • one's deliverance from God's judgment through the substitute sacrifice **"And if his offering be a goat, then he shall offer it before the LORD" (Le.3:12).**	We must look to the Person symbolized by the sacrifice of the goat, the Lord Jesus Christ. Jesus Christ is the Sin-Bearer and the Judgment-Bearer for us. When He died upon the cross, Christ bore our sins and the judgment of God against sin—all for us.	*"So Christ was once offered to bear the sins of many; and unto them that look for him shall he appear the second time without sin unto salvation" (He.9:28).* *"Christ hath redeemed us from the curse of the law, being made a curse for us: for it is written, Cursed is every one that hangeth on a tree" (Ga.3:13).* *"But we see Jesus, who was made a little lower than the angels for the suffering of death, crowned with glory and honour; that he by the grace of God should taste death for every man" (He.2:9).* *"Who his own self bare our sins in his own body on the tree, that we, being dead to sins, should live unto righteousness: by whose stripes ye were healed" (1 Pe.2:24; see Is.53:5).*
18. The Sin Offering (Le.4:1-5:13. See also Le. 6:24-30; 8:14-17; 9:2; 9:15; 10:17; 16:3-22)	The Sin Offering is a type of Christ, a symbol or picture of Christ. This offering was to secure the forgiveness of sins. **"Speak unto the children of Israel, saying, If a soul shall sin through ignorance against any of the**	Jesus Christ is the Savior of the world, the One who provides the way of forgiveness for us. This He does through His sacrifice upon the cross. Through His blood we are cleaned from sin, cleansed from all unrighteousness.	*"If we confess our sins, he is faithful and just to forgive us our sins, and to cleanse us from all unrighteousness" (1 Jn.1:9).* *"But we see Jesus, who was made a little lower than the angels for the suffering of death, crowned with glory and honour; that he*

Historical Term	Type or Picture (Scriptural Basis for Each)	Life Application for Today's Believer	Biblical Application
The Sin Offering (continued) (Le.4:1-5:13. See also Le. 6:24-30; 8:14-17; 9:2; 9:15; 10:17; 16:3-22)	**commandments of the LORD** *concerning things* **which ought not to be done, and shall do against any of them: If the priest that is anointed do sin according to the sin of the people; then let him bring for his sin, which he hath sinned, a young bullock without blemish unto the LORD for a sin offering"** (Le.4:2-3).		*by the grace of God should taste death for every man"* (He.2:9). *"Who his own self bare our sins in his own body on the tree, that we, being dead to sins, should live unto righteousness: by whose stripes ye were healed"* (1 Pe.2:24). *"For Christ also hath once suffered for sins, the just for the unjust, that he might bring us to God, being put to death in the flesh, but quickened by the Spirit"* (1 Pe.3:18).
19. *Young Bull Without Defect: The Sacrifice Used In The Sin Offering For The Anointed Priest Or Minister* (Le.4:3-12; See also Le.1:3)	*This sacrifice is a symbol of Christ, and the bull with no defect was a symbol of the sinlessness and perfection of Christ.* **"If the priest that is anointed do sin according to the sin of the people; then let him bring for his sin, which he hath sinned, a young bullock without blemish unto the LORD for a sin offering"** (Le.4:3).	Jesus Christ is the Perfect, Sinless Sacrifice. As such, He stands before God as the Perfect, Ideal Man. As the Ideal, Perfect Man, He can represent us before God. This is the reason the sinner (all of us) has to approach God through Christ. We have no other way to secure forgiveness of sin. Priest, minister, and layperson alike—we all have to approach God through the Perfect, Sinless Sacrifice of the Lord Jesus Christ Himself.	*"For we have not an high priest which cannot be touched with the feeling of our infirmities; but was in all points tempted like as we are, yet without sin"* (He.4:15). *"For such an high priest became us, who is holy, harmless, undefiled, separate from sinners, and made higher than the heavens"* (He.7:26). *"Forasmuch as ye know that ye were not redeemed with corruptible things, as silver and gold, from your vain conversation received by tradition from your fathers; But with the precious blood of Christ, as of a lamb without blemish and without spot"* (1 Pe.1:18-19).
20. *Blood Sprinkled Seven Times In Front Of The Inner Curtain Of The Most Holy Place: During The Sin Offering For The Anointed Priest Or Minister* (Le.4:5-12)	*The blood sprinkled seven times in front of the inner curtain symbolized that a sinning priest (minister) was shut out from God's presence (the Most Holy Place), and could not be readmitted until he was cleansed by the blood. Remember, seven is the number of completion, of fulfillment. The priest was fully, completely cleansed by the blood.* **"And the priest shall dip his finger in the blood, and sprinkle of the blood seven times before the LORD, before the vail of the sanctuary"** (Le.4:6).	It is the death or the blood of the Lord Jesus Christ that cleanses the priest or minister, that cleanses all of us from sin. He died that we might be completely and fully cleansed. His death, His blood alone, cleanses us. Forgiveness of sins is found in Christ and Christ alone.	*"For this is my blood of the new testament, which is shed for many for the remission of sins"* (Mt.26:28). *"Much more then, being now justified by his blood, we shall be saved from wrath through him"* (Ro.5:9). *"For he hath made him to be sin for us, who knew no sin; that we might be made the righteousness of God in him"* (2 Co.5:21). *"In whom we have redemption through his blood, the forgiveness of sins, according to the riches of his grace"* (Ep.1:7).
21. *Blood Put Upon The Altar Of Incense During The Sin Offering For The Anointed Priest Or Minister* (Le.4:7)	*The blood put upon the altar of incense symbolized that the prayers of a sinning priest were shut out, rejected. They could not be heard and answered until he was cleansed by the blood.*	The believer who is living in unconfessed sin cannot be heard until he is cleansed by the blood of the Lamb, the shed blood of Jesus Christ.	*"Forasmuch as ye know that ye were not redeemed with corruptible things, as silver and gold, from your vain conversation received by tradition from your fathers; But with the precious blood of Christ, as of a*

Historical Term	Type or Picture (Scriptural Basis for Each)	Life Application for Today's Believer	Biblical Application
Blood Put Upon The Altar Of Incense During The Sin Offering For The Anointed Priest Or Minister (continued) (Le.4:7)	"And the priest shall put *some* of the blood upon the horns of the altar of sweet incense before the LORD, which *is* in the tabernacle of the congregation: and shall pour all the blood of the bullock at the bottom of the altar of the burnt offering, which *is at* the door of the tabernacle of the congregation" (Le.4:7).		*lamb without blemish and without spot" (1 Pe.1:18-19).* "But if we walk in the light, as he is in the light, we have fellowship one with another, and the blood of Jesus Christ his Son cleanseth us from all sin" (1 Jn.1:7).
22. *The Poured-Out Blood At The Bottom Of The Altar Of Burnt Offering* (Le.4:7)	*This poured-out blood is a symbol that appeases and satisfies the justice and demand of God for righteousness. The blood poured out at the foot of the altar fulfilled the judgment of God against sin.* "And the priest shall put *some* of the blood upon the horns of the altar of sweet incense before the LORD, which *is* in the tabernacle of the congregation: and shall pour all the blood of the bullock at the bottom of the altar of the burnt offering, which *is at* the door of the tabernacle of the congregation" (Le.4:7).	The only thing that can cleanse us from sin is the shed, poured-out blood of Jesus Christ. It is the blood of Christ... • that appeases and satisfies the justice and demands of God • that justifies us • that brings us near to God, being reconciled to Him.	"But God commendeth his love toward us, in that, while we were yet sinners, Christ died for us. Much more then, being now justified by his blood, we shall be saved from wrath through him. For if, when we were enemies, we were reconciled to God by the death of his Son, much more, being reconciled, we shall be saved by his life. And not only so, but we also joy in God through our Lord Jesus Christ, by whom we have now received the atonement" (Ro.5:8-11). "But now in Christ Jesus ye who sometimes were far off are made nigh by the blood of Christ" (Ep.2:13).
23. *The Ash Heap* (Le.4:12; 9:11)	*The ash heap is a symbol of God's feelings and judgment against sin. The priest was to take the rest of the sacrifice—all of it—outside the camp and burn it upon the ash heap.* "Even the whole bullock shall he carry forth without the camp unto a clean place, where the ashes are poured out, and burn him on the wood with fire: where the ashes are poured out shall he be burnt" (Le.4:12).	Sin cannot be allowed in God's presence; sin must be removed, judged, and condemned in order for the believer to be forgiven, whether priest, minister, or layperson.	"For the bodies of those beasts, whose blood is brought into the sanctuary by the high priest for sin, are burned without the camp. Wherefore Jesus also, that he might sanctify the people with his own blood, suffered without the gate. Let us go forth therefore unto him without the camp, bearing his reproach" (He.13:11-13). "He that covereth his sins shall not prosper: but whoso confesseth and forsaketh them shall have mercy" (Prov.28:13). "If we confess our sins, he is faithful and just to forgive us our sins, and to cleanse us from all unrighteousness" (1 Jn.1:9).
24. *The Bull Sacrificed For Society: During The Sin Offering* (Le.4:21)	*The bull sacrificed for society during the sin offering symbolized the condemnation of sin*	A community or nation of people stands just as guilty of sin before God as individuals do. Whole communities...	"By the blessing of the upright the city is exalted: but it is overthrown by the mouth of the wicked" (Pr.11:11).

Historical Term	Type or Picture (Scriptural Basis for Each)	Life Application for Today's Believer	Biblical Application
The Bull Sacrificed For Society: During The Sin Offering (continued) (Le.4:21)	**"And he shall carry forth the bullock without the camp, and burn him as he burned the first bullock: it *is* a sin offering for the congregation"** (Le.4:21).	• can become involved in sinful or evil acts of terrorism, war, lawlessness, violence, immoral behavior, abuse, drunkenness, and a host of other evils. • can become guilty by keeping silent and doing nothing. In such cases, the very ground of a community or nation becomes polluted and corrupt in God's eyes. When the day of judgment comes, leaders and citizens alike will give an account for their sinful acts and/or cowardly silence and inaction.	*"Righteousness exalteth a nation: but sin is a reproach to any people"* (Pr.14:34). *"And I will bring an everlasting reproach upon you, and a perpetual shame, which shall not be forgotten"* (Je.23:40). *"For our transgressions are multiplied before thee, and our sins testify against us: for our transgressions are with us; and as for our iniquities, we know them"* (Is.59:12). *"If my people, which are called by my name, shall humble themselves, and pray, and seek my face, and turn from their wicked ways; then will I hear from heaven, and will forgive their sin, and will heal their land"* (2 Chr.7:14).
25. *The Guilt Offering* (Le.5:14-6:7)	*The Guilt Offering symbolized Jesus Christ. He is the way for a person to be set free from the weight and anguish of guilt, the pricking of conscience.* **"And the priest shall offer them, the one *for* a sin offering, and the other *for* a burnt offering; and the priest shall make an atonement for him before the LORD for his issue"** (Le.15:15).	Jesus Christ bore our guilt, bore the judgment and condemnation of our guilt. His sacrifice has made atonement with God, forgiving the guilty person.	*"Who gave himself for our sins, that he might deliver us from this present evil world, according to the will of God and our Father"* (Ga.1:4). *"Christ hath redeemed us from the curse of the law, being made a curse for us: for it is written, Cursed is every one that hangeth on a tree"* (Ga.3:13). *"Having a good conscience; that, whereas they speak evil of you, as of evildoers, they may be ashamed that falsely accuse your good conversation in Christ"* (1 Pe.3:16).
26. *Ram Without Defect And Of True Value Was The Sacrifice Used In The Guilt Offering* (Le.5:15, 18; 6:6)	*The Ram without defect was a type of Christ who was sinless, without blemish or defect.* **"If a soul commit a trespass, and sin through ignorance, in the holy things of the LORD; then he shall bring for his trespass unto the LORD a ram without blemish out of the flocks, with thy estimation by shekels of silver, after the shekel of the sanctuary, for a trespass offering"** (Le.5:15).	Jesus Christ was the sinless, perfect sacrifice who gave Himself for us. As the Perfect Sacrifice, He bore our guilt, bore the judgment and condemnation of our guilt. We can now be set free from guilt by approaching God through the Perfect Sacrifice of Christ. If we believe God, approach Him exactly as He says—through Christ—then God counts the sacrifice of Christ… • on our behalf • in our place • in our stead • as our substitute The result is wonderful: through Christ, we are set free from the guilt of our	*"Who gave himself for our sins, that he might deliver us from this present evil world, according to the will of God and our Father"* (Ga.1:4). *"Christ hath redeemed us from the curse of the law, being made a curse for us: for it is written, Cursed is every one that hangeth on a tree"* (Ga.3:13). *"Having a good conscience; that, whereas they speak evil of you, as of evildoers, they may be ashamed that falsely accuse your good conversation in Christ"* (1 Pe.3:16). *"That which we have seen and heard declare we unto you, that ye also may*

Historical Term	Type or Picture (Scriptural Basis for Each)	Life Application for Today's Believer	Biblical Application
Ram Without Defect And Of True Value Was The Sacrifice Used In The Guilt Offering (continued) (Le.5:15, 18; 6:6)		sin against God. We are able to stand before God free, set free from sin and guilt—all through the sacrifice of Christ.	*have fellowship with us: and truly our fellowship is with the Father, and with his Son Jesus Christ" (1 Jn.1:3).*
27. *The Perpetual Fire Of The Burnt Offering (Le.6:8-13)*	*The perpetual fire of the burnt offering is a clear symbol of the sacrifice of Christ. His sacrifice is lasting; it is permanent, sufficient, adequate. The priests were to offer the sacrifice of the Burnt Offering every morning and every evening (Nu.28:3-8). The sacrifice of the Burnt Offering was never to cease. The priests were always to keep the fire of the Burnt Offering ablaze, even through the night. They were never to let the sacrifice cease from being offered.* **"Command Aaron and his sons, saying, This is the law of the burnt offering: It is the burnt offering, because of the burning upon the altar all night unto the morning, and the fire of the altar shall be burning in it" (Le.6:9).**	The sacrifice that Jesus Christ made is... • perpetual, lasting and permanent • timeless, not bound by time • abiding, always present • enduring, never exhausting its power • immutable, never changing • durable, never wearing out • everlasting, for each and every generation of believers The sacrifice of Jesus Christ was once and for all.	*"Who needeth not daily, as those high priests, to offer up sacrifice, first for his own sins, and then for the people's: for this he did once, when he offered up himself" (He.7:27).* *"For Christ also hath once suffered for sins, the just for the unjust, that he might bring us to God, being put to death in the flesh, but quickened by the Spirit" (1 Pe.3:18).* *"By the which will we are sanctified through the offering of the body of Jesus Christ once for all" (He.10:10).* *"For by one offering he hath perfected for ever them that are sanctified" (He. 10:14).*
28. *The Priestly Clothing (Le.6:8-13)*	*The priestly clothing symbolizes the clothing of righteousness, the righteousness of Christ. Jesus Christ removes the ashes or dirt of sin and clothes a person in righteousness. The priests were to put on the special linen clothing and undergarments—the priestly clothing—for removing the ashes.* **"And the priest shall put on his linen garment, and his linen breeches shall he put upon his flesh, and take up the ashes which the fire hath consumed with the burnt offering on the altar, and he shall put them beside the altar" (Le.6:10).**	Jesus Christ is our righteousness, the only One who can cleanse us from sin and clothe us in righteousness. Jesus Christ is the only one who can make us acceptable to God, acceptable in His righteousness.	*"But we are all as an unclean thing, and all our righteousnesses are as filthy rags; and we all do fade as a leaf; and our iniquities, like the wind, have taken us away" (Is.64:6).* *"For he hath made him to be sin for us, who knew no sin; that we might be made the righteousness of God in him" (2 Co.5:21).* *"And to her was granted that she should be arrayed in fine linen, clean and white: for the fine linen is the righteousness of saints" (Re.19:8).* *"For Christ is the end of the law for righteousness to every one that believeth" (Ro.10:4).*
29. *The Priest's Regular Clothing Worn When Taking The Ashes Of The Sacrifice Outside The Camp (Le.6:8-13)*	*The priest's regular clothing symbolized the human body or human flesh that Jesus Christ took upon Himself. Jesus Christ became man in order to bear and take away the sins of man. As stated, this He did as a man, clothed in the regular flesh of man.*	Jesus Christ clothed Himself in human flesh— became a man—so that He might die and bear the penalty for mans sin. Through Him and Him alone, sin is removed and taken away—far, far away.	*"Forasmuch then as the children are partakers of flesh and blood, he also himself likewise took part of the same; that through death he might destroy him that had the power of death, that is, the devil; And deliver them who through fear of death were all their lifetime subject to*

LEVITICUS - TYPES, SYMBOLS, AND PICTURES

Historical Term	Type or Picture (Scriptural Basis for Each)	Life Application for Today's Believer	Biblical Application
The Priest's Regular Clothing Worn When Taking The Ashes Of The Sacrifice Outside The Camp (continued) (Le.6:8-13)	"And he shall put off his garments, and put on other garments, and carry forth the ashes without the camp unto a clean place" (Le.6:11).		bondage. For verily he took not on him the nature of angels; but he took on him the seed of Abraham. Wherefore in all things it behooved him to be made like unto his brethren, that he might be a merciful and faithful high priest in things pertaining to God, to make reconciliation for the sins of the people. For in that he himself hath suffered being tempted, he is able to succour them that are tempted" (He.2:14-18; see 1 Pe.2:24). "And ye know that he was manifested to take away our sins; and in him is no sin" (1 Jn.3:5).
30. Laying The Grain Upon The Burnt Offering (Le.6:14-18)	Laying the grain upon the Burnt Offering symbolized two things: 1. It symbolized giving thanks to God for the atonement (reconciliation) secured by the Burnt offering. It also symbolized giving thanks for all else that God provided—crops, food, livelihood. 2. It symbolized dedication, the laying of one's life—all one is and has—upon the sacrifice lying upon the altar. God had reconciled His people to Himself through the sacrifice; therefore, the people owed their lives to God. "And he shall take of it his handful, of the flour of the meat offering, and of the oil thereof, and all the frankincense which is upon the meat offering, and shall burn it upon the altar for a sweet savour, even the memorial of it, unto the LORD" (Le.6:15).	Once we are saved, by trusting the sacrifice of Jesus Christ, we are compelled to offer thanksgiving to God. Our hearts just break forth thanking God for everything He has so graciously provided, things such as... • salvation • food • clothing • shelter • livelihood Once we are saved, we are to dedicate our lives to God. Nothing is to be withheld from Him, nothing	"Enter into his gates with thanksgiving, and into his courts with praise: be thankful unto him, and bless his name" (Ps.100:4). "Giving thanks always for all things unto God and the Father in the name of our Lord Jesus Christ" (Ep.5:20). "In every thing give thanks: for this is the will of God in Christ Jesus concerning you" (1 Th.5:18). "I beseech you therefore, brethren, by the mercies of God, that ye present your bodies a living sacrifice, holy, acceptable unto God, which is your reasonable service. And be not conformed to this world: but be ye transformed by the renewing of your mind, that ye may prove what is that good, and acceptable, and perfect, will of God" (Ro. 12:1-2).
31. Yeast Or Leaven Withheld From The Grain Offering (Le.6:14-18)	Yeast or Leaven is a symbol of corruption, evil, and worldliness. "It shall not be baken with leaven. I have given it unto them for their portion of my offerings made by fire; it is most holy, as is the sin offering, and as the trespass offering" (Le.6:17).	A believer—minister and layperson alike—must approach God with no yeast or leaven in his heart. He must have a pure, clean heart. He must give thanks and dedicate himself with a pure, clean heart. God does not accept a half-hearted dedication or praise. He does not accept a person who still seeks to live a sinful, corrupt life.	"Wherefore come out from among them, and be ye separate, saith the Lord, and touch not the unclean thing; and I will receive you, And will be a Father unto you, and ye shall be my sons and daughters, saith the Lord Almighty" (2 Co.6:17-18). "And have no fellowship with the unfruitful works of darkness, but

Historical Term	Type or Picture (Scriptural Basis for Each)	Life Application for Today's Believer	Biblical Application
Yeast Or Leaven Withheld From The Grain Offering (continued) (Le.6:14-18)			*rather reprove them. And this is the confidence that we have in him, that, if we ask any thing according to his will, he heareth us"* (Ep.5:11). *"Depart ye, depart ye, go ye out from thence, touch no unclean thing; go ye out of the midst of her; be ye clean, that bear the vessels of the LORD"* (Is.52:11).
32. *The Aroma Of The Grain Offering Laid Upon The Burnt Offering (Le.6:14-18; 6:19-23)*	*The aroma is most likely a symbol of the person's faith in the sacrifice ascending up like a sweet aroma to the LORD. The aroma of the Grain Offering ascending up symbolized that the thanksgiving and dedication pleased the LORD. God accepted the thanksgiving and dedication.* **"And he shall take of it his handful, of the flour of the meat offering, and of the oil thereof, and all the frankincense which** *is* **upon the meat offering, and shall burn** *it* **upon the altar** *for* **a sweet savour,** *even* **the memorial of it, unto the LORD"** (Le.6:15). **"In a pan it shall be made with oil;** *and when it is* **baken, thou shalt bring it in:** *and* **the baken pieces of the meat offering shalt thou offer** *for* **a sweet savour unto the LORD"** (Le.6:21).	God accepts our faith in the sacrifice of the Lord Jesus Christ. He accepts our faith as atonement or reconciliation by which we become acceptable to God (see Ge.15:6; Ro.4:9; 2 Co. 5:21).	*"And walk in love, as Christ also hath loved us, and hath given himself for us an offering and a sacrifice to God for a sweetsmelling savour"* (Ep. 5:2). *"For God so loved the world, that he gave his only begotten Son, that whosoever believeth in him should not perish, but have everlasting life"* (Jn.3:16). *"Forasmuch as ye know that ye were not redeemed with corruptible things, as silver and gold, from your vain conversation received by tradition from your fathers; But with the precious blood of Christ, as of a lamb without blemish and without spot"* (1 Pe.1:18-19).
33. *The Sin Offering: During The Special Duties Of The Priests In Conducting The Offerings (Le.6:24-30. See also Le. 4:1-5:13)*	*The sacrifice of the Sin Offering was most holy to God because it symbolized the death of His Son for the sins of the world.* **"Speak unto Aaron and to his sons, saying, This** *is* **the law of the sin offering: In the place where the burnt offering is killed shall the sin offering be killed before the LORD: it** *is* **most holy"** (Le.6:25).	Jesus Christ was the Perfect, Sinless Sacrifice. As such, He stands before God as the Perfect, Ideal Man. As the Ideal, Perfect Man, He can represent us before God. This is the reason the sinner (all of us) has to approach God through Christ. We have no other way to secure forgiveness of sin. Priest, minister, and layperson alike—we all have to approach God through the Perfect, Sinless Sacrifice of the Lord Jesus Christ Himself.	*"For we have not an high priest which cannot be touched with the feeling of our infirmities; but was in all points tempted like as we are, yet without sin"* (He.4:15; see He.7:26). *"Forasmuch as ye know that ye were not redeemed with corruptible things, as silver and gold, from your vain conversation received by tradition from your fathers; But with the precious blood of Christ, as of a lamb without blemish and without spot"* (1 Pe.1:18-19). *"Who did no sin, neither was guile found in his mouth"* (1 Pe.2:22).

Historical Term	Type or Picture (Scriptural Basis for Each)	Life Application for Today's Believer	Biblical Application
34. *The Guilt Offering: During The Special Duties Of The Priests In Conducting The Offerings* (Le.7:1-10. See also Le.5:14-6:7)	*The sacrifice is a symbol of Christ's dying for the guilt of the world.* **"In the place where they kill the burnt offering shall they kill the trespass offering: and the blood thereof shall he sprinkle round about upon the altar" (Le.7:2).**	The only permanent deliverance from the weight and anguish of guilt is through the LORD Jesus Christ. The only way we can ever be set free from the condemnation and judg-ment of sin is to be forgiven our sin through the blood of Jesus Christ. Jesus Christ alone can set us free from the weight and anguish of sin and guilt.	*"Who gave himself for our sins, that he might deliver us from this present evil world, according to the will of God and our Father" (Ga.1:4).* *"Christ hath redeemed us from the curse of the law, being made a curse for us: for it is written, Cursed is every one that hangeth on a tree" (Ga.3:13; see 1 Pe.1:18-19).* *"That which we have seen and heard declare we unto you, that ye also may have fellowship with us: and truly our fellowship is with the Father, and with his Son Jesus Christ" (1 Jn.1:3).*
35. *Washing In Water* (Le.8:6; 11:25)	*Washing in water is a symbol of the need to be spiritually cleansed.* **"And Moses brought Aaron and his sons, and washed them with water" (Le.8:6).**	No person can cleanse himself, not spiritually, not from sin. Only God's mediator, Jesus Christ, can wash and cleanse a person spiritually. This He does through the blood of His cross.	*"And now why tarriest thou? arise, and be baptized, and wash away thy sins, calling on the name of the Lord" (Ac.22:16).* *"In whom we have redemption through his blood, the forgiveness of sins, according to the riches of his grace" (Ep.1:7).* *"How much more shall the blood of Christ, who through the eternal Spirit offered himself without spot to God, purge your conscience from dead works to serve the living God?" (He.9:14).*
36. *The Putting On Of The High Priest's Special Clothing* (Le.8:7-9)	*The High Priest's Special Clothing is a symbol of Christ's righteousness and of bringing dignity and honor to the name of God. Remember: the High Priest symbolized the High Priesthood of Jesus Christ; and the clothing symbolized the righteousness of Jesus Christ.* **"And he put upon him the coat, and girded him with the girdle, and clothed him with the robe, and put the ephod upon him, and he girded him with the curious girdle of the ephod, and bound it unto him therewith. And he put the breastplate upon him: also he put in the breastplate the Urim and the Thummim. And he put the mitre upon his head; also upon the mitre, even upon his forefront, did he put the golden plate, the holy crown; as the LORD commanded Moses" (Le.8:7-9).**	A person must put on and be covered with the right-eousness of Jesus Christ in order to be acceptable to God.	*"For he hath made him to be sin for us, who knew no sin; that we might be made the righteousness of God in him" (2 Co.5:21).* *"Even as Abraham believed God, and it was accounted to him for righteousness" (Ga.3:6).* *"And be found in him, not having mine own righteousness, which is of the law, but that which is through the faith of Christ, the righteousness which is of God by faith" (Ph.3:9).* *"And he believed in the LORD; and he counted it to him for righteousness" (Ge.15:6).*

Historical Term	Type or Picture (Scriptural Basis for Each)	Life Application for Today's Believer	Biblical Application
37. *The Linen Tunic* (Le.8:7)	*Linen is symbolic of righteousness. The linen tunic (a long coat-like garment that essentially covered the whole body) is symbolic of putting on God's righteousness.* **"And he put upon him the coat [tunic], and girded him with the girdle, and clothed him with the robe, and put the ephod upon him, and he girded him with the curious girdle of the ephod, and bound** *it* **unto him therewith"** (Le.8:7).	What the Linen Tunic taught: If a person wishes to live in God's presence, he must put on the righteousness of Christ. A person is depraved and totally inadequate, having no righteousness of his own. Therefore, a person cannot walk before God or serve God unless he puts on the righteousness of Christ.	*"For he hath made him to be sin for us, who knew no sin; that we might be made the righteousness of God in him"* (2 Co.5:21). *"I put on righteousness, and it clothed me: my judgment was as a robe and a diadem"* (Jb.29:14). *"I will greatly rejoice in the* LORD, *my soul shall be joyful in my God; for he hath clothed me with the garments of salvation, he hath covered me with the robe of righteousness, as a bridegroom decketh himself with ornaments, and as a bride adorneth herself with her jewels"* (Is.61:10; see 1 Co.1:30).
38. *The Sash* (Le.8:7)	*The multi-colored sash of fine linen is symbolic of truth, the truth of God's Word. It is comparable to the belt of truth in the armor of God that the believer is to put on (Ep.6:14). The Word of God enlightens and wraps together everything in the believer's spiritual wardrobe.* **"And he put upon him the coat [tunic], and girded him with the girdle, and clothed him with the robe, and put the ephod upon him, and he girded him with the curious girdle of the ephod, and bound** *it* **unto him therewith"** (Le.8:7).	What the Sash taught: 1. Jesus Christ is the Truth, the Living Word of God. It is the Word of God that holds everything together. 2. A person needs help and support in life because he does not have the strength to conquer the terrible trials and temptations of life, the trials and temptations that drag him ever downward toward the grave and eternal separation from God. Only the Word of God can strengthen and hold us together as we walk through life.	*"Jesus saith unto him, I am the way, the truth, and the life: no man cometh unto the Father, but by me"* (Jn.14:6). *"Stand therefore, having your loins girt about with truth, and having on the breastplate of righteousness"* (Ep.6:14). *"Sanctify them through thy truth: thy word is truth"* (Jn.17:17). *"All scripture is given by inspiration of God, and is profitable for doctrine, for reproof, for correction, for instruction in righteousness"* (2 Ti.3:16). *"For the word of God is quick, and powerful, and sharper than any twoedged sword, piercing even to the dividing asunder of soul and spirit, and of the joints and marrow, and is a discerner of the thoughts and intents of the heart"* (He.4:12).
39. *The Robe Of The Ephod* (Le.8:7)	*The Robe of the Ephod was worn by the High Priest as he entered through the Veil and ministered to the Lord in the Sanctuary. It had small bells in the shape of pomegranates sewed to its hem. The Robe of the Ephod is symbolic of two things:* *1. The Robe of the Ephod symbolized the sounding forth of the intercessory ministry of the High Priest*	What the Robe of the Ephod taught: 1. Jesus Christ is our Great High Priest who sounds forth the glorious truth that His intercession never ends, never stops. This is a strong lesson for us: we too must pray without	*"But this man, because he continueth ever, hath an unchangeable priesthood. Wherefore he is able also to save them to the uttermost that come unto God by him, seeing he ever liveth to make intercession for them"* (He.7:24-25). *"The next day John seeth Jesus coming unto him, and saith, Behold the Lamb of God, which taketh away the sin of the world"* (Jn.1:29). *"Wherefore God also hath highly exalted him,*

Historical Term	Type or Picture (Scriptural Basis for Each)	Life Application for Today's Believer	Biblical Application
The Robe Of The Ephod (continued) (Le.8:7)	2. *The Robe of the Ephod symbolized the sounding forth of a wonderful fact, that God accepted the offering of the High Priest, that he had not been stricken dead.* **"And he put upon him the coat [tunic], and girded him with the girdle, and clothed him with the robe, and put the ephod upon him, and he girded him with the curious girdle of the ephod, and bound** *it* **unto him therewith"** (Le.8:7).	ceasing. We must become intercessors—great intercessors—for our loved ones and for the lost of the world. 2. We should rejoice in the fact that the sacrifice and intercessory ministry of Jesus Christ is perfectly acceptable to God the Father. Once we have been saved, we no longer have to worry about being condemned to death.	*and given him a name which is above every name"* *(Phil.2:9).* *"Who is he that condemneth? It is Christ that died, yea rather, that is risen again, who is even at the right hand of God, who also maketh intercession for us" (Ro.8:34).* *"Therefore will I divide him a portion with the great, and he shall divide the spoil with the strong; because he hath poured out his soul unto death: and he was numbered with the transgressors; and he bare the sin of many, and made intercession for the transgressors" (Is.53:12).*
40. *The Ephod* (Le.8:7)	*Remember, the Ephod was a linen garment worn on the chest by the High Priest. It had twelve stones sewn on it that represented God's people, the twelve tribes of Israel. The Ephod symbolized that the High Priest represented and carried the names of God's people before the LORD.* **"And he put upon him the coat [tunic], and girded him with the girdle, and clothed him with the robe, and put the ephod upon him, and he girded him with the curious girdle of the ephod, and bound** *it* **unto him therewith"** (Le.8:7).	What the Ephod taught: 1. Man cannot represent himself before God because he is a sinner. Man needs an Advocate, an Intercessor, a Mediator, a Savior who can approach God legally and perfectly. Man cannot do any of this; therefore, man needs someone who can. 2. Jesus Christ is the One who represents and carries the names of believers before the Father. No matter what our burden, no matter how terrifying, we can cast it upon Christ. He will bring us to God. He will relieve us, strengthen us, and give us rest and peace from the burden.	*"Come unto me, all ye that labour and are heavy laden, and I will give you rest. Take my yoke upon you, and learn of me; for I am meek and lowly in heart: and ye shall find rest unto your souls. For my yoke is easy, and my burden is light" (Mt.11:28-30).* *"Who is he that condemneth? It is Christ that died, yea rather, that is risen again, who is even at the right hand of God, who also maketh intercession for us" (Ro.8:34).* *"Casting all your care upon him; for he careth for you" (1 Pe.5:7).* *"Who is he that condemneth? It is Christ that died, yea rather, that is risen again, who is even at the right hand of God, who also maketh intercession for us" (Ro.8:34).* *"Wherefore in all things it behooved him to be made like unto his brethren, that he might be a merciful and faithful high priest in things pertaining to God, to make reconciliation for the sins of the people. For in that he himself hath suffered being tempted, he is able to succour them that are tempted" (He.2:17-18).*

Historical Term	Type or Picture (Scriptural Basis for Each)	Life Application for Today's Believer	Biblical Application
41. *The Urim And Thummim* (Le.8:8)	*The Urim and Thummim were two stones that symbolized the special revelation or guidance that God gave the High Priest. Imagine the scene as the High Priest entered into the Holy Place. The Urim and Thummim reminded him and the people that God would speak and give His direction to His people. The High Priest was there on behalf of the people of God; therefore, God would hear and answer him. God would make His will and direction known to the High Priest. How? God would speak and move upon the heart of the High Priest.* **"And he put the breastplate upon him: also he put in the breastplate the Urim and the Thummim"** (Le.8:8).	We are to pray and seek God's face for the needs of others. The world reels under the weight of suffering and evil, of death and judgment to come. The only hope is God. God's help is needed. We must therefore seek His face, seek Him day and night for the needs of people.	*"But if from thence thou shalt seek the LORD thy God, thou shalt find him, if thou seek him with all thy heart and with all thy soul"* (De.4:29). *"Seek the LORD and his strength, seek his face continually"* (1 Chr.16:11). *"He shall call upon me, and I will answer him: I will be with him in trouble; I will deliver him, and honour him"* (Ps.91:15). *"Seek ye the LORD while he may be found, call ye upon him while he is near"* (Is.55:6). *"And it shall come to pass, that before they call, I will answer; and while they are yet speaking, I will hear"* (Is.65:24; see Je.33:3; Lu.11:9).
42. *The Linen Turban* (Le.8:9)	*Linen is symbolic of righteousness. The mind and thoughts of the High Priest had to be subjected to God and His righteousness. The linen turban (a headdress cloth or cap) is symbolic of putting on God's righteousness.* **"And he put the mitre [turban] upon his head; also upon the mitre [turban], even upon his forefront, did he put the golden plate, the holy crown; as the LORD commanded Moses"** (Le.8:9).	What the Linen Headband taught: The believer must willingly submit his mind and will, his thoughts and agenda to God. He must subject every thought, every idea, every agenda to Christ.	*"Casting down imaginations, and every high thing that exalteth itself against the knowledge of God, and bringing into captivity every thought to the obedience of Christ;"* (2 Co. 10:5) *"I will greatly rejoice in the LORD, my soul shall be joyful in my God; for he hath clothed me with the garments of salvation, he hath covered me with the robe of righteousness, as a bridegroom decketh himself with ornaments, and as a bride adorneth herself with her jewels"* (Is.61:10). *"But of him are ye in Christ Jesus, who of God is made unto us wisdom, and righteousness, and sanctification, and redemption"* (1 Co.1:30).
43. *The Gold Plate [Medallion] Or Sacred Diadem* (Le.8:9)	*The gold plate (medallion) or sacred diadem was attached with a blue ribbon to the head of the High Priest and was the crowning piece of the High Priest's wardrobe. The words "HOLINESS TO THE LORD" were written upon the medallion. The Gold Medallion...* • *symbolized that the High Priest bore the guilt for the shortcomings of the people*	What the Gold Plate or Medallion taught: 1. We are ever so short of the glory and holiness of God. We desperately need Someone to bear the guilt for our shortcoming. That person is	*"Who gave himself for us, that he might redeem us from all iniquity, and purify unto himself a peculiar people, zealous of good works"* (Tit.2:14).

Historical Term	Type or Picture (Scriptural Basis for Each)	Life Application for Today's Believer	Biblical Application
The Gold Plate [Medallion] Or Sacred Diadem (continued) (Le.8:9)	• *symbolized that the people must seek the acceptance of a holy God* "**And he put the mitre upon his head; also upon the mitre, *even* upon his forefront, did he put the golden plate [medallion], the holy crown; as the LORD commanded Moses**" (Le.8:9).	Jesus Christ. It is Jesus Christ who bore the shortcomings and errors of the people. A person needs a perfect sacrifice, and that Sacrifice is Jesus Christ, who died upon the cross for our sins. 2. We are guilty of sin. Our sin indicts us and places us at the mercy of a holy and righteous Judge. God beckons each person to come to Him based upon the merit of Christ and His righteousness. We must seek the approval of God by approaching God through Christ and Christ alone.	"*For Christ also hath once suffered for sins, the just for the unjust, that he might bring us to God, being put to death in the flesh, but quickened by the Spirit*" (1 Pe.3:18). "*Jesus saith unto him, I am the way, the truth, and the life: no man cometh unto the Father, but by me*" (Jn.14:6). "*Neither is there salvation in any other: for there is none other name under heaven given among men, whereby we must be saved*" (Ac.4:12).
44. *The Altar Of Burnt Offering Anointed With Oil Seven Times* (Le.8:10-13)	*The altar was anointed with oil seven times to symbolize that a complete, full, and perfect sacrifice was being made for man's atonement (reconciliation) and redemption. Throughout the Bible, the number seven symbolizes the idea of completion, fullness, and perfection.* "**And he sprinkled thereof upon the altar seven times, and anointed the altar and all his vessels, both the laver and his foot, to sanctify them**" (Le.8:11).	Why was the altar anointed seven times? Remember, the altar was where the atoning sacrifice was offered, the place where the payment or ransom for sin was made. The sacrifice or payment for sin was full and complete. It provided a perfect redemption for man.	"*Wherefore he is able also to save them to the uttermost that come unto God by him, seeing he ever liveth to make intercession for them*" (He.7:25). "*For it became him, for whom are all things, and by whom are all things, in bringing many sons unto glory, to make the captain of their salvation perfect through sufferings*" (He. 2:10). "*And being made perfect, he became the author of eternal salvation unto all them that obey him*" (He.5:9). "*But ye shall receive power, after that the Holy Ghost is come upon you: and ye shall be witnesses unto me both in Jerusalem, and in all Judaea, and in Samaria, and unto the uttermost part of the earth.*" (Ac.1:8)
45. *Anointing Aaron (The High Priest) With Oil* (Le.8:10-13)	*The anointing with oil is a symbol of Aaron being dedicated or consecrated by the Holy Spirit.* "**And he poured of the anointing oil upon Aaron's head, and anointed him, to sanctify him**" (Le.8:12).	A person being ordained to the ministry must be anointed by the Spirit of God. He must be called by God and led to the point of dedication and consecration to God. The person must be totally dedicated to the service of God through the presence and power of the Holy Spirit.	"*But ye shall receive power, after that the Holy Ghost is come upon you: and ye shall be witnesses unto me both in Jerusalem, and in all Judaea, and in Samaria, and unto the uttermost part of the earth.*" (Ac.1:8; see Lu.9:23). "*And when they had prayed, the place was shaken where they were assembled together; and they were all filled with the Holy Ghost, and they spake the word of God with boldness*" (Ac.4:31; see Ac.13:2; Ro.8:14).

LEVITICUS - TYPES, SYMBOLS, AND PICTURES

Historical Term	Type or Picture (Scriptural Basis for Each)	Life Application for Today's Believer	Biblical Application
46. *The Taking Of Certain Parts Of The Sin Offering Outside The Camp And Burning Them. This Included The Hide, The Flesh, And The Offal (Waste, Filth).* (Le.8:17)	*This is a symbol of Christ taking away the sins of the world. By this act, the sins of the priests were pictured as being removed, taken off, and taken away from them. A substitute sacrifice died for them and took away their sins.* **"But the bullock, and his hide, his flesh, and his dung, he burnt with fire without the camp; as the LORD commanded Moses"** (Le.8:17).	When a person believes or identifies with the sacrifice of Jesus Christ, his sins… • are removed • are taken off • are taken away from him	*"And now why tarriest thou? arise, and be baptized, and wash away thy sins, calling on the name of the Lord"* (Ac.22:16). *"Who gave himself for our sins, that he might deliver us from this present evil world, according to the will of God and our Father"* (Ga.1:4; see He. 9:14; 1 Jn.1:7).
47. *The Ordination Offering* (Le.8:22-32)	*The Ordination Offering symbolized the sacrifice and death of the Lord Jesus Christ. Through the Ordination Offering, God accepted a person's dedication to God through the blood of the substitute sacrifice.* **"And Moses took of the anointing oil, and of the blood which was upon the altar, and sprinkled it upon Aaron, and upon his garments, and upon his sons, and upon his sons' garments with him; and sanctified Aaron, and his garments, and his sons, and his sons' garments with him"** (Le.8:30).	It is Christ who challenges us to dedicate all that we are and do to God.	*"I beseech you therefore, brethren, by the mercies of God, that ye present your bodies a living sacrifice, holy, acceptable unto God, which is your reasonable service. And be not conformed to this world: but be ye transformed by the renewing of your mind, that ye may prove what is that good, and acceptable, and perfect, will of God"* (Ro.12:1-2). *"Therefore, my beloved brethren, be ye stedfast, unmoveable, always abounding in the work of the Lord, forasmuch as ye know that your labour is not in vain in the Lord"* (1 Co.15:58).
48. *The Dedication Or Setting Apart Of One's Whole Being To God Through The Blood Of The Sacrifice* (Le.8:23-24)	⇒ *The Dedication was symbolized in two ways:* 1. *It was symbolized by placing blood on Aaron's right ear, thumb, and big toe. His hearing and the work of his hands and the direction of his feet were all sanctified, set apart, and dedicated to the service of God. His ear was set apart to listen and hear the Word of God, to hear and listen only to clean and holy conversation. His thumb or hand was set apart to touch and do only clean and holy things. His big toe or foot was set apart to walk after God and only where good, clean, and holy things were done.* 2. *It was also symbolized by placing blood on Aaron's sons, on their right ears, thumbs, and*	The commitment of a person's right ear, thumb, and big toe is a descriptive picture of just how dedicated a believer must be. It is a lesson not only for ordained servants of God but also for every believer. 1. The believer is to dedicate and set apart his ears to God: he is to listen and hear only clean and holy conversation. 2. He is to dedicate and set apart his thumb or hand to God: he is to touch and do only that which is clean and holy. 3. He is to dedicate and set apart his feet to God: he is to walk only where good, clean, and holy things are done.	*"But blessed are your eyes, for they see: and your ears, for they hear"* (Mt.13:16). *"The heart of the prudent getteth knowledge; and the ear of the wise seeketh knowledge"* (Pr.18:15). *"And every one that heareth these sayings of mine, and doeth them not, shall be likened unto a foolish man, which built his house upon the sand"* (Mt.7:26). *"Labour not for the meat which perisheth, but for that meat which endureth unto everlasting life, which the Son of man shall give unto you: for him hath God the Father sealed"* (Jn.6:27). *"This I say then, Walk in the Spirit, and ye shall not fulfil the lust of the flesh….Now the works of the flesh are manifest, which are these; Adultery,*

Historical Term	Type or Picture (Scriptural Basis for Each)	Life Application for Today's Believer	Biblical Application
The Dedication Or Setting Apart Of One's Whole Being To God Through The Blood Of The Sacrifice (continued) (Le.8:23-24)	*big toes.* "And he slew *it;* and Moses took of the blood of it, and put *it* upon the tip of Aaron's right ear, and upon the thumb of his right hand, and upon the great toe of his right foot. And he brought Aaron's sons, and Moses put of the blood upon the tip of their right ear, and upon the thumbs of their right hands, and upon the great toes of their right feet: and Moses sprinkled the blood upon the altar round about" (Le.8:23-24).		*fornication, uncleanness, lasciviousness, Idolatry, witchcraft, hatred, variance, emulations, wrath, strife, seditions, heresies, Envyings, murders, drunkenness, revellings, and such like: of the which I tell you before, as I have also told you in time past, that they which do such things shall not inherit the kingdom of God" (Ga.5:16, 19-21).*
49. *The Dedication Of The Altar Of Sacrifice: During The Ordination Offering* (Le.8:24)	*This is a picture of dedication. The dedication of the altar of sacrifice was symbolized by the sprinkling of blood against all sides of the altar.* "And he brought Aaron's sons, and Moses put of the blood upon the tip of their right ear, and upon the thumbs of their right hands, and upon the great toes of their right feet: and Moses sprinkled the blood upon the altar round about" (Le.8:24).	The minister of God, yea every believer, is to be totally dedicated to God. He is to set apart his whole being to God.	*"I beseech you therefore, brethren, by the mercies of God, that ye present your bodies a living sacrifice, holy, acceptable unto God, which is your reasonable service. And be not conformed to this world: but be ye transformed by the renewing of your mind, that ye may prove what is that good, and acceptable, and perfect, will of God"* (Ro.12:1-2). *"Therefore, my beloved brethren, be ye stedfast, unmoveable, always abounding in the work of the Lord, forasmuch as ye know that your labour is not in vain in the Lord"* (1 Co.15:58). *"And thou shalt love the LORD thy God with all thine heart, and with all thy soul, and with all thy might"* (De.6:5).
50. *The Sweet Aroma Of The Roasted Meat Of The Ordination Offering Ascended Up Toward Heaven* (Le.8:28)	*The sweet aroma is a symbol of pleasing the LORD. The dedication of the priest's lives to God was acceptable to Him.* "And Moses took them from off their hands, and burnt *them* on the altar upon the burnt offering: they *were* consecrations for a sweet savour: it *is* an offering made by fire unto the LORD" (Le.8:28).	It must be the goal of every believer to have a life that pleases the Lord. How does a believer please the LORD? By obeying Him, by dedicating his life to the LORD and doing everything He says.	*"My son, give me thine heart, and let thine eyes observe my ways"* (Pr.23:26). *"This book of the law shall not depart out of thy mouth; but thou shalt meditate therein day and night, that thou mayest observe to do according to all that is written therein: for then thou shalt make thy way prosperous, and then thou shalt have good success"* (Jos.1:8). *"Not every one that saith unto me, Lord, Lord, shall enter into the kingdom of heaven; but he that doeth the will of my Father which is in heaven"* (Mt.7:21).

Historical Term	Type or Picture (Scriptural Basis for Each)	Life Application for Today's Believer	Biblical Application
51. *The Ordination Service Repeated For Seven Days* (Le.8:33)	*The ordination service repeated for seven days symbolizes that the ordained person must complete his ministry. This is the very commandment of God. Remember that seven is the number of completion, of fulfillment, of perfection.* **"And ye shall not go out of the door of the tabernacle of the congregation in seven days, until the days of your consecration be at an end: for seven days shall he consecrate you" (Le.8:33).**	Whatever we do for God, we must do our best, we must complete and finish it. Far too many people have not offered God their best nor have they completed what they started. The charge is clear: we must do our very best for God, and we must finish the task, complete it to the fullest..	*"Jesus saith unto them, My meat is to do the will of him that sent me, and to finish his work" (Jn.4:34).* *"I have glorified thee on the earth: I have finished the work which thou gavest me to do" (Jn.17:4).* *"When Jesus therefore had received the vinegar, he said, It is finished: and he bowed his head, and gave up the ghost" (Jn.19:30).* *"Take heed to the ministry which thou hast received in the Lord, that thou fulfil it" (Col.4:17).*
52. *Pouring Out The Remaining Blood Of The Sin Offering: During The First Worship Service Of The Priest* (Le.9:9; See also Le. 4:7)	*Pouring out the remaining blood of the substitute sacrifice symbolized the complete and full forgiveness of sin.* **"And the sons of Aaron brought the blood unto him: and he dipped his finger in the blood, and put it upon the horns of the altar, and poured out the blood at the bottom of the altar" (Le.9:9).**	It is only through the blood of Jesus Christ that our sins are forgiven—all our sins. The blood of Jesus Christ forgives us… • completely • fully • entirely • wholly • sufficiently • through and through	*"If we confess our sins, he is faithful and just to forgive us our sins, and to cleanse us from all unrighteousness" (1 Jn.1:9).* *"Much more then, being now justified by his blood, we shall be saved from wrath through him" (Ro.5:9).* *"And, having made peace through the blood of his cross, by him to reconcile all things unto himself; by him, I say, whether they be things in earth, or things in heaven" (Col.1:20).* *"But if we walk in the light, as he is in the light, we have fellowship one with another, and the blood of Jesus Christ his Son cleanseth us from all sin" (1 Jn.1:7).*
53. *The Washing Of The Inner Parts And Legs Of The Burnt Offering During The First Worship Service Of The Priest* (Le.9:14)	*The washing of the inner parts and legs of the sacrifice symbolized that only a clean and pure sacrifice (sinless, perfect) could be offered to God.* **"And he did wash the inwards and the legs, and burnt them upon the burnt offering on the altar" (Le.9:14).**	Whatever we do for God must be offered as a clean and pure sacrifice. The best gift that we can give to God is our own personal holiness, a life that is marked with purity. Our personal witness of Christ is more authentic to the lost when our hearts have been cleansed, washed by the Word of God.	*"Having therefore these promises, dearly beloved, let us cleanse ourselves from all filthiness of the flesh and spirit, perfecting holiness in the fear of God" (2 Co.7:1).* *"That he might sanctify and cleanse it with the washing of water by the word" (Ep.5:26).* *"Draw nigh to God, and he will draw nigh to you. Cleanse your hands, ye sinners; and purify your hearts, ye double minded" (Js.4:8).* *"Wash me throughly from mine iniquity, and cleanse me from my sin" (Ps.51:2).* *"Wherewithal shall a young man cleanse his way? by taking heed thereto*

Historical Term	Type or Picture (Scriptural Basis for Each)	Life Application for Today's Believer	Biblical Application
The Washing Of The Inner Parts And Legs Of The Burnt Offering: During The First Worship Service Of The Priest (continued) (Le.9:14)			*according to thy word" (Ps.119:9).* *"If we confess our sins, he is faithful and just to forgive us our sins, and to cleanse us from all unrighteousness" (1 Jn.1:9).*
54. *A Goat Offered For The Sins Of A Ruler (the Sin Offering): During The First Worship Service Of The Priest (Le.9:15. See also Le. 3:12-16)*	*The sacrifice of the goat is a symbol of Jesus Christ, of His dying for the sins of the world.* **"And he brought the people's offering, and took the goat, which *was* the sin offering for the people, and slew it, and offered it for sin, as the first" (Le.9:15).**	Jesus Christ died for the sins of the world. We must prepare to meet God, prepare by seeking forgiveness of sin.	*"The next day John seeth Jesus coming unto him, and saith, Behold the Lamb of God, which taketh away the sin of the world" (Jn.1:29).* *"Him hath God exalted with his right hand to be a Prince and a Saviour, for to give repentance to Israel, and forgiveness of sins" (Ac.5:31).* *"Be it known unto you therefore, men and brethren, that through this man is preached unto you the forgiveness of sins" (Ac.13:38).* *"In whom we have redemption through his blood, the forgiveness of sins, according to the riches of his grace" (Ep.1:7).*
55. *The Odor Of The Burning Grain and The Roasting Meat That Ascending Up Toward Heaven During The First Worship Service Of The Priest (Le.9:17)*	*The odor of the burning grain and the roasting meat that ascended up toward Heaven symbolizing two things:* *1. The odor symbolized the offering up of thanksgiving for the atonement (for one's reconciliation) and for God's provision of one's livelihood (food crops).* *2. The laying of grain upon the sacrifice pictured the dedication, the laying of one's life upon God.* **"And he brought the meat offering, and took an handful thereof, and burnt *it* upon the altar, beside the burnt sacrifice of the morning" (Le.9:17).**	The lesson is clear: we must prepare to meet God… • prepare by giving thanks for the atonement (reconciliation with God) and for all His goodness in providing for us • prepare by dedicating our lives to God, by giving ourselves totally to Him	*"When thou hast eaten and art full, then thou shalt bless the LORD thy God for the good land which he hath given thee" (De.8:10).* *"Enter into his gates with thanksgiving, and into his courts with praise: be thankful unto him, and bless his name" (Ps.100:4).* *"And let them sacrifice the sacrifices of thanksgiving, and declare his works with rejoicing" (Ps.107:22).* *"Giving thanks unto the Father, which hath made us meet to be partakers of the inheritance of the saints in light" (Col.1:12).* *"And he said to them all, If any man will come after me, let him deny himself, and take up his cross daily, and follow me" (Lu.9:23).* *"And they that are Christ's have crucified the flesh with the affections and lusts" (Ga.5:24).*
56. *The Offering Of Strange, Unauthorized Fire To The LORD. (Le.10:1)*	*The offering of strange, unauthorized fire to the LORD is a symbol of approaching God in the wrong way.* **"And Nadab and Abihu, the sons of Aaron,**	We must always remember that the true worship and religion of God are a *revealed worship* and a *revealed religion*. God has revealed through His Son and the Holy Scriptures exactly how	*"Jesus saith unto him, I am the way, the truth, and the life: no man cometh unto the Father, but by me" (Jn.14:6).* *"Judas saith unto him, not Iscariot, Lord, how is it*

Historical Term	Type or Picture (Scriptural Basis for Each)	Life Application for Today's Believer	Biblical Application
	took either of them his censer, and put fire therein, and put incense thereon, and offered strange fire before the LORD, which he commanded them not" (Le.10:1).	His people are to worship Him. But these two priests (Nadab and Abihu) ignored and rejected God's way. They created and developed their own way to approach God. How like so many today who approach God as they think and as they wish, ignoring God's way and His clear instructions.	*that thou wilt manifest thyself unto us, and not unto the world? Jesus answered and said unto him, If a man love me, he will keep my words: and my Father will love him, and we will come unto him, and make our abode with him. He that loveth me not keepeth not my sayings: and the word which ye hear is not mine, but the Father's which sent me"* (Jn.14:22-24). *"Neither is there salvation in any other: for there is none other name under heaven given among men, whereby we must be saved"* (Ac.4:12).
57. *Death: A Person who came in Contact with the Dead was Counted Unclean, Defiled.* (Le.10:4-5)	*The death of Aaron's two sons is a picture of defilement, uncleanness, corruption, and decay. Note that Aaron was not allowed to take care of his two dead sons. Priests were forbidden to touch or go near dead corpses because death symbolized defilement and uncleanness, corruption and decay. Defilement and corruption disqualified a priest from performing his service for God. For this reason, Aaron was forbidden to touch the two dead bodies despite the fact that they were his sons. Note that Moses had the two nephews of Aaron remove the dead bodies (the defilement) outside the camp (v.5).* *"And Moses called Mishael and Elzaphan, the sons of Uzziel the uncle of Aaron, and said unto them, Come near, carry your brethren from before the sanctuary out of the camp"* (Le.10:4).	The lesson to us is clear: ministers and believers alike must do all they can to prevent the judgment of God, prevent His judgment from falling upon them or upon any other believer. The way to escape the judgment of God is the same for us as it was for Aaron and the Israelites. We must guard against defilement if we wish to escape the judgment of God.	*"All these evil things come from within, and defile the man"* (Mk.7:23). *"Having therefore these promises, dearly beloved, let us cleanse ourselves from all filthiness of the flesh and spirit, perfecting holiness in the fear of God"* (2 Co.7:1). *"Looking diligently lest any man fail of the grace of God; lest any root of bitterness springing up trouble you, and thereby many be defiled"* (He.12:15). *"Draw nigh to God, and he will draw nigh to you. Cleanse your hands, ye sinners; and purify your hearts, ye double minded"* (Js.4:8). *"If a man therefore purge himself from these, he shall be a vessel unto honour, sanctified, and meet for the master's use, and prepared unto every good work"* (2 Ti.2:21).
58. *The Laws Of Cleanliness And Defilement* (Le.11:1-47)	*The laws of cleanliness and defilement are symbolic of spiritual truth, of being spiritually clean and undefiled.* *"This is the law of the beasts, and of the fowl, and of every living creature that moveth in the waters, and of every creature that creepeth upon the earth: To make a difference between the*	God cares for His people physically and spiritually; therefore, He wants them to take care of their bodies and spirits. God had more than health in mind when He gave the food laws. God had a spiritual purpose in mind. The laws of cleanliness set God's people apart as a clean, holy people. This is the reason for these laws, that His people might have strong bodies and	*"Know ye not that your bodies are the members of Christ? shall I then take the members of Christ, and make them the members of an harlot? God forbid"* (1 Co.6:15). *"And the very God of peace sanctify you wholly; and I pray God your whole spirit and soul and body be preserved blameless unto the coming of our Lord Jesus Christ"* (1 Th.5:23).

Historical Term	Type or Picture (Scriptural Basis for Each)	Life Application for Today's Believer	Biblical Application
The Laws Of Cleanliness And Defilement (continued) (Le.11:1-47)	**unclean and the clean, and between the beast that may be eaten and the beast that may not be eaten"** **(Le.11:46-47).**	strong spirits.	*"Know ye not that ye are the temple of God, and that the Spirit of God dwelleth in you?" (1 Co.3:16).* *"What? know ye not that your body is the temple of the Holy Ghost which is in you, which ye have of God, and ye are not your own?" (1 Co.6:19).* *"In whom ye also are builded together for an habitation of God through the Spirit" (Ep.2:22).*
59. *The Clean And Unclean Animals* (Le.11:2-8)	*The clean and unclean animals are symbols of being ceremonially clean or unclean, of being spiritually clean or unclean. This is to say that God had two purposes in giving these laws governing food:* *1. The purpose of keeping His people physically healthy and clean* *2. The purpose of keeping His people ceremonially, spiritually clean and healthy* **"Speak unto the children of Israel, saying, These are the beasts which ye shall eat among all the beasts that are on the earth" (Le.11:2).**	The application and lesson for the believer is clear: 1. The believer must keep his body clean and healthy. 2. The believer must keep his spirit clean and healthy.	*"What? know ye not that your body is the temple of the Holy Ghost which is in you, which ye have of God, and ye are not your own?" (1 Co.6:19).* *"And the very God of peace sanctify you wholly; and I pray God your whole spirit and soul and body be preserved blameless unto the coming of our Lord Jesus Christ" (1 Th.5:23).* *"Beloved, I wish above all things that thou mayest prosper and be in health, even as thy soul prospereth" (3 Jn.1:2).*
60. *Washing* (Le.11:24-40)	*Washing is a symbol of being spiritually, ceremonially cleansed.* **"And whosoever beareth ought of the carcase of them shall wash his clothes, and be unclean until the even" (Le.11:25).**	No person can cleanse himself, not spiritually, not from sin. Only God's mediator—Jesus Christ—can wash and cleanse a person spiritually.	*"And now why tarriest thou? arise, and be baptized, and wash away thy sins, calling on the name of the Lord" (Ac.22:16).* *"In whom we have redemption through his blood, the forgiveness of sins, according to the riches of his grace" (Ep.1:7; see He.9:14).* *Unto him that loved us, and washed us from our sins in his own blood" (Re.1:5).*
61. *Egypt* (Le.11:44-47. See also Le.19:33-34)	*Egypt is a symbol of the world. God had saved His people from the slavery of the world (Egypt), from the slavery of its sin and death. Note why:* *1. He saved them to be their God.* *2. He saved them to set them apart as His holy people.* **"For I am the LORD that bringeth you up out of the land of Egypt, to be**	The application and lesson for us is clear: 1. We must be holy because God is holy. As believers, we have no choice: the command is direct and forceful. We must be like God: consecrated—set apart—holy. 2. We must declare that God is the Savior of the world, the Savior who delivered us from the	*"That he would grant unto us, that we being delivered out of the hand of our enemies might serve him without fear, In holiness and righteousness before him, all the days of our life" (Lu.1:74-75).* *"Having therefore these promises, dearly beloved, let us cleanse ourselves from all filthiness of the flesh and spirit, perfecting holiness in the fear of God" (2 Co.7:1).*

Historical Term	Type or Picture (Scriptural Basis for Each)	Life Application for Today's Believer	Biblical Application
Egypt (continued) (Le.11:44-47. See also Le.19:33-34)	**your God: ye shall therefore be holy, for I *am* holy" (Le.11:45).**	world (Egypt). We must bear testimony, strong testimony, that God is building a new race of people, a people… • who will let Him be their God • who will be set apart and live as the holy people of God 3. We must learn to discern more and more between the clean and unclean, the holy and unholy. We must sharpen our power to discern, learn to distinguish between right and wrong, the just and unjust, the moral and immoral, the kind and unkind, the unselfish and selfish.	*"Follow peace with all men, and holiness, without which no man shall see the Lord" (He.12:14).* *"But sanctify [set apart as holy, pure] the Lord God in your hearts: and be ready always to give an answer to every man that asketh you a reason of the hope that is in you with meekness and fear" (1 Pe.3:15).* *"But the natural man receiveth not the things of the Spirit of God: for they are foolishness unto him: neither can he know them, because they are spiritually discerned" (1 Co.2:14).* *"But strong meat belongeth to them that are of full age, even those who by reason of use have their senses exercised to discern both good and evil" (He.5:14).* *"Give therefore thy servant an understanding heart to judge thy people, that I may discern between good and bad: for who is able to judge this thy so great a people?" (1 K.3:9).*
62. *Laws That Protect Mother And Child After Childbirth* (Le.12:1-8)	*Laws that protect mother and child after childbirth symbolized the need for cleansing from the sinful nature.* **"Speak unto the children of Israel, saying, If a woman have conceived seed, and born a man child: then she shall be unclean seven days; according to the days of the separation for her infirmity shall she be unclean" (Le.12:2).**	Childbirth is one way God is able to teach the truth of human depravity. God has created man to live with Him forever in perfection. But sin has disrupted this relationship, alienated man from God. Sin has brought about death, terrible separation, and judgment to come. Teaching this truth was one of the purposes for the law of ceremonial uncleanness governing childbirth.	*"By man came death" (1 Co.15:21).* *"Wherefore, as by one man sin entered into the world, and death by sin; and so death passed upon all men, for that all have sinned" (Ro.5:12).* *"For the wages of sin is death" (Ro.6:23).* *"Behold, I was shapen in iniquity; and in sin did my mother conceive me" (Ps.51:5).* *"The wicked are estranged from the womb: they go astray as soon as they be born, speaking lies" (Ps.58:3).*
63. *Circumcision* (Le.12:1-4)	*Circumcision symbolized that a person was a member of God's people. Circumcision meant…* • *that a baby son was to be reared as a follower of God* • *that he was to be taught the covenant of God* • *that he would inherit the promises of God—if he truly obeyed and followed God* • *that God covered the baby under His cove-*	God covers the child of the believer with His marvelous grace through the covenant of the Lord Jesus Christ. By Christ, God gives great assurance and security to the parents: He will look after their children.	*"But Jesus said, Suffer little children, and forbid them not, to come unto me: for of such is the kingdom of heaven" (Mt.19:14).* *"Honour thy father and thy mother, as the Lord thy God hath commanded thee; that thy days may be prolonged, and that it may go well with thee, in the land which the Lord thy God giveth thee." (Deut. 5:16)* *"When my father and my mother forsake me,*

Historical Term	Type or Picture (Scriptural Basis for Each)	Life Application for Today's Believer	Biblical Application
Circumcision (continued) (Le.12:1-4)	*nant and grace until he reached the age of responsibility.* **"And in the eighth day the flesh of his foreskin shall be circumcised"** (Le.12:3).		*then the Lord will take me up"* (Ps.27:10). *"He shall feed his flock like a shepherd: he shall gather the lambs with his arm, and carry them in his bosom, and shall gently lead those that are with young." (Is.40:11)* *"For the promise is unto you, and to your children, and to all that are afar off, even as many as the Lord our God shall call" (Ac.2:39).*
64. *Leprosy Or Infectious Skin Disease* (Le.13:1-59)	*These contagious diseases symbolize the disease of sin, how contagious it is, and the need to prevent the spread of sin.* **"And the leper in whom the plague *is*, his clothes shall be rent, and his head bare, and he shall put a covering upon his upper lip, and shall cry, Unclean, unclean. All the days wherein the plague *shall be* in him he shall be defiled; he *is* unclean: he shall dwell alone; without the camp *shall* his habitation *be*"** (Le.13:45-46).	God gave Israel the law governing leprosy or infectious skin disease because He loves His people. God loves us and cares for us; therefore He wants us healthy. He wants us experiencing the fullness of life, worshipping and serving Him. He wants us bearing strong testimony to a world lost and reeling under the weight of desperate need. This is the reason He wants all of His people throughout all generations healthy. This was the purpose behind the laws governing leprosy or infectious skin disease.	*"The Spirit of the Lord is upon me, because he hath anointed me to preach the gospel to the poor; he hath sent me to heal the brokenhearted, to preach deliverance to the captives, and recovering of sight to the blind, to set at liberty them that are bruised" (Lu.4:18).* *"When Jesus heard it, he saith unto them, They that are whole have no need of the physician, but they that are sick: I came not to call the righteous, but sinners to repentance" (Mk.2:17).* *"Beloved, I wish above all things that thou mayest prosper and be in health, even as thy soul prospereth" (3 Jn.1:2).* *"And said, If thou wilt diligently hearken to the voice of the LORD thy God, and wilt do that which is right in his sight, and wilt give ear to his commandments, and keep all his statutes, I will put none of these diseases upon thee, which I have brought upon the Egyptians: for I am the LORD that healeth thee" (Ex.15:26).*
65. *Clothing* (Le.13:47-59)	*Throughout Scripture, clothing is either a symbol of righteousness or unrighteousness.* *1. Clean clothing is a symbol of righteousness.* *2. Unclean clothing is a symbol of unrighteousness.* **"The garment also that the plague of leprosy [infectious mildew] is in,** *whether it be* **a woollen**	A person must make sure, absolutely sure, that he is clothed in the righteousness of Jesus Christ. If not, then the mildew of sin will rot his clothing. He will stand before God clothed in unrighteousness.	*"For the wrath of God is revealed from heaven against all ungodliness and unrighteousness of men, who hold the truth in unrighteousness" (Ro.1:18).* *"Neither yield ye your members as instruments of unrighteousness unto sin: but yield yourselves unto God, as those that are alive from the dead, and your members as instruments of righteousness unto God" (Ro.6:13).*

Historical Term	Type or Picture (Scriptural Basis for Each)	Life Application for Today's Believer	Biblical Application
Clothing (continued) (Le.13:47-59)	garment, or a linen garment; Whether *it be* in the warp, or woof; of linen, or of woollen; whether in a skin, or in any thing made of skin; And if the plague be greenish or reddish in the garment, or in the skin, either in the warp, or in the woof, or in any thing of skin; it *is* a plague of leprosy [infectious mildew], and shall be showed unto the priest" (Le.13:47-49).		*"But these [the unrighteous], as natural brute beasts, made to be taken and destroyed, speak evil of the things that they understand not; and shall utterly perish in their own corruption; And shall receive the reward of unrighteousness, as they that count it pleasure to riot in the day time. Spots they are and blemishes, sporting themselves with their own deceivings while they feast with you"* (2 Pe.2:12-13). *"All unrighteousness is sin"* (1 Jn.5:17).
66. *Infectious Mildew Or A Plague Of Leprosy* (Le.13:47-59)	*Infectious mildew or a plague of leprosy is a symbol of sin and the rot it causes in the life of a person.* "This *is* the law of the plague of leprosy [infectious mildew] in a garment of woollen or linen, either in the warp, or woof, or any thing of skins, to pronounce it clean, or to pronounce it unclean" (Le.13:59).	Scripture declares that the infectious mildew or rot of sin must be washed away by the blood of Christ. Only the blood of Christ can cleanse a person from sin and make him acceptable to God.	*"And now why tarriest thou? arise, and be baptized, and wash away thy sins, calling on the name of the Lord"* (Ac.22:16). *"In whom we have redemption through his blood, the forgiveness of sins, according to the riches of his grace"* (Ep.1:7). *"How much more shall the blood of Christ, who through the eternal Spirit offered himself without spot to God, purge your conscience from dead works to serve the living God?"* (He.9:14). *"If we confess our sins, he is faithful and just to forgive us our sins, and to cleanse us from all unrighteousness"* (1 Jn.1:9).
67. *Laws That Cleanse And Restore People From Leprosy, From All Forms Of Infectious Skin Disease* (Le.14:1-57)	*These laws (laws that cleanse and restore people from leprosy, from all forms of infectious skin disease) symbolize the need for spiritual cleansing.* "This shall be the law of the leper in the day of his cleansing: He shall be brought unto the priest" (Le.14:2).	God loves and cares for His people, so he naturally cares about their health. He wants His people to be healthy so they can enjoy the fullness of life, so they can be productive and fruitful in life. Stated simply, God wants His people strong so that they can live lives that are strong in work, play, and worship. God wants His people conquering throughout all of life, being victorious over all the trials and temptations of life. He wants them physically and mentally strong so that they can bear strong testimony to His glorious goodness and saving grace.	*"The thief cometh not, but for to steal, and to kill, and to destroy: I am come that they might have life, and that they might have it more abundantly"* (Jn. 10:10). *"And God is able to make all grace abound toward you; that ye, always having all sufficiency in all things, may abound to every good work"* (2 Co.9:8). *"They shall be abundantly satisfied with the fatness of thy house; and thou shalt make them drink of the river of thy pleasures"* (Ps.36:8). *"Now unto him that is able to do exceeding abundantly above all that we ask or think, according to the*

Historical Term	Type or Picture (Scriptural Basis for Each)	Life Application for Today's Believer	Biblical Application
Laws That Cleanse And Restore People From Leprosy, From All Forms Of Infectious Skin Disease (continued) (Le.14:1-57)			*power that worketh in us"* (Ep.3:20). *"But my God shall supply all your need according to his riches in glory by Christ Jesus"* (Ph. 4:19).
68. *The Cleansing That Took Place Outside The Camp* (Le.14:2-9)	*The cleansing that took place outside the camp is a symbol of being outside, separated from God's people, but of being healed of infectious skin disease (a symbol of sin)* **"This shall be the law of the leper in the day of his cleansing: He shall be brought unto the priest: And the priest shall go forth out of the camp; and the priest shall look, and, behold, *if* the plague of leprosy be healed in the leper"** (Le.14:2-3).	When a person walks in sin he is "outside" Christ, separated from Christ. He is living "outside the camp," not in "the camp of the righteous." If he is to be reached and cleansed, he has to be reached and cleansed "outside the camp." Once he has been cleansed, he can then enter the camp of believers.	*"He that covereth his sins shall not prosper: but whoso confesseth and forsaketh them shall have mercy"* (Pr.28:13). *"For God shall bring every work into judgment, with every secret thing, whether it be good, or whether it be evil"* (Ec.12:14). *"The night is far spent, the day is at hand: let us therefore cast off the works of darkness, and let us put on the armour of light"* (Ro.13:12). *In the name of our Lord Jesus Christ, when ye are gathered together, and my spirit, with the power of our Lord Jesus Christ, To deliver such an one unto Satan for the destruction of the flesh, that the spirit may be saved in the day of the Lord Jesus"* (1 Co.5:4-5).
69. *The Priest's Going Outside The Camp To Cleanse The Diseased Person* (Le.14:3)	*The priest's going outside the camp to cleanse the diseased person is a picture of Jesus Christ and His work. Jesus Christ left the camp and glory of heaven to come to this sin diseased world. He came to cleanse the world of sin.* **"And the priest shall go forth out of the camp; and the priest shall look, and, behold, *if* the plague of leprosy be healed in the leper"** (Le.14:3).	Jesus Christ left the camp and glory of heaven to come to this sin-diseased world. He came forth from heaven's glory to cleanse all who are infected with the disease of sin. Cleansing us from our sins took place outside of heaven. He had to go outside the community of heaven with all its glory and come to where we are in order to cleanse us.	*"But we see Jesus, who was made a little lower than the angels for the suffering of death, crowned with glory and honour; that he by the grace of God should taste death for every man. For it became him, for whom are all things, and by whom are all things, in bringing many sons unto glory, to make the captain of their salvation perfect through sufferings"* (He.2:9-10). *"For verily he took not on him the nature of angels; but he took on him the seed of Abraham. Wherefore in all things it behooved him to be made like unto his brethren, that he might be a merciful and faithful high priest in things pertaining to God, to make reconciliation for the sins of the people"* (He.2:16-17). *"But when the fulness of the time was come, God sent forth his Son, made of*

Historical Term	Type or Picture (Scriptural Basis for Each)	Life Application for Today's Believer	Biblical Application
The Priest's Going Outside The Camp To Cleanse The Diseased Person (continued) (Le.14:3)			*a woman, made under the law, To redeem them that were under the law, that we might receive the adoption of sons" (Ga.4:4-5).*
70. *The Person Being Cleansed Through The Sacrifice Of The Shed Blood—Outside The Camp* (Le.14:4-7)	*The person being cleansed through the sacrifice of the shed blood—outside the camp—is a symbol or picture of two things:* 1. *This is a picture of the sacrifice of Jesus Christ. Note that the blood of the sacrificed bird was sprinkled over a person seven times; then he was pronounced clean. The number seven symbolized completeness, fullness. The person was completely, fully cleansed by the blood of the sacrifice.* 2. *Note that the live bird was dipped into the blood and then released, set free. This was a symbol that the person's disease was gone, taken away. He was free to live with God and His people.* **"As for the living bird, he shall take it, and the cedar wood, and the scarlet, and the hyssop, and shall dip them and the living bird in the blood of the bird *that was* killed over the running water: And he shall sprinkle upon him that is to be cleansed from the leprosy seven times, and shall pronounce him clean, and shall let the living bird loose into the open field"** (Le.14:6-7).	There are two pictures that apply to the believer in this ritual: 1. There is the picture of a believer being fully and completely cleansed through the blood of the Lord Jesus Christ. 2. The live bird, of course, is a picture of the believer's sin being taken away: the believer is free of sin, free to live with God and the people of God.	*"For this is my blood of the new testament, which is shed for many for the remission of sins"* (Mt.26:28). *"Take heed therefore unto yourselves, and to all the flock, over the which the Holy Ghost hath made you overseers, to feed the church of God, which he hath purchased with his own blood"* (Ac.20:28). *"Much more then, being now justified by his blood, we shall be saved from wrath through him"* (Ro.5:9). *"How much more shall the blood of Christ, who through the eternal Spirit offered himself without spot to God, purge your conscience from dead works to serve the living God?"* (He.9:14). *"Forasmuch as ye know that ye were not redeemed with corruptible things, as silver and gold, from your vain conversation received by tradition from your fathers; But with the precious blood of Christ, as of a lamb without blemish and without spot"* (1 Pe.1:18-19).
71. *The Washing Of A Diseased Person's Clothes, Shaving His Body, And Bathing* (Le.14:8)	*This is a picture of being completely washed and cleansed of sin. This, of course, exposed a person's whole body, revealing that he was completely cleansed of the contagious disease.* **"And he that is to be cleansed shall wash his clothes, and shave off all his hair, and wash himself in water, that he may be clean: and after that he shall come into the camp,**	The person who is afflicted with the disease of sin can be completely washed and cleansed. The blood of Jesus Christ, God's son, cleanses us from sin—completely and fully.	*"But if we walk in the light, as he is in the light, we have fellowship one with another, and the blood of Jesus Christ his Son cleanseth us from all sin"* (1 Jn.1:7). *Unto him that loved us, and washed us from our sins in his own blood"* (Re.1:5). *"And I said unto him, Sir, thou knowest. And he said to me, These are they which came out of great*

LEVITICUS - TYPES, SYMBOLS, AND PICTURES

Historical Term	Type or Picture (Scriptural Basis for Each)	Life Application for Today's Believer	Biblical Application
The Washing Of A Diseased Person's Clothes, Shaving His Body, And Bathing (continued) (Le.14:8)	**and shall tarry abroad out of his tent seven days"** (Le.14:8).		*tribulation, and have washed their robes, and made them white in the blood of the Lamb"* (Re.7:14).
72. *The Cleansing That Took Place Inside The Camp* (Le.14:10-20)	*The cleansing that took place inside the camp is the symbol of being fully reconciled and restored through Jesus Christ.* **"And on the eighth day he shall take two he lambs without blemish, and one ewe lamb of the first year without blemish, and three tenth deals of fine flour *for* a meat offering, mingled with oil, and one log of oil"** (Le.14:10).	The believer who has sinned needs to come to Christ. Coming to Christ is the only way to make sure… • that he is fully reconciled to God • that he has no hidden sin in his life • that he is not suffering under the weight and anguish of guilt • that he receives an infusion of God's strength, assurance and of God's guidance	*"And all things are of God, who hath reconciled us to himself by Jesus Christ, and hath given to us the ministry of reconciliation"* (2 Co.5:18). *"And that he might reconcile both unto God in one body by the cross, having slain the enmity thereby"* (Ep.2:16). *"And, having made peace through the blood of his cross, by him to reconcile all things unto himself; by him, I say, whether they be things in earth, or things in heaven"* (Col.1:20). *"Wherefore in all things it behooved him to be made like unto his brethren, that he might be a merciful and faithful high priest in things pertaining to God, to make reconciliation for the sins of the people"* (He.2:17).
73. *Some Blood Placed On The Cleansed Person's Right Ear, Thumb, And Toe During The Guilt Offering* (Le.14:10-20)	*Some blood placed on the cleansed person's right ear, thumb, and toe symbolized that the person's whole being was cleansed and dedicated to God through the blood of the sacrifice:* 1. *He was dedicating his ear to listen to the voice of God and to allow God to guide him day by day.* 2. *He was dedicating his thumb or hand to serve God as he labored day by day.* 3. *He was dedicating his toe or feet to walk where God wanted him to walk, following God day by day.* **"And the priest shall take *some* of the blood of the trespass offering, and the priest shall put *it* upon the tip of the right ear of him that is to be cleansed, and upon the thumb of his right hand, and upon the great toe of his right foot"** (Le.14:14).	When we come to God through the sacrifice of the Lord Jesus Christ, we are to dedicate our whole beings to God. • We are to dedicate our ears to God, listening only to the voice of God and to the things of righteousness. We are not to listen to the voices of this world, not to the foul language, immoral talk, off-colored jokes, false teachings, and worldly philosophies. We are to listen only to those things that will build up and benefit ourselves and society. • We are to dedicate our thumbs and hands to serve God in our work, play, and activities throughout the day. We are only to touch and handle the things of righteousness. We are not to touch the things of unrighteousness. • We are to dedicate our toes or feet to God. We are to go only where He	*"For Moses had said, Consecrate yourselves to day to the LORD, even every man upon his son, and upon his brother; that he may bestow upon you a blessing this day"* (Ex.32:29). *"The gold for things of gold, and the silver for things of silver, and for all manner of work to be made by the hands of artificers. And who then is willing to consecrate his service this day unto the LORD?"* (1 Chr.29:5). *"My son, give me thine heart, and let thine eyes observe my ways"* (Pr.23:26). *"I beseech you therefore, brethren, by the mercies of God, that ye present your bodies a living sacrifice, holy, acceptable unto God, which is your reasonable service"* (Ro.12:1). *"But what things were gain to me, those I counted loss for Christ. Yea doubtless, and I count all things but loss for the excellency of the knowledge of Christ Jesus my Lord: for whom I have suffered the loss of all*

Historical Term	Type or Picture (Scriptural Basis for Each)	Life Application for Today's Believer	Biblical Application
Some Blood Placed On The Cleansed Person's Right Ear, Thumb, And Toe During The Guilt Offering (continued) (Le.14:10-20)		would want us to go. We are not to walk into the bright lights and places of sinful behavior. We are to walk only into the places that will build up and benefit us and society.	*things, and do count them but dung, that I may win Christ" (Ph.3:7-8).*
74. *Oil* (Le.14:16-18)	*Oil is a symbol of the Holy Spirit and of God's strength and guidance throughout the Scripture. This is symbolized in two ways:* 1. *The oil that was sprinkled before the Lord seven times was symbolizing the request for God's complete, perfect strength and guidance.* 2. *The oil that was then placed upon the cleansed person was symbolizing that the person was being infused with the Spirit of God. He was being given the complete, perfect strength and guidance of God's Spirit as he walked day by day. He needed a special infusion of God's Spirit and strength just in case some people still rejected him because of his infectious disease. They possibly would not believe that he was fully cleansed. Only God's strength could overcome the sense of rejection and isolation that the diseased person might sense.* **"And the priest shall dip his right finger in the oil that *is* in his left hand, and shall sprinkle of the oil with his finger seven times before the LORD: And of the rest of the oil that *is* in his hand shall the priest put upon the tip of the right ear of him that is to be cleansed, and upon the thumb of his right hand, and upon the great toe of his right foot, upon the blood of the trespass offering: And the remnant of the oil that *is* in the priest's hand he shall pour upon the head of him that is to be cleansed: and the priest shall make an**	When a person has been infected with the disease of sin—especially for a long time—he often needs a special infusion of God's Spirit. He needs the strength and guidance of God's Spirit to combat whatever rejection and ridicule might be thrown against him by his former worldly friends. He needs God's strength and guidance to combat the onslaught of trials and temptation that will confront him day by day.	*"But ye shall receive power, after that the Holy Ghost is come upon you: and ye shall be witnesses unto me both in Jerusalem, and in all Judaea, and in Samaria, and unto the uttermost part of the earth" (Ac.1:8).* *"Then he answered and spake unto me, saying, This is the word of the LORD unto Zerubbabel, saying, Not by might, nor by power, but by my spirit, saith the LORD of hosts" (Zec.4:6).* *"And I will put my spirit within you, and cause you to walk in my statutes, and ye shall keep my judgments, and do them" (Eze.36:27).* *"Even the Spirit of truth; whom the world cannot receive, because it seeth him not, neither knoweth him: but ye know him; for he dwelleth with you, and shall be in you" (Jn.14:17).* *"For the bread of God is he which cometh down from heaven, and giveth life unto the world" (Jn.6:33).* *"But if the Spirit of him that raised up Jesus from the dead dwell in you, he that raised up Christ from the dead shall also quicken your mortal bodies by his Spirit that dwelleth in you" (Ro.8:11).* *"Who also hath made us able ministers of the new testament; not of the letter, but of the spirit: for the letter killeth, but the spirit giveth life" (2 Co.3:6).* *"Howbeit when he, the Spirit of truth, is come, he will guide you into all truth: for he shall not speak of himself; but whatsoever he shall hear, that shall he speak: and he will show you things to come" (Jn.16:13).*

Historical Term	Type or Picture (Scriptural Basis for Each)	Life Application for Today's Believer	Biblical Application
Oil *(continued)* (Le.14:16-18)	**atonement for him before the LORD"** (Le.14:16-18).		
75. *The Cleansing Of Mildew In Houses* (Le.14:33-53)	*The cleansing of mildew in houses is a symbol of sin in houses or within one's environment* **"When ye be come into the land of Canaan, which I give to you for a possession, and I put the plague of leprosy in a house of the land of your possession"** (Le.14:34).	Believers—in fact, every human being—should naturally keep their houses and their environment clean. No believer is to allow sin nor do sinful things within his house or environment. His house is to be dedicated to God. If sinful behavior is found within the house or environment of the believer, he needs to go before God and ask God for His cleansing power. God has the power to cleanse any of our homes; He even has the power to cleanse our environment.	*"Depart ye, depart ye, go ye out from thence, touch no unclean thing; go ye out of the midst of her; be ye clean, that bear the vessels of the LORD"* (Is.52:11). *"If ye were of the world, the world would love his own: but because ye are not of the world, but I have chosen you out of the world, therefore the world hateth you"* (Jn.15:19). *"And with many other words did he testify and exhort, saying, Save yourselves from this untoward generation"* (Ac.2:40). *"Be ye not unequally yoked together with unbelievers: for what fellowship hath righteousness with unrighteousness? and what communion hath light with darkness? And what concord hath Christ with Belial? or what part hath he that believeth with an infidel? And what agreement hath the temple of God with idols? for ye are the temple of the living God; as God hath said, I will dwell in them, and walk in them; and I will be their God, and they shall be my people"* (2 Co.6:14-16). *"Wherefore come out from among them, and be ye separate, saith the Lord, and touch not the unclean thing; and I will receive you, And will be a Father unto you, and ye shall be my sons and daughters, saith the Lord Almighty"* (2 Co.6:17-18).
76. *Laws That Protected & Cleansed People From Sexual Diseases and Impurity* (Le.15:1-33)	*These laws symbolize how defiling sexual sin is and the need to be cleansed.* **"Thus shall ye separate the children of Israel from their uncleanness; that they die not in their uncleanness, when they defile my tabernacle that is among them"** (Le.15:31).	God cares about the sexual behavior of His people. He wants them sexually healthy, free from venereal or sexual disease. He wants them living moral, pure, and clean lives. He wants His people to handle sex with appreciation and enjoyment, but with honor and respect, and always keeping sex pure within marriage. Sex is only for husband and wife, given as a gift to them and only to them.	*"For ye know what commandments we gave you by the Lord Jesus. For this is the will of God, even your sanctification, that ye should abstain from fornication: That every one of you should know how to possess his vessel in sanctification and honour; Not in the lust of concupiscence, even as the Gentiles which know not God"*(1 Th.4:2-5). *"Flee fornication. Every sin that a man doeth is*

Historical Term	Type or Picture (Scriptural Basis for Each)	Life Application for Today's Believer	Biblical Application
Laws That Protected & Cleansed People From Sexual Diseases and Impurity (continued) (Le.15:1-33)			*without the body; but he that committeth fornication sinneth against his own body" (1 Co.6:18).* *"Mortify therefore your members which are upon the earth; fornication, un-cleanness, inordinate affec-tion, evil concupiscence, and covetousness, which is idolatry" (Col.3:5).*
77. *Washing Clothes And Bathing In Water For The Bodily Discharges And Cleansing Of Men And Women* (Le.15:2-18; 19-30)	*Washing clothes and bath-ing in water is a symbol of being cleansed through Christ, the water of life.* **"Speak unto the chil-dren of Israel, and say unto them, When any man hath a running issue out of his flesh, because of his is-sue he is unclean"** (Le.15:2). **"And if a woman have an issue, *and* her issue in her flesh be blood, she shall be put apart seven days: and whosoever toucheth her shall be un-clean until the even"** (Le.15:19).	A sexually impure person must come to Jesus Christ for washing and cleansing. He or she needs to be cleansed from sin and rec-onciled with God. Immoral-ity—sexual impurity—sepa-rates and alienates a person from God. A person who is sexually impure must ap-proach God through Jesus Christ for reconciliation and forgiveness of sins.	*"And all things are of God, who hath reconciled us to himself by Jesus Christ, and hath given to us the ministry of reconcilia-tion; To wit, that God was in Christ, reconciling the world unto himself, not im-puting their trespasses unto them; and hath committed unto us the word of recon-ciliation. Now then we are ambassadors for Christ, as though God did beseech you by us: we pray you in Christ's stead, be ye recon-ciled to God"(2 Co.5:18-20).* *"For God sent not his Son into the world to con-demn the world; but that the world through him might be saved" (Jn.3:17).* *"In whom we have re-demption through his blood, the forgiveness of sins, ac-cording to the riches of his grace" (Ep.1:7).* *"Who his own self bare our sins in his own body on the tree, that we, being dead to sins, should live unto right-eousness: by whose stripes ye were healed" (1 Pe.2:24).* *"For Christ also hath once suffered for sins, the just for the unjust, that he might bring us to God, be-ing put to death in the flesh, but quickened by the Spirit" (1 Pe.3:18).*
78. *The Person Who Suf-fered From A Sexual Disease: Defiled Any Clay Pot Or Wood He Touched. The Item Had To Be Washed And Cleansed With Water* (Le.15:12)	*This is a symbol of the defil-ing, polluting nature of sin. The washing and cleansing of the pot or wood is a sym-bol of Christ cleansing all things. Any clay pot or wood that was defiled [touched] by an unclean person had to be rinsed with water.*	It is the blood of Jesus Christ that cleanses us from the defilement of sin. His blood cleanses us from all things, no matter how terri-ble the sin—if we just repent and confess our sins.	*"For this is my blood of the new testament, which is shed for many for the remission of sins"* (Mt.26:28). *"In whom we have re-demption through his blood, the forgiveness of sins, ac-cording to the riches of his grace" (Ep.1:7).* *"If we confess our sins, he is faithful and just to*

Historical Term	Type or Picture (Scriptural Basis for Each)	Life Application for Today's Believer	Biblical Application
The Person Who Suffered From A Sexual Disease: Defiled Any Clay Pot Or Wood He Touched. The Item Had To Be Washed And Cleansed With Water (Le.15:12)	**"And the vessel of earth, that he toucheth which hath the issue, shall be broken: and every vessel of wood shall be rinsed in water" (Le.15:12).**		*forgive us our sins, and to cleanse us from all un-righteousness." (1 Jn.1:9)*
79. *The Cleansing Of A Person From Sexual Impurity. He Had To Wash His Clothes and Himself With Fresh Water For Seven Days* (Le.15:13)	*Washing with water for seven days is a symbol of complete and full cleansing.* **"And when he that hath an issue is cleansed of his issue; then he shall number to himself seven days for his cleansing, and wash his clothes, and bathe his flesh in running water, and shall be clean" (Le.15:13).**	The believer has absolute confidence in the cleansing power of Christ. He knows that *God will* forgive Him—completely and fully. God will complete the work He began in him.	*"Who forgiveth all thine iniquities; who healeth all thy diseases" (Ps.103:3).* *"Be it known unto you therefore, men and brethren, that through this man is preached unto you the forgiveness of sins" (Ac.13:38).* *"Being confident of this very thing, that he which hath begun a good work in you will perform it until the day of Jesus Christ" (Phil.1:6).* *"Jesus saith unto them, My meat is to do the will of him that sent me, and to finish his work" (Jn.4:34).* *"I have glorified thee on the earth: I have finished the work which thou gavest me to do" (Jn.17:4).*
80. *A Sacrifice Of Two Doves Or Two Young Pigeons* (Le.15:14-15)	*A sacrifice of two doves or two young pigeons on the eighth day is a symbol of Christ cleansing a man from sexual impurity. Note how clearly the sacrifice symbolizes Jesus Christ. Christ died as our substitute: in our behalf, in our stead, in our place. He died to cleanse a person from sexual impurity.* **"And on the eighth day he shall take to him two turtledoves, or two young pigeons, and come before the LORD unto the door of the tabernacle of the congregation, and give them unto the priest" (Le.15:14).**	There is only one way any of us can be forgiven—whether priest, minister, or layperson: we must present ourselves to God in the substitute sacrifice, in the Lord Jesus Christ. Christ is the only sacrifice acceptable to God. He is the only sacrifice that can cleanse a person from sexual sin. Forgiveness of sins comes only through Him: He is the one and only acceptable sacrifice.	*"For he hath made him to be sin for us, who knew no sin; that we might be made the righteousness of God in him" (2 Co.5:21).* *"To whom it [righteousness] shall be imputed, if we believe on him that raised up Jesus our Lord from the dead; who was delivered for our offences, and was raised again for our justification" (Ro.4:24-25).*
81. *The Normal Bodily Discharges [Excretion] Of A Man: Had To Bathe With Water* (Le.15:16)	*Bathing with water is a symbol of being cleansed from disease in Christ, the water of life.* **"And if any man's seed of copulation go out from him, then he shall wash all his flesh in water, and be unclean until the even" (Le.15:16).**	It is the shed blood of Jesus Christ that washes the believer and cleanses him from the stain of sin.	*"Wash me throughly from mine iniquity, and cleanse me from my sin" (Ps.51:2).* *"Purge me with hyssop, and I shall be clean: wash me, and I shall be whiter than snow" (Ps.51:7).* *"There is a generation that are pure in their own eyes, and yet is not washed from their filthiness" (Pr.30:12).*

Historical Term	Type or Picture (Scriptural Basis for Each)	Life Application for Today's Believer	Biblical Application
The Normal Bodily Discharges [Excretion] Of A Man: Had To Bathe With Water (continued) (Le.15:16)			*"Jesus saith to him, He that is washed needeth not save to wash his feet, but is clean every whit: and ye are clean, but not all"* (Jn.13:10).
82. *Clothing With Semen On It: Had To Be Washed With Water* (Le.15:17)	*Washing soiled clothes with water is a symbol of being clothed with purity.* **"And every garment, and every skin, whereon is the seed of copulation, shall be washed with water, and be unclean until the even"** (Le.15:17).	God wants us to keep ourselves clean and pure, both physically and spiritually.	*"Let us draw near with a true heart in full assurance of faith, having our hearts sprinkled from an evil conscience, and our bodies washed with pure water"* (He.10:22). *"Wash you, make you clean; put away the evil of your doings from before mine eyes; cease to do evil"* (Is.1:16). *"Having therefore these promises, dearly beloved, let us cleanse ourselves from all filthiness of the flesh and spirit, perfecting holiness in the fear of God"* (2 Co.7:1).
83. *The Day Of Atonement* (Le.16:1-34. See also Le.23:27)	*The Day Of Atonement symbolizes the only way to approach God: through the shed blood of the atoning sacrifice of the Lord Jesus Christ. A person is forgiven his sins and reconciled to God only through the atoning sacrifice of Christ.* **"For on that day shall** *the priest* **make an atonement for you, to cleanse you,** *that* **ye may be clean from all your sins before the LORD"** (Le.16:30). **"Also on the tenth** *day* **of this seventh month** *there* **shall be a day of atonement: it shall be an holy convocation unto you; and ye shall afflict your souls, and offer an offering made by fire unto the LORD"** (Le.23:27).	The penalty for sin has been paid. How? By Jesus Christ. Jesus Christ died as our atoning sacrifice, reconciling us to God. Hanging upon the cross, Jesus Christ... • bore our sins, taking them away • allowed the justice and judgment of God to be executed against Him, suffering the punishment due us • paid the penalty of sin and death, bearing the alienation and separation from God for us	*"Having therefore, brethren, boldness to enter into the holiest by the blood of Jesus, By a new and living way, which he hath consecrated for us, through the veil, that is to say, his flesh; And having an high priest over the house of God; Let us draw near with a true heart in full assurance of faith, having our hearts sprinkled from an evil conscience, and our bodies washed with pure water"* (He.10:19-22). *"Therefore being justified by faith, we have peace with God through our Lord Jesus Christ: By whom also we have access by faith into this grace wherein we stand, and rejoice in hope of the glory of God"* (Ro.5:1-2).
84. *The High Priest* (Le.16:3-10; 16:11-14. See also Le. 21:10-15)	*The High Priest is a symbol of Jesus Christ. The High Priest himself had to approach God through the Sin Offering and Burnt Offering. He himself had to be cleansed from sin before he could make sacrifice for the sins of the people. Once his sins had been forgiven, he stood sinless and perfect before God: he was able to offer sacrifice for the sins of the people. This is a symbol of Jesus Christ, the High*	Sin has separated and alienated man from God. Sin has created a veil, a curtain, between God and man. The curtain of sin cannot be removed by man, no matter how much he tries. No matter how righteous man seeks to be, his righteousness cannot break through the curtain of sin that separates him and God. But thank God! Jesus Christ—our Great High Priest—has ripped the curtain of sin	*"But your iniquities have separated between you and your God, and your sins have hid his face from you, that he will not hear"* (Is.59:2). *"Jesus, when he had cried again with a loud voice, yielded up the ghost. And, behold, the veil of the temple was rent in twain from the top to the bottom; and the earth did quake, and the rocks rent"* (Mt.27:50-51).

Historical Term	Type or Picture (Scriptural Basis for Each)	Life Application for Today's Believer	Biblical Application
The High Priest (continued) (Le.16:3-10; 16:11-14. See also Le.21:10-15)	*Priest of God, who stood sinless and perfect before God, offering Himself as the sacrifice for sin.* **"Thus shall Aaron come into the holy *place*: with a young bullock for a sin offering, and a ram for a burnt offering"** (Le.16:3). **"And Aaron shall offer his bullock of the sin offering, which *is* for himself, and make an atonement for himself, and for his house"** (Le.16:6).	from top to bottom, opening the way into God's presence. Man now has access into the presence of God. All of us—without exception—can now enter the presence of God, all because of what Jesus Christ has done.	*"Having therefore, brethren, boldness to enter into the holiest by the blood of Jesus, By a new and living way, which he hath consecrated for us, through the veil, that is to say, his flesh; And having an high priest over the house of God; Let us draw near with a true heart in full assurance of faith, having our hearts sprinkled from an evil conscience, and our bodies washed with pure water"* (He.10:19-22).
85. *The Pure White Linen Clothing Of The High Priest* (Le.16:3-10)	*The pure white linen clothing of the high priest symbolized the clothing of righteousness, the righteousness of Jesus Christ.* **"He shall put on the holy linen coat, and he shall have the linen breeches upon his flesh, and shall be girded with a linen girdle, and with the linen mitre shall he be attired: these *are* holy garments; therefore shall he wash his flesh in water, and *so* put them on"** (Le.16:4).	Jesus Christ stands before God clothed in perfect righteousness. As perfect, His righteousness is the Ideal righteousness, the Pattern of all righteousness. As the Ideal and Pattern, His righteousness can cover all men everywhere and present them righteous before God. No person stands before God in his own righteousness: he can stand before God only in the righteousness of Jesus Christ.	*"For Christ is the end of the law for righteousness to every one that believeth"* (Ro.10:4). *"But of him are ye in Christ Jesus, who of God is made unto us wisdom, and righteousness, and sanctification, and redemption"* (1 Co.1:30). *"For he hath made him to be sin for us, who knew no sin; that we might be made the righteousness of God in him"* (2 Co.5:21). *"And be found in him, not having mine own righteousness, which is of the law, but that which is through the faith of Christ, the righteousness which is of God by faith"* (Ph.3:9).
86. *The Scapegoat: Symbolized the Removal and Taking Away of Sin* (Le.16:3-10; 16:20-22. See also Le. 3:12-16)	*The scapegoat (the goat that was sent away alive bearing the sins of the people) symbolized the removal and taking away of sin—all through the atoning sacrifice of Christ.* **"And Aaron shall bring the goat upon which the LORD'S lot fell, and offer him *for* a sin offering. But the goat, on which the lot fell to be the scapegoat, shall be presented alive before the LORD, to make an atonement with him, *and* to let him go for a scapegoat into the wilderness"** (Le.16:9-10).	It is Jesus Christ who has forgiven our sins. It is Jesus Christ who bore the sins of the world and who removes and takes them away—far, far away.	*"Who gave himself for our sins, that he might deliver us from this present evil world, according to the will of God and our Father"* (Ga.1:4). *"Who gave himself for us, that he might redeem us from all iniquity, and purify unto himself a peculiar people, zealous of good works"* (Tit.2:14). *"For Christ also hath once suffered for sins, the just for the unjust, that he might bring us to God, being put to death in the flesh, but quickened by the Spirit"* (1 Pe.3:18). *"So Christ was once offered to bear the sins of many; and unto them that look for him shall he appear the second time without sin unto salvation"* (He.9:28). *"Who his own self bare our sins in his own body on*

Historical Term	Type or Picture (Scriptural Basis for Each)	Life Application for Today's Believer	Biblical Application
The Scapegoat: Symbolized the Removal and Taking Away of Sin (continued) (Le.16:3-10; 16:20-22. See also Le.3:12-16)			*the tree, that we, being dead to sins, should live unto righteousness: by whose stripes ye were healed" (1 Pe.2:24).*
87. *The Sprinkling Of The Atonement Cover Or Mercy Seat Of The Ark Seven Times: With The Shed Blood Of The Sacrifice* (Le.16:11-14)	*In this act, the High Priest was symbolizing that a full, perfect mercy and forgiveness was being made for the sins of the people. Remember, the number seven in Scripture symbolizes fullness, completion, perfection.* **"And he shall take of the blood of the bullock, and sprinkle it with his finger upon the mercy seat eastward; and before the mercy seat shall he sprinkle of the blood with his finger seven times" (Le.16:14).**	Jesus Christ lived a sinless life, securing righteousness and perfection for man. Therefore He could stand before God sinless and perfect, offering Himself as the substitute sacrifice for the sins of man. This He did.	*"For he hath made him to be sin for us, who knew no sin; that we might be made the righteousness of God in him" (2 Co.5:21).* *"For we have not an high priest which cannot be touched with the feeling of our infirmities; but was in all points tempted like as we are, yet without sin" (He.4:15).* *"For such an high priest became us, who is holy, harmless, undefiled, separate from sinners, and made higher than the heavens" (He.7:26).* *"Forasmuch as ye know that ye were not redeemed with corruptible things, as silver and gold, from your vain conversation received by tradition from your fathers; But with the precious blood of Christ, as of a lamb without blemish and without spot" (1 Pe.1:18-19).* *"Who did no sin, neither was guile found in his mouth" (1 Pe.2:22).*
88. *The Only Person [The High Priest] Who Could Secure Atonement For The People* (Le.16:17)	*The only person [The High Priest] who could secure atonement for the people symbolized that Christ alone can make atonement for man; He alone can reconcile a person to God.* **"And there shall be no man in the tabernacle of the congregation when he goeth in to make an atonement in the holy place, until he come out, and have made an atonement for himself, and for his household, and for all the congregation of Israel" (Le.16:17).**	Jesus Christ—our High Priest—is the only One who can make atonement for us. Christ and Christ alone can reconcile a person to God.	*"Wherefore in all things it behooved him to be made like unto his brethren, that he might be a merciful and faithful high priest in things pertaining to God, to make reconciliation for the sins of the people" (He.2:17).* *"Seeing then that we have a great high priest, that is passed into the heavens, Jesus the Son of God, let us hold fast our profession. For we have not an high priest which cannot be touched with the feeling of our infirmities; but was in all points tempted like as we are, yet without sin" (He.4:14-15).* *"Whither the forerunner is for us entered, even Jesus, made an high priest for ever after the order of Melchisedec" (He.6:20).* *"For such an high priest became us, who is holy, harmless, undefiled,*

Historical Term	Type or Picture (Scriptural Basis for Each)	Life Application for Today's Believer	Biblical Application
The Only Person [The High Priest] Who Could Secure Atonement For The People (continued) (Le.16:17)			*separate from sinners, and made higher than the heavens" (He.7:26).* *Now of the things which we have spoken this is the sum: We have such an high priest, who is set on the right hand of the throne of the Majesty in the heavens" (He.8:1).*
89. *Atonement Being Made For The Altar Of Burnt Offering By Sprinkling Blood On The Altar Seven Times (Le.16:18-19)*	*Sprinkling blood on the altar of Burnt Offering seven times is a symbol of a full, perfect cleansing: The High Priest was to take some blood from the bull and from the goat and put it on the horns of the altar (v.18). He was then to sprinkle blood on the altar seven times, symbolizing that a full, perfect cleansing was being made. The altar was being cleansed for the same reason that the Mercy Seat had been cleansed: the sins of the people had contaminated the entire Tabernacle and its furnishings.* **"And he shall sprinkle of the blood upon it with his finger seven times, and cleanse it, and hallow it from the uncleanness of the children of Israel" (Le.16:19).**	There were insincere, hypocritical people who approached God in that day just as there are today. Insincere, hypocritical people do not have their sins forgiven. In fact, their hypocrisy contaminates their very approach to God. The same was true of insincere, hypocritical Israelites who approached God with their sacrifices. Their hypocrisy contaminated the very Tabernacle and altar upon which they made their sacrifices. The point is obvious: everything contaminated by sin has to be cleansed by the blood of Christ before God can forgive sins.	**"Take heed therefore unto yourselves, and to all the flock, over the which the Holy Ghost hath made you overseers, to feed the church of God, which he hath purchased with his own blood" (Ac.20:28; see Mt.26:28).** **"Much more then, being now justified by his blood, we shall be saved from wrath through him" (Ro.5:9).** **"How much more shall the blood of Christ, who through the eternal Spirit offered himself without spot to God, purge your conscience from dead works to serve the living God?" (He.9:14).** **"Forasmuch as ye know that ye were not redeemed with corruptible things, as silver and gold, from your vain conversation received by tradition from your fathers; But with the precious blood of Christ, as of a lamb without blemish and without spot" (1 Pe.1:18-19).**
90. *The Goat That Was Slaughtered For The Sin Offering Of The People (Le.16:15. See also Le. 3:12-16)*	*The goat that was put to death is a symbol of the death of Christ.* **"Then shall he kill the goat of the sin offering, that is for the people, and bring his blood within the vail, and do with that blood as he did with the blood of the bullock, and sprinkle it upon the mercy seat, and before the mercy seat" (Le.16:15).**	Jesus Christ gave Himself as an offering and sacrifice to God so that we might be forgiven our sins. Jesus Christ died as the perfect offering for sin. His death cleanses everything contaminated by sin. Just keep in mind, it was the blood that made sacrifice for sin; it was not the Tabernacle nor any of the furnishings within the Tabernacle. Thus it is with Christ: it is Christ, His blood, that is important and that cleanses from sin.	**"And walk in love, as Christ also hath loved us, and hath given himself for us an offering and a sacrifice to God for a sweetsmelling savour" (Ep.5:2).** **"Who gave himself for us, that he might redeem us from all iniquity, and purify unto himself a peculiar people, zealous of good works" (Tit.2:14).** **"Who gave himself for our sins, that he might deliver us from this present evil world, according to the will of God and our Father" (Ga.1:4).** **"But he was wounded for our transgressions, he was bruised for our iniquities: the chastisement of our peace was upon him; and with his stripes we are healed" (Is.53:5).**

Historical Term	Type or Picture (Scriptural Basis for Each)	Life Application for Today's Believer	Biblical Application
91. *The Tabernacle And Its Worship* (Le.17:3-9)	*The Tabernacle and its worship symbolized the coming of the Savior of the world and the great sacrifice He was to make upon the cross for the world.* **"And thou shalt say unto them, Whatsoever man** *there be* **of the house of Israel, or of the strangers which sojourn among you, that offereth a burnt offering of sacrifice, And bringeth it not unto the door of the tabernacle of the congregation, to offer it unto the LORD; even that man shall be cut off from among his people"** (Le.17:8-9).	There was only one place that God wanted people approaching Him, the place appointed by Him. For the Israelites, that place was the Tabernacle. For us, that place is the Lord Jesus Christ Himself. Jesus Christ is the fulfillment of the Tabernacle. When a person approaches God, he must approach God at the designated place appointed by God; at the foot of the cross of His Son, the Lord Jesus Christ.	*"For God so loved the world, that he gave his only begotten Son, that whosoever believeth in him should not perish, but have everlasting life"* (Jn.3:16). *"I said therefore unto you, that ye shall die in your sins: for if ye believe not that I am he, ye shall die in your sins"* (Jn.8:24). *"Jesus saith unto him, I am the way, the truth, and the life: no man cometh unto the Father, but by me"* (Jn.14:6). *"Neither is there salvation in any other: for there is none other name under heaven given among men, whereby we must be saved"* (Ac.4:12). *"That if thou shalt confess with thy mouth the Lord Jesus, and shalt believe in thine heart that God hath raised him from the dead, thou shalt be saved. For with the heart man believeth unto righteousness; and with the mouth confession is made unto salvation"* (Ro.10:9-10).
92. *The Sacrifice Of The Fellowship and Peace Offering* (Le.19:5)	*The sacrifice of the Fellowship or Peace Offering is a symbol of Christ and His sacrifice upon the cross. By His sacrifice a believer is able to grow in the peace and fellowship of God.* **"And if ye offer a sacrifice of peace offerings unto the LORD, ye shall offer it at your own will"** (Le.19:5).	The believer must seek to grow in the peace and fellowship of God thru the sacrifice of the Lord Jesus Christ.	*"That which we have seen and heard declare we unto you, that ye also may have fellowship with us: and truly our fellowship is with the Father, and with his Son Jesus Christ"* (1 Jn.1:3). *"The LORD is nigh unto them that are of a broken heart; and saveth such as be of a contrite spirit"* (Ps.34:18). *"The LORD is nigh unto all them that call upon him, to all that call upon him in truth"* (Ps.145:18). *"Therefore being justified by faith, we have peace with God through our Lord Jesus Christ: By whom also we have access by faith into this grace wherein we stand, and rejoice in hope of the glory of God"* (Ro.5:1-2).
93. *Keeping God's Laws And Living A Life Of Total Separation, A Life That Is Distinct And Different From The Immoral And Lawless Of This World* (Le.19:19)	*Keeping God's laws and living a life of total separation is a symbol of not being mixed with the things of the world. This commandment was symbolized by keeping all things separate in the daily lives of God's people.*	Note the great lessons of this symbol: There was to be... • no mixture of truth and error • no mixture of godliness and ungodliness • no mixture of morality and immorality	*"Wherefore come out from among them, and be ye separate, saith the Lord, and touch not the unclean thing; and I will receive you"* (2 Co.6:17). *"And have no fellowship with the unfruitful works of*

Historical Term	Type or Picture (Scriptural Basis for Each)	Life Application for Today's Believer	Biblical Application
Keeping God's Laws And Living A Life Of Total Separation, A Life That Is Distinct And Different From The Immoral And Lawless Of This World (continued) (Le.19:19)	*The truth of spiritual separation was driven into their hearts and minds through everything they did. God wanted His people separated, set apart to Him and not to the world and its sinful ways. Therefore God commanded...* • *that there be no cross-breeding of animals* • *that there be no mixing of seed when sowing a field* • *that no person wear any clothing woven of two kinds of material* **"Ye shall keep my statutes. Thou shalt not let thy cattle gender with a diverse kind: thou shalt not sow thy field with mingled seed: neither shall a garment mingled of linen and woollen come upon thee"** (Le.19:19).	This law was to protect God's people from becoming mixed with the immoral and lawless people of this world. God's people were to remain distinct and different, totally separated and set apart to God.	*darkness, but rather reprove them" (Ep.5:11).* *"I beseech you therefore, brethren, by the mercies of God, that ye present your bodies a living sacrifice, holy, acceptable unto God, which is your reasonable service. And be not conformed to this world: but be ye transformed by the renewing of your mind, that ye may prove what is that good, and acceptable, and perfect, will of God" (Ro.12:1-2).* *"Love not the world, neither the things that are in the world. If any man love the world, the love of the Father is not in him. For all that is in the world, the lust of the flesh, and the lust of the eyes, and the pride of life, is not of the Father, but is of the world" (1 Jn.2:15-16).*
94. *Foreigners Or Strangers In Egypt* (Le.19:33-34; See also Le. 11:44-47; Le, 22:33)	*Foreigners or strangers in Egypt is a picture of how God's people are to treat those who are different. They are to love people...* • *who are from another culture* • *who are of another race or color* • *who speak another language* • *who are of a different social status* **"But the stranger that dwelleth with you shall be unto you as one born among you, and thou shalt love him as thyself; for ye were strangers in the land of Egypt: I am the LORD your God"** (Le.19:34).	The picture teaches a strong lesson for all believers. Believers of all generations are to love those who are different, including foreigners. Believers are never to mistreat those who are different. Their love is to be as strong as the love for oneself. Why? Because the believer was an alien in Egypt (the world) before God freed him.	*"Love ye therefore the stranger: for ye were strangers in the land of Egypt" (De.10:19).* *"And the second is like unto it, Thou shalt love thy neighbour as thyself" (Mt.22:39).* *"By this shall all men know that ye are my disciples, if ye have love one to another" (Jn.13:35).* *"This is my commandment, That ye love one another, as I have loved you" (Jn.15:12).* *"Let love be without dissimulation. Abhor that which is evil; cleave to that which is good" (Ro.12:9).* *"And the Lord make you to increase and abound in love one toward another, and toward all men, even as we do toward you" (1 Th.3:12).*
95. *The Promised Land* (Le.20:24)	*The promised land is a symbol of heaven, of the new heavens and earth. God has set apart the obedient to be His people and to inherit the promised land, the land that flows with milk and honey, the land that once belonged to the immoral and lawless of the world.* **"But I have said unto you, Ye shall inherit their**	The obedient person is the person who lives a life of separation, a life that is entirely different from the immoral and lawless people of the earth. It is the obedient who will receive the inheritance of God, the promised land that flows with milk and honey.	*"In my Father's house are many mansions: if it were not so, I would have told you. I go to prepare a place for you. And if I go and prepare a place for you, I will come again, and receive you unto myself; that where I am, there ye may be also." (Jn. 14:2-3)* *"For our conversation [citizenship] is in heaven; from whence also we look*

Historical Term	Type or Picture (Scriptural Basis for Each)	Life Application for Today's Believer	Biblical Application
The Promised Land (continued) (Le.20:24)	**land, and I will give it unto you to possess it, a land that floweth with milk and honey: I *am* the LORD your God, which have separated you from *other* people" (Le.20:24).**		*for the Saviour, the Lord Jesus Christ:"* (Ph.3:20; see 2 Co.5:1; 1 Pe.1:3-4; 2 Pe.3:10-13)
96. *The Perfect Priest, The Priest Without Any Deformity Or Defect* (Le.21:16-24)	*The Priest is a symbol of Jesus Christ, the perfect High Priest. Because the priest was to represent the perfection of the coming Savior, he was not allowed to serve as a priest if he had any deformity or physical defect whatsoever.* **"No man that hath a blemish of the seed of Aaron the priest shall come nigh to offer the offerings of the LORD made by fire: he hath a blemish; he shall not come nigh to offer the bread of his God" (Le.21:21).**	Any person who comes to God through the Lord Jesus Christ is accepted by God. The person is accepted by God because Jesus Christ stands before God as the perfect High Priest, interceding in behalf of the person. God accepts the person in Christ. Jesus Christ is the perfect, sinless High Priest and sacrifice who stands before God for the human race.	*"For he hath made him to be sin for us, who knew no sin; that we might be made the righteousness of God in him"* (2 Co.5:21). *"Seeing then that we have a great high priest, that is passed into the heavens, Jesus the Son of God, let us hold fast our profession. For we have not an high priest which cannot be touched with the feeling of our infirmities; but was in all points tempted like as we are, yet without sin"* (He. 4:14-15; see He.7:24-27).
97. *Dead, Overly Mourning For The* (Le.21:1-4)	*This law symbolized the need to focus upon life not death. The priest was allowed to show the utmost love, comfort, and hope by mourning for his immediate family and for a sister or brother who was dependent upon him. But he was not to defile himself by overly mourning for other relatives who died. This would interrupt his service for God, and this he was not allowed to do.* **"And the LORD said unto Moses, Speak unto the priests the sons of Aaron, and say unto them, There shall none be defiled for the dead among his people:" (Le.21:1).**	The believer is not to set his attention upon death but upon the One who gives life, the Lord Jesus Christ.	*"Verily, verily, I say unto you, He that heareth my word, and believeth on him that sent me, hath everlasting life, and shall not come into condemnation; but is passed from death unto life"* (Jn.5:24). *"The thief cometh not, but for to steal, and to kill, and to destroy: I am come that they might have life, and that they might have it more abundantly"* (Jn..10:10). *"Jesus saith unto him, I am the way, the truth, and the life: no man cometh unto the Father, but by me"* (Jn.14:6). *"He that hath the Son hath life; and he that hath not the Son of God hath not life"* (1 Jn.5:12).
98. *Defilement* (Le.22:1-9)	*Defilement is a symbol of sin, a symbol of being ceremonially and spiritually unclean. The picture is this: if a priest or minister sins, he becomes unclean, that is unfit to carry out the ministry of God.* **"Say unto them, Whosoever *he be* of all your seed among your generations, that goeth unto the holy things, which the children of Israel hallow**	The application is clear: the minister of God must treat the ministry with great respect. He must not abuse the ministry nor profane or shame God's name in the ministry.	*"But I keep under my body, and bring it into subjection: lest that by any means, when I have preached to others, I myself should be a castaway"* (1 Co.9:27). *"Take heed therefore unto yourselves, and to all the flock, over the which the Holy Ghost hath made you overseers, to feed the church of God, which he hath purchased with his own blood"* (Ac.20:28).

Historical Term	Type or Picture (Scriptural Basis for Each)	Life Application for Today's Believer	Biblical Application
Defilement (continued) (Le.22:1-9)	**unto the LORD, having his uncleanness upon him, that soul shall be cut off from my presence: I** *am* **the LORD" (Le.22:3).**		*"Be thou diligent to know the state of thy flocks, and look well to thy herds" (Pr.27:23).* *"Feed the flock of God which is among you, taking the oversight thereof, not by constraint, but willingly; not for filthy lucre, but of a ready mind" (1 Pe.5:2; see Pr.27:23; Je.3:15).*
99. *The Holy Food Of God* (Le.22:10-16)	*The holy food is a symbol of Christ the holy sacrifice or holy food of God. The sacrifice was holy in the sight of God—all of it, including the portion given to the priest as holy food.* **"There shall no stranger eat** *of* **the holy thing: a sojourner of the priest, or an hired servant, shall not eat** *of* **the holy thing" (Le.22:10).**	The sacrifice of Jesus Christ was presented to God as the holy, perfect sacrifice. This sacrifice is the perfect sacrifice offered to God on behalf of man. The minister of God must protect this message, that Jesus Christ is the holy, perfect sacrifice offered to God for the sins of the world.	*"The next day John seeth Jesus coming unto him, and saith, Behold the Lamb of God, which taketh away the sin of the world" (Jn.1:29; see Mt.28:19-20; mk.16:15).* *"And straightway he preached Christ in the synagogues, that he is the Son of God" (Ac.9:20).* *"And ye know that he was manifested to take away our sins; and in him is no sin" (1 Jn.3:5).*
100. *The Sabbath* (Le.23:3)	*The Sabbath is a symbol of the spiritual rest that God promises to those who believe and follow him. The Sabbath rest is a symbol of redemption, of God's deliverance from the heavy burdens and trials of this life.* **"Six days shall work be done: but the seventh day** *is* **the sabbath of rest, an holy convocation; ye shall do no work** *therein:* **it** *is* **the sabbath of the LORD in all your dwellings" (Le.23:3).**	The Sabbath is a picture of the perfect rest that Jesus Christ brings to a person. The Sabbath gives a person a day to rest and worship, but... • Jesus Christ gives a person rest itself, a complete rest, a perfect rest of mind and soul. • Jesus Christ gives a person the perfect assurance that we are acceptable to God. A person is to be faithful to worship and rest on the Sabbath, as God has ordained. It is only through obedience to God's command that we are able to receive the perfect rest that only God can give.	*"There remaineth therefore a rest to the people of God. For he that is entered into his rest, he also hath ceased from his own works, as God did from his. Let us labour therefore to enter into that rest, lest any man fall after the same example of unbelief" (He.4:9-11).* *"Come unto me, all ye that labour and are heavy laden, and I will give you rest" (Mt.11:28).* *"But they that wait upon the LORD shall renew their strength; they shall mount up with wings as eagles; they shall run, and not be weary; and they shall walk, and not faint" (Is.40:31).* *"For the Son of man is Lord even of the sabbath day" (Mt.12:8).*
101. *The Passover* (Le.23:5)	*The Passover is a symbol of Christ our Passover who was sacrificed for us.* **"In the fourteenth** *day* **of the first month at even** *is* **the LORD'S passover" (Le.23:5).**	Jesus Christ is the perfect fulfillment of the Passover Lamb that was slain in behalf of God's people. Through the blood of Jesus Christ, a person escapes the judgment of God. God accepts the blood of His Son—the blood of the substitute sacrifice—as full payment for a person's sin and rebellion against God.	*"The next day John seeth Jesus coming unto him, and saith, Behold the Lamb of God, which taketh away the sin of the world" (Jn.1:29).* *"...For even Christ our passover is sacrificed for us" (1 Co.5:7).* *"He was oppressed, and he was afflicted, yet he opened not his mouth: he is brought as a lamb to the slaughter, and as a sheep before her shearers is*

Historical Term	Type or Picture (Scriptural Basis for Each)	Life Application for Today's Believer	Biblical Application
The Passover (continued) (Le.23:5)			*dumb, so he openeth not his mouth" (Is.53:7).* "Who gave himself for our sins, that he might deliver us from this present evil world, according to the will of God and our Father" (Ga.1:4).
102. *The Festival Of Unleavened Bread* (Le.23:6)	*The Feast or Festival of Unleavened Bread symbolizes the need for a person to be free from the world and its enslavement to sin and death, the urgency for a person to begin the march to the promised land.* **And on the fifteenth day of the same month is the feast of unleavened bread unto the LORD: seven days ye must eat unleavened bread" (Le.23:6).**	There is a need—an urgent, desperate need— to be delivered from all the oppression and pollution of this world, from all the sin and evil, immorality and lawlessness, corruption and death of this world. There is a need and urgency to be set free and liberated to live for God, a desperate need and urgency to begin the march to the promise land of heaven.	"...behold, now is the day of salvation (2 Co.6:2). "Seek ye the LORD while he may be found, call ye upon him while he is near" (Is.55:6). "But this I say, brethren, the time is short: it remaineth, that both they that have wives be as though they had none" (1 Co.7:29). "For our conversation [citizenship] is in heaven; from whence also we look for the Saviour, the Lord Jesus Christ" (Ph.3:20; see 2 Ti.4:8).
103. *The Festival Of Firstfruits* (Le.23:9-14)	*The Festival Of Firstfruits is a symbol of Christ's resurrection: He is the first of the harvest, the first to arise from the dead.* **"Speak unto the children of Israel, and say unto them, When ye be come into the land which I give unto you, and shall reap the harvest thereof, then ye shall bring a sheaf of the firstfruits of your harvest unto the priest" (Le.23:10).**	Christ is the first of the harvest, the first to arise from the dead. It is Jesus Christ and His resurrection that gives the believer hope of arising from the dead and living eternally with God. The prophetic picture of salvation is this: the Passover symbolized the believers deliverance or redemption from the world; the Festival of Unleavened Bread symbolized the urgency of the believer to leave the world and begin his march to the promise land; and now, the Festival of Firstfruits symbolizes the glorious hope the believer has as he marches toward the promise land, the hope of being raised from the dead and living eternally with God—all because of the resurrection of Christ.	"That Christ should suffer, and that he should be the first that should rise from the dead, and should show light unto the people, and to the Gentiles" (Ac.26:23). "But now is Christ risen from the dead, and become the firstfruits of them that slept. For since by man came death, by man came also the resurrection of the dead. For as in Adam all die, even so in Christ shall all be made alive. But every man in his own order: Christ the firstfruits; afterward they that are Christ's at his coming" (1 Co. 15:20-23). "Knowing that he which raised up the Lord Jesus shall raise up us also by Jesus, and shall present us with you" (2 Co.4:14). "Blessed be the God and Father of our Lord Jesus Christ, which according to his abundant mercy hath begotten us again unto a lively hope by the resurrection of Jesus Christ from the dead, To an inheritance incorruptible, and undefiled, and that fadeth not away, reserved in heaven for you" (1 Pe.1:3-4).

Historical Term	Type or Picture (Scriptural Basis for Each)	Life Application for Today's Believer	Biblical Application
104. *The Aroma Of The Burning Sacrifice And Grain Offering That Ascending Up: During The Festival Of Firstfruits* (Le.23:13)	*The aroma of the burning sacrifice and Grain Offering symbolized God's acceptance. He was pleased with the aroma of the sacrifice, the obedience of the people.* **"And the meat offering thereof** *shall be* **two tenth deals of fine flour mingled with oil, an offering made by fire unto the LORD** *for* **a sweet savour: and the drink offering thereof** *shall be* **of wine, the fourth** *part* **of an hin"** (Le.23:13).	What can we do to please God? We must… ⇒ approach God as He says, approach Him through the sacrifice of the Lord Jesus Christ ⇒ commit ourselves to God, thanking Him for the atoning sacrifice of Christ, for so great a salvation	*"This day the LORD thy God hath commanded thee to do these statutes and judgments: thou shalt therefore keep and do them with all thine heart, and with all thy soul"* (De.26:16). *"And Samuel said, Hath the LORD as great delight in burnt offerings and sacrifices, as in obeying the voice of the Lord? Behold, to obey is better than sacrifice, and to hearken than the fat of rams"* (1 S. 15:22). *"Not every one that saith unto me, Lord, Lord, shall enter into the kingdom of heaven; but he that doeth the will of my Father which is in heaven"* (Mt.7:21).
105. *The Festival Of Harvest Or Pentecost* (Le.23:15-22)	*The Festival of Harvest or Pentecost is a symbol of Pentecost, of the great harvest of souls and of people giving their lives to God. The Festival of Harvest symbolized the great day of Pentecost that took place fifty days after the resurrection of Christ, the great day when the Holy Spirit came upon the disciples and gave a great harvest of souls.* **"Even unto the morrow after the seventh sabbath shall ye number fifty days; and ye shall offer a new meat offering unto the LORD"** (Le.23:16).	As the believer marches to the Promised Land, he is to be filled with God's Spirit and bear strong testimony, seeking a great harvest of souls.	*"And when the day of Pentecost was fully come, they were all with one accord in one place. And suddenly there came a sound from heaven as of a rushing mighty wind, and it filled all the house where they were sitting. And there appeared unto them cloven tongues like as of fire, and it sat upon each of them. And they were all filled with the Holy Ghost, and began to speak with other tongues, as the Spirit gave them utterance"* (Ac.2:1-4). *"Now when they heard this, they were pricked in their heart, and said unto Peter and to the rest of the apostles, Men and brethren, what shall we do? Then Peter said unto them, Repent, and be baptized every one of you in the name of Jesus Christ for the remission of sins, and ye shall receive the gift of the Holy Ghost"* (Ac.2:37-38). *"Then they that gladly received his word were baptized: and the same day there were added unto them about three thousand souls"* (Ac.2:41).
106. *The Sacrifice Of Seven Male Lambs, One Young Bull And Two Rams—All With No Defect—In The Festival Of Harvest* (Le.23:18)	*The sacrifice of seven male lambs, one young bull and two rams—all with no defect—in the Festival of Harvest is a symbol of Christ, His perfect and sinless sacrifice. Remember that the number seven symbolizes*	Jesus Christ is the perfect and sinless sacrifice. His death upon the cross was the perfect solution to the problem of sin: The finished work of a perfect and sinless Man has secured our salvation	*"And being made perfect, he became the author of eternal salvation unto all them that obey him"* (He.5:9). *"And he made his grave with the wicked, and with the rich in his death;*

Historical Term	Type or Picture (Scriptural Basis for Each)	Life Application for Today's Believer	Biblical Application
The Sacrifice Of Seven Male Lambs, One Young Bull And Two Rams—All With No Defect—In The Festival Of Harvest (continued) (Le.23:18)	*completion, fulfillment and perfection.* **"And ye shall offer with the bread seven lambs without blemish of the first year, and one young bullock, and two rams: they shall be** *for* **a burnt offering unto the LORD, with their meat offering, and their drink offerings,** *even* **an offering made by fire, of sweet savour unto the LORD"** (Le.23:18).		*because he had done no violence, neither was any deceit in his mouth"* (Is.53:9). *"For he hath made him to be sin for us, who knew no sin; that we might be made the righteousness of God in him"* (2 Co.5:21). *"For we have not an high priest which cannot be touched with the feeling of our infirmities; but was in all points tempted like as we are, yet without sin"* (He.4:15). *"For such an high priest became us, who is holy, harmless, undefiled, separate from sinners, and made higher than the heavens"* (He.7:26).
107. *The Festival Of Trumpets* (Le.23:23-25)	*The Feast of Trumpets is a picture of salvation and of the rapture, the glorious day when Christ will return and take believers—both the living and the dead—to live with Him forever.* **"Speak unto the children of Israel, saying, In the seventh month, in the first** *day* **of the month, shall ye have a sabbath, a memorial of blowing of trumpets, an holy convocation"** (Le.23:24).	As the believer marches to the promised land, he is to focus upon God, learning to trust God more and more and to heed the message of joy over the atonement or reconciliation with God. God has saved him; consequently, the believer is to joy in his salvation, joy in the atonement and reconciliation with God. Moreover, he is to focus upon God more and more and learn to trust God more and more. Simply stated, the believer is to grow in his trust and joy; he is to be ever maturing, learning to focus upon the Lord.	*"But I would not have you to be ignorant, brethren, concerning them which are asleep, that ye sorrow not, even as others which have no hope. For if we believe that Jesus died and rose again, even so them also which sleep in Jesus will God bring with him. For this we say unto you by the word of the Lord, that we which are alive and remain unto the coming of the Lord shall not prevent them which are asleep. For the Lord himself shall descend from heaven with a shout, with the voice of the archangel, and with the trump [the trumpet call] of God: and the dead in Christ shall rise first: Then we which are alive and remain shall be caught up together with them in the clouds, to meet the Lord in the air: and so shall we ever be with the Lord. Wherefore comfort one another with these words"* (1 Th.4:13-18).
108. *The Festival Of Tabernacles Or Booths Or Shelters* (Le.23:33-34)	*The Festival Of Tabernacles is a symbol of the believer's short, temporary life and march through this world to the promised land of heaven.* **"Speak unto the children of Israel, saying, The fifteenth day of this seventh month** *shall be* **the feast of tabernacles** *for*	As the believer marches through this world to the promised land of heaven, his dwelling is only temporary. No matter what kind of house he lives in, it is temporary. It is made out of decaying, corruptible materials. It will waste away and some day, perhaps decades or even a few centuries, it will cease to be. Earthly	*"For we know that if our earthly house of this tabernacle were dissolved, we have a building of God, an house not made with hands, eternal in the heavens"* (2 Co.5:1). *"Of old hast thou laid the foundation of the earth: and the heavens are the work of thy hands. They shall perish, but thou shalt*

Historical Term	Type or Picture (Scriptural Basis for Each)	Life Application for Today's Believer	Biblical Application
The Festival Of Taber-nacles Or Booths Or Shelters (continued) (Le.23:33-34)	seven days unto the LORD" (Le.23:34). "Ye shall dwell in booths seven days; all that are Israelites born shall dwell in booths: That your generations may know that I made the children of Is-rael to dwell in booths, when I brought them out of the land of Egypt: I *am* the LORD your God" (Le.23:42-43).	homes are only temporary structures. Moreover, the believer is living in a tem-porary body, a body that the Bible describes as a tempo-rary tent or tabernacle. The body is corruptible and will decay and cease to exist. The believer's journey or pilgrimage through this world is only temporary. He is marching to his perma-nent and eternal home in heaven where he will live forever in the presence of God.	*endure: yea, all of them shall wax old like a gar-ment; as a vesture shalt thou change them, and they shall be changed"* (Ps. 102:25-26). *"And they that use this world, as not abusing it: for the fashion of this world passeth away"* (1 Co.7:31). *"While we look not at the things which are seen, but at the things which are not seen: for the things which are seen are tempo-ral; but the things which are not seen are eternal"* (2 Co.4:18; see 2 Pe.3:10; Re.21:1).
109. *The Lampstand* (Le.24:1-4)	*The Lampstand is a symbol that the way into God's presence always shines brightly—is always open for people to approach God. The Lampstand is a symbol of Christ, the light of the world. Jesus Christ gives a clear light, and open access into the presence of God.* **"Command the children of Israel, that they bring unto thee pure oil olive beaten for the light, to cause the lamps to burn continually"** (Le.24:2).	The way into God's pres-ence can be clearly seen through Jesus Christ. In fact, the brightest light ever lived is the light of Christ that shows the way into God's presence. Through Christ, the way into God's presence has been lit so brightly that it is wide open. There is not a single barrier, not even the slightest shadow of a barrier, be-tween man and God. Again, the most brightly lit light every created has been set ablaze by Christ Jesus, the Son of God himself. He is the light of the universe, giving light into God's pres-ence.	*"In him was life; and the life was the light of men"* (Jn.1:4). *"Then spake Jesus again unto them, saying, I am the light of the world: he that followeth me shall not walk in darkness, but shall have the light of life"* (Jn.8:12). *"I am come a light into the world, that whosoever believeth on me should not abide in darkness"* (Jn. 12:46). *"For God, who com-manded the light to shine out of darkness, hath shined in our hearts, to give the light of the knowledge of the glory of God in the face of Jesus Christ"* (2 Co.4:6). *"And the city had no need of the sun, neither of the moon, to shine in it: for the glory of God did lighten it, and the Lamb is the light thereof"* (Re.21:23).
110. *Pure Olive Oil That Kept The Lampstand Burning Continually* (Le.24:2)	*Pure olive oil that kept the Lampstand burning continu-ally is a symbol of the Holy Spirit. The oil had to be pure, a representation of perfection in order to sym-bolize the Holy Spirit of God. Note that the people had a part in keeping the light burning in the Taber-nacle. The people were just as responsible as the priest or ministers for keeping the way into God's presence shining brightly.*	Believers are responsible for keeping the light of Christ burning ever so brightly be-fore the eyes of people. Be-lievers are to bring the oil, the power of the Holy Spirit, to the worship of God, proclaiming the mes-sage of Christ the light of the world. Scripture declares that believers themselves are the light of the world. Ever since Jesus Christ ascended into heaven, they are the rep-resentatives of Christ upon the earth. They are now the lights of the world proclaim-	*"Ye are the light of the world. A city that is set on an hill cannot be hid"* (Mt.5:14). *"For so hath the Lord commanded us, saying, I have set thee to be a light of the Gentiles, that thou shouldest be for salvation unto the ends of the earth"* (Ac.13:47). *"For ye were sometimes darkness, but now are ye light in the Lord: walk as children of light"* (Ep.5:8). *"That ye may be blame-less and harmless, the sons*

Historical Term	Type or Picture (Scriptural Basis for Each)	Life Application for Today's Believer	Biblical Application
Pure Olive Oil That Kept The Lampstand Burning Continually (continued) (Le.24:2)	**"Command the children of Israel, that they bring unto thee pure oil olive beaten for the light, to cause the lamps to burn continually" (Le.24:2).**	ing the saving light of Jesus Christ	*of God, without rebuke, in the midst of a crooked and perverse nation, among whom ye shine as lights in the world" (Ph.2:15).*
111. *The High Priest Tending The Lampstand Continually* (Le.24:4)	*The High Priest tending the Lampstand continually is a symbol of Christ, the Light of the World.* **"He [Aaron, the High Priest] shall order the lamps upon the pure candlestick before the LORD continually" (Le.24:4).**	Believers are *now* the light of the world. Jesus said, "As long as I am in the world, I am the light of the world" (John 9:5). Jesus is no longer in the world, not bodily. His light is now in the lives of believers. Believers are *reflections* of Him.	*"For ye were sometimes darkness, but now are ye light in the Lord: walk as children of light" (Ep.5:8).* *"The night is far spent, the day is at hand: let us therefore cast off the works of darkness, and let us put on the armour of light" (Ro.13:12).* *"That ye may be blameless and harmless, the sons of God, without rebuke, in the midst of a crooked and perverse nation, among whom ye shine as lights in the world" (Ph.2:15).*
112. *The Holy Bread* (Le.24:5-9)	*There are three symbols associated with the Holy Bread:* *1. The Holy Bread is a symbol of Christ as the Bread of Life—God fulfills His covenant, satisfies man's hunger.* *2. The Holy Bread is a symbol of God's people (the twelve tribes of Israel)—setting their lives before the face of God, offering and placing themselves under the care of God.* *3. The aroma of the burning incense that ascended up symbolizes that God was accepting the offering of their lives to Him.* **"Every sabbath he shall set it [the holy bread] in order before the LORD continually, *being taken* from the children of Israel by an everlasting covenant" (Le.24:8).**	The Holy Bread paints two strong lessons for us: 1. The believer is to offer himself to God, setting himself before the face of God and trusting God to take care of him. If a person so offers himself to God, God promises that he will enter a covenant with the person. God will take care and look after the person who trusts him; moreover, God will lead him to the promise land of heaven. 2. The person who sets his life before God will be given the Bread of Life: his spiritual hunger will be met. God gave his Son, the Lord Jesus Christ, to be the Bread who will satisfy the spiritual hunger of man.	*"And he said to them all, If any man will come after me, let him deny himself, and take up his cross daily, and follow me" (Lu.9:23).* *"I beseech you therefore, brethren, by the mercies of God, that ye present your bodies a living sacrifice, holy, acceptable unto God, which is your reasonable service. And be not conformed to this world: but be ye transformed by the renewing of your mind, that ye may prove what is that good, and acceptable, and perfect, will of God" (Ro.12:1-2).* *"Blessed are they which do hunger and thirst after righteousness: for they shall be filled" (Mt.5:6).* *"For the bread of God is he which cometh down from heaven, and giveth life unto the world" (Jn.6:33).* *"And Jesus said unto them, I am the bread of life: he that cometh to me shall never hunger; and he that believeth on me shall never thirst" (Jn.6:35; see Jn.6:58).*
113. *The Laying Of Hands On The Person Who Cursed God* (Le.24:10-23)	*The laying of hands on the person who cursed God symbolized the removal of guilt from the hearers. This is critical to note: in God's eyes, the cursing of His name is so serious that the people who hear His name*	Profanity, vulgarity, and cursing God are serious matters in the eyes of God. Taking the name of the Lord God in vain is even one of the Ten Commandments. The person who curses God and uses profanity of	*"Thou shalt not take the name of the LORD thy God in vain; for the LORD will not hold him guiltless that taketh his name in vain" (Ex.20:7).* *"But above all things, my brethren, swear not,*

Historical Term	Type or Picture (Scriptural Basis for Each)	Life Application for Today's Believer	Biblical Application
The Laying Of Hands On The Person Who Cursed God (continued) (Le.24:10-23)	*taken in vain are just as guilty as the curser until they correct him. The hearers had to have their guilt removed: this was done by laying their hands on the offender who was to be executed.* "**Bring forth him that hath cursed without the camp; and let all that heard** *him* **lay their hands upon his head, and let all the congregation stone him**" (Le.24:14).	any sort will face the judgment of God.	*neither by heaven, neither by the earth, neither by any other oath: but let your yea be yea; and your nay, nay; lest ye fall into condemnation*" (Js.5:12). "*And all people of the earth shall see that thou art called by the name of the* LORD; *and they shall be afraid of thee*" (De.28:10). "*As he loved cursing, so let it come unto him: as he delighted not in blessing, so let it be far from him*" (Ps.109:17). "*Wherefore laying aside all malice, and all guile, and hypocrisies, and envies, and all evil speakings*" (1 Pe. 2:1; see 1 Ti.1:20).
114. *The Kinsman-Redeemer Law* (Le.25:23-34)	*The Kinsman-Redeemer Law is a symbol of Christ, our Kinsman-Redeemer.* "**If thy brother be waxen poor, and hath sold away** *some* **of his possession, and if any of his kin come to redeem it, then shall he redeem that which his brother sold**" (Le.25:25).	Note two striking lessons: 1. The Kinsman—Redeemer is a symbol of the Lord Jesus Christ. Christ is our Kinsman in that he took our nature upon himself and came to earth as a man. Jesus Christ shared in our humanity, became flesh and blood, in order to redeem us. 2. The Kinsman-Redeemer bought back the land that his relative had forfeited or lost because of debt. This is what Jesus Christ has done for us. This is a symbol of free grace. Through sin we have forfeited and lost our possession and the promised land of heaven. But Jesus Christ has paid the debt for our sin; He has redeemed or bought back our inheritance or possession in the Promised Land of heaven.	"*For all have sinned, and come short of the glory of God; Being justified freely by his grace through the redemption that is in Christ Jesus*" (Ro.3:23-24). "*Christ hath redeemed us from the curse of the law, being made a curse for us: for it is written, Cursed is every one that hangeth on a tree*" (Ga.3:13). "*In whom we have redemption through his blood, the forgiveness of sins, according to the riches of his grace*" (Ep.1:7; Col.1:14). "*Blessed be the God and Father of our Lord Jesus Christ, which according to his abundant mercy hath begotten us again unto a lively hope by the resurrection of Jesus Christ from the dead, To an inheritance incorruptible, and undefiled, and that fadeth not away, reserved in heaven for you*" (1 Pe.1:3-4). "*For our conversation [citizenship] is in heaven; from whence also we look for the Saviour, the Lord Jesus Christ: Who shall change our vile body, that it may be fashioned like unto his glorious body, according to the working whereby he is able even to subdue all things unto himself*" (Ph.3:20-21).

THE
OUTLINE & SUBJECT INDEX

REMEMBER: When you look up a subject and turn to the Scripture reference, you have not just the Scripture but also an outline and a discussion (commentary) of the Scripture and subject.

This is one of the GREAT FEATURES of *The Preacher's Outline & Sermon Bible*®. Once you have all the volumes, you will have not only what all other Bible indexes give you, that is, a list of all the subjects and their Scripture references, but in addition you will have...

- an outline of every Scripture and subject in the Bible
- a discussion (commentary) on every Scripture and subject
- every subject supported by other Scripture, already written out or cross referenced

DISCOVER THE UNIQUE VALUE for yourself. Quickly glance below to the first subject of the Index:

> **AARON**
> Anointing of.
> With oil, a symbol of the Holy Spirit.
> 8:10-13; Types chart, pt.45

Turn to the first reference. Glance at the Scripture and the outline, then read the commentary. You will immediately see the TREMENDOUS BENEFIT of the INDEX of *The Preacher's Outline & Sermon Bible*®.

OUTLINE AND SUBJECT INDEX

AARON
Anointing of.
  With oil, a symbol of the Holy Spirit.
  8:10-13; Types chart, pt.45
Blessing of. Pronounced upon God's people. 9:22-24
Discussed.
  Aaron's public confession of sin. 9:7-14
  How the Christian enjoys far greater privileges than Aaron. 16:29-34, pt.6, Thgt.4
Fact. The only time in Leviticus that God speaks directly to **A**. 10:4-11, pt.3
High Priesthood of.
  Clothing of. 8:7-9
  Ordination of. 8:1-36
Type - Symbol of
  Christ as the High Priest. 8:7-9

ABIHU
Discussed. Approached God in the wrong way. 10:1-20

ABOMINATION
Meaning of. 18:20-23

ABUNDANT - ABUNDANCE (See OF-FERINGS)
Discussed. The blessing of having more than enough. 26:4-13, pt.2

ABUSE
Discussed.
  Of a slave: sexual abuse. 19:9-22, pt.9
  Of children. 18:6-18
  Of parents. 20:9
  Of spouse. 18:6-18

ACCESS (See APPROACH--APPROACHABLE)
Discussed. Into God's presence. 24:1-4

ACCEPTANCE
Discussed. How a person is accepted by God: through the sacrifice of an animal. 1:2

ADULTERY (See SEX)
Discussed. Commandment against--
Prohibitions against. 26:1-3; 18:20-23, pt.1
Results.
  Defiles both parties. 18:20-23, pt.1
  In death. 20:10-21

AGE OF ACCOUNTABILITY
Discussed. 12:1-4, Thgt.3

ALTAR OF BURNT OFFERING
Anointing of. Anointed w/ oil seven times: to prepare for a complete, full, & perfect sacrifice. 8:10-13; Types chart, pt.44
Discussed. Blood poured out at the bottom of. 4:7; Types chart, pt.22

ALTAR OF INCENSE
Discussed. Blood put upon the Altar of Incense. 4:7; Types chart, pt.21

ANIMALS
Discussed.
  Law governing **a**. that live on land. 11:2-8
  Law governing **a**. that live in water. 11:9-12
  Vow to dedicate an **a**. to God. 27:9-13
  Way **a**. defiled a person & the required treatment. 11:24-40
Kinds of.
  Clean. 11:2-8, pt.1
  Defective. 27:9-13
  Land. 11:2-8
  Sea. 11:9-12
  Unclean. 11:2-8, pt.2

Type - Symbol of. Clean & unclean **a**.: a person being ceremonially,. 11:2-8, Types chart, pt.59 spiritually clean & unclean
Inedible birds: a person being spiritually unclean. 11:13-19
Warnings against. Eating an animal found dead. 17:10-16, pt.5

ANIMAL SACRIFICE (See SACRIFICE, ANIMAL)
Facts.
  Had to be male. 1:3
  Had to be perfect, w/out defect or blemish. 1:3; 4:3-12
Type - Symbol of.
  Male sacrifice: symbol of strength. 1:3; Types chart, pt.3
  Perfect sacrifice: symbol of the righteousness & sinlessness of Christ. 1:3; 4:3-12; Types chart, pt.4

ANOINT - ANOINTING
Discussed.
  A. Aaron w/ oil. 8:10-13
  The altar and its utensils, basin, and stand. 8:10-13
  The Tabernacle and its furnishings. 8:10-13

APPROACH--APPROACHABLE
Discussed.
  Approaching God in the wrong way. 10:1-2
  Judgment of a man who failed to **a**. God. 24:10-23
Duty. Must **a**. God correctly. 16:1-3; 22:17-30
Fact. A mother was protected by approaching God for cleansing. 12:6-7
Typed - Symbolized - Pictured. By the Burnt Offering: the only way to **a**. God. 1:1-17

Strange or unauthorized fire: symbolized approaching 10:1; Types chart, God in the wrong way. pt.56

FIRSTFRUITS, FESTIVAL OF
Chart of. Prophetic picture of salvation. 23:1-44
Purpose of. 23:4-14, pt.3
Type - Symbol of. Christ's resurrection. 23:9-14; Types chart, pt.103

FIRSTFRUITS, OFFERING OF
Discussed. 2:14-16
Duty. To give our best to God. 19:23-36, pt.1

FOOD (See **DIET**)
Discussed. The blessing of. 26:4-13, pt.1
Kinds of.
Clean. 11:2-8, 11:9-12
Unclean. 11:2-8; 11:9-12; 11:13-19

FOOD LAWS (See **LAWS; DIET**)
Discussed.
Importance of. 11:41-43
Purpose for. 11:44-47

FOOD, THE HOLY
Discussed. No outsider was allowed to eat the holy food. 22:10-16, pt.1
Duty. Must protect the holy food of God. 22:10-16
Type - Symbol of. Christ, the holy Sacrifice or Food. 22:10-16

FOREIGNER, THE
Duty. Must not mistreat the **f**. 19:23-36, pt.7
Type - Symbol of. How God's people are to treat people who are different. 19:33-34; Types chart, pt.94

FORGIVE - FORGIVENESS
Discussed.
The reason we must seek **f**. 4:2
The way to secure **f**. of sin. 4:1-5:13
Fact. The guilty person will be **f**. for anything he had 6:1-7, Thgt.1 done that makes him guilty.
Instructions on how a person is forgiven.
The way for a guilty person to be **f**. 5:14-6:7
The way for a leader to be **f**. 4:22-26
The way for a person to be **f**. for a specific, terrible sins 5:1-6
The way for an anointed priest (minister) to be **f**. 4:3-12
The way for an individual person to be **f**. 4:27-35
The way for society to be **f**. 4:13-21
The way for the poor person to be **f**. 5:7-13
Typed - Symbolized - Pictured. By the Day of Atonement: a symbol of the **f**. of sins. 16:1-34

FORTUNE TELLING
Duty. Must reject fortune telling & sorcery (witchcraft). 19:23-36, pt.2

FREEWILL OFFERING
Discussed. 22:17-30

FUNGUS (See **MILDEW**)

GIVE - GIVING
Duty. To give our best to God. 19:23-36, pt.1

GLORY OF GOD
Discussed. The Shekinah Glory, the glory of God, fell upon the people. 9:22-24, pt.4

GOAT
Discussed.
Offered for the sins of a ruler. 9:15; Types chart, pt.54
Slaughtered for the sin offering for the people. 16:15; Types chart, pt.90
Why were two goats used in the Sin Offering? 16:3-10, Thgt.2
Kinds of.
As an idol. 17:3-9, pt.4
Sacrifice. 3:12-16; 4:14-26; 4:27-35; 5:1-6; 9:1-6; 9:15-21; 10:16-20; 16:3-10, Thgt.2; 16:15-22; 16:23-28; 17:3-9; 22:17-30; 23:15-22
Scapegoat. 16:3-10, pt.5; 16:15-22, pt.2
Type - Symbol of. Christ on the cross, bearing the judgment of God. 3:12-16; 16:15-22, pt.2; Types chart, pt.17

GOD
Access to. 24:1-4
Care of. 10:12-15
Compassion of **G**. 5:7-13
Discipline of. 26:14-15
Discussed.
Face of. 24:5-9
Source of Laws. 17:1-2
Duty to. (Man's duty to.)
Must acknowledge God & acknowledge Him as holy. 22:31-33, pt.2
Must approach God in the right way. 10:1
Must be holy. 19:1-8
Must not profane God's holy **n**. 22:31-33
Must not turn to idols or false gods. 19:1-8
Must respect God's appointed order within the family. 19:1-8
Must worship on the Sabbath. 19:1-8
Fact. Blood is sacred to God. 17:10-16, pt.3; 17:10-16, pt.5, Thgt.1
Faithfulness of. 26:40-46
Forgiveness of **G**. 5:7-13
Glory of. 9:22-24, pt.4
Grace of. 10:12-15
Holiness of. 11:44-47; 16:1-2; 22:31-33
Judgment of. 10:1-20; 26:16-39
Love of **G**. 5:7-13
Mercy of. 10:16-20; 12:8
Presence of. 9:1-6; 26:4-13, pt.6
Promises of. 26:1-46
Revelation of. 9:1-6
Tenderness of. 10:16-20

GOLD MEDALLION (See **MEDALLION, GOLD**)

GRACE
Discussed. God's **g**. in the face of judgment. 10:12-15

GRAIN OFFERING (See **MEAL OFFERING**)
Chart of. Lev.6:8-7:38
Discussed. 2:1-16; 6:14-18, 6:19-23; 9:15-21, pt.3; 10:12-15, pt.1
Duty. The priests were to make a daily offering of thanksgiving & 6:19-23, pt.1 dedication to God.
Elements. Grain, fine flour, oil, incense, salt 2:1-16
Facts.
Had to be eaten within the courtyard of the Tabernacle. 6:14-18
Three purposes or reasons for. 2:1-3
Three ways to cook the Grain Offering. 2:4-7
Results of. Met man's need for joy & thanksgiving & for dedication to God. 7:37-38, pt.1b
Type - Symbol of.
Christ, the Bread of Life. 2:1-3, pt.3, Thgt.2; Types chart, pt.11
The way to give thanks & to show one's dedication to God. 2:1-16; 6:14-18; Types chart, pt.11

GUILT
Discussed. How a person is set free from the weight of **g**. 5:14-16; 5:17-19; 6:1-7, pt.3
Meaning of. What **g**. is. 5:14-6:7, Intro.

GUILT OFFERING
Chart of. Symbols pointing to Christ. 6:8-7:38
Discussed. 5:14-6:7; 7:1-10; 14:12-18
Elements.
A ram without defect and of proper value. 5:14-16
Restitution plus 20 %. 5:17-19
Instructions for. 5:14-6:7; 7:1-10
Results of. Met man's need for deliverance from the weight & anguish of guilt. 7:37-38, pt.1d
Type - Symbol of.
Christ dying for the guilt of the world. 7:1-10; Types chart, pt.34
The sacrifice of Christ, the way to be set free from the weight of guilt. 5:14-6:7; Types chart, pt.25

HANDICAPPED, THE
Duty. Must not mistreat the **h**. 19:9-22, pt.5

HARVEST
Discussed. Drought & poor **h**. 26:16-39, pt.2

HARVEST, FESTIVAL OF
Chart of. Prophetic picture of salvation. 23:1-44
Discussed. Purpose of. 23:15-22

HEALTH
Fact. God wants us healthy. 13:1, Thgt.1

HEART
Duty. To give the LORD's offering with a pure **h**. 2:11-13

RECONCILE - RECONCILIATION (See ATONEMENT)
Duty.
Must be an acknowledgment that cleansing & sacrifice are necessary. 16:23-28
The people were to seek **r**. through the sacrifice of an animal. 1:2
Fact. The greatest need in the world is for forgiveness of sin & **r**. with God. 16:1-34, Intro.
Typed - Pictured - Symbolized. By the substitutionary sacrifice making atonement for us. 8:18-21

REJECTION
Of God. 24:10-23

REPENT - REPENTANCE
Duty. A person must **r**. in order to be saved. 26:40-46, pt.1

REST, SPIRITUAL
Typed - Symbolized - Pictured. By the Sabbath: a symbol of spiritual rest, of redemption, of God's deliverance from burdens. 23:3

RESTITUTION
Meaning. 6:1-7, pt.3

RESTORATION
Conditions for.
One must confess his sins 26:40-46, pt.1
One must humble his hard heart. 26:40-46, pt.1
One must repent. 26:40-46, pt.1
Discussed.
How a person is restored with God's people. 14:2-9
The promise of. 26:40-46

RESTLESSNESS
Facts. We live in an age of **r**. 3:1-17, Intro.

RETURN- RETURNING
Discussed. To God. 26:40-46

REVERENCE
Duty. Must **r**. God's sanctuary. 26:1-3, pt.3

RICH, THE
Instructions on how God was to be approached. Through the symbol of the Burnt Offering. 1:3-9

RIGHTEOUSNESS
Typed - Symbolized - Pictured.
By the priest's special linen clothing & undergarments for removing ashes. 6:8-13, pt.2
By clean clothing. 13:47-59, Thgt.1
By the clothing of the High Priest. 16:3-10

ROBE OF THE EPHOD
Type - Symbol of. The intercessory or mediatorial ministry of the High Priest. 8:7-9, pt.1; Types chart, pt.39

ROT (See MILDEW)

SABBATH
Duty.
Must keep the **S**. 19:1-8; 26:1-3
To work six days; rest on the seventh day. 23:3
Purpose of. The LORD'S day, a day set aside for rest & worship. 23:3; Types chart, pt.100

SABBATICAL YEAR
Purpose of. 25:2-7

SACRED ASSEMBLIES
Discussed. Appointed or set by God. 23:1-2

SACRIFICE - SACRIFICES (See OFFERINGS)
Chart of. Symbols pointing to Christ. 6:8-7:38
Discussed.
Abuse of. 17:1-16, Intro.
Not holding anything back from God by sacrificing 3:17
ourselves totally to God.
Of children to idols. 18:20-23
Of the poor. 12:8
Duty. Must be offered to the LORD, without defect, perfect. 22:17-30
Kinds of.
Animal. 22:17-30
Burnt Offering. 1:1-17; 6:8-13; 8:18-21; 16:24
Grain Offering. 2:1-15; 6:14-23
Guilt Offering. 5:14-6:7; 7:1-6
Human (See **HUMAN SACRIFICE**)
Ordination Offering. 6:19-23
Peace or Fellowship Offering. 3:1-17; 7:11-34
Sin Offering. 4:1-5:13; 6:24-30; 8:14-17; 16:3-22
Fact. No **s**. was to be made except in the Tabernacle, the place appointed by God. 17:3-9
List.
Bull or cow, an animal of service. 3:1-5; 4:3-12; 4:21; Types chart, pt.14,19,24
Goat. 3:12-16; 4:14-26; 4:27-35; 5:1-6; 9:1-6; 9:15-21; 10:16-20; 16:3-10, Thgt.2; 16:15-22; 16:23-28; 17:3-9; 22:17-30; 23:15-22
Female goat. 4:27-35, pt.3
Lamb. 3:6-11; 4:27-35, pt.6; 5:6; 9:3; 12:6; 14:10,13,21,24-25; 23:12; Types chart, pt.15
Ram, perfect without blemish or defect. 5:14-16; 5:17-19; 6:6;Types chart, pt.26
Two doves or two young pigeons. 15:14-15; Types chart, pt.80
Young bull without defect. 4:3-12; 4:13-21
Type - Symbol of.
Bearing the judgment of God. 3:12-16
God's feelings toward sin & judgment against sin. 4:3-12, pt.4
Judgment--sin can never be allowed in God's presence. 4:13-21, pt.6
The blood of Christ. 17:10-16, pt.3b
The sinlessness & perfection of Christ. 4:3-12
Typed - Pictured - Symbolized.
As the Lamb of God. 3:6-11
As the Servant of God. 3:1-5

SALT
Discussed. Qualities of **s**. 2:11-13

SALVATION
Discussed.
Conditions of. 26:40-46, pt.1
Purpose for. 11:44-47
Remembrance of. 23:3
The great harvest of souls. 23:15-22

SANCTIFY - SANCTIFICATION
Discussed. The justice of God demands **s**. 20:7-8

SANCTUARY
Discussed. Reverence for. 19:23-36, pt.4
Duty. Must reverence God's sanctuary. 26:1-3, pt.3

SASH
Type- Symbol of. Truth, the truth of God's Word. 8:7-9, pt.1; Types chart, pt.38

SCAPEGOAT
Discussed. 16:3-10, pt.5
Type - Symbol of. The people being reconciled to God by the removal of their sins. 16:3-10, pt.5; 16:15-22, pt.2; Types chart, pt.86

SEEK - SEEKING
Discussed. **S**. after God. 3:1-16

SEPARATION
Discussed. Purpose: to keep God's people pure, separate from defilement. 15:31-33
Duty. Must live a life of **s**. 18:1-5, pt.1a; 18:24-30; 19:9-22, pt.8; 20:22-27, pt.2; Types chart, pt.93

SEVEN, THE NUMBER
Type- Symbol of. Completion, fullness, & perfection. 8:1-13, pt.2; 14:2-9; 16:11-14, pt.3; Types chart, pt.20, 79, 51, 87

SEX
Discussed.
Laws that govern sexual behavior. 18:1-30
S. disease. (See **SEXUAL DISEASE**)
S. prohibited during a wife's period. 18:19
Fact. God cares about the sexual behavior of His people. 15:1
Perversions of.
Sexual abuse of a slave. 19:9-22, pt.9
Adultery.
Results: Defiles both parties. 18:20-23, pt.1
Bestiality. Results: Perverts & defiles a person. 18:20-23, pt.4
Child sacrifice to idols. Results: Profanes God's name. 18:20-23, pt.2
Homosexuality. Discussed: Is detestable. 18:20-23, pt.3
Incest. Duty: Not to sexually approach any close family member or relative. 18:6-18
Warning.
God will vomit out the worldly, the sexually deviant. 18:24-30, pt.4
Justice will be executed upon various sexual sins. 20:10-21

INDEX

SEXUAL DISEASES
Discussed.
    Are infectious & contagious. 15:2-18;
    Types chart, pt.78
    Laws that protect & cleanse people
    from sexual disease & impurity.
    15:1-33; Types chart, pt.76

SEXUAL IMPURITY
Discussed.
    The purpose for the laws that protect
    people from sexual impurity.
    15:31-33
    Hope for the sexually impure person.
    15:2-18, Thgt.2
    Purpose for the laws that protect peo-
    ple from sexual impurity. 15:31-33
Duty. Must not sexually approach any
    close family member or relative.
    18:6-18
Facts.
    Immorality and sexual misbehavior are
    severely condemned by God. 15:2-
    18, Thgt.1
    Society's wrong emphasis upon sex is
    eating away 15:1-33, Intro. at the
    foundation of society.

SHEKEL, TABERNACLE
Discussed. Weight of. 27:14-25, pt.3

SHELTERS (See **BOOTHS**)

SHOWBREAD (See **BREAD, HOLY**)

SIN
Discussed. Cleansing of. 23:26-32
Duty. At the first sign of s. must immedi-
    ately go to the High Priest of God.
    13:2-46, pt.1, Thgt.1
Fact.
    Burns a person. 13:2-46, pt.4, Thgt.1
    S. can reappear. 13:2-46, pt.3, Thgt.1
Kinds of.
    Against one's neighbor. 6:1-7
    Blasphemy against the Holy Spirit.
    4:2, D.S. #1
    Breaking the commandments of God.
    5:17-19
    Defiant **s.** 4:2, D.S. #1
    Human & personal defilement. 5:1-13
    National **s.** 4:13-21, pt.1
    Profaning & shaming God's Name.
    22:1-9
    Religious defilement. 5:1-13
    Sexual. 15:1-33
    S. through ignorance. 4:2, D.S. #1
    Secret or unknown. 13:2-46, pt.5,
    Thgt.1
    Social & civil injustice. 5:1-13
    Terrible **s.** 5:1-13
    Unintentional **s.** 4:2, D.S. #1
    Verbal **s.** or sins of the tongue. 5:1-13
Meaning of. 4:1-5:13, Intro.
Remedy for. Discussed. 5:1-13, pt.2;
    13:2-46, pt.8, Thgt.1
Results. When a priest or minister sins.
    4:3-12, pt.1
Seriousness of.
    Against one's neighbor—a sin against
    God Himself. 6:1-7, pt.1
    Every person is held accountable for
    all **s.** 5:17-19

SIN OFFERING, THE
Chart of. Symbols pointing to Christ.
    6:8-7:38
Discussed. 4:1-5:13; 6:24-30; 8:14-17;
    9:7-14, pt.2; 9:15-21, pt.1; 10:16-20;
    15:2-18, Thgt.2; Types chart, pt.18
Elements of.
    A female goat or lamb without defect
    offered for the individual person.
    4:27-35
    A male goat without defect offered for
    the leader. 4:22-26
    A tenth of an ephah (two quarts/two li-
    ters) of fine flour for the poorest.
    5:7-13, pt.4
    A young bull without defect offered
    for the anointed priest. 4:3-12
    A young bull without defect offered
    for society. 4:13-21
    Two doves or two young pigeons of-
    fered for the poor. 5:7-13
Results of.
    Met man's need for forgiveness of sin.
    7:37-38, pt.1c
Type - Symbol of.
    Christ securing the forgiveness of sin.
    4:1-5:13; 6:24-30

SLAVE - SLAVERY
Discussed.
    No human being is to be enslaved.
    25:35-55, Thgt.2
    Savage abuse of. 25:35-55
    Sexual abuse of. 19:9-22, pt.9

SOCIETY
Discussed. The way for **s.** to be forgiven.
    4:13-21

SORCERY (See **FORTUNE TELLING**)

SPIRITISTS (See **PSYCHICS**)

SPIRITUAL HUNGER
Discussed. Of man. 24:5-9

SPIRITUAL REST (See **REST, SPIR-
ITUAL**)

STEALING
Duty. Must not **s.** 19:9-22, pt.2

STEWARD - STEWARDSHIP
Discussed. Three things that already be-
    long to the LORD & cannot be vowed or
    dedicated. 27:26-33
Duty. To offer God our very best. 2:4-7

SUBSTITUTE - SUBSTITUTION (See
IDENTIFICATION)
Fact. Christ became our **s.** 1:3-9, pt.2

SYMBOL
Discussed. How a person must identify
    with a **s.** 1:3-9, pt.2
List of. Types Chart. Introductory Mate-
    rials

TABERNACLE
Discussed.
    Cleansing of. 16:15-22
    Worship of. 17:3-9, Thgt.3; Types
    chart, pt.91

TABERNACLES, FESTIVAL OF
Chart of. Prophetic picture of salvation.
    23:1-44
Purpose of. 23:33-44
Type - Symbol of. The believer's march
    through the world to heaven. 23:33-34;
    Types chart, pt.108

TENDER - TENDERNESS
Of God. 10:16-20

TESTIFY - TESTIMONY
Discussed. Aaron's public confession of
    sin. 9:7-14

THANKS - THANKSGIVING
Discussed. The Grain Offering was an act
    of joy & **t.** to God. 2:1; 2:8; 6:14-18;
    6:19-23

THIRST, SPIRITUAL
Discussed. **T.** for God. 3:1-16

THUMMIM
Type - Symbol of. The High Priest seek-
    ing the will of God for the people. 8:7-
    9, pt.2; Types chart, pt.41

TITHE
Discussed. A person must not pledge the
    t. or a vow: already belonged to the
    LORD. 27:26-33, pt.3
Duty. A believer must **t.** 27:26-33, pt.3,
    Thgt.1

TRUMPETS, FESTIVAL OF
Chart of. Prophetic picture of salvation.
    23:1-44
Purpose of. 23:23-25
Type - Symbol of. Salvation & of the rap-
    ture. 23:23-25; Types chart, pt.107

TRUST
Discussed. Growing in. 23:23-25

TUNIC, LINEN
Type - Symbol of. Righteousness, the
    putting on of God's righteousness. 8:7-
    9, pt.1; Types chart, pt.37

TURBAN, LINEN
Type - Symbol of. The need for right-
    eousness of mind & thoughts. 8:7-9,
    pt.3; Types chart, pt.42

TYPES (See **SYMBOL**)

UNBELIEVER - UNBELIEVERS
Practices of. 19:23-36, pt.2

UNCLEAN
Discussed.
    What being **u.** meant to a mother who
    had just delivered a son. 12:1-4, pt.1
    Why a mother's uncleanness is dou-
    bled with a girl. 12:5

UNLEAVENED BREAD, FESTIVAL OF
Chart of. Prophetic picture of salvation.
    23:1-44
Discussed. Purpose of. 23:4-14, pt.2
Type - Symbol of. The need & urgency
    for the believer to be free from the
    world & its enslavement to sin &
    death. 23:6; Types chart, pt.102

INDEX

UNINTENTIONAL SIN (See **SIN**)

UNRIGHTEOUSNESS
Discussed. Unclean clothing is a symbol
of **u**. 13:47-59, Thgt.1

URIM
Type - Symbol of. The High Priest seeking the will of God for the people. 8:7-
9, pt.2; Types chart, pt.41

VALUE
Discussed. Of persons dedicating their
lives to God. 27:1-8

VICTORY
Discussed. The blessing of **v**. over the
enemy. 26:4-13, pt.2

VOW -VOWS (See **COMMIT - COM-
MITMENTS**)
Discussed.
Dedicating animals to God. 27:9-13
The Fellowship Offering given as a **v**.
7:11-36, pt.2
The law governing **v**. & commitments
made to God. 27:1-34
Three things that already belong to the
LORD and cannot be vowed or dedi-
cated. 27:26-33
List. Three **v**. of dedication to the LORD.
27:1-25

VULGARITY (See **CURSE - CURSING;
PROFANITY**)

WAR
Discussed. Punishment of 26:16-39, pt.4

WARN - WARNING
Discussed. The **w**. of judgment & pun-
ishment to the disobedient. 26:16-39
Duty. Must heed God's **w**. 8:33-36

WASH - WASHING
Discussed.

Of a person's clothes, shaving his
body, & bathing. 14:8; Types chart,
pt.71
Of the inner parts & legs of the substitute sacrifice. 9:14; Types chart,
pt.53
Type - Symbol of.
Being clothed with purity. 8:6;
15:2-18
Being spiritually, ceremonially
cleansed. 11:24-40; 14:2-9; Types
chart, pt.60

WATER
Type - Symbol of. Spiritual cleansing.
8:6; Types chart, pt.35

WAVE OFFERING
Discussed. 7:11-36; 10:12-15, pt.1

WAY, THE
Fact. God, not man, appointed & determined the **w**. 1:1-17

WEEKS, FESTIVAL OF (See **HAR-
VEST, FESTIVAL OF**)

WILDERNESS WANDERING
Discussed. Celebrated with the Festival
of Tabernacles. 23:33-44

WITCHCRAFT (See **FORTUNE TELL-
ING**)

WITNESS - WITNESSING
Discussed. The great harvest of souls.
23:15-22

WOMEN
Discussed.
Childbirth laws to protect mother &
child. 12:1-8
Menstrual period of. 18:19

WORLDLINESS (See **CORRUPTION**)
Discussed. Symbolized by yeast &
honey. 2:11-13; Types chart, pt.12

Duty.
Must keep God's decrees & laws.
18:24-30, pt.2
Must not allow any person to commit
any acts of perversion. 18:24-30,
pt.3
Must not defile oneself in any illicit,
sexual act. 18:24-30, pt.1
Must not follow any of the detestable
customs of the worldly. 18:24-30,
pt.5
Warning.
Against **w**., against sexual impurity &
deviancy. 18:24-30
God will vomit out the worldly, the
sexually deviant. 18:24-30, pt.4

WORSHIP
Purpose of. 23:3
Typed - Symbolized - Pictured. By the
Tabernacle & its **w**.: symbolized the
coming of the Savior of the world &
the great sacrifice upon the cross. 17:3-9,
Thgt.3; Types chart, pt.91

WORSHIP, FALSE (See **FALSE WOR-
SHIPPERS**)

YEAR OF JUBILEE (See **JUBILEE,
YEAR OF**)

YEAR, SABBATICAL (See **SABBATI-
CAL YEAR**)

YEAST
Discussed. Why it was withheld from the
grain offering. 6:14-18; Types chart,
pt.31
Type - Symbol of. Corruption or worldliness. 2:11-13; 6:14-18, pt.2-3; Types
chart, pt.12

YOM KIPPUR (See **DAY OF ATONE-
MENT**)

LEADERSHIP MINISTRIES WORLDWIDE

PURPOSE STATEMENT

LEADERSHIP MINISTRIES WORLDWIDE exists to equip ministers, teachers, and laypersons in their understanding, preaching, and teaching of God's Word by publishing and distributing worldwide *The Preacher's Outline & Sermon Bible*® and derivative works to reach & disciple all people for Jesus Christ.

MISSION STATEMENT

1. To make the Bible so understandable – its truth so clear and plain – that men and women everywhere, whether teacher or student, preacher or hearer, can grasp its message and receive Jesus Christ as Savior, and…

2. To place the Bible in the hands of all who will preach and teach God's Holy Word, verse by verse, precept by precept, regardless of the individual's ability to purchase it.

The Preacher's Outline & Sermon Bible and derivative works have been given to LMW as LMW Resources for printing and distribution worldwide at/below cost, by those who remain anonymous. One fact, however, is as true today as it was in the time of Christ:

THE GOSPEL IS FREE, BUT THE COST OF TAKING IT IS NOT

LMW depends on the generous gifts of believers with a heart for Him and a love for the lost. They help pay for the printing, translating, and distributing of LMW Resources into the hands of God's servants worldwide, who will present the Gospel message with clarity, authority, and understanding beyond their own.

LMW was incorporated in the state of Tennessee in July 1992 and received IRS 501 (c)(3) non-profit status in March 1994. LMW is an international, nondenominational mission organization. All proceeds from USA sales, along with donations from donor partners, go directly to underwrite translation and distribution projects of LMW Resources to preachers, church and lay leaders, and Bible students around the world.

LMW Resources

This material, like similar works, has come from imperfect man and is thus susceptible to human error. We are nevertheless grateful to God for both calling us and empowering us through His Holy Spirit to undertake this task. Because of His goodness and grace, ***The Preacher's Outline & Sermon Bible®*** New Testament and the Old Testament volumes have been completed.

LMW Resources include *The Minister's Personal Handbook, The Believer's Personal Handbook,* and other helpful resources available in printed form as well as electronically on various digital platforms.

God has given the strength and stamina to bring us this far. Our confidence is that as we keep our eyes on Him and remain grounded in the undeniable truths of the Word, we will continue to produce other helpful resources for God's dear servants to use in their Bible study and discipleship.

We offer this material, first, to Him in whose name we labor and serve and for whose glory it has been produced and, second, to everyone everywhere who studies, preaches, and teaches the Word.

Our daily prayer is that each volume will lead thousands, millions, yes even billions, into a better understanding of the Holy Scriptures and a fuller knowledge of Jesus Christ the Incarnate Word, of whom the Scriptures so faithfully testify.

You will be pleased to know that Leadership Ministries Worldwide partners with Christian organizations, printers, and mission groups around the world to make LMW Resources available and affordable in many countries and foreign languages. It is our goal that *every* leader around the world, both clergy and lay, will be able to understand God's holy Word and present God's message with more clarity, authority, and understanding—all beyond his or her own power.

Leadership Ministries Worldwide
1928 Central Avenue • Chattanooga, TN 37408
1(800) 987-8790
Email: info@lmw.org
lmw.org

11/22

Product Listing

THE PREACHER'S OUTLINE & SERMON BIBLE® (POSB)

Available in KJV (44 vols) & NIV (40 vols)

OLD TESTAMENT

- Genesis I: Chs. 1–11
- Genesis II: Chs. 12–50
- Exodus I: Chs. 1–18
- Exodus II: Chs. 19–40
- Leviticus
- Numbers
- Deuteronomy
- Joshua
- Judges, Ruth
- 1 Samuel
- 2 Samuel
- 1 Kings
- 2 Kings
- 1 Chronicles
- 2 Chronicles
- Ezra, Nehemiah, Esther
- Job
- Psalms I: Chs. 1-41
- Psalms II: Chs. 42-106
- Psalms III: Chs. 107-150
- Proverbs
- Ecclesiastes, Song of Solomon
- Isaiah I: Chs. 1-35
- Isaiah II: Chs. 36-66
- Jeremiah I: Chs. 1-29
- Jeremiah II: Chs. 30-52, Lamentations
- Ezekiel
- Daniel, Hosea Joel, Amos, Obadiah, Jonah, Micah, Nahum
- Habakkuk, Zephaniah, Haggai, Zechariah, Malachi

NEW TESTAMENT

- Matthew I: Chs. 1–15
- Matthew II: Chs. 16–28
- Mark
- Luke
- John
- Acts
- Romans
- 1 & 2 Corinthians
- Galatians, Ephesians, Philippians, Colossians
- 1 & 2 Thessalonians, 1 & 2 Timothy, Titus, Philemon
- Hebrews, James
- 1 & 2 Peter, 1, 2, & 3 John, Jude
- Revelation
- Master Outline & Subject Index

Handbooks

- **What the Bible Says to the Believer** —
  The Believer's Personal Handbook
  11 Chapters. – Over 500 Subjects, 300 Promises, & 400 Verses Expounded - Gift leatherette or paperback options

- **What the Bible Says to the Minister** —
  The Minister's Personal Handbook
  12 Chapters. - 127 Subjects - 400 Verses Expounded - Gift leatherette or paperback options

- **What the Bible Says to the Business Leader**—The Business Leader's Personal Handbook
  12 Chapters – Over 100 topics plus hundreds of scriptural values for conducting business in a 21st-century world — Paperback

- **What the Bible Says About Series** —
  Various Subjects

everyWORD

Scripture, Outline, Commentary of the Gospels with ESV Scripture

- everyWORD: Matthew 1–16:12

- everyWORD: Matthew 16:13–28:20

- everyWORD: Mark

- everyWORD: Luke 1–13:21

- everyWORD: Luke 13:22–24:53

- everyWORD: John

- **The Teacher's Outline & Study Bible™** - Various New Testament Books
  Complete 30 - 45 minute lessons – with illustrations and discussion questions
- *Practical Illustrations — Companion to the POSB Arranged by topic and Scripture reference*
- *LMW Resources on various digital platforms Learn more on our website at lmw.org*
- *Contact for resources in other languages*

Contact Us

LEADERSHIP MINISTRIES WORLDWIDE
1928 Central Avenue • Chattanooga, TN 37408
1(800) 987-8790 • E-mail - info@lmw.org
Order online at lmw.org

Made in the USA
Columbia, SC
31 January 2025